Tourism Geography

Tourism Geography

SECOND EDITION

Philip G. Davidoff, CTC
Doris S. Davidoff, CTC
J. Douglas Eyre, PhD

Prentice Hall
Englewood Cliffs, New Jersey 07632

Library of Congress Cataloging-in-Publication Data

Davidoff, Philip G.
    Tourism geography / Philip G. Davidoff, Doris S. Davidoff, J.
Douglas Eyre. — 2nd ed.
      p.   cm.
    Includes index.
    ISBN 0–13–148735–3
    1. Tourist trade.   I. Davidoff, Doris S.   II. Eyre, John D. (John
Douglas).   III. Title.
G155.A1D35   1995   94–47027
338.4′791—dc20   CIP

Acquisitions Editor: Robin Baliszweski
Production Editors: Rose Kernan and Fred Dahl
Copy Editor: Jean Babrick
Cover Designer: Melissa Hayden/Photonica
Designer: Fred Dahl
Production Coordinator: Ed O'Dougherty

© 1995, 1988, Philip G. Davidoff, Doris S. Davidoff, and
J. Douglas Eyre
Published By Prentice-Hall, Inc.
A Simon & Schuster Company
Englewood Cliffs, NJ 07632

Printed in the United States of America

1 2 3 4 5 6 7 8 9 10

ISBN 0-13-148735-3

Prentice-Hall International (UK) Limited, *London*
Prentice-Hall of Australia Pty. Limited, *Sydney*
Prentice-Hall Canada Inc., *Toronto*
Prentice-Hall Hispanoamericana, S.A., *Mexico*
Prentice-Hall of India Private Limited, *New Delhi*
Prentice-Hall of Japan, Inc., *Tokyo*
Simon & Schuster Asia Pte. Ltd., *Singapore*
Editora Prentice-Hall do Brasil, Ltda., *Rio de Janeiro*

nghia tran

Contents

8 Caribbean, 235

9 Western Europe, 275

10 Eastern Europe and the Former Soviet Union, 355

11 The Middle East and North Africa, 407

Acknowledgments

We would like to thank the following individuals and organizations for their contributions to this text:

Our copy editor, Jean Babrick, who always goes way beyond just copy editing and adds greatly to the quality of the book.

The Hotel and Travel Index and Official Hotel Guide, published by Reed Travel Group, for their permission to reprint some of the country maps.

The Bureau of Public Affairs, United States Department of State, whose *Background Notes* provided some of the detailed country maps.

The United States Travel and Tourism Administration, which provided the regional definitions used in the Eastern and Western United States chapters and whose regional maps are also used in these chapters.

The following tour operators and cruise lines, who graciously granted permission to reprint their tour and cruise itineraries within these pages, allowing us to demonstrate some of the most popular types of tours of the various regions of the world:

Brendan Tours

Carnival Cruise Lines

Collette Tours

General Tours and Delta Dream Vacations

Globus and Cosmos

Holland America Line/Westours

Insight International Tours

Mayflower Tours

Official Airline Guide

Pacific Delight Tours

Sanborn's Tours

SITA World Travel

Tauck Tours

TBI Tours

Trafalgar Tours

The various government tourist offices throughout the world who provided many of the pictures used in this book. Photo credits are given on the pages containing the photos that were used.

We would also like to thank the editorial staff of Prentice Hall for their assistance, Robin Baliszewski of Prentice Hall who has helped us make this book a success, and our staffs at Belair Travel, VALU Travel Marketing, Inc. and the Geography Department of the University of North Carolina, as well as our families for bearing with us through the development of this text.

Philip G. Davidoff, CTC
Doris S. Davidoff, CTC
J. Douglas Eyre, PhD

About the Authors

Phil and Doris Davidoff are leading travel industry professionals who are also active in travel and tourism education and training. They are the co-founders and co-owners of Belair Travel Consultants in Maryland, and have served as travel and tourism educators for more than twenty years. Both are Certified Travel Counselors and Master Cruise Counselors and both are Life Members of ICTA. They have also served as members of the tourism faculties of The George Washington University and Northern Virginia Community College. They are co-authors of five books—*Sales and Marketing for Travel and Tourism, Air Fares and Ticketing, Financial Management for Travel Agencies, Worldwide Tours—A Travel Agent's Guide to Selling Tours,* and *Tourism Geography Workbook.*

Phil Davidoff is currently President of Belair Travel Consultants, VALU Travel Marketing, Inc. and of Davidoff Associates, Inc., a travel industry education and consulting organization. He was (1990–1992) President of the American Society of Travel Agents (ASTA) and was previously ASTA's Staff Vice-President, Education and Training. He was also President of ASTA's Central Atlantic Chapter as well as Vice-

Chairman of its National Education and Training Committee. He holds Bachelor's and Master's degrees from the University of Pennsylvania and has completed extensive studies in Human Resource Development at The George Washington University.

Doris Davidoff is Vice-President of Belair Travel Consultants, VALU Travel Marketing, Inc. and of Davidoff Associates, Inc. She wrote a monthly column, "The Agency Manager," for *Travel Weekly* magazine for several years and has been a columnist for *Travel Trade* since 1989. She is a former national trustee of the Institute of Certified Travel Agents and a former officer of the Central Atlantic Chapter of the American Society of Travel Agents. Doris is a well-known seminar presenter in the travel industry. She earned a Bachelor of Business Administration degree from Adelphi University and a Master of Arts in Education degree with specialization in Tourism Development and Travel Administration from The George Washington University.

Professor J. Douglas Eyre was born at Silverside, Delaware, in 1922, attended Wilmington public schools, and received the A.B. degree from the University of Michigan in Ann Arbor. Following four years of military service as a Japanese language officer during World War II, Dr. Eyre returned to Michigan for graduate study. After a year of additional field research in Japan, he was awarded the Ph.D. in Geography in 1951. He served on the faculty of the University of Washington in Seattle 1951–1957, then moved to the University of North Carolina at Chapel Hill, his present post and residence. At Chapel Hill, Dr. Eyre has served as a departmental chairman, academic advisor, and director of international programs in addition to his regular teaching and research activities. A specialist in the urban and economic geography of East Asia, especially Japan, he has conducted field research in Japan, South Korea, and Micronesia, and has traveled widely in Eurasia and other world areas. He has published a number of books, monographs, scholarly articles, and encyclopedia entries, and was listed in *Who's Who in America.*

Introduction

Geography is a very broad topic—it literally includes the world. Traditionally, geography is concerned with the study of places and locations, emphasizing both the physical environment and the characteristics and arrangement of the people there, and how their environment affects the way they live.

From a systematic viewpoint, geography is divided into two primary branches—physical and human (cultural). Physical geography includes the study of landforms and climate. Cartography, or map making, is the graphic representation of the physical or human world on maps and globes. Human geography centers on the interactions among people and the places where they live. Cultural and economic activities are the primary areas of study in human geography. These two branches can be analyzed on a regional basis as well as a global one. Regional geography looks at all aspects of physical and human geography with respect to a specifically defined, small or large, area of the world.

In developing this tourism geography text, the authors have attempted to follow the basic concepts of geography, while at the same time providing an emphasis that differs from traditional approaches to the subject. Instead of concentrating on the needs of the people in an area, this text is written with great concern for the needs of people who may visit the area. Although the physical and cultural attributes of a country or region are covered, primary emphasis is given to areas of touristic importance and the places and activities of greatest interest to potential tourists visiting the area.

This text is not a travel guide. It does provide extensive information on what to see and where to see it; however, its primary purpose is to provide a broad overview of tourism throughout the world rather than to direct travelers in specific areas.

■ ORGANIZATION

A brief summary of the most basic concepts of physical geography is a framework for understanding the specific conditions that affect tourism. The psychological and sociological factors affecting travel are also summarized. Only when we understand why people travel can we determine why specific attractions and experiences found throughout the world appeal to travelers. Basic information on immigration, customs, and health requirements for international travel is also covered.

The tourism geography of the world is discussed by region. The Western Hemisphere is covered first, starting in North America and moving through Central and South America and the Caribbean. This is followed by the Eastern Hemisphere, beginning in Europe and moving through the Middle East, sub-Saharan Africa, Asia, and the South Pacific.

An area map is at the beginning of each regional chapter. Within each chapter, a consistent format is followed.

At the beginning of the material for each state or country, capital, area in square miles, and population are listed. For sovereign nations, this listing also includes:

- language(s)
- currency
- time zone
- national airline (if applicable)
- documentation (for example, passport and visa) required for travel to the country by a United States citizen*

*Information pertaining to documentation can change. The information in this book was correct at time of printing, but check with appropriate sources to be sure of accuracy at time of travel.

A map of each state and most countries is included to show its location and neighbors. A more detailed map is included for major tourism countries.

Following this material, a general description of each area and state or country is provided. This includes important physical features, climate, the cultural background and heritage of the people, and important historical developments. Areas of touristic importance are then presented for each state or country. This text contains the geographic and touristic information which, in the judgment of the authors, is most important to the needs of travel advisors and travelers. Volumes can be written on this subject and limitations of space prevent a more detailed approach.

At the end of each regional chapter, several examples of tour itineraries within each area are provided. The itineraries are for programs operated by some well-known tour companies and demonstrate common ways in which travelers tour an area. They provide additional touristic information as well.

A glossary of major geographical terms is provided at the back of the book. An in-depth index is also provided.

■ INFORMATION SOURCES

The spelling of all international place names conforms to that used by the United States State Department. Populations and areas are from the 1994 *World Almanac* and *Book of Facts*. Documentation requirements were verified with the Summer 1994 editions of the OAG Travel Planners. The regions of the United States are those designated by the United States Travel and Tourism Administration.

2

The Physical World

A basic knowledge of physical geography is essential in understanding the geography of tourism. This chapter briefly discusses the water and landforms found on the Earth. It also describes cartography—the science of representing our planet. Finally, this chapter explains the concepts of longitude and latitude, as well as world time and climate.

■ LANDFORMS AND WATER

A description of the physical features of a locality or region contains the characteristics of the landform, including types of water, if any, in the area. The terrain of the area (for example, mountains, hills, valleys, plateaus, etc.) and its vegetation may affect the activities possible in that area. Similarly, the type of surface water, if any, affects potential activities.

Most geography texts concentrate on the relationship of landforms to economic enterprises such as manufacturing or transportation, and on the cultural activities of the people living in the area. In contrast, we will concentrate on potential activities for visitors. Specifically, we will show how land and water interact to meet the varying needs of the traveler.

Students of tourism geography should always look for ways in which land and water may attract the traveler. The most obvious are for sports and other outdoor activities—for example, mountains provide hiking spring through fall and may permit skiing in winter; rivers and lakes offer opportunities for boating and fishing. Less obvious, perhaps, is the allure of the natural beauty of green countrysides. Fall foliage also attracts the traveler. Making the best use of this knowledge requires an understanding of climatic patterns. Because beauty is truly in the eye of the beholder, all areas of natural beauty cannot be covered in one text; however, the major areas that all travel professionals should know will be included.

■ CARTOGRAPHY

Cartography is the science of map making. If the earth were flat, it would be easy to develop a map on paper. Distances could be easily shown to scale. If the earth were a cylinder or even a cone, a flat map could be developed by cutting and unrolling a picture of its surface.

Because the earth is a sphere, however, the only totally accurate map of the world is spherical in form—a globe. Through the years, cartographers have developed many different ways of depicting or projecting the spherical earth on a flat surface.

FIGURE 2–1. Mercator projection.

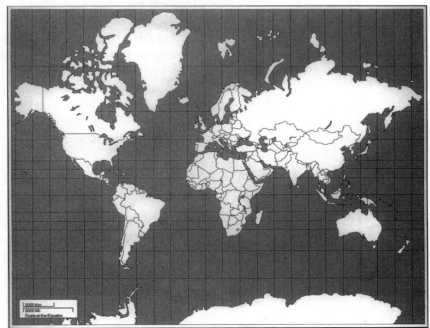

FIGURE 2–2. Robinson projection.

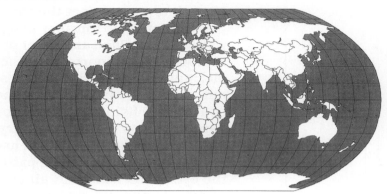

The most common type of map is the Mercator projection (Figure 2–1). The Mercator projection is a flat map that usually has the equator at its center. On this map, parallels (lines of latitude) and meridians (lines of longitude) cross at right angles. Most classroom maps of the world are Mercator projections.

However, all world areas are not equal on a Mercator world map. The Arctic and Antarctic areas are extremely distorted. Thus Greenland, an area one-eighth the size of South America, appears to be larger than that continent. The distortion of the Mercator projection is not critical when viewing smaller areas in mid and low latitudes. Most maps in this book are Mercator projections.

A newer, more accurate projection, which has gained some popularity is the Robinson projection (Figure 2–2). This provides a more accurate view of the world, especially the higher latitudes.

The azimuthal or polar projection (Figure 2–3) shows true distance and direction along its meridians, but distorts as distance increases from the pole. Only half the earth can be seen in a single projection.

The Goode's Homolosine projection looks like a flattened orange peel. This type of map (Figure 2–4) does the most accurate job of depicting spherical information on a flat surface. Distortion is at a minimum.

■ DETERMINING POSITION: LONGITUDE AND LATITUDE

Because the earth is spherical, geographers and navigators measure position in terms of degrees of longitude and latitude. For exact positioning, there are divisions of one degree (60 minutes) and subdivisions of one minute (60 seconds).

Lines of longitude, called meridians, run north and south between the North Pole and the South Pole. The zero degree meridian has been established at the Greenwich Observatory in England and is called the prime meridian, or Greenwich

FIGURE 2–3. Azimuthal equidistant projection.

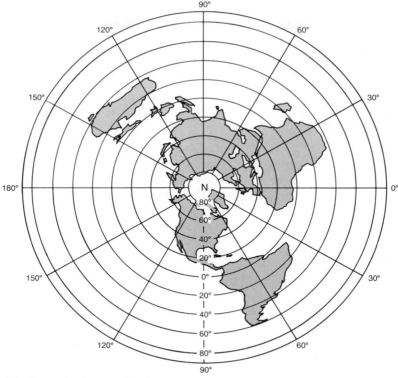

FIGURE 2–4. Goode's Homolosine projection.

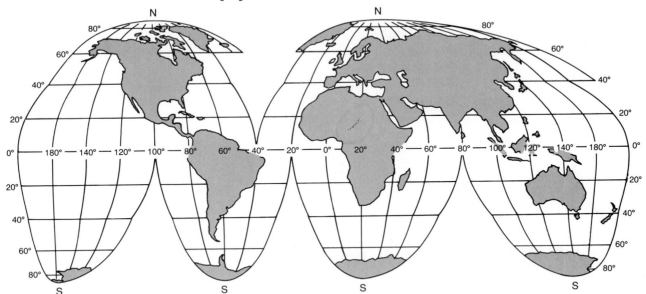

meridian. Longitude is measured east and west from this prime meridian to 180° (exactly halfway around the world). The 180° meridian is the place where east and west meet. It serves as the International Date Line over most of its length.

All meridians start at one pole, spread to their widest separation at the equator, and converge at the opposite pole. For this reason, distances between meridians are not equal at all

FIGURE 2–5.

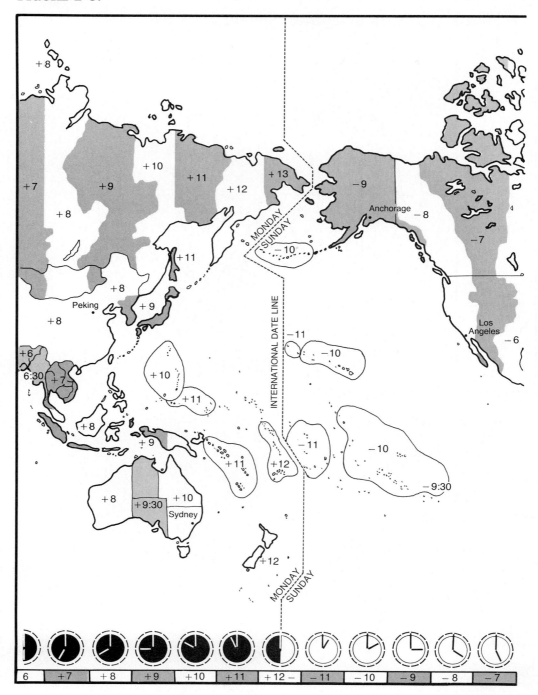

points. For example, ten degrees of longitude is a much smaller distance in northern Europe than in equatorial Africa.

Lines of latitude, called parallels, express relative position north or south of the equator (0° degrees latitude). Latitude is measured from 0° to 90° north or south. 90° North

FIGURE 2–5.

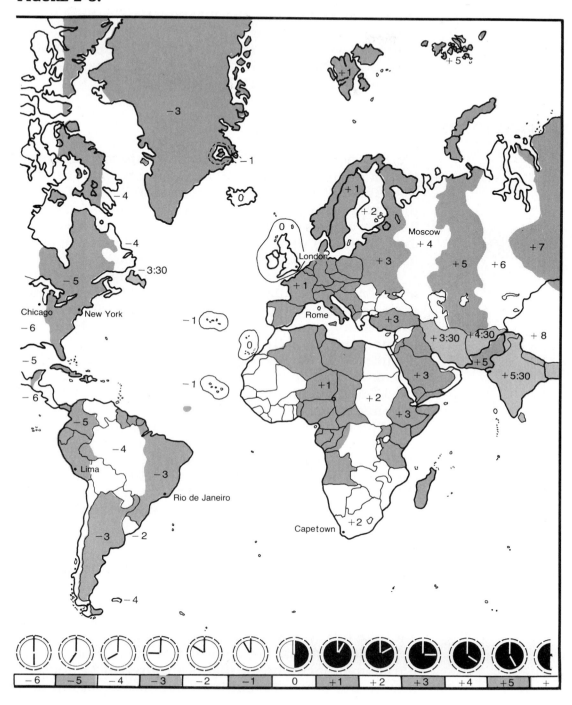

Latitude is the North Pole; 90° South Latitude is the South Pole. Latitudinal distances are equal over the world, with one degree equaling approximately 70° statute miles.

The world can be split into hemispheres (halves) in two primary ways—Eastern/Western and Northern/Southern. The

Eastern Hemisphere includes all meridians of East Longitude from 0° to 180°; while the Western Hemisphere includes all meridians of West Longitude. The Northern/Southern division splits the world at the equator with all parallels of North Latitude in the Northern Hemisphere and all parallels of South Latitude in the Southern Hemisphere.

■ DETERMINING TIME

World time varies in a direct relationship to longitudinal location of a point, adjusted as necessary by political decisions. There are 360 degrees of longitude (180 East and 180 West) on the earth and 24 hours in a day. Dividing 360 degrees by 24 hours produces a result of 15 degrees per hour. Thus, for even distribution of time, there should be a difference of one hour for each 15 degrees difference in longitude.

Where meridians at 15° intervals cross over empty spaces of water or unpopulated land, one hour time differences have been established on each side of the meridian. However, because straight meridians cut across populated areas, time differences are usually established along political boundaries (Figure 2–5). For example, the boundary between Eastern Standard and Central Standard Time (one hour difference) runs along the Illinois/Indiana border with Illinois on Central time and Indiana on Eastern time.

The International Date Line (normally 180°) literally zigzags so that all of Russia is in the same day and all of Alaska, including the Aleutian Islands, is in the same day. Thus, Uelen, Russia, located at 170° West Longitude, retains an Eastern Hemisphere date and time and Attu, Alaska, located at 172° East Longitude, maintains a Western Hemisphere date and time.

The 24-Hour Clock

The 24-hour clock is used as the standard time system in many parts of the world. The travel industry frequently uses it to avoid confusion and reduce errors in identifying AM and PM times. Many international airlines use the 24-hour clock to show flight times, and all flight times in the *International Official Airline Guide* are shown in 24-hour time. Often schedule changes for domestic flights are given in 24-hour time even though the original flight information was shown on the 12-hour clock.

The 24-hour clock is always shown in four digits, including both hours and minutes. The cycle begins at one minute past midnight (0001), progressing through the day and ending at midnight (2400). Table 2–1 below shows 24-hour time and the corresponding AM or PM time on the 12-hour clock: Figure 2–6 shows a clock face indicating both 12-hour and 24-hour

TABLE 2-1. 24-hour and 12-hour times

	AM		PM
24-Hour Clock	*12-Hour Clock*	*24-Hour Clock*	*12-Hour Clock*
0100	1:00 AM	1300	1:00 PM
0245	2:45 AM	1425	2:25 PM
0300	3:00 AM	1515	3:15 PM
0420	4:20 AM	1600	4:00 PM
0540	5:40 AM	1700	5:00 PM
0600	6:00 AM	1800	6:00 PM
0710	7:10 AM	1900	7:00 PM
0800	8:00 AM	2000	8:00 PM
0930	9:30 AM	2100	9:00 PM
1000	10:00 AM	2200	10:00 PM
1135	11:35 AM	2300	11:00 PM
1200	(12:00 noon)	2400	(12:00 midnight)

FIGURE 2–6. 24-hour clock.

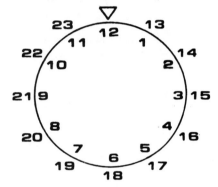

time systems. Converting morning time to the 24-hour clock can be accomplished simply by removing the ":" and "AM." To convert afternoon time, remove the ":" and add 1200 to the time. For example, to convert 1:00 PM:

$$
\begin{array}{r}
0100 \\
+1200 \\
\hline
1300
\end{array}
$$

To convert the 24-hour clock to the 12-hour clock, subtract 1200 from the PM times, insert the ":" and add "PM." For example:

$$
\begin{array}{r}
2045 \\
-1200 \\
\hline
845 \text{ (becomes 8:45 PM)}
\end{array}
$$

Time Differences Between Cities

Knowing time differences between cities is helpful both in planning communications and in determining actual length of transportation time. For example, if we know that Paris local

INTERNATIONAL STANDARD TIME CHART

Standard Time: Legal time for each country fixed by law and based on the theoretical division of the world's surface into 24 zones each of 15° longitude with certain deviations due to frontiers or local option.

Daylight Saving Time (DST): Modified (advanced) legal time adopted by certain countries for part of year, especially during local summer.

△ — Arizona and parts of Indiana do not observe DST.
‡ — Province of Saskatchewan and certain Canadian cities remain on Standard Time all year.
★ — Except Broken Hill, N.S.W.; follows South Australia times.
■ — Certain States of Brazil do not observe DST.
E — Estimated Date Based On Previous Year.
* — Listed are MAJOR cities for each zone.
▽ — All ports not in Croatia or Slovenia.

Country	Standard Time — Hours from GMT	Time at 1200 hrs GMT	Daylight Saving Time — Hours from GMT	Effective Period (first and last day)
Afghanistan	+4 1/2	16 30		
Albania	+1	13 00	+2	Mar. 28, 1993—Sep. 25, 1993
Algeria	+1	13 00		
American Samoa	−11	01 00		
Andorra	+1	13 00	+2	Mar. 28, 1993E—Sep. 25, 1993E
Angola	+1	13 00		
Argentina — Except provinces below	−3	09 00		
Buenos Aires, Santa Cruz, Tierra Del Fuego	−3	09 00	−2	Oct. 17, 1993E—Mar. 5, 1994E
Armenia	+4	16 00		
Aruba	−4	08 00		
Australia				
Lord Howe Is.	+10 1/2	22 30	+11	Oct. 31, 1993—Mar. 5, 1994
New South Wales, Victoria, Australian Capitol Territory (A.C.T.), HIS, HTI, LDC ★	+10	22 00	+11	Oct. 31, 1993—Mar. 5, 1994
Northern Territory	+9 1/2	21 30		
Queensland (except HIS, HTI, LDC)	+10	22 00		
South Australia and Broken Hill	+9 1/2	21 30	+10 1/2	Oct. 31, 1993—Mar. 5, 1994
Tasmania	+10	22 00	+11	Oct. 3, 1993—Mar. 26, 1994
Western Australia	+8	20 00		
Austria	+1	13 00	+2	Mar. 28, 1993—Sep. 25, 1993
Azerbaijan	+4	16 00		
Bahamas (excluding Turks and Caicos Islands)	−5	07 00	−4	Apr. 4, 1993—Oct. 30, 1993
Bahrain Island	+3	15 00		
Bangladesh	+6	18 00		
Barbados	−4	08 00		
Belarus	+2	14 00	+3	Mar. 28, 1993—Sep. 25, 1993
Belgium	+1	13 00	+2	Mar. 28, 1993—Sep. 25, 1993
Belize	−6	06 00		
Benin Peoples Rep. (Dahomey)	+1	13 00		
Bermuda	−4	08 00	−3	Apr. 4, 1993—Oct. 30, 1993
Bhutan	+6	18 00		
Bolivia	−4	08 00		
Bosnia Herzegovina	+1	13 00	+2	Mar. 28, 1993—Sep. 25, 1993
Botswana	+2	14 00		
Brazil ■ — East (Including All Coast and Brasilia)	−3	09 00	−2	Oct. 17, 1993—Feb. 20, 1994
West	−4	08 00	−3	Oct. 17, 1993—Feb. 20, 1994
Territory of Acre	−5	07 00		
Fernando De Noronha	−2	10 00		
British Virgin Islands	−4	08 00		
Brunei Darussalam	+8	20 00		
Bulgaria	+2	14 00	+3	Mar. 28, 1993—Sep. 25, 1993
Burkina Faso	GMT	12 00		
Burundi	+2	14 00		
Cambodia	+7	19 00		
Cameroon. Republic Of	+1	13 00		
Canada ‡ — Newfoundland (Island of)	−3 1/2	08 30	−2 1/2	Apr. 4, 1993—Oct. 30, 1993
Atlantic	−4	08 00	−3	Apr. 4, 1993—Oct. 30, 1993
Eastern	−5	07 00	−4	Apr. 4, 1993—Oct. 30, 1993
Central	−6	06 00	−5	Apr. 4, 1993—Oct. 30, 1993
Mountain	−7	05 00	−6	Apr. 4, 1993—Oct. 30, 1993
Pacific	−8	04 00	−7	Apr. 4, 1993—Oct. 30, 1993
Yukon Territory	−8	04 00	−7	Apr. 4, 1993—Oct. 30, 1993
Cape Verde Islands	−1	11 00		
Cayman Islands	−5	07 00		
Central African Republic	+1	13 00		
Chad	+1	13 00		
Chile				
Continental	−4	08 00	−3	Oct. 10, 1993—Mar. 12, 1994
Easter Island	−6	06 00	−5	Oct. 10, 1993—Mar. 12, 1994
China, People's Republic Of	+8	20 00		
Cocos (Keeling) Islands	+6 1/2	18 30		
Colombia	−5	07 00		
Comoros	+3	15 00		
Congo	+1	13 00		
Cook Islands	−10	02 00		
Costa Rica	−6	06 00		
Cote D'Ivoire	GMT	12 00		
Croatia	+1	13 00	+2	Mar. 28, 1993—Sep. 25, 1993
Cuba	−5	07 00	−4	Apr. 4, 1993—Oct. 9, 1993
Cyprus	+2	14 00	+3	Mar. 28, 1993—Sep. 25, 1993
Czech Republic	+1	13 00	+2	Mar. 28, 1993—Sep. 25, 1993
Denmark	+1	13 00	+2	Mar. 28, 1993—Sep. 25, 1993
Djibouti	+3	15 00		
Dominican Republic	−4	08 00		
Ecuador				
Continental	−5	07 00		
Galapagos Is.	−6	06 00		
Egypt	+2	14 00	+3	May 1, 1993—Sep. 30, 1993
El Salvador	−6	06 00		
Equatorial Guinea	+1	13 00		
Eritrea	+3	15 00		
Estonia	+2	14 00	+3	Mar. 28, 1993—Sep. 25, 1993
Ethiopia	+3	15 00		
Falkland Islands	−4	08 00	−3	Sep. 12, 1992E—Apr. 17, 1993E
Faroe Island	GMT	12 00	+1	Mar. 28, 1993—Sep. 25, 1993
Fiji	+12	23 59		
Finland	+2	14 00	+3	Mar. 28, 1993—Sep. 25, 1993
France	+1	13 00	+2	Mar. 28, 1993—Sep. 25, 1993
French Guiana	−3	09 00		
French Polynesia				
Gambier Is.	−9	03 00		
Marquesas Is.	−9 1/2	02 30		
Society Is., Tubuai Is., Tuamotu Is., Tahiti	−10	02 00		
Gabon	+1	13 00		
Gambia	GMT	12 00		
Germany	+1	13 00	+2	Mar. 28, 1993—Sep. 25, 1993
Georgia	+3	15 00	+4	Mar. 28, 1993—Sep. 25, 1993
Ghana	GMT	12 00		
Gibraltar	+1	13 00	+2	Mar. 28, 1993—Sep. 25, 1993
Greece	+2	14 00	+3	Mar. 28, 1993—Sep. 25, 1993
Greenland				
Except Scoresbysund and Thule	−3	09 00	−2	Mar. 28, 1993—Sep. 25, 1993
Scoresbysund	−1	11 00	GMT	Mar. 28, 1993—Sep. 26, 1993
Thule	−4	08 00		
Guadeloupe (incl. St. Barthelemy, Northern St. Martin)	−4	08 00		
Guam	+10	22 00		
Guatemala	−6	06 00		
Guinea	GMT	12 00		
Guinea-Bissau	GMT	12 00		
Guyana	−4	08 00		
Haiti	−5	07 00	−4	Apr. 4, 1993—Oct. 30, 1993
Honduras	−6	06 00		
Hong Kong	+8	20 00		
Hungary	+1	13 00	+2	Mar. 28, 1993—Sep. 25, 1993
Iceland	GMT	12 00		
India (incl. Andaman Is.)	+5 1/2	17 30		
Indonesia				
Central	+8	20 00		
East	+9	21 00		
West (Jakarta)	+7	19 00		
Iran (The Islamic Rep. of)	+3 1/2	15 30	+4 1/2	Mar. 21, 1993—Sep. 22, 1993
Iraq	+3	15 00	+4	Apr. 1, 1993E—Sep. 30, 1993E
Ireland, Rep. Of	GMT	12 00	+1	Mar. 28, 1993—Oct. 23, 1993
Israel	+2	14 00	+3	Apr. 2, 1993—Sep. 4, 1993
Italy	+1	13 00	+2	Mar. 28, 1993—Sep. 25, 1993
Jamaica	−5	07 00		
Japan	+9	21 00		
Johnston Is.	−10	02 00		
Jordan	+2	14 00	+3	Apr. 2, 1993—Sep. 30, 1993E
Kampuchea, Dem. (see Cambodia)				
Kazakhstan	+6	18 00	+7	Mar. 28, 1993—Sep. 25, 1993
Kenya	+3	15 00		
Kiribati, Rep. Of	+12	23 59		
Canton, Enderbury Islands	−11	01 00		
Christmas Is.	−10	02 00		
Korea, Democratic People's Rep. Of	+9	21 00		
Korea, Republic Of	+9	21 00		
Kuwait	+3	15 00		
Kyrgyzstan	+5	17 00	+6	Mar. 28, 1993—Sep. 25, 1993
Laos	+7	19 00		
Latvia	+2	14 00	+3	Mar. 28, 1993—Sep. 25, 1993
Lebanon	+2	14 00	+3	Mar. 28, 1993—Sep. 25, 1993
Leeward Islands				
Antigua, Dominica, Montserrat, St. Christopher, St. Kitts, Nevis, Anguilla	−4	08 00		
Lesotho	+2	14 00		
Liberia	GMT	12 00		
Libyan Arab Jamahiriya	+2	14 00		
Lithuania	+2	14 00	+3	Mar. 28, 1993—Sep. 25, 1993
Luxembourg	+1	13 00	+2	Mar. 28, 1993—Sep. 25, 1993
Macedonia	+1	13 00	+2	Mar. 28, 1993E—Sep. 25, 1993E
Madagascar	+3	15 00		
Malawi	+2	14 00		
Malaysia	+8	20 00		
Maldives	+5	17 00		
Mali	GMT	12 00		
Malta	+1	13 00	+2	Mar. 28, 1993—Sep. 25, 1993
Martinique	−4	08 00		
Mauritania	GMT	12 00		
Mauritius	+4	16 00		
Mexico*				
Except Baja California Norte, Baja California Sur, Nayarit, Sinaloa, Sonora	−6	06 00		
Baja California Sur and N. Pacific Coast (States of Nayarit, Sinaloa and Sonora) — Culican, La Paz, Mazatlan	−7	05 00		
Baja California Norte (Above 28th Parallel) — Mexicali, Tijuana	−8	04 00	−7	Apr. 4, 1993—Oct. 30, 1993
Midway Island	−11	01 00		
Moldova	+2	14 00	+3	Mar. 28, 1993—Sep. 25, 1993
Monaco	+1	13 00	+2	Mar. 28, 1993E—Sep. 25, 1993E
Mongolia (Ulan Bator)	+8	20 00	+9	Mar. 28, 1993—Sep. 25, 1993
Morocco	GMT	12 00		
Mozambique	+2	14 00		
Myanmar	+6 1/2	18 30		
Namibia	+2	14 00		
Nauru, Republic Of	+12	23 59		
Nepal	+5 3/4	17 45		
Netherlands	+1	13 00	+2	Mar. 28, 1993—Sep. 25, 1993
Netherlands Antilles (incl. Southern St. Maarten)	−4	08 00		
New Caledonia	+11	23 00		
New Zealand (Excluding Chatham Is.)	+12	23 59	+13	Oct. 3, 1993—Mar. 19, 1994
Chatham Is.	+12 3/4	00 45	+13 3/4	Oct. 3, 1993—Mar. 19, 1994
Nicaragua	−6	06 00	−5	Jan. 1, 1992—Unknown
Niger	+1	13 00		
Nigeria	+1	13 00		
Niue Island	−11	01 00		
Norfolk Island	+11 1/2	23 30		
Norway	+1	13 00	+2	Mar. 28, 1993—Sep. 25, 1993
Oman	+4	16 00		
Pacific Islands Trust Territory				
Caroline Is. (Excluding Ponape Is., Kusaie, and Pingelap)	+11	22 00		
Kusaie, Pingelap, Marshall Is. (Excluding Kwajalein)	+12	23 59		
Kwajalein	−12	00 01		
Mariana Island (Excluding Guam)	+10	22 00		
Palau Island	+9	21 00		
Ponape Island	+11	23 00		
Pakistan	+5	17 00		
Panama	−5	07 00		
Papua New Guinea (And Bougainville Is.)	+10	22 00		
Paraguay	−4	08 00	−3	Oct. 1, 1993—Feb. 26, 1994
Peru	−5	07 00	−4	Jan. 1, 1994E—Mar. 31, 1994E
Philippines, Republic Of	+8	20 00		
Poland	+1	13 00	+2	Mar. 28, 1993—Sep. 25, 1993

INTERNATIONAL STANDARD TIME CHART

Standard Time: Legal time for each country fixed by law and based on the theoretical division of the world's surface into 24 zones each of 15° longitude with certain deviations due to frontiers or local option.
Daylight Saving Time (DST): Modified (advanced) legal time adopted by certain countries for part of year, especially during local summer.

△ — Arizona and parts of Indiana do not observe DST.
‡ — Province of Saskatchewan and certain Canadian cities remain on Standard Time all year.
★ — Except Broken Hill, N.S.W.; follows South Australia times.
■ — Certain States of Brazil do not observe DST.
E — Estimated Date Based On Previous Year.
* — Listed are MAJOR cities for each zone.
▽ - All ports not in Croatia or Slovenia

Country	Standard Time			Daylight Saving Time
	Hours from GMT	Time at 1200 hrs GMT	Hours from GMT	Effective Period (first and last day)
Portugal				
Azores	GMT	12 00		
Madeira	GMT	12 00	+1	Mar. 28, 1993—Sep. 25, 1993
Mainland	+1	13 00	+2	Mar. 28, 1993—Sep. 25, 1993
Puerto Rico	−4	08 00		
Qatar	+3	15 00		
Reunion	+4	16 00		
Romania	+2	14 00	+3	Mar. 28, 1993—Sep. 25, 1993
Russian Federation*				
Zone 1 Moscow, St. Petersburg, Murmarsk, Astrakhan, Volrograd—(Moscow time)	+3	15 00	+4	Mar. 28, 1993—Sep. 25, 1993
Zone 2 Samara, Izhevsk	+4	16 00	+5	Mar. 28, 1993—Sep. 25, 1993
Zone 3 Chelyabinsk, Ekatrinburg, Perm, Nizhnevartovsk	+5	17 00	+6	Mar. 28, 1993—Sep. 25, 1993
Zone 4 Omsk	+6	18 00	+7	Mar. 28, 1993—Sep. 25, 1993
Zone 5 Novosibirsk, Krasnojarsk, Nonilsk	+7	19 00	+8	Mar. 28, 1993—Sep. 25, 1993
Zone 6 Irkutsk, Ulan-ude, Bratsk	+8	20 00	+9	Mar. 28, 1993—Sep. 25, 1993
Zone 7 Chita, Yakatsk	+9	21 00	+10	Mar. 28, 1993—Sep. 25, 1993
Zone 8 Khabarovsk, Vladivostok	+10	22 00	+11	Mar. 28, 1993—Sep. 25, 1993
Zone 9 Magadan	+11	23 00	+12	Mar. 28, 1993—Sep. 25, 1993
Zone 10 Petropavlovsk-Kamchatsky	+12	23 59	+13	Mar. 28, 1993—Sep. 25, 1993
Rwanda	+2	14 00		
Saint Pierre and Miquelon	−3	09 00	−2	Apr. 4, 1993—Oct. 30, 1993
Saint Vincent and the Grenadines	−4	08 00		
Samoa	−11	01 00		
San Marino	+1	13 00	+2	Mar. 28, 1993E—Sep. 25, 1993E
Sao Tome Island and Principe Is.	GMT	12 00		
Saudi Arabia	+3	15 00		
Senegal	GMT	12 00		
Seychelles	+4	16 00		
Sierra Leone	GMT	12 00		
Singapore	+8	20 00		
Slovenia	+1	13 00	+2	Mar. 28, 1993E—Sep. 25, 1993E
Slovakia	+1	13 00	+2	Mar. 28, 1993—Sep. 25, 1993
Solomon Islands (Excluding Bougainville Is.)	+11	23 00		
Somalia	+3	15 00		
South Africa	+2	14 00		
Spain				
Canary Is.	GMT	12 00	+1	Mar. 28, 1993—Sep. 25, 1993
Continental, Balearic and Mallorca Islands	+1	13 00	+2	Mar. 28, 1993—Sep. 25, 1993
Melilla	+1	13 00	+2	Mar. 28, 1993—Sep. 25, 1993
Sri Lanka	+5 1/2	17 30		
St. Helena	GMT	12 00		
Sudan	+2	14 00		
Suriname, Republic Of	−3	09 00		
Swaziland	+2	14 00		

Country	Standard Time			Daylight Saving Time
	Hours from GMT	Time at 1200 hrs GMT	Hours from GMT	Effective Period (first and last day)
Sweden	+1	13 00	+2	Mar. 28, 1993—Sep. 25, 1993
Switzerland	+1	13 00	+2	Mar. 28, 1993—Sep. 25, 1993
Syria	+2	14 00	+3	Apr. 1, 1993—Sep. 30, 1993
Taiwan	+8	20 00		
Tajikistan	+5	17 00		
Tanzania	+3	15 00		
Thailand	+7	19 00		
Togo	GMT	12 00		
Tonga	+13	01 00		
Trinidad and Tobago	−4	08 00		
Tunisia	+1	13 00		
Turkey	+2	14 00	+3	Mar. 28, 1993—Sep. 25, 1993
Turkmenistan	+5	17 00		
Turks and Caicos Is.	−5	07 00	−4	Apr. 4, 1993—Oct. 30, 1993
Tuvalu	+12	23 59		
Uganda	+3	15 00		
Ukraine	+2	14 00	+3	Mar. 28, 1993—Sep. 25, 1993
United Arab Emirates (Abu Dhabi, Dubai, Sharjah, Ras Al Khaimah)	+4	16 00		
United Kingdom	GMT	12 00	+1	Mar. 28, 1993—Oct. 23, 1993
U.S.A.—Eastern Time△	−5	07 00	−4	Apr. 4, 1993—Oct. 30, 1993
Central Time	−6	06 00	−5	Apr. 4, 1993—Oct. 30, 1993
Mountain Time△	−7	05 00	−6	Apr. 4, 1993—Oct. 30, 1993
Pacific Time	−8	04 00	−7	Apr. 4, 1993—Oct. 30, 1993
Alaska (except Aleutian Islands W. 169.30 Deg.)	−9	03 00	−8	Apr. 4, 1993—Oct. 30, 1993
Aleutian Islands 169.30 long. W. to Western tip	−10	02 00	−9	Apr. 4, 1993—Oct. 30, 1993
Arizona△	−7	05 00		
Hawaiian Islands	−10	02 00		
Indiana (East)△	−5	07 00		
U.S. Virgin Islands	−4	08 00		
Uruguay	−3	09 00	−2	Oct. 17, 1993—Mar. 5, 1994
Uzbekistan	+5	17 00		
Vanuatu	+11	23 00		
Venezuela	−4	08 00		
Vietnam, Socialist Rep. of	+7	19 00		
Wake Is.	+12	23 59		
Wallis and Futuna Is.	+12	23 59		
Windward Islands				
Grenada, St. Lucia	−4	08 00		
Yemen, Republic of	+3	15 00		
Yugoslavia (Former) ▽	+1	13 00	+2	Mar. 28, 1993—Sep. 25, 1993
Zaire				
Kinshasa Mbandaka	+1	13 00		
Kasai, Kivu, Haut-Zaire, Shaba	+2	14 00		
Zambia	+2	14 00		
Zimbabwe	+2	14 00		

time is 6 hours later than New York local time, we are aware that a phone call should be made before 11:00 AM in New York to reach an office in Paris before the close of business. Similarly, a call from Paris must be made after 3:00 PM to reach an office in New York that opens at 9:00 AM.

If a flight leaves Washington, DC at 5:30 PM and arrives in Los Angeles at 8:30 PM, we cannot determine that the actual travel time is 6 hours (rather than the 3 shown on the clock) unless we know that local time in Los Angeles is 3 hours earlier than in Washington, DC. Similarly, unless we can determine that local time in London is 5 hours later than in Washington, DC, we might think that a flight departing Washington, DC at 8:00 PM and arriving in London at 7:00 AM takes 11 hours. Subtracting the 5 hours time difference from the 11 hours shown on the clock provides flying time of 6 hours.

FIGURE 2–7. Time line for determining time differences.

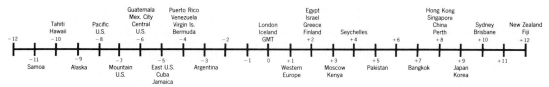

INTERNATIONAL TIME ZONES (STANDARD TIME)

World time is measured in terms of relationships to the time at the Greenwich Observatory. The time at the prime meridian is often called Greenwich or Greenwich Mean Time (GMT) or Zulu (Z) time. An International Standard Time Chart is shown on page 12. The chart lists countries, number of hours later (+) or earlier (−) than GMT, and the time in the country when it is 1200 hours GMT. Also shown is Daylight Saving Time where it exists, the number of hours + or − from GMT, and the dates during which daylight time is in effect.

A time line is a simplified way to measure time differences between world cities. A sample time line is shown in Figure 2–7. To determine the number of hours of time difference between listed locations, count the appropriate number of ticks on the line. (Please note that the time line does not provide adjustments for daylight saving time.)

Most computer reservations systems can display local time for different cities. If you have access to a system, display the local time for the specific cities and add or subtract as necessary to determine differences.

■ CLIMATE AND WEATHER

One of the most important factors affecting where people choose to travel is climate. This is especially true for pleasure travel. For example, the beaches in the northeastern United States are among the finest in the world. However, the area's climate limits their use for sunning and swimming to the summer months.

The difference between climate and weather should also be noted. Weather is the current state or condition of temperature, barometric pressure, and precipitation in an area. It can only be predicted on a short-term basis. Climate is the average state or condition over a long period of time in an area. Climate is quite predictable. For example, the climate of Hawaii makes it attractive for beach activities throughout the year. Weather (rain) on a specific day keeps sunbathers off the beach. Climate allows one to generalize. Weather prevents guarantees.

Temperature distributions depend on the radiant energy received from the sun. The amount of radiant energy depends mainly on latitude as well as on the distribution of land masses and oceans, prevailing winds and ocean currents, and topography and altitude. Four primary factors affect the climate of a location:

1. Latitude (location north or south of the equator)
2. Mountains (altitude lowers temperature and prevents weather patterns from crossing)
3. Proximity to major bodies of water
4. Prevailing wind and ocean current patterns

■ CLIMATIC ZONES

The earth is divided into five basic climatic zones, based upon latitudinal position. Figure 2–8 depicts these climatic zones.

The equator (0°) is the line of latitude that splits the world into the Northern and Southern Hemispheres. The lines of latitude at 23°27′ North Latitude and 23°27′ South Latitude are called the Tropic of Cancer and the Tropic of Capricorn, respectively. The area between these two lines is usually referred to as the tropics or the area of tropical climate, which means that there are only minimal changes in the warm temperatures that exist in this area throughout the year.

FIGURE 2–8. Climate zones.

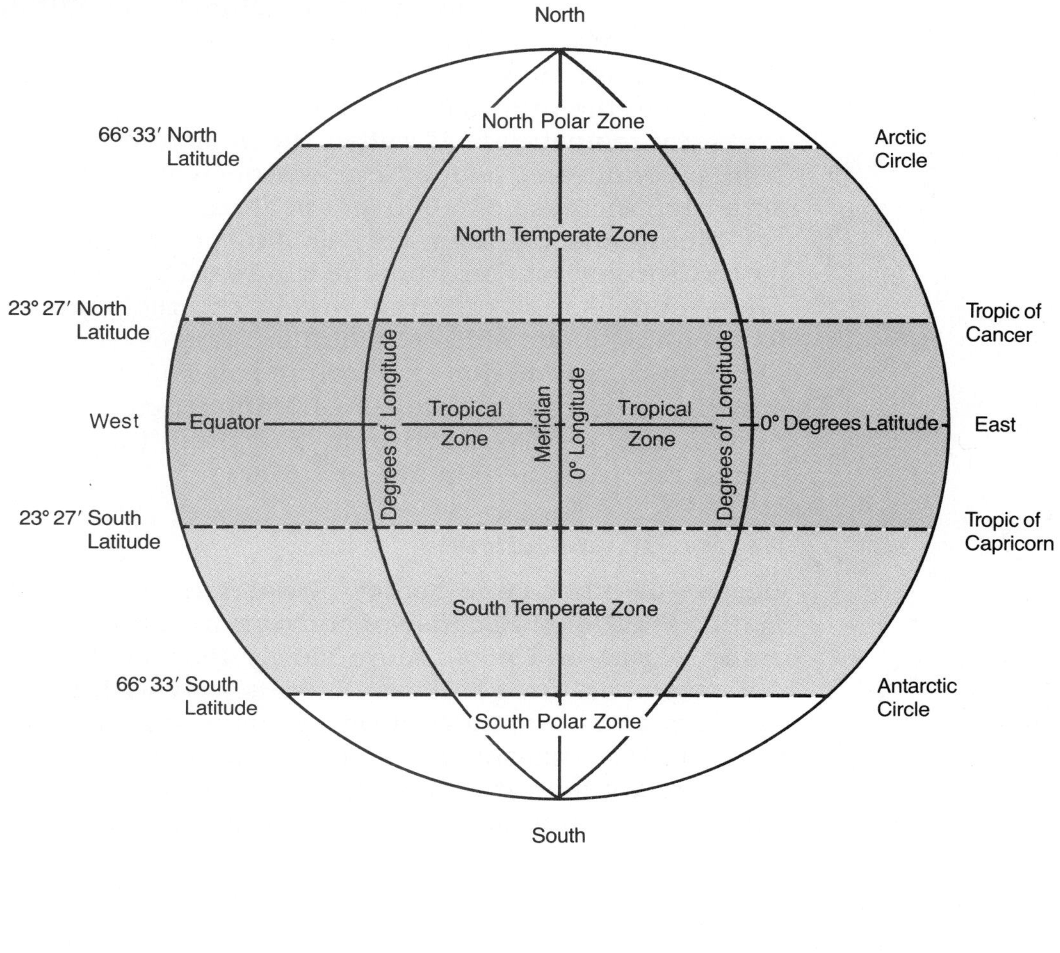

The Caribbean islands, for example, lie within the tropics. Advertisements for the United States Virgin Islands guarantee 80° weather on a year-round basis. Miami and the Bahamas, on the other hand, are located just north of the Tropic of Cancer. Their climate is considered subtropical. Although many travelers expect to find weather similar to the Caribbean Islands in Miami, for example, winter days are often cool, and a very occasional snow flurry has been seen in January or February.

The lines of latitude at 66°33′ North Latitude and 66°33′ South Latitude are called the Arctic Circle and the Antarctic Circle, respectively. The area between the Arctic Circle and the Tropic of Cancer is the North Temperate Zone; the area between the Antarctic Circle and the Tropic of Capricorn is the South Temperate Zone. Locations within the temperate zones are characterized by changes in temperature through the four seasons. Generally, the farther north of the Tropic of Cancer and the farther south of the Tropic of Capricorn, the colder the climate.

The areas between the North and the South Poles and the Arctic and Antarctic Circles, respectively, are called the North Polar and the South Polar Zones. Polar climate is normally below freezing at all times.

Altitude and Climate

Altitude has a cooling effect on climatic conditions. The higher the location, the cooler the climate. For example, there is often winter snow in the mountains near Los Angeles, California, but the valleys below rarely see a flake. The rate of decrease of temperature is called the adiabatic rate: assuming similar conditions, temperature will decrease by three degrees with each increase of 1,000 feet of altitude.

Mountains, by their very height, prevent many weather patterns from crossing from the windward to the leeward side. Thus, considerably different levels of precipitation can be found on opposite sides of mountain ranges. A classic example of this phenomenon exists on the big island of Hawaii. Hilo and the northeastern slopes of Mauna Kea get substantial rainfall and are green and lush. Kona and the southwestern slopes receive little rain and are arid.

Water, Air, and Climate

Oceans or other large bodies of water tend to moderate climatic conditions. Because of convection currents, water generally warms and cools more slowly than land. As a result, ocean temperatures will drop more slowly with the approach of winter and warm more slowly with the approach of summer than will land masses. Thus, it is cooler at the beach on a hot summer day than it is inland. It is also usually warmer near the shore on a winter day than farther inland. Coastal areas generally have more moderate climates than interior areas at similar latitudes.

Minneapolis, for example, is located on a latitude actually south of Seattle. Yet, Minneapolis has warmer summers and colder winters than Seattle. Minneapolis is landlocked in the center (east to west) of the United States. Seattle is on the west coast, bounded by Puget Sound and not far from the Pacific Ocean; these bodies of water moderate temperatures.

Prevailing wind patterns are different in the Northern and Southern Hemispheres. North of the equator, winds (and weather patterns) tend to move from west to east. The weather in Chicago today can often portend conditions in New York tomorrow. In the Southern Hemisphere, winds generally move from east to west. Toward the poles, the winds move west to east.

Air and water currents affect climatic conditions. For example, the jet stream (air currents) brings cold, arctic air down from Canada into the central United States and the Gulf Stream (water currents) brings warm water from the Gulf of Mexico northward and eastward across the Atlantic. Thus, Bermuda is warm in winter (springlike temperatures prevail) while North Carolina, directly west, has freezing temperatures. Similarly, Reykjavik, Iceland is considerably warmer in winter than locations in Greenland and Canada on the same line of latitude.

Seasons

The relative positions of the sun and the earth throughout the year determine the seasons. Twice each year, on approximately March 21 and September 21, the sun is directly overhead at noon on the equator. On these equinox dates, virtually all points on the earth receive 12 hours of sunlight. Day and night are equal in length throughout the world.

Twice each year, on approximately June 21 and December 21, the in length between night and day reaches its maximum amount difference. At noon on these solstice dates, the sun is at its most northerly or southerly position, providing the longest day of the year in the Northern Hemisphere in June and the shortest in December. In the Southern Hemisphere the opposite is true.

Seasons are opposite in the Northern and Southern Hemispheres. The chart below shows the approximate date on which each season begins:

Date	Northern Hemisphere	Southern Hemisphere
March 21	Spring	Autumn
June 21	Summer	Winter
September 21	Autumn	Spring
December 21	Winter	Summer

Climates of the World

Geographers have adopted the Koppen Classification System, named after its originator, to identify climates according to temperature and precipitation values. Koppen classification includes five basic climatic types.

1. **Tropical Rain Forest Climates**, in which average monthly temperature is above 18°C (64.4°F) throughout the year. There is no real winter. Rainfall is high and precipitation exceeds evaporation, producing lush vegetation.

2. **Dry Climates**, where evaporation exceeds precipitation. Dry climates include the steppe climate, a semiarid environment with less than 30 inches of precipitation in tropical latitudes and less than 15 inches in midlatitudes, and the desert climate, an arid environment with less than 10 inches of annual precipitation.

3. **Warm Midlatitude Forest Climates**, which have pronounced changes of seasons. The temperature in the coldest month is between 18°C (64.4°F) and freezing (0°C or 32°F).

4. **Snow Climates**, which have average temperatures during the coldest month below freezing (0°C or 32°F) and during the warmest month average 10°C (50°F).

5. **Ice Climates**, which have no true summer. With average temperatures during the warmest month below 10°C (50°F), trees do not grow in these areas. Included in the ice climates are the tundra climate, with the warmest month between 10°C (50°F) and freezing, and the perpetual frost climate, with no month having an average temperature above freezing.

Western Hemisphere Climatic Conditions. Nearly all of North America falls within middle (temperate) and northern latitudes. The northwestern United States has mild summer temperatures as contrasted with the interior. Its winter is mild in coastal areas as contrasted with more severe conditions in the Great Lakes areas.

Tropical climates are found in the West Indies (Caribbean) as well as southern Mexico, Central America, and much of northern South America. Southern-moving Brazilian currents from tropical waters exert a warming effect on the Atlantic shores of South America.

Eastern Hemisphere Climatic Conditions. Within Europe there are only gradual changes from west to east because there is no major north to south mountain range. Precipitation is heaviest on the west coast. The Mediterranean countries are characterized by dry summers.

Because of its vast land area, Asia has a variety of conditions. India has its monsoon season because of barometric pressure distributions and its proximity to the ocean. The heavy rainfall cannot, however, penetrate very far beyond the Himalayan mountains into China.

Much of central Africa is tropical rain forest. Except for the northwest, where the Atlas Mountains set up a barrier and produce rainfall from the trade winds, desert conditions prevail from the Atlantic Ocean to the Red Sea and from the Mediterranean southward to the latitudes of southern Arabia. South of the Sahara, rainfall increases.

Australia has freezing temperatures only at high elevations in the south. Its interior is arid and is characterized by high summer temperatures. Heavy summer rains occur in the south of Australia.

Specific conditions that affect travel will be discussed more fully in the chapters covering the regions of the world.

■ REVIEW—THE PHYSICAL WORLD

1. Give three examples of ways landforms or water provide attractions for the traveler and affect tourism in an area.

2. Why can't east to west distances between two points be determined by knowing their respective longitudes?

3. For each date and time in the city in column A, determine the date and time in city B:

City A	City B
a. New York, 1:00 PM, July 16	Rome _____
b. Chicago, 8:00 PM, December 4	Bangkok _____
c. Sydney, 7:00 AM, January 3	London _____
d. Washington, DC, noon, February 4	Honolulu _____

4. Distinguish between climate and weather.

5. Identify three factors that influence the climate of a region and describe their effects.

6. Describe the major climatic characteristics of the Tropical, Temperate, and Polar Zones.

3

Why People Travel

Understanding tourism geography is a twofold process. It is not enough to understand only the geography of various areas of the world. A travel professional must also understand the motivations of travelers; that is, why they choose to go where they go. Knowing why people travel gives the professional the insights into what a specific destination offers a specific traveler.

It is this interaction of traveler and destination that distinguishes tourism geography from other forms of geography. Knowledge of the psychological and sociological factors affecting the traveler helps develop a sense of the types of travel that exist. With this background, we can then analyze geographic areas in terms of what these areas offer the traveler.

The human need for travel has persisted throughout history. However, until recent times, most people traveled out of necessity rather than for pleasure. In early times, travel was both difficult and dangerous. It is no coincidence that the root word for both travel and travail (heavy labor) is the same. Travel was hard. Today it is pleasurable (or at least it is supposed to be) and looked forward to by most people.

Travel destinations are in the business of marketing or selling themselves to prospective travelers. It is impossible to market or sell a product or service without some understanding of the psychology of the prospective purchaser. What motivates a particular traveler to go to a particular place? What motivates a traveler to avoid a particular place? Most of the balance of this chapter will focus on what motivates travelers—the forces that cause people to take specific actions.

People from every income and educational level engage in travel. Differences occur in the type of travel they choose. Those in lower income and education brackets tend to travel more by automobile and stay with friends and relatives. Low air fares have resulted in a great increase in flying and a great decrease in intercity bus travel by persons of lower income. As we go up the income and educational ladder, the use of air transportation increases, as does the tendency to use hotels for lodging. International travelers are primarily upscale in terms of education and income.

For many people, travel has been and continues to be one of the symbols of the good life. Travel professionals must understand what people are looking for when they plan to visit different destinations. In addition, the communities within travel destinations must understand travelers if they are to meet their needs. Several theories have been developed that are useful for determining consumer (traveler) motivation.

■ NEED SATISFACTION THEORY

All consumer purchases, including choice of travel destination, are made to satisfy some need of the consumer. An individual has a desire for something. Depending on circumstances, the desire may grow to an actual need. For example, people do not buy bicycles just to buy bicycles unless they are bicycle collectors. Perhaps they buy bicycles for transportation because they are too young or cannot afford to drive cars. Perhaps they desire exercise or recreation. Perhaps a neighbor just bought one and the purchaser wants to keep up with the Joneses. If the desire becomes strong enough, it becomes a need and is satisfied by the actual purchase. Notice that in all cases, the bicycle was the means to satisfy different needs.

The same is true of travel. People do not travel just to travel. Travel fills some need in each consumer. Travelers' needs differ just as bicycle buyers' needs differ. Some of the most popular reasons given by people for why they travel are:

■ to visit friends and relatives
■ to conduct business

■ to see new places and learn new things

■ to learn how other people live, work, and play

■ to see how their ancestors lived

■ to do things they can't do at home (skiing, for example)

■ to rest and relax

■ to improve their health

The list can go on and on, for there is an almost infinite number of specific reasons why people travel. For organization and continuity, it is necessary to group travel motivations more compactly. We believe it is essential that the travel professional fully understand three major categories of travel activities:

1. business travel
2. rest and relaxation (R and R) travel
3. cultural travel

Virtually every reason for travel can be grouped within one of these major categories.

The traveler's state of mind differs greatly for each travel category. In addition, the resources of the travel destination also differ greatly for each travel category. Yet, there is great commonality of traveler needs and destination resources within each category, no matter which region of the world is visited.

It is important that travel professionals look at tourism geography as more than names, places, and activities segmented by political and physical borders. Many destinations throughout the world are far more similar than they are different.

By understanding the similarities of resources in different parts of the world, it is possible to take a global approach to meeting travelers' needs. Thus, skiers who go to Vail, Colorado or Innsbruck, Austria in February and March can also go to Portillo, Chile or Mount Cook, New Zealand in July and August. Students of Moslem culture should visit not only the Arab Mideast, but also consider India, Pakistan, Indonesia, and Malaysia.

A brief look at the similarities of needs and resources within the business, R and R, and cultural travel categories will provide an overview of these concepts.

■ THE PSYCHOLOGY AND GEOGRAPHY OF BUSINESS TRAVEL

Business travel is nondiscretionary in nature. Business travelers take their trips, not because they want to, but because they have to. Although some business travelers enjoy traveling, many do not, and even those who enjoy many trips do not enjoy all trips or the frequency of their travels. As a result, they prefer the fastest flights with the fewest stops or connections consistent with their company's travel policies.

Business travelers often seek frequency and convenience more than price. They are more likely than leisure travelers to fly in the first class or business class sections of an airplane, especially on long trips. However, do not assume that the business traveler is not looking for low fares. Many business firms operate on tight budgets and have strict policies determining who can fly on business or first class and on which trips, or for which employees classes higher than economy fares are authorized.

Most of the world's business centers have excellent transportation and accommodation facilities. Actually, the growth of a business center and its travel facilities are symbiotic in nature. As either grows, it attracts the development of the other.

For example, the growth of the Dallas-Fort Worth area as a business center helped with the decision to build the Dallas-Fort Worth International Airport complex. The existence of the new airport has, in turn, attracted new business. The natural harbor of Hong Kong plus its central Asian location attracted businesses dependent on international shipping. These, in turn, attracted banking and other industries as well as further harbor development.

Every industry has its own "geography." For example, the geography of the oil industry includes Texas, Ohio, Pennsylvania, and California as well as the Middle East, Mexico, and Venezuela. The diamond industry includes mines primarily in South Africa and processing and sales centers in Antwerp, Amsterdam, Israel, and New York City.

Information on major business activities will be included as we discuss each region. Travel professionals working with specific corporate accounts should learn the specific business geography of those accounts.

■ THE PSYCHOLOGY AND GEOGRAPHY OF REST AND RELAXATION TRAVEL

Rest and relaxation (R & R). . . . The very thought of R & R elicits a variety of images. To some, the first thought is of lying on a white sand beach on a tranquil island; to others it is watching a sporting event; to still others it is participating in sports or recreational activities. The determination of what R & R is depends on an individual's personality and mind-set.

Travelers, like all people, have differing personalities. Some are leaders and some are followers. Allocentric personality types are the leaders and psychocentric personality types are the followers. See Figure 3–1.

The allocentric person is a trendsetter—the first person in a community to go to a new destination. The psychocentric person doesn't go anywhere until they are sure of what the destination has to offer. The psychocentric waits for friends to go and then follows the fashion. It is necessary to judge the traveler's position on the personality scale to recommend the proper travel experience. Most people, of course, fall somewhere in the middle.

Each season, different destinations rise and fall in popularity. When selling travel to an allocentric person, the travel professional would recommend the new and exciting destination. On the other hand, when working with a psychocentric client, it is necessary to go with a known travel product. The psychocentric does not want to experiment and is more comfortable with the tried and true.

The main principle of the geography of rest and relaxation travel is this: similar activities that meet travelers' needs can usually be found in a number of different places throughout the world. One must concentrate on specific activities and the geographic requirements for such activities. With an understanding of the geographic requirements for an activity, it should be possible to identify similar locations throughout the world where the activity can or could be supported.

For example, skiing requires mountains, temperatures below freezing for extended periods, and snow. We first think of the Rockies and the Alps as places for skiing. However, there are many other possibilities as well. When it is too warm in the Northern Hemisphere, it is possible to ski in the Southern Hemisphere. June to September skiing is available in Chile and New Zealand.

It is important for travelers to be aware of such geographic conditions as weather patterns, since a rainy or stormy season could ruin chances for a successful vacation experience.

FIGURE 3–1. Allocentric and psychocentric personality types.

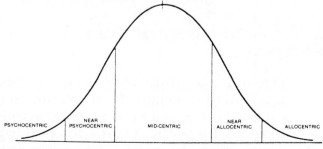

From an article originally published in the February, 1974 issue of *The Cornell Hotel and Restaurant Administration Quarterly*. Reprinted here with the permission of the Cornell University School of Hotel Administration. © 1974.

■ THE PSYCHOLOGY AND GEOGRAPHY OF CULTURAL TRAVEL

An interest in the similarities and differences among peoples throughout the world makes culture a primary motivation for some travelers. Many persons travel to return to their roots. Others travel to see how people with different heritages live, work, and play.

Our nation is populated by people whose cultural background, with the exception of the American Indians, can be easily traced to another continent. The vast majority of white Americans are descended from immigrants from Europe. This fact, coupled with the natural desire to see where earlier generations lived, makes Europe the major overseas destination for United States travelers.

Similarly, black, Hispanic, Asian, and other groups within our population usually will visit first those areas of common heritage before venturing into the unknown. Specialized, "ethnic" markets are an important part of the travel industry.

The comparison of one's own cultural background with that of others is a normal part of human behavior. It is natural to make both factual and judgmental comparisons. The opportunity to make these comparisons by seeing how others live, work, and play gives great impetus to international travel.

Typical travelers begin their culturally oriented touring by visiting either the country of their family's origin or the United Kingdom. The United Kingdom visit precedes other European countries because, while English culture is somewhat different from American, it is close and there is no real language barrier.

France, Italy, and other parts of Europe are most often next on the list. The cultural renaissance of the 15th through 18th centuries with emphasis on art and literature is well-known to Americans. The museums of Paris, Rome, Florence, and Amsterdam attract many visitors from the United States.

Having been fully bitten by the cultural travel bug, our travelers now become more adventurous and seek to broaden their knowledge even farther. The Moslem world of the Middle East and North Africa may beckon next. India, Asia, South America, the Orient and South Pacific, and sub-Saharan Africa will follow as travelers gain personal insight into the populated world.

Recent years have seen impressive growth in international travel by high school and college students. In addition to large numbers of young individuals traveling alone, group travel by language and other culturally oriented travel clubs, school orchestras and glee clubs, and sports teams has become very popular. Indeed, the opportunity for international travel has led many students to participate in these activities.

An in-depth view of the cultural aspects of each region of the world will be found in the chapters which follow. Knowledge of the world's cultures helps travel professionals become even more effective in guiding clients.

■ REVIEW—WHY PEOPLE TRAVEL

1. Identify five major reasons why people travel. For each reason, give an example of a destination travelers might choose and explain how the destination meets the travelers' needs.

2. Describe the primary needs and desires of the business traveler.

3. Describe three types of R & R destinations.

4. How has travel changed since early times?

5. How might differences in income or education levels affect travel desires?

6. Discuss the differences between allocentric and psychocentric travelers. What destinations or types of travel might appeal to each extreme?

7. Discuss some of the places you might visit to trace your own roots.

4

North America—Eastern United States

North America, as defined here, is the large continent occupied by the United States and Canada, sometimes called Anglo-America, as opposed to Latin America. Some classifications also include Mexico, Central America, and the Caribbean area, but these areas are discussed separately in this book. Canada and the United States both were once British colonies and in their early growth had expanding east-to-west frontiers.

Although they have followed different national courses since then, both nations have become highly urban, economically advanced, part of the so-called "developed world," and politically stable. Both have benefited from rich supplies of energy, food, and raw materials, and both have had to cope with the problems of long distances and physical obstacles in integrating and developing their large territories. The United States' physical environment is much more permissive and supports the world's fourth largest national population, in contrast to the more hostile, lightly occupied northern areas of Canadian territory. Almost all of Canada's major cities are within 100 miles of the United States border.

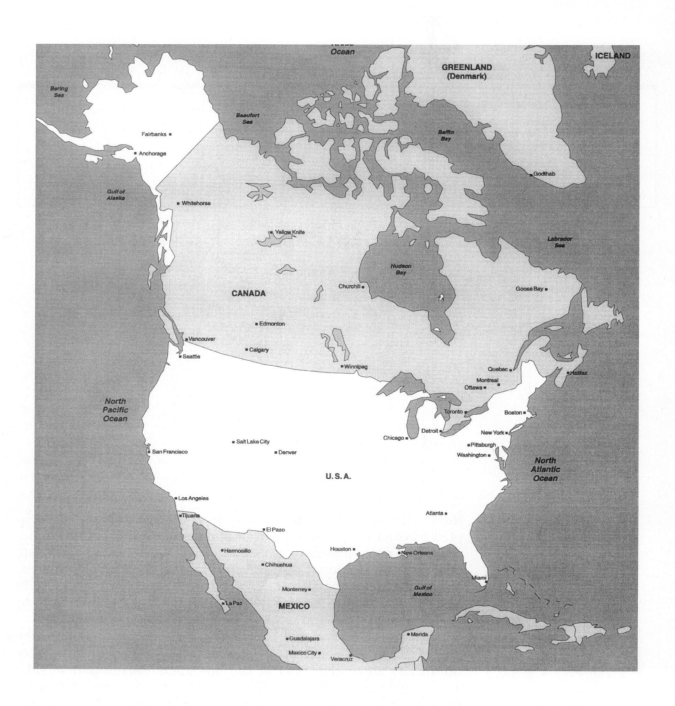

UNITED STATES

Official Name: United States
of America
Language: English
Area: 3,618,770 square miles
Time Zone: GMT −5 through
−8 (except Alaska −9 (−10

for Aleutian Islands) and
Hawaii −10)
National Airline: Many
Capital: Washington, DC
Currency: US dollar (USD)
Population: 248,709,873

The Land

The United States mainland, roughly rectangular in form, extends 2,600 miles east-west between Canada to the north and Mexico and the Gulf of Mexico to the south. The widest north-south extent, 1,600 miles, is along the Atlantic coast between New England, which juts to the northeast, and the Florida Peninsula, which juts to the south. There are two major unattached portions: the state of Alaska, which lies far to the northwest off the Canadian coast, and the state of Hawaii, in the Pacific Ocean west of the mainland.

The territory of the United States is marked by a diversity of landforms and climate over broad areas. The eastern United States is topographically shaped around the Appalachian Mountain system, which extends from the northeast to deep into the southeast. East and south of the mountains is a broad apron of coastal plains and interior hills, or Piedmont.

The central United States is dominated by a vast interior lowland that rises gradually to the west in the Great Plains. This region is drained by the south-flowing Mississippi River system, including the two largest of its many tributaries, the Ohio River from the east and the Missouri River from the west.

The world's largest network of lakes is located on the northern border with Canada. Known as the Great Lakes—Lake Superior, Lake Huron, Lake Michigan, Lake Erie, and Lake Ontario—their waters flow eastward to the Atlantic Ocean via the St. Lawrence River. On the south, the long Rio Grande River forms part of the boundary with Mexico.

Climatically, the United States has hot summers and cold, snowy winters in the north that become milder to the south. The eastern half is humid; the interior, from the Great Plains westward, is dry, with desert conditions in the western portion, and the Pacific coast receives Pacific Ocean moisture.

The People

American society is decidedly pluralistic, formed of people who come from remarkably diverse ethnic backgrounds and who practice many different religions. In number, the population is heaviest in the humid eastern half of the nation. There, the main clusters are found in the northeast, especially along the Atlantic coast and the southern margins of the Great Lakes. There are many lightly populated and unpopulated areas in the dry western interior.

Americans are highly mobile. Their lifestyle is shaped around the privately owned automobile, and a high standard of living provides opportunity for travel and recreation. They are mobile, too, often changing their places of residence for economic, retirement, or other reasons. Consequently, United States population geography undergoes constant modification. During the past decades, for instance, there have been large shifts of people from the northeastern one-quarter ("snow belt") to the south and west ("sun belt") and is the world's leading exporting nation.

The Economy

Americans are predominantly an urban people. Few are farmers, although agriculture has great regional importance. Large and small cities, with the full range of urban facilities and amenities, are found in all regions. The United States is a world economic power, a leader in the output of manufactured goods and foodstuffs. It is also the world's greatest market for goods and raw materials from other nations and is the world's leading exporting nation.

■ REGIONAL CLASSIFICATIONS

There are many different ways to classify the 50 American states into component regions. The underlying problem is that many states incorporate parts of two or more regions and hence are transitional in character. The regional classifications used here are those used by the United States Travel and Tourism Administration, the Department of Commerce administration responsible for promoting travel to the United States from foreign countries.

The Eastern United States

The eastern United States is the more densely populated half of the nation. Because the United States was settled and developed from east to west, the eastern states have older cities and towns and are generally more historic. The United States Travel and Tourism Administration divides the eastern United States into six regions: New England, Eastern Gateway, Historic Washington Country, Southeast Sun Country, Southland USA, and the Great Lakes Region.

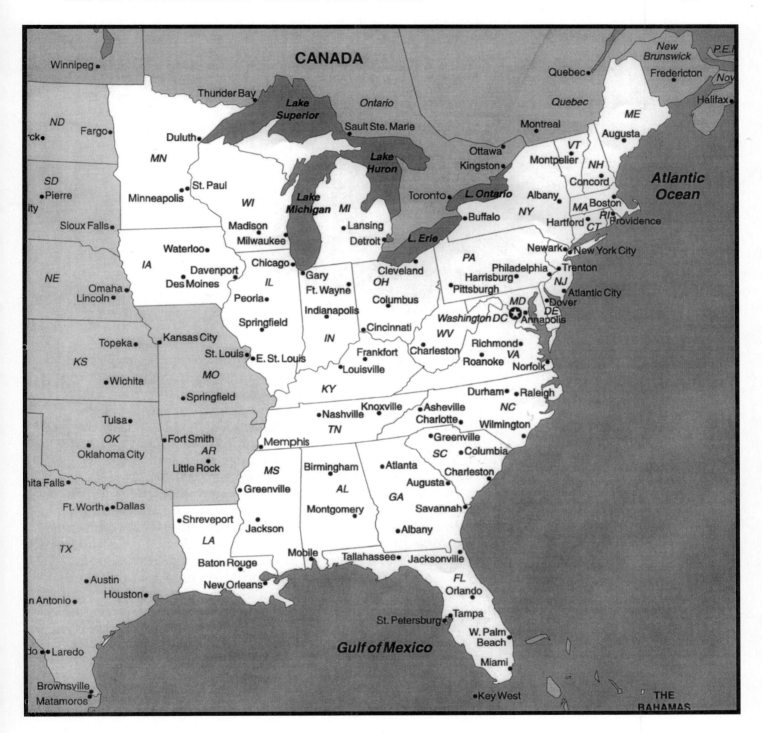

■ NEW ENGLAND—AN OVERVIEW

New England, located in the northeastern United States, consists of Maine, New Hampshire, Vermont, Massachusetts, Rhode Island, and Connecticut. Important in the colonial and early independence periods, New England's towns and cities

abound in reminders of their illustrious past. Boston is the largest city and the regional economic hub. Maine and the mountainous northern halves of Vermont and New Hampshire are more rural and lightly populated. Southern Maine is served by Portland and southern New Hampshire by Manchester.

In southern New England, much of Connecticut falls within commuter radius and the long economic shadow of New York City. However, the interior Connecticut River Valley which runs southward between New Hampshire and Vermont and through central Massachusetts and Connecticut, has many flourishing cities. Included are Springfield, Massachusetts, and Hartford and New Haven, Connecticut. Little Rhode Island is the smallest state but has a major city, Providence.

New England has a national reputation for educational excellence. It has some of America's oldest and most distinguished preparatory schools and colleges. In addition, it has good recreational facilities in its mountains and along the coast in areas such as Cape Cod and on such offshore islands as Nantucket and Martha's Vineyard.

The southern, more urban and prosperous, two-thirds of New England must be viewed in two other broad regional contexts. First, along with the Middle Atlantic states to the south and the Midwest states to the west, it is part of the American core region, or the industrial heartland where so much of the productive capacity of the nation grew and remains concentrated. Second, from Boston southward to Washington, DC, it is part of the most heavily urbanized area in the United States, a massive strip of cities whose suburbs blend together.

MAINE

Area: 33,215 square miles
Capital: Augusta
Population: 1,227,928

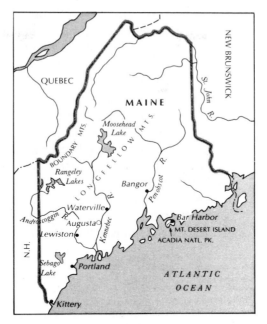

Maine, the northernmost and largest state in New England, has Canada as its neighbor on the north, New Hampshire on the west, Massachusetts on the south, and the mighty Atlantic Ocean all along the craggy east coast. The shoreline is long and heavily indented. Maine's winters are cold. Summers are temperate, attracting visitors from warmer areas who want to get away from the heat. The terrain is a mixture of mountains, valleys, and seashore. Much of the state is heavily forested. The population and main towns and cities are in the southern fringe of Maine.

Areas of Touristic Importance. Nature's moods fascinate visitors to Maine. The intensity of ocean waves pounding against rocky cliffs contrasts with the solitude and stillness deep in the North Woods. Explore the Maine coast by land or sea. Ocean swimming is best along the southern coast below Portland. Maine's famed North Woods region is sprinkled with lakes, ponds, and rushing streams. Canoe adventures are available along the Allagash Wilderness Waterway. White-water rafting along the Kennebec and Penobscot Rivers, hiking along the renowned Appalachian Trail, and fishing in the many lakes and streams and the Atlantic surf are quite popular in summer.

Bangor is the gateway to the North Woods. Once a brawling lumber and seafaring center, today, despite its small population of 33,000, it is the commercial and financial center for northern and central Maine. The Rangeley Lakes area, Baxter State Park, and Sebago Lake are popular attractions in the area.

Portland, Maine's largest city, lies at the head of the beautiful Casco Bay. Its Old Fort section and waterfront feature boutiques and restaurants. Wadsworth-Longfellow House was the childhood home of the poet, Henry Wadsworth Longfellow.

Bar Harbor is at the entrance to Acadia National Park. Sea, mountain, lake, and forest scenery make this region a famous summer resort. Acadia National Park on the Atlantic Ocean offers an unusual combination of ocean and mountain scenery, which is some of the most beautiful in the country. Acadia features a 20-mile scenic drive along the Park Loop Road.

Maine boasts numerous summer resort areas such as Kennebunkport and Bath (the home of the Maine Maritime Museum). For winter tourists, Sugarloaf is a popular ski resort.

NEW HAMPSHIRE

Area: 9,304 square miles
Capital: Concord
Population: 1,109,252

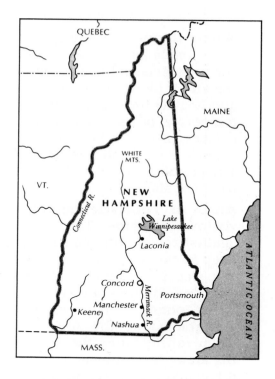

New Hampshire is bordered by Vermont on the west, Massachusetts on the south, Canada on the north, and Maine on the east along with a short length of Atlantic Ocean coast. The White Mountains run from north to south in the western part of the state. The state is heavily forested. Most population and cities are in the south.

Areas of Touristic Importance. New England's mountain ranges exhibit their majestic beauty in the granite peaks of northern New Hampshire. Towering above the state is Mount Washington in the Presidential Range of the White Mountains. A narrow-gauge cog railway takes visitors to the top for a panoramic view that includes part of Canada. Nearby is Franconia Notch, which pierces the mountains in a dramatic 8-mile gorge. An aerial tramway whisks visitors to the top of Cannon Mountain, a popular ski area, in 5 minutes. Fall foliage is spectacular throughout New Hampshire's mountains.

From lofty Mount Washington to the ocean beaches near Hampton, the scenery of this small state changes considerably. The central part of New Hampshire features idyllic lakes. The popular resort town of Laconia is squeezed between two beautiful lakes—Winnipesaukee and Winnisquam. New Hampshire provides abundant recreational activities including fishing, camping, hiking, boating, and skiing.

VERMONT

Area: 9,609 square miles
Capital: Montpelier
Population: 562,758

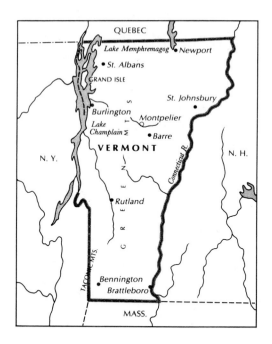

Vermont lies inland to the west of New Hampshire and is bordered by Canada on the north, New York on the west, and Massachusetts on the south. Lake Champlain forms the northern one-half of the western boundary. The Green Mountains run north and south, overlooking lovely valleys and quiet, crystal clear lakes and streams. Summer is temperate and winter cold.

Areas of Touristic Importance. No state is more park-like throughout its area than Vermont. The Green Mountains overlook picture-postcard villages and placid valley farms. Winter snow attracts world class skiers, both alpine and cross-country, to its many quality resorts including Stowe, Sugarbush, Killington, Mount Snow, Smuggler's Notch, and Boylton Valley. Vermont is maple sugar country; the sap is tapped in March and April. Camping, hiking, and fishing are popular spring through fall, with exquisite multicolor foliage from September to mid-October.

Burlington, Vermont's largest city, commands magnificent views of Lake Champlain, which is shared by New York, Canada, and Vermont. The lake is 12 miles wide and 119 miles long. Ferry service connects Vermont and New York and provides excellent views of mountains in both states. Vermont is the only New England state without a seacoast, but its Lake Champlain shore makes up for this.

Rutland is the home of Norman Rockwell Museum and the Marble Exhibition.

MASSACHUSETTS

Area: 8,257 square miles

Capital: Boston

Population: 6,016,425

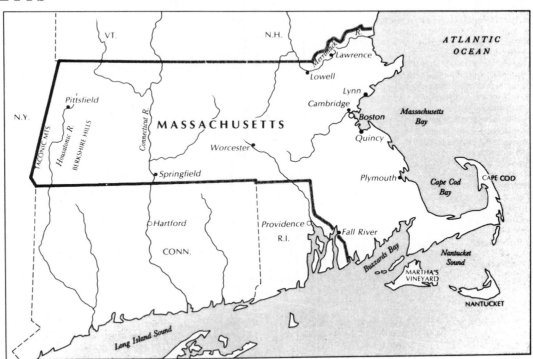

Massachusetts lies between New Hampshire and Vermont on the north, New York on the west, and Connecticut and Rhode Island on the south. The Berkshire Hills, a section of the Appalachian Mountains, cut across western Massachusetts, while the eastern two-thirds of the state gradually rolls eastward to the sea. The two regions are divided by the north-south Connecticut River, forming the Pioneer Valley. Cape Cod, the state's most prominent coastline feature, extends like a flexed arm into the Atlantic. Nantucket Island, Martha's Vineyard, and the Elizabeth Islands are south of the Cape. Summer temperatures attract thousands to the shore. Winter temperatures are ideal for skiing, sledding, and ice skating. Most of the population and cities are in the eastern part of the state. Boston is New England's largest city.

Areas of Touristic Importance. The contrast of preservation and progress characterizes the state capital, Boston. Modern skyscrapers tower above the spires and cupolas of historic structures. The Freedom Trail is a 2-mile walk through the city's most important historic points of interest, including the Boston Common, the Old North Church from which the invasion of the British was signaled to Paul Revere, and "Old Ironsides," the USS *Constitution*. The Bunker Hill Monument on Breed's Hill is a reminder of the first battle of the American revolution.

Boston and the towns surrounding it are homes to some of the finest preparatory schools, colleges and universities in the United States, including Harvard, Wellesley, and the Massachusetts Institute of Technology (MIT). The John F. Kennedy Library, designed by I. M. Pei, is considered one of the most striking examples of modern architecture in America.

Boston's shopping and entertainment facilities are among the best in New England. Faneuil Hall and the Quincy Market, in 150-year-old buildings, contain many restaurants and boutiques. There are also several major department stores, including Filene's, noted for its bargain basement. The Boston Symphony and Boston Pops are world famous. Boston also has teams in almost all professional sports.

Outdoor recreation is plentiful in Massachusetts. The sand dunes and beaches of Cape Cod National Seashore Park attract beach buggy enthusiasts and swimmers. Ocean swimming, sailing, and beach fun are favorite summer pastimes on the Cape as well as on the islands of Martha's Vineyard and Nantucket to the south. Plymouth Rock, the site of the landing of the first Pilgrim settlers in 1620, is on the Cape.

Fishing and camping are popular in the Pioneer Valley and in the Berkshires. Old Sturbridge Village, in the rolling Berkshire Hills, is an outdoor, living museum with buildings and costumed guides showing New England life in the early

1800s. The Witch Museum is found in Salem, site of the historic witch trials in the late 1600s.

RHODE ISLAND

Area: 1,214 square miles
Capital: Providence
Population: 1,003,464

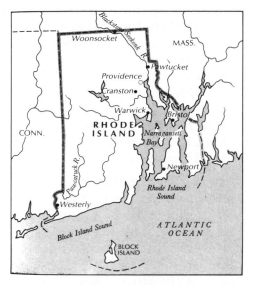

Rhode Island, the smallest of the 50 states, is 48 miles long and 37 miles wide, but within its borders are hundreds of miles of coastline and many beautiful parks. It is in the heart of the northeast industrial corridor, and is bordered by Connecticut on the west, Massachusetts on the north and east, and Rhode Island Sound on the south. Deep-cut Narragansett Bay occupies its southeastern portion.

Belcourt Castle, Newport, Rhode Island
Photo: Courtesy Rhode Island Department of Economic Development

CHAPTER 4 / NORTH AMERICA—EASTERN UNITED STATES

Areas of Touristic Importance. Providence and Newport are two of New England's most interesting cities. Arts and cultural attractions abound. The historic east side of Providence contains many buildings preserved from pre-Revolutionary times. The architectural heritage of the state mirrors the development of the nation. Colonial homes, mansions, and churches, with styles ranging from clapboard to Gothic revival, show its historic development. Slater Mill in nearby Pawtucket was built in 1793 and ushered the Industrial Revolution into the United States.

Newport overlooks the sea from lofty cliffs. Its Ocean Drive, a 10-mile stretch along the oceanfront, offers incomparable vistas of the ocean and views of many of Newport's fabled mansions. Newport's summer music and jazz festivals are world renowned. Newport is a mecca for yachting and sailing, and has hosted many America's Cup races. Newport is also the home of the Naval War College Museum and the International Tennis Hall of Fame, as well as Touro Synagogue, the first synagogue in the United States.

CONNECTICUT

Area: 5,009 square miles
Capital: Hartford
Population: 3,287,116

Connecticut is a state of two faces. Approach it from neighboring New York and pass through a series of "bedroom communities" where New York executives live among golf courses and yacht clubs, close to corporate headquarters. Come from Rhode Island and see its New England face with farms, lakes, forests, steeples, and quiet colonial village greens. The state is bordered by Massachusetts on the north, Rhode Island on the east, New York on the west, and Long Island Sound on the south. The Connecticut River, New England's longest, bisects the state from north to south, passing through the beautiful village of Old Saybrook as it nears Long Island Sound.

Areas of Touristic Importance. Hartford, the state's largest city and capital, has an impressive downtown complex with stylish shops, fine restaurants, and a modern Civic Center. It is the "capital" of the insurance industry, serving as headquarters for many national companies. Hartford was also the home of Samuel Clemens (Mark Twain), Harriet Beecher Stowe, and Noah Webster.

New Haven attracts visitors to highly regarded Yale University and the Peabody Museum of Natural History. Mystic Seaport, with its whaling history, is one of America's most fascinating outdoor museums. It features sailing ships with soaring masts and old-time shops and other buildings evoking memories of the era of the clipper ships. The United States Coast Guard Academy is in New London.

■ THE EASTERN GATEWAY—AN OVERVIEW

The Eastern Gateway region consists of New York, New Jersey, and Pennsylvania. It is rich in contrasts—from skyscrapers to small towns; from casinos to woodland trails. This is one of the most heavily populated and urbanized parts of the United States. Historically, it has been the entry place for most Europeans planning to become Americans. It continues to occupy a prominent place in American manufacturing and commercial economy.

NEW YORK

Area: 49,576
   square miles
Capital: Albany
Population:
   17,990,455

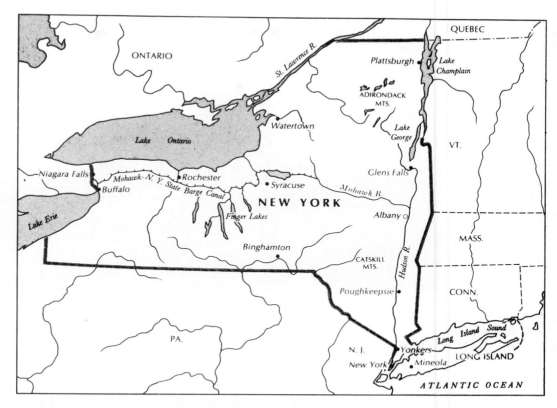

New York, one of the most populous states, has a varied physical geography. The eastern part of the state is marked by the north-south Hudson River Valley. In the northern valley, Lake Champlain is crossed by the Canadian border. At mid-point, the Hudson Valley is joined by an east-west lowland, the Mohawk River Valley, which provides easy access to Lake Ontario and Lake Erie. Along the valley are such cities as Albany, Schenectady, Utica, Syracuse, and Rochester. Buffalo is on Lake Erie, only a short distance from Niagara Falls.

North of the Mohawk Valley are the Adirondack Mountains and to the south is rough hill and mountain country, part of the northern Appalachian Mountain system that continues southward through central and western Pennsylvania. At the mouth of the Hudson River is the nation's largest city, New York, famed for its financial, communications, fashion, entertainment, and manufacturing activities. Part of New York spills eastward on Long Island.

New York is bordered by Canada on the North; Lake Ontario, Lake Erie, and a small part of Pennsylvania on the west; Pennsylvania and New Jersey on the south; and Vermont, Connecticut, Massachusetts, and the Atlantic Ocean on the east.

Areas of Touristic Importance. New York City lives up to its nickname—the Big Apple. Everything about it is big: the build-

Manhattan Skyline, New York

ings, the crowds of people, the overall size of the city. New York offers an abundance of everything—shopping, sightseeing, dining, theater, sports, cultural events, and more. Most visitors think of New York City only as Manhattan Island, supposedly bought from the Indians by the Dutch for 24 dollars worth of trinkets, but Manhattan is just one of the five boroughs that comprise the city. Legendary Brooklyn contains many ethnic neighborhoods plus Coney Island and beaches. Queens is the site of John F. Kennedy (JFK) and LaGuardia airports. The Bronx houses one of the best zoos in America and is also the home of the New York Yankees. Staten Island is primarily residential.

Most tourist attractions, however, are in or near Manhattan. The Statue of Liberty and Ellis Island (a museum commemorating the history of immigration to the United States), in New York harbor, can be reached by ferry shuttle from lower Manhattan. The financial center of the world, Wall Street, the twin towers of the World Trade Center, and the artists' colony of Greenwich Village are in lower Manhattan.

Midtown Manhattan is the location of the Empire State Building, with observation platforms at the 96th and 102nd floors. St. Patrick's Cathedral and the headquarters of the United Nations are also here. The Broadway theater district, Rockefeller Center, and the fabulous Fifth Avenue shops are in this area also.

Manhattan hosts many of the world's finest museums and cultural activities. The Metropolitan Museum of Art covers the history of art from ancient civilizations to the present. The

Museum of Modern Art features modern paintings and sculptures as well as architecture, films, and industrial and graphic designs. The Solomon R. Guggenheim Museum features a great modern art collection, and, with its unique Frank Lloyd Wright design, is an art form in itself. The Intrepid Sea-Air-Space Museum is on the retired aircraft carrier *Intrepid,* docked at Pier 86. The American Museum of Natural History and Hayden Planetarium present exhibits on almost everything about our world and the plant and animal life on it. Lincoln Center and the Metropolitan Opera House are both recognized through the world for their musical performances.

New York has one of the largest and busiest harbors in the world. From spring through fall it is also a major passenger cruise port for ships sailing to Bermuda, Canada, and the Caribbean. The Cunard *Queen Elizabeth 2,* the last remaining transatlantic passenger liner, sails regularly from New York to England.

Brooklyn and Queens are located on the western third of Long Island, separated from Manhattan Island by the East River and from the Bronx (part of the mainland) by the Harlem River. The remainder of Long Island serves primarily as bedroom communities for New York City. The south-shore beaches of Long Island, especially Jones Beach and Fire Island, are among the finest white sand beaches in the world. Climate limits the area to a summer swimming season.

The area west and north of New York City is known as Upstate New York. The summer climate here is ideal for all outdoor activities and winters are tailor-made for skiing and skating.

The Hudson Valley, just north of the city, includes the United States Military Academy at West Point. The Catskill Mountains have fine year-round resorts as well as Ice Cave Mountain and the famed Catskill Game Farm. North of Poughkeepsie is Hyde Park, the home of Franklin Delano Roosevelt. Farther north is the state capital, Albany, and Saratoga Spa State Park, noted for its Performing Arts Center.

Between Albany and Canada are the Adirondack Mountains with a large forest preserve. Lake Placid, which hosted Olympic Games in 1932 and 1980, is in the area. Lake George provides good resorts in an area of exceptional beauty. At the far north of the state are the Thousand Islands (actually more than 2,000) in the St. Lawrence River between New York and Canada.

The Finger Lake region, west of Albany, is graced by 11 long, narrow glacier-formed lakes stretching southward from Lake Ontario. It is an area of lakes, waterfalls, steep gorges, and wooded glens. Rochester features the Eastman Kodak Corporation and the International Museum of Photography. Syracuse, home of the New York State Fair, is also home of the Salt Museum. Cooperstown houses the Baseball Hall of Fame. Watkins Glen State Park at the south end of Seneca Lake includes 18 waterfalls, of which Rainbow Falls is the most impressive.

Although Buffalo houses several interesting restorations and museums, it is best known as the gateway to Niagara Falls. Niagara Falls, although not the highest in the world, is one of the broadest, most spectacular, and most acessible. The *Maid of the Mist* riverboats cruise at the base of the falls, providing unique views.

Ausable Chasm, New York

NEW JERSEY

Area: 7,836 square miles
Capital: Trenton
Population: 7,730,188

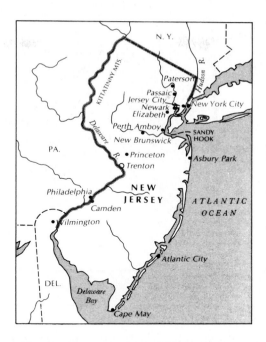

Amazingly compact, New Jersey has the highest population density of any state in the nation. Yet, it is also packed with beauty, entertainment, and excitement. With its wooded waterways, its rich colonial history, its sandy Atlantic beaches, and legalized gambling in Atlantic City, New Jersey thrives with tourism activity.

West and south of New York City, New Jersey extends southward along the Atlantic Ocean until its southern tip juts into Delaware Bay. In addition, New Jersey is bordered on the north by New York, on the west by Pennsylvania, and on the south by Delaware. Although there are some small mountains in the northwestern portion of the state, New Jersey is basically flat. Most of the population and cities are in the northern one-half of the state.

Areas of Touristic Importance. New Jersey's coastal communities and resorts offer deep-sea fishing and surfcasting, scuba diving and shell collecting, swimming, water surfing, and power boating. From Sandy Hook to Asbury Park and south to Long Beach Island, Atlantic City, Wildwood, and Cape May, beach resorts cater to the summer trade. The Atlantic City casinos offer gambling, cabaret and nightclub shows, and theater spectaculars with top-name entertainers. These activities have made Atlantic City a year-round attraction. West central New Jersey hosts the state capital complex at Trenton and the Princeton University campus in Princeton.

PENNSYLVANIA

Area: 45,333
   square miles
Capital: Harrisburg
Population:
   11,881,643

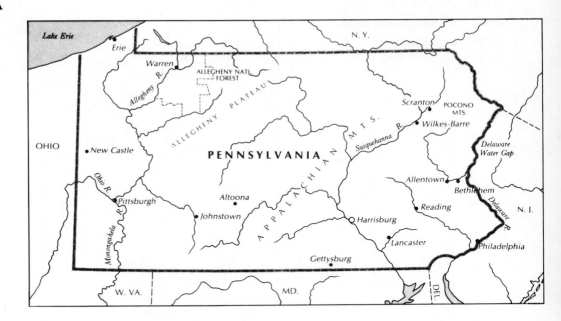

Pennsylvania is mountainous except in its southeastern one-third, part of the broader Atlantic coastal plain, which is drained by the south-flowing Delaware River and Susquehanna River. Philadelphia, on the Delaware River, is one of America's most historic cities. Along with Harrisburg in the center of the state and Pittsburgh in the west, it has been one of the focal points of Pennsylvania's development. Pittsburgh is the hub of a great network of heavily industrialized cities in southwestern Pennsylvania, northern West Virginia, and eastern Ohio. It is the largest such concentration in the Americas.

Pennsylvania is diverse in both its geography and its people. It enjoys an extensive agricultural industry, yet two of the largest cities in the United States are at opposite ends of the state. Its people represent a rich variety of ethnic backgrounds. It is a landlocked state, yet waterways are important to it. The Delaware River on the east and the Ohio River in the west are of critical importance. Lake Erie on the north sends and receives shipping through the St. Lawrence Seaway.

As the state stretches westward toward the nation's heartland, it is pierced by two mountain ranges, the Poconos in the northeast and the Allegheny Mountains in the center and southwest of the state. A long hot summer supports agricultural activities, while winter snows encourage skiing and other winter activities. Pennsylvania is bordered by Ohio and West Virginia to the west, Lake Erie and New York to the north, New Jersey to the east, and West Virginia, Delaware, and Maryland to the south.

Areas of Touristic Importance. Philadelphia was the geographical center of the original 13 colonies—delegates met here both to sign the Declaration of Independence and to draft

Liberty Bell, Philadelphia
Photo: Courtesy Philadelphia Convention & Visitors Bureau

and sign the Constitution of the United States. Philadelphia was the first capital of the new nation and the center of political and cultural activity in the late 1700s and early 1800s. Independence Hall and Independence National Historical Park with the Liberty Bell Pavilion preserve buildings and papers of that era. Franklin Court is a tribute to Benjamin Franklin's activities. The Delaware River brings ocean shipping to the city.

Not far from the city is Valley Forge National Historical Park, where the Continental Army under George Washington spent a desperate winter. About an hour's drive from the city is Longwood Gardens, where exotic plant collections are displayed in one of America's leading botanical and horticultural exhibitions.

The Pocono Mountains offer year-round resort vacation facilities. Major ski areas include Big Boulder, Camelback, and Jack Frost Mountain. Hiking, fishing, hunting, horseback riding, and boating are available spring through fall.

Pennsylvania Dutch Country (actually the area was settled by Germans) is in the southeastern part of the state. Retaining the customs and strict religious beliefs of their forefathers, the Amish lifestyle attracts many visitors. Barns are decorated with colorful hex signs, and the people ride in horse-drawn buggies. The Amish towns of Lititz, Strasburg, Ephrata, Bird-in-Hand, and Intercourse are not far from Lancaster.

Hershey, famous for the chocolate company, and the state capital, Harrisburg, are west of the Amish country. Hershey offers resort facilities, a plant tour, and a large theme amusement park.

Gettysburg, site of one of the most famous battles of the Civil War, is in the south-central part of the state. The National Military Park provides a definitive documentary of the battle. The home of former President Dwight Eisenhower is also at Gettysburg.

Pittsburgh presents a clean and sparkling array of towering skyscrapers and landscaped parks. The terrain is a mix of hillsides and plateaus. Ravines and rivers are spanned by many bridges. The center of the city is at the point where the Allegheny and Monongahela Rivers meet to form the Ohio River, the major west-flowing tributary of the Mississippi. The Fort Pitt Museum concentrates on early western Pennsylvania history and the French and Indian War. Science and technology are featured at the Buhl Science Center.

■ HISTORIC WASHINGTON COUNTRY—
AN OVERVIEW

The Historic Washington Country consists of Delaware, Maryland, the District of Columbia (Washington, DC), Virginia, and West Virginia. It is an exciting blend of contemporary living and American heritage. The nation's capital provides a sense of history in the making, while the surrounding states offer a mix of history and new development.

DELAWARE

Area: 2,057 square miles
Capital: Dover
Population: 666,168

Little Delaware lies in the Delmarva Peninsula, a coastal projection between Delaware Bay and the Atlantic Ocean on one side and Chesapeake Bay on the other, that also includes territory belonging to Maryland and Virginia. Southern Delaware remains rural, but the urbanized northern part, including Wilmington, has close ties with Philadelphia.

Delaware is the second smallest state in the nation and has only three counties. Its Atlantic coastline features excellent summer resort facilities. It is bounded by the Delaware River, Delaware Bay, and Atlantic Ocean on the east; Pennsylvania on the north; and Maryland on the south and west.

Areas of Touristic Importance. Wilmington is the state's metropolis. Located in the north, not far from Philadelphia, Wilmington is the capital of the chemical industry. The DuPont company began its chemical production business here in 1802. The Winterthur Museum and Gardens is a historic house and exotic garden exhibition. The Nemours Mansion and Gardens and the DuPont Estate and Gardens also display antique period furnishings and exquisite landscapes.

Rehoboth and Bethany Beaches along with Cape Henlopen State Park provide white sand and active surf to thousands of vacationers each year. Summer is swim season, while spring and fall are pleasant for sunning and strolling.

MARYLAND

Area: 10,577 square miles
Capital: Annapolis
Population: 4,781,468

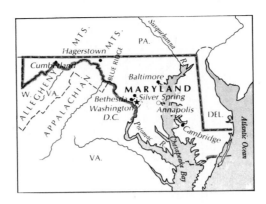

Maryland includes both shores of Chesapeake Bay, which is noted for its fisheries, and extends westward into the Appalachians. Its southern boundary with Virginia lies along the Potomac River. Most of the state's population as well as Baltimore and historic Annapolis are located on the west coast of the Chesapeake Bay. The area east of the bay, known as the Eastern Shore, is heavily rural. Bordered on the west by West Virginia; the south by West Virginia, the District of Columbia, and Virginia; on the north by Pennsylvania; and on the east by Delaware and the Atlantic Ocean, Maryland slopes from the Allegheny and Blue Ridge Mountains in the western part of the state to the Atlantic Ocean in the east. The fabled Mason-Dixon line separating North from South is the Maryland-Pennsylvania border.

Areas of Touristic Importance. Baltimore is Maryland's major city. It is one of America's busiest freight shipping ports. The rebuilt and revitalized Inner Harbor area has many shops, restaurants, and attractions including an excellent aquarium. The USS *Constellation,* the first ship in the US Navy (1797) and the oldest ship in the world still afloat, is open to visitors. Another unique Baltimore attraction is the B & O Railroad Museum. The museum is the site of the nation's first railroad station and contains engines and cars dating back to 1829.

South from Baltimore along the western shore of the Chesapeake Bay is Annapolis, capital of the state and home of the United States Naval Academy. Its State House, completed in 1779, is the oldest state capitol in continuous legislative use.

Other tourist-attracting areas in Maryland are the Eastern Shore and the western mountains. Ocean City, on the Eastern Shore, is a major summer resort. Deep Creek Lake in western Maryland is excellent for camping and hiking.

THE DISTRICT OF COLUMBIA
Also Called: Washington, DC

Area: 67 square miles
Capital: Washington
Population: 606,900

Facing on the middle course of the Potomac River is Washington, DC. Washington is bordered by Maryland on the north, east, and west and by Virginia across the Potomac River on the south. The metropolitan area spills over into both neighbors.

Washington, a custom-built city, became the seat of United States government in 1800. The master plan of French engineer Pierre Charles L'Enfant is still evident in the wide boulevards and designated green park areas. The city's centerpiece is the Mall, an open grassy area a mile long between the Capitol and the Lincoln Memorial. Clustered around or near the Mall are the Washington Monument, the Jefferson Memorial, the Vietnam Memorial, and the many museums of the Smithsonian Institution, including the most popular Air and Space Museum and the Museum of History and Technology. Other popular museums in Washington are the National Museum of Natural History, the Freer Gallery of Art, and the Hirschhorn Museum and Sculpture Garden. The Holocaust Museum, which opened in 1993, has drawn record-breaking crowds to this historical record of the Nazi era and the destruction of millions of people because of their religion and/or nationality. The National Archives, in which the Declaration of Independence and the US Constitution are displayed, and many other major government buildings also border on the Mall. The White House, residence of the President, backs onto the Mall.

The Capitol Hill area is at the east end of the Mall. Tours of the Capitol include both the House of Representatives and the Senate. The Supreme Court, Library of Congress, and several House and Senate office buildings are also in the area.

Washington is also home to the John F. Kennedy Center, where operas, plays and other cultural events take place. In addition there are other theaters, such as the National Theater and the Arena Stage.

On the outskirts of the city are attractions such as the National Zoo and the National Arboretum.

Tomb of the Unknown Soldiers, Arlington, Virginia
Photo: Courtesy Virginia Division of Tourism

Arlington County in Northern Virginia was part of the District of Columbia until it was ceded back to Virginia in the mid-1800s. The Pentagon, one of the world's largest office buildings, houses the Department of Defense. Arlington Cemetery is known for the Tomb of the Unknown Soldiers and the John F. Kennedy Memorial. Old Town, Alexandria, just be-low Arlington, has restored the atmosphere of an early Amer-ican port city. Mount Vernon, farther south on the Potomac River, was the home of George Washington, Virginia's most fa-mous resident. Although in Virginia, it is usually visited by tourists coming to the Washington, DC area.

VIRGINIA

Area: 40,817 square miles

Capital: Richmond

Population: 6,187,358

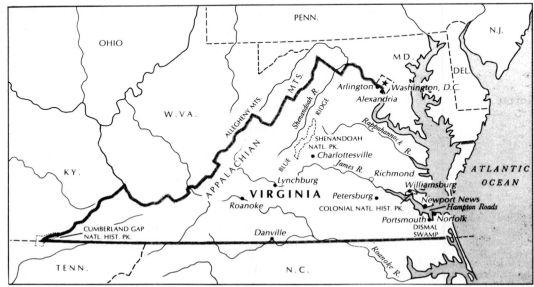

Virginia has two large metropolitan clusters: the suburbs of Washington, DC, including Alexandria, in the north; and the Norfolk area in the southeast at the mouth of Chesapeake Bay and the James River. The latter urbanization continues west-ward through historic Williamsburg to Richmond. This area is commonly known as the Tidewater. Lynchburg and Roanoke are major inner Piedmont cities.

Virginia's topography ranges from ocean beaches in the east to mountain crests in the west. Its Tidewater coastal plain makes up the eastern part of the state. A physically iso-lated part on the southern tip of the Delmarva Peninsula (Vir-ginia's Eastern Shore) is linked to the Norfolk area by an engineering wonder, the Chesapeake Bay Bridge-Tunnel. The Piedmont plateau rises out of the Tidewater and stretches across the middle part of the state to the Blue Ridge Moun-tains, which run from northeast to southwest in the western section. Virginia is bounded by the Atlantic Ocean on the east, North Carolina on the south, Kentucky and West Vir-ginia on the west, and Maryland and the District of Columbia on the north. The climate is marked by hot summers and chilly to cold winters.

Called the Old Dominion, Virginia was the home of the first permanent English settlers in the New World. The state was also the home of eight United States Presidents, among them George Washington and Thomas Jefferson.

Areas of Touristic Importance. Points of interest in northern Virginia, near Washington, DC, are described in the District of Columbia section above.

Richmond, Virginia's capital, was also the capital of the Confederacy during the Civil War. The State Capitol was designed by Thomas Jefferson. St. John's Church, built in 1741, was the scene of Patrick Henry's "Give me liberty or give me death" speech. The Civil War is documented from the southern point of view in the Museum of the Confederacy. Richmond is also the location of some of the largest tobacco processing plants in the country. Factory tours are available.

Sixty miles east of Richmond is the Historic Triangle of Williamsburg, Jamestown, and Yorktown. Yorktown was the site of the British surrender at the end of the Revolutionary War. The Yorktown Victory Center documents activities at that time. Jamestown was the location of the first permanent English settlement.

Colonial Williamsburg is the most notable restored community in the United States. It is the most extensive restoration of an eighteenth century village and is composed of public buildings, shops, homes, taverns, and gardens. Costumed townspeople are employed in the shops and taverns. Expert artisans demonstrate colonial crafts. Busch Gardens Old Country theme park is just east of Williamsburg.

Farther east, Norfolk and Newport News serve as home ports for the largest group of United States Navy ships in the east. Virginia Beach, on the Atlantic coast, is a summer playground.

The Shenandoah and Blue Ridge Mountains begin at Front Royal in the northwest part of the state and run southwest to the North Carolina border. The Skyline Drive runs for one hundred miles through Shenandoah National Park. Nearby, the Luray Caverns and Crystal Caves display many natural formations. The erosion-carved limestone arch called "Natural Bridge" is also located in this area.

Charlottesville lies between Richmond and the mountains. It is the home of the University of Virginia and the closest town to Monticello, an architectural masterpiece which was designed and built by Thomas Jefferson in 1769. He lived there until his death in 1824.

Ship reproductions, Jamestown

WEST VIRGINIA

Area: 24,181 square miles
Capital: Charleston
Population: 1,793,477

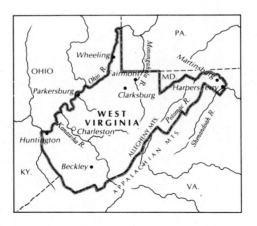

Most of mountainous West Virginia's population live in or near the Ohio River valley in the west. Its small cities, including Charleston and Huntington, are in or near the Ohio River valley and have strong ties with southern Ohio and western Pennsylvania. Few states are as mountainous. Besides scenic beauty, West Virginia contains vast mineral resources, especially coal.

West Virginia is bordered by Virginia and Maryland on the east, Pennsylvania and Maryland on the north, Ohio on the west, and Kentucky and Virginia on the south. Originally part of Virginia, it split off during the Civil War to remain part of the Union.

Areas of Touristic Importance. West Virginia offers visitors the opportunity to hike, camp, fish, ski, and climb mountains. Its many rivers provide opportunities for white-water rafting. West Virginia offers more than 40 state parks and forest areas. White Sulphur Springs and Berkeley Springs are popular areas.

Harpers Ferry, in the state's eastern panhandle, is most famous as the scene of abolitionist John Brown's attempt to seize the United States Arsenal and free the slaves. Several town buildings are open to the public.

■ SOUTHEAST SUN COUNTRY—AN OVERVIEW

The Southeast Sun Country region includes North Carolina, South Carolina, Georgia, and Florida. All have important vacation areas on the coast of the Atlantic Ocean. Florida also features extensive Gulf of Mexico coastal areas on its west side and on the southern border of its panhandle. The coasts of the Carolinas, Georgia, and Florida have the finest sandy beaches in the United States. Winter climate becomes progressively milder southward, while summers are hot and humid. There is a heavy inflow of retired persons from more northern states, especially into Florida.

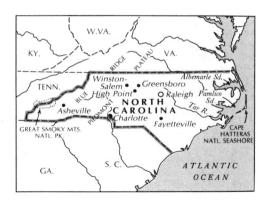

NORTH CAROLINA

Area: 52,586 square miles
Capital: Raleigh
Population: 6,628,637

North Carolina contains three physical units: the coastal plain in the east, the Piedmont in the center, and the Appalachian Mountains in the west. The bulk of North Carolina's people and urban-based activities are clustered in a crescent-shaped Piedmont area from Raleigh westward through Durham, Greensboro, Winston-Salem, and Charlotte. Asheville serves the mountainous west; the port city of Wilmington, the southeastern coast. Off the North Carolina coast, projecting eastward into the Atlantic Ocean, lies a great stretch of barrier islands, the Outer Banks, which culminate in Cape Hatteras. The northeast-flowing Gulf Stream is a short distance offshore and contributes to the coastal area's relatively mild winters.

The state is bordered on the north by Virginia, on the west by Tennessee, on the south by Georgia and South Carolina, and on the east by the Atlantic Ocean. Great Smoky Mountains National Park in the west contains Mount Mitchell, the tallest mountain in the eastern United States. Agriculture, textiles, and cigarettes are among the state's leading industries. North Carolina leads the nation in furniture production. Textile and furniture factory outlet stores attract many visitors.

Areas of Touristic Importance. The Atlantic seashore is the state's most popular tourist area. Nags Head is the largest resort in the area. Nearby is Kitty Hawk, site of the Wright brothers' first flight in 1903. The Cape Hatteras and Cape Lookout National Seashores contain vast stretches of undeveloped, white sand beaches. The Cape Hatteras Lighthouse, at the southeastern tip of the National Seashore, is the tallest such brick structure in the nation.

Charlotte is the largest city, and Raleigh, in the Piedmont area, is the political center of the state. Discovery Place in Charlotte is a hands-on participatory museum of science. The North Carolina Museums of Art and History can be found in Raleigh. Nearby Southern Pines and Pinehurst host some of the best golf facilities in the world as well as the Golf Hall of Fame. The Research Triangle Park, bounded by Raleigh, Durham and Chapel Hill, is one of America's leading research parks.

The Great Smoky Mountains National Park is evenly divided between North Carolina and Tennessee. The park hosts a pioneer farmstead which depicts pioneer life with reconstructed log buildings and exhibits. Cades Cove and Cataloochee provide excellent fishing. The park also contains some of the most varied plant life in the nation.

SOUTH CAROLINA

Area: 31,055 square miles
Capital: Columbia
Population: 3,486,703

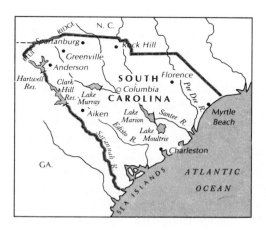

South Carolina is formed by a coastal plain, central Piedmont and small western mountain sections. South Carolina is home to historic Charleston on the coast, Columbia in the center,

Middleton Place Gardens and Plantation Stableyards, South Carolina
Photo: Courtesy South Carolina Department of Parks, Recreation & Tourism

and Spartanburg and Greenville in the inner Piedmont. It is bounded on the north by North Carolina, on the south and west by Georgia, and on the east by the Atlantic Ocean. The state enjoys a moderate winter climate and hot summers.

Areas of Touristic Importance. Myrtle Beach and Hilton Head Island, on the state's ocean coast, offer wide, sandy beaches and excellent resort facilities. Golf and fishing are among the most popular activities. Other island resort areas include Kiawah, Seabrook, and Wild Dunes.

Although Charleston is a gateway to many of the state's seaside resorts, it is also an attraction itself. More than 800 pre-Civil War homes and buildings have been preserved in the city's downtown historic district. The first shots of the Civil War were fired at Fort Sumter in Charleston harbor. Charleston is also well-known for its landscaped gardens. Magnolia and Cypress Gardens are among the most popular. Middleton Place Gardens and Plantation Stableyards are the oldest landscaped gardens in the nation. Camden, north of Columbia, is noted for its colonial homes and equestrian activities.

GEORGIA

Area: 58,876 square miles
Capital: Atlanta
Population: 6,478,216

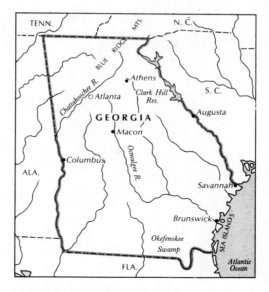

Georgia is the largest state east of the Mississippi River. Like its Carolina neighbors, Georgia consists of a coastal plain, Piedmont and interior mountain sections. In the first two sections, summers are hot and humid and winters moderate. The mountains have cooler summers and colder winters. Both coastal and mountain areas have many summer resorts. Atlanta, in northern Georgia, is not only the largest Georgian city, but the largest in the Southeast and the region's commercial and air transportation hub. Augusta and Savannah are important coastal plain cities. The state is bounded by South Carolina and the Atlantic Ocean on the east, Florida on the south, Alabama on the west, and Tennessee and North Carolina on the north.

Areas of Touristic Importance. With a metropolitan area population of more than 2 million, Atlanta most dramatically expresses the transition from Old South to New South. Its older residential areas are lined with magnolia and dogwood trees that surround handsome Georgian homes, typifying the graciousness of the Old South. The downtown area features some of the nation's most contemporary skyscrapers. Atlanta offers excellent shopping and dining as well as a variety of theatrical and cultural activities. Nearby Stone Mountain features a giant carving of Confederate heroes. Other attractions in the Atlanta area include the Martin Luther King, Jr. National Historical Site and Calloway Gardens at Pine Mountain.

Savannah, on the Atlantic coast, is America's first planned city. More than one thousand pre-Civil War buildings are considered historically significant. Downtown squares feature live oaks draped with Spanish moss. Pubs and boutiques dot Savannah's 9-block Riverfront Plaza. The Telfair

Mansion and Art Museum and the Great Savannah Exposition document the area's rich history.

The "golden isles" south of Savannah include Sea Island, Jekyll Island, and St. Simons Island, which are known for their leisurely paced resort life and expansive, white sand beaches as well as fine golf, tennis, and fishing. Inland from the coast is the Okefenokee Swamp, which includes a large park and wildlife refuge.

FLORIDA

Area: 58,560 square miles
Capital: Tallahassee
Population: 12,937,926

The large, low-lying peninsula of Florida has the mildest winter weather in the United States, a feature that has made it one of the several most important meccas for retirees, especially from the Northeast and Midwest. It is the most populous and fastest growing Southern state. Urban growth is spreading rapidly along the east coast from Miami in the south to Jacksonville in the north, in the central interior around Orlando, around Tampa-St. Petersburg on the west (Gulf of Mexico) coast, and around Pensacola in the western panhandle. Florida is also one of the great tourist magnets of the eastern United States. Millions flock to see its natural wonders, including the Everglades; unusual recreational facilities, including Disney World; and beaches on both the east and west coasts of the state.

Florida is a large, low-lying peninsula nearly 500 miles long and 150 miles wide. Surrounded on three sides by the Atlantic Ocean and the Gulf of Mexico, it is bordered on the north by Georgia and Alabama. The east coast is warmed by the Gulf Stream and the west coast by the Gulf of Mexico. Countless deep bays and islands can be found on its perimeter. The famous Florida Keys are a string of islands running

Kennedy Space Center, Cape Canaveral
Photo Courtesy Florida Department of Commerce, Division of Tourism

basically southwest from the southern part of the mainland south of Miami.

Most of Florida is flat land, barely a few meters above sea level. Much of the interior from Lake Okeechobee southward, including the Everglades, is a labyrinth of waterways zigzagging through cypress and mangrove swamps. More than four hundred species of birds as well as deer, bear, cougar, and fox inhabit the region. The alligator population, once an endangered species, is growing and is no longer considered endangered.

Areas of Touristic Importance. Miami is the southern gateway to the United States. Its population of more than 1.7 million includes many persons of Cuban and other Latin

American backgrounds. Miami is the largest cruise origination port in the world, with thousands of passengers embarking each week. Hundreds of wild animals roam uncaged at the city's large Metrozoo. The city's Seaquarium, Monkey Jungle, Parrot Jungle and Orchid Jungle provide opportunities to view exotic fauna and flora. Little Havana provides Latin American atmosphere with its Cuban restaurants and cafes.

Miami Beach is an 8-mile-long island separated from Miami by Biscayne Bay. Its recently restored, nearly 100-yard-wide, white sand beach is lined by both luxury and family-style resorts. The world's largest concentration of 1930s art deco architecture is found here.

Everglades National Park offers opportunities to view wildlife in their natural habitat. Airboats skim along the shallow waters. There are also Seminole Indian villages in the area. The Florida Keys provide opportunities for viewing additional wildlife as well as beaches and harbors for sailing and yachting. Excellent beaches and golf courses can also be found on Sanibel and Captiva Islands off Fort Myers on the west coast.

Hollywood and Fort Lauderdale, north of Miami Beach, offer more "sun and fun" resort areas. In addition, Fort Lauderdale serves as a major cruise port. Palm Beach, 30 miles farther north, is known as the playground of millionaires.

Florida's (and the world's) biggest tourism drawing card is Walt Disney World near Orlando in central Florida. The Magic Kingdom, Epcot Center, and the Disney-MGM Studios are among the most popular theme parks in the world. Other major attractions in the area include Universal Studios; Sea World; Cypress Gardens, with its famous waterskiing show; and the Kennedy Space Center at Cape Canaveral, east of Orlando.

Tampa and St. Petersburg, on the west coast of central Florida, provide additional beach resort facilities. Busch Gardens, outside of Tampa, has an African theme, including a train ride through a wild animal park.

One of America's first permanent European settlements, St. Augustine was founded in 1565 by the Spanish. Its historic district preserves Spanish and British colonial architecture. South of St. Augustine, Daytona Beach has white sand beaches on the Atlantic Ocean. The Daytona 500 is a world-famous stock car race.

One of the finest beaches in the nation can be found along the Gulf coast on Florida's panhandle in the area between Pensacola and Panama City Beach. Golf and tennis resorts abound, providing activities in addition to soaking up the sun on clean, soft, white sand beaches. Pensacola, itself, is a center of historic restoration with charming shops and galleries.

■ SOUTHLAND USA—AN OVERVIEW

From vibrant cities and historical, stately mansions, to traditional towns and rural landscapes, from misty lowland bayous to rolling green mountains, Southland USA presents a wide variety of customs and scenery accompanied by the deep-rooted tradition of gracious southern hospitality. Southland USA includes the states of Kentucky, Tennessee, Alabama, Mississippi, and Louisiana. Summers are hot and humid, while winters become more moderate from north to south. The Appalachian Mountains of eastern Kentucky, Tennessee and Alabama have cooler summers and snowier winters. The region is heavily forested.

Many of the states along the Mississippi River have taken advantage of laws passed in the late 1980s and early 1990s allowing gambling on riverboats. One by one, almost all eligible states have passed laws permitting such activities as an additional source of tax income.

KENTUCKY

Area: 40,395 square miles
Capital: Frankfort
Population: 3,685,296

Kentucky has a short Mississippi River boundary on its west; its northern boundary is formed by the Ohio River; and mountains dominate its east and south. Lexington is the center of the famed Bluegrass region in northern Kentucky, and a short distance westward, Louisville is a port city on the Ohio River. Kentucky is a transitional, "border" state. It is essentially southern in history and character, yet its main centers face, and its economic life is oriented, northward toward Ohio and the Midwest.

Lincoln's boyhood home, near Hodgenville, Kentucky
Photo: Courtesy Commonwealth of Kentucky, Department of Travel Development

Kentucky is bordered by Ohio, Indiana, and Illinois on the north, Missouri on the west, Tennessee on the south, and Virginia and West Virginia on the east. The heavily forested mountains in the southeast create rugged scenery, whereas rolling hills dominate the Bluegrass region.

Areas of Touristic Importance. Lexington and Louisville are in the heart of horse country. There are about 250 horse farms in the area and several race tracks. The world-famous Kentucky Derby horse race is held on the first Saturday in May at Churchill Downs.

One of the world's largest cave systems—nearly 300 miles long—is found at giant Mammoth Cave National Park. Echo River can be toured underground for closeup views of colorful stalactites and stalagmites.

Other interesting attractions in Kentucky include Abraham Lincoln's log cabin birthplace, Boonesboro with its reconstructed fort and pioneer crafts center, and the Cumberland Gap historical monument. The airport at Covington, on the south side of the Ohio River, serves Cincinnati, a major Ohio city across the river.

TENNESSEE

Area: 42,244 square miles

Capital: Nashville

Population: 4,877,185

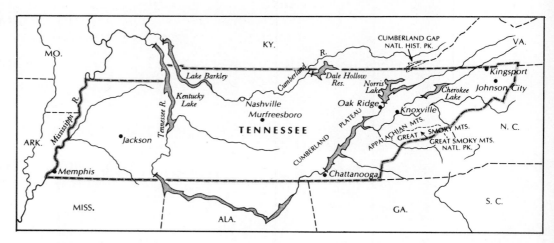

Tennessee, lying west of North Carolina, has a mountainous east, a hilly center, and plains on the west. Knoxville and Chattanooga serve the populous Great Valley in the east; Nashville, central Tennessee; and the Mississippi River port city of Memphis, the west. The state has greatly benefited from the river development works and electricity generated by the Tennessee Valley Authority (TVA).

The state is bordered by Kentucky and Virginia on the north; North Carolina on the east; Georgia, Alabama and Mississippi on the south; and Missouri and Arkansas on the west.

Areas of Touristic Importance. Nashville is rightly known as "Music City, USA." More than half of all the musical recordings in the nation are made here. Country and western music's Grand Ole Opry is presented and broadcast from Nashville. The Opryland USA theme park has been designed with this show as a focal point. The Country Music Hall of Fame also attracts many visitors. The Hermitage, President Jackson's home, is near Nashville as well.

Knoxville, surrounded by Tennessee Valley Authority dams, is a center for outdoor recreation with abundant fishing, boating, and waterskiing on the lakes made by the dams. Nearby Gatlinburg is the Tennessee gateway to the Great Smoky Mountains National Park (see North Carolina, page 57, for description).

Chattanooga lies on the Moccasin Bend of the Tennessee River at the base of Lookout Mountain, which towers over the city. Union victories at Lookout Mountain and Missionary Ridge sealed the fate of the Confederacy. Much of the battlefield is preserved in Chickamauga-Chattanooga National Military Park. An incline railway takes visitors to the top of Lookout Mountain.

Memphis has been the center for two types of American music—blues and rock and roll. This was Elvis Presley's hometown and his famous Graceland Mansion is open to the public and is one of Memphis' major attractions. The Beale Street Historic District is the home of blues music.

ALABAMA

Area: 51,609 square miles
Capital: Montgomery
Population: 4,040,587

Alabama, Mississippi, and Louisiana face on the Gulf of Mexico. In Alabama, the port of Mobile is on the narrow Gulf frontage; Montgomery and Tuscaloosa are in mid-state; and Birmingham is in the northeastern Piedmont. Manufacturing has expanded in Gadsden and other northern Alabama localities, attracted by river transportation along the Tennessee River and electric power generated by the Tennessee Valley Authority (TVA). Alabama is bordered by Georgia on the east, Tennessee on the north, Mississippi on the west, and the Gulf of Mexico and Florida on the south.

Areas of Touristic Importance. Forest-covered ridges and hills spread over the northern part of the state. The many dams on creeks and rivers have created excellent recreation facilities. The Mobile delta has swamps and bayous, and sandy beaches dot Mobile Bay and the Gulf of Mexico in the southernmost part of Alabama. The state's winter climate is quite mild.

The state capital of Montgomery was the home of Jefferson Davis and housed the White House of the Confederacy. The home of Helen Keller is in Tuscumbia.

Huntsville is the home for NASA's Marshall Space Flight Center, and the Alabama Space and Rocket Center has America's largest Space Museum. Montgomery, the state capital, was the first capital of the Confederacy.

Mobile is one of the country's largest and busiest seaports. Gulf Shores and other Gulf Coast resort areas provide miles of sandy beaches.

MISSISSIPPI

Area: 47,716 square miles
Capital: Jackson
Population: 2,573,216

Bordered on the west by the Mississippi River, Mississippi is a rural state with small cities, among them Biloxi on the coast, Natchez and Vicksburg on the Mississippi River, and Jackson in the interior. Its neighboring states are Alabama on the east, Tennessee on the north, Arkansas and Louisiana on the west, and Louisiana and the Gulf of Mexico on the south.

Areas of Touristic Importance. Mississippi is known for its pre-Civil War mansions, riverboating, Gulf coast beaches, and scenery. Natchez has nearly 500 antebellum homes and other structures, many of which are open to the public. Along with Vicksburg, it is a port for Mississippi River steamboat cruises. Vicksburg is the site of a National Military Park preserving the history of the Civil War battle. The Gulf Coast beaches offer sun and swimming activities.

LOUISIANA

Area: 48,523 square miles
Capital: Baton Rouge
Population: 4,219,973

Louisiana is shaped around the lower Mississippi River, its plains, and fan-shaped delta where the river flows into the Gulf of Mexico. The historic port city of New Orleans sits on the delta. Upstream is Baton Rouge. Northwestern Louisiana is served by Shreveport. Louisiana benefits from natural gas and oil deposits, which are also found in adjacent Texas and Oklahoma.

Louisiana is bordered on the north by Arkansas and Mississippi, on the east by Mississippi, on the south by the Gulf of Mexico, and on the west by Texas.

Much of southern Louisiana is dominated by French culture and language even though nearly two centuries have passed since Napoleon sold the vast Louisiana Territory, including New Orleans, to the United States. French-speaking residents fall into two groups: Creoles, who primarily reside

Mardi Gras, New Orleans

in New Orleans; and Cajuns, who live in the bayou country out-side of New Orleans. Northern Louisiana, however, is predominantly of English-speaking culture.

Areas of Touristic Importance. New Orleans holds a high position in the culinary world because of its famed Creole cuisine. Creole cooking is basically a combination of French and Spanish styles, enhanced with spices.

New Orleans' Cajun style of cooking, which uses even more spices and features dishes blackened in an iron skillet, is famous well beyond Louisiana.

New Orleans has long been an important commercial link between the north, via the Mississippi, and the south, as well as between Latin America and the east via the Gulf and the Atlantic. Its unique French history and culture make it one of the largest tourist-drawing areas in the south. New Orleans' Garden District is the site of many old southern mansions, and dinner cruises on the Mississippi are popular with New Orleans visitors.

The French Quarter, or Vieux Carre, encompasses 70 blocks of the city. Royal Street and Magazine Street contain fascinating boutiques and shops. Jackson Square, in the center of the quarter, is an artists' gathering place. Bourbon Street is the home and founding location of Dixieland Jazz music. Many excellent French restaurants and quaint cafes dot the quarter. In the evening, part of Bourbon Street is closed to automobiles and is the scene of fun-loving crowds enjoying the spirited party atmosphere. New Orleans is most famous for its huge annual Mardi Gras celebrations.

Baton Rouge, the capital, is at the heart of the southern plantation region. Louisiana's swamp tours are adventures to another place and time. Cajun country is the area settled by the Acadians who fled Nova Scotia in the 1700s. Cajun towns are primarily located south and west of New Orleans. The most interesting of these are Lafayette, New Iberia, and St. Martinville.

■ THE GREAT LAKES REGION—AN OVERVIEW

Commonly known as the Midwest, the Great Lakes Region includes the states of Ohio, Indiana, Illinois, Michigan, Wisconsin, Minnesota, and Iowa. With Southern New England and the Middle Atlantic states, this is the American industrial heartland, the "manufacturing belt." In addition, the region is an agricultural leader especially noted for its corn, beef, and pork output. Its climate features hot summers and cold winters, with pleasant but short springs and falls.

OHIO

Area: 41,222 square miles
Capital: Columbus
Population: 10,847,115

Ohio, Indiana, and Illinois all face two ways, north to the Great Lakes and south to the Ohio River valley. Eastern and southeastern Ohio are mountainous, part of the Allegheny Plateau. Rolling, glaciated terrain is typical elsewhere in the state. In northern Ohio, Toledo and Cleveland are major Lake Erie ports. Nearby interior cities, such as Akron, Canton, and Youngstown, are heavily industrialized. Columbus serves central Ohio, and Cincinnati, situated on the Ohio River, serves southwestern Ohio and northern Kentucky, across the river.

Ohio is bordered by Kentucky to the south, Pennsylvania to the east, Michigan and Lake Erie on the north, and Indiana on the west.

Areas of Touristic Importance. Cincinnati, Cleveland, and Columbus are the commercial and cultural centers for their respective parts of the state. Cincinnati, on the Ohio River, has a variety of excellent museums, a great zoo, and a historic floating restaurant, the *Mike Fink.* King's Island, northeast of the city, is an amusement park with six theme areas and the largest roller coaster in the nation.

Cleveland, on Lake Erie, is known for the quality of its symphony orchestra and its Museum of Art. Columbus is the state capital and home of one of the largest universities in the nation, Ohio State University. Columbus also hosts the interesting Center of Science and Industry.

Dayton was the home of the Wright brothers, who built the first successful airplane in their bicycle shop. It is now home to Wright-Patterson Air Force Base and the Air Force Museum. The museum houses more than 150 historic aircraft as well as displays on the history of flight.

Other attractions include the Pro Football Hall of Fame at Canton and national landmarks, which include the homes of several United States presidents.

INDIANA

Area: 36,291 square miles
Capital: Indianapolis
Population: 5,544,159

Indiana is in America's east-central lowland. The southern part of the state has deep valleys, piercing ridges, and rolling foothills. Central Indiana has a glacial heritage of plains and shallow river valleys. The northern part of the state has interior lakes and borders on scenic Lake Michigan. Indiana is bordered by Illinois to the west, Michigan and Lake Michigan to the north, Ohio to the east, and Kentucky to the south. The Wabash River forms the southern part of the Indiana-Illinois boundary.

Areas of Touristic Importance. Indianapolis, Indiana's capital, is at the geographic center of the state and serves as the center of commerce, culture, and industry. The famous Indianapolis 500 automobile race has been held almost every year since 1909. The Indy Hall of Fame Museum is a tribute to auto development and racing. The Auburn-Cord-Duesenberg Museum in Auburn houses over 125 classic motor cars.

To the north, the Indiana Dunes National Lakeshore on the south coast of Lake Michigan is alive with native and migratory birds and hundreds of species of wildflowers. Swimming and camping facilities are available. In southern Indiana, the French Lick and West Baden resorts are also popular with tourists, as is New Harmony, the restored site of a 19th century Utopian community.

ILLINOIS

Area: 56,400 square miles
Capital: Springfield
Population: 11,430,602

Northern Illinois is dominated by the Chicago metropolitan area on Lake Michigan. Peoria and Springfield are in central Illinois. East St. Louis is on the Mississippi River across from St. Louis, Missouri and Cairo is at the Ohio and Mississippi River junction.

Glaciers planed most of Illinois into relatively flat prairie land, except for the southern part of the state that contains the hills and valleys of the Illinois Ozarks. Illinois is bordered by Wisconsin on the north, Iowa and Missouri on the west, and Indiana and Lake Michigan on the east.

Areas of Touristic Importance. Chicago, clearly the largest city in the Midwest, is the third largest city in the nation. A sprawling giant of commerce and industry, Chicago also has more than 15 miles of Lake Michigan beaches. Shopping, entertainment, and recreation are readily available. The Chicago Symphony Orchestra and the Lyric Opera Company are among the best in the nation.

The city skyline includes hundreds of tall buildings, with the tallest building in the world, the Sears Tower, among them. North Michigan Avenue, dubbed the Magnificent Mile, is the center of shopping. The Old Water Tower at Michigan and Chicago Avenues survived the Chicago fire of 1871.

Major museums include the Field Museum of Natural History, the Museum of Science and Industry, the Shedd Aquarium, and the Art Institute of Chicago with a world-class collection of Impressionist paintings. The Brookfield Zoo was the first in America to exhibit animals in natural surroundings instead of cages.

Sears Tower, Chicago, Illinois
Photo: Courtesy Chicago Convention and Tourism Bureau, Inc.

Other attractions in northern Illinois include Galena, a Victorian city, which was the home of Ulysses S. Grant, and Rockford, home of the Time Museum, which houses a large collection of clocks and watches. The western part of the state contains the Dickson Mounds, site of Mississippian Indian culture of 1000 BC, and Fort Crevecoeur, a replica of the French explorer LaSalle's outpost. Nauvoo, a center of Morman history, is on the Mississippi at the western edge of Illinois.

Central Illinois includes the state capital, Springfield, where Abraham Lincoln started his legislative career. *A Sound and Light Show* depicting his life is presented during the summer months. Southern Illinois, settled by the French, retains some of its culture and heritage in such sites as Fort de Chartres. The Shawnee National Forest, at the southern tip of the state, includes large wilderness and outdoor recreation areas.

MICHIGAN

Area: 58,216 square miles
Capital: Lansing
Population: 9,295,297

Michigan has an unusual shape. A Great Lakes state, it has a larger Lower Peninsula that lies between Lake Erie, Lake Huron, and Lake Michigan, and a smaller Upper Peninsula (called the U.P.) between Lake Superior, Lake Michigan, and Lake Huron. Most of the population is in the former, concentrated in the southeast around Detroit, Flint, Saginaw, and Lansing and in the southwest around Kalamazoo and Grand Rapids.

Ohio and Indiana are to the south of the Lower Peninsula, and Wisconsin is to the south and west of the Upper Peninsula. The remainder of the state is bounded by the Great Lakes, except for a small portion of the east, which is bounded by Canada. The Lower Peninsula is low and slightly rolling with many lakes. The Upper Peninsula is rugged and hilly, with streams, and waterfalls. Both portions of the state have extensive forested recreational area. Winter recreational facilities are better developed in the colder and snowier U.P.

Areas of Touristic Importance. Detroit is the cultural and commercial center of the state. It is also synonymous with automobile production, and the Detroit metropolitan area is home to General Motors, Ford, and Chrysler, the "Big Three" of United States auto production. Detroit's redeveloped downtown includes the Renaissance Center, the Civic Center, Philip Hart Plaza, and the Riverfront.

Greenfield Village and the Henry Ford Museum in Dearborn is a leading indoor and outdoor museum with over one hundred structures including the original homes and workshops of Thomas Edison and Henry Ford, and the Wright Brothers bicycle shop. The museum also houses more than two hundred antique autos and thousands of vintage machines. In Frankenmuth, Bavarian hospitality and charm abound in the town's restaurants and shops.

Holland, Michigan is the scene of an annual tulip festival. Traverse City, on the west side of Michigan, offers excellent opportunities for golf, skiing, and fine resorts.

Mackinac Island, off the Upper Peninsula, is a popular resort area. No cars or mechanized vehicles are allowed on the island. Unique and colorful, the island's shops feature antiques, curios, and fudge. Fort Mackinac is a restored British and American military outpost with 13 period buildings. Pictured Rocks National Lakeshore rises directly from Lake Superior with a 40-mile expanse of water-carved rocks.

WISCONSIN

Area: 56,154 square miles
Capital: Madison
Population: 4,891,769

Wisconsin has a long eastern frontage on Lake Michigan and a short stretch on Lake Superior. Much of its western boundary with Minnesota and Iowa is formed by the Mississippi River. Its northern border is the Upper Peninsula of Michigan and its southern border is Illinois. Wisconsin is dotted with lakes; Lake Oshkosh is the largest. Most of the population live in the southeast, around the main cities of Milwaukee, facing on Lake Michigan, and Madison. Prehistoric glaciers carved the variegated face of the state, leaving it with more than 15,000 lakes. Steep ridges are found in the southwest corner, an area never covered by glaciers. Skiing and ice fishing are important in winter.

Areas of Touristic Importance. Milwaukee is a city of rich ethnic heritage. German, Polish, Irish, and Italian traditions remain intact in the city's neighborhoods, restaurants, and festivals. Partly because of its German heritage the city is the beer capital of the United States. The Wisconsin Dells are the state's foremost natural attraction. The seven-mile stretch of the Wisconsin River features sculptured cliffs rising nearly one hundred feet above the river. Fort Dells is a replica of a pioneer fort. Lake Geneva is another popular resort area. Door County, in northeast Wisconsin, is popular for its rural, "New England" atmosphere. Taliesin, the home of world-famous architect Frank Lloyd Wright, is open to visitors.

MINNESOTA

Area: 84,068 square miles
Capital: St. Paul
Population: 4,375,099

The westernmost Great Lakes state, Minnesota, faces on Lake Superior. The Mississippi River originates in Minnesota and forms its southeastern boundary, while much of the state's western boundary lies along the north-flowing Red River of the north. Bordering states are North and South Dakota on the west, Iowa on the south, and Wisconsin on the east. Canada borders on the north. Lightly populated northern Minnesota is known for its many lakes, iron-ore mining, the port city of Duluth on the western tip of Lake Superior, and outstanding wheat production in the Red River valley. In the agricultural and more heavily populated south, Minneapolis-St. Paul is a large metropolitan center on the Mississippi River.

Minnesota is a land of prairies, farmland, bluffs, forests, and over eleven thousand lakes. Lake of the Woods on the Minnesota-Ontario border is the headwater for the mighty Mississippi River.

Areas of Touristic Importance. Minneapolis and St. Paul, commonly known as the Twin Cities, have a metropolitan area population of more than two million. The area was a mecca for German, Irish, and Scandinavian immigrants. More recently, it has seen an influx of H'mong immigrants from southeast Asia. St. Paul, the state capital, is more historic and earthy, while Minneapolis is more contemporary and modern. They share excellent cultural activities including orchestras and theater. Both offer interesting museums and festivals.

Minneapolis is the site of the Mall of America, a huge shopping and entertainment complex. Visitors come in just for the day to visit the Mall; some Europeans come for the weekend.

Downtown Minneapolis, Minnesota
Photo: Courtesy Minneapolis Convention & Tourism Commission

The North Woods is an area of lakes and vast wilderness. Voyageurs National Park follows the waterways of the early French explorers along the Minnesota-Canadian border. Boundary Waters Canoe Area offers more than 1,200 miles of canoe routes and over 2,000 campsite areas in northeastern Minnesota. Duluth is a major port on Lake Superior.

IOWA

Area: 56,290 square miles
Capital: Des Moines
Population: 2,776,755

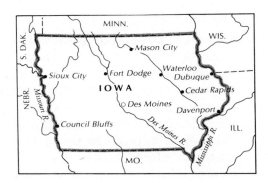

Iowa is west of and faces on the Mississippi River. It is bordered by the Missouri River on the west. States bordering on Iowa are Minnesota to the north, Wisconsin and Illinois to the east, Missouri to the south, and South Dakota and Nebraska to the west. Its main cities are Davenport and Cedar Rapids in the east and Des Moines in the center. Iowa has important agricultural and industrial economies. It is in the heartland of American agriculture; corn and wheat are its main crops. Nearly 95 percent of the state's land is under cultivation.

Areas of Touristic Importance. The Amana Colonies were settled in the 1840s by a religious sect from Germany, Switzerland, and France. Once communal, the colonies are now organized as a member-owned manufacturing cooperative. Living History Farms in Des Moines is an open air museum featuring authentic, working farms, including an Indian site from the 1700s, an 1840 pioneer farm, a 1900 horse farm, and a "farm of today." The vintage Boone and Scenic Valley Railroad provides a 10-mile train ride across the Des Moines River Valley.

■ TYPES OF TOURISM

Independent touring is the most popular form of travel in the Eastern United States. However, escorted and hosted group tours are quite popular as well. The following tour programs are samples of those available within the region:

- Historic East
- Kentucky and Tennessee
- New Orleans and the Deep South
- Florida Resorts Plus Walt Disney World
- Grand Autumn New England

GLOBUS· *First Class* ESCORTED

The Historic East

Washington D.C., Williamsburg, Monticello, Charlottesville, Gettysburg, Valley Forge, Philadelphia

Tour **AHE** – 8 days from Washington D.C. to Washington D.C.

Maximum elevation on tour: 4,000 ft.

ALL THIS IS INCLUDED

- Services of a professional tour director
- First-class hotels listed below or equivalent (see page 9). Twin-bedded rooms with private bath or shower, hotel taxes, service charges and tips for baggage handling
- 7 American breakfasts (B); and 5 three-course dinners offering choice of entree (D), with a special welcome dinner in Washington DC and a farewell dinner in Philadelphia
- Private deluxe air-conditioned motorcoach
- Sightseeing with local guide in

Washington D.C., Gettysburg National Military Park and Philadelphia
- Visits to Mount Vernon, Yorktown, Jamestown, Colonial Williamsburg, Richmond, Monticello, Charlottesville, Harpers Ferry, Lancaster, Valley Forge, Philadelphia, Annapolis
- Other scenic highlights: the Skyline Drive, Shenandoah National Park, Pennsylvania Dutch countryside
- Inside visits as shown in UPPER-CASE LETTERS in the tour description, including admission charges where applicable
- Globus travel bag and travel documents

▼ *JEFFERSON MEMORIAL, WASHINGTON D.C.*

Day 1 WASHINGTON D.C. Today all tour members check in on independent schedules. The tour begins at 5:30 pm with a sightseeing tour of the capital. A stop en route to visit the LINCOLN MEMORIAL before reaching the restaurant. This evening your tour director hosts a welcome dinner, the perfect occasion to get acquainted with your traveling companions. (D)

Day 2 WASHINGTON D.C. The nation's capital city is a sightseeing treasure and a full-day tour shows off its many landmarks: the U.S. CAPITOL BUILDING and the ARLINGTON NATIONAL CEMETERY, where the Kennedy gravesites and the TOMB OF THE UNKNOWN SOLDIER are located. Also on the agenda is the Supreme Court Building, the Library of Congress and parts of the vast SMITHSONIAN INSTITUTE. Our suggestion for this evening is the optional outing to Alexandria. Visit the historic colonial town and enjoy dinner in the heart of Old Town at one of Alexandria's oldest restaurants. (B)

Day 3 WASHINGTON D.C.-MOUNT VERNON-YORKTOWN-JAMESTOWN-WILLIAMSBURG. South this morning to MOUNT VERNON, the wonderfully restored home of George Washington; tour the estate and visit the gravesite. Then into Virginia to YORKTOWN, the little village on the shores of the Chesapeake Bay where the British commander, Lord Cornwallis, surrendered to Washington's troops in 1781, bringing the American Revolution to an end. Last stop before reaching Williamsburg is JAMESTOWN, the first permanent English settlement in the New World. To complement the day, your tour director hosts a special "Virginia Colony" dinner. (B,D)

Day 4 WILLIAMSBURG. This morning tour COLONIAL WILLIAMSBURG'S HISTORIC AREA, where costumed villagers add to the authenticity and enchantment of the reconstructed areas. Take a stroll down its quaint streets and browse through the Historic Trade Shops or visit such exhibits as the Public Gaol, where Blackbeard the Pirate's crew were once imprisoned; and Raleigh Tavern, the meeting place for Jefferson, Patrick Henry and other patriots. The balance of the day is free. (B)

Day 5 WILLIAMSBURG-MONTICELLO-CHARLOTTESVILLE. Today's first stop is Richmond, Virginia's capital, once the Capital of the Confederacy. Visit the CAPITOL BUILDING and ST. JOHN'S CHURCH where Patrick Henry proclaimed "give me liberty or give me death". On the way to Charlottesville, tour MONTICELLO, Thomas Jefferson's estate, with its beautiful gardens and imposing mansion, designed by Jefferson himself. He died here and lies buried in the family graveyard near the home. (B,D)

Day 6 CHARLOTTESVILLE-GETTYSBURG. Enjoy panoramic vistas from the Skyline Drive cresting the Blue Ridge Mountains in the beautiful SHENANDOAH NATIONAL PARK. HARPERS FERRY, West Virginia is next, where John Brown and his "army of liberation" staged their famous raid on a U.S. arsenal. A short drive across Maryland to Gettysburg in Pennsylvania. Upon arrival, view the ELECTRIC MAP program to prepare for the battlefield tour tomorrow. (B,D)

Day 7 GETTYSBURG-PENN DUTCH COUNTRY-VALLEY FORGE-PHILADELPHIA. Start the day with a guided tour of THE GETTYSBURG NATIONAL MILITARY PARK, site of the decisive Civil War battles of 1863, the same year Abraham Lincoln delivered his famous speech at the dedication of the Gettysburg National Cemetery. Before leaving, visit THE FARM of the late President Dwight D. Eisenhower, adjoining the national park. East across the Susquehanna River into Pennsylvania Dutch Countryside – land of the religious Amish and Mennonite sects who shun

58 US

Reprinted courtesy of Globus and Cosmos.

the use of all modern conveniences. After a lunch break in Lancaster County, continue to VALLEY FORGE, the camp where Washington and his troops endured the harsh winter of 1777/78. This evening, a festive farewell dinner, an appropriate finale to a great touring adventure of America's Historic East. (B,D)

Day 8 PHILADELPHIA-ANNAPOLIS-WASHINGTON D.C. Visits to three of the country's most treasured shrines this morning: CONGRESS HALL, where Washington and Adams were inaugurated; the LIBERTY BELL PAVILION; and INDEPENDENCE HALL, where the Declaration of Independence and the U.S. Constitution were both signed. Drive through Delaware and Maryland before reaching Annapolis on the Chesapeake Bay. Enjoy a short orientation tour of this picturesque one-time

capital of the U.S. before returning to Washington D.C. A stop at National Airport for tour members with connecting flights; the coach then continues to the Washington Vista Hotel where the tour ends this afternoon. (B)

FALL FOLIAGE

Enjoy the spectacular fall colors of the mid-Atlantic states on our special fall foliage departures:

Fridays from September 16 to October 14
Saturdays from September 17 to October 15.
Sundays from September 18 to October 16.

(Please do not schedule return flights earlier than 6 p.m.)

➤ *This tour combines neatly with many of our other tours of The East. You pay less for your second tour: see page 3.*

Tour AHE: DATES & PRICES

Tour Code	Start Washington D.C.		End Washington D.C.		8 days US$
AHE0320	Sun	20-Mar	Sun	27-Mar	828
AHE0327	Sun	27-Mar	Sun	03-Apr	828
AHE0403	Sun	03-Apr	Sun	10-Apr	838
AHE0410	Sun	10-Apr	Sun	17-Apr	838
AHE0416	Sat	16-Apr	Sat	23-Apr	838
AHE0417	Sun	17-Apr	Sun	24-Apr	838
AHE0423	Sat	23-Apr	Sat	30-Apr	858
AHE0424	Sun	24-Apr	Sun	01-May	858
AHE0430	Sat	30-Apr	Sat	07-May	858
AHE0501	Sun	01-May	Sun	08-May	858
AHE0507	Sat	07-May	Sat	14-May	858
AHE0508	Sun	08-May	Sun	15-May	858
AHE0514	Sat	14-May	Sat	21-May	858
AHE0515	Sun	15-May	Sun	22-May	858
AHE0521	Sat	21-May	Sat	28-May	858
AHE0522	Sun	22-May	Sun	29-May	858
AHE0528	Sat	28-May	Sat	04-Jun	858
AHE0529	Sun	29-May	Sun	05-Jun	858
AHE0605	Sun	05-Jun	Sun	12-Jun	858
AHE0612	Sun	12-Jun	Sun	19-Jun	858
AHE0619	Sun	19-Jun	Sun	26-Jun	858
AHE0626	Sun	26-Jun	Sun	03-Jul	858
AHE0703	Sun	03-Jul	Sun	10-Jul	858
AHE0710	Sun	10-Jul	Sun	17-Jul	858
AHE0717	Sun	17-Jul	Sun	24-Jul	858
AHE0724	Sun	24-Jul	Sun	31-Jul	858
AHE0731	Sun	31-Jul	Sun	07-Aug	858
AHE0807	Sun	07-Aug	Sun	14-Aug	848
AHE0814	Sun	14-Aug	Sun	21-Aug	848
AHE0821	Sun	21-Aug	Sun	28-Aug	848
AHE0828	Sun	28-Aug	Sun	04-Sep	848
AHE0904	Sun	04-Sep	Sun	11-Sep	858
AHE0910	Sat	10-Sep	Sat	17-Sep	858
AHE0911	Sun	11-Sep	Sun	18-Sep	858
AHE0916	Fri	16-Sep	Fri	23-Sep	858
AHE0917	Sat	17-Sep	Sat	24-Sep	858
AHE0918	Sun	18-Sep	Sun	25-Sep	858
AHE0923	Fri	23-Sep	Fri	30-Sep	858
AHE0924	Sat	24-Sep	Sat	01-Oct	858
AHE0925	Sun	25-Sep	Sun	02-Oct	858
AHE0930	Fri	30-Sep	Fri	07-Oct	858
AHE1001	Sat	01-Oct	Sat	08-Oct	858
AHE1002	Sun	02-Oct	Sun	09-Oct	858
AHE1007	Fri	07-Oct	Fri	14-Oct	858
AHE1008	Sat	08-Oct	Sat	15-Oct	858
AHE1009	Sun	09-Oct	Sun	16-Oct	858
AHE1014	Fri	14-Oct	Fri	21-Oct	858
AHE1015	Sat	15-Oct	Sat	22-Oct	858
AHE1016	Sun	16-Oct	Sun	23-Oct	858
AHE1022	Sat	22-Oct	Sat	29-Oct	838
AHE1023	Sun	23-Oct	Sun	30-Oct	838
AHE1030	Sun	30-Oct	Sun	06-Nov	828

Prices are for all land arrangements. Air fare to and from Washington D.C. is additional. Your travel agent can help you find the best available air fare.

Single room supplement: $277

Triple room reduction per person: $53

Reduction for joining on day 3 upon departure from Washington D.C.: $127

Reduction for leaving on day 7 upon arrival in Philadelphia: $70

For additional accommodations in Washington D.C. before and after the tour, see our special rates on page 11.

APOLLO: TD*GG, **PARS:** G/PTS/GGX, **SABRE:** Y/TUR/QGG

GLOBUS HOTELS

WASHINGTON D.C. Washington Vista,
WILLIAMSBURG Fort Magruder Inn,
CHARLOTTESVILLE Omni Charlottesville Hotel,
GETTYSBURG Holiday Inn Battlefield,
PHILADELPHIA Philadelphia Hilton & Towers

▼ *ELDERLY AMISH MAN*

▼ *THE LIBERTY BELL*

▼ *COLONIAL WILLIAMSBURG*

■ For a longer vacation in the Mid-South, combine this tour with The Ozarks.

🍁 🍁 **8 Days (7 Nights)** **$1190**

Extra Highlights: *Blue Ridge Parkway* □ *Chimney Rock* □ *Churchill Downs* □ *Appalachian Mountains* □ *"My Old Kentucky Home"* *Keeneland Race Track* □ *Grand Ole Opry* □ *Opryland USA* □ *The Hermitage* — *7 Breakfasts, 5 Lunches, 7 Dinners*

Kentucky and Tennessee
Plus Smoky Mountains National Park

Welcome to the Bluegrass State of Kentucky, where the finest thoroughbreds in the world are raised. This is the pioneer land of Daniel Boone and Appalachia. Drive through the spectacular scenery of the Great Smoky Mountains. And tap your toes to the foot stompin' country music in Tennessee! This part of America has a culture all its own!

See the famous horse farms of Kentucky

1. CHARLOTTE / LAKE LURE
Fly to Charlotte, North Carolina. **Tour departs: Charlotte Airport, 1:00 P.M.** Meet your tour director near the US Air baggage claim area after 12:00 noon. It is an easy drive into the Blue Ridge Mountains for a visit to Chimney Rock with its breathtaking vista of verdant valleys, lakes and forest-clad hills and mountains. Overnight on nearby Lake Lure, one of the prettiest spots in the Carolinas. Meals included **D**

2. BILTMORE HOUSE / SMOKY MTNS
Motor to historic Asheville to visit the palatial Biltmore House, the last of the great mansions constructed by the flamboyantly wealthy Vanderbilt family. You travel the picturesque Blue Ridge Parkway with a stop at Cherokee for lunch and a visit to the Oconaluftee Indian Village (seasonal). Here the trail leads skyward through cool mountain passes into Great Smoky Mountains National Park. Mile high peaks covered with virgin forests provide a spectacular panorama. At times the mountains are veiled in ghostly mists rising like smoke from which comes the name "Great Smokies." Descend into the mountain town of Gatlinburg and continue to Knoxville, Tennessee, for overnight. Meals included **BLD**

3. BLUEGRASS KENTUCKY
This morning you visit the Museum of Appalachia, a living mountain village which preserves the way of life of our pioneers. Then, wind through the Cumberland Mountains, that vast wilderness which sealed off the infant American coastal colonies from the interior. Follow in the footsteps of Daniel Boone who, with 30 axmen, cut a 208-mile swath through the forest to open his legendary "Wilderness Road." Cross into the Bluegrass State of Kentucky. Lunch is at Boone Tavern on the campus of Berea College where student waiters serve you as part of the school's Student Work Program. Continue this afternoon to Lexington, in the very heart of Central Kentucky's bluegrass region. Visit Ashland, the Henry Clay Estate, before arriving at your hotel. Meals included **BLD**

4. LEXINGTON HORSE FARMS
When you think of Kentucky, you think of bourbon whiskey or horses in fields of bluegrass. The latter image will come to life today as you tour Lexington's horse farm country. First stop is at Keeneland Race Track where you may see thoroughbreds being exercised as part of their morning workout. This is one of the most beautiful, traditional racetracks in America. Then, take to back roads and sightsee some of the famous horse farms. After lunch visit the fascinating Kentucky Horse Park which offers a close-up view of a real horse farm. Return to the hotel with time to visit the nearby shops, or take a walking tour of historic downtown Lexington. Meals included **BLD**

The Biltmore House

5. LOUISVILLE / CHURCHILL DOWNS

Begin this morning with a visit to Frankfort's beautiful state capitol building. Then travel to Louisville, the home of Churchill Downs and the Kentucky Derby. The name elicits feelings of tradition and prestige that have become legendary. After lunch, visit the Kentucky Derby Museum depicting horse racing's colorful history and featuring a 360° multi-media presentation. Overnight in Louisville. Meals included **BLD**

6. NASHVILLE / GRAND OLE OPRY

Travel south to Bardstown, the location of the 18th-century plantation known as "My Old Kentucky Home," where Stephen Foster was inspired to compose his best-loved song. Next, visit an authentic distillery of Kentucky bourbon whiskey. After lunch, cross into Tennessee for a short drive to Nashville, the capital of Tennessee. Nashville is best known as the "Athens of the South" and "Music City, USA." This evening visit the world-famous Grand Ole Opry in Nashville.

The Opry has given birth to an entire industry and offers you the very best in live country music. Meals included **BLD**

7. HERMITAGE / OPRYLAND

This morning see the state capitol, Printer's Alley and the Parthenon – the world's only full-size reproduction of the Athenian original. Continue to Hermitage, the magnificent 625-acre estate that was the home of Andrew Jackson, soldier, senator, president. Then, visit nearby Opryland USA, a 118-acre entertainment complex featuring American music from jazz and blues to pop and country and western, all in appropriate settings. This is more than a theme park; it's an opportunity to see 350 young entertainers play and sing and kick up their heels making more music than you could hear on Broadway in a week. Whatever your taste in music, you'll find it here with more than 70 productions presented daily. This evening, join us for a farewell reception and dinner. Meals included **BD**

Opryland

8. JOURNEY HOME

Tour ends: Nashville Airport, 11:00 A.M. Our motorcoach returns to the airport to connect with various flights departing after 12 Noon. (Independent shuttles are available at an additional cost of about $9 per person.) Meals included **B**

Departure Dates:

SUNDAYS – Mar. 27 to Oct. 30

Price Per Person:

Twin $1190   Single $1414   Triple $1113
Twin with roll-away

See "Tour Prices Include," page 122.
19 Meals Included.

Air Fare to Charlotte and from Nashville is additional

Contact your booking agent for special low fares which are usually available.

Stay at the best available hotels

Night 1	**Lake Lure Inn**	Lake Lure, NC
Night 2	**Hyatt Regency Knoxville**	Knoxville, TN
Night 3,4	**Hyatt Regency Lexington**	Lexington, KY
Night 5*	**Seelbach Hotel**	Louisville, KY
Night 6,7	**Loews Vanderbilt Plaza Hotel**	Nashville, TN

* *Tours of May 1, 2 will spend three nights at Hyatt Regency Lexington.*

APOLLO ACCESS TD*28034
WORLDSPAN ACCESS .... G/PTS/TTX/KY

Pioneer life in Appalachia

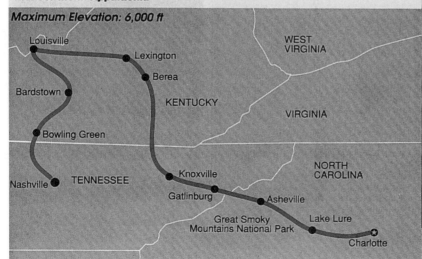

Maximum Elevation: 6,000 ft

Louisville
Lexington
Berea
Bardstown
Bowling Green
Nashville   TENNESSEE
Knoxville
Gatlinburg
Asheville
Great Smoky Mountains National Park
Lake Lure
Charlotte
KENTUCKY
WEST VIRGINIA
VIRGINIA
NORTH CAROLINA

■ For a longer vacation in the South, combine this tour with Charleston, Kentucky or The Ozarks.

9 Days (8 Nights) $1190

Extra Highlights: *Natchez Antebellum Homes* ☐ *Mississippi River Cruise* ☐ *Vicksburg Battlefield* ☐ *Natchez Trace* ☐ *French Quarter* ☐ *Cajun Country* ☐ *Atchafalaya Basin Cruise* — *8 Breakfasts, 6 Lunches, 7 Dinners*

New Orleans and the Deep South

Cajun Country Bellingrath Gardens

1. ARRIVE NEW ORLEANS / BILOXI

Fly to New Orleans. **Tour departs: New Orleans Intl. Airport, 3:00 P.M.,** Meet outside Delta Airlines baggage claim area, lower level. Here in the "Heart of Dixie," you begin an intriguing adventure through the Deep South. Take a spectacular 24-mile drive across Lake Pontchartrain on the "longest causeway in the world" en route to Biloxi, located on Mississippi's Gulf Coast. This evening you are invited to a reception and dinner to get acquainted with your fellow travelers. Meals included **D**

2. BELLINGRATH GARDENS

Today see the 65 landscaped acres of Bellingrath Gardens. Every season at Bellingrath brings new visual delights and transforms the garden into a floral wonderland. Also visit the home of Mr. and Mrs. Walter Bellingrath to see their prized furnishings. Then drive to Mobile, Alabama, for lunch and a tour of the city before returning to Biloxi. Enjoy a swim in the warm waters of the Gulf or in the pool at your hotel. Tonight, dinner out provides a sampling of local fare. Meals included **BLD**

3. BILOXI BAY CRUISE / NATCHEZ

Embark on an interesting and entertaining cruise of the Mississippi Sound. Watch your captain set his trawl and demonstrate the trade of the Biloxi fishermen. Then proceed north through Hattiesburg, the home of the University of Southern Mississippi, to Natchez for the next two nights. This historic town, perched on the east bank of the Mississippi River, is one of the most charming in our nation. Located in the heart of downtown, the historic Eola Hotel stands as a reminder of the faded elegance of the Old South. Meals included **BLD**

4. VICKSBURG BATTLEFIELD

Today is steeped in history. Begin by traveling north through Washington, Miss., home of Jefferson College, where renowned figures such as Jefferson Davis, John James Audubon and Aaron Burr played a role. Travel on part of the Natchez Trace, perhaps the first highway in the United States, before arriving in Vicksburg, scene of one of the most decisive Civil War battles. Enjoy a brief tour of the city and a comprehensive tour of the battlefield before lunch. Return to Natchez in the afternoon. Meals included **BLD**

5. ANTEBELLUM NATCHEZ

Today you explore Natchez, much of which has been restored to its antebellum grandeur. A member of the Garden Club

Nottoway Plantation – the largest plantation home in the South

Cajun wilderness

Fine cuisine at Arnaud's

Reprinted courtesy of Tauck Tours.

Bellingrath Gardens – brilliantly aflame with thousands of flowers

takes you into the interior of several dignified private homes. On display are some of the finest furniture, china, silver and paintings to be found in the South. Lunch is amid the charming atmosphere of the Garden Club's Carriage House. Continue to Louisiana for overnight. Meals included **BLD**

6. CAJUN COUNTRY / EVANGELINE

Motor south through the farmlands and cotton fields of Louisiana to Lafayette. Explore the land of Henry Wadsworth Longfellow's poem "Evangeline." Cruise into the Atchafalaya River Basin, one of the South's scenic semi-wilderness areas. A Cajun guide entertains you with local folklore and seeks out the wildlife. Overnight is in Lafayette. Meals included **BLD**

7. NEW ORLEANS / BRENNAN'S

Travel the bayou country to Nottoway Plantation to visit the largest plantation house in the South. At midday arrive at Brennan's for brunch, a tradition in New Orleans. Today you'll tour the city and see the Mississippi River, St. Louis Cathedral, the Napoleon House, Pirates' Alley, the French Market and many other points of interest. Soon arrive at your hotel in the heart of the French Quarter. You will enjoy the narrow streets and age-old buildings, iron-trellised balconies and sweeping fan windows. Meals included **BL**

8. RIVER STEAMBOAT CRUISE

Sleep late if you wish or stroll the quaint French Quarter and visit the specialty shops of Royal Street and the open-air galleries of Jackson Square. Lunch is not included today. This afternoon board the stern-wheeler steamboat "Natchez" for a sightseeing cruise of New Orleans-On-The-River. Along these river banks, some 250 years ago, "cotton was king" and "slow and easy" was a way of life. Tonight you are invited to a farewell dinner at famed Arnaud's. Meals included **BD**

9. JOURNEY HOME

The final morning is for leisure. **Tour ends: New Orleans. Fly home any time.** Since persons leave at different times, it is not practical to include a transfer to the airport. Limo/van fare is about $10 per person, cabs about $32 per car for up to four persons. Check out time is 12:00 Noon. (For those who wish additional time in New Orleans, a post-tour stay may be arranged at time of booking.) Meals included **B**

Departure Dates:

Feb. 14, 22
Mar. 6, 10, 14, 18, 22, 26, 30
April 3, 7, 11, 15, 19, 23, 27
May 1, 5, 9, 13, 21, 29
June 6, 14, 22, 30
July 8, 16, 24
Aug. 1, 9, 17, 25
Sept. 2, 10, 18, 22, 26, 30
Oct. 4, 8, 12, 16, 20, 28
Nov. 5

Price Per Person:

Twin $1190   Single $1414   Triple $1102
                                        Twin with roll-away

See "Tour Prices Include," page 122.
21 Meals Included.

Air fare to and from New Orleans is additional

Contact your booking agent for special low fares which are usually available.

Stay at the best available hotels

Night 1,2	**Treasure Bay Hotel** Biloxi, MS
Night 3,4	**Natchez Eola Hotel** Natchez, MS
Night 5	**Hotel Bentley** Alexandria, LA
Night 6	**Lafayette Hilton** Lafayette, LA
Night 7,8	**Bourbon Orleans Hotel** New Orleans, LA

Note: The sightseeing features of the Deep South are relatively remote. Also, hotels and services, although chosen from the best available, may not compare with facilities found in more populated areas.

APOLLO ACCESS TD*28035
WORLDSPAN ACCESS .... G/PTS/TTX/NO

Maximum Elevation: 200 ft.

Vicksburg
Natchez Trace
MISSISSIPPI
ALABAMA
Alexandria   Natchez
Hattiesburg
LOUISIANA
Lafayette
Lake Pontchartrain
Mobile
Atchafalaya Basin
MISSISSIPPI RIVER
New Orleans
Nottoway Plantation
Biloxi
Bellingrath Gardens
GULF OF MEXICO

Florida Resorts Tour ... **7 Days (6 Nights) From $1195**
With Walt Disney World ... **10 Days (9 Nights) From $1740**

Extra Highlights: *Edison Home ☐ Key West ☐ Everglades ☐ Palm Beach ☐ Kennedy Space Center*
☐ MAGIC KINGDOM® Park/EPCOT® Center/Disney-MGM Studios Theme Park **— 9 Breakfasts, 4 Lunches, 8 Dinners**

Florida Resorts Plus Walt Disney World®

This tour features some of the finest coastal resorts in all of Florida...the posh Boca Raton Hotel, Hawks Cay Resort, Marco Island Resort and the fabulous Walt Disney World Swan. In addition, see the fabulous Florida Keys, the Everglades and Kennedy Space Center. Those who do not wish to visit Walt Disney World may take just the first 7 days, ending their tour in Boca Raton.

1. TAMPA / YBOR CITY
Fly to Tampa. **Tour departs: Tampa Airport, TWA baggage claim area (blue area), 1:30 PM.** Claim your luggage and meet your tour director. Begin with a sightseeing tour of Tampa on the Gulf of Mexico. This afternoon visit Ybor City, Tampa's historic district. See Spanish Courtyards, artisans' workshops, and visit the State Museum before arriving at your waterfront hotel. Tonight enjoy a welcome dinner at one of Tampa's landmark restaurants. Meals included **D**

2. FORT MYERS / MARCO ISLAND
Head south along the west coast. After luncheon in Ft. Myers, visit the winter

home of Thomas A. Edison, situated in a botanical garden and remaining as it was when he died. Soon arrive in the resort community of Marco Island for the next two nights. Your hotel overlooks a magnificent white sand beach along the Gulf of Mexico. Meals included **BLD**

3. MARCO ISLAND BEACH RESORT
You will like the tasteful elegance of Marco Island and the many resort facilities available. There are pools and beach for swimming and sunbathing, tennis, golf, shopping, or you can just plain relax. The entire day is free to enjoy your visit here. Keep your fingers crossed for good weather. Meals included **BD**

4. EVERGLADES / KEY BISCAYNE
This morning, drive into the silent Everglades. Pause for an interesting excursion through the Everglades waterways, where it is possible to see an occasional alligator basking on the banks and snowy white egrets poised to take flight. Lunch is on Key Biscayne, an exclusive island suburb of Miami nestled between the Atlantic and Biscayne Bay. After lunch, drive out along the Florida Keys, a series of coral reef islands strung

Beautiful sunsets in the Keys

Kennedy Space Center

out in a long, westward arc from the tip of Florida's Atlantic coast to the Gulf of Mexico. Arrive at Hawk's Cay for a relaxing two-night stay. You will like the gracious, informal ambience of this island resort. Wicker furniture, rambling patios; it's a relaxing place in a magnificent island setting. Meals included **BLD**

5. FLORIDA KEYS / KEY WEST
Sleep late, or linger over a sumptuous breakfast. Sunbathe, swim, play a game of tennis or take it easy. You may even enjoy a walk along the hotel's private lagoon. Marathon, Key Largo, Islamorada, Sugarloaf, 7-Mile Bridge, Key West, are places synonymous with the Keys. You

The Boca Raton Hotel – one of America's most elegant resorts

Reprinted courtesy of Tauck Tours.

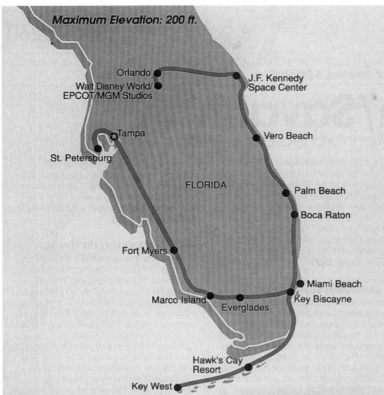

Maximum Elevation: 200 ft.

Orlando
Walt Disney World/
EPCOT/MGM Studios

J.F. Kennedy
Space Center

Tampa

Vero Beach

St. Petersburg

FLORIDA

Palm Beach

Boca Raton

Fort Myers

Miami Beach

Marco Island

Key Biscayne

Everglades

Hawk's Cay
Resort

Key West

will see them all. This afternoon motor south along the ocean causeway to the end of the chain, Key West. Sightsee this quaint, historic port city and have time to enjoy the museums and boutiques at Mallory Square on harbor's edge. Dinner is in Key West before returning to Hawk's Cay. Meals included **BD**

6. BOCA RATON HOTEL

Leave the Keys and the relaxed island lifestyle and drive north through Florida's Gold Coast. Arrive at the famous Boca Raton Hotel for lunch and an afternoon at leisure. Rich in history and tradition, this is one of America's most elegant, water-side properties. Your accommodations will be in the Cloisters, where old-world charm has enchanted privileged guests since the 1920's. This evening, we will host a farewell reception for those leaving tomorrow. Meals included **BLD**

7. SPACE CENTER / ORLANDO

7-day tour ends: Boca Raton. Fly home anytime. Since persons leave at different times, it is not practical to include an airport transfer to the Fort Lauderdale Airport. Airport limousines are available at about $13 per person, cabs about $50 for up to four passengers. Those opting for the 10-day tour will continue north to Cape Canaveral for a NASA tour of the Kennedy Space Center. Then, it's on to WALT DISNEY WORLD® Resort. You will have an experience of a lifetime visiting this fantastic entertainment mecca for the

EPCOT® Center

next two days. We provide a 4-day Bonus Passport which allows four days admission to MAGIC KINGDOM® Park, EPCOT® Center, Disney-MGM Studios Theme Park and transportation between the parks, plus one admission to Pleasure Island or River Country. Meals included **BLD**

8/9. WALT DISNEY WORLD® RESORT

Today and tomorrow you discover the fabulous attractions at the WALT DISNEY WORLD Resort. Visit the MAGIC KINGDOM Park, a world of fun and fantasy. Take an exciting look into the future at EPCOT Center, the "Experimental Prototype City of Tomorrow." Step into the world of Hollywood at the Disney-MGM Studios

Theme Park. Reminisce as you ride through scenes of Hollywood's most classic movies. See current films and TV shows actually being made. Witness breathtaking stunts and special effects. On your final evening, we invite you to a dinner party to bid farewell to your fellow travelers. Meals included **B8/BD9**

10. JOURNEY HOME

10-day tour ends: Orlando. Fly home anytime. Since persons leave at different times, it is not practical to include an airport transfer. Limousine fare is about $12 per person, cabs about $38 per car for up to 4 passengers. Meals included **B**

Departure Dates:

Jan 1, 10, 19, 29	July 6, 16
Feb 7, 16, 25	Aug 3, 13, 31
Mar 7, 16, 26	Sept 10, 19, 28
Apr 4, 13, 23	Oct 8, 17, 26
May 2, 11, 21, 30	Nov 5, 14, 23
Jun 8, 18, 27	Dec 3, 13, 16, 22

Price Per Person: 7 Days

Departures: Apr 24 – Dec 31
Twin $1195   Single $1555   Triple $1087
Twin with roll-away

Departures: Jan 1 – Apr 23
Twin $1380   Single $1914   Triple $1212
Twin with roll-away

See "Tour Prices Include," page 122.
15 Meals Included.

Price Per Person: 10 Days

Departures: Apr 24 – Dec 31
Twin $1740   Single $2352   Triple $1551
Twin with roll-away

Departures: Jan 1 – Apr 23
Twin $1940   Single $2750   Triple $1679
Twin with roll-away

See "Tour Prices Include," page 122.
21 Meals Included.

Air fare is additional

Contact your booking agent for special low fares which are usually available.

Stay at the best available hotels

Night 1	**Wyndham Harbour Island Hotel** Tampa, FL
Night 2,3*	**Marriott Marco Island Resort** Marco Island, FL
Night 4,5	**Hawk's Cay Resort** Marathon, FL
Night 6**	**Boca Raton Hotel** Boca Raton, FL
Night 7,8,9	**Walt Disney World Swan** Lake Buena Vista, FL

* Tour of Feb 25, May 21 stay at Marco Beach Hilton.
** Tour of Dec 22 will stay at Boca Raton Marriott.

APOLLO ACCESS..................................... TD*28037
WORLDSPAN ACCESS........................ G/PTS/TTX/FR

🍁 🍁 🍁 **11 Days (10 Nights) $1895**

Extra Highlights: *Lake Placid Cruise ☐ Shelburne Museum ☐ White Mts. ☐ Green Mts. ☐ Franconia Notch ☐ Plimoth Plantation ☐ Boothbay Harbor Cruise ☐ The Breakers* — ***10 Breakfasts, 8 Lunches, 8 Dinners***

Grand Autumn New England

WHAT'S THE DIFFERENCE?...
It's called Grand Autumn New England because it includes more days than other Autumn tours. There are more visits to attractions, more time to browse and absorb in each area visited and less of a feeling of being on-the-go. 8 of the 10 overnights are spent at two-night destinations.

1. **LAKE GEORGE / LAKE PLACID**
Tour departs: Waldorf-Astoria Hotel, 49th St., 8:00 A.M. Travel north along the New York Thruway. Take a meander through Albany and follow the Northway into the Adirondacks for luncheon. Continue through the mountains to the village of Lake Placid. This was the home of the 1932 and 1980 Winter Olympics. Meals included **LD**

2. **ADIRONDACKS LEISURE**
Sleep late if you wish. Enjoy a boat ride around Lake Placid to see many of the homes and estates of this resort community.

The remainder of the afternoon is free to explore this quaint village or just sit back and enjoy the quiet view of Mirror Lake from your hotel. Meals included **BD**

3. **LAKE CHAMPLAIN / SHELBURNE**
Today autumn coloring takes on its full splendor. It's a sight to behold. You wind along the Ausable River through Wilmington Notch to Lake Champlain where you board a ferry for Vermont. Visit Shelburne Museum, a remarkable 45-acre reconstruction of three centuries of Early American life. Continue on to Stowe, Vermont, your home for the next two nights. Meals included **BLD**

4. **STOWE / TRAPP FAMILY LODGE**
Enjoy the serenity of Vermont life! A morning tour will orient you to this picturesque area. Lunch is included at the famous Trapp Family Lodge. The remainder of the day is free. You may wish to meander about Stowe and do a bit of shopping, take pictures or visit a Cider Mill. Meals included **BLD**

Boston - The old and the new

Reprinted courtesy of Tauck Tours.

5. VERMONT / NEW HAMPSHIRE

We're on-the-go again. Traverse winding roads to Montpelier, where Vermont's capitol stands framed against the hills in a picturebook setting. Continue into New Hampshire's White Mountains. The foliage takes on a beautiful hue as we climb to Franconia Notch to see the Old Man of the Mountain, a natural rock profile. After lunch against the backdrop of spectacular Mount Washington, arrive at your hotel in North Conway for overnight. Meals included **BLD**

6. MAINE'S ROCKY COAST

Today it's down to the rockbound coast. Artists for centuries have flocked to the Maine/New Hampshire shore. It's a rugged, rocky shore, salt-sea air, lobstermen, shipbuilding, boatyards and magnificent summer homes...a place where tradition is a way of life. Visit the Maine Maritime Museum in Bath, depicting the shipbuilding heritage of Maine. Arrive in Boothbay Harbor for a delightful cruise (weather permitting) among the islands of this popular coastal town. Overnight overlooking the rockbound coast of Maine. Meals included **BLD**

Lobster buoys

7. KENNEBUNKPORT / BOSTON

Journey south to Kennebunkport. Stroll the narrow streets of this picturesque village. Our coach will pass Walker Point for a view of George and Barbara Bush's home. Enjoy luncheon on the Maine Coast. Continue to Portsmouth, NH, once the home of John Paul Jones. Wind along the 17-mile coastline of New Hampshire before crossing into Massachusetts. Your home for the next two nights is the Marriott Hotel-Copley Place, ideally located in the heart of Boston. Meals included **BLD**

8. BOSTON / FREEDOM TRAIL

In recent years our country has been on a binge to restore the past. As a result, there is more to see in Boston today than ever before. There is the Freedom Trail, a walk through historic Boston...the new Quincy Market Place beside Faneuil Hall, the Charles Street antique shops, the Common, Museums and historic shrines ...and all in a relatively compact, easily accessible area. We will do a sightseeing tour to orient you to the city, then drop

"American as Apple Pie"

you off at either the Quincy Market Place, the Common or Copley Square so that you may pursue your own interests. Meals included **B**

9. PLYMOUTH / SANDWICH

South of Boston is Plymouth. Here, visit the Plimoth Plantation, a restoration depicting the times, life and crafts of 17th-century Plymouth. See Plymouth Rock. Cross the Cape Cod Canal to the historic village of Sandwich for a luncheon at the Daniel Webster Inn. Then continue on to Newport, RI, for the next two nights. Meals included **BL**

10. NEWPORT / 10 MILE DRIVE

When the sun's up, it will shine on your yachting cap and bounce off your binoculars as you browse and explore America's yachting capital. This morning you slowly wind along the famed "10-Mile Drive" which boasts many of the homes and exquisite estates of the "400." You pause to visit The Breakers, the most palatial of them all. See Newport's famed harbor and Bowen's Wharf. The afternoon is yours to explore Newport on your own. In early evening, visit Hammersmith Farm, the waterfront estate where Jacqueline Kennedy Onassis spent her summers as a child. End the day with a memorable farewell dinner on the town. Meals included **BD**

11. MYSTIC SEAPORT, CONN.

En route to New York, visit Mystic Seaport a nationally acclaimed "living" museum depicting 19th century life in coastal New England. Step aboard tall ships that once braved the Seven Seas in the great Age of Sail. And marvel at extensive exhibits of ship models, scrimshaw, figureheads and other items from the whaling era.

Tour ends: La Guardia Airport 4:45 PM and Waldorf-Astoria Hotel 5:45 PM (Traffic permitting). To JFK Airport there is a Carey bus shuttle that departs from La Guardia every half hour, fare $9.50 per person. Allow 1 hour for shuttle connection and transfer. Taxis to JFK are approx. $15 per car. Allow 45 min. It is risky to book LGA flights prior to 6 PM or JFK flights prior to 6:30 PM. Meals included **BL**

Departure Dates:

DAILY – Sept. 3 to Oct 16

Price Per Person:

Twin $1895   Single $2415   Triple $1715
Twin with roll-away

See "Tour Prices Include," page 122.
26 Meals Included.

Air Fare to New York additional

Contact your booking agent for special low fares which are usually available.

Stay at the best available hotels

Night 1,2	**Mirror Lake Inn** Lake Placid, NY
Night 3,4	**Stoweflake Resort** Stowe, VT
Night 5	**Red Jacket Mountain View** North Conway, NH
Night 6	**Spruce Point Inn** Boothbay Harbor, ME
Night 7,8	**Marriott Copley Place** Boston, MA
Night 9,10	**Newport Harbor Hotel** Newport, RI

APOLLO ACCESS TD*28007
WORLDSPAN ACCESS .... G/PTS/TTX/GR

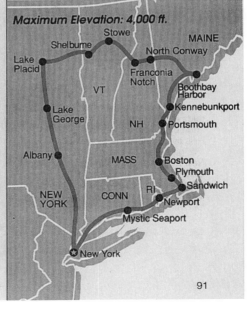

Maximum Elevation: 4,000 ft.

■ **REVIEW—NORTH AMERICA: EASTERN UNITED STATES**

1. How does the American climate change from north to south and east to midwest?

2. Which area of the country has the most concentrated population?

3. What features make New England distinctive among American regions? Name the New England states.

4. Why might the term "Eastern Gateway" be applied to the region formed by New York, New Jersey, and Pennsylvania?

5. What is distinctive about New Orleans?

6. What are the major ski areas of the eastern United States? Where are they located?

7. Where are the major beach areas located in the eastern United States?

8. Where are the major golf resort areas in the eastern United States?

9. Describe four areas of scenic beauty in the eastern United States.

10. Choose three destinations in the eastern United States and describe why you would recommend that someone visit each of them.

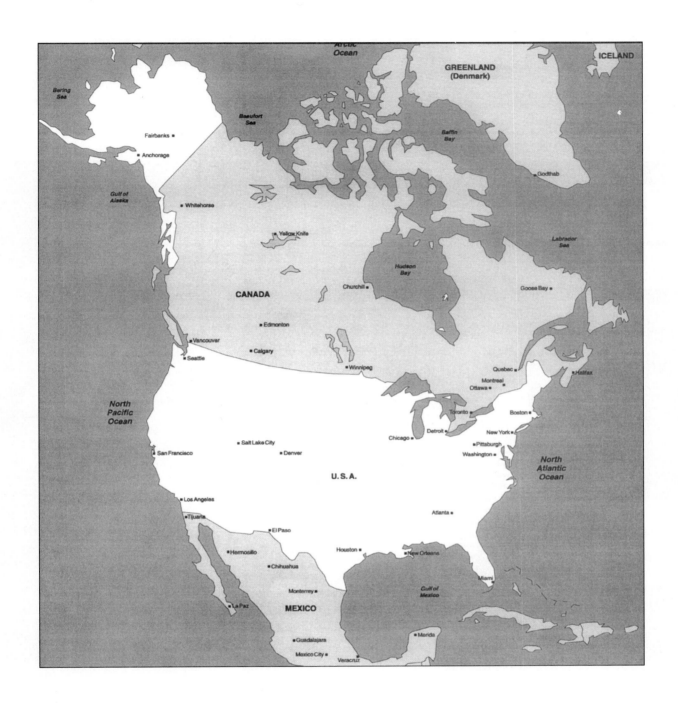

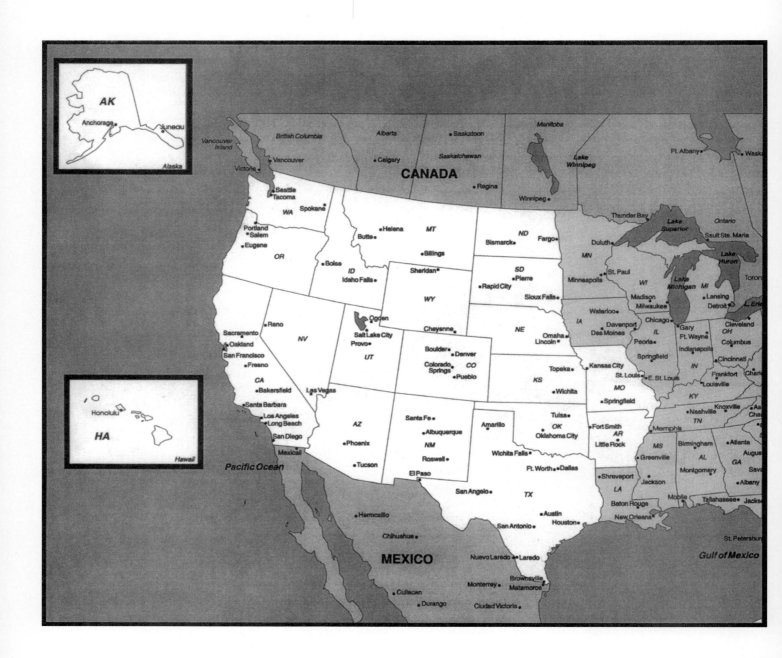

5

North America—Western United States

■ **THE LAND**

Mountains and rough terrain characterize much of the western United States. The Rocky Mountains, trending north to east southeast, border the Great Plains. On their western flanks is a zone of rugged plateaus, large basins, and short ranges. The mountain heights form the Continental Divide, separating the east-flowing and west-flowing river systems. Among the latter is the southwest-flowing Colorado River. Along its course is the spectacular Grand Canyon.

In the northwest, the Snake-Columbia River system eventually flows into the Pacific Ocean. In the northern interior is Great Salt Lake, a saline water body that has no outlet. The western fringe of the United States has still another formidable north-south mountain chain formed by the Cascade Mountains in the north and the Sierra Nevada Mountains farther south. The lower Coast Ranges lie along the Pacific coast.

Major lowlands within these ranges include the Puget Sound lowland and the Willamette River Valley in the northwest and the massive Central Valley of California. The combined American landforms have a distinct north-south grain across which the historic tide of settlement and national development have flowed.

More moderate climate conditions are found along the west coast than along the east coast, and local climates are modified by elevation. The western half of the United States is marked by varying degrees of dryness, or aridity. From the Great Plains westward, rainfall lessens and much of the western interior is semiarid or desert.

■ THE PEOPLE

In contrast to the east, the dry west is lightly populated. Only in the extreme west, in the lowlands near the Pacific Coast, are there large concentrations of people.

The western United States has been divided into six regions by the United States Travel and Tourism Administration. The Trails West and Western Gateways regions are the states immediately west of the Mississippi, that were the jumping off points for pioneer western settlers. The Great Southwest is Indian and national park country. The Pacific Northwest and Golden West regions represent the far western contiguous states. Alaska and Hawaii are the newest states and are separated geographically from the other 48.

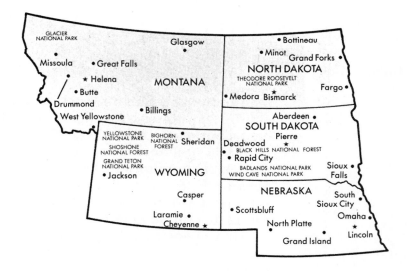

■ TRAILS WEST—AN OVERVIEW

This is the *Old West*, a land that stretches from the banks of the Missouri River to the towering heights of the Rocky Mountains. North Dakota, South Dakota, Nebraska, Montana, and Wyoming are the areas where Buffalo Bill Cody, Wild Bill Hickok, Sitting Bull, and Crazy Horse became famous. As with other western states, state boundaries tend to be straight and state shapes more rectangular, a result of the rectangular land survey system, the settlement process, and boundary decisions made at the time of state admissions. All of the Great Plains states are agricultural, raising crops in the better watered east and grazing livestock in the west where the climate is much drier. This is a region of seasonal contrasts—hot summers and long, cold and snowy winters. State populations are relatively small.

NORTH DAKOTA

Area: 70,665 square miles
Capital: Bismarck
Population: 638,800

North Dakota is rich in frontier history and natural scenic beauty. The spirit of fur trappers, cowboys, homesteaders, and cavalry soldiers, active in the state's development, can be felt today. The fertile Red River Valley is in the east; hill-laden, drift prairie is in the center of the state; and the rugged Missouri Valley Plateau is in the southwest. Bismarck, the capital, is centrally located on the Missouri river. North Dakota is bordered by Canada on the north, Montana on the west, South Dakota on the south, and Minnesota on the east.

Areas of Touristic Importance. Theodore Roosevelt National Park is located in the "Badlands," an area of fantastically eroded topography in the western part of the state. The Little Missouri River runs through the park, which is home to deer, antelope, buffalo, and bighorn sheep. Historic Medora, south of the park, has been rebuilt as it was in frontier days. Lake Sakakawea, in the central part of the state, is the largest lake and recreational area in North Dakota. Fargo, largest city in the state, is in the northeast, and is the home of Bonanzaville, USA, a pioneer recreation facility. Fort Union and Jamestown also host pioneer frontier recreations facilities.

SOUTH DAKOTA

Area: 77,047 square miles
Capital: Pierre
Population: 696,004

Pierre (pronounced "peer") is located centrally on the Missouri River, and Sioux Falls is in the southeast. In western South Dakota, the forested peaks of the Black Hills, shared with Wyoming, rise unexpectedly from the plains. Nearby are the severely eroded and desolate Badlands. The state features rolling hills and high plains. It is bisected by the north-south course of the Missouri River. There is fertile farmland in the east and the plains rise to the Badlands and pine-covered mountains, the Black Hills, in the west. South Dakota is bordered by North Dakota on the north, Montana and Wyoming on the west, Nebraska on the south, and Minnesota and Iowa on the east.

Areas of Touristic Importance. Mount Rushmore National Memorial, also known as the "Shrine of Democracy," honors four presidents with 60-foot high stone carvings of their faces on the mountain. Washington, Jefferson, Lincoln, and Theodore Roosevelt's faces were carved by Gutzon Borglum in the 1930s. Rapid City is the gateway to this unique park. A nearby mountain is currently being carved into a representation of Crazy Horse, a Native American leader.

Badlands National Park is east of the Black Hills. It is a maze of jagged spines, pinnacles, buttes, and gorges worn by millions of years of wind and water. Wind Cave National Park and Jewel Cave National Monument, south of Rapid City, provide cave explorers with hundreds of miles of caverns and passageways. Custer State Park holds the largest publicly owned herd of buffalo as well as elk, mountain goats, and antelope.

Deadwood began as a Wild West gold rush-town and still holds the nation's largest gold mine. The city was home to historical western characters including Wild Bill Hickok and Calamity Jane, whose likenesses are preserved in a wax museum. It now houses gambling casinos, and there are ski resorts nearby.

"Shrine of Democracy," Mount Rushmore, South Dakota
Photo: Courtesy South Dakota Tourism/by Bill Goring

NEBRASKA

Area: 77,227 square miles
Capital: Lincoln
Population: 1,578,385

Nebraska faces eastward on the Missouri River. In southeastern Nebraska are Omaha and Lincoln, the state's largest cities. Several smaller cities lie along the Platte River, which flows eastward along a course through central Nebraska to union with the Missouri River. Farmland in the east merges into cattle ranges in the center to pine-covered ridges and buttes in the north and west. Nebraska is bordered by South Dakota on the north, Wyoming and Colorado on the west, Kansas on the south, and Iowa and Missouri on the east.

Areas of Touristic Importance. Omaha is the commercial and cultural center of the state. The Joslyn Art Museum features European and American art. The Strategic Air Command Museum includes aircraft and missiles. Lincoln, the state capital, hosts the Nebraska State Museum and the Sheldon Art Gallery. West of Omaha is Boys Town, a famous community for homeless boys founded by Father Flanagan.

Stuhr Museum of the Prairie Pioneer near Grand Island recreates a pioneer village. Buffalo Bill State Historical Park includes much of his Scott's Rest Ranch. Near Chadron, the Museum of the Fur Trade recreates the days of the fur trappers. Pioneer Village has one of the largest private collections of Americana. Fort Robinson and Lake McConaughy offer outdoor recreational activities. Scotts Bluff National Monument and Chimney Rock are located in Nebraska.

MONTANA

Area: 147,138 square miles
Capital: Helena
Population: 799,065

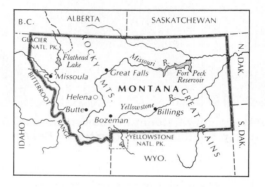

Eastern Montana lies within the Great Plains, and has the urban centers of Great Falls on the upper Missouri River and Billings on the Yellowstone River. The east is supported by farming and grazing, but mining drew people to mountainous western Montana, especially to the areas around Missoula, Helena, and Butte. Montana is bordered by Canada to the north, Idaho to the west, Idaho and Wyoming to the south, and North and South Dakota to the east. Because of its northerly location and mountainous terrain, it is often the coldest place in the nation in winter.

Areas of Touristic Importance. Glacier National Park, often called "The Crown of the Continent," is one of the nation's largest parks. It is a rugged, wilderness area with glaciers, mountain lakes, and pine-covered forests. Sheer cliffs, moun-

Swiftcurrent Lake, Glacier National Park, Montana
Photo: Courtesy State Advertising Unit, Montana Department of Highways

tain streams that can be fished, and wildlife of all kinds are abundant throughout the park. Montana also includes other wilderness areas, such as Red Rock Lakes National Refuge, Charlie Russell National Refuge, and the Bob Marshall Wilderness Area.

Ski resorts include Big Sky and Bridger Bowl near Bozeman, the Big Mountain near Kalispell, and Red Lodge Mountain near Billings.

The Little Big Horn National Monument, 53 miles southeast of Billings, is a tribute to the Indian victory over Lt. Colonel George Custer at the Little Bighorn.

Virginia City and Nevada City, 150 miles south of the state capital, Helena, are both restored Old West boom towns from the gold rush days. They are restored to recreate the 19-century wild west. The Grant-Kohrs Ranch National Historic Site shows how an early-day western ranch was operated.

Yellowstone National Park, shared with Wyoming, is described in the Wyoming section (see next page).

WYOMING

Area: 97,914 square miles
Capital: Cheyenne
Population: 453,588

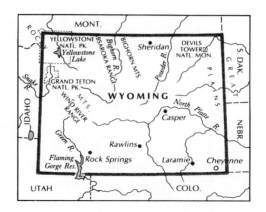

Wyoming is essentially a mountain state, but it does contain a small segment of the Great Plains and the flanks of the Black Hills in the east. The South Pass is the only main interruption in, and easy east-west passageway through, the Rocky Mountains. Through it have passed early migrations to Oregon and California, later came transcontinental telegraph and rail services, and, more recently, modern highways.

Sheridan in the north, Casper in the center on the North Platte River, and Cheyenne in the southeast are the main cities. Cold winters and mountainous countryside provide excellent downhill and cross-country skiing as well as snowmobiling and iceskating. Wyoming is bordered by Montana on the north, Idaho and Utah on the west, Utah and Colorado to the south, and South Dakota and Nebraska to the east.

Areas of Touristic Importance. Yellowstone National Park, established in 1872 as America's first national park, is also the largest of the national parks. With constant thermal activity, it is a wonderland of thundering geysers, steaming hot springs, deep canyons, scenic lakes, and roaring waterfalls. There are more than 200 major geysers and 10,000 other thermal features. Old Faithful, the park's most famous attraction, spouts more than 45,000 gallons of steaming water into the air nearly every hour. Yellowstone Lake, formed by volcanoes and glaciers, has a 100-mile shoreline. The Grand Canyon of the Yellowstone is nearly 35 miles long and a quarter of a mile deep.

Grand Teton National Park is just a few miles south of the Yellowstone border. Jagged, snow-covered mountains dominate the park, rising over 1.5 miles above the valley floor. Jackson Lake offers a spectacular view. The nearby town of Jackson is an "Old West adventure." Art galleries and shops offer western items. In winter, Jackson Hole is a major ski resort area.

Devil's Tower National Monument rises sharply about 280 yards above the flat prairie in remote northeastern Wyoming. The jutting monument, which changes colors with the time of day, is the core of a now extinct volcano.

Other attractions include the Buffalo Bill Historical Center with four western museums in Cody, the Fort Laramie National Historic Site (a former trading post), Old Trail Town, and the Bighorn Canyon National Recreation Area. Flaming Gorge and Fossil Butte Monument provide unforgettable scenery.

Cheyenne's Frontier Days, the last week in July, is the nation's oldest and biggest rodeo, and throughout the state, rodeos, roundups, and dude ranches attract tourists.

■ WESTERN GATEWAYS—AN OVERVIEW

Kansas, Missouri, Arkansas, Oklahoma, and Texas provide gateways from the southern half of the nation to the west. In pioneer days, as eastern railroads reached the Mississippi and Missouri Rivers, towns and cities sprang up to outfit travelers heading west. Many of today's cities have grown from towns that served old cattle trails. Most of the region lies within the Great Plains and its eastern flanks, with mountainous terrain in parts of Missouri, Oklahoma, and Arkansas. Like other Great Plains states, this area has a climate marked by hot summers and cold winters. Well watered and forested in the east, it is dry grassland in the west.

KANSAS

Area: 82,264 square miles
Capital: Topeka
Population: 2,477,574

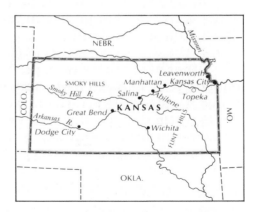

Rolling hills and valleys dominate the northeastern corner of the state; in contrast, the southwest is relatively flat. Fertile pastures and hills are in the south-central region, with the elevation gradually rising toward the Rocky Mountains. Along the western border are sharp hills and the prairie-grass-covered dunes of the high plains. The state has a well-balanced agricultural and urban-based industrial economy. Most of the population and the largest city, Kansas City, Kansas on the Missouri River, are in eastern Kansas. Bordered by Missouri to the east, Nebraska to the north, Colorado to the west, and Oklahoma to the south, Kansas is at the geographic center of the nation.

Areas of Touristic Importance. The urban centers of Kansas are Kansas City and Topeka in the east and Wichita in the central part of the state. Dodge City is a restored cattle town that includes the famous Boot Hill Cemetery and the Long Branch Saloon. Wagon train rides are available at El Dorado, not far from Wichita. The home and library of former President Dwight Eisenhower is at the Eisenhower Center at Abilene.

MISSOURI

Area: 69,686 square miles
Capital: Jefferson City
Population: 5,117,073

Missouri, which is crossed by the Missouri River, has some of the roughest topography in the region in the Ozark Plateau in the southwest. The main cities are St. Louis, in the east near the confluence of the Missouri and Mississippi Rivers, and Kansas City, in the northwest across the Missouri River from Kansas City, Kansas. Northern Missouri resembles the rolling farming country of adjacent Iowa and Illinois. Missouri is bordered by Illinois, Kentucky, and Tennessee to the east, Iowa to the north, Nebraska, Kansas, and Oklahoma to the west, and Arkansas to the south.

Areas of Touristic Importance. St. Louis was founded in 1764 and quickly became a booming midwestern metropolis. Because of its position near the confluence of the Missouri and Mississippi Rivers, it became the most important stop for pioneers heading west. The 634-foot-high Gateway Arch was erected as a monument to those pioneers who passed through St. Louis on their journey. Visitors may ride to its observation tower.

The Missouri Botanical Gardens and the St. Louis Zoological Park are among the best in the central states. Mississippi River excursions are available and the city is a major port stop for the Delta Queen and Mississippi Queen steamboat cruises.

Kansas City was a key departure point for pioneers heading west. The Oregon, California, and Santa Fe trails began here. Country Club Plaza, established in 1922, is America's oldest shopping center. The Nelson-Atkins Museum of Art is best known for its large Oriental collection. Independence, 10 miles east, home of former President Harry S. Truman, houses the Truman Library and Museum.

Other Missouri attractions include Lake of the Ozarks with more than 100 miles of shoreline, three excellent state parks, and many resorts. Northeast Missouri is Mark Twain country. Hannibal was his hometown and the setting for *Tom Sawyer* and *Huckleberry Finn*. St. Joseph was the starting point for the Pony Express and many westward-bound wagon trains. The original stables have been converted to a museum commemorating the Express and frontier history.

Missouri is also famous for its contribution to American music. In Kansas City, ragtime, Dixieland, and Kansas City jazz may be enjoyed. In the Ozarks, bluegrass and other traditional folk music is popular. In the early 1990s, Branson became a mecca for country music fans, rivaling Nashville, Tennessee. Most well-known country singers have built theaters in Branson.

ARKANSAS

Area: 53,104 square miles
Capital: Little Rock
Population: 2,350,725

Arkansas is a state of ridgelike mountains, cool pine-forested valleys, and freeflowing rivers. Excellent fresh-water fishing is available in the streams of the Ozark and Ouachita Mountains. It is bordered by the Mississippi River on the east and is bisected by the east-flowing Arkansas River. Its principal city is its capital, Little Rock, in the center of the state. Arkansas is bordered by Missouri on the north, Oklahoma and Texas on the west, Louisiana on the south, and Tennessee and Mississippi on the east.

Areas of Touristic Importance. Hot Springs National Park is a resort city, park, and international spa. Even before statehood, people were coming to bathe in the thermal, mineral springs. Eureka Springs is a picturesque Victorian spa town literally built into the mountainside. More than 300 artists and craftspeople work and sell their goods here. The Ozark Folk Center at Mountain View presents the arts, crafts, customs, and music of the Ozark Mountain people. Underground tours are available at Blanchard Springs Caverns, north of Mountain View. Crater of Diamonds State Park is the only diamond-bearing field in North America that is open to the public.

OKLAHOMA

Area: 69,919 square miles
Capital: Oklahoma City
Population: 3,145,585

Oklahoma has unusually rough topography for a Great Plains state—a share of the Ozark Plateau in the northeast, part of the Ouachita Mountains in the southeast, and the Wichita Mountains in the southwest. The Red River of the South forms part of its southern border with Texas. The main cities are Tulsa in the northeast and Oklahoma City in the west. Oklahoma shares (with neighboring Texas and Louisiana), and has benefited economically from, extensive oil and natural gas deposits. Oklahoma is bordered by Kansas and Colorado to the north, New Mexico and Texas to the west, Texas to the south, and Missouri and Arkansas to the east.

Areas of Touristic Importance. The National Cowboy Hall of Fame and Western Heritage Center, sponsored by 17 western states, is located in Oklahoma City. It is one of the nation's finest museums featuring the art and history of the Old West and a national memorial to those who contributed to the building of the west. Oklahoma's State Capitol building sits atop a producing oil field.

Tulsa is the center of the state's cultural activity with the Philbrook Art Center and the Gilcrease Institute of American History and Art. The many lakes in the state, of which Eufaula Lake and Lake Texoma are the most prominent, offer a wide variety of recreational opportunities. Bartlesville houses an exotic game reserve and the Tom Mix Museum.

Other interesting Oklahoma attractions include the Will Rogers Memorial and Museum and the Cherokee Heritage Center with its Tsa-La-Gi Village, a re-creation of a 17th-century Indian village.

TEXAS

Area: 267,338
  square
  miles

Capital:
  Austin

Population:
  16,986,510

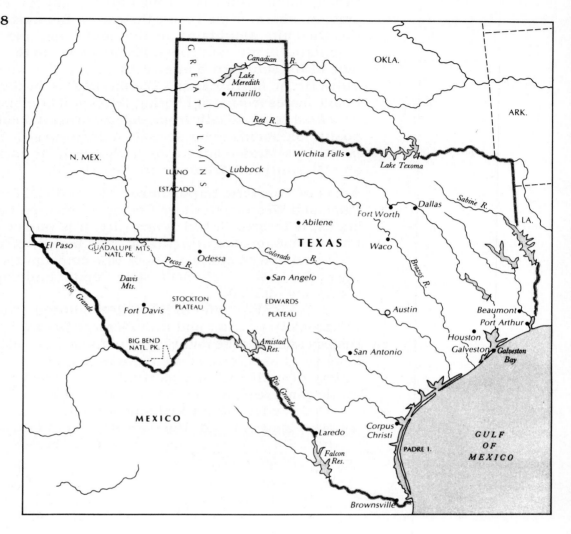

Texas is a hybrid, resulting in part from its large size. Eastern Texas is southern in climate, vegetation, and culture. It has large local and offshore oil and natural gas deposits. Houston is Texas' largest city. Other nearby cities include Galveston, Beaumont, and Port Arthur. Dallas, in Texas' agricultural northeast, is the main commercial city in the state. Adjoining it in a sprawling metropolitan area is Fort Worth. South from Dallas-Fort Worth, Waco, San Antonio, and smaller cities have developed from earlier cattle-ranching centers. Austin, the state capital, is growing rapidly.

The Rio Grande River forms the American boundary with Mexico. The main portal cities are Laredo in the southeast and El Paso in the extreme west, where Texas extends a narrow arm between New Mexico and Mexico. The Hispanic popula-

Chisos Mountains, Big Bend National Park, Texas
Photo: Courtesy Texas Tourist Development Agency

tion is large and culturally important. Dry west Texas has irrigated farming in the Panhandle, oil and natural gas fields in the center, and sheep and goat raising in the dry Edwards Plateau. Texas is bordered by New Mexico to the west; New Mexico and Oklahoma to the north; Arkansas, Louisiana, and the Gulf of Mexico to the east; and Mexico and the Gulf of Mexico to the south.

Areas of Touristic Importance. Texas, second only to Alaska in size, is often considered bigger than life. Houston epitomizes all that is big and bustling in this huge state. The skyline is filled with award-winning modern buildings. The Astrodome was the first enclosed, climate-controlled stadium in the nation. The Lyndon B. Johnson Space Center is headquarters for the manned space program. The San Jacinto Battleground was the site of the final battle for Texas' independence. Just 30 miles south is Galveston Island on the Gulf of Mexico where the weather is warm all year and the beach invites sunning and swimming.

San Antonio, in south-central Texas, is a modern city which retains much of the flavor of its historic past. The Paseo Del Rio (Riverwalk) in the city center is a unique, modern shopping and entertainment area. The city's best known monument is the Alamo, a small adobe fort that was the site of the famous 1836 independence battle. Across the street from the

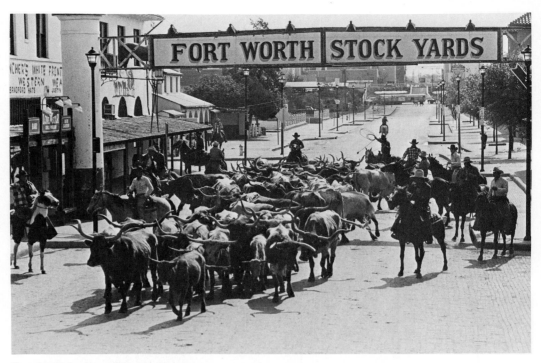

Stockyards, Fort Worth, Texas
Photo: Courtesy Texas Tourist Development Agency

Alamo, the Heart of Texas provides an in-depth look at the region's history.

Separated by only 30 miles, Dallas and Fort Worth have become a vast metroplex, yet each city has maintained its own flavor and character. Dallas is a leading commercial, banking, and shopping center and one of the country's leading fashion centers. Fort Worth retains its Old West heritage with rodeos, stockyards, and museums. Dallas-Fort Worth Regional Airport, one of the busiest in the nation, serves both cities from a point midway between them.

El Paso, in far western Texas, is directly across the Rio Grande from Juarez, Mexico. The Tigua Indian Reservation is a major source of native crafts. An 1840s cavalry fort can be viewed at Fort Bliss Replica. Most visitors do not leave without a shopping spree across the border in Mexico.

Many resorts can be found along the Gulf coast. Padre Island National Seashore offers 90 miles of coastal beaches. Malaquite Beach offers a recreational pavilion and restaurants.

Austin, 90 miles northeast of San Antonio, is the state capital. The Lyndon B. Johnson Presidential Library is on the campus of the University of Texas. Austin also hosts the Texas Confederate Museum.

The Rio Grande Valley is characterized by palm-lined highways and lush citrus groves. Big Bend National Park, named for the U-shaped turn of the Rio Grande, features the Chisos Mountains and three rugged canyons carved by the river. The Fort Davis National Historical Site, north of Big Bend Park, is one of the best surviving examples of a southwestern frontier cavalry post. The Confederate Air Force Museum in Harlingen houses a large collection of World War II aircraft.

■ THE GREAT SOUTHWEST—AN OVERVIEW

The Great Southwest is a magnificent area of glittering cities and wide-open spaces where modern-day cowboys and American Indians may be seen, as well as retirement communities and large-scale recreation facilities. It is a region of long distances, small and scattered population, dry climate where water availability is the key to development, and some of America's most forbidding and scenic mountainous topography, exemplified by the Rocky Mountains of Colorado and northern New Mexico. New Mexico, Arizona, Colorado, and Utah all have many attractions for the visitor.

NEW MEXICO

Area: 121,666 square miles
Capital: Santa Fe
Population: 1,515,069

New Mexico shares the mountains and plateaus of the Rocky Mountain system and the aridity of western Texas and neighboring Arizona. However, it is bisected by the south-flowing Rio Grande River and its valley. The valley is the state's most habitable area and contains its main cities, Santa Fe and Albuquerque. The large Hispanic and Indian population has been joined in recent decades by large numbers of immigrants, especially retirees, from other states. New Mexico is bordered by Texas to the south and east, Colorado to the north, and Arizona to the west. A portion of the state's southern border is with Mexico.

Areas of Touristic Importance. The Pueblo Indian culture, dating back 1600 years, is very much alive in New Mexico. The Indian Pueblo Cultural Center is in Albuquerque. Taos and the Taos Pueblo are on a low plateau above the Rio Grande River. Taos is also a major ski resort as well as an artists' colony. Examples of Indian cliff dwellings can be found near Albuquerque and Santa Fe.

Albuquerque was founded in 1706. Old Town is the site of the original settlement, centering around a plaza and the Church of San Felipe de Neri. The Albuquerque Museum and adjacent New Mexico Museum of Natural History trace the physical and cultural history of the region. Sandia Park, to the north, is a ski resort.

Santa Fe was settled by the Spanish in 1610, and is the nation's oldest capital city. Its narrow streets and adobe architecture have an old-world atmosphere. Nearby Fort Union was the western terminal of the Santa Fe Trail.

Carlsbad Caverns National Park is in southern New Mexico, near the Texas border. Ground water seeping through limestone for millions of years has created eerie and magical

Taos Pueblo, New Mexico
Photo: Courtesy New Mexico Tourism & Travel, Commerce and Industry

rock formations. Its main attraction, the Big Room, has a ceiling over 80 feet high.

A large, thriving Navajo Indian Reservation is located in the northwest corner of the state. Also in the area are three prehistoric Indian ruins—the Salmon Ruins, Chaco Canyon, and the Aztec Ruins National Monument, which features the only fully restored kiva, an underground ceremonial chamber. Four Corners Monument at Shiprock is the only point in the country where four states meet (New Mexico, Arizona, Colorado, and Utah).

ARIZONA

Area: 113,909 square miles
Capital: Phoenix
Population: 3,665,228

Northern Arizona is dominated by the rough topography of the western Colorado Plateau. The Colorado River rises in Colorado, passes through southeastern Utah, and forms Arizona's western boundary with Nevada and California. On the Arizona-Nevada border, the river water is impounded in Lake Mead by Hoover Dam (Boulder Dam). Flagstaff serves central and northern Arizona, where the Indian population is concentrated. The main settled areas in the south are along the course of the Gila River, a primary water source. Phoenix is the main center for a booming retirement and agricultural area. Tucson, in the south, shares in the retirement boom.

Sunny weather and a dry climate plus modern-day air conditioning contribute to Arizona's reputation as a vacation wonderland. Arizona borders on Mexico to the south, New Mexico on the east, Utah on the north, and California and Nevada on the west.

Areas of Touristic Importance. Phoenix, the capital in south-central Arizona, is the commercial and cultural center of the state. It has fine museums, galleries, shopping, and recreational facilities. Its Desert Botanical Gardens and Zoo feature unique displays. Heritage Square, part of the original city, has turn-of-the-century Victorian houses open to view. Suburban Scottsdale is a major tourist area with some of the finest resorts and golf courses in the nation. The town of Scottsdale features art galleries and craft shops.

Sedona, north of Phoenix, offers a variety of unusual and beautiful desert rock formations. It provides an excellent side-trip to a Phoenix vacation.

Tucson is a year-round resort center with guest ranches, hotels, spas, and golf courses nestled in the hills. Nearby Saguaro National Monument is known for the giant saguaro cacti, which can grow to a height of nearly 50 feet and live for 200 years. Old Tucson is a theme park with an Old West motif.

Legendary Tombstone is one of the best known old western towns. It was founded in 1877 as a mining town. The O.K. Corral and Tombstone Epitaph Building are a memorial to the western frontier.

Grand Canyon National Park, in the north part of the state, contains the largest, most spectacular and awe-inspiring of the continent's gorges. Located above Flagstaff, the canyon is more than 220 miles long, 2 miles wide, and more than 1 mile deep. Its layers of yellow, red, green, magenta, and gold document the earth's history with open rock strata dating back 2 billion years. Many trails have been developed for visitors on both the North and South Rims of the canyon. The best facilities are at Grand Canyon Village at the South Rim. Airplane and helicopter tours are available, as are hiking and mule trips into the canyon.

Petrified Forest National Park-Painted Desert is near the New Mexico border. The park features giant petrified logs that are millions of years old.

Like New Mexico, Arizona is Indian country. The Hopi and Navajo reservations are open to visitors, but Indian rights must be respected. The Canyon de Chelly National Monument has spectacular rock formations as well as cliff dwellings abandoned by Indians nearly 700 years ago.

Arizona also has several major lake resort areas. Lake Mead, formed at the Nevada border by the Hoover Dam, offers opportunities for boating and fishing. Giant Lake Powell in the Glen Canyon National Recreation Areas, with nearly 2,000 miles of shoreline and 96 side canyons, is the second largest constructed lake in the nation. Lake Havasu, more than 40 miles long, is now the site of the original London Bridge. The bridge, which formerly spanned the Thames River, was dismantled in England and rebuilt across an inlet of the Colorado River.

COLORADO

Area: 104,247 square miles
Capital: Denver
Population: 3,294,394

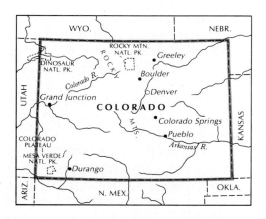

The main part of the Southern Rockies, and the highest peaks in the entire mountain system, are found in Colorado. From the heights, the North Platte, South Platte, and Arkansas Rivers flow eastward; the Colorado River flows to the southwest; and the Rio Grande River flows to the south. Eastern Colorado shares part of the Great Plains and there, within sight of the imposing Front Range of the Rockies, is a north to south string of cities—large Denver and smaller Boulder, Colorado Springs, and Pueblo. Mining opened the mountains to settlement and helped bring prosperity to the nearby Plains cities. Today, government services, retirement, and recreation are economic mainstays. The mountains have some of the finest ski facilities in the United States. Colorado is bordered by Wyoming and Nebraska to the north, Nebraska and Kansas to the east, Utah to the west, and New Mexico and Oklahoma to the south.

Areas of Touristic Importance. "Ski the Rockies" is Colorado's prime claim to tourism fame. Many of this nation's best ski areas are found here. Aspen offers skiing down four different mountains plus apres-ski activities in an old western mining town. Vail offers a wide variety of skiing opportunities including the Beaver Creek development. Vail Village, developed primarily in the 1960s, is a charming European-flavored ski village. Other major ski areas include Telluride, Purgatory, Breckenridge, Keystone, Copper Mountain, Loveland, Arapahoe, Steamboat Springs, and Winter Park. Snow season is usually from Thanksgiving through Easter. In the off season, the ski resorts offer summer recreation along the lakes and trails and sightseeing among the scenic mountains.

Denver, the Mile High City, is a major metropolis on the eastern flank of the Rocky Mountains. Once a mining boom town, Denver is now the commercial and cultural center of the region. The Denver Mint conducts tours showing how coins are made.

Cliff Palace, Mesa Verde National Park, Colorado

Colorado Springs is the home of the United States Air Force Academy. Pikes Peak is 14 miles west of the city. Both a cog railway and a well-maintained road bring visitors to the summit of this tall mountain. The Garden of the Gods is another breathtaking scenic area renowned for its many beautiful sandstone formations.

Rocky Mountain National Park in northwest Colorado is one of the nation's most spectacular mountain areas. Hiking, camping, and fishing are popular during the summer months.

Mesa Verde National Park in the southwest corner of the state is the site of 8th-century Indian cliff dwellings. The cliff dwellings and mesa-top pit houses are easily accessible to visitors. The comprehensive Chapin Mesa Museum depicts Pueblo Indian life.

Remarkably beautiful canyons are found at Royal Gorge in central Colorado. Multicolored cliffs rise nearly 1,500 feet above the Arkansas River. The cliffs are spanned by one of the world's highest suspension bridges.

The Colorado National Monument features unique rock monoliths and rugged canyons near the state's west-central border. Gunnison River Gorge and the Black Canyon of the Gunnison National Monument offer spectacular views and geological displays, also in the west-central part of the state. Dinosaur National Monument, on the northwestern Colorado border, is a quarry from which more than 2,000 fossilized bones as old as 140 million years have been unearthed.

UTAH

Area: 84,916 square miles
Capital: Salt Lake City
Population: 1,722,850

Utah, Nevada, southern Idaho, southeastern Oregon, and part of southern California form the Great Basin, so-called because of its lower elevation among adjacent mountains. The Great Basin is situated between the Rockies on the east and the Cascade-Sierra Nevada Mountains on the west. It is the driest part of the United States, and in many places is hostile desert. It is all the more remarkable, therefore, that northern Utah has a large population concentration on plains between Great Salt Lake and the Wasatch Mountains, whose snowfields provide meltwater that flows into the land-bound saline lake.

Salt Lake City, Ogden, and Provo lie in this flourishing area, which is the creation of a distinctive American religious group, the Mormons (Church of Jesus Christ of Latter Day Saints). In the 1840s, the Mormons selected an isolated site in the Great Basin, to escape persecution in the East. With great zeal, they developed irrigation agriculture and urban facilities. The Wasatch Mountains have some of the West's best skiing grounds.

Utah is bordered by Wyoming and Idaho on the north, Nevada on the west, Arizona on the south, and Colorado on the east.

Areas of Touristic Importance. Salt Lake City is the international center for the Mormon Church, as well as the capital and largest city in Utah. The Great Salt Lake, only minutes from downtown, is the world's largest inland saltwater body. The famous ski resorts of Alta, Park City, and Snowbird are within 30 miles of the city.

The Mormon Temple is a majestic six-spired structure which took 40 years to build. Although non-Mormons are not permitted inside, tours of the Tabernacle are offered. This acoustically perfect hall serves as home to the Mormon Tabernacle Choir. The Assembly Hall is also open to the public. Beehive House, one block east of Temple Square, was built by Brigham Young as his official residence.

Utah is a state of great canyons, colorful towns, and five incomparable national parks. Bryce Canyon National Park in southern Utah is a series of amphitheaters filled with natural pillars, bridges, and windowed tunnels of sandstone. Just west of Bryce Canyon is Zion National Park, centered around the Virgin River Canyon, with formations which resemble temples and cathedrals. The Great White Throne is Zion's most commanding rock formation. Capitol Reef National Park is possibly the most colorful of Utah's parks. Gigantic red and orange formations are interspersed with rainbow-rock cliffs of blue and green stripes.

To the east, along the Colorado River, are Canyonlands National Park and Arches National Park. Canyonlands is filled with magnificent arches and awesome spires. Arches contains the world's largest concentration of natural stone arches.

■ THE PACIFIC NORTHWEST—AN OVERVIEW

The Pacific Northwest region, which includes the states of Idaho, Washington, and Oregon, is an area of rugged natural beauty. The west-flowing Snake River and Columbia River and the majestic Cascade Mountains, with their snow-clad volcanic peaks, are among the scenic wonders of the West. Modern cities provide a contrast of commercial and cultural activities. The western, Pacific-facing part of the region is better watered and more urbanized.

IDAHO

Area: 83,557 square miles
Capital: Boise
Population: 1,006,749

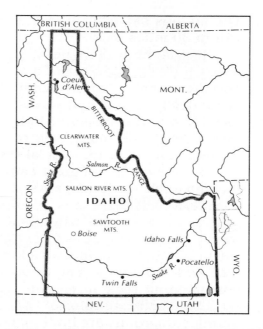

Idaho has the most difficult terrain in the Northern Rockies, and most of the population is found in the irrigated plains region in the south near the Snake River, which flows northward to form the Idaho-Oregon boundary. Boise, in the southwest, is the largest city. Coeur d'Alene is an important lead-zinc mining and east-west transportation center in extreme northern Idaho. Idaho's mountains and snow are ideal for skiing. The state has more than 2,000 lakes and more than 200 mountain peaks over 7,500 feet high. Idaho is bordered by Montana and Wyoming in the east, Canada on the north, Washington and Oregon on the west, and Utah and Nevada on the south.

Areas of Touristic Importance. Sun Valley, in central Idaho, offers a variety of both winter and summer outdoor activities. It is a world-class ski resort. The Birds of Prey National Area is home to thousands of eagles, falcons, ospreys, owls, and hawks. The Shoshone Indian Ice Caves maintain freezing conditions even in warm summer. Hell's Canyon, shared with Oregon, contains North America's deepest gorge, cut by the Snake River. Craters of the Moon National Monument is a large volcanic area resembling ground conditions on the moon. Fort Hall preserves a major landmark on the Oregon Trail. Coeur d'Alene has the largest silver production in the world.

WASHINGTON

Area: 68,192 square miles
Capital: Olympia
Population: 4,866,692

Washington and Oregon both have well-watered Pacific coasts with relatively mild year-round climates, the forested Cascade Range, and dry eastern regions. Washington's west coast is marked by deep-cut Puget Sound and the Olympic Peninsula, lying between the Sound and the Pacific Ocean. The lowlands around Puget Sound have most of the state's population and the cities of Seattle (the largest), Tacoma, and Olympia.

The Cascades feature towering peaks, including Mt. Rainier. The irregular topography of eastern Washington is traversed by the Columbia River. After it is joined by its major tributary, the Snake River, the Columbia forms part of the Washington-Oregon boundary before reaching the Pacific coast. Spokane is the main city of eastern Washington; Walla Walla serves an important wheat-growing area in the southeast; and Yakima is the hub of an irrigated apple-growing area southeast of the Cascades.

The state has two distinct climates. Eastern Washington has hot summers and cold winters, while the western part of the state has both milder summers and winters because of the moderating effects of air off the Pacific Ocean. Washington is bordered by Canada to the north, the Pacific Ocean to the west, Oregon to the south, and Idaho to the east.

Areas of Touristic Importance. Seattle, the Emerald City, is virtually surrounded by water and mountains. The city lies between Puget Sound and Lake Washington and commands excellent views of the Olympic and Cascade Mountains. Its most prominent landmark, the Space Needle, was built for the 1962 Seattle World's Fair. The Pike Street Market, Seattle Center, Pioneer Square, and International District all offer a variety of experiences. Ferry service is available through the San Juan Islands and to Victoria, B.C. Day excursions are also available to Mt. Rainier. Boating and other water activities are popular. Crossing Lake Washington are two bridges, one a famous floating, or pontoon, bridge.

Olympic National Park is a wilderness with rain forests, lakes, and streams as well as rugged mountains and Pacific seashore. The park, on the Olympic Peninsula, is accessible by ferry or by driving around the southern end of Puget Sound. Mount Rainier National Park, home of one of the most beautiful mountains in the nation, is 75 miles southeast of Seattle. Mount St. Helens, which erupted in a grand manner in 1980, is in the southern part of the state. It is now a National Volcanic Park.

Mount St. Helens, Washington
Photo: Courtesy Washington State Tourism Division

The Grand Coulee Dam, in northeastern Washington, captures the Columbia River for power and irrigation, forming 150-mile-long Lake Roosevelt. Spokane's Riverfront Park is a legacy of its 1974 World's Fair. Other eastern Washington attractions include the Yakima River Valley and its thriving apple orchards.

OREGON

Area: 96,981 square miles
Capital: Salem
Population: 2,842,321

The most habitable part of Oregon is the Willamette River Valley, located in the west between the Coast Ranges and the Cascades. Most of the state's population and the cities of Portland (the largest), Salem, and Eugene are found here. Mount Hood, east of Portland, and Crater Lake, in the southwest, are striking features of volcanic origin in the Cascades. Eastern Oregon, used for sheep-grazing, is drier, has rougher topography and fewer people than eastern Washington. Like Washington, Oregon enjoys a milder climate in the western part of the state than in the east. Oregon is bordered by Washington on the north, Idaho on the east, Nevada and California on the south, and the Pacific Ocean on the west.

Areas of Touristic Importance. Portland is the gateway to Oregon. The city is known for its rose gardens and jazz music. The Columbia River Highway parallels the scenic Columbia River both east and west of the city. Most scenic is the Columbia River Gorge with cliffs nearly 2,000 feet high. Snow-capped Mount Hood overlooks the city. The Mount Hood National Forest stretches from the Columbia River along the Cascade Mountains to Mount Jefferson and from the foothills outside Portland to the central Oregon Plateau.

Crater Lake National Park is to the east of the Cascade Mountains in southwestern Oregon. The lake, nearly 2,000 feet deep, and, in fact, the deepest of any lake in the country, was formed after Mount Mazama erupted so much ash and lava that it hollowed out and collapsed, eventually filling with water. Cave Junction and the Oregon Cave National Monument provide underground caverns, chambers, and corridors with fascinating rock formations.

Oregon offers the visitor deep forests, mountains, fishing, camping, and boating. The state has 296 miles of Pacific Ocean coastline and 230 state parks. Central Oregon is blessed with more than 220 lakes and many miles of rivers and streams. The Rogue River crisscrosses the region and offers adventurers a challenge in river rafting.

■ THE GOLDEN WEST—AN OVERVIEW

California and Nevada comprise the Golden West region. California is a rich mixture of sun-drenched Pacific beaches, Sierra Nevada Mountains, sophisticated cities, and majestic redwoods. Lit by neon and desert sunshine, Nevada lures the visitor with recreation, entertainment, and excitement 24 hours every day.

NEVADA

Area: 110,540 square miles
Capital: Carson City
Population: 1,201,833

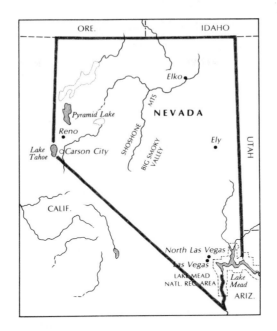

Nevada is, except on its western fringes, a desolate, arid, unpopulated state, part of the Great Basin. However, several small cities lie along the Humboldt River in the north. In the extreme south, Las Vegas is a major gambling and recreation center. In the west, water from the eastern slopes of the Sierra Nevada Mountains supports urban growth at Reno and Carson City, which are at the eastern end of the main highway and railway passage through the Sierras connecting Nevada with central California and San Francisco. Southern Nevada enjoys mild winters and hot summers. The state borders on Oregon and Idaho to the north, California to the west, Utah to the east, and Arizona at its southern tip.

Areas of Touristic Importance. Tourism is the number one industry in the state, primarily because of legalized gambling. Las Vegas is one of the world's most prominent gambling areas, with large numbers of casinos that operate 24 hours a day. Exciting nightclubs and cabaret shows are also a major part of the city's entertainment. Lake Mead and Hoover (Boulder) Dam are not far from the city and provide interesting sightseeing as well as boating and fishing.

Reno is somewhat smaller than Las Vegas, but offers the same types of gambling and nightlife. Virginia City, south of Reno, is an Old West town with renovated saloons, dance halls, and grand mansions. Lake Tahoe, on the California-Nevada border, is the largest mountain lake in the United States. Ski resorts can be found on all sides of the lake. Casino gambling is popular on the Nevada side.

CALIFORNIA

Area: 158,693 square miles

Capital: Sacramento

Population: 29,760,021

California, the nations's most populous state, is physically diverse. Its northern two-thirds is shaped around several large-scale features. The towering north-south Sierra Nevada Mountains form much of the state's eastern border. The lower Coast Ranges are found along the Pacific coast, and a massive depression, the Central Valley, is located between the two mountain chains.

The main rivers of the Central Valley, the Sacramento and San Joaquin, join to flow through a prominent break in the Coast Ranges into deep-cut San Francisco Bay. One of America's most specialized commercial agricultural areas, the Central Valley is served by such cities as Sacramento, Stockton, Fresno, and, in the extreme south, Bakersfield.

The San Francisco metropolitan area surrounds San Francisco Bay, including Berkeley and Oakland, and extends northward across Golden Gate Bridge, and southward through Palo Alto and San Jose. Monterey is nearby on the coast south of the Bay. Coastal northern California has the wet winters and splendid forest stands of western Washington and Oregon. Northeastern California is arid, and the Sierras have heavy snowfall that ultimately melts to provide water for the Central Valley.

Southern California has a different personality. At the southern end of the Sierras, arid Great Basin conditions prevail. Death Valley is the driest place in the United States. Along the coast, the Coast Ranges are broken into a number of small ranges. Between them and the ocean on narrow lowlands is the great metropolitan area of Los Angeles. "LA," like San Francisco, has one of the largest concentrations of people and wealth in the United States. Its economic activities include filmmaking in Hollywood, aircraft manufacturing, and many governmental and military facilities. It has a very diverse ethnic mix, including large Hispanic, Asian, and black populations.

Santa Barbara is on the scenic coast west of Los Angeles, and the seaport of San Diego is just north of the Mexican border. In the southern interior, the irrigated Imperial Valley is a highly specialized vegetable growing area.

California is bordered by Mexico to the south, the Pacific Ocean to the west, Oregon to the north, and Nevada and Arizona to the east. The state is the most populous in the nation and one of the largest in area. It features 840 miles of Pacific Ocean coastline. California is also the home of Mount Whitney, the highest mountain peak in the 48 contiguous states at 14,495 feet above sea level, and Death Valley, the lowest point in the nation at 282 feet below sea level. The state is also the home of six national parks—Channel Islands, Kings Canyon, Lassen Volcanic, Redwood, Sequoia, and Yosemite. It is a destination with something for everyone.

Areas of Touristic Importance. Established by Spanish missionaries and settled during the California Gold Rush, San Francisco has an international flavor all its own. One of the nation's most charming, cosmopolitan, and sophisticated cities, its fabled hills slope down to the Golden Gate Bridge and the protected deep-water harbor. Intriguing Sausalito with colorful yachts and houseboats is just across the bay. Golden Gate Park includes museum buildings dating back to the Columbian Exposition of 1893.

The city is known for its restaurants, shopping areas and attractions. The famous and convenient cable cars cut across the downtown area, traveling up and down steep hills and providing panoramic views of the city. Two of the lines connect Union Square in the fashionable downtown area with Fisherman's Wharf at the beginning of the Embarcadero section of the waterfront. Ghiradelli Square, the Cannery, and Pier 39, located near the wharf, provide interesting restaurants and shopping boutiques. Harbor cruises and tours to the former federal maximum security prison on Alcatraz Island begin from piers on the wharf.

Chinatown, along Grant Avenue, offers pagoda-style roofs, lanterns, Buddhist temples, exotic gift shops, and fascinating restaurants. North Beach, just above Chinatown, is the Italian-American section of the city. The area features art galleries, restaurants, and is also known for its exotic nightclub shows. Japan Center is a complex of restaurants, shops, fountains, tearooms, and baths.

Hearst Castle, San Simeon, California
Photo: Courtesy Carl Goodman

Muir Woods National Monument, less than 20 miles north of the city, features trails winding through a magnificent stand of centuries-old redwood trees. The Napa Valley, northeast of San Francisco, produces fine California wines. Winetasting tours are available at over 100 wineries in Napa, Sonoma, and Mendocino counties.

Northern California contains the scenic splendors of Redwood and Lassen Volcanic National Parks. Located near Eureka and Crescent City, Redwood National Park includes a majestic redwood forest with freshwater streams and rivers and a coastal zone with abrupt cliffs, beaches, lagoons, and tidepools. Dominated by 10,000-foot Mount Lassen, Lassen Volcanic National Park features lava flows, hot springs, and mud pots. Located near Mineral and Red Bluff, the park offers numerous hiking trails, lake swimming, boating, and packsaddle trips.

Yosemite National Park in Eastern California is natural beauty on a grand scale. Located on the western slopes of the Sierra Nevadas, the park features sculpted peaks and domes, groves of majestic sequoias and forests of pine, mountain meadows strewn with wild flowers, and scenic drives and trails. Yosemite has a wide variety of plant and wildlife and many thundering waterfalls. Lake Tahoe, nestled in a valley of the eastern Sierras, is shared with Nevada and described in the Nevada section.

Sacramento, California's capital, is rich in frontier history, having been the state's first pioneer outpost, Sutter's Fort. With the discovery of gold in 1848, Sacramento became a booming gold-rush town. Old Sacramento is a re-creation of the original city with a fascinating railroad museum.

The area between San Francisco and Los Angeles is rich with visitor attractions. The Monterey Peninsula offers a picturesque view of gnarled cypress trees clinging to a rocky coastline. The peninsula surrounds the historic city of Monterey with its spectacular modern aquarium and the artist colony town of Carmel. The scenic 17-Mile Drive takes travelers past white beaches, expansive golf courses, dramatic cypress groves, and some of the most magnificent estates in the west.

The Hearst Castle at San Simeon was built in the 1920s as a summer house for publishing tycoon William Randolph Hearst. In addition to the main mansion, the estate features acres of gardens, pools, terraces, and guest houses. Not far from Los Angeles is Santa Barbara, known for its gentle climate, picturesque beaches, and beautiful Spanish mission.

Inland in central California, Sequoia and Kings Canyon National Parks feature large groves of giant sequoia trees and magnificent forests of ponderosa and sugar pine, white and red fir, and cedar. The 4,000-year-old General Sherman Tree, towering nearly 150 feet, is the largest. Mount Whitney borders Sequoia National Park.

Los Angeles is the second most populous United States city. Cradled between the San Gabriel Mountains and the Pacific Ocean, Los Angeles is the gateway to the Southern California region. Founded in 1781, greater Los Angeles, which includes neighboring Orange County, is actually a collection of many large and small cities, each with its own identity and character. Popular visitor destinations in the area include Pasadena, Beverly Hills, Santa Monica, Hollywood, Long Beach, Burbank, and Anaheim.

The Los Angeles beaches begin in the north at Zuma Beach and continue south to Malibu, Santa Monica, Venice, Manhattan, Hermosa, Redondo, Huntington, Newport, and Laguna. Farther south is Long Beach, home of the ocean liner *Queen Mary*, which is now a hotel and museum, and Howard Hughes' famous Spruce Goose seaplane. San Pedro, adjacent to Long Beach, is Los Angeles' port and home to several cruise ships. Ferry and seaplane service is also available to Catalina Island, 26 miles off shore. Catalina is a quiet resort area with mountains, secluded coves, and undersea gardens.

Hollywood and Burbank are the centers of the movie and television industries. Tours of NBC and Burbank studios can be arranged. Mann's Chinese Theater has the footprints of the stars in its front sidewalk. Universal Studios features a tram tour of its huge lot, including demonstrations of how movies are made. Nearby Beverly Hills is home to the rich and famous as well as a center of high fashion shopping.

Disneyland and Knott's Berry Farm are in the Anaheim area. Home of Mickey Mouse, Disneyland is the original theme park created by Walt Disney. Its success led to the development of Walt Disney World in Florida. Started as a fruit farm, Knott's Berry Farm is a theme park with a western motif, including a Ghost Town and a Fiesta Village.

Once a sleepy little coastal town, San Diego is now the second largest city in California. Its clear and sunny weather and 80 miles of sandy beaches have attracted both residents and visitors. The state's oldest city, San Diego has a distinctly Spanish flavor. Old Town, the oldest European settlement in California, dates from 1769; its restored buildings feature specialty shops, art galleries, and restaurants. San Diego's missions provide a glimpse of early-day Spanish California.

The San Diego Zoo in Balboa Park houses over 3,000 creatures representing more than 750 species of wildlife. Its natural setting, with lush tropical vegetation, has earned it great praise. Balboa Park, itself, offers museums, art galleries, theaters, and sports facilities. Sea World, on Mission Bay, features sea animal shows including dolphins, sea lions, whales, and walruses as well as marine life exhibits and the world's largest collection of penguins. The San Diego Wild Animal Park, north of the city in Escondido, is a game preserve viewed on a 50-minute monorail ride.

Disneyland, Anaheim, California
Photo: Courtesy California Office of Tourism

■ HAWAII AND ALASKA—AN OVERVIEW

Hawaii and Alaska both attained statehood in 1959. Although very different in character, they share the common problems of locations separate and distant from the American mainland.

ALASKA

Area: 586,412 square miles
Capital: Juneau
Population: 550,043

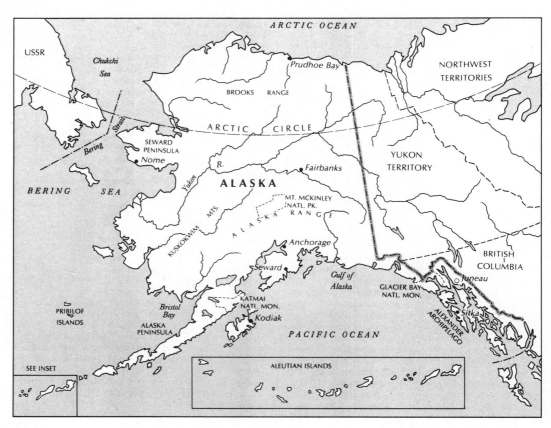

Alaska is a large territorial block bordering northwestern Canada between the Arctic Ocean on the north, the Bering Sea on the west, and the Pacific Ocean on the south. A long southern coastal strip composed of fjords and offshore islands and the territory farther south along the Canadian border have milder, wet winters. Sitka and Juneau, the southernmost cities, are in this strip. For the rest of Alaska, the long and bitterly cold winters are an enormous obstacle to attracting a large resident population.

Much of the interior is also mountainous—the Brooks Range in the north and the Alaskan Range and the Klondike Region in the south—with lowlands in the west and along the coasts. Between the highlands, the Yukon River flows westward to the Bering Sea.

Main urban centers include Anchorage and Seward on the south coast, Fairbanks in the central interior, and Nome on the west coast just south of narrow Bering Strait, which separates North America and Asia. Anchorage is the state's largest city and chief freight port. From the southwestern mainland, a long arc of volcanic islands, the Aleutian Islands, extends westward between the Bering Sea and the Pacific Ocean.

Gold strikes in the 1870s and later attracted a large number of prospectors to Alaska, but permanent settlers, since the 1930s, have been supported by military and other federal funding and, more recently, oil strikes in northern Alaska. Oil, which is piped to the south shore port of Valdez for shipment, is the main source of income for the Alaskan government. About 20 percent of the population of 500,000 are Indians and Eskimos (Aleuts and Inuit) whose lifestyle has been heavily modified by the imported American culture.

Alaska has spectacular natural scenery on a grand scale, including Mount McKinley, the highest peak in the United States, glaciers, and unusual birds and animals. Huge areas are held by the federal government, some in national forests, parks, and wildlife refuges.

Areas of Touristic Importance. Alaska is a northern wonderland where travelers can still encounter untamed nature and feel a sense of frontier adventure. There is pristine wilderness here where wild animals including polar bears, brown Kodiak bears, black bears, caribou, moose, walrus, sea lions, mountain goats, and wolves roam. Airplanes and ships make it possible for the traveler to experience much of Alaska's scenic splendor without trekking into far-off primeval wilderness. Most of Alaska's visitors come during a 4-month prime season from mid-May to mid-September. The state is very popular for hunting, fishing, and camping.

Anchorage is the gateway to the routes leading into internal Alaska. Although Eskimo and Indian settlements have been discovered in the area, Anchorage is a relatively new city. Founded in 1913 as a base camp for the Alaska Railroad, it is now Alaska's largest city. Its historical museum has excellent displays that trace the settlement and development of the state. The Chugach National Forest, only 20 miles from downtown, offers the photographer and sport hunter a variety of wildlife including moose, bear, goat, and sheep. The Alyeska resort area and Portage Glacier are within 1 hour of the city. Anchorage International Airport is a major transit stop for international airlines flying the polar route between Europe and Asia.

Air tours to arctic Kotzebue and Nome originate from Anchorage. Kotzebue, above the Arctic Circle, is an Inupiate (Eskimo) village north of the Arctic Circle. Its native museum

Chugach National Forest, Alaska
Photo: Courtesy Alaska DOT/photo by Mark Skok

offers a fascinating diorama of arctic life. Nome, developed as a gold-rush town, has preserved its frontier atmosphere.

The main line of the Alaska railroad connects Anchorage with Fairbanks. The tracks run through Denali National Park. Denali provides spectacular scenery including Mount McKinley, the nation's (and North America's) highest peak. The park is rich with wildlife.

Fairbanks, Alaska's second largest city, is a central location for exploring northern Alaska. Fairbanks was a gold-rush boomtown, and its main attractions include old gold camps, tours on an old sternwheel riverboat to an Indian village, and Alaskaland, a pioneer theme park. Fairbanks is also considered one of the best places from which to view the Aurora Borealis or Northern Lights, especially in winter when it is extremely cold. Air excursions to arctic Prudhoe Bay, hub of the Alaskan oil fields and starting point of the Alaska pipeline, and to Point Barrow, begin in Fairbanks.

The Katmai National Park and Preserve in southwest Alaska is the home of the Valley of Ten Thousand Smokes, an eerie, moonlike landscape created in 1912 by the eruption of nearby Novarupta Volcano. The Pribilof Islands in the Bering Sea feature nesting grounds for shorebirds and northern fur seals. Kodiak, south of the Kenai Peninsula, is a top world fishing port and Alaska's "Crab Capital." The Aleutian Islands extend into the Eastern Hemisphere, almost touching Russian territory. Populated primarily by Aleut Indians, Russian influence is apparent in these islands.

Southeastern Alaska is a major destination for cruise ships. The Inside Passage runs from Vancouver, Canada, along the Canadian Pacific coast to Skagway and Haines, Alaska. A few smaller ships continue to Whittier. Primary ports of call are Juneau, Sitka, and Ketchikan. The cruise ships bring visitors close to many glaciers and into the fjords along the coastline. Juneau, Alaska's capital, is close to the Mendenhall glacier. Its Russian Orthodox church, built in 1894, displays many beautiful icons. Sitka features an onion-domed Russian church and is much influenced by its Russian heritage.

HAWAII

Area: 6,450 square miles

Capital: Honolulu

Population: 1,108,229

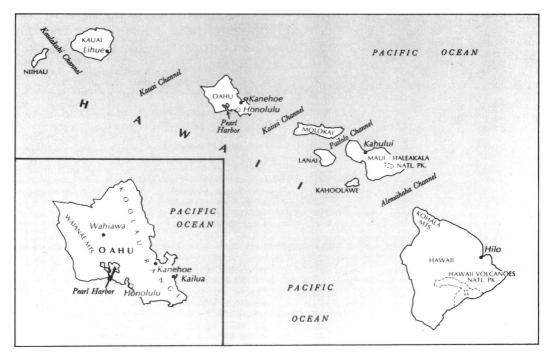

Hawaii, lying 2,400 miles west of San Francisco, is a chain of volcanic islands. Eight main islands in a 400-mile stretch of ocean contain most of the state's land area and its population of over 1 million persons. From east to west, the islands are Hawaii, the largest with two-thirds of the state's territory; Maui; uninhabited Kahoolawe, the smallest; Lanai; Molokai; Oahu, the most populated and best developed; Kauai; and Niihau.

Spectacular volcanic landscapes, including active volcanoes on the "Big Island" of Hawaii, rugged coastlines, and sheltered valleys abound. The prevailing climate, as in most other Pacific islands, is warm, breezy, and sunny, qualities that make the islands attractive to mainlanders in all seasons.

The original inhabitants were Polynesians, but they now form only a small part of the population because of the influx of outside groups and intermarriage. Some 40 percent of the population is Caucasian or part-Caucasian. People of Japanese and Chinese ancestry follow in numbers, and Filipino, Portuguese, and other ethnic groups are also present in substantial numbers. There has been considerable intermarriage between groups.

The population is found mainly on Oahu, where Honolulu, the largest city, continues to attract migrants from the American mainland, many of them retirees. The economy is supported by military and other federal government expenditures, a declining agriculture (sugar cane and pineapples), and tourism. Honolulu remains the main tourist magnet with its famed Diamond Head landmark and hotel-rimmed Waikiki Beach. However, resort development has spread to the outer islands as well. Honolulu attracts real estate investment and large tourist flows from Japan as well as the American mainland.

Areas of Touristic Importance. The island of Oahu, home of Honolulu and Waikiki Beach, is known as the "Gathering Place," because it was once the meeting place for members of Hawaiian royalty. Today, it is the hub of the state and of the Pacific. Honolulu, Hawaii's capital, is the business and cultural center of the state as well a major port. It is the home port for 1-week cruises throughout the Hawaiian islands. The Bishop Museum has vast collections of Pacific arts and crafts and fine examples of Hawaiiana. The Iolani Palace, the only royal palace in the United States, was used by Hawaiian royalty and also, until 1969, as the first capitol of the territory, and, later, the state of Hawaii.

Waikiki Beach is one of the most famous resort areas in the world. Deluxe hotels occupy beachfront positions. Because all beaches in the state are public property, visitors staying at less expensive, off-beach hotels have full access to the sand and surf. Diamond Head, an extinct volcano, is at the eastern end of Waikiki.

Oahu is far more than the city of Honolulu and Waikiki Beach. Just outside of Honolulu is the vast naval facility at Pearl Harbor, the nerve center and home of the Pacific fleet. Pearl Harbor's Arizona Memorial salutes the sunken battleship, Arizona, destroyed with its crew during the December 7,

Iolani Palace, Honolulu
Photo: Courtesy Hawaii Visitors Bureau

1941 Japanese attack. Paradise Park, in the Manoa Valley, is a lush showcase of tropical vegetation featuring hundreds of rare birds.

Rural areas with pineapple and sugar cane fields can be found within 20 miles of Honolulu and Waikiki. The north and west shores of Oahu are known for high surf beaches and host national and world surfboard championships. High surf occurs in the winter. In the summer, the surf at the northern Oahu beaches is calm.

Waimea Falls, also on the north shore, is an area of unspoiled beauty, with an expansive valley that is home to tropical growth and exotic birds. The Polynesian Cultural Center at Laie presents the cultures and crafts of six South Seas peoples in six recreated villages situated among landscaped gardens and waterways. The evening Polynesian revue is one of the best in Hawaii. The center is staffed primarily by students of the Laie campus of Brigham Young University. Mormon missionaries are active in the Pacific and the church provides many scholarships for students from Pacific nations.

Maui is called the "Valley Isle" because of the central valley formed between two major volcanoes, Haleakala and Puu Kukui. Major resort developments have been built from Lahaina and Kaanapali to Na Pali and from Kihei to Wailea. Lahaina is a preserved and protected old port town which once was Hawaii's capital and the center of Hawaii's whaling industry. It still shows the influence of missionaries, monarchs, and whalers.

Haleakala National Park, more than 10,000 feet in altitude, includes the crater of a dormant volcano. Seeing the sun rise over this "House of the Sun" is a breathtaking experience. The park encompasses the crater and extends down the eastern slope almost to Hana. The Seven Pools, south of Hana on the eastern end of Maui, were, according to legend, once the bathing spots of the Hawaiian kings. Hana is noted for its retention of old-style Hawaiian customs and pace.

The island of Hawaii is called the "Big Island" because it is the largest in the chain and also the "Orchid Isle" because more varieties of orchids are grown and sold here than anywhere else in the world. Ka Lae on the southern tip of the island is the southernmost point in the nation. The state's highest peaks, Mauna Kea and Mauna Loa, both more than 12,000 feet high, straddle the island. Limited skiing is available on Mauna Kea during the winter. Because of the mountains, Hilo and the east side of Hawaii are lush, green, and tropical, while Kailua-Kona and the west side of Hawaii are dry. Cattle raising is popular on the north slope of Mauna Kea, home of the Parker Ranch, second largest under the American flag.

Hawaii Volcanoes National Park, on the southeastern side of the island, is the site of the live Kiluea volcano which frequently spews lava high into the air. The park also has an array of other volcanic features including steaming craters, lava tubes, and forests of giant tree ferns.

Kailua town on the Kona coast hosts resort hotels with a Hawaiian-Western atmosphere. Puuhonua o Honaunau, the Place of Refuge, is south of Kailua on the western coast. It was built in the 12th century as a place of asylum for Hawaiians escaping battles and political persecution. Kailua and the Kona coast are the site of the yearly Ironman Triathalon swim-bike-running marathon.

Kauai is called the "Garden Isle" for the lush greenery that covers its canyons and valleys. Mount Waialeale, in its center, is perpetually covered by clouds. Its record rainfalls each year make it the wettest spot on earth. Resort hotels dot the south, east, and eastern part of the north coasts of the island.

The Fern Grotto, reached only by a boat trip up the lovely Wailua River, is a large cave thickly hung with ferns. It provides a romantic setting for weddings, and guides often entertain their groups with a rendition of the Hawaiian Wedding Song. The Waimea canyon, known as the "Grand Canyon of the Pacific," resembles its Arizona namesake in coloration.

The gorge is more than 2,500 feet deep and boasts vivid blues and greens contributed by tropical vegetation.

The north coast features the rugged Na Pali cliffs and the beautiful Hanalei Valley. The lower part of the valley is a bird sanctuary and refuge for endangered species. The Princeville area features hotels, condominiums, and a championship golf course. Helicopter tours of the mountains, canyons, and secluded beaches are an excellent method of sampling the contrasting conditions on Kauai.

Molokai, the "Friendly Isle," is a peaceful and easygoing island of unspoiled beauty. Hunting, fishing, golf, and swimming are popular activities. The Kalaupapa Peninsula at the bottom of 1,900 foot cliffs is a beautifully scenic area that once housed the leper colony founded in the 18th century by Father Damien. Molokai receives fewer visitors than the four islands described above.

Lanai is primarily a pineapple plantation. Although it has picturesque coves, bays, and beaches, until recently tourist facilities were limited. Two deluxe resort hotels are now available for visitors.

Niihau is a private island reserved for those of Hawaiian descent. Visits to this island are by invitation only. Kahoolawe is uninhabited, has no fresh water, and has been used by the Navy for target practice.

■ TYPES OF TOURISM

Independent touring is the most popular form of travel in the western United States. However, escorted and hosted group tours are quite popular as well. The following tour programs are samples of those available within the region:

- Parks and Canyons Spectacular
- Focus on California
- Yellowstone, Grand Teton and Glacier National Parks
- The Pacific Northwest
- Alaska
- Hawaii—Four Island
- Branson Music and the Ozarks
- Canyonlands

GLOBUS *First Class* ESCORTED

Parks & Canyons Spectacular

Las Vegas, Grand Canyon, Lake Powell, Zion and Bryce Canyon,
Salt Lake City, Jackson, Grand Tetons, Yellowstone, Cody,
The Black Hills, Mt Rushmore, Rapid City, Denver

Tour APC – 13 days from Las Vegas to Denver

Maximum elevation on tour: 8,860 ft.

ALL THIS IS INCLUDED

- Services of a professional tour director
- First-class hotels listed below or equivalent (see page 9). Twin-bedded rooms with private bath or shower, hotel taxes, service charges and tips for baggage handling
- Welcome reception; 11 American breakfasts (B); 10 three-course dinners offering choice of entree (D), with a special farewell dinner in Denver
- Private deluxe air-conditioned motorcoach
- Cruise on Lake Powell

- Visits to Las Vegas, Grand Canyon, Lake Powell, Zion and Bryce Canyon, Salt Lake City, Jackson, Grand Tetons, Yellowstone, Cody, Sheridan, Devils Tower, Lead, Deadwood's Mt Moriah Cemetery, Mount Rushmore, Rapid City, Cheyenne, Denver
- Other scenic highlights: Kaibab National Forest, Painted Desert, the Bighorn Mountains
- Inside visits as shown in UPPER-CASE LETTERS in the tour description, including admission charges where applicable
- Globus travel bag and travel documents

▼ *GRAND TETON NATIONAL PARK*

Day 1 LAS VEGAS. The tour begins at the splendid Golden Nugget Hotel, and this evening your tour director hosts a welcome reception and buffet dinner, a perfect occasion to get acquainted with your traveling companions. (D)

Day 2 LAS VEGAS-GRAND CANYON. Depart at 8 a.m. by deluxe air-conditioned motorcoach and it's a short drive south to the first stop in Arizona – the colossal Hoover Dam on Lake Mead. Via Kingman and Williams to the GRAND CANYON, one of the seven natural wonders of the world. Time still to view the spectacular sunset, for which the area is justly famous. (B,D)

Day 3 GRAND CANYON-PAINTED DESERT-LAKE POWELL. For a once-in-a-life-time experience – take our optional helicopter flight through the heart of the Grand Canyon. In the late morning motor along the East Rim Drive to Desert View Point for more stunning sights. Then on through Kaibab National Forest and the Painted Desert north to Lake Powell, one of the world's largest man-made lakes, arriving by late afternoon. The majestic beauty of this vast lake can be appreciated on our afternoon lake cruise: see gigantic Glen Canyon Dam, the "tapestry" walls of Antelope Canyon and the sheer red cliffs of Navajo Canyon. (B)

Day 4 LAKE POWELL-ZION NATIONAL PARK-BRYCE CANYON. Before leaving this morning, we highly recommend the optional "flightseeing" excursion: a thrilling flight from Lake Powell over Monument Valley. Later in the morning, head for Utah to visit ZION NATIONAL PARK, a spectacle of massive stone formations resembling temples and cathedrals whose colors change with the light of day and the season. Continue through Dixie National Forest to BRYCE CANYON NATIONAL PARK. (B,D)

Day 5 BRYCE CANYON-SALT LAKE CITY. Though much smaller than Zion, Bryce has a beauty of its own – startling pink cliffs and other weird-looking formations, which also undergo constant changes in color. From the rim drive, the oddly shaped rocks and cliffs appear like castles, animals, people and houses. The next two nights are in Salt Lake City, the Mormon capital of Utah. (B,D)

Day 6 SALT LAKE CITY. This city was founded by Brigham Young and his Mormon followers in 1847. Morning sightseeing focuses on its many historical monuments, each of which has a story to tell of the Mormon pioneer days. First, Temple Square with its imposing Temple and the Tabernacle; next, "This is the Place" monument, celebrating the words pronounced when Young first eyed this site. Complete the tour with a drive past the State Capitol and the University of Utah. As the remainder of the day is free, perhaps explore Trolley Square, an authentic old trolley car barn converted into a colorful shopping mall. (B)

Day 7 SALT LAKE CITY-JACKSON. Drive by Great Salt Lake this morning before heading north via Ogden and Logan. The journey continues through the southern tip of Idaho with a brief photo stop along the shores of Bear Lake. After a lunch break at Montpelier, proceed northward into Wyoming and through the town of Afton with its 3,000 elk horns adorning an arch over Main Street. Final destination today is all-western Jackson. Why not take a wander along the boardwalks of downtown Jackson and enjoy a drink in one of the rowdy swing-door saloons? (B,D)

Day 8 JACKSON-GRAND TETON NATIONAL PARK-YELLOWSTONE NATIONAL PARK. The morning is at leisure, and highly recommended is our optional rafting excursion on the Snake River. A 10-mile float trip in a comfortable rubber raft with spectacular views of the Grand Teton range.

36 US

Reprinted courtesy of Globus and Cosmos.

Then head north through GRAND TETON NATIONAL PARK and on to YELLOWSTONE NATIONAL PARK. Be sure to see the famous Old Faithful geyser that has been erupting consistently for over 100 years. (B,D)

Day 9 YELLOWSTONE NATIONAL PARK-CODY. A scenic drive on the loop road with views of plunging waterfalls, lakes, paint pots and mud volcanoes. Taking the east exit of the park, watch for elk, moose, antelope and buffalo – all are abundant in this area. A short drive from Yellowstone and by mid-afternoon arrive in Cody, named after the dashing frontiersman, Buffalo Bill Cody. The remainder of the day is at leisure. Tonight we offer an optional excursion to the Buffalo Bill Historical Center and Old Trail Town, a reconstruction of cabins used by such characters as Butch Cassidy and the Sundance Kid, with a comprehensive display of authentic western artifacts. (B,D)

Day 10 CODY-DEVILS TOWER-LEAD. An early start today with the climb high up into the Bighorn Mountains. Make a lunch stop in Sheridan, the town where many battles were fought between U.S. Cavalry troopers and the Sioux, Cheyenne and Crow Indian tribes. Some 75 miles north of here, Custer was defeated by Crazy Horse. Before crossing into South Dakota, visit the "flying-saucer haunted" DEVILS TOWER NATIONAL MONUMENT – a gigantic volcanic neck rising from the prairie. Overnight is in Lead. (B,D)

Day 11 LEAD-DEADWOOD-MT. RUSHMORE-RAPID CITY. Into the Black Hills this morning to Deadwood, once a wild and brawling gold-mining town where Jack McCall shot Wild Bill Hickok. Visit nearby MT. MORIAH CEMETERY on Boot Hill where Wild Bill lies buried with Calamity Jane. At the BORGLUM HISTORICAL CENTER in Keystone hear the Rushmore-Borglum story, a fascinating account on the sculptor and his famous work of art. And next ... behold the work of art: MOUNT RUSHMORE NATIONAL MEMORIAL, the enormous busts of four great American Presidents – Washington, Jefferson, Lincoln and Theodore Roosevelt carved on the face of the mountain that took 14 years to complete. A short drive from here to Rapid City, once a gold-rush boom town. (B,D)

▼ *DEVILS TOWER*

Day 12 RAPID CITY-CHEYENNE-DENVER. Early departure this morning and re-enter Wyoming heading south to Cheyenne, the state capital. A short orientation drive to see the city's landmarks: the state capitol and the governor's mansion. Next state is Colorado and reach its capital, Denver, in the early evening. Tonight your tour director hosts a delightful farewell dinner, a last get-together to celebrate the success of a great touring adventure. (B,D)

Day 13 DENVER. Tour ends this morning with tour members departing on independent schedules.

➤ *Many departures of this tour connect with SCENIC COLORADO & NEW MEXICO (page 40). You pay less for your second tour: see page 3.*

Tour APC: DATES & PRICES

Tour Code	Start Las Vegas	End Denver	13 days US$	Tour Code	Start Las Vegas	End Denver	13 days US$
APC0501	Sun 01-May	Fri 13-May	1318	APC0726	Tue 26-Jul	Sun 07-Aug	1348
APC0502	Mon 02-May	Sat 14-May	1318	APC0727	Wed 27-Jul	Mon 08-Aug	1348
APC0503	Tue 03-May	Sun 15-May	1318	APC0728	Thu 28-Jul	Tue 09-Aug	1348
APC0504	Wed 04-May	Mon 16-May	1318	APC0731	Sun 31-Jul	Fri 12-Aug	1348
APC0505	Thu 05-May	Tue 17-May	1318	APC0801	Mon 01-Aug	Sat 13-Aug	1348
APC0508	Sun 08-May	Fri 20-May	1338	APC0802	Tue 02-Aug	Sun 14-Aug	1348
APC0509	Mon 09-May	Sat 21-May	1338	APC0803	Wed 03-Aug	Mon 15-Aug	1348
APC0510	Tue 10-May	Sun 22-May	1338	APC0804	Thu 04-Aug	Tue 16-Aug	1348
APC0511	Wed 11-May	Mon 23-May	1338	APC0807	Sun 07-Aug	Fri 19-Aug	1348
APC0512	Thu 12-May	Tue 24-May	1338	APC0808	Mon 08-Aug	Sat 20-Aug	1348
APC0515	Sun 15-May	Fri 27-May	1348	APC0809	Tue 09-Aug	Sun 21-Aug	1348
APC0516	Mon 16-May	Sat 28-May	1348	APC0810	Wed 10-Aug	Mon 22-Aug	1348
APC0517	Tue 17-May	Sun 29-May	1348	APC0811	Thu 11-Aug	Tue 23-Aug	1348
APC0518	Wed 18-May	Mon 30-May	1348	APC0812	Fri 12-Aug	Wed 24-Aug	1348
APC0519	Thu 19-May	Tue 31-May	1348	APC0814	Sun 14-Aug	Fri 26-Aug	1348
APC0522	Sun 22-May	Fri 03-Jun	1348	APC0815	Mon 15-Aug	Sat 27-Aug	1348
APC0523	Mon 23-May	Sat 04-Jun	1348	APC0816	Tue 16-Aug	Sun 28-Aug	1348
APC0524	Tue 24-May	Sun 05-Jun	1348	APC0817	Wed 17-Aug	Mon 29-Aug	1348
APC0525	Wed 25-May	Mon 06-Jun	1348	APC0818	Thu 18-Aug	Tue 30-Aug	1348
APC0526	Thu 26-May	Tue 07-Jun	1348	APC0819	Fri 19-Aug	Wed 31-Aug	1348
APC0529	Sun 29-May	Fri 10-Jun	1348	APC0821	Sun 21-Aug	Fri 02-Sep	1348
APC0530	Mon 30-May	Sat 11-Jun	1348	APC0822	Mon 22-Aug	Sat 03-Sep	1348
APC0531	Tue 31-May	Sun 12-Jun	1348	APC0823	Tue 23-Aug	Sun 04-Sep	1348
APC0601	Wed 01-Jun	Mon 13-Jun	1348	APC0824	Wed 24-Aug	Mon 05-Sep	1348
APC0602	Thu 02-Jun	Tue 14-Jun	1348	APC0825	Thu 25-Aug	Tue 06-Sep	1348
APC0603	Fri 03-Jun	Wed 15-Jun	1348	APC0826	Fri 26-Aug	Wed 07-Sep	1348
APC0605	Sun 05-Jun	Fri 17-Jun	1348	APC0828	Sun 28-Aug	Fri 09-Sep	1348
APC0606	Mon 06-Jun	Sat 18-Jun	1348	APC0829	Mon 29-Aug	Sat 10-Sep	1348
APC0607	Tue 07-Jun	Sun 19-Jun	1348	APC0830	Tue 30-Aug	Sun 11-Sep	1348
APC0608	Wed 08-Jun	Mon 20-Jun	1348	APC0831	Wed 31-Aug	Mon 12-Sep	1348
APC0609	Thu 09-Jun	Tue 21-Jun	1348	APC0901	Thu 01-Sep	Tue 13-Sep	1348
APC0610	Fri 10-Jun	Wed 22-Jun	1348	APC0902	Fri 02-Sep	Wed 14-Sep	1348
APC0612	Sun 12-Jun	Fri 24-Jun	1348	APC0904	Sun 04-Sep	Fri 16-Sep	1348
APC0613	Mon 13-Jun	Sat 25-Jun	1348	APC0905	Mon 05-Sep	Sat 17-Sep	1348
APC0614	Tue 14-Jun	Sun 26-Jun	1348	APC0906	Tue 06-Sep	Sun 18-Sep	1348
APC0615	Wed 15-Jun	Mon 27-Jun	1348	APC0907	Wed 07-Sep	Mon 19-Sep	1348
APC0616	Thu 16-Jun	Tue 28-Jun	1348	APC0908	Thu 08-Sep	Tue 20-Sep	1348
APC0617	Fri 17-Jun	Wed 29-Jun	1348	APC0909	Fri 09-Sep	Wed 21-Sep	1348
APC0619	Sun 19-Jun	Fri 01-Jul	1348	APC0911	Sun 11-Sep	Fri 23-Sep	1348
APC0620	Mon 20-Jun	Sat 02-Jul	1348	APC0912	Mon 12-Sep	Sat 24-Sep	1348
APC0621	Tue 21-Jun	Sun 03-Jul	1348	APC0913	Tue 13-Sep	Sun 25-Sep	1348
APC0622	Wed 22-Jun	Mon 04-Jul	1348	APC0914	Wed 14-Sep	Mon 26-Sep	1348
APC0623	Thu 23-Jun	Tue 05-Jul	1348	APC0915	Thu 15-Sep	Tue 27-Sep	1348
APC0624	Fri 24-Jun	Wed 06-Jul	1348	APC0916	Fri 16-Sep	Wed 28-Sep	1348
APC0626	Sun 26-Jun	Fri 08-Jul	1348	APC0918	Sun 18-Sep	Fri 30-Sep	1348
APC0627	Mon 27-Jun	Sat 09-Jul	1348	APC0919	Mon 19-Sep	Sat 01-Oct	1338
APC0628	Tue 28-Jun	Sun 10-Jul	1348	APC0920	Tue 20-Sep	Sun 02-Oct	1338
APC0629	Wed 29-Jun	Mon 11-Jul	1348	APC0921	Wed 21-Sep	Mon 03-Oct	1338
APC0630	Thu 30-Jun	Tue 12-Jul	1348	APC0922	Thu 22-Sep	Tue 04-Oct	1338
APC0703	Sun 03-Jul	Fri 15-Jul	1348	APC0925	Sun 25-Sep	Fri 07-Oct	1338
APC0704	Mon 04-Jul	Sat 16-Jul	1348	APC0926	Mon 26-Sep	Sat 08-Oct	1318
APC0705	Tue 05-Jul	Sun 17-Jul	1348				
APC0706	Wed 06-Jul	Mon 18-Jul	1348				
APC0707	Thu 07-Jul	Tue 19-Jul	1348				
APC0710	Sun 10-Jul	Fri 22-Jul	1348				
APC0711	Mon 11-Jul	Sat 23-Jul	1348				
APC0712	Tue 12-Jul	Sun 24-Jul	1348				
APC0713	Wed 13-Jul	Mon 25-Jul	1348				
APC0714	Thu 14-Jul	Tue 26-Jul	1348				
APC0717	Sun 17-Jul	Fri 29-Jul	1348				
APC0718	Mon 18-Jul	Sat 30-Jul	1348				
APC0719	Tue 19-Jul	Sun 31-Jul	1348				
APC0720	Wed 20-Jul	Mon 01-Aug	1348				
APC0721	Thu 21-Jul	Tue 02-Aug	1348				
APC0724	Sun 24-Jul	Fri 05-Aug	1348				
APC0725	Mon 25-Jul	Sat 06-Aug	1348				

Prices are for all land arrangements. Air fare to Las Vegas and from Denver is additional. Your travel agent can help you find the best available air fare.

Single room supplement: $506
Triple room reduction per person: $79

Reduction for joining on day 2 upon departure from Las Vegas: $57
Reduction for leaving on day 12 upon arrival in Denver: $61

For additional accommodations in Las Vegas before the tour and additional accommodations in Denver after the tour, see our special rates on page 11.

APOLLO: TD*GG, **PARS:** G/PTS/GGX, **SABRE:** Y/TUR/QGG

GLOBUS HOTELS

LAS VEGAS Golden Nugget Hotel, **GRAND CANYON** Grand Canyon Lodges, **LAKE POWELL** Wahweap Lodge & Marina, **BRYCE N.P.** Ruby's Inn, **SALT LAKE CITY** Salt Lake City Hilton, **JACKSON** Wagon Wheel Village, **YELLOWSTONE N.P.** Yellowstone Lodges, **CODY** Holiday Inn, **LEAD** Golden Hills Resort, **RAPID CITY** Hotel Alex Johnson, **DENVER** Westin Tabor Center

GLOBUS   *First Class*   ESCORTED

Focus on California

San Francisco, Lake Tahoe, Yosemite
National Park, Monterey, Carmel, San
Simeon, Santa Maria, Los Angeles

Tour **ACA** – 9 days from San
Francisco to Los Angeles

Maximum elevation on tour: 9,940 ft.

ALL THIS IS INCLUDED

- Services of a professional tour director
- First-class hotels listed below or equivalent (see page 9). Twin-bedded rooms with private bath or shower, hotel taxes, service charges and tips for baggage handling
- 6 American breakfasts (B); 1 lunch (L); and 5 three-course dinners offering choice of entree (D), with a special welcome dinner in San Francisco and farewell dinner in Los Angeles
- Private deluxe air-conditioned motorcoach
- Cruise of San Francisco Bay; tram tour of

Yosemite National Park
- Sightseeing tours of San Francisco and Los Angeles
- Visits to a famous vineyard, Old Sacramento, Lake Tahoe, Yosemite National Park, Carmel Mission, Monterey Peninsula, San Simeon's Hearst Castle, Santa Maria, Solvang, Santa Barbara
- Other scenic highlights: Seventeen-Mile Drive, Big Sur, the Santa Inez Mountains
- Inside visits as shown in UPPER-CASE LETTERS in the tour description, including admission charges where applicable
- Globus travel bag and travel documents

▼ *LOS ANGELES AT NIGHT*

Day 1 SAN FRANCISCO. Our tour director will be on hand at the host hotel throughout the afternoon to give assistance upon arrival. This evening, a welcome dinner at the Fairmont Hotel's splendid Crown Room, the perfect occasion to get acquainted with your fellow travelers. (D)

Day 2 SAN FRANCISCO. This harbor-city's charm comes to life while sightseeing its steep hills, parks, cable-cars and bustling docks. Highlight visits include THE JAPANESE TEA GARDENS, Golden Gate Park, Seal Rocks, Twin Peaks, with the tour ending at Fisherman's Wharf. Lunch at a famed harbor-front restaurant before enjoying a cruise of the bay. Still plenty of time in the day for shopping and other leisure time activities. Highly recommended for this evening is the optional outing to San Francisco's vibrant Chinatown, "a city within a city", including a lavish four-course Chinese dinner at a specially selected restaurant. (B,L)

Day 3 SAN FRANCISCO-WINE COUNTRY-LAKE TAHOE. From the Pacific coast to the lush gentle slopes of California wine country, with more than 60 wineries in the famous valleys of Sonoma and Napa. Today visit the vineyards of one of the well-known labels for an inspection of the PROCESSING FACILITIES and a sample of a prized vintage. Sacramento, the state capital, is next. Enjoy a short stop in Old Sacramento, an area of the city where the days of the Pony Express and the gold rush have been recreated. Reach Lake Tahoe by late afternoon. This evening you may wish to join an optional dinner cruise on Lake Tahoe, with music and dancing. (B)

Day 4 LAKE TAHOE-YOSEMITE. Southward through the Sierra Nevada to YOSEMITE NATIONAL PARK. When inside the park descend to the valley floor (still some 3,000 feet above sea level). The scenery is nothing short of spectacular – views of sheer granite walls, ice-sculptured domes, thundering waterfalls, alpine peaks, glaciers and flowered meadows. A two-hour tram tour of the park shows off its unique sites, including El Capitan, Cathedral Spires, Yosemite Falls and Half Dome. (B,D)

Day 5 YOSEMITE-CARMEL-MONTEREY. Back to the Pacific coast and the rugged beauty of the Monterey Peninsula. A highpoint on today's journey is the spectacular Seventeen-Mile Drive, stretching from Pacific Grove to Carmel with views along the way of Cypress Point, the famous Pebble Beach golf course and the amazing Lone Cypress. Enjoy a visit at the posh resort of Carmel which has become a popular retreat for writers, artists and celebrities. Then on to Monterey, whose famous landmark – Cannery Row, was the locale of John Steinbeck's novel. Dinner tonight will be at a well-known restaurant along Fisherman's Wharf. (B,D)

Day 6 MONTEREY-SAN SIMEON-SANTA MARIA. Before leaving the peninsula this morning drive past the quaint colorful homes, the historic buildings, old Fisherman's Wharf to CARMEL MISSION. Besides its architectural appeal and religious significance, this particular mission is noted as the burial place of the founder of the Californian mission chain, Father Junipero Serra. Continue southward along the panoramic, rocky coastline of Big Sur. Next is San Simeon, where the wealthy newspaper tycoon William Randolf Hearst built his massive CASTLE-LIKE MANSION which houses antiques, art treasures and exotic possessions purchased from around the world at an estimated cost of 50 million dollars. The tour of two hours covers only a portion of the impressive 123-acre estate! Reach Santa Maria by late afternoon. (B,D)

26 US

Reprinted courtesy of Globus and Cosmos.

Day 7 SANTA MARIA-SOLVANG-SANTA BARBARA-LOS ANGELES. First stop this morning is Solvang, where Denmark has been re-created with picturesque buildings and windmills. Free time to browse through the charming shops featuring Danish imports and rich Danish pastries. Through the Santa Inez mountains, past Lake Cachuma to beautiful Santa Barbara where Spanish influence is apparent in its quaint white-washed and tile-roofed buildings. Marvel at the elegant beach homes of Hollywood celebrities which dot the shoreline from Malibu through Santa Monica, en route to Los Angeles, the motion-picture capital of the world. (B)

Day 8 LOS ANGELES. Morning sightseeing of this gigantic metropolis takes you from Olvera Street – the oldest thoroughfare in the city – to Hollywood, with an opportunity to step into the shoeprints of famous movie stars at Mann's Chinese Theatre. See Sunset Strip and Rodeo Drive before returning to your hotel. As the afternoon is free, why not join the optional excursion to Universal Studios, the world's largest motion-picture and television studio. This evening your tour director hosts a festive farewell dinner to celebrate the success of a great touring adventure of California. (D)

Day 9 LOS ANGELES. The tour ends this morning with tour members departing on individual schedules.

➤ *This tour combines neatly with many of our other tours of The West. You pay less for your second tour: see page 3.*

▲ *CRUISING ON LAKE TAHOE*

SAN FRANCISCO'S FAMOUS LOMBARD STREET ▼

Tour ACA: DATES & PRICES

Tour Code	Start San Francisco		End Los Angeles		9 days US$
ACA0305	Sat	05-Mar	Sun	13-Mar	968
ACA0319	Sat	19-Mar	Sun	27-Mar	968
ACA0402	Sat	02-Apr	Sun	10-Apr	978
ACA0409	Sat	09-Apr	Sun	17-Apr	978
ACA0416	Sat	16-Apr	Sun	24-Apr	988
ACA0423	Sat	23-Apr	Sun	01-May	998
ACA0430	Sat	30-Apr	Sun	08-May	998
ACA0507	Sat	07-May	Sun	15-May	998
ACA0514	Sat	14-May	Sun	22-May	998
ACA0521	Sat	21-May	Sun	29-May	998
ACA0528	Sat	28-May	Sun	05-Jun	998
ACA0603	Fri	03-Jun	Sat	11-Jun	998
ACA0604	Sat	04-Jun	Sun	12-Jun	998
ACA0610	Fri	10-Jun	Sat	18-Jun	998
ACA0611	Sat	11-Jun	Sun	19-Jun	998
ACA0617	Fri	17-Jun	Sat	25-Jun	998
ACA0618	Sat	18-Jun	Sun	26-Jun	998
ACA0624	Fri	24-Jun	Sat	02-Jul	998
ACA0625	Sat	25-Jun	Sun	03-Jul	998
ACA0701	Fri	01-Jul	Sat	09-Jul	998
ACA0702	Sat	02-Jul	Sun	10-Jul	998
ACA0708	Fri	08-Jul	Sat	16-Jul	998
ACA0709	Sat	09-Jul	Sun	17-Jul	998
ACA0715	Fri	15-Jul	Sat	23-Jul	998
ACA0716	Sat	16-Jul	Sun	24-Jul	998
ACA0717	Sun	17-Jul	Mon	25-Jul	998
ACA0722	Fri	22-Jul	Sat	30-Jul	998
ACA0723	Sat	23-Jul	Sun	31-Jul	998
ACA0724	Sun	24-Jul	Mon	01-Aug	998
ACA0729	Fri	29-Jul	Sat	06-Aug	998
ACA0730	Sat	30-Jul	Sun	07-Aug	998
ACA0731	Sun	31-Jul	Mon	08-Aug	998
ACA0805	Fri	05-Aug	Sat	13-Aug	998
ACA0806	Sat	06-Aug	Sun	14-Aug	998
ACA0807	Sun	07-Aug	Mon	15-Aug	998
ACA0812	Fri	12-Aug	Sat	20-Aug	998
ACA0813	Sat	13-Aug	Sun	21-Aug	998
ACA0814	Sun	14-Aug	Mon	22-Aug	998
ACA0819	Fri	19-Aug	Sat	27-Aug	998
ACA0820	Sat	20-Aug	Sun	28-Aug	998
ACA0821	Sun	21-Aug	Mon	29-Aug	998
ACA0826	Fri	26-Aug	Sat	03-Sep	998
ACA0827	Sat	27-Aug	Sun	04-Sep	998
ACA0902	Fri	02-Sep	Sat	10-Sep	998
ACA0903	Sat	03-Sep	Sun	11-Sep	998
ACA0909	Fri	09-Sep	Sat	17-Sep	998
ACA0910	Sat	10-Sep	Sun	18-Sep	998
ACA0916	Fri	16-Sep	Sat	24-Sep	998
ACA0917	Sat	17-Sep	Sun	25-Sep	998
ACA0923	Fri	23-Sep	Sat	01-Oct	998
ACA0924	Sat	24-Sep	Sun	02-Oct	998
ACA0930	Fri	30-Sep	Sat	08-Oct	998
ACA1001	Sat	01-Oct	Sun	09-Oct	998
ACA1008	Sat	08-Oct	Sun	16-Oct	998
ACA1015	Sat	15-Oct	Sun	23-Oct	998
ACA1022	Sat	22-Oct	Sun	30-Oct	998
ACA1029	Sat	29-Oct	Sun	06-Nov	988
ACA1105	Sat	05-Nov	Sun	13-Nov	978
ACA1112	Sat	12-Nov	Sun	20-Nov	978
ACA1119	Sat	19-Nov	Sun	27-Nov	968

Prices are for all land arrangements. Air fare to San Francisco and from Los Angeles is additional. Your travel agent can help you find the best available air fare.

Single room supplement: $434

Triple room reduction per person: $55

Reduction for joining on day 3 upon departure from San Francisco: $192

Reduction for leaving on day 7 upon arrival in Los Angeles: $97

For additional accommodations in San Francisco before the tour and additional accommodations in Los Angeles after the tour, see our special rates on page 11.

APOLLO: TD*GG, **PARS:** G/PTS/GGX, **SABRE:** Y/TUR/QGG

GLOBUS HOTELS

SAN FRANCISCO Sheraton Palace, **LAKE TAHOE** Horizon Hotel and Casino, **YOSEMITE N.P.** Yosemite Park Lodges, **MONTEREY** Hyatt Regency, **SANTA MARIA** Santa Maria Inn, **LOS ANGELES** Hyatt Regency

Yellowstone, Grand Teton & Glacier National Parks

12 DAYS

Two fabulous ways to experience the glorious west. Take a 12 day Amtrak tour from Chicago, or a very special 10 day tour which begins in Salt Lake City!

DEPARTURES

June: 24, 28
July: 15, 19, 26
August: 2, 9, 12, 16, 23

LODGING

SALT LAKE CITY, UT
　Little America Hotel

JACKSON, WY
　The 49'er Inn

YELLOWSTONE NATIONAL PARK
　Grant Village or Canyon Lodge

BUTTE, MT
　War Bonnet Inn

WHITEFISH, MT
　Kandahar Lodge

GLACIER NAT'L PARK
　Many Glacier Lodge and
　East Glacier Park Lodge

Old Faithful - Yellowstone National Park

PER PERSON RATES

FROM CHICAGO VIA AMTRAK
12 DAYS

$1679 two to a room
$1975 one to a room
$1661 three to a room

Prices listed above are for coach seating

BEDROOM ACCOMMODATIONS – *Bedroom accommodations between Chicago and Salt Lake City and between Glacier National Park and Chicago are available on a limited basis at an additional cost. The additional cost includes 8 meals on the train.*
　$285 per person, round trip, two to an economy bedroom.
　$608 per person, round trip, two to a deluxe bedroom.
AIR FARE – Add cost of air fare from your city to Chicago and return.
EXTRA NIGHTS – Rooms for the night before and after the tour are available at the Sheraton Plaza in downtown Chicago - $109 per night or Quality Inn O'Hare near O'Hare Airport - $79 per night. Cost includes tax.

FROM SALT LAKE CITY
10 DAYS

$1398 two to a room
$1694 one to a room
$1380 three to a room

SPECIAL 10 DAY PROGRAM - This special air tour begins one day later than train departure. Fly into Salt Lake City on DAY TWO of below itinerary. Begin your tour on Day 3 at 9:30 am with Salt Lake City touring. Your tour ends on Day 11 in Great Falls, Montana.
AIR FARE – Add cost of air fare from your city to Salt Lake City and return from Great Falls, Montana.

HIGHLIGHTS

◆ Round trip transfers from airport to pre-night hotel or Amtrak station
◆ 1 night aboard Amtrak in each direction for 12 day tour
◆ 9 nights hotel accommodations
◆ 9 meals, including 7 dinners with chuckwagon supper, 2 lunches
◆ Tour Grand Teton, Yellowstone and Glacier National Parks
◆ Salt Lake City sightseeing tour including Mormon Tabernacle Choir rehearsal
◆ Western Show
◆ Jenny Lake boat ride
◆ Visit Virginia City
◆ Old Montana Prison visit
◆ Grant-Kohr Ranch tour
◆ St. Ignatius Mission
◆ Scenic drive through Glacier National Park
◆ Swiftcurrent boat ride
◆ Museum of the Plains Indian
◆ $5 per day in future travel credits

Enjoy the countryside travelling by rail!

ITINERARY

DAY ONE ◆ Home/Amtrak

Have you always wanted to visit three of this nations most famous National Parks? Then this is the holiday for you. We gather at Union Station, CHICAGO, ILLINOIS, at 1:30 pm, with our Tour Director to board the *California Zephyr* Amtrak train for our cross country journey to Salt Lake City, Utah.

DAY TWO ◆ Amtrak/Salt Lake City

As we pass DENVER, COLORADO, we begin a scenic climb through the magnificent Rocky Mountains. Later this evening we arrive in SALT LAKE CITY, UTAH.

DAY THREE ◆ Salt Lake City

This morning we sightsee in beautiful Salt Lake City. We'll visit historic Temple Square and a local guide will take you through city attractions. The afternoon

Reprinted courtesy of Tauck Tours.

The amazing Grand Tetons

is free to explore the area on your own. After dinner we hear the famed Mormon Tabernacle Choir rehearse. (Dinner)

DAY FOUR ◆ Salt Lake/Jackson
Today we travel through Wasatch National Forest before crossing into JACKSON, WYOMING. We'll enjoy western style entertainment and a rib stickin' cowboy meal at the Bar J Cattle Ranch. (Dinner)

DAY FIVE ◆ Jackson/Yellowstone National Park
Travel through GRAND TETON NATIONAL PARK and take a boat cruise on Jenny Lake, located in the heart of the mountains. We'll view Hidden Falls and gaze at the beautiful Teton Mountain range which appears to be keeping watch over our boat ride. Later, we arrive in YELLOW-STONE NATIONAL PARK for two nights at Grant Village. (Lunch)

DAY SIX ◆ Yellowstone Nat'l Park
Today we tour majestic Yellowstone National Park, known for its natural wonders. You'll see famous Old Faithful go off like clockwork, as well as the Grand Canyon of Yellowstone, the Lower Falls, Paint Pots and West Thumb. Don't forget to keep your eyes open for bears and other wildlife along the road! (Dinner)

DAY SEVEN ◆ Yellowstone/Butte
We say goodbye to Yellowstone and cross into the vast state of

MONTANA. Tonight stay in BUTTE, a copper mining city called the "Richest Hill on Earth." (Dinner)

DAY EIGHT ◆ Butte/Whitefish
Next we move on to Deer Lodge, where we tour the Old Montana Prison, built in 1871. Later we arrive in WHITEFISH for the night, where we enjoy dinner. (Dinner)

DAY NINE ◆ Glacier National Park
Today experience Montana's Rocky Mountains in GLACIER NATIONAL PARK. We travel on spectacular Going to the Sun Road, one of the outstanding scenic roadways of the world. Our lodging for the night is at Many Glacier Lodge, located in the park. Tonight dine on an included meal. (Dinner)

DAY TEN ◆ Glacier National Park
Our highlights this morning are a cruise on Swiftcurrent Lake and the Grinnell Glacier area. Following lunch, we travel through the Blackfeet Indian Reservation and visit the Museum of the Plains Indian. We overnight in western style at East Glacier Park Lodge and enjoy dinner. (Lunch, Dinner)

DAY ELEVEN ◆ Glacier National Park/ Amtrak
All aboard! We start our journey home on Amtrak's *Empire Builder*, passing the beautiful mountains of Montana and the Northern plains of North Dakota.

DAY TWELVE ◆ Arrive Home
We arrive at Union Station in the late afternoon and are transferred to our pre-arranged hotel or the airport with wonderful memories of our journey through three of our nation's most famous National Parks.

Full refund less $100 per person Cancellation Fee. Bedroom charges have separate cancellation fees ranging from 25% to 100% within 72 hours of departure.

Glacier Park Lodge

21

GLOBUS.   *First Class*   ESCORTED

The Pacific Northwest

Vancouver, Seattle, Portland, Newport, Gold Beach, Redwood National Park, Eureka, California Wine Country, San Francisco

BRITISH COLUMBIA
Vancouver
Victoria
WASHINGTON
Pacific Ocean
Seattle
Mt. Rainier
Mt. St. Helens
Portland
Bonneville Dam
Newport
Coos Bay   **OREGON**
Gold Beach
Redwood National Park
Eureka
CALIFORNIA
Wine Country
San Francisco

Tour **ANW** – 12 days from Vancouver to San Francisco

Maximum elevation on tour: 1,635 ft.

ALL THIS IS INCLUDED

- Services of a professional tour director
- First-class hotels listed below or equivalent (see page 9). Twin-bedded rooms with private bath or shower, hotel taxes, service charges and tips for baggage handling
- 11 American breakfasts (B); 1 lunch (L); 8 three-course dinners offering choice of entree (D), with a special welcome dinner in Vancouver and farewell dinner in San Francisco
- Private deluxe air-conditioned motorcoach
- Mailboat ride on the Rogue River; ferry crossing to Victoria; cruise through the Gulf Islands; cruise of San Francisco Bay
- Sightseeing tour of Vancouver, Victoria, Seattle, Portland, San Francisco

- Visits to Victoria's Butchart Gardens, Mt. St. Helens Visitor Center, Portland's International Rose Test Gardens, Oregon winery, Newport's Oregon Coast Aquarium, Coos Bay and the Myrtlewood Factory, Gold Beach, Redwood National Park, Eureka
- Other scenic highlights: Columbia River Gorge, Multnomah Falls and the Bonneville Dam, Siuslaw National Forest, Oregon's Pacific coastline
- Inside visits as shown in UPPER-CASE LETTERS in the tour description, including admission charges where applicable
- Tips for baggage handling and to hotel personnel, and all local taxes
- Globus travel bag and portfolio of travel documents

Day 1 VANCOUVER. Today all tour members check in on independent schedules. The tour begins with an evening sightseeing of some important city landmarks. Then a special welcome dinner at a well-known restaurant, located at the Capilano Suspension Bridge – the famous swinging footbridge spanning a 230-foot-deep gorge. (D)

Day 2 VANCOUVER. A full day at leisure to explore cosmopolitan Vancouver, Canada's "Gem of the Pacific". Our suggestion for today: an optional excursion aboard the MV Brittania cruising through English Bay and up breathtaking Howe Sound. The return journey is by the last operational "Royal" Hudson train in a cliff-hugging tour of North Vancouver. (B)

Day 3 VANCOUVER-VICTORIA. A morning transfer to the ferry terminal for the scenic crossing to Swartz Bay on Vancouver Island. Major sights on the afternoon tour of the provincial capital include Beacon Hill Park, the Empress Hotel, Bastion Square and Thunderbird Park with its unusual collection of totem poles. The balance of the day is free for independent sightseeing and shopping. See Government Street with its many elegant shops carrying English tweeds and fine China; or browse through Market Square with its vast collection of specialty stores in beautifully-restored buildings. (B,D)

Day 4 VICTORIA-GULF ISLANDS-SEATTLE. Start the day with a visit to the world-famous BUTCHART GARDENS covering over 35 acres in an abandoned limestone quarry and divided into the English Gardens, Rose Garden, Japanese Garden, formal Italian Garden and the Sunken Garden. At Swartz Bay, board the ferry and cruise through the narrow waterways of the picturesque Gulf Islands and then by coach head south to Seattle. (B,D)

Day 5 SEATTLE. This city – built upon hills between Lake Washington and Puget Sound – is the metropolis of the Pacific Northwest and a major center of America's huge aerospace industry. Main attractions on the morning sightseeing: Seattle Center, site of the 1962 World's Fair and the 605-foot-high Space Needle. As the balance of the day is free, we recommend the optional outing to the site of the Boeing aircraft plant, the largest building in the world. The guided tour covers the assembly plant for the 747 and 767 aircraft. (B)

Day 6 SEATTLE-PORTLAND. Shortly after leaving this great seaport, Mount Rainier, a towering ice-clad volcano, can be seen to the east. Head south, tracing the route pioneered by Lewis and Clarke, to the VOLCANO VISITOR'S CENTER for a stop to view a presentation of the dramatic eruption of Mount St. Helens in 1980. One more attraction

▼ *SEATTLE SKYLINE*

▲ *THE RUGGED OREGON COASTLINE*

▲ *CALIFORNIA REDWOODS*

Tour ANW: DATES & PRICES

Tour Code	Start Vancouver		End San Francisco		12 days US$
ANW0513	Fri	13-May	Tue	24-May	1458
ANW0520	Fri	20-May	Tue	31-May	1468
ANW0527	Fri	27-May	Tue	07-Jun	1478
ANW0603	Fri	03-Jun	Tue	14-Jun	1488
ANW0610	Fri	10-Jun	Tue	21-Jun	1488
ANW0617	Fri	17-Jun	Tue	28-Jun	1488
ANW0624	Fri	24-Jun	Tue	05-Jul	1488
ANW0701	Fri	01-Jul	Tue	12-Jul	1488
ANW0708	Fri	08-Jul	Tue	19-Jul	1488
ANW0715	Fri	15-Jul	Tue	26-Jul	1488
ANW0722	Fri	22-Jul	Tue	02-Aug	1488
ANW0729	Fri	29-Jul	Tue	09-Aug	1488
ANW0805	Fri	05-Aug	Tue	16-Aug	1488
ANW0812	Fri	12-Aug	Tue	23-Aug	1488
ANW0818	Thu	18-Aug	Mon	29-Aug	1488
ANW0819	Fri	19-Aug	Tue	30-Aug	1488
ANW0825	Thu	25-Aug	Mon	05-Sep	1488
ANW0826	Fri	26-Aug	Tue	06-Sep	1488
ANW0901	Thu	01-Sep	Mon	12-Sep	1488
ANW0902	Fri	02-Sep	Tue	13-Sep	1488
ANW0908	Thu	08-Sep	Mon	19-Sep	1488
ANW0909	Fri	09-Sep	Tue	20-Sep	1488
ANW0915	Thu	15-Sep	Mon	26-Sep	1488
ANW0916	Fri	16-Sep	Tue	27-Sep	1488
ANW0923	Fri	23-Sep	Tue	04-Oct	1488
ANW0930	Fri	30-Sep	Tue	11-Oct	1478
ANW1007	Fri	07-Oct	Tue	18-Oct	1468
ANW1014	Fri	14-Oct	Tue	25-Oct	1458

Prices are for all land arrangements. Air fare to Vancouver and from San Francisco is additional. Your travel agent can help you find the best available air fare.

Single room supplement: $606
Triple room reduction per person: $109

Reduction for joining on day 4 in Seattle before dinner: $236

Reduction for leaving on day 10 upon arrival in San Francisco: $203

For additional accommodations in Vancouver before the tour and additional accommodations in San Francisco after the tour, see our special rates on page 11.

APOLLO: TD*GG, **PARS:** G/PTS/GGX, **SABRE:** Y/TUR/QGG

GLOBUS HOTELS

VANCOUVER Georgian Court, **VICTORIA** Harbor Towers, **SEATTLE** Stouffer Madison, **PORTLAND** Red Lion Lloyd Center, **NEWPORT** Hotel Newport, **GOLD BEACH** Gold Beach Resort, **EUREKA** Eureka Inn, **SAN FRANCISCO** Sheraton Palace

before reaching Portland: a scenic drive along the Columbia River Gorge to see the spectacular Multnomah Falls and the Bonneville Dam. (B,D)

Day 7 PORTLAND-NEWPORT. Portland is known as the City of Roses and prides itself in having more than 150 parks. Before leaving this morning, a visit to one of its most famous, WASHINGTON PARK, home of the INTERNATIONAL ROSE TEST GARDENS. Oregon's vineyards are now producing some very fine wines; a stop at A LOCAL WINERY will allow you to judge for yourself. Head west to Lincoln City and motor southward hugging the rugged Pacific coastline interspersed with numerous beaches en route to Newport, one of Oregon's most popular seaside resorts. At the OREGON COAST AQUARIUM, explore indoor exhibits and a vast outdoor acreage of natural habitat where seals, sea lions, puffins and otters make their home. (B,D)

Day 8 NEWPORT-COOS BAY-GOLD BEACH. Continuing south through the Siuslaw National Forest, the Oregon sand dunes come into view, some reaching a height of 300 feet! Upon arrival in Coos Bay visit a MYRTLEWOOD FACTORY to see craftsmen at work carving attractive dishes, jewelry and other decorative items from this native hardwood. Back to the scenic coastal highway and on to Gold Beach for overnight accommodations. (B,D)

Day 9 GOLD BEACH-REDWOOD NATIONAL PARK-EUREKA. A thrilling experience in store this morning! A ride on the Rogue River Mailboat up the fast-flowing rapids of the Rogue, an area abundant with a variety of wildlife. Cameras ready... as you may spot a bald eagle in flight. Into California and proceed along the coastal route through Redwood National Park whose trees are recognized to be the world's tallest and a

species that evolved millions of years ago. Entering Eureka, California's lumber center, see one of the city's most noted landmarks, the Carson Mansion, once the dwelling of a west coast lumber baron. (B,D)

Day 10 EUREKA-SAN FRANCISCO. From the rugged Pacific coastline to the lush gentle slopes of California wine country. A short stop in the Mendocino Valley to sample a local vintage. Cross the bay via the magnificent Golden Gate Bridge and proceed to downtown San Francisco. Learn more of the city and its Oriental heritage on this evening's optional outing to Chinatown. A lavish four-course dinner in an authentic Chinese restaurant is followed by a special-effects movie highlighting the historic events that have shaped San Francisco. (B)

Day 11 SAN FRANCISCO. This harbor-city's charm comes to life while sightseeing its steep hills, parks, cable-cars and bustling docks. Highlight visits include THE JAPANESE TEA GARDENS, Golden Gate Park, Seal Rocks, Twin Peaks, with the tour ending at Fisherman's Wharf. Lunch at a famed harbor-front restaurant before enjoying a cruise of the bay. Still plenty of time in the day for shopping and other leisure time activities. This evening your tour director hosts a farewell dinner, a festive finale to a great touring adventure. (B,L,D)

Day 12 SAN FRANCISCO. The tour ends this morning with tour members departing on individual schedules. (B)

➤ *This tour is planned to connect with "FOCUS ON CALIFORNIA" (page 26) and with "CALIFORNIA COAST VACATION" (page 30). You pay less for your second tour: see page 3.*

13 Days (12 Nights) From $4265

Extra Highlights: *Space Needle* □ *Sternwheeler Cruise* □ *Wildlife Tour* □ *Portage Glacier* □ *Columbia Glacier Flightseeing* □ *Days of '98 Show* □ *Lynn Canal Cruise* □ *Alaskaland* — ***12 Breakfasts, 8 Lunches, 12 Dinners***

Alaska
Fairbanks / Denali National Park / Anchorage
Inside Passage Cruise / Glacier Bay

1. SIGHTSEE SEATTLE
Fly to Seattle. **Tour begins: Seattle Airport 2:00 P.M., United Airlines Baggage Claim Area.** Meet your tour director and commence a brief sightseeing tour of Seattle. See the downtown area, the waterways and residential parks. This evening be our guest for a get-acquainted reception and dinner. Meals included **D**

2. FLY TO FAIRBANKS
Start the day with breakfast at the revolving Space Needle Restaurant. Enjoy the endless 360° panorama of the mountains, the city and the sea. In mid-morning, fly to Fairbanks, Alaska's frontier city. Fairbanks was the supply post for the Alaska pipeline project, and is the hub of the interior. A gold-rush town born at the turn of the century, Fairbanks lies only 120 miles south of the Arctic Circle. Arrive in time to take a drive to see the massive Alaska pipeline which connects the oil fields of the Arctic to the port of Valdez. Meals included **BLD**

Wildlife in Denali Park

3. GOLDMINING / ARCTIC OPTION
You have a choice today. Take an optional flight to Barrow on the Arctic Ocean (see below) or join us for a trip to the Little El Dorado Gold Camp. You will pan for gold and learn about gold mining techniques. Also, visit the University of Alaska with its impressive museum. This evening join us for a salmon bake dinner and Palace Theater show at Alaskaland. Meals included **BLD**

BARROW ARCTIC OPTION
$415 EXTRA

Situated on the northernmost point of land on the North American continent 330 miles north of the Arctic Circle, Barrow is Alaska's largest Eskimo village. It is the whaling capital of the Arctic and many age-old traditions linger, including expressive dancing and handcrafting of fur clothing, ivory and baleen. Instead of the day in Fairbanks, you may choose this full day (9 AM - 9 PM) excursion by jet to the "top of the world" where you enjoy a ceremonial dance program and an Eskimo blanket toss. Learn about the rich cultural heritage of the Eskimo, the great whale hunts and see how mukluks, dolls and ceremonial masks are made from caribou and sealskin. Return to Fairbanks. You'll receive a handsome certificate to commemorate your crossing of the Arctic Circle. (Lunch is included in Barrow. Dinner is not included but credited to you in the option price.) To insure availability, arrangements for this option should be made at the time of booking.

Point Barrow

Maximum Elevation: 3,290 ft.

Arctic Circle

ALASKA

Fairbanks

YUKON

Denali National Park

Anchorage

Columbia Glacier

Skagway

Glacier Bay

Juneau

Sitka

Inside Passage

BRITISH COLUMBIA

Vancouver

Seattle

- ■ ■ ■ ■ Optional Air
- ——— Motorcoach
- ——— Boat/Ship
- ——— Air

Reprinted courtesy of Tauck Tours.

Sitka — a colorful community on Baranof Island

4. RIVERBOAT / DENALI

A must in Fairbanks is a trip on the sternwheel riverboat, *Discovery* on the Chena and Tanana Rivers. (Note: Tour of May 19 will cruise on the *Discovery* on day 3.) At one time, the riverboat was the only transportation in Alaska and the Yukon. End the cruise with lunch at the Pump House Restaurant, originally built to pump water to the Fairbanks area gold fields. Continue to Denali National Park. Meals included **BLD**

5. DENALI NAT'L PK / MT. McKINLEY

The highest mountain in North America, Mt. McKinley in Denali National Park, soars up 20,320 feet. It's an awesome sight, if weather permits. Take an eight-hour wildlife tour deep into the park's interior. Limited vehicular traffic into the park minimizes man's effect on this habitat. The morning is the best time to find moose, Dall sheep and maybe a grizzly bear or two. (Don't forget your binoculars!) Later today relax at the pool or take an optional raft ride. This evening you are invited to an Alaska cabin dinner. Meals included **BLD**

6. PRIVATE GLACIER FLIGHTS

This should be one of the most exciting days of your trip. Keep your fingers crossed for good weather. Drive through woodlands of spruce, birch and aspen to Anchorage. This stretch of highway provides you with a respect for the vast interior. The route parallels the Alaska railroad from Anchorage to Fairbanks. This is a delightful drive which, unlike the train, offers the flexibility to stop to take photos, enjoy the countryside and observe the wildlife that occasionally is seen. This

drive allows for viewing Mt. McKinley. As you approach the coast, the forest gives way to the lush Matanuska River valley. Tour Anchorage, the state's largest city, and check into your centrally located hotel. Then, flightseeing! In late afternoon or early evening when the light is best, join us for a three-hour floatplane trip over some of the most spectacular scenery in North America. Your pilot gains altitude as you approach Turnagain Arm and Portage Glacier. Fly up to its source to see the five glaciers fed by the ever-present snowfields.

Flightseeing!

Then fly through Portage Pass where suddenly the mountains drop to the sea. This is Prince William Sound studded with forested islands and flanked by white-capped mountains. Your pilot banks to the left and there, coming at you is the massive Columbia Glacier. It's an awesome sight! Meals included **BLD**
(This flight may be scheduled or rerouted to take advantage of the best forecast weather.)

7. ANCHORAGE / MT. ALYESKA

Start the day with a drive along Turnagain Arm, a fjord of rushing tidal water flanked by inspiring glacial-hewn mountains. Here occur the third-highest tides in the world.

At the head of the Arm is Portage Glacier. Here the glacial activity sets icebergs adrift and the winds frequently guide them to within your reach. En route back to Anchorage, visit Mt. Alyeska where you view alpine meadows ablaze with wildflowers against a backdrop of the snowcapped Chugach and Kenai Mountains. Meals included **BD**

8. MENDENHALL / SKAGWAY

You have now tasted Alaska's great interior, so it's time to head for the sea. Fly to Juneau, Alaska's capital. See the famed Mendenhall Glacier, boarding the mv Fairweather and cruise the Lynn Canal to Skagway, a frontier, gay-90s town which served as a gateway to the Yukon during the gold rush of 1898. This era is preserved in the town's wooden sidewalks and colorful saloons. Tonight, join us for the famous "Days of '98" show. Meals included **BD**

9. FLY TO JUNEAU / START CRUISE

Start the day with a sightseeing tour of Skagway including a drive up White Pass, a notorious obstacle for gold miners leaving Skagway. Later, stroll the wooden sidewalks and browse the shops of Skagway before taking a small plane flight to Juneau to board your Holland America cruise ship for a relaxing four-night Inside Passage cruise. We sail at midnight so the remainder of the evening is yours to get to know the ship or further explore Juneau. Don't miss the Red Dog Saloon. Meals included **BD**

10. GLACIER BAY

Awake to find your cruise ship gliding through Glacier Bay National Monument. Seals, eagles, whales, bears and other wildlife are often seen. Before you, glacier-ice cliffs of white and blue seem to rise from the sea. Your ship drifts a short distance from the ice fall. You may see giant slabs of ice break away and crash into the sea. It can be a thundering spectacle. You linger most of the day here. Meals included **BLD**

11. SITKA / ARCHANGEL DANCERS

Alaska once belonged to the Russians. It was their fur-trading empire which extended south to northern California. For years Sitka reigned as the capital of

Cruise on Holland America Lines

this Russian outpost. Sitka is a colorful little community on Baronof Island that today shelters fishing and pleasure craft. Here, you have an opportunity to see the New Archangel Dancers and their Russian ethnic folk dances. You will also have a chance to examine and understand more of the Tlingit Indian culture. Meals included **BLD**

12. INSIDE PASSAGE CRUISE

Holland America Lines is famous for its Dutch captains and officers and their attentive Indonesian crew. This is an entire day to relax and enjoy the amenities of your ship... the finest continental cuisine, gracious lounges, gymnasiums, two swimming pools, a movie theater, a casino and the choice of a Broadway revue or disco. There are many scheduled activities throughout the day. All this is yours to enjoy as you cruise through the rugged beauty of the Inside Passage. In addition, your on board naturalist is available to help you spot pods of killer whales, porpoises and soaring bald eagles. Relax and enjoy nature's awesome beauty at your own pace today. Meals included **BLD**

13. VANCOUVER / SEATTLE

In early morning, arrive in Vancouver to clear Canadian Customs (see Canadian Immigration, page 122), and take a final motorcoach transfer to Seattle. **Tour ends: Seattle Airport at 2:00 PM.** For persons

who wish an overnight in Vancouver or Seattle before connecting with home-bound flights, we can make arrangements at reduced rates at selected hotels. Meals included **B**

Departure Dates:

THURSDAY – May 12 to Sept. 1
Cruise on ms Maasdam

MONDAYS – May 30 to Aug. 22
Cruise on ms Westerdam

Air Fare to Seattle is additional

Contact your booking agent for special low fares which are usually available.

Stay at the best available hotels

Night 1	**Westin Hotel Seattle** Seattle, WA
Night 2,3	**Westmark Fairbanks** Fairbanks, AK
Night 4,5	**McKinley Chalet Resort** Denali National Park, AK
Night 6,7	**Anchorage Hilton** Anchorage, AK
Night 8	**Westmark Inn** Skagway, AK
Night 9 -12	**Aboard Your Holland America Ship**

APOLLO ACCESS TD*28040
WORLDSPAN ACCESS .... G/PTS/TTX/AL

Price Per Person:

THURSDAYS – MS MAASDAM

	TWIN	SINGLE	TRIPLE
Base Inside (M) Two beds, shower, cozy	$4315	$5437	3938
Large Inside (J) Two beds, shower	$4405	$5572	N/A
Outside (G) Two beds, shower, porthole	$4645	$5932	N/A
Better Outside (D) Two beds, bath & shower, porthole	$4825	$6202	$4278
Deluxe Outside/Verandah (B) Sitting area, 2 beds, bath & shower, private verandah and floor to ceiling windows	$5215	$6787	N/A

MONDAYS – MS WESTERDAM

Base Inside (M) Two beds, shower, cozy	$4265	$5357	N/A
Better Inside (J) Higher deck, two beds, shower	$4355	$5492	N/A
Outside (G) Two beds, shower, porthole	$4595	$5852	N/A
Large Outside (D) Two beds, bathtub and shower, porthole	$4775	$6122	$4245
Deluxe Outside (B) Sitting area, 2 beds, bathtub and shower, porthole	$5105	$6617	N/A

SAVE $100 per person twin or triple and $125 single if you choose a departure before June 15.

POINT BARROW OPTION .... ADD $415

The Price Includes

Everything in General Information (page 122) PLUS:

• Same tour director throughout*	
• Air from Seattle to Fairbanks	$594 value
• Air from Anchorage to Juneau	$397 value
• Four nights Southbound Cruise Fare	$1340 value
• A flightseeing excursion on Day 6	$200 value
• Flightseeing, Skagway to Juneau	$121 value
• Sitka shore excursion	$28 value
• All port taxes	$55 value
• All shipboard gratuities	$24 value

*When comparing different Alaska tours, one must note that this Tauck Alaska Tour is fully escorted from Seattle back to Seattle. The same escort and group travel together from beginning to end. In contrast, many other tours merely involve a linking of various travel components into an individual, unescorted package with different persons joining and leaving the itinerary throughout.

It pays to recognize that all of the above items are included on a Tauck Tour. On many other tours, some or all of these items are extra. Compare what Tauck includes with that which others exclude and you will see clearly that Tauck is by far the best value to Alaska.

Cancellation Fees

for Tauck's Alaska tour supersede those fees and conditions under General Information in this brochure. The following cancellation assessments apply: $100 per room if cancelled prior to 60 days before departure. $200 per person if cancelled within 60 to 30 days before departure. $650 if cancelled 29 to 15 days before departure. $1300 per person if cancelled within 14 days of departure. No refunds will be made for non-appearance. Time of cancellation will be when notice is received at Tauck Tours Westport office. Cancellation Protection may be purchased for $60 from Tauck Tours as per General Information, page 122.

13 Days (12 Nights)   From $2590

Extra Highlights: *Wailua River Cruise* □ *Old Hanalei* □ *City of Refuge* □ *Parker Ranch* □ *Royal Hawaiian* □ *Punchbowl* □ *Helicopter flight on Kauai* □ *Bishop Museum* □ *Iao Valley* — *12 Breakfasts, 4 Lunches, 11 Dinners*

Hawaii – 4 Islands
Oahu / Kauai / Maui / Hawaii

1. **LIMO ARRIVAL / HONOLULU**
Fly to Hawaii. Most flights arrive in the late afternoon. A private limousine is waiting to take you immediately to the Royal Hawaiian Hotel where your tour director will meet you upon arrival. The Royal Hawaiian is located in the heart of Waikiki Beach. You have a choice of either ocean view or garden view rooms, see "price per person." Meals included **D**

2. **PEARL HARBOR / WAIKIKI**
Enjoy a beachside breakfast on the terrace of the Surf Room. Later this morning visit Pearl Harbor and board the memorial of the *U.S.S. Arizona.* The afternoon is free for you to sun and swim at Waikiki Beach or to shop in the fashionable Kalakaua shopping district. As an end to a perfect day, you are invited to a cocktail party followed by dinner. This is a perfect time to become better acquainted with the members of your tour and your Tauck Tour director. Meals included **BD**

3. **OAHU SIGHTSEEING**
This morning sightsee the island of Oahu. Travel through the fashionable Kahala residential district before weaving along the rugged lava rock coast past Hanauma Bay, Koko Head and Makapuu Point. Ascend to the windy cliffs of the Nuuanu Pali for a magnificent view of the Kailua and Kaneohe coast. Wind through the Mount Tantalus Rain Forest to Punchbowl, an extinct volcano crater and the site of the National Memorial Cemetery of the Pacific. While at the Royal, we invite you to an exciting dinner show in the famous Monarch Room. Meals included **BD**

4. **FLY TO KAUAI**
Leave fast-paced Honolulu for nine relaxing days in the Neighbor Islands. This morning fly to Kauai, the Garden Isle. Upon arrival drive north past the Sleeping Giant of Kapaa to your hotel overlooking lovely Hanalei Bay. After lunch the afternoon is at leisure to relax and enjoy the gracious surroundings of the resort. For those who wish, we provide a tour by van into Hanalei Valley. Meals included **BLD**

5. **KAUAI / POIPU BEACH**
This morning is free to enjoy Hanalei Bay Resort. After lunch embark on a boat ride on the palm-fringed Wailua River

The Pink Palace - Hawaii's most famous hotel

to Kauai's Fern Grotto, a volcanic cave where numerous Hawaiian weddings have been performed. This afternoon arrive at Kauai's South Shore and Poipu Beach for two nights at the magnificent Hyatt Regency Kauai. Meals included **BLD**

6. **NA PALI BY HELICOPTER**
This day could be one of the most exciting and unforgettable experiences of your vacation! By helicopter, you will sightsee the most spectacular scenery on Kauai including Waimea Canyon and the beaches, cliffs and valleys of the inaccessible Na Pali Coast (conditions permitting). Then fly into the wild unexplored mysterious Kalalau Valley and the Valley of the Lost Tribe. Meals included **BD**

7. **FLY TO THE BIG ISLAND**
This is a long but fascinating day. Fly to Hilo on the Big Island of Hawaii, an island created by five volcanoes. Mt. Kilauea has been active since 1983. Visit Hawaii Volcanoes National Park then drive along the Hamakua Coast. Continue through the grazing lands of the Parker Ranch, the largest privately owned ranch in America. From volcanoes to lush valleys to snow-capped peaks and expansive

pasturelands, Hawaii has more variety than any other island it's size. Arrive at the Royal Waikoloan, your home for the next three nights. Meals included **BLD**

Tropical Flowers

118

Reprinted courtesy of Tauck Tours.

8. BIG ISLAND AT LEISURE

There is much to see and do on the Big Island. The entire day is at leisure to enjoy the resort or explore the island on your own. Tauck has arranged special rates for those who wish to take a volcano helicopter flight, a jeep safari or charter a sportfishing boat. Meals included **BD**

9. CITY OF REFUGE / HALE KEA

On this day you have a choice. Remain at the resort or join us for a morning tour to the historical City of Refuge and the harborside village of Kailua. This evening we return to the pastoral ranchlands for an elegant dinner at the Hale Kea Estate, once the home of the Parker Ranch Manager. Meals included **BD**

*Kauai's Na Pali Coast —
inaccessible except by helicopter*

10. FLY TO MAUI / LAHAINA

The Valley Island, Maui now awaits you. After a morning flight, visit the peaceful Iao Valley, hidden amid towering peaks. It's called the Yosemite of the Pacific. Enjoy a delightful luncheon at Maui Tropical Plantation, then skirt the Pacific shore past sugarcane fields to the historic capital of Lahaina. Lahaina was once the winter rendezvous of the world's whaling fleets and is now a shopping mecca. Soon arrive at modern Kaanapali Beach where your home for the next three

Hanalei Bay, Kauai

nights is the Hyatt Regency Maui. For dinner this evening, choose among the hotel's restaurants. Meals included **BLD**

11. AT LEISURE MAUI

Today is at leisure. Play tennis, golf, shop, visit the nearby marketplaces, or spend the day at the Hyatt's magnificent pool …a wonderland of waterfalls, gardens and grottoes. Lunch and dinner are not included so you may choose among the many dining spots available in Lahaina and Kaanapali. Meals included **B**

12. MT. HALEAKALA

Today enjoy a trip to the 10,023 ft. summit of Maui's giant Mt. Haleakala… the house of the sun. This is the world's largest dormant volcano crater, a huge basin of ash and lava in rich, reddish-brown colors. Return to your hotel in the early afternoon. Tonight enjoy a farewell reception followed by gourmet dining in the Hyatt's elegant Swan Court Restaurant. Meals included **BD**

13. JOURNEY HOME FROM MAUI

You are now a *kamaaina*, an old-timer in the islands. Soon your limousine and chauffeur will drive you to the airport on Maui. **Tour ends: Anytime on Maui.** Check out time is 12 Noon. A courtesy room is available until 6 PM. Meals included **B**

Departure Dates:

SUNDAYS, TUESDAYS, THURSDAYS – January 2 through December 29

Price Per Person:

Since there is a meaningful price difference between ocean view and garden view at the Royal Hawaiian we leave that choice to you. All other rooms are ocean view.

♦ With **garden view** at the Royal Hawaiian:
Twin $2590   Single $3396   Triple $2434
Twin with roll-away

♦ With **ocean view** at the Royal Hawaiian:
Twin $2765   Single $3746   Triple $2554
Twin with roll-away

See "Tour Prices Include," page 122.
27 Meals Included.
3 Inter-island Flights Included.

Air Fare to Hawaii is additional

Contact your booking agent for special low fares which are usually available. Tauck has blocked space on United Airlines from certain cities.

Stay at the best available hotels

Night 1,2,3	**Royal Hawaiian Hotel**	Honolulu, HI
Night 4*	**Hanalei Bay Resort**	Hanalei, Kauai
Night 5,6	**Hyatt Regency Kauai**	Poipu Beach, Kauai
Night 7,8,9	**The Royal Waikoloan**	Waikoloa, HI
Night 10,11,12	**Hyatt Regency Maui**	Kaanapali Beach, Maui

* *Tours of Jan. 2,4,6,9,11,13,14,16,18,20,21,23,25,27,28 will stay at the Sheraton Princeville Hotel.*

APOLLO ACCESS TD*28001
WORLDSPAN ACCESS .... G/PTS/TTX/HW

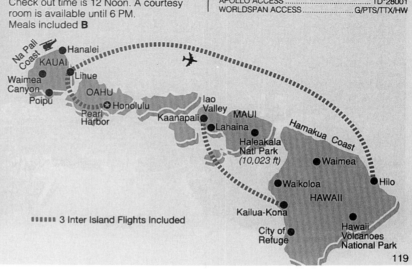

••••••• 3 Inter Island Flights Included

Branson Music & the Ozarks

6 DAYS

Everybody's talkin' about Branson! Top name musical entertainment, the rolling hills of Missouri, and The Great Passion Play are waiting for you!

DEPARTURES

May: 3, 10, 17, 24, 28, 31
June: 7, 14, 21, 28
July: 5, 12, 19, 26
August: 9, 16, 23
September: 6, 10, 13, 17, 20, 22, 24, 27
October: 1, 4, 8, 11, 15, 18, 22, 25, 29
November: 15

LODGING

ST. LOUIS, MO
 Regal Riverfront Hotel
BRANSON, MO
 The Edgewood
EUREKA SPRINGS, AR
 Inn of the Ozarks
LAKE OZARK, MO
 Inn at Grand Glaize

PER PERSON RATES

$739 two to a room
$927 one to a room
$729 three to a room

AIR FARE – Add cost of air fare from your city to St. Louis and return.

EXTRA NIGHTS – Rooms for the night before and after the tour are available at the Regal Riverfront, St. Louis, Missouri. Cost for a single or double room is $79 per night, tax included.

Silver Dollar City Jail

HIGHLIGHTS

- Airport transfers to and from St. Louis Hotel
- 5 nights accommodations
- 5 meals – 4 dinners, including dinner cruise and 1 lunch on excursion train
- St. Louis city tour
- Cruise on the Mississippi River
- Silver Dollar City
- 3 top name Branson variety music shows - Shoji Tabuchi, Wayne Newton, Bobby Vinton, Tony Orlando, Andy Williams and Jim Stafford are among our selected shows
- Eureka Springs, Arkansas guided tour
- Ozark countryside steam train ride
- The Great Passion Play
- Lake Ozark cruise
- $30 in future travel credits

Shoji Tabuchi

ITINERARY

DAY ONE ◆ Home/St. Louis
Arriving in ST. LOUIS, MISSOURI, we transfer to our downtown lodging overlooking the Mississippi River. Our American music adventure begins as we meet at 4 pm in the hotel lobby for a guided tour of this old French city. The spectacular Gateway Arch, celebrating the growth of our country, dominates the exciting riverfront. With our traveling friends we board a paddlewheeler for a get-acquainted dinner hosted by our Tour Director. We cruise the Mississippi with lively Dixieland entertainment in the background. The city lights create an attractive skyline as we return to the dock at dusk. (Dinner)

DAY TWO ◆ St. Louis/Branson
This morning we depart for BRANSON, MISSOURI for music, music, music at two shows today! After we check into our hotel for two nights we hit the downtown streets of this musical capital. We enjoy an afternoon matinee before dinner together. The talented musicians are ready for us as we visit another of Branson's top musical performances this evening. (Dinner)

Reprinted courtesy of Mayflower Tours.

MISSOURI

St. Louis

Lake
Ozark

Branson

Eureka Springs

ARKANSAS

Enjoy Ozark crafts

Aerial view of Eureka Springs

DAY THREE ◆ Branson Shows

The music continues at popular Silver Dollar City. Enjoy hours of live music, see crafts made by hand, and delight in home-cooked food - all part of the many treasures in Silver Dollar City. After dinner we find our toes tapping at another downtown Branson performance. This booming community hosts more than 30 theatres with live performances by some of the greatest names in music and entertainment. (Dinner)

DAY FOUR ◆ Branson/ Eureka Springs

This morning we travel to EUREKA SPRINGS, ARKANSAS, the Little Switzerland of the Ozarks. Our guided tour includes lunch on a vintage steam train excursion through the countryside. See the beautiful Victorian homes and walk the downtown shopping district that is now on the National Register of Historic Places in America. Tonight we are captivated by an evening performance of *The Great Passion Play*, an outdoor drama depicting Christ's last week on earth. (Lunch)

DAY FIVE ◆ Eureka Springs/ Lake Ozark

We ride through the beautiful Ozark hills of Arkansas and Missouri traveling to the resort community of LAKE OZARK, MISSOURI for our overnight. We see this beautiful area

from a new viewpoint on a lake cruise. Bagnell Dam created a recreational reservoir with over 1,000 miles of irregular shoreline, now known as Lake of the Ozarks. This evening we enjoy a farewell dinner with our fellow travelers. (Dinner)

See Andy Williams Live

DAY SIX ◆ Lake Ozark/ St. Louis/Home

We cross the Missouri River twice on our return trip to St. Louis. We are transferred to the St. Louis Airport for flights after 2 pm or to our pre-arranged hotel. Share the memories of musical fun in the fastest growing entertainment destination in America.

The Great Passion Play

■ For a longer vacation in the West, combine this tour with Colorado, New Mexico or Salt Lake/Yellowstone.

8 Days (7 Nights) $1270

Extra Highlights: *Navajo Indian Reservation* □ *Museum of No. Arizona* □ *Flagstaff* □ *Heard Museum* □ *Rainbow Bridge* □ *Lake Powell — 7 Breakfasts, 6 Lunches, 7 Dinners*

Canyonlands

Grand Canyon
Zion National Park
Oak Creek Canyon
Bryce National Park
Las Vegas

1. PHOENIX / SCOTTSDALE

Fly to Phoenix. **Tour departs: Phoenix Airport, 1:00 P.M.** Here, in the Valley of the Sun, meet your tour director in Terminal #3 at the group meeting area located near carousel #4. Begin with a brief tour of Phoenix. Visit the Heard Museum before arriving in Scottsdale, famed for its dry, desert climate. Overnight is at the foot of Camelback Mountain. Browse the grounds of your hotel or enjoy a swim before dinner. Meals included **D**

2. MONTEZUMA / SEDONA

Visit Montezuma National Monument and see the deserted cliff dwellings of one of the oldest known civilizations. Lunch is in Sedona surrounded by towering red rock formations that have provided back-grounds for hundreds of western movies. Then wind through magnificent Oak Creek Canyon to Flagstaff. Finally, Grand Canyon awaits you. Nature's most spectacular example of erosion, 277 miles long and over a mile deep, is truly the ultimate in silent majesty and beauty. Overnight on the rim of the Canyon. Meals included **BLD**

Glen Canyon - Colorado River

3. GRAND CANYON / NAVAJO LANDS

Grand Canyon captures the imagination. It is easy to be mesmerized by its grandeur, by its chameleon-like colors, and by the unbelievable realization that its vastness is a result of simple water erosion. The morning is free for you to browse the canyon rim and Canyon Village. After lunch tour the East Rim with stops to photograph the myriad colors

Bryce National Park

spread before you. See Moran Point, Lipan Point and Desert View Lookout. The canyon ends and green pine forests give way to open desert. Travel through the Navajo Indian Reservation en route to Page, Arizona, where your hotel overlooks the watery canyonlands of Lake Powell. Meals included **BLD**

4. LK POWELL / RAINBOW BRIDGE

When the Glen Canyon Dam was completed in 1964, it transformed the Colorado River into a massive lake, 186 miles long. Lake Powell, fringed by fjord-like canyons and splendid grottos aflame with color, is accessible only by boat. For sheer spectacle there is no lake like it on earth. To see this properly we have scheduled two trips today. The first is an early morning, 30-minute flight over the remote reaches of the lake. Below, colorful patterns of water are surrounded by unusual red rock formations including Rainbow Bridge, a natural rock arch rising 309 feet in the air. (You may take this flight and continue to Monument Valley – see "Monument Valley Option.") The second trip is an afternoon boat trip to the dam and into the canyon grottos. Meals included **BLD**

Maximum Elevation: 8,300 ft.

UTAH
NEVADA
Bryce National Park
Zion National Park (4,000 ft)
Kanab
Glen Canyon Dam
Monument Valley
Lake Powell
Las Vegas
Grand Canyon (8,300 ft)
Oak Creek Canyon
CALIFORNIA
Sedona
NEW MEXICO
ARIZONA
Montezuma National Monument
Phoenix/Scottsdale
TEXAS
MEXICO

54

5. GLEN CANYON RAFT TRIP

Today is filled with the excitement of a half-day float trip through Glen Canyon, one of the more scenic parts of the Colorado River. It's a peaceful, fun experience. Continue to Kanab, Utah, for overnight. This is a real outback kind of western town; the real thing, and the best location for our coming visits to

Monument Valley

Bryce and Zion. This evening we invite you to a cocktail party and western cookout. You will find western or casual attire most comfortable. Take your cameras. Meals included **BLD**

Persons wishing Monument Valley flight . . . add $110

This enchanted earthscape of monumental red rock formations is the ultimate symbol of western scenery. This optional 4-hour trip includes the flight itinerary described in fourth day above plus a continuing flight on to Monument Valley Tribal Park. Here you land and meet your Navajo Indian tour guide to tour this extraordinary land of monoliths. Then fly back to Page in time for lunch and the scheduled afternoon boat trip. Arrangements for this optional flight/tour should be made at the time of booking. We highly recommend this. It is a spectacular experience.

6. BRYCE NATIONAL PARK

Today you see Utah's Bryce Canyon National Park, a land of pines and pinnacles. Bryce is one of the most amazing and fascinating sights on earth, an immense semi-circular amphitheatre where countless, weirdly sculptured rock formations form tableaus of extraordinary beauty. Travel the length of the rim road where before you lies a city of stone cathedral spires carved by nature's chisel, delicately tinted in shades of pink, red and orange, and softened by gray and white. See Sunset Point and Inspiration Point. Then you are off to Zion National Park for overnight. Meals included **BLD**

7. ZION NAT'L PARK / LAS VEGAS

Today is a day of contrasts. Zion is noted for its narrow, tortuous canyons and isolated buttes and mesas. You wind deep into the canyon where great red precipices rise on either side and widen into a beautiful valley carpeted in green. Next pass through St. George where you will see the St. George Mormon Temple. Although a bit of a juxtaposition from the rest of the tour, Las Vegas is the nearest airport city for persons returning from Bryce and Zion. A bonus is that Vegas is also the Entertainment Capital of the World. See the casino areas and drive the length of the Las Vegas Strip. This evening we invite you to a farewell reception and dinner. You may wish to end the evening with a show or a flirt with Lady Luck in the casino. Meals included **BLD**

8. JOURNEY HOME

Tour ends: Las Vegas. Fly out any time. Check-out time is noon. From Las Vegas there are easy flight connections for persons joining our Colorado, New Mexico, Idaho, California and Salt Lake tours. Since individuals leave at different times, a transfer is not included. Taxi is the most practical transportation to the airport. Fares are about $11 per car for up to four persons. Meals included **B**

Departure Dates:

SATURDAYS – April 2 to Nov. 5
TUESDAYS – March 29 to Nov. 1
WEDNESDAYS – May 4 to Sept. 21
THURSDAYS – March 31 to Oct. 20

Price Per Person:

Twin $1270   Single $1536   Triple $1200
Twin with roll-away

Monument Valley flight . . . add $110

See "Tour Prices Include," page 122. Lake Powell flight, boat, and Glen Canyon Raft Trip all included. **20 Meals Included.**

Air Fare to Phoenix and from Las Vegas is additional

Contact your booking agent for special low fares which are usually available.

Stay at the best available hotels

Night 1	**Red Lion La Posada Resort** Scottsdale, AZ
Night 2*	**Kachina Lodge** Grand Canyon, AZ
Night 3,4	**Wahweap Lodge** Page, AZ
Night 5	**Four Seasons Motor Inn** Kanab, UT
Night 6	**Zion Lodge** Zion National Park, UT
Night 7	**Las Vegas Hilton** Las Vegas, NV

* Tours of Oct. 29, 30 will stay at Maswik Lodge.

Note: The canyon areas of the Southwest are relatively remote. Hotels and services, although chosen from the best available, may not compare with facilities found in more populated areas..

APOLLO ACCESS TD*28025
WORLDSPAN ACCESS .... G/PTS/TTX/CY

■ REVIEW—NORTH AMERICA: WESTERN UNITED STATES

1. Where are the Black Hills and why are they important?

2. Describe the importance of tourism in Colorado.

3. Identify three major regions of Texas and the major cities of each.

4. Which western states have a relatively large Hispanic population? A relatively large Indian (Native American) population?

5. What physical and human factors influenced the development of Salt Lake City?

6. Name the main cities of Washington and Oregon. Where are they located and why there?

7. Name the two main cities of Nevada. Where are they located and why there?

8. Name California's two great metropolitan areas. How do they differ in climate and character?

9. Where is Mount McKinley? Why is it important?

10. Identify the main ethnic groups in the population of Hawaii.

11. Name the major ski areas in the western United States. Where are they located? Where are the major beach resorts in the western United States located? Where are the major golf resorts of the western United States located? Describe four areas of scenic beauty in the western United States.

Canada

- —— International boundary
- ⊛ National capital
- ·—·— Railroad
- —— Road
- ·—·— Province boundary
- ✛ International airport

0 ⊢⊢⊢⊢⊢⊢⊢⊣ 500 Kilometers
0 ⊢⊢⊢⊢⊢⊢⊢⊣ 500 Miles

6

North America: Canada

Canada, the northern neighbor of the United States, is the second largest nation in area in the world, surpassed only by Russia. Canada and the United States have a friendly border that allows easy movement of people and goods and tightly intertwined economies, in keeping with the North American Free Trade Agreement (NAFTA). Yet, Canada is proud of its distinctive heritage and works to maintain a strong, independent identity while sharing a common lifestyle with its more populous and economically stronger North American neighbor.

■ THE LAND

Canada extends far to the north where long, cold winters and snow cover limit habitability over vast areas. From the northern coast, Hudson Bay protrudes deeply from the north into northeastern Canada. The far northern territories, lying north of the Arctic Circle, are broken into numerous islands. At the southern extreme, Canada borders the Great Lakes and contains most of the St. Lawrence River and its lowlands.

CANADA

Language: English, French
Area: 3,849,000 square miles
Time Zone: GMT −4 through −7
National Airline: Air Canada, Canadian Airlines Int'l

Capital: Ottawa
Currency: Canadian dollar (CAD)
Population: 26,835,500
Documentation: U.S. citizenship proof

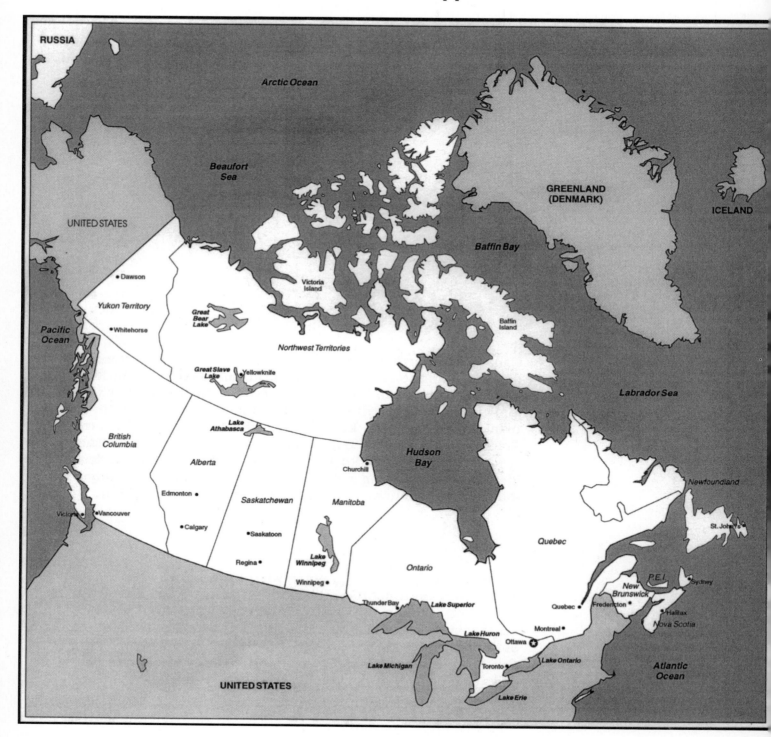

Canada juts eastward into the Atlantic Ocean, with large peninsulas north and south of the St. Lawrence River mouth and offshore islands, of which Newfoundland is the largest. In the west, the Pacific coast features more moderate winter weather, fjords, and offshore islands. Large Vancouver Island lies near the Canadian-American border. As in the United States, the topography is laid out on a grand scale with many common features. The east and southeast have rugged, glaciated topography, dense forests, and swift rivers.

Lowlands surround Hudson Bay and on their inner fringe is a grand arc of lakes, the legacy of retreating continental glaciers, that extends from the northeast and south across central Canada to the far north-northwest. The Great Plains of the United States continue into Canada, and northern portions of the Rocky Mountains and Coast Ranges dominate western Canada. The large Mackenzie River drains the northwest, and the Fraser River, the southwest.

■ THE PEOPLE

Politically, Canada is a federation of ten provinces and two territories. The four Maritime Provinces—Newfoundland, Nova Scotia, Prince Edward Island, and New Brunswick—are on the east coast. Between the Great Lakes and Hudson Bay are the two key provinces of Quebec and Ontario, where most of the population, manufacturing centers, and main cities are found. The three Prairie Provinces are Manitoba, Saskatchewan, and Alberta. British Columbia faces on the Pacific Ocean in the southwest. The Yukon Territory and Northwest Territories include a large Arctic fringe area in the northwest. In 1992, the Canadian government agreed to give political control of the eastern Northwest Territories, named Nunavut, to the local native (Inuit) people.

Most of Canada's relatively small population is concentrated in the south near the Canadian-American border in four distinct clusters. By far the largest, involving two-thirds of the total population, is in southern Ontario and Quebec near the Great Lakes and the St. Lawrence River. In Ontario are Toronto, the largest metropolitan area with 3 million persons and the nation's economic leader, and the federal capital, Ottawa. Quebec Province has Montreal, the second largest metropolitan area, and historic Quebec.

The second largest cluster is in the agricultural Prairie Provinces, where Winnipeg (Manitoba), Regina (Saskatchewan), and Edmonton (Alberta) are the main cities. A third, smaller cluster centers on Vancouver in British Columbia. The fourth is in the Maritime Provinces, where Halifax (Nova

Scotia), Canada's largest ice-free deep-water Atlantic port, and St. John's (Newfoundland), Canada's easternmost city, are located.

The population is 45 percent British and 29 percent French in extraction, with many ethnic minorities comprising the balance. Scattered Indian and Eskimo groups live in the north. As in the United States, Canada has opened its doors to large numbers of immigrants from Europe and Asia and is an increasingly complex pluralistic society. English and French are the two official languages. In Quebec Province, where a strong French-speaking nationalism exists, French has been declared the exclusive language.

■ THE ECONOMY

Canada has an advanced industrial economy based upon superb domestic natural resources, energy supplies, and surplus foodstuffs. Quebec is rich in minerals, forests, and hydroelectric power. Alberta has valuable oil and natural gas deposits. British Columbia has rich forest stands and a productive Pacific fishery. Canada is one of the world's leading wheat exporters. Four-fifths of the farmland and most of the grain production is in the Prairie Provinces.

■ THE EASTERN PROVINCES

NEWFOUNDLAND

Area: 143,510 square miles
Capital: St. John's
Population: 573,000

Newfoundland includes the easternmost point in North America. The province consists of the island of Newfoundland and Labrador on the mainland. Newfoundland has many minerals, a pulp and paper industry, and an excellent fishing industry.

Areas of Touristic Importance. Excellent fishing is available in the many lakes within the province and excellent hunting can be found in the mountains. The rugged coast is quite scenic. Signal Hill, the site of the first transatlantic radio transmission, offers a beautiful overview of the fishing town of St. John's. L'Anse aux Meadows, on the northern tip of Newfoundland Island, has the remains of the earliest European settlement in North America—a group of sod homes built around 1000 AD by Norsemen.

Labrador, because of its cold climate, is basically undeveloped.

NOVA SCOTIA

Area: 20,402 square miles
Capital: Halifax
Population: 892,000

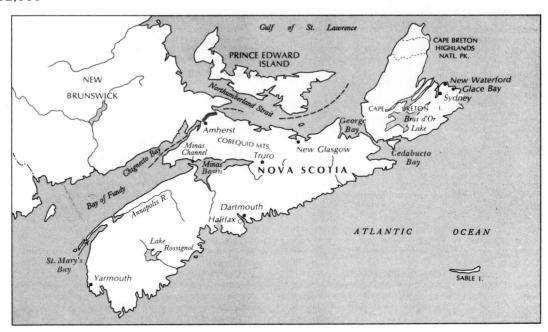

Nova Scotia is a leader in the Canadian fishing industry, and is rich in minerals. Its beaches and coastal resorts are excellent for summer vacations. Its mountainous coastline contrasts with the farming landscapes of the Annapolis Valley. It was from Nova Scotia that the early Acadian (Cajun) people were expelled. They traveled south and settled in the New Orleans area.

Areas of Touristic Importance. Lunenburg is the site of one of the world's most modern fish processing plants. The coast is dotted with charming fishing villages such as Peggy's Cove, Prospect, and Terence Cove. The fortress of Louisbourg was a French outpost. For scenic beauty, the Cabot Trail, which skirts Cape Breton Highlands National Park is hard to beat. Halifax, the capital, is the center of cultural and economic activities. Its best-known landmark is the Citadel, a star-shaped fortress which is now a museum. Overnight car ferry service across the Bay of Fundy connects Nova Scotia with Maine during the summer season.

Peggy's Cove, Nova Scotia
Photo: Courtesy Government of Canada, Regional Industry Expansion

PRINCE EDWARD ISLAND

Area: 2,185 square miles
Capital: Charlottetown
Population: 130,400

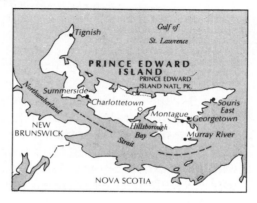

Prince Edward Island, affectionately known as "PEI," is the smallest Canadian province. The inhabitants of Prince County are primarily French-speaking Acadians.

Areas of Touristic Importance. Excellent swimming and sailing is available during the summer. Warm sea (nearly 70° Fahrenheit) meets the sandy beaches along the Gulf of St. Lawrence. PEI is a delightful patchwork of small farming communities, fishing villages, and parks. Prince Edward Island National Park, on the North Shore, has a good golf course along with 20 miles of beaches and dunes. The house made famous in L. M. Montgomery's Anne of Green Gables books is in the park.

NEW BRUNSWICK

Area: 27,834 square miles
Capital: Fredericton
Population: 724,300

New Brunswick is a quiet, peaceful province with more than 90 percent of its land covered by forest. It has an active commercial fishing industry, as well as paper and pulp and mining activities. Potatoes are the most important agricultural crop.

Areas of Touristic Importance. New Brunswick is one of the best sport fishing areas in North America, with a plentiful supply both in interior streams and along the Atlantic coast. The province boasts of two coastlines, one on the Gulf of St. Lawrence and the other on the Bay of Fundy. The dramatic tides at the Bay of Fundy are an impressive spectacle. The capital, Fredericton, houses the Beaverbrook Art Gallery, one of the best in Canada. Its collection includes a 10-foot-high painting by Salvador Dali. The Reversing Falls Rapids is an unusual sight. This province was once the capital of French Acadia and still has many French-speaking communities.

■ THE MAJOR PROVINCES

QUEBEC

Area: 523,859 square miles
Capital: Quebec City
Population: 6,770,800

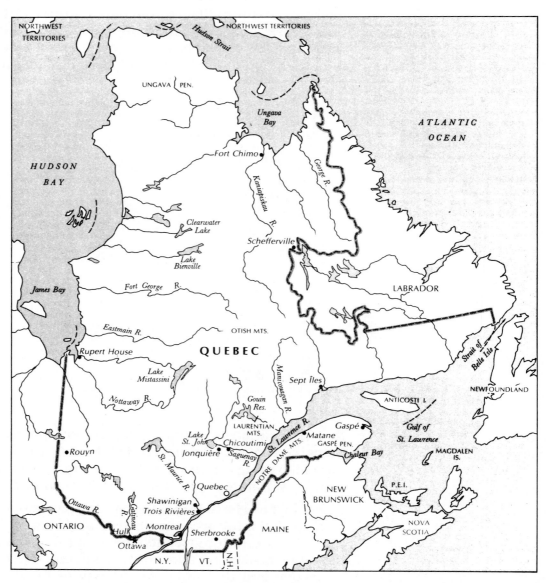

Quebec is the largest of Canada's ten provinces. Its area ranges from the icy waters of Hudson Bay to the New England border. The far north is treeless tundra. Toward the south, Quebec has forests and streams that offer excellent hunting, fishing and winter sports. Eighty percent of its population is French-speaking. Quebec contains most of Canada's French population as well as historic French colonial sites along the St. Lawrence River.

Areas of Touristic Importance. Montreal is Canada's second largest city. It is also the second-largest French-speaking city in the world. The city is located on an island in the St. Lawrence River about half-way between Lake Ontario and the Atlantic Ocean. Montreal is a bustling, cosmopolitan city and a major seaport, even though it is more than 1,000 miles from the Atlantic. Mount Royal is an almost rural oasis in the middle of the city. An excellent view of the city can be seen from its peak.

Montreal's architecture is a combination of old French and modern Canadian. The Chateau de Ramezay, a French mansion, was headquarters for the invading American army in 1775. Notre Dame de Montreal is the second-largest church in North America. Montreal has many interesting museums and parks. The city also has more than 4,000 restaurants and excellent shopping facilities. It is the center of culture and entertainment as well, offering many theater, music, and dance events.

Quebec City retains the old world charm and style created by its original French settlers. Narrow streets from the Lower Town twist and turn their way from the St. Lawrence River upwards through the walls of the Upper Town. A funicular rail-

Quebec City, Quebec
Photo: Courtesy Government of Canada, Regional Industrial Expansion

car makes the trip easier. A prominent sight in the Lower Town is the church of Notre Dame des Victoires built in 1688. The wall between Upper and Lower Towns is now a wide promenade overlooking the St. Lawrence. The city's atmosphere sometimes seems to be more French than France. Quebec's Winter Carnival fills the city with visitors.

Just north of Quebec city is the shrine of Ste Anne de Beaupre, which attracts more than a million pilgrims each year. Also in this region is the beautiful Montmorency Falls, higher than Niagara Falls.

The Laurentian Mountains north of Montreal offer abundant outdoor recreation. Fishing, camping, and hiking are popular in the summer while skiing attracts many in winter.

The Gaspé Peninsula in eastern Quebec features rugged hills, picturesque fishing villages, and rocky cliffs. The peninsula ends at Perce Rock, which juts nearly 300 feet out of the water. In summer, cruise ships from the northeastern United States sail through the St. Lawrence to see Gaspé and visit Quebec and Montreal.

ONTARIO

Area: 344,090 square miles
Capital: Toronto
Population: 9,747,600

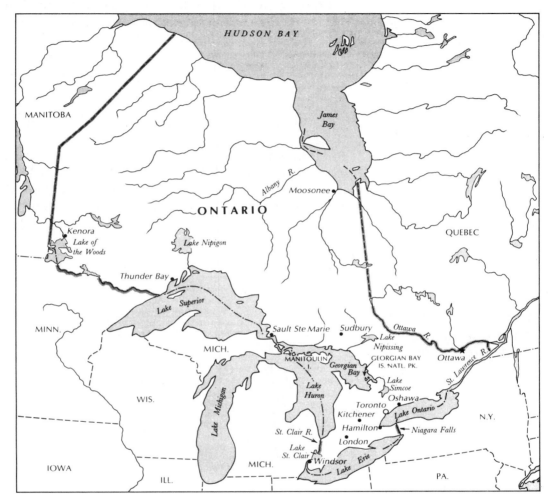

Canada's second largest province is also its most populous. Toronto, the provincial capital, is the largest city in the nation. Southern Ontario borders four of the Great Lakes and has strong international ties with Michigan and New York.

Areas of Touristic Importance. Toronto is in the heart of an urban area that spreads to Lake Ontario, Hamilton, and the national capital, Ottawa. Toronto is a dynamic city with excellent parks, museums, and theaters. The CN Tower, standing 1,815 feet high, is one of the world's tallest structures. St. Lawrence Hall and Mackenzie House are part of Toronto's heritage. The Casa Loma, a "castle" built in 1911, contrasts with the modern city. Canada's Wonderland is a 325-acre, family amusement park with its own artificial mountain.

Ottawa, Canada's capital, is a city of majestic beauty. The splendor of the Parliament buildings standing high on a hill is unique in North America. The guard is changed each morning during the summer months with pomp and ceremony. Museums and art galleries mingle with fine restaurants and shops. The Peace Tower features a 53-bell carillon.

Thunder Bay, at the western end of the St. Lawrence Seaway, is a well-known ski resort with one of the world's largest ski jumps.

Other areas of interest in Ontario include Stratford and Niagara Falls. Stratford, 95 miles west of Toronto, houses a Shakespeare Festival from June through October. The best views of Niagara Falls are from the Canadian side, about one hour from Toronto. In 1790, Niagara-on-the-Lake was the capital of Upper Canada (Ontario). The Thousand Islands area in the St. Lawrence River is a vacationland shared with neighboring New York in the United States.

MANITOBA

Area: 211,723 square miles
Capital: Winnipeg
Population: 1,090,700

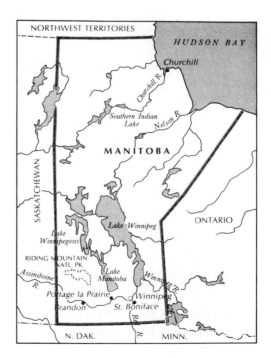

Like the heartland of the United States, Manitoba is a great fertile plain noted for production of wheat and other grains. In fact, like its United States counterpart, Manitoba is Canada's breadbasket. Manitoba also supports substantial manufacturing activities. It stretches between the American border and Hudson Bay.

Areas of Touristic Importance. Manitoba is dotted with thousands of lakes, the largest of which is Lake Winnipeg. Excellent fishing and other outdoor recreational activities are abundant. In addition to farmland, Manitoba has thousands of acres of forests and parks.

Winnipeg, midway between the Atlantic and Pacific coasts, is an important commercial center that houses more than half of the population of the province. The Royal Winnipeg Ballet and the Manitoba Theater exemplify the city's commitment to the arts. The Grain Exchange provides a view of its main industry. Indian Handicrafts of Manitoba shows the wares of Manitoba's original natives.

SASKATCHEWAN

Area: 220,348 square miles
Capital: Regina
Population: 1,000,300

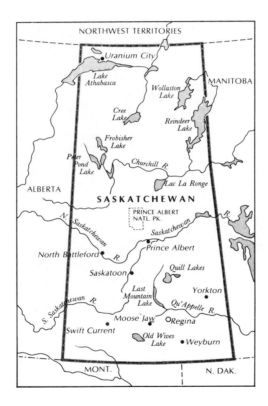

The southern half of this province is a continuation of the Canadian breadbasket. Wheat, truck farms, and cattle ranches are abundant. In contrast, the northern half is rugged lake country covered by tall evergreen trees growing from the granite of the Canadian Shield. Oil and mining also contribute to the Saskatchewan economy.

Areas of Touristic Importance. Regina, the capital, is a major commercial center. Often called "Home of the Mounties," Regina was the headquarters of the forerunners to the famous Royal Canadian Mounted Police.

Saskatoon is home to several interesting museums. The Western Development Museum shows life in the area nearly one hundred years ago. The Memorial Art Gallery displays the works of Canadian artists. The Mendel Gallery features Eskimo works. Saskatoon also houses the Ukrainian Museum of Canada.

Prince Albert is the main gateway to the northern wilderness with its hundreds of lakes. This region is popular for hunting, fishing and camping.

Prince Albert National Park, Saskatchewan
Photo: Courtesy Canadian Government Travel Bureau

ALBERTA

Area: 248,800 square miles
Capital: Edmonton
Population: 2,472,500

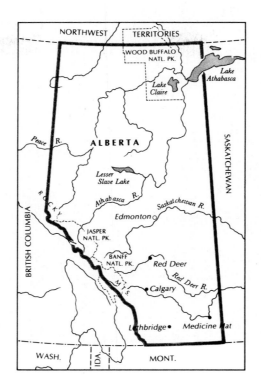

Alberta is the center of the Canadian Rockies. The province combines a growing agricultural and mining economy with the splendor of the mountains.

Areas of Touristic Importance. Edmonton's population exceeds 650,000. Edmonton is the home of the world's largest enclosed shopping mall, a complex more than a mile long with stores, offices, and recreational activities, including a miniature golf course, ice rink and swimming pool. Edmonton is also known for Fantasyland, the largest indoor amusement park and for Canada's largest planetarium.

Calgary, one of Canada's fastest growing cities, is the site of the world's most famous rodeo, the Calgary Stampede, a 10-day event each summer. Calgary's Glenhbow Museum is noted for historical and North American Indian displays. The city is also known for its Dinosaur Park and Zoo.

Banff, Jasper, and Waterton National Parks attract large numbers of visitors with their majestic beauty, excellent accommodations, and superb fishing, hiking, skiing, and other outdoor recreational activities. Lake Louise and Moraine Lake are not far from Banff and offer both scenic beauty and outdoor activities. The Columbia Icefields are a vivid reminder of earlier glacial periods.

Calgary Stampede, Alberta
Photo: Courtesy Government of Canada, Regional Industrial Expansion

BRITISH COLUMBIA

Area: 358,971 square miles
Capital: Victoria
Population: 3,138,900

British Columbia, or "BC" as it is fondly called, is the westernmost of Canada's ten provinces. Timber, mining, manufacturing, and tourism contribute most to BC's economy. Mountains and dense forests cover much of the area. The Fraser River is the largest salmon breeding ground in the world. The coastal areas are known for a wide variety of Indian totem art. Most of the population is in the southwest in and around Vancouver.

Areas of Touristic Importance. Vancouver, BC's largest city and Canada's third largest, is built on the shores of Burrard Inlet, an excellent natural harbor. It is a major cruise port, primarily for ships sailing the Inland Passageway to Alaska. Excellent recreation facilities are nearby. Vancouver hosted the 1986 World's Fair, which provided the city with excellent permanent facilities including a theater/concert hall, stadium, and Canada Place, its modern cruise ship pier. Vancouver's Chinatown is the second largest on the continent.

Victoria, the provincial capital, is located on Vancouver Island. It is most widely known for its British atmosphere and architecture and its beautiful parks and gardens. Butchart Gardens is both beautiful and exotic. The stately Parliament Buildings and the Empress Hotel, on the harbor, are classically British. Frequent ferry service connects Victoria to Port Angeles, Washington. Daily service is also available between Victoria and Seattle, Washington. BC Ferries also provides service between Vancouver Island and the Canadian mainland about 30 miles from Vancouver.

Prince Rupert, on the west coast, and Dawson Creek, on the Alaska Highway near the BC-Alberta border, are popular for hunting and fishing.

■ THE CANADIAN TERRITORIES

NORTHWEST TERRITORIES

Area: 1,271,442 square miles
Capital: Yellowknife
Population: 54,000

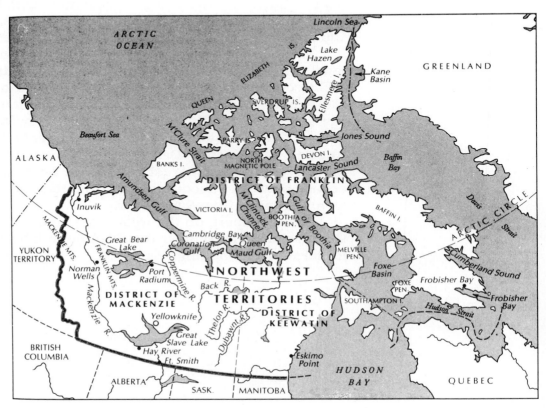

This vast land covers almost one third of Canada, yet supports a population of only slightly more than 50,000 people, two thirds of them native Indian or Eskimos (Inuit). Half of its area is north of the Arctic Circle. The territories have been the scene of attempts to find the Northwest Passage to the Orient. The area is basically undeveloped. The territories are administered by a government appointed commission, although the eastern part is scheduled for direct Inuit control in recognition of their precolonial land rights. There is some production of oil and minerals, but virtually no tourism. Eskimo craftsmen produce stone and ivory carving of high quality. Visitors to this area seek a wilderness atmosphere for hunting and fishing.

YUKON TERRITORY

Area: 184,931 square miles
Capital: Whitehorse
Population: 26,000

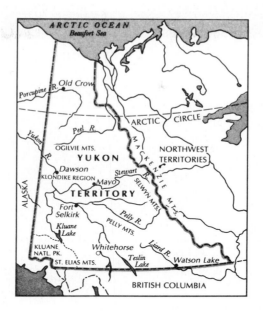

The Yukon is a land of rugged mountains and isolated lakes. It was made famous by tales of the Gold Rush of the 1890s. Mount Logan, Canada's highest peak at an altitude of 19,850 feet, is located in Kluane National Park. Dawson and Whitehorse both attract a substantial number of tourists in the summer season and are frequently part of an Alaskan tour. Mining still takes place in the territory.

■ TYPES OF TOURISM

Because of its long border with the United States, Canada attracts more visitors from the United States than any other nation in the world. The vast majority are independent travelers using personal automobiles. Package tours, including hotel accommodations and sightseeing in individual cities, are readily available. Escorted tours to different regions of the nation are also popular. Some are combined with visits to neighboring parts of the United States. The following are examples of the types of tour itineraries which are popular for United States visitors to Canada:

■ Heart of the Canadian Rockies
■ French Canada and Niagara Falls
■ Atlantic Canada

GLOBUS — *First Class* — ESCORTED

Heart of the Canadian Rockies

Seattle, Kelowna, Banff, Columbia Icefields, Jasper, Kamloops, Vancouver, Victoria

Tour **ACR** – 9 days from Seattle to Seattle

Maximum elevation on tour: 7,500 ft.

ALL THIS IS INCLUDED

- Services of a professional tour director
- First-class or best available hotels listed below or equivalent (see page 9). Twin-bedded rooms with private bath or shower, hotel taxes, service charges and tips for baggage handling
- 8 American breakfasts (B); 7 three-course dinners offering choice of entree (D), with a special Chinese dinner in Vancouver and farewell dinner in Victoria
- Private deluxe air-conditioned motorcoach
- Gondola ride up Banff's Sulphur Mountain; snowmobile ride on the

- Columbia Icefields; ferry crossing to Victoria; cruise through the Gulf Islands
- Visits to Kelowna on Lake Okanagan, Banff National Park, Lake Louise, Jasper National Park, Vancouver, Victoria and its famous Butchart Gardens
- Other scenic highlights: Steven's Pass, Glacier National Park, Rogers Pass, Bow Summit, Peyto Lake, Sunwapta Pass, and the Yellowhead Highway
- Inside visits as shown in UPPER-CASE LETTERS in the tour description, including admission charges where applicable
- Globus travel bag and travel documents

Day 1 SEATTLE-THE CASCADES-KELOWNA. Depart from the Stouffer Madison Hotel, at 8 a.m. Cross Steven's Pass in the towering Cascade Range and on into Canada. Today's extensive drive offers a myriad of exciting and contrasting vistas. Head north through British Columbia to Kelowna, nestled on the eastern shores of Lake Okanagan. Be sure to ask the locals to recount their tales of the Ogopogo, the Okanagan's legendary "loch" monster. (D)

Day 2 KELOWNA-BANFF. Along the shores of the lake, through the fertile valley of the Okanagan with its picturesque orchard lands and vineyards to Canada's Glacier National Park. Then over Rogers Pass, with magnificent vistas of peaks exceeding 10,000 feet, before reaching Kicking Horse Pass. View the Spiral Tunnels and Natural Bridge before crossing over into the province of Alberta to reach the scenic heart of the Canadian Rockies – BANFF NATIONAL PARK. (B,D)

Day 3 BANFF NATIONAL PARK. The morning sightseeing includes the Buffalo Paddocks where wood bison roam freely, a stop at famed Banff Springs Hotel, the Hoodoos – weirdly-shaped pillars along the Bow River, Bow Falls, and lastly, a thrilling ride up to Sulphur Mountain in a gondola lift. For the afternoon, maybe join our optional raft trip down the Bow River; or a 20-minute "flightseeing" by helicopter affords a unique perspective of the Rockies. The balance of the day is free to appreciate the tranquil setting of this resort renowned for its surrounding majestic mountains. Elk, deer, moose and coyote can frequently be seen and, with a little luck, a glimpse of a black bear. (B,D)

Day 4 BANFF-COLUMBIA ICEFIELDS-JASPER. Follow the Icefield Parkway today and head for JASPER NATIONAL PARK. First stop is Lake Louise, with its cold green-blue waters forming a perfect mirror reflection of 11,365-foot Mount Victoria and its glacier. Scale Bow Pass with splendid views from the summit of turquoise-blue Peyto Lake and then over Sunwapta Pass with vistas of alpine meadows,

▼ *BUTCHART GARDENS*

Reprinted courtesy of Globus and Cosmos.

waterfalls and glacier masses. Next is the highlight of the day: a stop at the 1000-foot thick Columbia Icefield for a thrilling ride aboard the snowmobile tour vehicles. Reach the resort village of Jasper by late afternoon. (B,D)

Day 5 JASPER-MT. ROBSON-KAMLOOPS. Plenty of free time this morning before leaving Jasper. Why not join our optional drive to Lake Maligne with a fully-narrated cruise of the glacial lake. Back into British Columbia via the base of 12,972-foot Mt. Robson, the highest point in the Rockies. Then descend the Yellowhead Highway hugging the North Thompson River – a route pioneered by fur trappers a century ago. Overnight in lakeside Kamloops renowned for cattle raising and excellent trout fishing. (B,D)

Day 6 KAMLOOPS-VANCOUVER. A short scenic drive back to the Pacific Coast. Upon arrival in Vancouver, enjoy an orientation drive of Canada's "Gem of the Pacific", with still plenty of time in the day for independent sightseeing. The program on this evening's optional outing includes a fascinating film at the IMAX Theatre, a sumptuous dinner at a top restaurant at Canada Place Pier, ending with a drive up to the Harbor Centre Lookout. (B)

Day 7 VANCOUVER. A full day at leisure to explore cosmopolitan Vancouver. Our suggestion for today is an optional excursion aboard the MV Brittania cruising through English Bay and up breathtaking Howe Sound. The return journey is by the last operational "Royal" Hudson train in a cliff-hugging tour to North Vancouver. Tonight, a chance to savor a local specialty – a Chinese dinner in Vancouver, home to the second largest Chinatown in North America after San Francisco. (B,D)

Day 8 VANCOUVER-VICTORIA. A morning transfer to the ferry terminal for the scenic crossing to Swartz Bay on Vancouver Island. This afternoon's tour of Victoria – the provincial capital of British Columbia – includes Beacon Hill Park, the largest of the city's gardens; the Empress Hotel; Bastion Square; and Thunderbird Park, with its unusual collection of totem poles. The balance of the afternoon is free for independent sightseeing and shopping. See Government Street with its many elegant shops carrying English tweeds and fine China; or browse through Market Square with its vast collection of specialty stores in beautifully-restored buildings. This evening your tour director hosts a farewell dinner, a festive finale to a great touring adventure in the Canadian Rockies. (B,D)

Day 9 VICTORIA-GULF ISLANDS-SEATTLE. Before leaving Victoria, a visit to the world-famous BUTCHART GARDENS covering over 35 acres in an abandoned limestone quarry and divided into the English Gardens, Rose Garden, Japanese Garden, formal Italian Garden and the Sunken Garden. At Swartz Bay, board the ferry and cruise through the narrow waterways of the picturesque Gulf Islands and then by coach along the coastal highway through Washington State. The tour ends this afternoon at the Stouffer Madison Hotel in downtown Seattle. Transfer to Seattle-Tacoma International Airport is available for tour members who have connecting flights. (B)

(Please do not schedule return flights earlier than 7 p.m.)

➤ *This tour combines neatly with many of our other tours of The West. You pay less for your second tour: see page 3.*

▲ *BANFF NATIONAL PARK*

Tour ACR: DATES & PRICES

Tour Code	Start Seattle		End Seattle		9 days US$	Tour Code	Start Seattle		End Seattle		9 days US$
ACR0430	Sat	30-Apr	Sun	08-May	1078	ACR0802	Tue	02-Aug	Wed	10-Aug	1118
ACR0507	Sat	07-May	Sun	15-May	1088	ACR0803	Wed	03-Aug	Thu	11-Aug	1118
ACR0514	Sat	14-May	Sun	22-May	1088	ACR0804	Thu	04-Aug	Fri	12-Aug	1118
ACR0515	Sun	15-May	Mon	23-May	1088	ACR0805	Fri	05-Aug	Sat	13-Aug	1118
ACR0519	Thu	19-May	Fri	27-May	1098	ACR0806	Sat	06-Aug	Sun	14-Aug	1118
ACR0520	Fri	20-May	Sat	28-May	1098	ACR0807	Sun	07-Aug	Mon	15-Aug	1118
ACR0521	Sat	21-May	Sun	29-May	1098	ACR0809	Tue	09-Aug	Wed	17-Aug	1118
ACR0522	Sun	22-May	Mon	30-May	1098	ACR0810	Wed	10-Aug	Thu	18-Aug	1118
ACR0526	Thu	26-May	Fri	03-Jun	1118	ACR0811	Thu	11-Aug	Fri	19-Aug	1118
ACR0527	Fri	27-May	Sat	04-Jun	1118	ACR0812	Fri	12-Aug	Sat	20-Aug	1118
ACR0528	Sat	28-May	Sun	05-Jun	1118	ACR0813	Sat	13-Aug	Sun	21-Aug	1118
ACR0529	Sun	29-May	Mon	06-Jun	1118	ACR0814	Sun	14-Aug	Mon	22-Aug	1118
ACR0531	Tue	31-May	Wed	08-Jun	1118	ACR0816	Tue	16-Aug	Wed	24-Aug	1118
ACR0602	Thu	02-Jun	Fri	10-Jun	1118	ACR0817	Wed	17-Aug	Thu	25-Aug	1118
ACR0603	Fri	03-Jun	Sat	11-Jun	1118	ACR0818	Thu	18-Aug	Fri	26-Aug	1118
ACR0604	Sat	04-Jun	Sun	12-Jun	1118	ACR0819	Fri	19-Aug	Sat	27-Aug	1118
ACR0605	Sun	05-Jun	Mon	13-Jun	1118	ACR0820	Sat	20-Aug	Sun	28-Aug	1118
ACR0607	Tue	07-Jun	Wed	15-Jun	1118	ACR0821	Sun	21-Aug	Mon	29-Aug	1118
ACR0609	Thu	09-Jun	Fri	17-Jun	1118	ACR0823	Tue	23-Aug	Wed	31-Aug	1118
ACR0610	Fri	10-Jun	Sat	18-Jun	1118	ACR0824	Wed	24-Aug	Thu	01-Sep	1118
ACR0611	Sat	11-Jun	Sun	19-Jun	1118	ACR0825	Thu	25-Aug	Fri	02-Sep	1118
ACR0612	Sun	12-Jun	Mon	20-Jun	1118	ACR0826	Fri	26-Aug	Sat	03-Sep	1118
ACR0614	Tue	14-Jun	Wed	22-Jun	1118	ACR0827	Sat	27-Aug	Sun	04-Sep	1118
ACR0616	Thu	16-Jun	Fri	24-Jun	1118	ACR0828	Sun	28-Aug	Mon	05-Sep	1118
ACR0617	Fri	17-Jun	Sat	25-Jun	1118	ACR0830	Tue	30-Aug	Wed	07-Sep	1118
ACR0618	Sat	18-Jun	Sun	26-Jun	1118	ACR0831	Wed	31-Aug	Thu	08-Sep	1118
ACR0619	Sun	19-Jun	Mon	27-Jun	1118	ACR0901	Thu	01-Sep	Fri	09-Sep	1118
ACR0621	Tue	21-Jun	Wed	29-Jun	1118	ACR0902	Fri	02-Sep	Sat	10-Sep	1118
ACR0622	Wed	22-Jun	Thu	30-Jun	1118	ACR0903	Sat	03-Sep	Sun	11-Sep	1118
ACR0623	Thu	23-Jun	Fri	01-Jul	1118	ACR0904	Sun	04-Sep	Mon	12-Sep	1118
ACR0624	Fri	24-Jun	Sat	02-Jul	1118	ACR0906	Tue	06-Sep	Wed	14-Sep	1118
ACR0625	Sat	25-Jun	Sun	03-Jul	1118	ACR0907	Wed	07-Sep	Thu	15-Sep	1118
ACR0626	Sun	26-Jun	Mon	04-Jul	1118	ACR0908	Thu	08-Sep	Fri	16-Sep	1118
ACR0628	Tue	28-Jun	Wed	06-Jul	1118	ACR0909	Fri	09-Sep	Sat	17-Sep	1118
ACR0629	Wed	29-Jun	Thu	07-Jul	1118	ACR0910	Sat	10-Sep	Sun	18-Sep	1118
ACR0630	Thu	30-Jun	Fri	08-Jul	1118	ACR0911	Sun	11-Sep	Mon	19-Sep	1118
ACR0701	Fri	01-Jul	Sat	09-Jul	1118	ACR0913	Tue	13-Sep	Wed	21-Sep	1118
ACR0702	Sat	02-Jul	Sun	10-Jul	1118	ACR0914	Wed	14-Sep	Thu	22-Sep	1118
ACR0703	Sun	03-Jul	Mon	11-Jul	1118	ACR0915	Thu	15-Sep	Fri	23-Sep	1118
ACR0705	Tue	05-Jul	Wed	13-Jul	1118	ACR0916	Fri	16-Sep	Sat	24-Sep	1118
ACR0706	Wed	06-Jul	Thu	14-Jul	1118	ACR0917	Sat	17-Sep	Sun	25-Sep	1118
ACR0707	Thu	07-Jul	Fri	15-Jul	1118	ACR0918	Sun	18-Sep	Mon	26-Sep	1118
ACR0708	Fri	08-Jul	Sat	16-Jul	1118	ACR0920	Tue	20-Sep	Wed	28-Sep	1098
ACR0709	Sat	09-Jul	Sun	17-Jul	1118	ACR0921	Wed	21-Sep	Thu	29-Sep	1098
ACR0710	Sun	10-Jul	Mon	18-Jul	1118	ACR0922	Thu	22-Sep	Fri	30-Sep	1098
ACR0712	Tue	12-Jul	Wed	20-Jul	1118	ACR0923	Fri	23-Sep	Sat	01-Oct	1088
ACR0713	Wed	13-Jul	Thu	21-Jul	1118	ACR0924	Sat	24-Sep	Sun	02-Oct	1088
ACR0714	Thu	14-Jul	Fri	22-Jul	1118	ACR0925	Sun	25-Sep	Mon	03-Oct	1088
ACR0715	Fri	15-Jul	Sat	23-Jul	1118	ACR1001	Sat	01-Oct	Sun	09-Oct	1078
ACR0716	Sat	16-Jul	Sun	24-Jul	1118						
ACR0717	Sun	17-Jul	Mon	25-Jul	1118						
ACR0719	Tue	19-Jul	Wed	27-Jul	1118						
ACR0720	Wed	20-Jul	Thu	28-Jul	1118						
ACR0721	Thu	21-Jul	Fri	29-Jul	1118						
ACR0722	Fri	22-Jul	Sat	30-Jul	1118						
ACR0723	Sat	23-Jul	Sun	31-Jul	1118						
ACR0724	Sun	24-Jul	Mon	01-Aug	1118						
ACR0726	Tue	26-Jul	Wed	03-Aug	1118						
ACR0727	Wed	27-Jul	Thu	04-Aug	1118						
ACR0728	Thu	28-Jul	Fri	05-Aug	1118						
ACR0729	Fri	29-Jul	Sat	06-Aug	1118						
ACR0730	Sat	30-Jul	Sun	07-Aug	1118						
ACR0731	Sun	31-Jul	Mon	08-Aug	1118						

Prices are for all land arrangements. Air fare to and from Seattle is additional. Your travel agent can help you find the best available air fare.

Single room supplement: $430

Triple room reduction per person: $80

For additional accommodations in Seattle before and after the tour, see our special rates on page 11.

APOLLO: TD*GG, **PARS:** G/PTS/GGX, **SABRE:** Y/TUR/QGG

GLOBUS HOTELS

KELOWNA Capri Hotel, **BANFF** Inns of Banff Park, Banff Park Lodge or Buffalo Mountain Lodge, **JASPER** Jasper Inn, **KAMLOOPS** Dome Motor Inn, **VANCOUVER** Georgian Court, **VICTORIA** Harbor Towers

French Canada & Niagara Falls

8 DAYS

Beautiful countryside, history and tradition are waiting to be explored in CANADA, America's "Neighbor to the North."

DEPARTURES

July: 9, 23
August: 6, 20
September: 10, 17, 24
*October: 1

*Autumn Foliage Departure

LODGING

TORONTO, ON
Royal York Hotel

OTTAWA, ON
Lord Elgin Hotel

QUEBEC CITY, PQ
Lowes Le Concorde

MONTREAL, PQ
Queen Elizabeth Hotel

NIAGARA FALLS, ON
Sheraton Fallsview

HIGHLIGHTS

◆ Airport transfers to and from hotels

◆ 7 nights hotel accommodations

◆ 7 meals - 5 dinners and 2 lunches, including dinners at CN Tower and Le Festin du Gouverneur

◆ Ottawa touring including the Parliament Buildings

◆ Quebec sightseeing - Montmorency Falls, Ste. Anne de Beaupre and the old "Walled City"

◆ Montreal's Mt. Royal Park, Notre Dame Basilica, Old Quarter, Place d'Armes, St. Joseph's Oratory and Olympic Park

◆ Niagara Falls with IMAX theatre and Maid of the Mist boat ride

◆ Toronto sightseeing

◆ CN Tower tour

◆ $40 in future travel credits

PER PERSON RATES

$1179 two to a room
$1549 one to a room
$1165 three to a room

AIR FARE – Add cost of air fare from your city to Toronto and return.

EXTRA NIGHTS – Rooms for the night before and after the tour are available at the Royal York Hotel in downtown Toronto. Cost for a single or double room is U.S. $119, tax included.

ITINERARY

SATURDAY ◆ Home/Toronto
Bonjour! Visit the old new world next door - CANADA. We start in TORONTO, ONTARIO with a get-acquainted dinner this evening after meeting in the hotel lobby at 6 pm. While dining, gaze on a panoramic view of the city and beyond while atop the CN Tower, the world's tallest freestanding structure. (Dinner)

SUNDAY ◆ Toronto/Ottawa
This morning glimpse the world's newest great city with its impressive Parliament Buildings and the futuristic city hall. Take a look at the flower-bedecked streets separating the wonderful variety of ethnic neighborhoods. Enjoy the lovely countryside scenery on our way to the nation's capital of OTTAWA. We check into our lodging in the downtown area before dining at Mother Tucker's Restaurant. (Dinner)

MONDAY ◆ Ottawa/Quebec City
Today, tour Ottawa's Parliament Buildings, which include three huge Gothic stone structures roofed with green copper. We'll tour the House of Commons and other government buildings. Canadian Mounties in their bright red uniforms stand guard at all times. Enjoy lunch before traveling to QUEBEC CITY, in QUEBEC Province, where we spend two nights.

Quaint outdoor cafe in Montreal

Enjoy the European flavor of Quebec

Reprinted courtesy of Mayflower Tours.

Canada's Parliament Building

TUESDAY ◆ Quebec City

There are many sights to see in Quebec City, known as the cradle of French civilization in Canada. We begin with a morning sightseeing tour of the Plains of Abraham Battlefield followed by a tour of Quebec's famous city wall. We see the fortifications, which make it the only walled city in North America. Our sightseeing also includes the historic Place Royale, where the city was born, and its surrounding streets, which represent a great concentration of 17th and 18th century buildings. Later today we are free to wander on our own. Stop to watch street musicians and artists who line the old city walls. This evening we dine at Aux Anciens Canadiens Restaurant. (Dinner)

WEDNESDAY ◆ Quebec City/ Montreal

Travel along the St. Lawrence River to the Basilica of Ste. Anne de Beaupre in the countryside where nearly 2 million people make a pilgrimage each year. Then we make a quick stop at Montmorency Falls, taller than Niagara, before arriving in MONTREAL and our lodging. Tonight we eat at Le Festin du Gouverneur where singing waiters and minstrels serve a 17th century feast which is to be eaten with a single utensil - a small dagger! Wine flows as musicians, jesters and actors add to the revelry of the evening. (Dinner)

THURSDAY ◆ Montreal

We continue our touring of Montreal. The city grew from a settlement which was established in the mid 1600's. Many of the historic buildings now lie within the boundaries of the original settlement. We stop at Mont Royal in the old city, which began as a fur-trading center. Now underground shopping centers line miles of subterranean pedestrian malls. After lunch together, we enjoy a tour of Notre Dame Basilica, Place d'Armes and St. Joseph's Oratory of Mt. Royal. See the site of the 1976 Summer Olympics. (Lunch)

FRIDAY ◆ Montreal/ Niagara Falls

We continue our travels along the St. Lawrence River to NIAGARA FALLS, ONTARIO. After checking into our lodging, we enjoy a farewell dinner in the dining room with a fantastic view of Niagara Falls. Our day is complete as we take an evening stroll to the illuminated falls. (Dinner)

SATURDAY ◆ Niagara Falls/Home

Today we view an IMAX movie of this spectacular area. See the churning Niagara Falls up close as we ride the exciting Maid of the Mist boat into the base of the falls. We don raincoats and hats to protect us from the water's spray! Traveling back to Toronto, we are transferred to Pearson International Airport for flights departing after 3 pm, or to our prearranged hotel.

Spectacular Niagara Falls

29

8 Days (7 Nights) $1530

Extra Highlights: Halifax Harbor Tour ☐ Round trip flight Halifax ☐ Northumberland Strait ☐ Land of Evangeline ☐ Digby Pines ☐ Fort Anne ☐ Cape Tormentine ☐ Lobster Supper — *7 Breakfasts, 8 Lunches, 6 Dinners*

Atlantic Canada

Prince Edward Island
New Brunswick
Nova Scotia

Includes round-trip air from New York (Newark) to Halifax.

1. FLY TO NOVA SCOTIA
Tour begins: Waldorf-Astoria, 49th Street, New York City, 8:30 A.M. (or join at Continental Air, Newark Airport at 9 A.M. Newark joins must be arranged at time of booking.) Board a comfortable flight with an early luncheon served over the beautiful New England/New Brunswick coastline to Halifax International Airport. (See Canadian Immigration, page 122.) Here, our motorcoach is waiting. You meet your fellow passengers and are soon traveling through the tidelands of the Bay of Fundy where occur the world's greatest rise and fall in tides. Visit Grand Pré Memorial Park, center of the ancient Acadian Village and dedicated to Longfellow's immortal poem, "Evangeline." Travel off the beaten path to Cape Blomidon

Bay of Fundy at low tide

overlooking the famed tidal waters of the Minas Basin before continuing via the Gasporeau Valley to Greenwich, N.S., for overnight. Meals included **LD**

2. DIGBY / ANNAPOLIS ROYAL
This morning you travel through apple orchards and the fertile farmlands of the lush Annapolis Valley to Annapolis Royal. Here you visit the Habitation at Port Royal, the oldest permanent settlement north of the Gulf of Mexico. Then visit

Fort Anne, one time protector of the first capitol of Nova Scotia. Continue to Digby, the scallop capital of the world, and arrive for lunch at the Digby Pines Hotel, overlooking the Annapolis Basin. The afternoon is free for golfing, tennis, swimming, shopping or just plain relaxing in the pleasant surroundings of the hotel. Meals included **BLD**

3. FERRY TO SAINT JOHN
The morning is at leisure to do what you like most. At mid-day, board a steamer ferry to cross the Bay of Fundy to Saint John, New Brunswick's largest city. The Bay of Fundy has the highest range of tides in the world. Sometimes the difference between high and low water is over 40 feet. On arrival in Saint John, enjoy a brief motor tour of this historic Canadian port city before arriving at your hotel. Meals included **BLD**

4. NEW BRUNSWICK
Today is a long but interesting day. Motor through the fertile farmland of the Kennebecasis River valley to Moncton and Shediac. After lunch, continue through quaint French towns along the Northumberland Strait, which separates New Brunswick and Nova Scotia from Prince Edward Island. Arrive in Cape Tormentine to board another ferry to traverse the strait to Borden, P.E.I. These are some of the warmest waters in the North Atlantic, one of the many reasons P.E.I. is one of the favorite

Lovely, unspoiled Prince Edward Island

110

Reprinted courtesy of Tauck Tours.

summer resorts for eastern Canadians. Soon you are in Charlottetown for the next two nights. Meals included **BLD**

5. PRINCE EDWARD ISLAND

A sunny day on Prince Edward Island is like nowhere else on earth. Summer or fall, the sun pours out warmth on this special island, igniting the fiery red soil, nurturing the green pastoral fields and warming over 500 miles of sandy beaches. Prince Edward Island is Canada's smallest province and one of the most beautiful. Situated in the Gulf of St. Lawrence, it is home to the farmer, fisherman, laborer

Anne of Green Gables

and businessman, a pleasing blend of life styles. Relax this morning before leaving for a tour of the Island. You will travel north through beautiful farm lands of rich red soil. After lunch visit the tiny fishing village of North Rustico Harbor. Next, travel along the magnificent beaches of Prince Edward Island National Park and visit Green Gables, the literary home of "Anne of Green Gables." End the day with a traditional maritime lobster dinner. Return to Charlottetown in mid-evening. Meals included **BLD**

Tranquil coves of Nova Scotia

6. HALIFAX, NOVA SCOTIA

Today you return to Nova Scotia via Wood Island where you board a ferry to Pictou, N.S. Continue through Truro to the capital city of Halifax for the next two nights. Enjoy a sightseeing orientation tour of the city to see the Citadel, Public Gardens, Northwest Arm and the bustling harbor. Dinner this evening is not included to allow you a choice of many nearby restaurants. Meals included **BL**

7. PEGGY'S COVE / HARBOR TOUR

This morning's drive is to Peggy's Cove. The quaint little fishing village stands on solid rock and reflects a character unique to North America…it's an artists dream …thousands are attracted here every year. The entire morning will delight all who love the ocean as it affords exquisite panoramas of countless islands and coves. Return to Halifax for a harbour tour in late afternoon. This evening you are invited to join us for a farewell reception and dinner at the hotel. Meals included **BLD**

8. JOURNEY HOME

The morning is at leisure for last-minute sightseeing or shopping. In late morning, depart for Halifax Airport where you enplane for New York/Newark. A light lunch is served aloft before arriving in New York. **Tour ends: Newark Airport, 3:15 P.M. - Waldorf-Astoria at 4:30 P.M.** Meals included **BL**

Departure Dates:

SATURDAYS – June 18 to Oct. 15
(Best Fall Foliage tours Sept. 10 to Oct. 15)

Price Per Person:

Twin $1530   Single $1789   Triple $1460
Twin with roll-away

See "Tour Prices Include," page 122, plus round-trip air to Nova Scotia included.
21 Meals Included.

Air Fare to New York is additional

Contact your booking agent for special low fares which are usually available.

Stay at the best available hotels

Night		Night/Reverse
1	**Old Orchard Inn** Greenwich, N.S.	7
2*	**Digby Pines Hotel** Digby, N.S.	6
3	**Saint John Hilton** Saint John, N.B.	5
4,5	**Prince Edward Hotel** Charlottetown, P.E.I.	3,4
6,7	**Delta Barrington** Halifax, N.S.	1,2

To avoid overcrowding when two tours depart on the same date, one tour, upon arrival at Halifax airport, operates in Reverse direction.

* *Tour of July 9 will stay at the Mountain Gap Inn for which there is a per person allowance of $20 single, $15 twin/triple.*

APOLLO ACCESS TD*28022
WORLDSPAN ACCESS .... G/PTS/TTX/AC

Maximum Elevation: 700 ft.

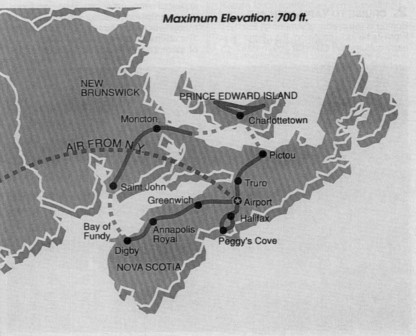

■ REVIEW—NORTH AMERICA: CANADA

1. What cultural features do Canada and the United States share?

2. What physical features are shared by southern Canada and the northern United States?

3. Where is the bulk of Canada's population concentrated? Why there?

4. What are the two official languages of Canada? Where are the minority language speakers most heavily concentrated?

5. Identify the main characteristics of Canada's Maritime Provinces.

6. What are the major ski areas of Canada? Where are they located?

7. Where are the major beach and resort areas of Canada?

8. Describe three areas of scenic beauty in Canada.

7

Mexico, Central America, and South America

The lands south of the United States are all popularly called Latin America. Unfortunately, this name perpetuates a widely held but incorrect stereotype of an overall cultural similarity derived from Iberia (Spain and Portugal). Latin America actually includes many non-Iberian peoples and cultures, and even nations that do share an Iberian heritage have different characteristics. Further differences are created by great regional and national variations in physical environment.

■ SUBDIVISIONS OF LATIN AMERICA

Central America and the Caribbean

Latin America is conventionally subdivided into Middle America, which lies between the United States and South America itself. In turn, Middle America consists of two very different units. One is a mainland portion, usually called Central America, that narrows southward from the United States to a slender land bridge link with South America. Its topography,

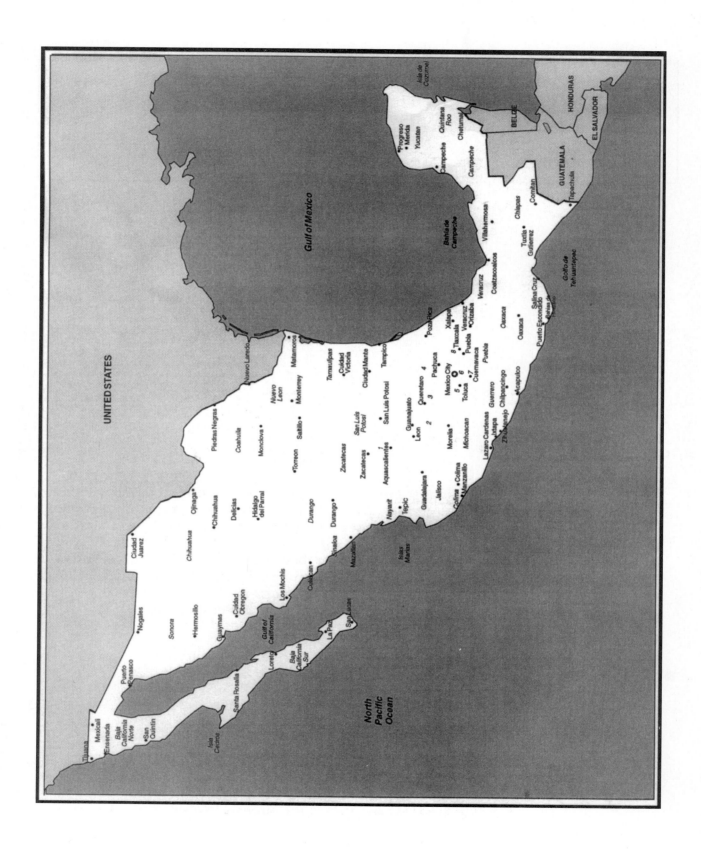

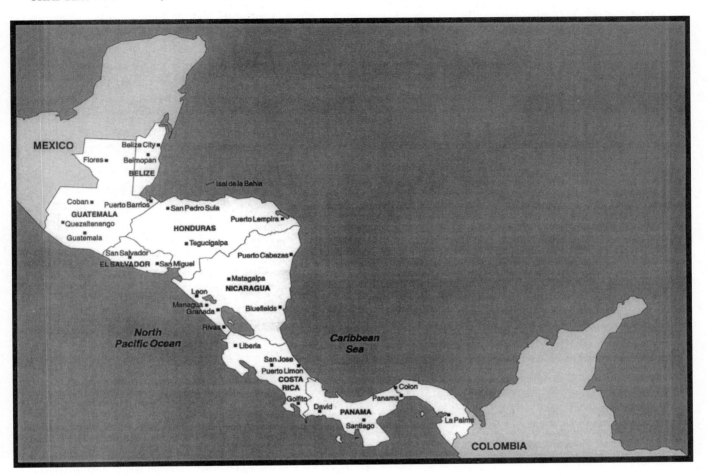

dominated by a mountainous spine with volcanic features, continues the western United States mountains southward into the Andes Mountains of South America. Narrow lowlands lie along the western (Pacific Ocean) and eastern (Caribbean Sea) coasts. Mexico borders on the United States; southward from Mexico are Guatemala, Belize, Honduras, El Salvador, Nicaragua, Costa Rica, and Panama. Although Mexico is frequently considered, at least politically, to be part of North America, it is geographically part of Central America.

The other part of Middle America is the Caribbean, which is shaped around the Antilles—groups of islands stretching from Florida to South America. Although the population here has some cultural characteristics in common with those found in Latin America, the region has great variety and is a tourist destination in itself. It is covered in Chapter 8. The island destinations of Bermuda and the Bahamas are also covered in the Caribbean chapter, even though they are located farther north in the Atlantic Ocean.

South America

South America is a continental landmass extending nearly 5,000 miles north-south. It extends much farther toward the South Pole than do Africa or New Zealand. The northern half of South America is more than 3,000 miles from east to west. Then the landmass narrows to a cone shape in the south. Most of the continent lies east of the United States. New York City, for example, lies west of most of the western South American coastline.

The Land. One of the world's great mountain ranges, the Andes, whose highest peaks exceed 21,000 feet elevation, runs parallel to the west coast of South America and extends inland over a distance of 200 to 600 miles. East of the mountains, two large river systems and the plains they cross are dominant features—the east-flowing Amazon River system in the north, and the south-flowing Paraná River system in the southeast. Between these river systems, mountains and plateaus dominate the interior of the eastern bulge of South America. In the north, small mountain ranges stand between the Amazon River system and the east-flowing Orinoco River.

The Equator passes through northern South America, hence most of the northern half of the continent has a tropical climate except where it is modified by the heights of the Andes, where snowfields lie at higher elevations, and other local physical conditions. Midlatitude climatic conditions prevail in the southeast and part of the southern west coast. However, deserts line the central west coast and dry conditions prevail along the eastern flank of the southern Andes.

The Andean area is shared from north to south by Colombia, Ecuador, Peru, landlocked Bolivia, and long, narrow Chile. Brazil occupies the eastern bulge and most of the Amazon Basin. The southern cone is dominated by Argentina and, on its northern flank, Uruguay and landlocked Paraguay. Off the southeastern tip of the continent are the British-held Falkland Islands (or, in Spanish, Islas Malvinas). East of Colombia in northern South America are Venezuela, which faces the Caribbean Sea, and the three units of Guyana, Suriname, and French Guiana.

History. Through 15th and 16th century explorations, the Spaniards and Portuguese initially claimed all of Latin America; the Portuguese gained control over present-day Brazil and Spain held the rest. Colonization by settlers from these nations was stimulated by a search for silver and gold, the desire to introduce Christianity to the native Indians, and a reward system that gave large land grants to favored individuals. Major attention was directed toward the main concentrations of Indians.

The colonial control of Spain and Portugal was terminated at a relatively early date. Brazil and most Spanish colonies in South America and Central America became independent during the first half of the 19th century. Belize, in Central America, and British Guiana and Dutch Guiana, in South America, did not become independent until after World War II. French Guiana and the Falkland Islands (claimed by the United Kingdom) are the last remaining colonies in South America.

Mexico City, currently growing at the rate of 400,000 per year, largely through in-migration, is the second largest city in the world. There and in other large Latin American cities, usually the capitals, government cannot provide for the flood of new arrivals, and depressing slums and shantytowns are the result. Emigration to the United States, legal or illegal, is another alternative. Migrants come to the United States from Cuba, Haiti, Mexico, and other nations in Central America, the Caribbean, and northern South America.

Political instability has been another Latin American characteristic. In earlier years, this meant one conservative group taking over control from another, usually some coalition of military, landholding, and church interests. More recently, however, the lack or slow pace of change has generated more radical political movements and outbreaks of antigovernment guerrilla warfare. This trend resulted in a Communist government in Cuba and, during the 1980s, a radical government in Nicaragua. The present trend, however, is toward stabler and less authoritarian governments.

The People. The Incas of the Andes Mountains and the Aztecs of central Mexico had reached high levels of development prior to the arrival of the Spaniards. While still numerous, the Maya of southern Mexico, Guatemala, and Honduras were already in decline. Elsewhere in Latin America, native peoples were few and scattered. Intermarriage between Europeans and Indians produced a hybrid, mestizo population.

In the late 19th and early 20th century, at about the same time as immigration to North America occurred, a wave of non-Iberian Europeans came to southern Brazil, Argentina, Uruguay, Paraguay, and central Chile in search of land and job opportunities. Japanese settlers also came in large numbers to southern Brazil.

As a result of these migrations, the racial and ethnic composition of Latin American nations is varied. African-American populations dominate in the Caribbean islands and the coastal areas of Brazil and northeastern South America; Indian, mestizo, and white populations are the rule in Central America; Indians and mestizos are most numerous in Andean South America; and southern and southeastern South America is predominantly white. Brazil has the greatest mixture of peoples. In most Latin American nations, Roman Catholicism is the main religion.

The higher elevations of Central America are home to most of the population. The Andes have surprisingly large populations, resulting from precolonial development and the peopling of the mountains by the Incas. Coastal and adjacent interior parts of eastern and northern South America are relatively densely settled.

The Amazon Basin, southern Chile, and southern Argentina (Patagonia) are sparsely populated because of their inhospitable climate and remoteness. Among nations, Brazil and Mexico are by far the largest in population, followed by Argentina and Colombia.

The Economy. As part of their colonial heritage, most Latin American nations remain economically undeveloped. Typically, they have agricultural economies that rely upon exports of foodstuffs, mineral ores, beef and other animal products, or timber. Dependence upon external markets keeps them at the mercy of changes in commodity markets. Land problems are often critical, stemming from the concentration of the best lands in the hands of a relatively few families. A large, landless class is hungry for land redistribution.

There are exceptions to the dominance of agriculture; Brazil, Mexico, and Argentina are making important strides toward industrialization through use of their raw material and energy resources. Venezuela, Mexico, and Ecuador earn income from oil exports.

One response to rural backwardness and poverty is flight to the large cities in search of employment. Consequently, Latin America is one of the fastest urbanizing parts of the world. One estimate is that three-fourths of all Latin Americans will be city dwellers by the end of this century, signalling a massive retreat from rural life. Rural poverty has also been a factor in the participation in illegal drug shipments by some groups in such nations as Colombia, Peru, and Bolivia.

■ CENTRAL AMERICA

MEXICO

Official Name: The United
  Mexican States
Language: Spanish
Area: 761,604 square miles
Time Zone: GMT –6
  through –8

National Airlines: Aeromexico,
  Mexicana
Capital: Mexico City
Currency: Peso
Population: 90,007,000
Documentation: Tourist card

Mexico is the leading nation of Central America. It has the largest land area and population, and the most advanced, diversified economy. About one fifth the size of the United States, with which it shares a common northern border, Mexico narrows to the south. There, the rectangular Yucatan Peninsula juts abruptly northward into the Gulf of Mexico. In the northwest, the long, narrow Baja California peninsula extends southward along the Mexican mainland, separated by the Gulf of California.

The topography includes north-south mountain ranges, the high Central Plateau between the ranges, and narrow plains along the Pacific and Gulf coasts. The climate is dry to desert in the north, and tropical with dry winters along the southern coasts.

The Spaniards were attracted to Mexico by the large number of Indians and their wealth. Principal groups were the Maya of the Yucatan Peninsula and the ruling Aztecs and other tribal units of the Central Plateau. The Indian heritage remains strong—Indians are 29 percent and mestizos 55 percent of the present population. The capital, Mexico City, is in the southern Central Plateau and is built on the site of the Aztec capital. Now the world's second largest city and still growing rapidly, it faces enormous problems of inadequate housing and services, traffic congestion, and air pollution.

West of Mexico City is Guadalajara, the second largest city (3 million), and in the northeast near Texas, Monterrey is only slightly smaller. Vera Cruz, east of Mexico City on the Gulf coast, is the chief port city. Acapulco, on the southwest coast, was an important colonial port and is Mexico's most celebrated west coast resort.

Agriculture, involving both subsistence and cash crops, is still the economic mainstay. Stable national governments have made good progress in redistributing farmland since the 1920s, yet a large segment of the rural population remains poor and uneducated. Manufacturing is growing and employs a large labor force in Mexico City and cities of the north and the Gulf coast. Petroleum and natural gas strikes along the Gulf coast have made Mexico one of the world's major energy producers. The United States is Mexico's main trading partner and is also the goal of hundreds of thousands of illegal migrants who cross, or attempt to cross, the American border each year in search of employment. The North American Free Trade Agreement (NAFTA), signed by Mexico, Canada and the United States in 1993, will increase commercial interaction. The nation has basic road, rail, and air service, but many southern areas remain relatively isolated.

Areas of Touristic Importance. Mexico is one of the most popular foreign destinations for American tourists. It offers a broad range of cultural and rest and relaxation activities. Attractions can be found on both the Pacific and Gulf of Mexico coasts as well as on the Central Plateau. Mexico's proximity to the United States makes travel both convenient and reasonably priced.

Mexico City, the capital, is one of the most exciting, beautiful, and cosmopolitan cities in the Western Hemisphere. The city is at an altitude of more than 7,300 feet. Its broad avenues and many monuments are reminiscent of Paris. Attractions range from bullfights and museums to native markets and international shopping. Evenings feature both native and world class restaurants and a wide variety of entertainment. Many tours begin in Mexico City and branch out in a variety of directions after 3 or 4 days.

Mexico City's Museum of Anthropology and History is one of the finest in the world. It shows the cultures that have shaped

Pyramids of Teotihurcan, Mexico
Photo: Courtesy FONATUR

Mexico from Aztec and Mayan through Spanish colonial to the modern day. Visitors should also see the Palace of Fine Arts, featuring brilliant murals and the famous Tiffany glass curtain, and the University of Mexico's Aztec-inspired mosaic walls.

The professional bullfight season fills arenas on Sundays from October to March. Amateurs can be seen during other parts of the year. Symphony orchestras and the National Folkloric Ballet as well as extravagant nightclub shows are available for visitors.

A most popular and interesting excursion from Mexico City visits the Shrine of Guadalupe and the Pyramids of Teotihuacan, about 30 miles outside the city. The Shrine of

Guadalupe is the most sacred Roman Catholic site in Mexico, attracting pilgrims from the entire country. The Pyramids of the Sun and Moon date back more than 2,000 years and rival those of Egypt.

Cuernavaca, 50 miles south of the city, can be visited as an excursion from Mexico City or en route to Taxco and Acapulco. With its lakes, pyramids, and quaint streets, Cuernavaca has attracted visitors seeking rest and relaxation since the days of Cortez.

Taxco, located halfway between Mexico City and Acapulco, is known as Mexico's silver city. A typically Spanish colonial-style town with stucco buildings, red tile roofs, and cobblestone streets, Taxco is home to hundreds of silver craftsmen producing unique, handmade jewelry.

Acapulco is a major resort destination, world-famous for its picturesque bay and excellent Pacific coast beaches. It has an excellent, modern convention center and many first class and deluxe hotels. Sun, swimming, and surfing are major daytime activities. Viewing the unique Acapulco cliff divers is a must for the first-time visitor.

Other Pacific coast resort destinations include Puerto Vallarta and Mazatlan. Both feature good hotels and sun and fun activities. Along with Acapulco, these cities are featured ports of call on 7- and 10-day cruises from Los Angeles. The Gulf of California, between the peninsula of Baja California and mainland Mexico, offers whale-watching and diving or snorkeling activities.

Guadalajara, Mexico's second largest city, is located inland from Mazatlan and west of Mexico City. It is one of the best areas in the country for shopping for native Mexican products. Best values are leather goods, ceramics, wood carvings, and silver products. South of the city is Lake Chapala, a popular resort area which has maintained an old world charm.

The Yucatan has grown greatly in popularity since the development of a new, planned resort area, Cancun, in the mid 1970s. Still growing, with new hotels being added each year, Cancun is the most popular Mexican destination for visitors from the East Coast of the United States. In addition to resort activities, tourists can visit nearby Mayan ruins.

Merida, Uxmal, and Chichen Itza on the Yucatan Peninsula provide extensive access to temples and ruins of the Mayan civilization. Cozumel Island serves as a cruise port for this area and also features beach resorts which are smaller and less extensively developed than Cancun.

Ixtapa, another new government developed resort area, is located near the small Pacific coast town of Zihuatenejo, north of Acapulco. It is most attractive to visitors from the western United States.

Huatulco is the newest government-developed resort area in Mexico. Located on the Pacific coast, southeast of Oaxaca, Huatulco will feature first class and deluxe resort hotels similar to those found in Cancun and Ixtapa. Sun and surf activities along with active nightlife will prevail.

Baja California, the peninsula jutting southward from the southern border of the state of California, has some resort areas, but is basically little developed. Encinada and Cabo San Lucas serve as ports for cruises from southern California.

Border cities like Tijuana (near San Diego) and Juarez (across the Rio Grande from El Paso) attract large numbers of tourists, very few of whom stay more than a few hours. The only major activity is shopping for native Mexican products and pharmaceutical items, which are available without prescription for very low prices. Prices for many goods are lower than in the United States, but generally higher than in other cities in Mexico. El Paso is also a starting point for tours to the remote Copper Canyon region of the Sierra Madre Mountains. A rail line traverses the edge of a complex of canyons four times larger than the Grand Canyon.

GUATEMALA

Official Name: Republic of Guatemala

Language: Spanish

Area: 42,042 square miles

Time Zone: GMT –6

National Airline: Aviateca

Capital: Guatemala City

Currency: Quetzal

Population: 9,266,000

Documentation: Passport, tourist card

South and east of Mexico is Guatemala, which has a small Caribbean frontage and a longer Pacific coastline. In the higher elevations of the interior are the capital, Guatemala City, and the bulk of the population. Volcanic peaks, among them, Tajumulco, the highest in Central America, abound. Guatemala is the most Indian of the Central American nations in its population composition. Although Indians are about one-half of the population, they have little political or economic power. The densely forested and lightly populated Peten region in the north has impressive Mayan archeological sites. Basically agricultural, Guatemala exports foodstuffs (coffee, cotton, sugar, bananas), timber, and meat.

Areas of Touristic Importance. Guatemala City is the major gateway for entry into the country. Its museums feature the relics of ancient Mayan civilizations. Guatemala City, historically, was the site of the beginning of the revolt against Spain in 1821. Its marketplace is an excellent source of Indian woven products.

Excursions from Guatemala City visit the Spanish colonial capital of Antigua known for its Spanish architecture. Nearby is Lake Atitlan, a mountain lake of spectacular scenic beauty, surrounded by three volcanos and many Indian villages.

Chichicastenango features a busy marketplace that attracts thousands of visitors each Sunday. Handcarved and handwoven Indian goods are the mainstays of the market. The Indian and Spanish heritage of the country is reflected in Chichicastenango's Church of Saint Thomas. Excursions to this area also begin in Guatemala City.

The ancient Mayan city of Tikal is 1 hour's flying time from Guatemala City. Because it is located in dense jungle, Tikal was not discovered for more than 1,000 years after its demise. Intricate carvings on its pyramids and monuments depict the history of the advanced civilization that flourished here. Day trips and overnight tours to Tikal are available.

Huchuetenango, in the northeast, is a favorite spot for tourists interested in archeological sites. It is noted for its temples, forts, and ballfields.

Because of political unrest, tourism to Guatemala has remained low.

BELIZE

Language: English, Spanish, Mayan

Area: 8,866 square miles

Time Zone: GMT–6

Capital: Belmopan

Currency: Belize dollar

Population: 228,000

Documentation: Passport

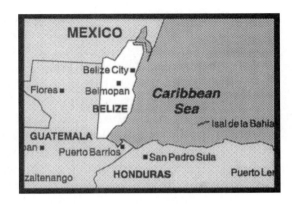

Sandwiched between Mexico and Guatemala, little Belize faces on the Gulf of Honduras in the western Caribbean. It was formerly British Honduras and the official language remains English. A relatively new nation, Belize gained its independence in 1981. More than one-fourth of the 175,000 population live in Belize City on the low-lying, swampy coast. In 1982, the capital was transferred from there to the small city of Belmopan in the higher interior. One-half of the Belize population is black or part-black. Negro-Carib Indians are the second largest ethnic group. Timber is the major export income earner.

Tourism is growing in Belize. There are beach resorts at Ambergris Cay and Turneffe Island. Adventurous, independent travelers also participate in hunting, fishing, and ecotourism activities. Belize has become a prime vacation spot for scuba divers because of its excellent reefs and reasonable prices. Also, Mayan ruins have been discovered. Among them are Altun Ha, where an immense jade head can be seen, and Xunantunich. A museum in Belize City contains many Mayan relics.

HONDURAS

Official Name: Republic of Honduras

Language: Spanish

Area: 43,277 square miles

Time Zone: GMT –6

National Airline: SAHSA

Capital: Tegucigalpa

Currency: Lempira

Population: 4,949,000

Documentation: Passport, visa

Honduras lies between Guatemala and Nicaragua. It has a 400-mile Caribbean coast, but on the Pacific the presence of El Salvador limits it to a small frontage. Its capital, Tegucigalpa, is in the south central highlands, about 60 miles inland from the Pacific coast. The population, about 90 percent mestizo, lives mostly in the interior highlands; the low-lying, swampy Caribbean coast is sparsely settled. Honduras is one of the two poorest nations in Central America. A once prosperous mining industry has declined, leaving agriculture the economic mainstay. Coffee and timber are exported.

Honduras fought a short war with El Salvador in 1969 over the illegal entry and use of land by Salvadoran squatters. In the 1980s, it experienced some spillover of the fighting between government and antigovernment forces in Nicaragua and government forces and radical guerrillas in El Salvador. The government faces severe domestic social and economic problems.

Areas of Touristic Importance. Copan, located northwest of Tegucigalpa is considered by many to be the most outstanding example of the ancient Mayan civilization. Restored areas include stone temples, courts, and an amphitheater.

Fine beaches can be found on the northern shores of Honduras on the Caribbean coast, but these areas are relatively undeveloped. Tegucigalpa, itself, is a picturesque, hillside city with winding cobblestone streets.

EL SALVADOR

Official Name: Republic of El Salvador
Language: Spanish
Area: 8,124 square miles
Time Zone: GMT –6
National Airline: TACA
Capital: San Salvador
Currency: Colon
Population: 5,418,000
Documentation: Passport

El Salvador is one of the two smallest Central America nations. Hemmed in by Guatemala and Honduras, it is the only one with only a Pacific coastline. It is more densely populated than its neighbors, and most of its people live in the volcanic uplands. Centrally located San Salvador is the capital. Basically agricultural with a small amount of manufacturing, El Salvador exports coffee and cotton. During the 1980s, national life was disrupted by intermittent fighting between American-supported government troops and antigovernment, leftist guerrillas. A cease fire was agreed upon in 1991.

El Salvador's capital, San Salvador, features palatial residential areas and large parks. Indian culture can be traced through ruins at Tazumal and San Andres. Tourism, however, is severely limited by internal problems.

NICARAGUA

Official Name: Republic of
   Nicaragua

Language: Spanish

Area: 50,193 square miles

Time Zone: GMT –6

National Airline: Nica Airlines

Capital: Managua

Currency: Cordoba

Population: 3,751,000

Documentation: Passport,
   visa

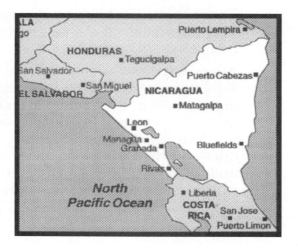

Nicaragua is the second largest Central American nation (after Mexico). It was also the center of political unrest in Central America in the 1980s. A Marxist (Sandinista) government came to power in 1979, and American military aid was given in support of antigovernment guerrillas (Contras). The Sandinista government was voted out of power in 1990. Most of the heavily mestizo population lives in the western highlands. The swampy and forested Caribbean coast, called the Mosquito Coast, has a small, mostly black population. A short distance inland from the Pacific in the highlands are large Lake Nicaragua and small Lake Managua. Near the latter is Managua, the nation's capital. Agriculture is the main source of employment. Economic conditions remain unsettled and tourism from the United States has been slow to revive.

COSTA RICA

Official Name: Republic of
   Costa Rica

Language: Spanish

Area: 19,575 square miles

Time Zone: GMT –6

National Airline: LACSA

Capital: San Jose

Currency: Colon

Population: 3,111,000

Documentation: Tourist card

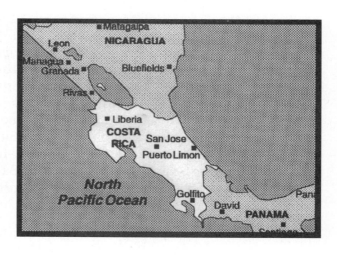

South of Nicaragua, Central America narrows in Costa Rica to a width of 75 miles and is even narrower in neighboring Panama. Most of Costa Rica's population, its capital (San Jose), and its agricultural economy are found in the central highlands. In contrast to the political and military turbulence in Nicaragua and El Salvador, Costa Rica is peaceful and stable. It operates without a national army, which was abolished in 1949, and is strongly allied with the United States. It is a regional leader in nature preservation and ecotourism.

Areas of Touristic Importance. San Jose is located in a valley and enjoys comfortable weather all year. Its National Theater is decorated with murals and sculpture. Other points of interest include the National University, the Metropolitan Cathedral, and the National Stadium. The Central Bank gold exhibition is the largest north of Peru.

San Jose can be a tourist's hub for visits to the Atlantic and Caribbean coasts. Daily rail service along a most interesting route through tropical jungle connects San Jose with Puerto Limón on the Caribbean coast.

Other interesting sights include the Irazu and Poas volcanos. The Sarachi Oxcart Factory features brightly painted, miniature to full size, oxcarts. Hand-tooled leather products are also popular with tourists.

Costa Rica has an international regulation for protecting its natural environment and is very popular with travellers interested in ecotourism.

PANAMA

Official Name: Republic of Panama

Language: Spanish

Area: 29,208 square miles

Time Zone: GMT –6

National Airline: Air Panama

Capital: Panama City

Currency: Balboa

Population: 2,426,000

Documentation: Passport or citizenship proof, visa

Panama links Costa Rica and the rest of Central America with Colombia and South America. Central mountains and hills are bordered by broad Pacific coast plains. The basically rural population is two-thirds mestizo, with the rest black, white, and Indian.

Originally part of Colombia, Panama got its independence in 1903 with American government support. The United States then built the Panama Canal across the narrow territory, between Balboa on the Pacific coast and Colon on the Caribbean coast, to link Pacific and Atlantic shipping lanes. Completed in 1914, the canal is one of the world's greatest transportation

Panama Canal
Photo: Courtesy Jim Woodman

facilities. In exchange for American subsidies, a 10-mile wide strip of land along the canal, the Canal Zone, was leased to the United States. Panamanian employment in the Canal Zone has been a vital source of national income. In 1977, the United States agreed to transfer its authority in the Canal Zone to Panama at the end of 1999. The capital, Panama City, is adjacent to the Pacific end of the Canal Zone.

Areas of Touristic Importance. The Panama Canal, with its locks taking ships from higher water to lower water or vice versa, is, of course, the main attraction in Panama. No trip to the country is complete without a canal visit. The canal can be viewed from Cristobal and Colon on the Atlantic end or Balboa on the Pacific. Although we think of traveling from the Atlantic to the Pacific as traveling from east to west, the Panama Canal, itself, runs from north (Atlantic) to south (Pacific).

Traversing the canal is a popular cruise experience, with ships operating in both directions between Florida and Caribbean ports and west coast ports. These voyages are generally 10 days or longer. A newer type of cruise, for the popular 1 week market, departs from ports such as Jamaica or Aruba, travels halfway through the canal to Gatun Lake, turns around and returns to its port of embarkation.

In Panama City, the visitor can see many of the treasures from 17th century colonialism and piracy. The Altar of Gold in the Church of San Jose is a most interesting sight.

The San Blas Islands, a short flight from Panama City in the Atlantic or a typical port stop on Canal cruises, attracts many visitors. The islands are home to the Cuna Indians, a tribe that has maintained its unique language and customs for hundreds, if not thousands, of years.

■ SOUTH AMERICA

COLOMBIA

Official Name: Republic of Colombia

Language: Spanish

Area: 439,735 square miles (COP)

Time Zone: GMT –5

National Airline: Avianca

Capital: Bogota

Currency: Colombian peso

Population: 33,777,000

Documentation: Passport

Located in northwestern South America, Colombia has both long Pacific and Caribbean coastlines; between them is the land link with Panama and Central America. Colombia has an interior as well as a Caribbean coast orientation. Its western portion is dominated by three mountain ranges, part of the northern Andes. Two major rivers, the Cauca and Magdalena, flow northward between them to the Caribbean. The Magdalena River valley is the main north-south transportation route. Most of the population lives within these mountains and valleys or along the coasts.

The capital, Bogota, is in the interior mountains at 8,700 feet elevation. Southwest of Bogota, the third largest city, Cali, services a flourishing hacienda district where sugar and cacao are main crops. Cali is linked to Buenaventura, the only Colombian port of consequence on the Pacific coast. There are many Indians in the southwest. Whites and mestizos predominate elsewhere. North of Bogota, Medellin, the second largest city, services one of the world's largest coffee-raising districts. Coffee is Colombia's most valuable export, not including illegal drugs.

The Caribbean lowlands are served by two port cities, Barranquilla and Cartagena. The coastal population is partially black, descendants of former slaves who worked in now-defunct plantations. Oil fields in the northeast provide Colombia with another valuable export. This area is also the source of illegal shipments of drugs, especially marijuana and cocaine, to North American destinations.

The eastern half of Colombia shares the rain forests of the Amazon Basin and, in the northeast, the seasonally wet-dry grasslands, llanos, that continue eastward into Venezuela. This region is sparsely populated, poorly developed, and remote from the main currents of Colombian life.

Areas of Touristic Importance. Bogota's most popular attraction is the Gold Museum (Museo del Oro) which contains more than 15,000 pre-Columbian gold pieces. The Church of Veracruz contains the remains of heroes who fought for independence from Spain. The Church of San Francisco La Tercera is known for its fine wood carvings. The Colonial Art Museum, Museum of Native Handicrafts and Traditions, and Archeology Museum preserve much of Colombia's heritage. The National Museum is located in an old prison.

At the edge of the city is the Quinta de Bolivar, the villa of South American liberator Simon Bolivar. A cable car nearby takes visitors to the top of Monserrate for a magnificent view of the city.

One of the wonders of South America, the Salt Cathedral of Zipaquira is 35 miles from Bogota. Carved by the Chibcha

Indians, the cathedral is one-half mile below ground and can hold more than 10,000 people.

Colombia's Caribbean coast was, during the colonial period, the famous Spanish Main. Barranquilla, Cartagena, and Santa Marta offer resort activities and beaches. Barranquilla is also Colombia's main port, because of its location on the north end of the Magdalena River, and its most modern industrial city.

San Andres Island is part of Colombia, although it is located off the coast of Nicaragua. The pirate, Morgan, is reported to have buried treasure here. San Andres features miles of sandy beaches and some of the most interesting underwater scenery in the world.

VENEZUELA

Official Name: Republic of Venezuela
Language: Spanish
Area: 352,143 square miles
Time Zone: GMT –4
National Airline: Viasa
Capital: Caracas
Currency: Bolivar (VBO)
Population: 20,189,000
Documentation: Passport

Venezuela, which lies east of Colombia, is the other large nation of northern South America. Its core area is in the northwest, where the northernmost arm of the Andes runs parallel to the Caribbean coast. Most of the population and the capital, Caracas, are in these highlands. Most Venezuelans are mestizo or white; there are also blacks in the coastal areas. Caracas, a city of more than 4 million, is served by the nearby coastal port of La Guaira. In the northwest, around Lake Maracaibo, is one of the world's largest producing oil fields, a main source of Venezuela's income. Maracaibo, Venezuela's second largest city, services this important region.

Southeastern Venezuela is occupied by the forested and remote Guiana Highlands. Between the core area and the highlands is a broad interior plain drained by the Orinoco River, which flows eastward into the Atlantic Ocean. A seasonally wet-dry climate produces grasslands (llanos). Lightly settled, the grasslands support cattle grazing.

The newest boom area in Venezuela is in the northeast, around the lower Orinoco plain. There are oil and natural gas fields, iron ore mining, and large-scale hydroelectric power generation. Such local resources represent one of Latin America's brightest potentials for future industrialization. Ciudad Bolivar, on the Orinoco River, is the regional service center.

Areas of Touristic Importance. Although Caracas is more than 400 years old, there are few remnants of the Spanish colonial period. The modern university, the Simon Bolivar Civic Center, and other new buildings dominate the city. Casa Natal, the birthplace of liberator Simon Bolivar, is preserved, as is the National Pantheon, his final resting place. Colonia Tovar, a German community reminiscent of Bavaria, is a short drive from the city.

Mount Avila overlooks the city. Visitors can reach the top by cable car and also descend to the seaside resort area of Macuto. La Guaira, located nearby, is a major cruise port.

Angel Falls, the highest waterfall in the world (more than 3,200 feet), is in the interior jungle of Venezuela. Visitors must fly to Ciudad Bolivar or Canaima to reach this most beautiful spot.

Beach resorts can be found near Caracas at Macuto and on Marguerita Island in the Caribbean. These resorts cater mainly to South American and European tourists.

■ THE GUIANAS

GUYANA

Official Name: Cooperative Republic of Guyana

Language: English, Hindi, Urdu

Area: 83,000 square miles

Time Zone: GMT –3

National Airline: Guyana Airways

Capital: Georgetown

Currency: Guyana Dollar (GYD)

Population: 748,000

Documentation: Passport

SURINAME

Official Name: Republic of Suriname

Language: Dutch, Hindustani, Javanese

Area: 63,037 square miles

Time Zone: GMT –3

National Airline: Suriname Airways

Capital: Paramaribo

Currency: Suriname guilder (SFL)

Population: 402,000

Documentation: Passport

FRENCH GUIANA

Official Name: French Guiana
Language: French
Area: 43,740 square miles
Time Zone: GMT –3
Capital: Cayenne

Currency: French franc (FFR)
Population: 101,000
Documentation: Passport, visa

Hemmed in along the Atlantic coast by Venezuela on the west and Brazil on the south are three political units with distinctive backgrounds. Westernmost Guyana was formerly British Guiana; central Suriname was formerly Dutch Guiana; and easternmost French Guiana remains under the control of France. Populations are small and coastal; the interior of each unit is forested and has few people.

The populations are complex, formed of blacks, Asians, and whites; Indonesians are also found in Suriname. Guyana exports plantation products and aluminum ore (bauxite). Bauxite also is the chief source of income for Suriname. French Guiana, which has a predominantly white population, is the least developed of the three, and depends on financial support from France. Because of lack of development and small populations, the area's touristic importance is somewhat limited. Found on few organized tour programs, the Guianas appeal primarily to the adventurous traveler.

Areas of Touristic Importance. Georgetown, Guyana, is the home of St. George's Cathedral, one of the tallest wooden structures in the world. Georgetown also hosts beautiful botanical gardens and a busy marketplace. One-day excursions take tourists to visit magnificent Kaietur Falls, plunging 741 feet from top to bottom.

Of the three Guineas, Suriname hosts the most tourists. Paramaribo is a surprisingly modern and cosmopolitan city. It has a diversity of cultures, and visitors will see Catholic cathedrals, Moslem mosques, and Hindu temples. Excursions by dugout canoe up the Suriname River take visitors to the bush country where natives still practice voodoo.

French Guiana is the most underdeveloped country on the continent. Cayenne, its capital, is the starting point for excursions into the untamed jungle or to the former French penal colony, Devil's Island.

ECUADOR

Official Name: Republic of Ecuador

Language: Spanish

Area: 109,483 square miles

Time Zone: GMT –5 (except Galapagos Islands)

National Airline: Ecuatoriana

Capital: Quito

Currency: Sucre (SUC)

Population: 10,751,000

Documentation: Passport

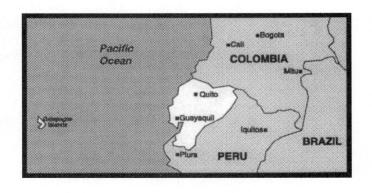

Western South America is physically dominated by the massive Andes Mountains, which run the full length of the continent. Much of the Andean area is culturally distinctive, peopled by large Indian and mestizo populations descended from the Incan and other precolonial groups. Ecuador, Peru, and Bolivia are most representative.

Small Ecuador faces on the Pacific coast between Colombia and Peru. It has a distinct north-south physical orientation, formed of a coastal plain, the Andes, and eastern slopes facing upon the Amazon Basin. The capital, Quito, lies in one of a number of high mountain basins. There is little mining, leaving agriculture the main support of the Indian and mestizo population. The eastern region (Oriente) is remote, yet in recent years has been the site of oil strikes that give Ecuador its chief source of wealth. Oil is shipped by pipeline to the west coast for export.

The west coast has the most vigorous and growing regional economy, based upon banana and cacao plantations and offshore fisheries. The main port, Guayaquil, has surpassed Quito in size. As in the entire region, Ecuador's population is mainly mestizo. Ecuador owns the Galapagos Islands (or Colon Archipelago), 600 miles westward in the Pacific Ocean.

Areas of Touristic Importance. Much of the Spanish colonial influence on the region remains in Quito and gives the city a special charm. At more than 9,000 feet above sea level, the altitude moderates the climate in this capital, which is located only a few miles from the equator. Santo Domingo, a village 85 miles west of the city, is a popular excursion. It is home to the Colorado Indians, known for their distinctive traditions in clothing and body painting.

Guayaquil, on the Pacific Ocean 300 miles south of Quito, is Ecuador's primary port. An unusual railway, full of hairpin turns and switchbacks, maneuvers an ascent or descent of nearly 10,000 feet, connecting the two cities. Again, the Spanish colonial influence is found in the city's architecture and its churches and cathedrals.

The Galapagos Islands are famous for their distinctive bird, mammal, and marine life, first described by Charles Darwin. The twelve islands are peaks of gigantic undersea volcanoes rising 7,000 to 10,000 feet above the sea floor. Darwin's studies of flora and fauna in this natural sanctuary became the basis for his monumental work, *Origin of Species*. A limited number of visitors flying from the mainland can be housed on one of the five inhabited islands. Cruises from Guayaquil also bring tourists to the area.

PERU

Official Name: Republic of Peru

Language: Spanish

Area: 496,222 square miles

Time Zone: GMT –5

National Airline: AeroPeru

Capital: Lima

Currency: Sol (SOL)

Population: 22,361,000

Documentation: Passport

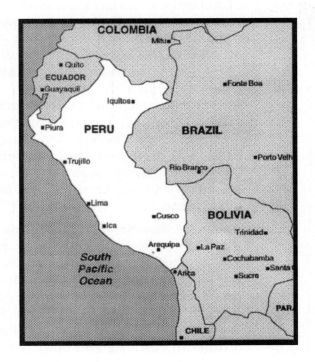

The Land and People. Peru extends southward from Ecuador for nearly 1,500 miles along the Pacific. It shares Ecuador's three-part physical layout, with the narrow coastal plain at its core. Although arid, the plain is irrigated by streams flowing from the Andes and supports a thriving agriculture. In a central location are the capital, Lima, a city of more than 5 million people, and its nearby port of Callao. The coastal population is mainly white and mestizo.

The high Andes occupy one third of Peru and contain about half of its population, mostly Quechua-speaking Indians, descendants of the Incas. The region is poor and economically undeveloped. Subsistence crops and pastoral activities are the main means of support. However, the mining of copper, silver, and lead for export provides some jobs in the cold mountain environment.

A large segment of the eastern mountain slopes (Oriente) and western Amazon Basin (Montana) are found in Peru. This region is isolated from west coast centers and poorly developed. In fact, the main growth center, Iquitos, on the upper Amazon River, makes external contacts via freighter service on the Brazilian Amazon River and by air. Local oil strikes have brought some growth, and a pipeline carries oil across the Andes to the west coast.

With eastern Bolivia, interior Peru is the main production area for coca, whose leaves are the raw material of the illegal drug cocaine. There is much rural upset over attempts to control this drug traffic. Also, the terrorist activities of radical guerrilla groups have kept travel hazardous in large interior areas since the early 1990s.

Areas of Touristic Importance. Lima is one of the largest cities on the continent. Like most other South American capitals, it presents a contrast of old and new, with Spanish colonial buildings and large modern skyscrapers. The Plaza de Armas was the site of Spanish conquistador Pizarro's palace. Inquisition trials took place in a hall at the Plaza de Bolivar.

Before the Spaniards arrived, Peru was a key part of the great Inca empire. Treasures and artifacts of the Inca empire attract visitors to Cuzco and Machu Picchu high in the Andes in southeastern Peru. Cuzco was the capital of the Inca Empire when the Spanish arrived. Its temples became Catholic churches, but still retain their Indian influence.

Machu Picchu is the legendary "Lost City of the Incas." It was so inaccessible and remote on top of a high mountain peak that the Spanish never discovered it. Thus saved from

Machu Picchu, Peru
Photo: Courtesy Jim Woodman

pillaging by the Spaniards, it is pure Incan, with its stone altars and terraced gardens. Machu Picchu is a 3-hour train journey from Cuzco.

Iquitos is located in northeastern Peru at the headwaters of the Amazon River. Boat cruises of varying durations sail into the "green hell" of the Amazon Jungle.

BOLIVIA

Official Name: Republic of Bolivia

Language: Spanish

Area: 424,165 square miles

Time Zone: GMT –4

National Airline: LAB

Capital: La Paz

Currency: Bolivian peso

Population: 7,156,000

Documentation: Passport

Southward from Peru the Andes broaden, become higher, and divide into two great ranges. Between them an extensive plateau, the Altiplano, at an average elevation of 12,000 feet, forms the physical core of landlocked Bolivia. On the boundary with Peru is Lake Titicaca, at 12,500 feet the highest large lake in the world. A short distance away is La Paz, Bolivia's capital, the highest (12,001 feet) national capital in the world. Some 80 percent of Bolivia's population lives in the Altiplano. As in Peru, the population is heavily Indian, with mestizos concentrated more to the east.

Bolivia is a leading minerals producer—silver, copper, zinc, and tin, currently the main export income earner. Bolivia has lost territory to Chile, Paraguay, and Brazil in earlier wars and must rely upon the Chilean ports of Arica and Antofagasta for shipping services. Its eastern lowlands are gradually playing a larger economic role since the discovery there of gas and oil; the latter is exported to Argentina and Brazil. Santa Cruz, an eastern boomtown, is now the second largest city in Bolivia.

Areas of Touristic Importance. Bolivia's high altitude makes breathing difficult for those not used to it. Limited tourism includes the modern city of La Paz and hydrofoil rides on Lake Titicaca. Also, the ruins of Tiahuanaco, near La Paz, are believed to be older than the Egyptian pyramids.

CHILE

Official Name: Republic of Chile

Language: Spanish

Area: 292,257 square miles

Time Zone: GMT –4 (except Easter Island)

National Airline: LAN Chile

Capital: Santiago

Currency: Chilean (CHE)

Population: 13,286,000

Documentation: Passport

Chile has a remarkable shape—less than 200 miles wide, it extends southward from Peru and Bolivia for 1,800 miles along the Pacific coast. The southern Andes forms a mountainous spine that separates Chile from Argentina to the east. Chile is composed of three very different regions. The northern coastal region is the Atacama Desert, a prime source of copper, the leading Chilean export. In the better watered, 700-mile-long plain of central Chile are most of the population, a mixture of whites and mestizos; the main agricultural areas; and the largest cities, including the capital, Santiago, and port, Valparaiso. In southern Chile, the coast is

Naval Museum, Vina del Mar, Chile
Photo: Courtesy Jim Woodman

fragmented into numerous islands and inlets created by glaciers, which still occur. There is virtually no settlement in this bleak and cold environment.

Chile's southern extreme is cut by the Strait of Magellan. On the strait is Punta Arenas, the southernmost city in the world. Beyond the strait is Tierra del Fuego, a large island shared with Argentina. On its southern tip (part of Chile) is Cape Horn, the southernmost point in South America. Chile also owns some distant Pacific islands, including Easter Island.

Areas of Touristic Importance. Santiago is Chile's largest city and the fourth largest on the continent. The contrast of old Spanish and modern buildings is further enhanced by the backdrop of high, snowcapped Andean mountains. Prime tourist sights include the Plaza de Armas, on which stands Santiago Cathedral, and Quinta National Park, home of the Museum of Modern Art and the Natural History Museum. The first Spanish fort built in Chile is at the top of Santa Lucia. Excellent views of the city are available from Santa Lucia and San Cristobal mountains. Valparaiso, Chile's main seaport, is 90 miles from Santiago.

Vina del Mar is a world-famous beach resort catering primarily to the wealthy. It is a city of flowers and trees, and houses the President's Summer Palace and the Naval Museum.

The Lake District is south of Vina del Mar near the seaport of Puerto Montt. The area features mountain and lake scenery and excellent rainbow and brown trout fishing.

Skiing is available in Portillo during June, July, and August. Lifts and trails are somewhat primitive by United States and European standards.

Easter Island, located 2,300 miles west of Santiago in the Pacific Ocean, is best known for its archeological sites, including seven huge stone heads crafted by a still-unknown civilization.

ARGENTINA

Language: Spanish

Area: 1,065,189 square miles

Time Zone: GMT –3

National Airline: Aerolineas Argentinas

Capital: Buenos Aires

Currency: Austral

Population: 32,663,000

Documentation: Passport

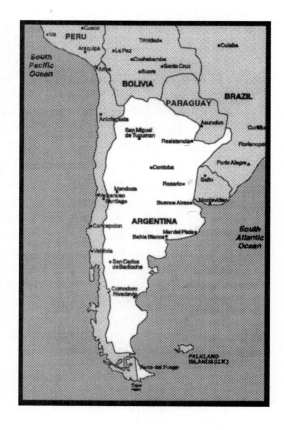

Chile's eastern neighbor in the narrow southern cone of South America is Argentina, one of the most economically advanced Latin American nations. It ranks second only to Brazil in size of territory and population in South America. The core area is in the northeast in the Pampas, a broad plain once covered with tall grass, much like the prairie of North America, now one of the world's largest expanses of commercial agriculture. Divided among large farming units, haciendas, the Pampas produces large surpluses of wheat, beef, mutton, wool, and other exportable commodities.

Buenos Aires, the capital, main port, manufacturing center, and dominant city of Argentina, is located on the flanking east coast of the Pampas where the southflowing Paraná River empties into a deep-cut estuary, Rio de la Plata, and the South Atlantic Ocean. Three-fourths of Argentina's population live in the Pampas; more than one-third are in Buenos Aires, one of the largest and most cosmopolitan cities of Latin America.

Most of the Pampas is within a radius of 350 miles from Buenos Aires and is linked to it by a dense network of railways and highways. Argentina's population is mainly of earlier Spanish and later European stock, including many immigrants from Germany and Italy. There remains a strong European orientation in national economic and cultural life.

In contrast to the Pampas, the rest of Argentina is lightly populated, largely because of its inhospitable, mostly dry, climate. In western Argentina, along the eastern flanks of the Andes, water is available for irrigated agriculture and urban development. Tucuman, Cordoba, and Mendoza are important agricultural and emerging manufacturing centers. The southern 40 percent of Argentina, Patagonia, narrows to the south. Semiarid and windswept, it has a large sheep population but few people. At the southern tip, eastern Tierra del Fuego is separated by the Strait of Magellan and Chilean territory.

Areas of Touristic Importance. Buenos Aires is a huge, cosmopolitan, and very sophisticated city, often called the "Paris of South America." It has the same high fashion and high level of cultural attractions as major European cities. Restaurants

Iguazú Falls
Photo: Courtesy Jim Woodman

cover the range from native to world-class French. Beef is a major specialty with home-raised steaks from the Pampas available at very reasonable prices. The Argentine liberator, Jose de San Martin, is commemorated throughout the city.

Beautiful parks abound along with wide, tree-lined streets and a colorful waterfront. Interesting museums feature art and artifacts from all over the world. Excursions to ranches on the Pampas give the tourist the chance to see the cattle herds and gauchos (cowboys) known for their use of the bolas (a rope with weighted ends.)

Mar del Plata, the Atlantic beaches, lie 250 miles south of Buenos Aires. The area is a summer playground with more than 1,500 hotels. The Bristol Beach Casino is the largest casino in the world. Most hotels are open only in the December through March summer season, as the water is cold during the balance of the year.

The Andes Mountains provide a number of resort area and numerous national parks, great scenery and excellent skiing opportunities. The village of Bariloche, on the Argentine side of the border with Chile, is a South American version of a Swiss alpine village and is famous for its skiing and its chocolate.

Iguazu Falls is 1,300 miles northeast of Buenos Aires on the Paraná River, where it forms the Brazilian border. One of the most impressive falls in the world, Iguazu measures 10,000 feet by 221 feet and is more massive than Niagara. More visitors come to its Brazilian side.

The southern area of Patagonia has become popular with eco-tourism travelers. This area is expected to enjoy a growth in tourism in the coming years.

Entre Rios and Cordoba in the north offer great beauty and interesting historical places for the tourist. Parana, capital of Entre Rios, is built on the river and has a great cultural life. Cordoba is both a city and a province. The city was founded more than 400 years ago and contains much colonial architecture including towers and churches.

The Falkland Islands. An Argentinian attempt to seize the Falkland Islands (known as the Islas Malvinas in Argentina), a British dependency 300 miles off the southern coast, was defeated in a short war in 1982. Islanders receive few visitors and depend on sheep ranching and British government programs for support. Britain maintains control over the Falklands for strategic purposes.

URUGUAY

Official Name: Oriental Republic of Uruguay
Language: Spanish
Area: 68,037 square miles
Time Zone: GMT –3
National Airline: PLUNA
Capital: Montevideo
Currency: Peso (URP)
Population: 3,121,000
Documentation: Passport

Northeast of the Pampas, across the Rio de la Plata, is Uruguay, a small nation with an Atlantic coastline and common borders with Argentina and Brazil. Physical conditions and commercial agriculture resemble those of the Pampas. Wheat, wool, beef, and hides are the main agricultural products. There is little manufacturing. More than half the population resides in the capital, Montevideo, on the coast. As in Argentina, the population is almost entirely of European descent. Uruguay has strong commercial interaction with Buenos Aires and cities of southeastern Brazil.

Areas of Touristic Importance. Montevideo is a charming capital city with an atmosphere of relaxed openness. The Plaza Independencia is the heart of the city. The Palacio Legislativo features pink granite pillars, mosaic floors, and historic wall murals. The Teatro Solis (Theater of the Sun) and the Museum of Natural History are most popular.

Eastward from Montevideo is the famous Riviera, more than 200 miles of beaches with deep sand and clean waters. The capital itself has eight beaches that attract both residents and tourists. More than 3 million tourists visit Uruguayan beaches each year.

Punta del Este, 90 miles east of Montevideo, is the brightest and most famous beach area and is most popular with the international set. Clear water and white sand as well as racetracks and casinos make this a most active summer resort area. The season is only slightly longer than that of Argentina's Mar del Plata.

PARAGUAY

Official Name: Republic of
   Paraguay
Language: Spanish, Guarani
Area: 157,047 square miles
Time Zone: GMT –4
National Airline: Air Paraguay
Capital: Asuncion
Currency: Guaranu (GUA)
Population: 4,798,000
Documentation: Passport

Sandwiched between Bolivia, Brazil, and Argentina, Paraguay lies east of the Andes. Most of its small population is Indian or mestizo, and Guarani is the main Indian language. National boundaries on the east, south, and west are drawn along rivers of the Paraná River systems. The capital, Asuncion, is in the southwest on the Paraguay River.

Most of the population lives in the eastern half where wet-dry grasslands support cattle grazing, the main economic activity. Western Paraguay consists of the Chaco, a forested and lightly settled region that is shared with Argentina. Relatively isolated and, like Bolivia, landlocked, Paraguay's easiest external contacts are with Buenos Aires, in Argentina, by river transportation. The recently completed Itaipu Dam on the Paraná River, a joint project with Brazil, produces large amounts of electricity that may stir improvement in a poor nation.

Northwestern Paraguay, the Chaco, was a 1932-1937 battlefield for military forces of Paraguay and Bolivia with heavy casualties. It has 60 percent of Paraguay's land area but only 2 percent of its population. Most economic development has been carried out by Mennonite settlers, now numbering 13,000, who came there between 1927-1947 from Canada and the Soviet Union to escape religious opposition. They have good relationships with local Indian groups and have made Filadelfia into their main town.

Areas of Touristic Importance. Tourism is not a major factor in Paraguay. Asuncion is a quiet town reminding the visitor of earlier times. Excursions include hunting and fishing expeditions. Iguazu Falls is also a popular excursion for visitors to Paraguay. Interest in ecotourism is increasing.

BRAZIL

Official Name: Federative Republic of Brazil

Language: Portuguese

Area: 3,286,470 square miles

Time Zone: GMT –3 through –4

National Airline: Varig

Capital: Brasilia

Currency: Cruzeiro

Population: 148,000,000

Documentation: Passport, visa

The Land. Located in eastern South America where the continent bulges prominently eastward, Brazil is the giant of Latin America—it is the largest in size on the continent, the fifth largest country in the world, and has the largest population in South America. In addition, it has an enormous supply of natural resources, thriving agriculture, and leads Latin America in industrialization. It occupies almost half of South America and measures 2,600 miles east-west and 2,700 miles north-south astride the equator. It has 4,600 miles of Atlantic Ocean coastline.

Brazil borders every South American nation except Chile and Ecuador. A nation of great distances, Brazil is a land of extensive hills and plateaus, with low mountains along the southeast coast. The climate and vegetation change from tropical rain forest in the north to tropical wet-dry grasslands (savannas) in the southwest to temperate midlatitude areas in the southeast.

Northern Brazil is shaped around the lightly populated and still relatively remote Amazon Basin, which is drained by the east-flowing Amazon River, one of the world's greatest rivers in drainage and volume of water. Ocean steamers can go upstream 2,300 miles to Iquitos, Peru. Midway is the main Brazilian city on the Amazon, Manaus. Coastal cities on the eastern bulge of Brazil date from the early Portuguese settlement. Inland, however, because the area of the bulge suffers from severe seasonal drought, it is among the poorest sections of Brazil, and the source of large-scale migration to the prosperous southeast.

Amazon River
Photo: Courtesy Brazilian Tourism Foundation

The Economy. The core area of Brazil, in the southeast, has most of the population, mining and manufacturing, excellent agriculture, and the major cities. On the coast, Rio de Janeiro long served as the capital and dominant city. However, the capital has been shifted to Brasilia, a planned city farther west, in an attempt to pull national development into the interior from the coastal districts. Still the national cultural center, "Rio" has been outstripped in size by Sao Paulo. About 300 miles north of Rio is Brazil's mining and heavy industrial district, large by world standards. Belo Horizonte is the main service center. Mining activities yield iron ore as well as precious and semiprecious stones, many of which are cut, polished, and set by jewelers for export or sale to visitors.

Sao Paulo, located 225 miles west of Rio, a short distance from the coast, is Brazil's urban dynamo. It ranks behind Mexico City as the second largest city of the Western hemisphere. It is the main manufacturing and commercial city and services the most prosperous agricultural area, where coffee, soybeans, and citrus are important export crops. Exports are shipped through the nearby port of Santos. Farther south, flourishing regional cities benefit from local coal supplies and electric power from the Itaipu Dam on the Parana River boundary with Paraguay.

After decades of neglect, Brazilians are restoring the decayed colonial cores of many of their historic coastal cities, following a national trend toward historic preservation and tourism encouragement.

The People. Overall, Brazil's population is 60 percent white, 26 percent mestizo, and 11 percent black. The southeast is heavily white, with many people of German and other European ancestry. There are also people of Japanese ancestry. The coastal districts are heavily black or mestizo, and the Amazon Basin has a small, scattered Indian population. Brazil faces serious problems in its fast-growing numbers, crowded urban slums, great regional differences in living standards, and its continuing reliance upon the export of food and raw materials. Its primary economic focus is with Europe and increasingly with the United States.

Areas of Touristic Importance. Rio de Janeiro is the most famous city in Brazil and one of the most well known in the world. The pre-Lenten Carnival in Rio is one of the most exciting events, and is popular even among those who will never travel. Copacabana and Ipanema beaches have been featured in song and story the world over. Although a wide variety of hotels are available, the image of Rio is one of opulence and luxury. Unfortunately, crime has been a major problem in Rio in recent years and tourists must be careful.

Emeralds, amethysts, topaz, and other precious and semiprecious stones, cut and polished from Brazilian mines and available at hundreds of jewelry shops throughout the city, add to the belief that Rio is for the rich and famous. In reality, Rio is quite affordable. Although Rio de Janeiro is often part of multicity itineraries, it is one of the few destinations on the continent that supports single-destination trips.

The beaches are the center of action day and night. Hotels, restaurants, and nightclubs line the beachfront. Discos and floorshows are often crowded with visitors.

The most prominent landmarks are Sugarloaf and Corcovado. Sugarloaf rises 1,380 feet almost straight up from the bay. A cable car whisks passengers to the restaurant and park at the top. Corcovado, a mountain behind the seashore city, is crowned by the impressive 1,200-ton, 130-foot statue of Christ the Redeemer. Both Sugarloaf and Corcovado provide excellent views of the city below.

Rio has many parks and cultural attractions as well. The Jardin Botanico contains more than 7,000 varieties of plants, including more than 600 types of orchids. The Quinta de Boa Vista is the largest park and features the National Museum, zoo, and a tropical aquarium. The Museum of Modern Art and War Memorial is almost all glass. The Museum of Fine Art features both contemporary artists and old masters.

South of Rio is Sao Paulo, Brazil's largest city and one of the leading industrial centers on the continent. It is a huge, urban, commercial center tastefully blending parks and gardens with modern skyscrapers. The unique Buhanta Snake Farm and Museum is located in the suburbs of the city. Beaches and resorts are also located nearby.

Brasilia is the modern capital of the nation. It is located 750 miles west of Rio de Janeiro. Inaugurated in 1960, Brasilia has been developed in an attempt to attract population and development inland from the coast. The public buildings were designed by architect Oscar Niemeyer. The governmental center is the Plaza of the Three Powers, with an array of marble buildings, reflecting pools, and contemporary metal sculpture. The top of the Television Tower provides the best view of this truly "new" city.

Recife, Belem, and Manaus to the north of Rio are interesting as well. Recife is the "Venice of South America," laced with waterways and graceful bridges. Belem is at the mouth of the Amazon, 90 miles from the open sea and just south of the Equator. Manaus is a frontier city 1,000 miles up the Amazon River in the middle of the Amazon rainforest.

■ TYPES OF TOURISM

Central and South America have a wide variety of travel programs. South America attracts primarily multicity hosted and escorted tour programs. Independent travel is mostly for business purposes and to the capital and industrial cities on the continent. Resort destinations such as Rio de Janeiro, the Caribbean resorts of Colombia and Venezuela, and the beach areas of Mexico and Central America also attract single-destination visitors.

Travel to much of Central America is limited by political unrest. Travel to South America is affected by perceptions of both high price and limited appeal. The potential for growth is great.

The following tour programs are examples of travel within the region:

- Costa Rica
- From the Amazon to the Andes
- Ecuador and the Galapagos Island Cruise
- Copper Canyon
- Colonial Mexico
- Mayan Empire

Costa Rica
9 Days - Escorted Tour CO

San Jose • Poas Volcano • Oxcart Factory • Villa Blanca • Monteverde Cloud Forest Reserve • Puntarenas • Gulf Cruise • Tortuga Island

15 Meals: 8 Breakfasts, 1 Lunch, 6 Dinners

Monteverde   Villa
                Blanca
Puntarenas
              San Jose
COSTA
RICA

Itinerary

Day 1: Arrive San Jose, Costa Rica
Costa Rica - a land rich in natural wonders, awaits you! Here you will find beautiful beaches, lush tropical rain forests, a wide variety of adventure sports, and plenty of relaxation. There are over 600 miles of beaches with coasts on both the Caribbean and Pacific Oceans. Costa Rica is dedicated to eco-tourism which sustains the delicate ecological balance of nature and tourism. You will arrive in SAN JOSE today, the capital city of Costa Rica. Meals included **D**

Day 2: San Jose - Local Sightseeing
This morning you will enjoy a comprehensive tour of San Jose and its surroundings hosted by a local guide. First you will travel to LANKESTER GARDENS which are world-renowned for their spectacular orchid collection boasting over 800 species. There are also tropical plants, a cactus garden and groves of bamboo, fruit and hardwood trees. You will return to San Jose to view the UNIVERSITY OF COSTA RICA, the NATIONAL THEATRE, the NATIONAL MUSEUM, and many other highlights of downtown San Jose. Following your visit, you will stop in the town of MORAVIA, where you will see stands of street vendors selling all types of leather goods and hand crafted items. This evening you will enjoy real Costa Rican hospitality at a HOME HOSTED DINNER. As the guest of a local family, you will have the opportunity to meet the local people and learn a little about their culture and lifestyle. Meals included **B D**

Day 3: San Jose
Today you will have an opportunity to enjoy a host of optional tours. Perhaps you would enjoy a visit to a local banana plantation along with a train ride on a historic Narrow Gauge Railroad. First, you will visit a banana plantation to learn how

the fruit is planted, harvested and shipped for exportation. Then you will board the historic Narrow Gauge Railroad, where you will journey slowly through coconut, banana and cocoa fields. Or, if you are adventurous, a thrilling optional whitewater rafting tour is available. For those who wish to spend the day in San Jose, there are a host of shops and boutiques or the many fine amenities at your hotel. Meals included **B**

Day 4: Poas Volcano - Sarchi - Oxcart Factory Tour - Villa Blanca
Today you will depart on a full day excursion to visit POAS VOLCANO NATIONAL PARK. You will travel northwest of San Jose through the city of Alajuela, past huge coffee plantations and many large flower greenhouses. Upon arrival at POAS VOLCANO NATIONAL PARK, you will have time to explore this volcano, one of the widest in the world. You will view the huge crater which features occasional geysers of ash and steam. Then you will travel to SARCHI, known as the predominant craft center of Costa Rica. Here you will visit an OXCART FACTORY where local artists hand paint oxcarts. You then travel to Villa Blanca, a charming lodge located in a pri-

TOUCAN

SARCHI, OXCART MAKER

Reprinted courtesy of Collette Travel Service, Inc.

ORCHIDS

PACIFIC COAST, SANDY BEACHES

vate cloud forest where you will enjoy accommodations in individual casitas. Meals included **B D**

Day 5: Villa Blanca - Puntarenas - Tortuga Island Cruise

This morning you will travel to the Pacific Coast, where you will be greeted by the long, sandy beaches of PUNTARENAS. Upon arrival, you will depart on a cruise to the GULF OF NICOYA. Your full day yacht excursion includes the magnificent scenery of the Gulf Islands as well as a stop on the deserted palm-shaded beach of TORTUGA ISLAND. Here you will have an included picnic lunch as well as time to snorkel and swim in the crystal clear waters of the Pacific. After your cruise, you will travel to a deluxe ocean front resort where you will overnight. Meals included **B L**

Day 6: Puntarenas

Today you will have a completely free day to relax and enjoy your beachfront resort hotel. Here you will have the opportunity to swim in the ocean, enjoy the hotel pool or participate in a host of activities. For those who wish, there will also be a number of optional tours available. One of the favorites is a visit to Carara Biological Reserve featuring a wide variety of

animals, flora and fauna. Whatever you choose, this is sure to be an enjoyable day. Meals included **B D**

Day 7: Puntarenas - Monteverde Cloud Forest Reserve

This morning you will travel to the MONTEVERDE CLOUD FOREST RESERVE. Here, nature, using the forces of wind, temperature and water, has created a unique environment which is usually covered by a haze of clouds. Here you will find over 2,000 plant species, 300 varieties of orchids, 400 different types of birds, and over 500 types of butterflies. The Cloud Forest is home of many exotic animals such as the toucanec, the world's largest population of quetzals, as well as the only known habitat of the golden toad. You will overnight in accommodations in the Cloud Forest Reserve. Meals included **B D**

Day 8: Monteverde - San Jose

Today you will return to San Jose where you will have an afternoon at leisure for any last minute sightseeing or shopping. This evening, you will enjoy a farewell dinner at your hotel. Meals included **B D**

Day 9: Depart San Jose

This morning you will depart Costa Rica with many pleasant memories of this beautiful country. Meals included **B**

COSTA RICA, CLOUD FOREST

YOUR HOTELS	
Day 1, 2, 3	Cariari Hotel, San Jose
Day 4	Villa Blanca Lodge, Villa Blanca
Day 5, 6	Fiesta Hotel, Puntarenas
Day 7	El Establo, Monteverde Cloud Forest
Day 8	Cariari Hotel, San Jose

On some dates, alternate hotels may be used.

Land Rates Per Person*

	Twin	Single	Triple	Child
Jan 1 - May 31	**$1149**	$1549	$1129	$749
Nov & Dec	**$1149**	$1549	$1129	$749
Rest of Year	**$999**	$1399	$979	$599

*Due to tour scheduling and limited air availability you are strongly advised to take advantage of Collette's air package on this tour.
*These prices are land only. Contact your agent for air fares.
*Sample air fares per person from Miami, effective at time of printing $425 varies seasonally (subject to change)
*Please note: Valid passports are required.
*All rates guaranteed upon deposit.
Departs — Most Thursdays

Jungle Odyssey

Add 3 nights for $399 Twin
land only

6 Meals: 2 Breakfasts, 2 Lunches, 2 Dinners

Extend your experience in Costa Rica with a jungle adventure to TORTUGUERO on the Caribbean Coast. Marvel at the jungle on a boat trip through a series of canals. You'll stay 2 nights at a tropical jungle lodge. Enjoy a day entirely free to view macaws, crocodiles, monkeys and many varieties of exotic plants. Giant turtles may also be seen June through October. Optional tours include a fishing expedition and a bird-watching/ natural history tour. The last night is spent in San Jose before departing for home.

AmericanAirlines®   5

GLOBUS. *First Class* ESCORTED

From the Amazon to the Andes

Brazil, Argentina, Chile

Maximum elevation on tour: SG:2,600ft SGX:11,800ft

Tour **SG** – 20 days

Tour **SGX** including 4-day Peru extension – 23 days

ALL THIS IS INCLUDED

- All scheduled flights if Globus issues the tickets
- All airport transfers, including baggage handling, for flights reserved as explained on page 9
- Services of a professional tour director (except days 20-22 on tour SGX, when you will be looked after by our local representatives in Peru)
- First-class hotels listed below or equivalent (see page 5). Twin-bedded rooms with private bath or shower, hotel taxes, service charges and tips for baggage handling
- 18 American breakfasts (B); 3 lunches (L); 9 dinners (D) with a special dinner at a

Churrascaria including a samba show in Rio, steak dinner and *gaucho* entertainment in Buenos Aires, and farewell dinner in Santiago
- Sightseeing with local guides in Manaus, Rio de Janeiro, Iguassu Falls, Buenos Aires, Santiago
- Cablecar ride up Sugarloaf Mountain; Corcovado Mountain by cog railway; Lake District cruise crossing
- Inside visits as shown in UPPER-CASE LETTERS in the tour description, including admission charges where applicable
- Globus travel bag and travel documents

Day 1, Mon. OVERNIGHT FLIGHT TO MANAUS, BRAZIL. The tour begins aboard a wide-bodied jet with an evening flight to Manaus.

Day 2, Tue. MANAUS. Arrive in Manaus in the early hours of the morning. Time to rest at the hotel before a late-morning city tour. Located in the densest part of the Amazon jungle, modern day Manaus still retains vestiges of its glory days of the rubber boom period. Visit the famous OPERA HOUSE which was built wholly from materials imported from Europe, the MUSEUM OF NATURAL SCIENCES and the INDIAN MUSEUM, displaying a fascinating way of life of a bygone era. (B,D)

Day 3, Wed. MANAUS. The highlight of your stay in Manaus: a full day "Meeting of the Waters" tour. The trip starts at the Porto Flutuante, the floating port of Manaus, where the English Custom House can be seen. Cruise from here to the confluence of the chocolate-colored Rio Negro and the yellow-grey Rio Solimoes, together forming the mighty Amazon. For four miles these two different colored rivers flow side by side but

never mix! After lunch on the river, a stop to explore a JUNGLE ISLAND with fascinating native flora and fauna. Return to the hotel late afternoon. (B,L)

Day 4, Thu. MANAUS-RIO DE JANEIRO. Some free time still in the morning before the transfer to Manaus airport. An evening arrival in Rio. (B)

Day 5, Fri. RIO DE JANEIRO. A full day dedicated to touring Rio's famous sights. First, a drive by its renowned beaches – Leblon, Ipanema and Copacabana – leading to the base of famous 1,300-foot SUGARLOAF MOUNTAIN. From here ascend by cable car to the summit, where spectacular vistas of the city can be enjoyed. Rio's landmark – STATUE OF CHRIST – crowns the mountain of Corcovado, a jagged peak rising 2,400 feet from the thronging city below. A scenic ride by cog railway leads to the top offering another perspective of Rio... a breathtaking 360-degree panorama of the bustling downtown area and Guanabara Bay. Lunch today is at Sol e Mar, one of Rio's well-known restaurants. (B,L)

Day 6, Sat. RIO DE JANEIRO. As the day is free, why not join our optional "tropical islands" excursion: a cruise along Rio's coast with a stop at one of the many islands dotting the shoreline. Buffet lunch included. This evening a visit to a "Churrascaria" for a feast of unlimited barbecued meats marinated and roasted over charcoal in true Brazilian style. Then, on to a Samba Show, where the color, animation and the sheer vitality of this city come to life in a highly-entertaining extravaganza. (B,D)

Day 7, Sun. RIO DE JANEIRO. No activities have been scheduled today to leave you completely free. Perhaps take our optional outing to visit the historic city of Petropolis: a mountain resort and site of the former summer palace of Emperor Dom Pedro II. For the shoppers: Rio is well-known for its jewelry, leather goods and lacework, and the many street markets across the city are fun to explore. For dinner this evening, try a local specialty in one of the many fine restaurants in downtown, or the Botafogo and Flamengo quarters. (B)

Day 8, Mon. RIO DE JANEIRO-IGUASSU FALLS. Arrive in Iguassu Falls by late morning, in time for lunch at your hotel. The afternoon is dedicated to touring the magnificent horseshoe of waterfalls. The spectacle of this 2.5 miles of torrential downpour – with some cataracts thundering down 250 feet to the basin – is nothing short of hypnotic. The clouds of spray, the incessant roar and the surrounding luxuriant tropical growth contribute to make this place a true natural wonder. (B,L)

Day 9, Tue. IGUASSU FALLS. A free day to further enjoy the sights and activites available in Iguassu. A highly recommended optional outing is the visit to Itaipu Dam, on the border with Paraguay. This massive hydroelectric plant – an impressive engineering feat – is a joint venture between Brazil and Paraguay. Another suggested activity: a thrilling helicopter ride offering a unique aerial perspective of the Falls... ideal for photography and video buffs. (B,D)

Day 10, Wed. IGUASSU FALLS-BUENOS AIRES, ARGENTINA. A morning transfer for the flight to Buenos Aires, with some free time in the afternoon to relax. Savor the atmosphere of this cosmopolitan city on the included evening excursion. Dinner at a popular restaurant, offering the best Argentinean steaks and regional specialties, is followed by a night club revue featuring Latin America's sensuous Tango and a thrilling performance by native gauchos. (B,D)

Day 11, Thu. BUENOS AIRES. On the first portion of the morning tour, your local expert focuses on the city's landmarks including the PLAZA DE MAYO, where the President's PINK HOUSE is located and the METROPOLITAN CATHEDRAL housing SAN MARTIN'S MAUSOLEUM. Also on the sightseeing agenda: historic San Telmo, the oldest neighborhood of Buenos Aires; the ornate COLON OPERA HOUSE; and lastly the elegant district of RECOLETA, which is the site of the famous cemetery where Argentina's eminent heroes are buried, including Eva Peron. The balance of the day is free. (B)

Day 12, Fri. BUENOS AIRES. A day at leisure for shopping or individual sightseeing. Also available is an optional excursion to the Pampas. An opportunity to experience the atmosphere of Argentinean country life with a visit to a working *estancia* (cattle ranch). Get acquainted with the lifestyle, folklore and traditions of the *gaucho* ranchhands. Then, enjoy a barbecue lunch and the warm hospitality of your hosts before returning to the city later in the afternoon. (B)

12 US

Day 13, Sat. BUENOS AIRES-BARILOCHE. Fly south to Bariloche today, set on the shores of fjord-like Nahuel Haupi, the center of Argentina's beautiful Lake District. With an early afternoon arrival, there is plenty of free time to start exploring Bariloche's pictureque town center. Stroll through the Municipality Square with its city hall and clock tower; and admire the famous chocolate factories – each built like a Swiss Chalet. (B,D)

Day 14, Sun. BARILOCHE. This chic alpine resort boasts some of the most glorious scenery in Argentina. Bring your cameras to capture the vistas of lakes and mountain peaks while touring the Llao Llao Peninsula, Lago Moreno and Lopez Bay. (B,D)

Day 15, Mon. BARILOCHE-PEULLA, CHILE. Board a boat for the cruise across Lake Nahuel Haupi, the first leg of the memorable journey – by boat and motorcoach – into Chile. The crossing today will take you through an area of pristine wilderness encompassing a myriad of emerald lakes, thick pine forests and snow-capped peaks. Overnight in the quaint village of Peulla. (B,D)

Day 16, Tue. PEULLA-PUERTO VARAS. The expedition continues with two scenic highlights punctuating the trip: the splendid Petrohue Falls and the white-crowned peak of Osorno Volcano. Arrive in Puerto Varas on Lake Llanquihue. Drive down the beautiful rosebush-lined streets of the lakeside town to reach your hotel. (B,D)

Day 17, Wed. PUERTO VARAS-PUERTO MONTT-SANTIAGO. A morning orientation tour of the nearby seaport of Puerto Montt – its harbor cluttered with fishing vessels and a busy waterfront lined with numerous fresh-seafood stalls. Transfer to the airport for the flight north to Santiago. Located in the center of the country and perched between the ocean and the Andes, it is no wonder that Santiago has evolved as the country's political, commercial and cultural capital. Step back into the 16th century as your local guide traces the city's history and heritage. During the morning tour visit LA MONEDA, the official Government Palace; the beautiful CLUB HIPICO RACETRACK; O'HIGGIN'S PARK, commemorating the country's first president; SAN CRISTOBAL HILL with its landmark statue of the Virgin Mary – a gift from France to Chile; and the main square – Plaza de Armas and the relic-filled CATHEDRAL. For dinner this evening, we highly recommend the local seafood – a rare treat; and be sure to sample the renowned Chilean wine. (B)

Day 18, Thu. SANTIAGO. The day is free for independent activities. The optional excursion to Valparaiso and Vina del Mar provides an opportunity to experience the country's coastal regions and countryside. A short drive from the bustling capital through the undulating hills of Chile's wine country to the historical port of Valparaiso and then nearby Vina del Mar. This chic resort with its spectacular coastline, palm tree-lined avenues and unique homes truly deserves its nickname, "The Pearl of the Pacific". Your tour director this evening hosts a special farewell dinner, a festive finale to a great touring adventure. (B,D)

Day 19, Fri. SANTIAGO-HOMEBOUND FLIGHT. A full day at leisure before the late evening transfer to the airport for your overnight flight back to Miami. (B)

Day 20, Sat. ARRIVE HOME. An early morning arrival in Miami to connect with your flight home.

▲ MANAUS. YAGUA INDIANS ALONG THE AMAZON

Tour SGX
PERU EXTENSION

Day 19, Fri. SANTIAGO-LIMA, PERU. A late evening flight to Lima. Upon arrival transfer to your hotel. (B)

Day 20, Sat. LIMA-CUZCO. A scenic early morning flight to Cuzco, the fascinating Andean city – once the center of the mighty Inca Empire. A short rest at your hotel is planned to acclimate to the 11,400-foot altitude. Learn of the mysteries surrounding the Incas with your local guide this afternoon. The tour visits the imposing CATHEDRAL, the SANTO DOMINGO MONASTERY, the nearby Inca Baths of TAMBOMACHAY and the semi-circular KENKO AMPHITHEATRE with it stone altars and labyrinth of passages. Stops will also be made at the ancient site of PUCA PUCARA and THE FORTRESS OF SACSAYHUAMAN, perched on a hillside overlooking Cuzco. It still remains unfathomable how and when this fortress of gigantic stones – with some blocks measuring more than 350 tons – was ever built. (B,D)

Day 21, Sun. CUZCO. MACHU PICCHU. Discover the treasures of legendary Machu Picchu – "The Lost City of the Incas". An early morning departure by train which zigzags its way through the lush Urubamba Valley. Then by coach for the last ascent to this sacred refuge, perched high above a steep valley coated in thick tropical jungle. Your local expert will recount the many accomplishments of this once sophisticated people as you tour the RUINS of towers, temples, a mausoleum, a prison and ceremonial baths. After the sightseeing, a buffet lunch at the Machu Picchu Inn before returning to Cuzco. (B,L)

Day 22, Mon. CUZCO-LIMA. A short flight back to Lima in the morning. A guided afternoon tour showcases the capital's colonial heritage. Visit the 11th-century SAN FRANCISCO MONASTERY with its unique cloisters, THE GOVERNMENT PALACE and THE CATHEDRAL both in the Plaza de Armas. A short drive south of the city to view the fine residential areas of San Isidro and Miraflores. Dinner this evening will be at a specially-selected restaurant before transferring to the airport for the flight home. (B,D)

Day 23, Tue. LIMA-HOMEBOUND FLIGHT. An early morning arrival in Miami.

Tours SG and SGX
DATES & PRICES

Departure number	Leave USA	Tour SG Air/land incl. US$	Tour SG Land only US$	Tour SGX Air/land incl. US$	Tour SGX Land only US$
0117	Mon 17-Jan	3662	2198	4657	2889
0131	Mon 31-Jan	3662	2198	4657	2889
0221	Mon 21-Feb	3662	2198	4657	2889
0314	Mon 14-Mar	3662	2198	4657	2889
0411	Mon 11-Apr	3633	2198	4628	2889
0509	Mon 09-May	3633	2198	4628	2889
0613	Mon 13-Jun	3633	2198	4628	2889
0711	Mon 11-Jul	3771	2198	4836	2889
0808	Mon 08-Aug	3633	2198	4628	2889
0905	Mon 05-Sep	3633	2198	4628	2889
0919	Mon 19-Sep	3633	2198	4628	2889
1003	Mon 03-Oct	3662	2198	4657	2889
1017	Mon 17-Oct	3662	2198	4657	2889
1107	Mon 07-Nov	3662	2198	4657	2889
1121	Mon 21-Nov	3662	2198	4657	2889
1219	Mon 19-Dec	3771	2198	4836	2889
1995					
0116	Mon 16-Jan	3771	2198	4836	2889
0130	Mon 30-Jan	3771	2198	4836	2889
0220	Mon 20-Feb	3771	2198	4836	2889

Inclusive Tour (IT) number: IT3RG1L007
Air/land inclusive price includes all flights from/to Miami

Land only price covers all land arrangements. For Tour SG: Manaus (day 2) to Santiago (day 19); Tour SGX: Manaus (day 2) to Lima (day 22)

Single room supplement: SG $1010; SGX $1184
Triple room reduction per person: SG $54; SGX $70

1995 departures are subject to itinerary and price modifications. Details will be available in August '94

APOLLO: TD*GG, **PARS:** G/PTS/GGX, **SABRE:** Y/TUR/QGG

ADD-ON AIR FARES

From	Add	From	Add
Chicago	$195	New Orleans	$335
Dallas/Ft. Worth	$385	New York	$150
Denver	$385	Phoenix	$420
Los Angeles	$240	Seattle	$520

All air fares are subject to change without notice. For travel from one of the cities listed above, add the roundtrip per person amount to the 'air/land' inclusive price. If your hometown is not listed, please check with your travel agent for the applicable add-on fare.

GLOBUS HOTELS

MANAUS Tropical Hotel de Manaus, **RIO DE JANEIRO** Sheraton Rio and Hotel and Towers, **IGUASSU FALLS** Tropical Hotel das Cataratas, **BUENOS AIRES** Sheraton Buenos Aires Hotel and Towers, **BARILOCHE** Crowne Plaza Resort Panamericano, **PEULLA** Hotel Peulla, **PUERTO VARAS** Hotel Cabanas del Lago, **SANTIAGO** Sheraton San Cristobal Hotel and Towers, **LIMA** El Pardo Hotel, **CUZCO** Libertador

GLOBUS *First Class* ESCORTED

Ecuador and the Galapagos Islands Cruise

Tour SE – 13 days

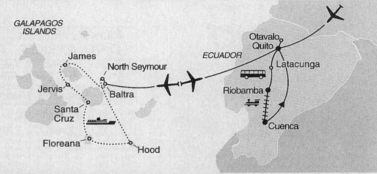

Maximum elevation on tour: 9,375ft

ALL THIS IS INCLUDED

- All scheduled flights if Globus issues the tickets
- All airport transfers, including baggage handling, for flights reserved as explained on page 9
- Services of a professional tour director
- First-class hotels on land listed below or equivalent (see page 5). Twin-bedded rooms with private bath or shower, hotel taxes, service charges and tips for baggage handling
- Cruise accommodations are based on Upper Deck outside cabins with 2 lower berths, each with private shower and toilet. Supplements for Boat Deck outside cabins are listed under "DATES & PRICES"
- 12 American breakfasts (B); 8 lunches (L); 10 dinners (D) with a special Ecuadorian dinner and folkore show, and a festive farewell dinner in Quito

- Train ride on the *Expreso Metropolitan* from Alausi to Cuenca; 5-day Galapagos Islands cruise aboard the *M.V. Santa Cruz* with visits to the islands of Baltra, North Seymour, Hood, Floreana, Santa Cruz and The Charles Darwin Research Station, Jervis and James. (Note: the itinerary and routing of the cruise is subject to change by the authorities of the Galapagos National Park)
- Sightseeing with local guides in Quito, Riobamba, Cuenca
- Visits to the Latacunga markets, the rug-making center of Guano, the Ingapirca Inca ruins, Otavalo, Calderon, Peguche, San Antonio del Ibarra
- Inside visits as shown in UPPER-CASE LETTERS in the tour description, including admission charges where applicable
- Globus travel bag and travel documents

Day 1, Thu. MIAMI-QUITO, ECUADOR. The tour begins with a comfortable jet flight to Quito, capital of Ecuador. After a late evening arrival, clear customs and transfer to your hotel.

Day 2, Fri. QUITO. Following the intense conflicts between the Incas and the Spanish during the early 16th century, a massive fire razed the city and ultimately destroyed its indigenous buildings. Quito soon became a pivotal city in Latin America for the conquistadores and numerous churches, monasteries and convents were built, in the lavish style of colonial baroque. Because of its well-preserved colonial legacy, the U.N. proclaimed Quito a World Cultural Heritage Site in 1978. On the morning tour, your local guide will showcase the city's treasures including: the LEGISLATIVE PALACE with its historic stone murals; the Independence Plaza bordered by The Cathedral and The Archbishop's Palace; La CAMPANIA CHURCH, with its stunning golden altars; and the BANCO CENTRAL ARCHEOLOGICAL MUSEUM. Lastly, a drive up Panecillo for a panoramic view over Quito and the surrounding Andean range. (B,D)

Day 3, Sat. QUITO-RIOBAMBA. Depart Quito early this morning and motor south along the Pan-American Highway. See the snow-capped cone of 19,613-foot Cotopaxi, the world's highest active volcano, before reaching the town of Latacunga. As today is market day, stroll the myriad stalls selling a variety of crafts... the hand-made ponchos and baskets here are magnificent! After lunch, continue to Ambato and visit the rug-making center of GUANO. Before reaching your hotel in Riobamba, a stop to visit the RELIGIOUS ART MUSEUM. (B,L,D)

Day 4, Sun. RIOBAMBA-EXPRESO TRAIN JOURNEY-CUENCA. At the Alausi rail station, board the *Expreso* train for a memorable journey through the Andean highlands. The trip, including lunch on board, starts with the ride down the Devil's Nose switchbacks to Sibambe. Leave the train in El Tambo for a visit to the INCA RUINS at the 15th-century settlement at Ingapirca. Then reboard the *Expreso* for Cuenca. (B,L,D)

Day 5, Mon. CUENCA. A full-day excursion, with lunch at a country inn, to visit Cuenca's most important COLONIAL BUILDINGS and fine CRAFT MARKETS. Also, a drive out to the Gualaceo Valley, Ecuador's main craft-producing center for ceramics, jewelery and the famous "Panama" hat. Before dinner this evening, take a leisurely stroll through Cuenca's public plazas, attractively lined with manicured flower beds, and explore the narrow cobblestone streets bordered by well-preserved white-washed buildings with large wooden doors and iron-work balconies. You will soon discover why Ecuadorians consider this city their most beautiful. (B,L,D)

Day 6, Tue. CUENCA-QUITO. Transfer today to Cuenca airport for the flight back to Quito. (B)

Day 7, Wed. QUITO. EXCURSION TO OTAVALO. Today's outing takes you into the beautiful "valley of the dawn" for a visit to OTAVALO. Cross the Equator Line this morning at Cayambe followed by a stop in CALDERON, where the famous "bread dolls" are made. Other visits include PEGUCHE, where local Indians weave beautiful scarves and ponchos. San Antonio del Ibarra, a WOODCARVING CENTER is also on the agenda. After lunch, return to Quito through the lush Tumbaco Valley with a stop at the SANCTUARY of El Quinche. For this evening's entertainment: a presentation of traditional dances and songs by the Jacchigua Folklore Ballet; and dinner will feature delectable dishes of Ecuadorian cuisine. (B,L,D)

Day 8, Thu. QUITO-BALTRA ISLE-GALAPAGOS CRUISE. A morning flight takes you out into the Pacific Ocean for your 5-day exploration of Charles Darwin's "natural zoo" – the remote archipelago of the Galapagos Islands. At Baltra Isle board the *M.V. Santa Cruz* and sail out to visit the first of these volcanic islands, Isla Seymour. This island is the best breeding grounds for seabirds – Darwin's finches, pelicans, red-pouched frigate birds and colonies of blue-footed boobies. (B,L,D)

Day 9, Fri. GALAPAGOS CRUISE. Step ashore at Punta Suarez this morning on Hood Island. Your naturalist will lead the way to observe a colony of red-spotted marine iguanas. Also on this island, you may spot the waved albatrosses acting out their vigorous mating dance. This afternoon drop anchor off the volcanic-cone-studded island of Floreana. The most famous inhabitants on Floreana are the magnificent pink flamingoes, whose favorite nesting grounds is the lagoon off Punta Cormorant. (B,L,D)

Day 10, Sat. GALAPAGOS CRUISE. The CHARLES DARWIN RESEARCH CENTER on Santa Cruz Island is one of the highpoints of today's activities. Visit the pens of giant tortoises located at the breeding and research section of the station. Plenty of time to tour the facility's museum, breeding-house, and perhaps take in a brief lecture given by one of the station guides. After a delightful lunch in the highlands, an opportunity to see these extraordinary giant tortoises in the wild. (B,L,D)

Day 11, Sun. GALAPAGOS CRUISE. Jervis Island's distinction is its red-sand beach. The morning walk leads to the island's interior lagoon full of bright pink flamingoes (the color derives from the shrimp they down for food). On the western shores of James Bay watch a colony of fur seals leap from the lava rocks of James Island into the cool waters of the Humbolt Current. Why not don a snorkel and swim around with these playful seals in their crystal pools and grottos... an experience you'll never forget! (B,L,D)

Day 12, Mon. GALAPAGOS CRUISE-BALTRA-QUITO. Return to Baltra, where your cruise adventure ends this morning and fly back to Quito. Your tour director hosts a festive farewell dinner this evening to celebrate the success of your tour and reminisce over a great "Galapagos expedition". (B,D)

Day 13, Tue. QUITO-MIAMI. After an early breakfast, transfer to Quito airport for the return flight to Miami to connect with your homebound flight. (B)

▶ *On the mainland the weather is surprisingly comfortable year-round. During the drier months, July to October, the temperatures will range from the 50s to the 70s F. The rest of the year: expect some afternoon showers. Pack comfortable light-weight clothes, plus a sweater or jacket for the cooler evenings – especially for the mountain regions. A light raincoat and/or umbrella is recommended for the wettest months. Good walking shoes are essential.*

The Galapagos Islands straddle the Equator, however, the tropical heat is tempered by the Pacific Ocean breezes. November through February are the slightly wetter months. The rest of the year, skies should be bright. Cruise clothing: essentials are sneakers, shorts, light-weight shirts, sunglasses, bathing suit, sunhat, a windbreaker or light jacket. And bring lots of film!

YOUR CRUISE SHIP

The 1500-ton **SANTA CRUZ** features broad sun decks, spacious lounge areas, a large dining room, cocktail lounge and bar, an observation deck for dolphin and whale watching, small speed boats (called *pangas*) for landing groups on the islands. The ship is fully-air conditioned and all cabins have private showers and toilets. Each evening, the ship's naturalist features a film/slide presentation and a briefing on upcoming activities.

▼ *MALE FRIGATE WITH INFLATED POUCH*

▼ *PORTRAIT OF AN IGUANA IN THE GALAPAGOS*

Tour SE: DATES & PRICES

Tour Code	Leave USA		Return USA		Air/land incl. US$	Land only US$
SE0120	Thu	20-Jan	Tue	01-Feb	2931	2198
SE0203	Thu	03-Feb	Tue	15-Feb	2931	2198
SE0224	Thu	24-Feb	Tue	08-Mar	2931	2198
SE0414	Thu	14-Apr	Tue	26-Apr	2931	2198
SE0519	Thu	19-May	Tue	31-May	2931	2198
SE0602	Thu	02-Jun	Tue	14-Jun	2931	2198
SE0630	Thu	30-Jun	Tue	12-Jul	2931	2198
SE0804	Thu	04-Aug	Tue	16-Aug	3008	2198
SE0818	Thu	18-Aug	Tue	30-Aug	2931	2198
SE0922	Thu	22-Sep	Tue	04-Oct	2931	2198
SE1117	Thu	17-Nov	Tue	29-Nov	2931	2198
SE1208	Thu	08-Dec	Tue	20-Dec	3008	2198

Air/land inclusive price includes all flights from/to Miami

Land only price covers land arrangements from Quito (day 1) to Quito (day 13) including domestic air fare from Cuenca to Quito

Our prices are based on twin "Upper Deck" outside cabins. Supplement for twin "Boat Deck" outside cabin: $115

Supplement for single room on land and single cabin (inside cabins only): $462

Reduction for triple room occupancy: available upon request.

Galapagos National Park Tax of $80 is additional and payable to your tour director.

APOLLO: TD*GG, **PARS:** G/PTS/GGX, **SABRE:** Y/TUR/QGG

ADD-ON AIR FARES

From	Add	From	Add
Chicago	$380	New Orleans	$260
Dallas/Ft. Worth	$315	New York	$150
Denver	$380	Phoenix	$395
Los Angeles	$410	Seattle	$455

All air fares are subject to change without notice. For travel from one of the cities listed above, add the roundtrip per person amount to the 'air/land' inclusive price. If your hometown is not listed, please check with your travel agent for the applicable add-on fare.

GLOBUS HOTELS

QUITO Hotel Colon, **RIOBAMBA** Hotel El Troje or La Andalusa, **CUENCA** Hotel Oro Verde la Laguna

▼ *FRIENDLY ECUADOREAN FOOD VENDORS*

COPPER CANYON RAIL TOURS

3

COPPER CANYON ROUND TRIP

Eight Days, Seven Nights—Escorted   IT3AM1ST05

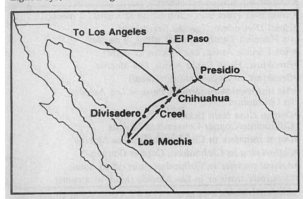

Tour begins and ends in Presidio, El Paso, Chihuahua or Los Angeles. Departs every Saturday except Christmas week (Dec. 18) and June, July and August which will depart on the following dates: June 12, 26; July 10, 24; and Aug. 14, 28. Escorted round trip Chihuahua to Chihuahua or Presidio to Presidio. Thirteen meals included.

ITINERARY:

FIRST DAY (Saturday): Upon arrival in Chihuahua, you will be met and transferred to Hotel San Francisco.

From Presidio: Meet at Sanborn's office at 1:00 p.m. (CDT). Ms. Stella McKeel will arrange car storage before your escort takes you to Chihuahua.

Note: During Standard Time (beginning Nov. 6 departure), meet at Sanborn's at noon CST.

SECOND DAY (Sunday): Morning sightseeing tour of Chihuahua, afternoon shopping tour. Accommodations at Hotel San Francisco. (BLD)

THIRD DAY (Monday): Depart from Chihuahua train station at 7:00 a.m. for ride into spectacular Sierra Madre. Arrive midafternoon at Divisadero for overnight at Hotel Divisadero, Posada Barrancas, or Mansion Tarahumara. Dinner included. (BD)

FOURTH DAY (Tuesday): Morning sightseeing along canyon rim. Board train after lunch for Los Mochis, arriving about 8:30 p.m. Transfer to Hotel Santa Anita. Breakfast and lunch at hotel are included. (BL)

FIFTH DAY (Wednesday): Sightseeing tour of Los Mochis and Topolobampo. Afternoon at leisure. (BL)

SIXTH DAY (Thursday): Board the train this morning for a ride through spectacular scenery. Arrive at Creel in late afternoon, and transfer to Parador de la Montana or Cascada Inn. Dinner tonight is included. (BD)

SEVENTH DAY (Friday): Plenty of time for sightseeing before boarding train to Chihuahua. Breakfast and lunch are included. Arrive Chihuahua in the evening and transfer to Hotel San Francisco. (BL)

EIGHTH DAY (Saturday): Departure transfer to the airport for your return flight, or to the bus station for return to Presidio.

TOUR INCLUDES:
- Full-time professional tour escort
- Hotel San Francisco, Chihuahua (3 nights, 3 meals)
- Hotel Divisadero, Posada Barrancas, or Mansion Tarahumara (1 night, 3 meals)
- Hotel Santa Anita, Los Mochis (two nights)
- Breakfast at Hotel Santa Anita, Los Mochis
- Two breakfasts on train (light box meals)
- Lunch in Los Mochis
- Parador de la Montana or Cascada Inn, Creel (1 night, 3 meals)
- Round trip bus transportation from Presidio, or
- Round trip air transportation between Los Angeles (AeroMexico) or El Paso (Leo Lopez Commuter Airlines) and Chihuahua
- Round trip deluxe class train tickets Chihuahua/Los Mochis/Chihuahua
- Depot transfers in Chihuahua and Los Mochis
- Airport transfers in Chihuahua
- Sightseeing in Chihuahua, Creel, Copper Canyon, Los Mochis, and Topolobampo
- All hotel taxes
- Meal taxes and gratuities on all included meals
- Luggage handling at Chihuahua airport, depots and hotels
- Complimentary copy of *Barranca Del Cobre*, definitive new 96 page illustrated book on the Copper Canyon, its history, culture, topography, and detailed railroad log

DEPARTURE GATEWAY	PRICE PER PERSON		
	Double	Triple	Single
Chihuahua	$1028	$859	$1289
Presidio	1093	934	1354
El Paso	1238	1084	1508
Los Angeles	1452	1299	1719
Optional Night:			
El Paso Hilton	42	38	84
Extra Night in Chihuahua:			
Hotel San Francisco	47	34	89

Approaching the 86th tunnel, over a mile long.

MEXICO'S HEARTLAND

15

COLONIAL MEXICO

Nine Days, Eight Nights—Escorted   IT3GU1STT170, IT3MX1SCOL9
                                    1T3C01SCOL9, IT3AM1SCOL9

Mexico City / San Miguel de Allende / Guanajuato /
Morelia / Uruapan / Guadalajara
Daily Arrivals

TOUR INCLUDES:

- One night hotel at Aristos or Galeria Plaza in Mexico City (EP)
- Airport arrival transfer in Mexico City
- One night hotel at Real de Minas in San Miguel (EP)
- Two nights hotel at Parador San Javier in Guanajuato (EP)
- One night hotel at Posada de la Soledad in Morelia (EP)
- One night hotel at Mansion de Cupatitzio in Uruapan (EP)
- Two nights hotel at De Mendoza or Hyatt Regency in Guadalajara (EP)
- All entrance and sightseeing fees including boat trip to Janitzio Island at Lake Patzcuaro
- Sightseeing in Tula, Tepotzotlan, San Juan del Rio, Queretaro, San Miguel de Allende, Guanajuato, Morelia, Patzcuaro, Uruapan, Lake Chapala, and Guadalajara
- Private car transportation with driver/guide
- Mexico tourism tax
- Departure transfer in Guadalajara

ITINERARY:

Day 1: Our representative will meet your flight in Mexico City and transfer you to your hotel.

Day 2: After breakfast, you will travel to Tepotzotlan and to Tula for sightseeing. Late afternoon arrival in San Miguel where you will overnight at the Real de Minas. Evening is for leisure.

Day 3: Early morning sightseeing in San Miguel; then on to Guanajuato with a brief visit to the Hidalgo Museum in Dolores Hidalgo. On the way to Guanajuato, you'll visit the Valenciana mines and church. Your host for the next two nights will be the Parador San Javier. Evening at leisure.

Day 4: After breakfast, you will visit the *Plaza de la Union*, Juarez Theater, Pantheon and statue of Pipila, the *Alhondiga de Granaditas*, a museum devoted to the state's history, and other points of interest, including the subterranean automobile passageway which once was the *Rio Guanajuato's* riverbed. Evening at leisure.

Day 5: Last minute sightseeing before departure to Morelia. Mexico's most famous living artist, Rufino Tamayo, calls Morelia the "best Mexican city," for by and large it has kept the architecture and traditions of the colonial period. You will visit the lovely *Plaza de los Martires*, the city cathedral, the College of San Nicolas, and the massive colonial aqueduct. Your host for tonight is the Posada de la Soledad in Morelia.

Day 6: Explore Patzcuaro, including a boat trip on Lake Patzcuaro to Janitzio Island, famous for the butterfly-net fishermen. Then you'll drive to Uruapan, one of the most beautiful cities in the state of Michoacan, and famous for its lacquerware. Your accommodations tonight are at the lovely colonial *Mansion del Cupititzio*, near the park.

Day 7: You're on the road today, past the south side of Lake Chapala for a brief visit to Ajijic before you enter Guadalajara, where you will spend the next two nights.

Day 8: You'll spend today sightseeing in romantic Guadalajara. Blessed with eternally Spring-like weather, this second-largest city in Mexico delights the senses with many inviting *plazas* and flower-lined boulevards. You will visit the famous pottery and ceramics center of Tlaquepaque, as well as other points of interest, such as the cathedral, *Libertad* (the nation's largest market), the government palace, and the museum.

Day 9: *Adios* to Mexico! Your escort will call for you in time to reach the airport for your flight home.

PRICE PER PERSON	Double	Triple	Single
Aristos/De Mendoza			
Two Passengers	$1597	N/A	$1999
Three Passengers	1293	$1232	1692
Four Passengers	1139	1077	1537
Galeria Plaza/Hyatt Regency			
Two Passengers	1783	N/A	2189
Three Passengers	1468	1299	1877
Four Passengers	1314	1147	1722

Reprinted courtesy of Sanborn Tours.

YUCATAN PENINSULA   23

MAYAN EMPIRE

Eleven Days, Ten Nights—Escorted   IT3GU1STT174, IT3MX1EMP11
                                     IT3CO1EMP11, IT3AM1EMP11

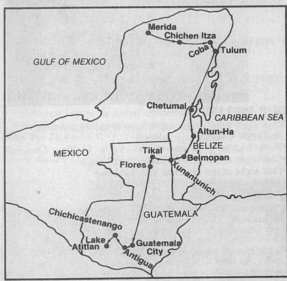

Mexico / Belize / Guatemala

Departures: First and third Saturdays of each month.

*Tour will also operate beginning in Guatemala City on first and third Tuesdays Jan., Apr., May, Jul., Oct. and Dec.; on second and fourth Tuesdays Feb., Mar., June, Aug., Sep. and Nov.

Note: When beginning tour in Guatemala, there will be one less night in Guatemala and one more night in Merida.

TOUR INCLUDES:

- *Airport transfers in Merida, Tikal and Guatemala*
- *Baggage assistance throughout*
- *One night in Merida at Hotel Los Aluxes or Conquistador*
- *One night in Coba at Villas Arqueologicas or Meson del Marquez in Valladolid*
- *One night in Chetumal, Hotel Los Cocos*
- *One night in San Ignacio (Belize), Hotel San Ignacio or Windy Hill Cottages*
- *Two nights in Flores (Guatemala), Hotel Villa Maya*
- *Two nights in Guatemala City, Hotel Conquistador Sheraton*
- *One night in Chichicastenango (Guatemala), Hotel Santo Tomas*
- *One night at Lake Atitlan at Del Lago or similar*
- *Six breakfasts, five lunches, five dinners*
- *Sightseeing: In Mexico— Merida city tour, Chichen Itza, Coba, Tulum; In Belize— Altun-Ha and Xunantinich; In Guatemala— Tikal, city tour of Guatemala City, Antigua, Chichicastenango, Lake Atitlan with motor launch excursion*
- *Air transportation— Flores (Tikal) / Guatemala City*
- *Hotel and included meal taxes·*

ITINERARY:

Day 1 *(Saturday):* Our representative will meet your flight in Merida, and transfer you to your hotel. Evening at leisure.

Day 2 *(Sunday):* After breakfast you will have a brief city tour of Merida before departing for the once great Mayan city of Chichen Itza. After exploring some of the magnificent buildings, you will continue to Coba, where ancient Mayan buildings stand between two large, green lakes. Accommodations tonight are at the charming Villa Arqueologicas or Meson del Marquez.   *(BLD)*

Day 3 *(Monday):* This morning, explore the castle, pyramid and ball court of Coba, then drive to the walled Mayan city of Tulum. Afterward you continue on to exotic Chetumal, on the border between Mexico and Belize. Your hotel for the night is Chetumal's finest, Los Cocos.   *(BLD)*

Day 4 *(Tuesday):* Crossing into the relatively unknown country of Belize early today, your first stop is at the ruins of Altun Ha, an ancient trading center where the largest piece of Mayan jade ever to be discovered was found, the spectacular carved head of the Maya sun god Kinich Ahav. After lunch, a visit to the archaeological museum in the capital city of Belmopan, then continue on to robust San Ignacio, where you will spend the night at the San Ignacio Hotel, or Windy Hill Cottages.   *(BLD)*

Day 5 *(Wednesday):* Today you will visit the 1400-year-old ruins of Xunantunich, a breathtakingly beautiful archaeological site towering above the Mopan River. Then it is across the Guatemalan border and on to Flores. Tonight's accommodations are at the Hotel Villa Maya in Flores.   *(BLD)*

Day 6 *(Thursday):* Today you will explore the unforgettable ruins of Tikal, set in the middle of 225 miles of jungle: thousands of intricately carved stelae and alters and pyramids, palaces and courtyards which create complex mazes that run for miles. In the late afternoon, return to Flores for the night.   *(BLD)*

Day 7 *(Friday):* This morning you will have a boat trip on the Peten Itza Lake, visiting the ruins of Tayazal, once a principal city of the Mayas. This city is located on an island in the lake and due to its inaccessibility, it was the last stronghold of the Mayas, not falling to the conquest of the Spaniards until 1697. In the afternoon, you will transfer to the airport in Flores for your flight to Guatemala City. Upon arrival, you will be transferred to the Hotel Conquistador Sheraton.   *(B)*

Day 8 *(Saturday):* Depart this morning from your hotel for a leisurely drive to Antigua, the old colonial capital of Guatemala. Visit the historic Colonial Museum, the Palace of the Captains General, old monasteries, beautiful ornate churches, and view the primitive pottery works and footlooms in this ancient city. This drive takes you through some of the world's most beautiful mountain areas. Arrive at the Santo Tomas Hotel in Chichicastenango for overnight stay.

Day 9 *(Sunday):* This is market day in "Chichi." You can browse and shop in the famous and colorful Indian open air marketplace— an ideal choice for bargain hunters. A short visit will follow to the 400-year-old church of Santo Tomas, where you can witness a most unusual local Indian ceremony which combines the worship of the old Mayan gods with the Christian religion. After this visit, you will transfer on to Lake Atitlan for an overnight stay at the Hotel Del Lago or similar.

Day 10 *(Monday):* This morning, you will have a launch excursion to the picturesque Indian village of Santiago de Atitlan. Return to Guatemala City and the Hotel Conquistador Sheraton for the night.

Day 11 *(Tuesday):* Your transfer escort will call for you at your hotel in time to reach the airport for the flight home.

PRICE PER PERSON	Double	Triple	Single
4/15-30; 5/28-6/1; 7/1-12/15	$2038	$1827	$2207
5/1-27; 6/2-30	1834	1644	1986

Note: This tour operates with a minimum of 2 passengers.

Reprinted courtesy of Sanborn Tours.

■ REVIEW—MEXICO, CENTRAL AMERICA, AND SOUTH AMERICA

1. Name the greatest river system of South America. Where does it flow?

2. Who were the Incan people? Where did they live? Where are the primary Incan sites that today's tourist may visit?

3. Where is the Yucatan Peninsula? Why is it touristically important?

4. What Central American nation has the greatest percentage of Indians in its population? Describe its touristic importance.

5. Where and what is the Panama Canal? What is its touristic importance?

6. Where are the three Guianas? What is their political status and touristic importance?

7. Where are Quito and La Paz? What do the two cities have in common?

8. Where was the Aztec culture concentrated? Describe its touristic importance.

9. Describe the factors that make Brazil the leading nation of Latin America.

10. Identify the major ethnic and racial differences in Brazil.

11. Where are the major ski areas in Latin America located?

12. Where are the major beach and resort areas in Latin America located?

13. Describe four areas of scenic beauty in Latin America.

8

Caribbean

■ ISLANDS IN THE SEA

The landform of the Caribbean region is a great arc of islands called the Antilles that stretch from Florida to northeastern South America and form the eastern border of the Caribbean Sea. On the west, the Caribbean blends into the Gulf of Mexico, bounded by the United States and Mexico.

The northern and larger Antilles, the Greater Antilles, include Cuba, Jamaica, the Cayman Islands, Hispaniola (shared by Haiti and the Dominican Republic), and Puerto Rico. The Lesser Antilles, a shorter chain of small islands, continue southward to the coast of South America. The northern part is known as the Leeward Islands and the southern part as the Windward Islands. Most of the Caribbean lies within the tropics, but the climate varies with the local topography and prevailing winds. The Caribbean islands are also known as the West Indies.

History

British and French interest in establishing tropical colonies, where sugar cane could be grown to yield sugar for export,

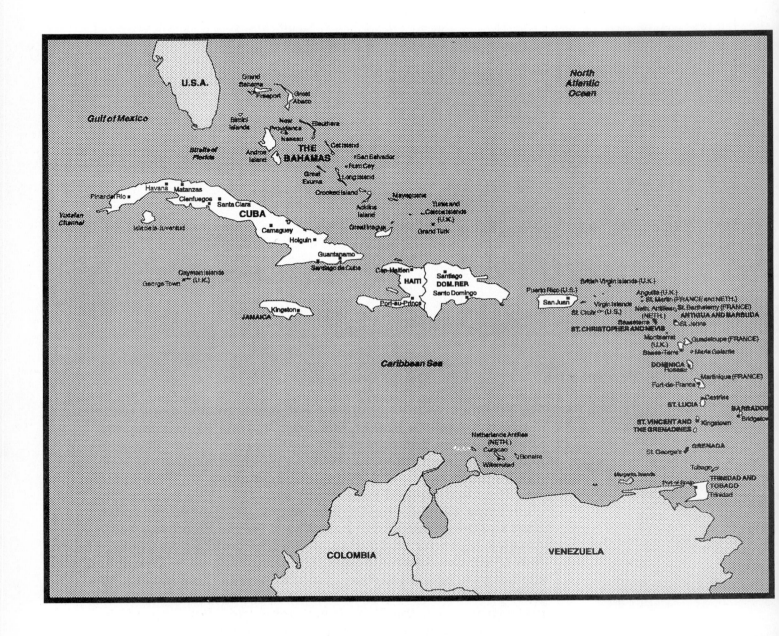

were realized at the expense of Spain during the 17th and 18th centuries. The British secured Jamaica, Trinidad, and a number of the Lesser Antilles, Belize (former British Honduras) on the Central American mainland, Guyana (former British Guiana) in northeastern South America, and the Falkland Islands. The French got Haiti, some of the Lesser Antilles, and French Guiana. The Dutch got some small islands and Suriname (former Dutch Guiana).

Later, in the present century, the United States acquired Puerto Rico, the adjacent American Virgin Islands, and the Panama Canal Zone. A sugar cane boom in the Caribbean islands and the coastal districts of northeastern South America was based upon the importation of large numbers of slaves from Africa as labor. Historians estimate that about half of all slaves shipped from Africa went to Brazil and the Guianas and another 40 percent to the Caribbean islands.

In the Greater Antilles, Haiti won its freedom in 1791, the Dominican Republic in the early 19th century, and Cuba in 1899. However, most other Caribbean islands, Belize, British Guiana, and Dutch Guiana did not become independent until after World War II. Scattered British, French, and Dutch colonial dependencies remain, especially in the Lesser Antilles.

Bermuda and the Bahamas—Islands in the Atlantic

Bermuda, still a British colony, and the Bahamas, a former colony, are not actually in the Caribbean Sea, but rather in the Atlantic Ocean. The Bahamas are at the northern end of the island chain described above, beginning just east of the Florida coast. Bermuda is an archipelago of seven main islands and many smaller ones. The archipelago is 26 miles long and 1 and one-half miles wide (at its widest point) and is located approximately 570 miles east of North Carolina. Both are covered in this chapter because their touristic activities are quite similar to those of Caribbean islands.

Climate

With the exception of Bermuda, climatic conditions in the region are subtropical and tropical. Winter temperatures at sea level throughout the Antilles are usually about 80° Fahrenheit, whereas summer conditions are somewhat warmer. The climate in the mountains is, of course, cooler. The rainy season (usually afternoon showers) is in late summer and fall. Sea breezes moderate the effects of the temperature on the beaches.

■ THE GREATER ANTILLES

CUBA

Official Name: Republic of
  Cuba

Language: Spanish

Area: 44,218 square miles

Time Zone: GMT –5

National Airline: Cubana

Capital: Havana

Currency: Cuban peso (CUP)

Population: 10,732,000

Documentation: Special
  permit

Cuba, which has the largest territory and population of any Caribbean island nation, lies only 90 miles south of Key West, Florida. A Communist nation since 1959, it has an agricultural economy shaped around the production of sugar from sugar cane for export.

The collapse of trade with and aid from the former Communist bloc has crippled the Cuban economy. As a partial remedy, the government ended its state monopoly of production, employment, and sales in 1993 by authorizing limited individual enterprise for profit. It also removed the ban on owning and using American dollars and other foreign hard currency. Foreign tourism is being promoted.

For political reasons, many Cubans have fled to the United States. The United States government curbs travel to Cuba, making it "off limits" to United States tourists. Paradoxically, the United States still maintains a strong naval base at Guantanamo, on the southeast coast, through an earlier treaty arrangement.

Areas of Touristic Importance. Cuba is expected to open up to United States tourists within the next few years. At that time, there will be a surge of interest, especially by cruise lines, in providing travel to Cuba. It will, however, be many years before Cuba can reach the quality or quantity of tourism opportunities available before 1959.

The capital, Havana, on the northwest coast, has a population of more than two million, about four times the number in Santiago de Cuba, the largest city of southeastern Cuba. Old Havana has maintained its Spanish colonial charm, flavor, and architecture. Cuba offers a magnificent coastline with deep bays and sandy beaches.

JAMAICA

Language: English
Area: 4,232 square miles
Time Zone: GMT –5
National Airline: Air Jamaica
Capital: Kingston
Currency: Jamaican dollar
Population: 2,489,000 million
Documentation: Citizenship proof

Ninety miles south of Cuba is Jamaica, a former British colony. It is somewhat small, about 150 miles east-west, and very mountainous. Its Blue Mountains are famous for their high-quality coffee, which is a favorite purchase of visitors.

Most of the population is black or black-white mixture. The capital, Kingston, on the south coast, is the largest city and main port. Montego Bay, on the northwest coast, is a well-developed resort area. The national economy depends on the export of sugar and bauxite (aluminum ore) and earnings from the tourist industry, mainly involving American tourists.

Areas of Touristic Importance. Jamaica offers a wider variety of activities than most island destinations. The mountainous terrain provides a beautiful backdrop for its beach resorts. Rivers and waterfalls, in addition to beaches and the sea, keep visitors interested and active. Excellent golf facilities are also available in most of the island's resort areas.

Many Jamaican hotels in the major resort areas feature an "all-inclusive" concept, in which rates include accommodations, all meals, wine with meals, free liquor, and the use of all sports equipment and facilities. Although this concept (without liquor) was pioneered by Club Mediterrannee and is featured at Club Med vacation villages throughout the world, the concentration of all-inclusive resorts is unique to Jamaica.

Jamaica also has a large number of villa rentals. Visitors choosing this type of property can rent a house, usually with private swimming pool, and have a private staff (maid/cook and gardener) to serve them. Jamaican villas vary from small 2-bedroom homes to large 5-bedroom facilities. Some of the most luxurious even have private tennis courts.

Montego Bay (or Mo'Bay as it is locally known) is the largest resort area, with sandy beaches and a variety of first class and deluxe hotels. Located on the northern coast, it is

Dunn's River Falls, Ocho Rios
Photo: Courtesy Jamaica Tourist Board

the site of Jamaica's largest international airport. Visitors destined for Negril, Ocho Rios, and Port Antonio also arrive at Montego Bay. It is also a major port of call for many Caribbean cruises.

Doctor's Cave Beach is an especially popular location. Another popular attraction is Rose Hall, a restored Great House once owned by the "White Witch," who killed three husbands before meeting a violent death herself.

Ocho Rios is Jamaica's second largest resort area. It is on the north shore of the island about 40 miles (one hour's drive) east of Montego Bay International Airport.

Walking up Dunn's River Falls near Ocho Rios, rafting on the Martha Brae River, enjoying Shaw Park Botanical Gardens, or sightseeing along beautiful mountain roads provide alternatives to the normal sun and fun of beach resorts.

Other, smaller resort areas on the island include Runaway Bay, Port Antonio, and Negril. Runaway Bay is located between Montego Bay and Ocho Rios, whereas Port Antonio is east of Ocho Rios. Negril is on Jamaica's west coast and originally gained fame for its appeal to the "alternative" life styles of the 60s and 70s with its nude beach. All these areas feature excellent beaches and a variety of resort hotels.

Kingston, Jamaica's capital, is located on the southern coast of the island. Known as Port Royal in the pirate days, when Kingston was known as a rich and wicked city, its natural harbor has made it Jamaica's largest city and commercial center. Its lack of good beaches prevents it from being a major tourist area.

THE CAYMAN ISLANDS

Language: English

Area: 102 square miles

Time Zone: GMT –5

National Airline: Cayman Airways

Capital: Georgetown

Currency: C. I. dollar (CID)

Population: 17,000

Documentation: Citizenship proof

This British colony includes three islands—Grand Cayman, Little Cayman, and Cayman Brac. They were first sighted by Columbus on his last voyage in 1503. He called them "Las Tortugas," the islands of the turtles. In 1788, ten ships were sunk at Gun Bay off Grand Cayman. Tourism and international banking are the only island industries.

Areas of Touristic Importance. The Caymans attract those seeking relaxation, sun, and sea. Grand Cayman attracts the largest numbers, and is noted for having the finest beaches in the Caribbean. West Bay Beach, stretching north from Georgetown, is better known as "Seven Mile Beach" because of its length. The many shipwrecks offshore serve as home for an abundance of tropical fish and attract both snorkelers and scuba divers. The Cayman Turtle Farm is the world's first commercial green turtle project.

A popular visit is to the post office in Hell—a village on Grand Cayman—to obtain cards and letters with its unique postmark.

HAITI

Official Name: Republic of Haiti

Language: French

Area: 10,579 square miles

Time Zone: GMT –5

National Airline: Air Haiti

Capital: Port-au-Prince

Currency: Gourde (GOU)

Population: 6,286,000 million

Documentation: Citizenship proof

Haiti occupies the western half of Hispaniola, the large island east of Cuba. It is one of the poorest and least developed nations in the Americas, a result, in part, of past repressive governments. Some American manufacturing plants have been attracted to Haiti in recent years by the cheap labor, and, alternatively, a large number of Haitians have emigrated to the United States, especially to Florida. A repressive government was ousted by American military intervention in 1994.

Most Haitians are black and speak the official language, French. The main population is on lowlands in western Haiti, where the capital, Port-au-Prince, is located. The interior is mountainous.

Areas of Touristic Importance. Although there are some beach resorts near Port-au-Prince, the area is not a prime tourist destination because of the poverty and most recent dictatorial government. Voodoo is still practiced in Haiti. Native handicrafts and wood carvings are readily available.

Port-au-Prince and Cap Haitien are on the itineraries of some cruise ships in peaceful political times. A visit to the Citadelle is a popular excursion for tourists visiting Cap Haitien. Located on top of a mountain, the Citadelle is a replica of a European palace from which King Henri ruled his poor nation with exaggerated pomp and splendor. Gambling casinos are available in Haiti.

DOMINICAN REPUBLIC

Language: Spanish
Area: 18,704 square miles
Time Zone: GMT –4
Capital: Santo Domingo
Currency: DR peso
Population: 7,384,000
Documentation: Citizenship
 proof

This nation is Haiti's neighbor, occupying two-thirds of the island of Hispaniola. The interior is mountainous; the fertile plains in the north and east contain most of the population. The capital, Santo Domingo, is on the south coast. Some 15 percent of the population is white; the rest are black or black-white mixture. Sugar, coffee, and nickel are principal exports.

Areas of Touristic Importance. Santo Domingo, the capital city, hosts several important historical sites. First among them is the Cathedral of Santa Maria La Menor. Founded in 1540, it is the oldest cathedral in the Americas. The remains of Christopher Columbus are buried here. The Alcazar of Diego Columbus was built in 1514 for Christopher's son, the second Spanish governor of the island. Recently restored, it provides an accurate reflection of life at the height of the Spanish Em-

Atlantic Coast, Dominican Republic
Photo: Courtesy Dominican Tourist Information Center

pire in the Americas. This is a thriving city with shopping, modern hotels, gambling casinos and cultural attractions.

Boca Chica, 19 miles from Santo Domingo, has one of the most beautiful harbors and beaches on the island. Swimming and fishing are excellent. The most popular seaside resort areas are Puerto Plata on the north coast and La Romana on the southeast coast. Puerto Plata is also the nation's third largest city and has its own international airport. La Romana is most noted for the deluxe Casa de Campo resort and for the village of Chavon, an artist colony built in medieval style.

PUERTO RICO

Language: Spanish, English
Area: 3,435 square miles
Time Zone: GMT –4
Capital: San Juan
Currency: United States dollar
Population: 3,566,000

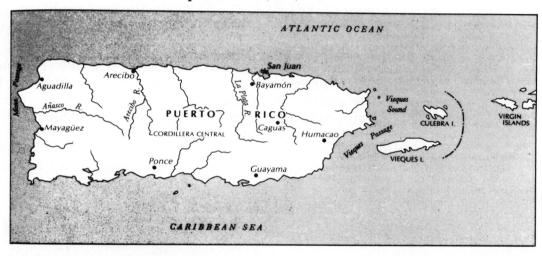

Puerto Rico, lying east of the Dominican Republic, is part of the United States. It was acquired from Spain in 1898, and in 1952 voted to become a Commonwealth in which Puerto Ricans are American citizens but have special taxation and political privileges.

With a population of about 3.5 million, Puerto Rico was formerly dependent on sugar exports to the United States mainland, but it now depends on American manufacturing investment, government support, and tourists. San Juan, 1,600 miles from New York, is the capital and largest city. Large numbers of Puerto Ricans have migrated to New York and other eastern American cities.

Areas of Touristic Importance. San Juan is both a commercial center and beach resort. Its historical quarter, Old San Juan, is a 35-block area that is now more than 450 years old. Musts for visitors are El Morro, Ft. San Cristobal, and the Great City Wall. El Morro, completed in 1785 is a fortress guarding access to San Juan's important, natural harbor. The old city is crammed with interesting shops and boutiques as well as native and continental restaurants. San Juan is quite cosmopolitan and its nightclubs attract European and South American star entertainment. Gambling casinos can be found in most major hotels and are open from late afternoon to early morning.

The main resort area stretches eastward along the Caribbean from downtown to the San Juan International Airport. Luquillo Beach, one of the finest in the area, is located a few miles east of the airport and is open to the public. Deluxe resort hotels and golf courses can also be found in the Dorado area, about 30 miles west of the city.

The island features a variety of scenery and vegetation ranging from beach to mountain and from rain forest to cactus-covered desert. El Yunque, a true tropical rain forest, is just 25 miles from San Juan.

Ponce and Mayaguez, on the south side of the island, attract relatively few visitors even though they offer pleasant alternatives to the hustle and bustle of busy San Juan. The Ponce Museum of Art, designed by Edward Durrell Stone, has one of the finest collections of art in Latin America. The

San Geronimo, San Juan, Puerto Rico
Photo: Courtesy Puerto Rico Tourism New Bureau

Mayaguez Institute of Tropical Agriculture contains the largest collection of tropical plants in the Americas.

■ THE LESSER ANTILLES

Many of the small islands and island groups east and south of Puerto Rico have achieved independence. These include the former British colonies of Antigua and Barbuda, St. Kitts and Nevis, Dominica, St. Lucia, St. Vincent and the Grenadines, Barbados, Grenada, and Trinidad and Tobago. The British Virgin Islands, Anguilla, and Montserrat remain British dependencies. Some form of political integration of St. Lucia, St. Vincent, Grenada, and Dominica is under discussion.

However, French political control persists in Martinique, Guadeloupe, and St. Martin; the Dutch still control Aruba, Bonaire, and Curacao as well as St. Maarten, Saba, and St. Eustatius. Interestingly, French St. Martin and Dutch St. Maarten share the same island. The Virgin Islands, due east of Puerto Rico, are divided into American and British portions.

Most islands have predominantly black populations, are poor, and rely on income from sugar or other export crops or materials and international tourism, especially from the United States. Trinidad is distinctive for its large Asian (Indian) population and its petroleum resource and exports.

UNITED STATES VIRGIN ISLANDS

Official Name: Virgin Islands of the United States

Language: English

Area: 133 square miles

Time Zone: GMT –4

Capital: Charlotte Amalie

Currency: United States dollar

Population: 101,809

Documentation: Citizenship proof

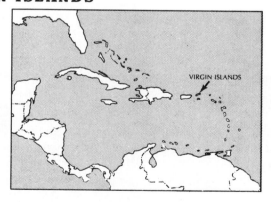

Located just east of Puerto Rico, the United States Virgin Islands consist of three main islands: St. Thomas, St. Croix, and St. John, plus 50 smaller, mostly uninhabited islands. The capital, Charlotte Amalie, is located on St. Thomas. The United States purchased these islands from Denmark in 1917, primarily because of the strategic value of the large natural harbor at Charlotte Amalie. With the purchase, the United

States gained ownership of some of the finest vacation territory in the Caribbean.

Areas of Touristic Importance. Each of the islands offers superb beaches as well as excellent boating, diving, and fishing. Magens Bay on St. Thomas is one of the world's most beautiful beaches. The majority of the islands' resorts are located on St. Thomas and St. Croix, the two largest islands. However, the world-class resort, Caneel Bay, is found on St. John. Nearly three fourths of St. John is a national park and campsites are available. Buck Island National Park, off the coast of St. Croix, is the only underwater national park in the United States park system. Coral World on St. Thomas contains an underwater observation tower from which fish and coral formations can be enjoyed.

Because these islands are United States possessions, visitors who are United States citizens receive larger duty-free allowances for purchases than they would when visiting other destinations. For this reason, shopping is a major tourist activity. Charlotte Amalie, on St. Thomas, and Christiansted, on St. Croix have become major cruise ports because of the attractive, duty-free shopping opportunities for visitors. International airports are also found on both St. Thomas and St. Croix with nonstop flights to United States east coast cities as well as San Juan and other Caribbean islands.

BRITISH VIRGIN ISLANDS

Language: English
Area: 59 square miles
Time Zone: GMT –4
Capital: Road Town
Currency: United States dollar
Population: 12,000
Documentation: Citizenship
  proof

Located northeast of Puerto Rico and adjacent to the United States Virgin Islands, the British Virgin Islands (BVI) include more than 40 small islands, 16 of which are inhabited. Road Town, the capital, is located on Tortola.

Areas of Touristic Importance. Tourism in the BVI is casual and relaxed in a secluded, uncommercialized atmosphere. Sand, surf, fishing, and excellent diving are the major attractions. The British Virgins are very popular with visitors sailing in the Caribbean.

Luxury hotels can be found on Tortola, where many of the best beaches are in the northern part, and Virgin Gorda, with its well- known grottoes and caves. Cottages and guest houses are available on these islands and on Anegada, Jost Van Dyke, Norman Island, and Peter Island as well. Norman Island was the model for Treasure Island in the Robert Louis Stevenson novel. Treasure was actually found there in the 19th century.

ANGUILLA

Language: English

Area: 35 square miles

Time Zone: GMT –4

Capital: The Valley

Currency: East Caribbean dollar

Population: 7,000

Documentation: Citizenship proof

Anguilla is a member of the West Indies Associated States and a voluntary member of the British Commonwealth. It is an island with many beaches but no larger towns. Tourist accommodations are limited to small, informal guest houses.

THE NETHERLANDS ANTILLES AND ST. MAARTEN

Language: Dutch, English, Patois

Area: 385 square miles

Time Zone: GMT –4

National Airline: ALM

Capital: Willemstad

Currency: Dutch guilder (DFL), Florin

Population: 187,000

Documentation: Passport

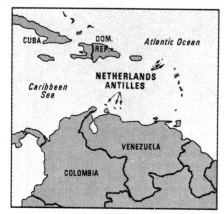

The Netherlands Antilles consists of two groups of three islands located in different parts of the Caribbean. St. Maarten, St. Eustatius, and Saba (the "Three S's") are located southeast of the Virgin Islands and are part of the Windward Island chain. Aruba, Bonaire, and Curacao (the "ABC Islands"), are less than 100 miles from the Venezuelan coast and are part of the Leeward Islands. Plans are being made for a constitutional conference by the mid-1990s to redefine their relationship with The Netherlands and with each other. In 1986, however,

Curacao, Netherlands Antilles

Aruba was granted independence with full status within The Netherlands equal to that of the Netherland Antilles. Both Aruba and Curacao have oil refineries, using imported crude oil from Venezuela and other sources.

Areas of Touristic Importance. A picturesque blend of Holland and the West Indies, these six islands offer a variety of excellent vacations. Casino gambling is available at many resorts on these islands. International flights serve St. Maarten, Aruba, and Curacao.

Aruba's Palm Beach is one of the broadest white sand beaches in the world. Aruba's northern coast provides an exciting opportunity to enjoy waves crashing against a rocky shore. The Natural Bridge, carved from the cliffs by the ocean, is Aruba's most famous natural wonder. Its capital, Oranjestad, blends modern architecture with quaint Dutch homes.

Bonaire is an unspoiled water paradise with excellent diving and deep sea fishing facilities. Its outstanding bird sanctuary is known for its flamingoes. Accommodations are somewhat limited, and Bonaire attracts fewer visitors than neighboring Aruba and Curacao.

Curacao is the largest and most populous of the Netherlands Antilles. Parts of its capital, Willemstad, look like exact replicas of streets in Amsterdam. Its varied shopping facilities attract many tourists. Curacao is a port of call for many cruise ships visiting the lower Caribbean.

St. Maarten, a Dutch colony, shares an island with St. Martin, a French dependency. Thus, the island is unique in offering two architectures, two languages, and two sets of customs. While Dutch St. Maarten occupies only one-third of the island, its tourist facilities are more developed than French St. Martin. Most visitors sightsee both the Dutch capital of Philipsburg and the French Marigot. Because of its uniqueness, the island also attracts many cruise ships.

St. Eustatius and Saba are both accessible from St. Maarten. They are uncommercialized and attract a small number of tourists who desire quiet relaxation. Saba's capital, Leverock, is called "The Bottom" because of its location at the bottom of an extinct volcano.

■ THE FRENCH ANTILLES

French dependencies in the Caribbean include St. Martin, St. Barthelemy, Guadeloupe, and Martinique. The features and facilities of St. Martin were discussed with the Netherlands Antilles because St. Martin shares the same island as St. Maarten.

St. Barthelemy, most popularly known as St. Barts, is a small island south of St. Martin. Visiting St. Barts is like visiting the French countryside, with sun, sand, and surf added.

GUADELOUPE

Language: French, Creole

Area: 660 square miles

Time Zone: GMT –4

Capital: Basse-Terre

Currency: French franc (FFR)

Population: 395,000

Documentation: Passport, visa

Guadeloupe is formed by two large islands, Grande-Terre and Basse-Terre, separated by the Salt River, and, when viewed from overhead, it resembles a huge butterfly. A drawbridge spans the narrow channel between the two. Guadeloupe is a mountainous island with dramatic contrasts among its beaches, coastline, lakes, waterfalls, volcanic peaks, and lush tropical forests.

Areas of Touristic Importance. Point-a-Pitre, on Grand-Terre, is the leading commercial center. The city has an international airport with flights from the East Coast of the United States, France, and other Caribbean islands. It is also a major cruise port. Guadeloupe's resorts are located on beaches adjoining Point-a-Pitre and Basse-Terre. The island boasts beautiful white or black sand beaches and scenic mountainous areas.

MARTINIQUE

Language: French
Area: 425 square miles
Time Zone: GMT –4
Capital: Fort-de-France
Currency: Caribbean franc
  (CFR)
Population: 365,000
Documentation: Passport,
  visa

To the south of Guadeloupe and separated from it by the island of Dominica, Martinique provides a combination of French atmosphere and Caribbean splendor.

Areas of Touristic Importance. Green rain forests, volcanic peaks, and beautiful beaches provide the visitor with a wide variety of activities. Fort-de-France has both an international airport and a seaport visited by many cruise ships.

Martinique is the birthplace of Napoleon's Josephine, and the site of Mt. Pelee, a volcano that erupted in 1902, burying the city of St. Pierre and 40,000 residents. A visit to the ruins reminds one of Pompeii.

ANTIGUA AND BARBUDA

Language: English
Area: 171 square miles
Time Zone: GMT –4
Capital: St. Johns
Currency: East Caribbean dollar
  lar
Population: 64,000
Documentation: Citizenship
  proof

Antigua, a former British colony, is located south of St. Maarten and St. Barthelemy.

Areas of Touristic Importance. Antigua has beautiful beaches and inlets, luxury hotels, and excellent water sports. Casino gambling is also available. Air service is available to San Juan and other Caribbean airports.

Forty miles to the north lies Barbuda, a small island which is part of this nation. Barbuda is accessible by ferry from St. Johns and offers informal, casual accommodations and one small luxury resort hotel. It is a coral island with long, sandy beaches.

ST. KITTS AND NEVIS

Language: English

Area: 101 square miles

Time Zone: GMT –4

Capital: Basseterre

Currency: East Caribbean dollar

Population: 40,293

Documentation: Citizenship proof

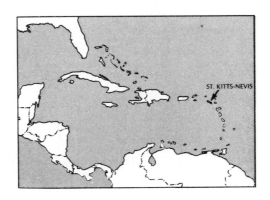

Located west of Antiqua and Barbuda, the two-island nation of St. Kitts-Nevis became independent in 1983. Like Anguilla, it is a member of the West Indies Associated States and a voluntary member of the British Commonwealth.

St. Kitts, still shown on many maps as St. Christopher, is the oldest British settlement in the Caribbean. It is a lush island, covered with sugar cane. Nevis is just a few miles from St. Kitts.

Areas of Touristic Importance. On St. Kitts, Frigate Bay provides fine beaches, a golf course and a casino. Brimstone Hill is an impressive fort, built on the peak of a prominence known as "The Gibraltar of the West Indies."

Nevis has become known for exclusive, deluxe resorts and spas.

MONTSERRAT

Language: English

Area: 32 square miles

Time Zone: GMT –4

Capital: Plymouth

Currency: East Caribbean dollar

Population: 11,600

Documentation: Citizenship proof

Located to the southwest of Antigua, Montserrat is a tiny, picturesque island, settled in 1692 by Irish (then British) immigrants. High peaks contrast with sandy beaches.

Areas of Touristic Importance. Small hotels and guest houses are available for tourists preferring a tranquil vacation. Rendezvous Bay is the only white sand beach. Most of the beaches are gray or golden, because of their volcanic origin. Excellent snorkeling is available.

DOMINICA

Official Name: Commonwealth of Dominica

Language: English, French, Patois

Area: 290 square miles

Time Zone: GMT –4

Capital: Roseau

Currency: East Caribbean dollar

Population: 86,000

Documentation: Citizenship proof

Dominica, the most northerly of the Windward Islands, is a mountainous, volcanic island with tropical rain forest cover. Its few beaches are almost all inaccessible except by boat.

Areas of Touristic Importance. Its dramatic scenery features wild, lush forests and many waterfalls. Points of interest include Boiling Lake and Sulphur Springs. Native birds and exotic flora attract wildlife enthusiasts.

The island has several small hotels. Day trips from Barbados, Guadeloupe, and Martinique are popular.

ST. LUCIA

Language: English, French, Patois

Area: 238 square miles

Time Zone: GMT –4

Capital: Castries

Currency: East Caribbean dollar

Population: 153,075

Documentation: Citizenship proof

During the colonial period, St. Lucia changed hands many times between the French and British. In the 20th century, it was a British colony before becoming independent. Its atmosphere, however, is primarily French and most natives speak a French Patois.

Areas of Touristic Importance. St. Lucia is a beautiful island with everything from beaches to jungles and rainforests. In addition to beach resorts, primarily near Castries, St. Lucia has a fuming volcano and hot sulphur springs. Its international airport is on the southern tip of the island. A smaller airport, near Castries in the northeast, is used for most flights within the Caribbean. Hotels vary from small guest houses to deluxe resort properties. St. Lucia is a popular cruise port.

BARBADOS

Language: English

Area: 166 square miles

Time Zone: GMT –4

Capital: Bridgetown

Currency: Barbados dollar

Population: 254,000

Documentation: Citizenship proof

Barbados, located east of St. Lucia and St. Vincent, is the most popular vacation destination in the Caribbean south of San Juan and St. Thomas. One of the oldest democracies in the Western Hemisphere, Barbados draws tourists from all over the world.

Areas of Touristic Importance. Great beaches, abundant nightlife, and a wide variety of accommodations and restaurants make the island a gem of the Caribbean.

Bridgetown, the nation's capital, in the southwest corner of the island, is its commercial center and seaport. It is a major Caribbean cruise port as well.

Most resort hotels are on the south and west coasts of the island, where the best beaches, such as St. James Beach, are located. The rugged but beautiful northeast coast is similar to the glens of Scotland.

Barbados' British heritage is obvious in many places of historic interest as well as in the accents of the population.

ST. VINCENT AND THE GRENADINES

Language: English

Area: 150 square miles

Time Zone: GMT –4

Capital: Kingstown

Currency: East Caribbean dollar

Population: 114,000

Documentation: Citizenship proof

The Grenadines include more than 100 islands stretching 35 miles southward between St. Vincent and Grenada. There are more than 600 if you count rocky tips jutting up from the sea. This area is heaven for tourists who enjoy yachting, fishing and snorkeling. The most frequented islands (none are truly crowded) are Bequia, Mustique, Canouan, Union, and Palm Islands. A few of the smallest Caribbean cruise ships sail among the Grenadines.

Areas of Touristic Importance. St. Vincent is also called "Breadfruit Island" because it was the first in the Caribbean to be planted with this bumpy-skinned fruit. Near the capital, Kingstown, are the Botanical Gardens where Captain Bligh, of *Bounty* fame, planted a breadfruit tree. The tree still flourishes today. In Kingstown, St. George's Cathedral and the Cathedral of St. Mary are fine examples of colonial architecture. Fort Charlotte, dating from the 18th century, sits above the town and is worth a visit.

Volcanic activity has produced black sand beaches that contrast with the white sand swimming areas. The slopes of 4,000-foot Mt. Soufriere are covered with tropical green. From the peak visitors can see St. Lucia to the north and the many tiny Grenadines to the south.

Mustique, known for its elegance, appeals to upscale clientele. Canouan provides some of the best beaches in the Caribbean. For those seeking high-class, out-of-the-way vacations, the Grenadines have much to offer.

GRENADA

Language: English

Area: 133 square miles

Time Zone: GMT –4

Capital: St. George's

Currency: East Caribbean dollar

Population: 84,000

Documentation: Citizenship proof

Grenada, on the southern end of the Windward Islands, 100 miles off the coast of Venezuela, was the scene of an American invasion in 1983 to drive out Cuban troops. That conflict has prevented this beautiful island from reaching its full touristic potential. Grenada is the smallest independent nation in the western hemisphere.

Areas of Touristic Importance. Nutmeg (the island produces 40 percent of the world's supply) and clove add a spice aroma to the tropical breezes. The spice towns of Grenville and Gouyave may be visited, and the route to Gouyave is particularly scenic. Excellent beaches can be found on all sides of its 2,700-foot volcanic center, Mount St. Catherine. St. George's, Grenada's capital, retains much of its English historical flavor. A wide range of tourist accommodations are available.

TRINIDAD AND TOBAGO

Official Name: Republic of Trinidad and Tobago

Language: English

Area: 1,980 square miles

Time Zone: GMT –4

National Airline: BWIA

Capital: Port-of-Spain

Currency: Trinidad/Tobago dollar

Population: 1,285,000

Documentation: Passport

Trinidad and Tobago's society is much more cosmopolitan than other Caribbean islands. Indian, British, French, and Chinese influences can be found. Calypso was first developed in Trinidad, and the steel drum as a musical instrument was invented here. Carnival in Port-of-Spain is one of the finest festivals in the hemisphere.

Muslin Mosque, Trinidad
Photo: Courtesy Tinidad and Tobago Tourist Board

Trinidad is a large, populous island only 7 miles off the coast of Venezuela. Port-of-Spain, a commercial center, sets the pace with exciting nightlife. The island was named by Columbus, himself, in 1498.

Tobago is sparsely populated compared to Trinidad, but has much natural beauty. Exotic tropical birds abound and there are more beaches than hotels. Many visitors prefer to stay on Trinidad and visit the Tobago beaches on a day excursion.

Areas of Touristic Importance. Trinidad is famous for its annual pre-Lenten Carnival celebration, which attracts visitors from around the world.

The finest beach near the capital city of Port-of-Spain is Maracas Beach. Trinidad provides opportunities for all the typical Caribbean vacation interests such as sun, golf and water sports.

Tobago is the quieter, more relaxing vacation spot with long stretches of white sand beaches.

■ BERMUDA, THE BAHAMAS, AND THE TURKS AND CAICOS ISLANDS

Three other islands are discussed with the Caribbean islands although they are in the Atlantic Ocean, not the Caribbean. However, from a tourism viewpoint, they are closely related to their Caribbean neighbors.

BERMUDA

Language: English
Area: 20.6 square miles
Time Zone: GMT –4
Capital: Hamilton
Currency: Bermuda dollar
Population: 59,800
Documentation: Citizenship proof

Bermuda is named for explorer Juan de Bermudez, who discovered the island in 1598. It has been a self-governing British colony since the original settlers, led by Sir George Somers, were shipwrecked there. Its close proximity to the

United States has made it a favorite tourist destination since the 1920s.

Bermuda's climate differs substantially from that of the other islands described in this chapter. Because Bermuda is east of Savannah, Georgia, it does not have tropical or sub-

Port Royal Golf Course, Southhampton, Bermuda
Photo: Courtesy Bermuda Department of Tourism

tropical conditions. The nearest continental land to Bermuda is Cape Hatteras, North Carolina. Whereas winter is "high season" throughout the Bahamas and the Caribbean, it is "low season" in Bermuda. The island's climate is moderated by its oceanic location along the Gulf Stream, however, and winter temperatures are usually quite springlike.

Areas of Touristic Importance. From the historic and quaint village of St. George's to the South Shore with its pink and white beaches, Bermuda is picturesque. The islands are hilly, but not mountainous. Roads are narrow and the speed limit throughout Bermuda is less than 30 miles per hour. The number of automobiles allowed is strictly controlled.

Visitors cannot rent cars. As a result, rented mopeds and motorbikes have become major means of tourist transportation. Busses traverse Bermuda and there is an ample supply of taxis.

Hamilton, the capital, is Bermuda's major commercial center and cruise port. Many international banks also maintain offices in Hamilton. St. George retains much of the flavor of an old English town.

From April through October, several cruise ships visit Bermuda on a weekly basis. Several follow a "linger longer" concept, remaining in port for as much as 3 days. Cruise ships dock at St. George's and at the Naval Dockyards in addition to Hamilton. Bermuda's airport receives daily flights from eastern United States cities and several flights each week from London.

Bermuda is a popular destination for honeymooners, and, throughout the island, you will see circular stone archways known as moongates. Legends say that honeymooners should walk through these gates for good luck.

Tourist accommodations, many on superb beaches, include guest houses, cottage colonies, small hotels, and large, luxury hotels. Snorkeling and diving among the coral reefs and multicolored waters is a favorite activity. Bermuda is also a golfer's paradise with several challenging courses. Bermuda's cleanliness and friendliness have made it a favorite of knowledgeable travelers for years.

THE BAHAMAS

Official Name: Commonwealth of the Bahamas

Language: English

Area: 5,380 square miles

Time Zone: GMT –5

National Airline: Bahamasair

Capital: Nassau

Currency: Bahamian dollar

Population: 251,000

Documentation: Citizenship proof

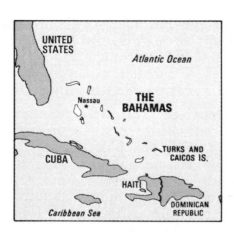

The Bahamas are a long string of hundreds of low-lying islands that stretch for more than 700 miles, from off southern Florida to north of Cuba. The 22 inhabited islands are relatively near, and have strong ties with, Miami, Florida. It is believed that when Columbus discovered the New World in 1492, he actually landed first on San Salvador Island. New Providence Island hosts the main city of Nassau.

A former British colony, the Bahamas have a predominantly black population. Banking and tourism are the principal sources of income and tax advantages have made it attractive to American commercial interests.

Areas of Touristic Importance. Nassau, the capital, is also the primary tourist destination in the Bahamas. Proximity to Miami, Florida makes Nassau a perfect spot for a quick getaway as well as a port for short 2- and 3-day cruises.

Nassau began to grow as a principal tourist destination in 1960 after Cuba became off-limits for American visitors. High-rise hotels were built and a bridge was constructed to connect the main part of New Providence Island to a small island with superb beaches not far from Nassau town. Originally called Hog Island, but now known as Paradise Island, this small island features a full casino and Las Vegas-type evening entertainment. Major hotels are also found in Nassau town and, along with another large casino, in the Cable Beach area of the island.

Grand Bahama Island, north of Nassau, attracts many visitors, primarily to the Freeport-Lucaya area. Three- and 4-day Freeport vacations are popular among visitors seeking beach and casino activities. Several ships sail on 3- and 4-day cruises from Miami to Nassau and Freeport.

Other islands in the Bahamas attract tourists who desire a quieter and more restful vacation. Hotels are smaller and more informal. Beach and water activities are emphasized and nightlife is limited. Called the "family islands," or simply the "out islands," these include Bimini, Eleuthera, Andros, Abaco, Exuma, Cat Island, Long Island, and San Salvador.

THE TURKS AND CAICOS ISLANDS

Language: English
Area: 193 square miles
Time Zone: GMT –5
Capital: Cockburn Town
Currency: United States dollar
Population: 9,000
Documentation: Citizenship proof

The Turks and Caicos Islands at the southern end of the Bahamas chain remain a British dependency. Six of the 30 islands are inhabited.

Areas of Touristic Importance. These islands are for the visitor who wants to get away to peace and quiet. Still unspoiled, they are popular for boating, fishing, and scuba diving and are becoming more popular and better known for vacation travelers.

■ TYPES OF TOURISM

Rest and relaxation is the primary motivation for visits to this region of the world. There are some historical and cultural activities, but these are secondary attractions for most tourists. Although the availability of these activities may help in choosing which island to visit, the history and culture of this region are not truly attractors.

Independent travel predominates in the area. Most group programs are for preformed groups such as church, professional, and social clubs. Most air travelers visit a single destination for 3 to 7 days. Very few island hop. Tourists desiring multiple island visits usually take a cruise. Cruise lengths vary, but the most popular are for 7 days. The following cruise itineraries are examples of typical offerings in the region:

■ 7 Day Eastern Caribbean

■ 7 Day Southern Caribbean

■ Western Caribbean

7 DAY EASTERN CARIBBEAN

SAN JUAN
PUERTO RICO

You can do it all in San Juan...the pearl of the Caribbean. There's a swirl of activities to enjoy, fashionable boutiques, delightful restaurants and the sites of "Old" San Juan, El Morro Castle and the fortress of San Geronimo.

The nights are awash with the lavish spectacle of stunning floor shows and elaborate casinos alive with action. The excitement flows through the streets with the pulsating heat of Latin music in a city that never sleeps.

ST. THOMAS
U. S. VIRGIN ISLANDS

St. Thomas offers the perfect combination...duty-free shopping and some of the best beaches in the world. Our full-

day stop allows you to make the most of this balmy haven. Stroll along the narrow streets of Charlotte Amalie with pastel-colored boutiques featuring jewelry, French perfumes and Scandinavian crystal. Relax on the powder-soft white beaches, then snorkel through a coral reef or take a raft cruise from the harbor. Sightsee at Bluebeard's Castle and catch the excitement of those swashbuckling buccaneer days!

CELEBRATION

ST. MAARTEN
NETHERLANDS ANTILLES

Some say it's the Dutch reception that wins their hearts on St. Maarten while others claim the French sophistication keeps them

ENDLESS SUMMER LOUNGE

THE TROLLEY BAR   HORIZON DINING ROOM

40

Reprinted courtesy of Carnival Cruise Lines.

CRUISES FROM MIAMI

Either way, this half Dutch, half French island is completely captivating from all angles. Swim cool emerald waters or snorkel off one of many secluded shores. Sprinkled about the island and especially around Simpson Bay are intimate stone cottages, French colonial homes and lovely duty-free shops.

ITINERARY:

DAY	PORT	ARRIVE	DEPART
Sat.	Miami		4:00 P.M.
Sun.	At Sea		
Mon.	San Juan	6:00 P.M.	
Tue.	San Juan		2:00 A.M.
Tue.	St. Thomas	8:00 A.M.	5:30 P.M.
Wed.	St. Maarten	7:00 A.M.	5:00 P.M.
Thur.	At Sea		
Fri.	At Sea		
Sat.	Miami	8:00 A.M.	

coming back time after time. To the south, Dutch hospitality reigns supreme in Philipsburg, where delicious chocolates, cheeses, dutch silver and Delftware are island specialties. The northern side is as French as Paris, with fashions, brandies and exquisite perfumes temptingly priced.

ON BOARD THE CELEBRATION

47,262 tons of fun/entered service March 14, 1987/Italian officers/international service staff/central air conditioning system throughout the entire ship, individually controlled in each stateroom/private facilities in each stateroom/closed circuit T.V., piped-in music, telephone, wall safe and 110 AC current in staterooms/3 outdoor pools including children's wading pool/Registered in Liberia.

WHEELHOUSE BAR & GRILL

ADMIRAL'S

RAINBOW CLUB CASINO

7 DAY SOUTHERN CARIBBEAN

Explore the glorious southern Caribbean on board Carnival's newest SuperLiner, the FASCINATION. From its spectacular seven-story atrium to its glittering casino, theme lounges and public areas, the FASCINATION's a magnificent floating resort just waiting to make your vacation unforgettable.

SAN JUAN
PUERTO RICO

Cobblestone streets and hidden courtyards characterize the charm of Old San Juan. Founded in 1508 by the Spanish explorer Ponce De Leon, this district has recently undergone a $200 million program to restore its priceless buildings. The new city dazzles the most sophisticated shoppers and sightseers.

ST. THOMAS
U. S. VIRGIN ISLANDS

Discovered by Columbus on his second trip to the New World in 1493, St. Thomas still rewards visitors today with pristine beaches, shopping and sightseeing. As the second largest of the Virgin Islands chain, St. Thomas' perennial popularity is due in good part to its friendly people and international shops, many duty-free, in its capital Charlotte Amalie. But it may be the island's lush coves, reefs and beaches that will linger in your memory.

GUADELOUPE
LESSER ANTILLES

It's no wonder that the Arawak Indians once called Guadeloupe *Karukera,* "island of beautiful waters," as you'll find when you explore this dramatic archipelago. Actually two islands separated by a strait, Basse-Terre and Grand-Terre offer vastly different terrains. For sightseeing or shopping, head for the rolling hills of Grand-Terre, where the main port, Point-a-Pitre, exudes all the elan of the French Riviera. Across the bridge, the volcanic peaks of Basse-Terre offer a rocky invitation for hikers.

GRENADA
WINDWARD ANTILLES

All the guidebooks agree — the port of St. George's boasts one of the most picturesque harbors in the Caribbean. With its red tiled roofs and soft green hills, this seaside city charms everyone with a mix of island hospitality and European sophistication. Sightseers will delight in

PASSAGE TO INDIA LOUNGE

PUTTING ON THE RITZ LOUNGE

Reprinted courtesy of Carnival Cruise Lines.

CRUISES FROM SAN JUAN

trendy boutiques and duty-free shops offering liquor, jewelry, cameras and decorative Italian glassware, shoppers will find a bonanza of souvenir choices. For an unforgettable view, take the city cable car to the summit of Mount Avila, almost 7,400 feet above the city. And if you like history, you'll discover fascinating sites associated with Venezuela's national hero, Simon Bolivar, in every corner of the city.

ARUBA
NETHERLANDS ANTILLES

There's a reason locals and international visitors have dubbed Aruba the "Turquoise Coast." With its miles of powdery beaches and sparkling aqua waters, this Dutch stronghold has long been a favorite of scuba divers, snorklers, wind surfers and other water sports enthusiasts.

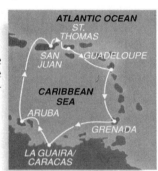

ITINERARY:

DAY	PORT	ARRIVE	DEPART
Sat.	San Juan		10:00 P.M.
Sun.	St. Thomas	8:00 A.M.	5:00 P.M.
Mon.	Guadeloupe	10:00 A.M.	4:00 P.M.
Tue.	Grenada	8:00 A.M.	1:00 P.M.
Wed.	La Guaira/Caracas	8:00 A.M.	6:00 P.M.
Thur.	Aruba	8:00 A.M.	6:00 P.M.
Fri.	At Sea		
Sat.	San Juan	8:00 A.M.	

the eighteenth century Fort George, where battlements are honeycombed with fascinating tunnels and offer a panoramic view of the city.

LA GUAIRA/CARACAS
VENEZUELA

We add a touch of South America to your cruise with a stop at this exotic port. Strolling down streets lined with

ON BOARD THE FASCINATION

70,367 tons of fun/enters service October 1, 1994/ Italian officers/international service staff/central air conditioning system throughout the entire ship, individually controlled in each stateroom/ private facilities in each stateroom/closed circuit T.V., piped-in music, telephone, wall safe and 110 AC current in each stateroom/3 outdoor pools including children's wading pool/Registered in Panama.

DIAMONDS ARE FOREVER DISCOTHEQUE

COCONUT GROVE BAR & GRILL

WESTERN CARIBBEAN

HOME OF THE BLUES, REGGAE AND MAYAN KINGS

Holland America's Western Caribbean offers yet a different realm, a different experience. For this is the Caribbean of spectacular beaches, world-class diving and ancient ruins. Where you can walk in the footsteps of Mayan kings and snorkel with blue angels one day, stroll the sprawling lawns of a sugar plantation and give sway to reggae the next. And all the while enjoy the good life aboard one of Holland America's luxurious sister ships, the Noordam or the Nieuw Amsterdam.

If paradise is lost, it must be found in Holland America's Western Caribbean. And we have three ways to find it. Sail from the sophisticated resort city of Ft. Lauderdale; or from the charming Gulf port of Tampa; or from our newest platform from which to dive into the Caribbean, New Orleans — part Creole, part Cajun, totally captivating. As you would expect, all New Orleans sailings will feature a Salute to Jazz. Come a little early or linger a while after your cruise and enjoy a mini vacation in this historic city. There's Bourbon Street and the French Quarter to explore, Mississippi riverboats, jambalaya and more jazz to sample.

Then, depending upon which itinerary you choose — a Saturday or Sunday 7-day cruise, 10 or 11 days aboard the Noordam or the Nieuw Amsterdam — you're off to different and fascinating island destinations.

Among them is Key West. It was in this distinctly American town with the look and feel of the Caribbean that Ernest Hemingway wrote nearly 30 of his novels; where John James Audubon painted the birds of the Florida Keys; and where President Harry Truman spent many a working vacation at the Little White House. How will you mark your time here? Watching the street musicians in Old Mallory Square? Riding the Conch Tour Train around the island? Looking at, but not touching, the gorgeous coral reef that took eons to create?

To make sure you get the most of your Caribbean cruise, Holland America offers a variety of excursions ashore. In Mexico's Yucatan the choices are many:

From the quaint village of **Playa del Carmen**, tour the famous archaeological sites at Chichen Itza and Tulum. As you sit at the foot of their ancient ruins,

In Jamaica, cool your heels at Dunn's River Falls.

Reprinted courtesy of   Holland America Lines

Tulum, only beachside resort of the Mayans.

A saxophonist belts out the blues in New Orleans.

you are awed into silence. And contemplation. Who were these people who lived here so very long ago? Why did they so mysteriously disappear? Questions perhaps that will never be answered, but certainly worthy topics of conversation over a Kahlúa coffee tonight in the Explorer's Lounge.

Or perhaps you'll remain on board as your elegant cruise ship ventures to the isle of **Cozumel** – ranked among the world's premier dive spots. While Palancar Reef is reserved for experts, the shallow waters of Chankanaub Lagoon are easily explored by novices. With just a few kicks of the flippers another world opens – the realm of blue angels, yellow butterfly fish, blue-green and red parrot fish.

Or dive into other island attractions: fiery Latin fiestas, shopping, a tennis outing at a premier resort.

Tonight in the elegant dining room, dessert choices will no doubt include crêpes Cozumel, flamed to perfection.

On **Grand Cayman** the big attraction is Seven Mile Beach...white as snow, soft as talcum powder. Name your game and you'll find it here. Snorkeling. Swimming. Fishing. Sailing. Windsurfing over rippling waves. Or gliding under them in a passenger submarine to see the shipwrecked *Carrie Lee*. Or perhaps shopping is your game. Duty-free bargains abound in Georgetown: crystal, perfume, jewelry fashioned of silver and prized pink coral.

WESTERN CARIBBEAN

Jamaica is for lovers and for lovers of nature. Here you can drift lazily down the Martha Brae on a gondola made of bamboo. Gaze into fields of shimmering sugar cane plumes as you share a Planter's Punch on the porch of a restored great house. Or spend a leisurely afternoon at Dunn's River Falls, where the cool water from the rain forest cascades over limestone terraces to the sea. Explore from the adjacent trail, or don your swimsuit and enjoy an easy, refreshing climb to the top. It's all possible from Montego Bay or Ocho Rios, depending upon the itinerary you select.

As you enjoy breakfast al fresco on the Lido you recall the interesting facts you learned about Aruba in yesterday's port lecture ...desert climate...dramatic coastline...a mélange of Latin and Dutch influences. You step ashore to shop Nassaustraat, brimming with luxury goods from around the world; and to venture into the countryside to see the unique rock gardens of **Casi Bari**, and the curious divi-divi tree, forever bending in the trade wind breezes.

Or perhaps you'll venture all the way to **Cartagena**, once the fortified bastion through which the treasures of the Spanish Main flowed — fabulous shipments of gold and silver and precious jewels. On a fascinating tour of the city, see San Felipe, the fortress that guarded it all from indefatigable sea dogs such as Sir Francis Drake. Perhaps shop for a treasure of your own — a prized Colombian emerald. ❧

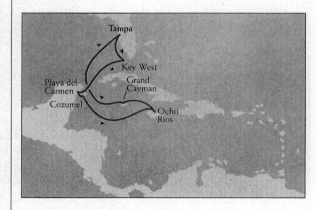

WESTERN CARIBBEAN DISCOVERY

MS NIEUW AMSTERDAM

7 DAYS	FROM $1,660

SAILING DATES FROM TAMPA

Economy 1993	Value 1994	Peak 1994
Oct 16*, 23*, 30*	Jan 8	Jan 15, 22, 29
Nov 6*, 13*, 20*♦, 27	Apr 2★, 9	Feb 5, 12, 19, 26
Dec 4		Mar 5, 12, 19, 26

DAY	PORT	ARRIVE	DEPART
SAT	TAMPA, FLORIDA		5:00PM
SUN	Key West, Florida	11:00AM	3:00PM
MON	Playa del Carmen, Mexico*	Noon	12:30PM
	Cozumel, Mexico	1:30PM	11:00PM
TUE	At sea		
WED	Ocho Rios, Jamaica	8:00AM	5:00PM
THU	Georgetown, Grand Cayman	8:00AM	5:00PM
FRI	At sea		
SAT	TAMPA, FLORIDA	8:00AM	

◦The Oct 16, 23, 30, Nov 6, 13 and 20 sailings will operate in reverse order. The Oct 16, 30 and Nov 13 sailings will call at Montego Bay instead of Ocho Rios. Otherwise, ports of call remain the same.

*Service call for shore excursion
♦Nov 20 Thanksgiving cruise
★Apr 2 Easter cruise

7-PLUS-7 COMBINATION CRUISE

By combining consecutive 7-day ms Nieuw Amsterdam Western Caribbean Discovery cruises and 7-day ms Westerdam Eastern Caribbean Getaway cruises (page 16), you save $500 per couple Cruise Only Credit. See page 34 for complete information and more special offers.

Drifting down the Martha Brae, a barefoot idea.

MS NIEUW AMSTERDAM

OUTSIDE DOUBLE STATEROOMS	ECONOMY 1993 OCT 16, 23, 30 NOV 6, 13, 20, 27 DEC 4	VALUE 1994 JAN 8 APR 2, 9	PEAK 1994 JAN 15, 22, 29 FEB 5, 12, 19, 26 MAR 5, 12, 19, 26
A Staterooms Deluxe	US $2,520	US $2,520	US $2,650
B Deluxe	2,220	2,220	2,335
C Deluxe	2,155	2,155	2,265
D Large	2,095	2,095	2,200
E Large	2,040	2,040	2,145
F Large	1,980	1,980	2,080
G Standard	1,915	1,915	2,015
INSIDE DOUBLE STATEROOMS			
H Large	1,915	1,915	2,015
I Large	1,885	1,885	1,980
J Large	1,855	1,855	1,950
K Standard	1,795	1,795	1,885
L Standard	1,740	1,740	1,830
M Standard	1,660	1,660	1,745
Each Guest Sharing Stateroom with Two Full-Fare Guests	795	795	795
Children Under Two Years Old Accompanied by Two Full-Fare Adults	250	250	250
Cruise Only Credit	250	250	250
Port Charges & Taxes	89	94	94
Deposit Requirements	300	300	300
Cancellation Fees Waiver	69	69	69

Refer to page 34 for single fare information.
Refer to deck plans on pages 42 and 43 for specific facilities in each stateroom.

MS NOORDAM

OUTSIDE DOUBLE STATEROOMS	VALUE 1994 JAN 9 APR 3	PEAK 1994 JAN 23 FEB 6, 20 MAR 6, 20
A Staterooms Deluxe	US $2,520	US $2,650
B Deluxe	2,220	2,335
C Deluxe	2,155	2,265
D Large	2,095	2,200
E Large	2,040	2,145
F Large	1,980	2,080
G Standard	1,915	2,015
INSIDE DOUBLE STATEROOMS		
H Large	1,915	2,015
I Large	1,885	1,980
J Large	1,855	1,950
K Standard	1,795	1,885
L Standard	1,740	1,830
M Standard	1,660	1,745
Each Guest Sharing Stateroom with Two Full-Fare Guests		795	795
Children Under Two Years Old Accompanied by Two Full-Fare Adults	250	250
Cruise Only Credit	250	250
Port Charges & Taxes	94	94
Deposit Requirements	300	300
Cancellation Fees Waiver	69	69

Refer to page 34 for single fare information.
Refer to deck plans on pages 42 and 43 for specific facilities in each stateroom.

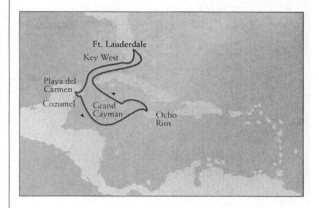

WESTERN CARIBBEAN SUNSET

MS NOORDAM   NEW SUNDAY SAILINGS

7 DAYS   FROM $1,660

SAILING DATES FROM FT. LAUDERDALE

Value 1994	Peak 1994
Jan 9	Jan 23
Apr 3♦	Feb 6, 20
	Mar 6, 20

DAY	PORT	ARRIVE	DEPART
SUN	FT. LAUDERDALE, FLORIDA		5:00PM
MON	Key West, Florida	7:00AM	1:00PM
TUE	Playa del Carmen, Mexico*	11:00AM	11:30AM
	Cozumel, Mexico	12:30PM	11:00PM
WED	At sea		
THU	Ocho Rios, Jamaica	8:00AM	5:00PM
FRI	Georgetown, Grand Cayman	8:00AM	5:00PM
SAT	At sea		
SUN	FT. LAUDERDALE, FLORIDA	8:00AM	

*Service call for shore excursion
♦Apr 3 Easter cruise

7-PLUS-7 COMBINATION CRUISE

By combining consecutive 7-day ms Noordam Eastern Caribbean Sunrise cruises (page 17) and 7-day Western Caribbean Sunset cruises, you save $500 per couple Cruise Only Credit. See page 34 for complete information and more special offers.

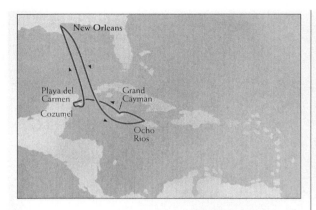

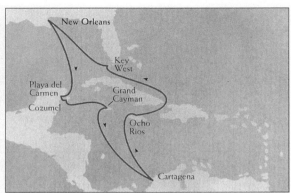

Western Caribbean Discovery

ms Noordam   FALL SUNDAY SAILINGS

7 Days   FROM $1,660

SAILING DATES FROM NEW ORLEANS

Economy 1993	Value 1994
Oct 24, 31	Apr 20 (Wed.)
Nov 7, 14, 21♦	

DAY	PORT	ARRIVE	DEPART
0	NEW ORLEANS, LOUISIANA		5:00PM
1	At sea		
2	At sea		
3	Ocho Rios, Jamaica	8:00AM	4:00PM
4	Georgetown, Grand Cayman	7:00AM	1:00PM
5	Playa del Carmen, Mexico*	7:30AM	8:00AM
	Cozumel, Mexico	9:00AM	4:00PM
6	At sea		
7	NEW ORLEANS, LOUISIANA	8:00AM	

*Service call for shore excursion
♦Nov 21 Thanksgiving cruise

*Grand Cayman,
blessed by the sun,
lapped by the sea.*

Western Caribbean Discovery

ms Noordam

11 Days   FROM $2,525

SAILING DATE FROM NEW ORLEANS			OCT 13, 1993	
DAY	DATE	PORT	ARRIVE	DEPART
WED	OCT 13	NEW ORLEANS, LOUISIANA		5:00PM
THU	OCT 14	At sea		
FRI	OCT 15	Playa del Carmen, Mexico*	7:00AM	7:30AM
		Cozumel, Mexico	8:30AM	3:30PM
SAT	OCT 16	Georgetown, Grand Cayman	Noon	6:00PM
SUN	OCT 17	At sea		
MON	OCT 18	Cartagena, Colombia	8:00AM	5:00PM
TUE	OCT 19	At sea		
WED	OCT 20	Ocho Rios, Jamaica	8:00AM	5:00PM
THU	OCT 21	At sea		
FRI	OCT 22	Key West, Florida	9:00AM	5:00PM
SAT	OCT 23	At sea		
SUN	OCT 24	NEW ORLEANS, LOUISIANA	8:00AM	

SAILING DATE FROM NEW ORLEANS			NOV 28, 1993	
DAY	DATE	PORT	ARRIVE	DEPART
SUN	NOV 28	NEW ORLEANS, LOUISIANA		5:00PM
MON	NOV 29	At sea		
TUE	NOV 30	Key West, Florida	8:00AM	2:00PM
WED	DEC 1	At sea		
THU	DEC 2	Ocho Rios, Jamaica	8:00AM	5:00PM
FRI	DEC 3	At sea		
SAT	DEC 4	Cartagena, Colombia	8:00AM	5:00PM
SUN	DEC 5	At sea		
MON	DEC 6	Georgetown, Grand Cayman	7:00AM	1:00PM
TUE	DEC 7	Playa del Carmen, Mexico*	7:30AM	8:00AM
		Cozumel, Mexico	9:00AM	4:00PM
WED	DEC 8	At sea		
THU	DEC 9	NEW ORLEANS, LOUISIANA	8:00AM	

*Service call for shore excursion

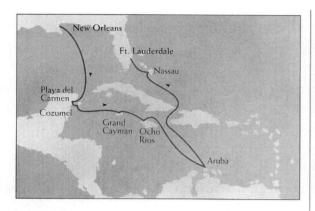

WESTERN CARIBBEAN DISCOVERY

MS NOORDAM

10 DAYS				FROM $2,295

SAILING DATE FROM NEW ORLEANS				DEC 9, 1993

DAY	DATE	PORT	ARRIVE	DEPART
THU	DEC 9	NEW ORLEANS, LOUISIANA		5:00PM
FRI	DEC 10	At sea		
SAT	DEC 11	Playa del Carmen, Mexico*	7:00AM	7:30AM
		Cozumel, Mexico	8:30AM	3:30PM
SUN	DEC 12	Georgetown, Grand Cayman	NOON	6:00PM
MON	DEC 13	Ocho Rios, Jamaica	9:00AM	6:00PM
TUE	DEC 14	At sea		
WED	DEC 15	Oranjestad, Aruba	8:00AM	11:45PM
THU-FRI	DEC 16-17	At sea		
SAT	DEC 18	Nassau, Bahamas	8:00AM	5:00PM
SUN	DEC 19	FT. LAUDERDALE, FLORIDA	8:00AM	

*Service call for shore excursion

WESTERN CARIBBEAN DISCOVERY

MS NOORDAM

10 DAYS				FROM $2,295

SAILING DATE FROM FT. LAUDERDALE				APR 10, 1994

DAY	DATE	PORT	ARRIVE	DEPART
SUN	APR 10	FT. LAUDERDALE, FLORIDA		5:00PM
MON	APR 11	Nassau, Bahamas	8:00AM	5:00PM
TUE-WED	APR 12-13	At sea		
THU	APR 14	Oranjestad, Aruba	8:00AM	11:30PM
FRI	APR 15	At sea		
SAT	APR 16	Ocho Rios, Jamaica	7:00AM	4:00PM
SUN	APR 17	Georgetown, Grand Cayman	7:00AM	1:00PM
MON	APR 18	Playa del Carmen, Mexico*	7:30AM	8:00AM
		Cozumel, Mexico	9:00AM	4:00PM
TUE	APR 19	At sea		
WED	APR 20	NEW ORLEANS, LOUISIANA	8:00AM	

*Service call for shore excursion

MS NOORDAM – SALUTE TO JAZZ CRUISES

		7-DAY ECONOMY 1993 OCT 24, 31 NOV 7, 14, 21	7-DAY VALUE 1994 APR 20	11-DAY FROM NEW ORLEANS OCT 13, NOV 28, 1993	10-DAY FROM NEW ORLEANS DEC 9, 1993	10-DAY FROM FT. LAUDERDALE APR 10, 1994
OUTSIDE DOUBLE STATEROOMS						
A	Staterooms Deluxe	US $2,520	US $2,520	US $3,950	US $3,590	US $3,590
B	Deluxe	2,220	2,220	3,420	3,110	3,110
C	Deluxe	2,155	2,155	3,300	3,000	3,000
D	Large	2,095	2,095	3,225	2,930	2,930
E	Large	2,040	2,040	3,125	2,840	2,840
F	Large	1,980	1,980	3,065	2,785	2,785
G	Standard	1,915	1,915	3,005	2,730	2,730
INSIDE DOUBLE STATEROOMS						
H	Large	1,915	1,915	3,005	2,730	2,730
I	Large	1,885	1,885	2,905	2,640	2,640
J	Large	1,855	1,855	2,795	2,540	2,540
K	Standard	1,795	1,795	2,715	2,470	2,470
L	Standard	1,740	1,740	2,620	2,380	2,380
M	Standard	1,660	1,660	2,525	2,295	2,295
Each Guest Sharing Stateroom with Two Full-Fare Guests		795	795	985	925	925
Children Under Two Years Old Accompanied by Two Full-Fare Adults		250	250	250	250	250
Cruise Only Credit		250	250	250	250	250
Port Charges & Taxes		89	94	109	109	109
Deposit Requirements		300	300	400	400	400
Cancellation Fees Waiver		69	69	89	89	89

Refer to page 34 for single fare information.
Refer to deck plans on pages 42 and 43 for specific facilities in each stateroom.

■ REVIEW—THE CARIBBEAN

1. Historically, what sparked European colonial interest in the Caribbean islands?

2. What is the current political and touristic status of Cuba?

3. Name the capital and largest city in Jamaica. What areas of Jamaica are most important to tourism?

4. Where are Port-au-Prince and Santo Domingo? What do the two cities have in common?

5. What is the current political status of Puerto Rico? Where are the major tourist areas and what do they offer the visitor?

6. Climatically, what is the best season for visiting the Caribbean islands? Why is it best?

7. What is the major racial group in the Lesser Antilles? Why is it most prominent?

8. Where is Bermuda? How does it differ from the other islands discussed in this chapter?

9. Which islands covered in this chapter are not in the Caribbean?

9

Western Europe

■ A WORLD INFLUENCE

Designated a continent by cartographers, Europe is actually a relatively small, irregularly shaped peninsula on the western edge of the enormous Asian landmass. Yet, for the past 300 years, it has occupied center stage in world affairs. European nations sent forth exploring expeditions that filled in the world map, led to overseas colonial empires, and through colonialism spread European values and practices into many distant parts of the world.

The migration of millions of Europeans to the Americas, Australia, New Zealand, and certain colonies in Africa and Southeast Asia furthered this massive cultural transfer. At home, European nations led the way in the development of manufacturing technology and developed a large-scale import-export trade that made Europe the focal point of the world's commercial network.

It is true that two draining world wars, the collapse of colonialism, the emergence of the American and other power centers, and the increase in the number of manufacturing

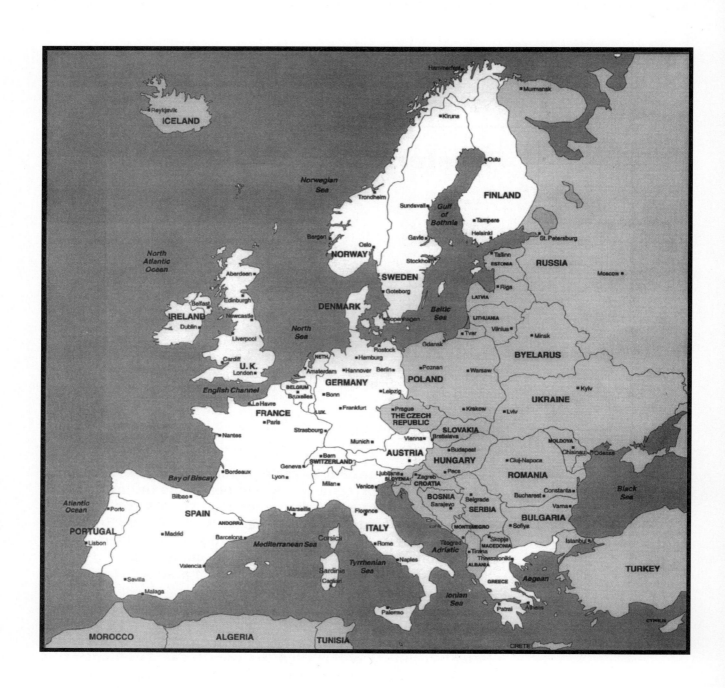

and international trading nations have reduced the relative importance of Europe during the last half of the present century. However, the European nations collectively remain a potent global force in the cultural, political, economic, and military spheres.

Western Europe was home to the ancestors of many Americans and the source of many of the social institutions that were reshaped into a distinctively American mold. It is the place where Americans traveling outside of North America go with the greatest frequency and in the largest numbers.

■ WESTERN AND EASTERN EUROPE

Europe can be divided into two segments, western and eastern. Western Europe has been maritime, outward-oriented, and economically advanced, and has led Europe to the peak of its international prestige. Eastern Europe has been more inner-oriented, slow to modernize, and more preoccupied with internal and regional affairs and relations with its stronger western European neighbors and Russia (the former USSR) on its eastern flank.

In all of Europe, the competition among ethnic groups and nations for the limited space has been intense and, as a result, Europe is divided into a relatively large number of nations, some of which have small territories.

Western Europe—Three Tiers of Nations

Western Europe can be subdivided into northern (Scandinavia or Norden), central, and southern (Mediterranean) tiers of nations. The northern tier consists of Iceland, an island in the North Atlantic Ocean; Norway, Sweden, and Finland on the Scandinavian Peninsula; and, on the opposite side of the intervening Baltic Sea, Denmark.

In the central tier, the British Isles are separated from the continent by the North Sea and the narrow English Channel. Politically, the main island of Great Britain (England, Scotland, and Wales) and Northern Ireland form the United Kingdom, while the larger, southern part of Ireland is the independent Republic of Ireland. Immediately east on the mainland are the three small nations of Belgium, Netherlands, and Luxembourg, known collectively as the Benelux nations. Large Germany (Federal Republic of Germany) and France and smaller, landlocked Switzerland and Austria as well as tiny Liechtenstein, on the Swiss-Austria border, and Monaco, on the Mediterranean coast between France and Italy, are also part of the central tier.

The southern, or Mediterranean, tier consists of Spain and Portugal on the Iberian Peninsula (even though Portugal faces on the Atlantic Ocean); peninsular, boot-shaped Italy and Greece, as well as such tiny nations as Andorra, on the Spanish-French border; San Marino in northeastern Italy; and Malta in the Mediterranean Sea, south of Italy.

Extending some 2,300 miles east-west, the Mediterranean separates Europe from North Africa and the Middle East. Yet, historically, its easily navigated waters have linked together and promoted interaction among these culturally different areas.

Language. Just as there are many nations, so there are many European linguistic and cultural groups. In Western Europe, the Germanic languages (German, Dutch, Danish, Flemish, Icelandic, Norwegian, and Swedish) predominate in the north. The southern, Romance languages (French, Spanish, Portuguese, and Italian) are derived from Latin. Greece has a language of its own. Regional dialects abound in both groups.

Whereas one main language for each national culture is the rule, Switzerland has four formally recognized languages and Belgium, two. English resulted from a fusion of the two language families—Anglo-Saxon, a Germanic language, overlaid with French, which was introduced after the Norman Conquest of 1066. Celtic languages, which predate the others, are represented by Irish, Scottish, and Welsh in Great Britain, and Breton in France.

In religion, the northern tier is predominantly Protestant, the Mediterranean is Roman Catholic and Orthodox, and the central tier has a blend of both Protestant and Roman Catholic.

The Land. One reason for Europe's historical development and importance is that overall it is, topographically and climatically, the most habitable of the continents. It contains many habitable plains and river valleys. The largest continuous plain stretches west to east from France and the Benelux nations, through Germany, Poland, and into the former USSR. Exceptions are the stark glaciated, rocky uplands of northern Scandinavia and northern Great Britain. Farther south, the Pyrenees of Spain and France, and the Alps of France, Italy, Switzerland, West Germany, Austria, and southeastern Europe have more substantial populations and are popular for recreational and tourist use in winter and summer.

The Climate. In latitude, most of Europe has the same location as the northern United States and Canada. New York City is at about the same latitude as Madrid, Spain and Rome, Italy, two of the southernmost European capitals. Fortunately, however, Europe is in the path of the prevailing westerlies, the general belt of west-to-east air movements that cross the United States and other mid-latitude nations.

The Atlantic Ocean, which does not warm or cool as fast or as fully as the adjacent landmasses, moderates the westerlies as they pass over it. Accordingly, winters are relatively milder in Western Europe than might be expected or are experienced in North America at the same latitude, although they are generally cold and have occasional severe storms.

Winter conditions are most extreme in Scandinavia and at higher altitudes and most moderate in the southern Mediterranean area. Winter daylight hours are of relatively short duration. However, during the cool summers daylight hours are relatively long. The central and southern Mediterranean has a distinctive climate marked by cool, rainy winters and hot, dry summers, with rainfall decreasing to the south. The summer conditions attract millions of vacationers to the Mediterranean beaches, but they pose problems to farmers, who commonly must irrigate to offset the summer drought.

The People. Overall, Europe is densely populated and has one of the world's principal population clusters. The four most populous nations, all in Western Europe, have also played key roles in modern history. Germany has the largest population, and Italy, the United Kingdom, and France follow in that order. At the other extreme, Norway, Sweden, Denmark, Ireland, and Switzerland each have fewer than 10 million people, and little Iceland has fewer than 300,000 people. Annual population growth rates are generally low.

The Economy. Western Europe is heavily urbanized, reflecting its diversified and advanced industrial economy. Each nation has a primary city, usually the capital, as well as smaller cities. A swath of urbanization extends across southeastern England, the three Benelux nations, western Germany, and northeastern France, with small clusters elsewhere. The large number of port cities, such as London, Rotterdam, and Copenhagen, are evidence of Europe's long, and still-important, tradition of maritime trade.

The historical centers of many old European cities have been carefully preserved and their earlier architectural styles stand in sharp contrast to the contemporary high-rise office buildings and housing units in other parts of the city. Living standards are among the highest in the world, but in the Mediterranean, Spain, Portugal, southern Italy, and Greece remain relatively poorer, have fewer employment opportunities, and suffer from unemployment. Workers from these and other Mediterranean fringe nations have proved willing to migrate temporarily to jobs in Germany, France, Switzerland, and elsewhere if economic conditions warrant.

Agriculture remains important in Western Europe even though the farming population is relatively small, usually 10 to 15 percent of the labor force. Farms tend to be small. Much of the vitality in agriculture is a result of cash income earned by members of the farming household and subsidies by individual governments and the European Union that keep farm income higher and stabler than it would be if left strictly to market forces.

France is the largest producer of farm goods and has surpluses to sell elsewhere. On the other hand, many nations depend heavily upon food imports from the other European nations or from outside the continent. Farming is basically commercial in character, shaped around grains, dairying, fruits, and vegetables that find ready markets. The Mediterranean area has such distinctive crops as grapes grown for wine, olives, citrus fruits, dry grains, and rice. Farmers there are generally poorer, less productive, and less technically advanced than their northern counterparts.

The Industrial Revolution began in Europe, and the combined European manufacturing capacity and output is one of the four largest in the world. Germany is the industrial leader, followed by the United Kingdom, France, and Italy. Originally based upon local supplies of coal, iron ore, and other natural resources, Western European manufacturing increasingly must reach abroad for much of its energy, now largely oil, and resources. The discovery of extensive oil and natural gas deposits in the North Sea has greatly benefited the British, Norwegian, and Dutch economies.

The greatest industrial concentrations are found in the Ruhr area of western Germany, central and southeastern England, northeastern France, and the Po Valley of northern Italy. However, smaller pockets of manufacturing are widespread elsewhere. The lowest industrial development levels are in the Mediterranean area, where large-scale manufacturing is limited to northern Spain and northern Italy.

Western Europe has a superb network of modern transportation facilities—railways, canals, shipping, auto expressways, and airlines—that allows the swift movement of people and goods within and between nations. Distances are relatively short. North to south in Germany, France, and Spain is about 500 to 550 miles; London-Paris is 375 miles; London-Madrid, 750 miles; and London-Rome, 1,000 miles. At their nearest points, the Baltic and Mediterranean Seas are only 600 miles apart. West Europeans are highly mobile and travel in great numbers for business, recreation, tourism, and other reasons.

Growth of Cooperation. Before World War II, Western European nations were basically intent upon protecting and enhancing their own national interests, with few gestures toward international cooperation, except for defensive military alliances. Since the devastation of the war, however, there has been an extraordinary turnabout, with nations, organizations, and businesses working together across national lines.

Among the large formal international organizations that illustrate this newfound cooperation is the European Union (EU), with headquarters in Brussels, Belgium. Twelve nations are members, and others have applications pending. The original members were West Germany, France, Belgium, Netherlands, Luxembourg, and Italy. The United Kingdom, Ireland, Denmark, Greece, Spain, and Portugal were added later. Finland, Sweden and Austria were added in 1995. By eradicating barriers to free trade, the EU has created a single Western European market area with enormous financial assets, and has succeeded in bringing some of the world's strong economies into friendly working relations. On the other side of the coin, nationalism remains strong and Western European national personalities and interests remain sharply drawn.

■ THE CENTRAL TIER

The central tier of nations includes the United Kingdom, Ireland, France, Germany, Austria, and the Benelux nations (Belgium, the Netherlands, and Luxembourg). It forms the modern core of Western Europe's greatest grouping of people and cities, has the most commercial and manufacturing activities, and has a great collection of cultural, artistic, scientific, and educational centers as well as Europe's major political centers.

UNITED KINGDOM

Official Name: United Kingdom of Great Britain and Northern Ireland

Language: English, Welsh, Gaelic

Area: 94,226 square miles

Time Zone: GMT

National Airline: British Airways

Capital: London

Currency: Pound (UKL)

Population: 55,486,800

Documentation: Passport

The British Isles, consisting of the United Kingdom and Ireland, are separated from the European mainland by the North Sea and the narrow English Channel. They are close enough, 21 miles at the nearest point, to be participants in European affairs, yet separated enough to retain their distinctive character and national interests. The United Kingdom (UK) is formed of Great Britain, which in turn consists of England, Scotland, and Wales; Northern Ireland; and hundreds of small islands, including the Channel Islands off the French coast, the Isle of Man in the Irish Sea between Great Britain and Ireland, and the Outer Hebrides, Orkney, and Shetland Islands off northern Scotland.

History. Historically, England has been the organizing center and London its seat of government. Celtic Scotland and Wales were absorbed centuries ago. The British also long controlled all of Ireland, but in 1921 the southern three-fourths got its independence as Eire, or the Irish Free State, now the Republic of Ireland. The Protestant majority of northern Ireland preferred not to be a part of Catholic Ireland and remains under British rule as Northern Ireland. The term, United Kingdom, refers to the union of Northern Ireland with Great Britain.

British history in modern times is remarkable. By the 19th century, London was the political nerve center for the world's largest colonial empire and trading network. Millions of British and Irish migrated to many parts of the globe, carrying with them the English language and culture and a distinctive system of parliamentary democracy. The British have lost their colonies and position of international dominance, but the United Kingdom remains a major European force.

The Land, People, and Economy. Most of Great Britain consists of habitable plains and hills. Mountains prevail in Wales, northern England (the Pennines), and Scotland. Farming and herding are widespread, yet the British must import a large portion of their foodstuffs and raw materials. Most of the population is urban and works in city-based commercial, manufacturing, and service jobs.

Historically, manufacturing developed in the coal-rich Midlands of central England, southern Wales, northeastern England, and the lowlands of southern Scotland. In the postwar era, many industries in these areas have declined as a result of the shift of emphasis from coal as a fuel, the obsolescence of older factories, worldwide overproduction and cutbacks in heavy industry, and competition from newer industrial nations.

Fortunately, the discovery of oil and natural gas fields in the North Sea has made Britain self-sufficient in energy, and newer industries are developing to replace older ones. The southeast, centered on London, with its outstanding financial, commercial, and shipping facilities via the Thames River, is the most prosperous part of the United Kingdom. The Chan-

nel Tunnel (the "Chunnel"), opened in 1994, provided an undersea link with France.

In southern England, outside the London metropolitan region, more rural areas are in East Anglia to the east, the south coast, the peninsular, scenic southwest, and the upper Thames valley. The Midlands have a large number of large and medium-size industrial centers, including Birmingham, Manchester, and the port of Liverpool in the west, and Sheffield and Leeds in the east. Newcastle is the main industrial city of the north, which is predominantly mountain and lake country. Wales, like the Midlands, is going through a period of difficult industrial change, especially in and around Swansea in the south.

Scotland's economic life centers in industrial Glasgow and cultural and administrative Edinburgh. Mountainous Scotland is one of the most lightly populated parts of the British Isles. In Wales and, to a greater degree, Scotland, there has been a modest revival of Celtic language and culture, long dominated by English.

Northern Ireland is politically tense because of the unyielding opposition of the Protestants, who comprise the majority of the population, to union with Ireland. The Catholic minority favors union. Belfast, the administrative seat and chief economic center, must face both the political and religious strife and declining older industries.

Changing Guard at Buckingham Palace, London
Photo: Courtesy The British Tourist Authority

Areas of Touristic Importance. London is one of the most interesting and exciting cities in the world. Historically, it is one of the most important cities to Americans because of the impact of actions taken there on the cultural development of the United States. There are more flights to London from more cities in the United States than to any other foreign destination. Thus, London is a most logical starting point for multi-city trips to Europe as well as for regional tours through the United Kingdom.

It is possible to spend weeks in London without seeing all its attractions. Space will only permit brief descriptions of the major points of interest.

Westminster Abbey has been the site of the coronation of English kings and queens for centuries. It is also a shrine to British poets, writers, and statesmen, and houses the tombs of many famous figures.

The Houses of the British Parliament can be found on the embankment of the Thames River. Tourists may visit the House of Commons, but the House of Lords does not permit visitors. Big Ben, the most famous clock in the world, stands atop the East Tower of the Parliament Buildings.

Buckingham Palace is the in-town residence of the reigning monarch. Watching the daily changing of the guard is a most popular morning activity. Visitors are welcomed at Hampton Court, which is noted for its royal residences and its elegant gardens. Windsor Castle, 20 miles outside of the city, is open to the public and often serves as a royal residence. Parts of Buckingham Palace have recently been open to public tours.

The Tower of London houses the Crown Jewels. It also has historical significance as a jail for political prisoners and as the site of many famous executions, including those of two wives of King Henry VIII. The Tower is the home of the elegantly costumed "Beefeater" guards. Nearby is the famous Tower Bridge which spans the Thames.

St. Paul's Cathedral, designed by Sir Christopher Wren, was built after the great London fire of 1666. Visitors can climb to the "whispering gallery" at the top of the dome.

London is also the home of many fascinating museums. Probably the most famous is the British Museum with its excellent collection of Egyptian antiquities. The National Gallery features a variety of European paintings, while the Tate Gallery specializes in modern British art. The Victoria and Albert Museum features applied art of all periods. The Science and Imperial War Museums are also of interest. The Royal Air Force Museum at Hendon, on the outskirts of London, centers on the development of British aviation and includes the Battle of Britain Museum.

Hyde Park and Kensington Gardens are centers of daytime activities. Speakers' Corner in Hyde Park is famous for "soapbox" orators talking about anything and everything, especially on Sunday mornings. Boating on the Serpentine is popular from spring through fall.

World-class shopping can be found on Oxford and Kensington Streets. Bargains and the unusual can be found on Portobello Road and at the weekend fleamarket at Maiden Lane.

Entertainment of all types is available in London. The West End theaters are as well known and popular as New York's Broadway. Casino gambling in a club atmosphere and cabaret shows are also popular.

Although London can be a destination in itself, the United Kingdom offers the visitor much more. England, Scotland, Wales, and Northern Ireland have a variety of touristic areas. Of the four primary parts of the United Kingdom, England attracts the most visitors to its many areas.

The south of England features Canterbury, Dover, Brighton, and Southampton. Canterbury is best known for its cathedral and retains many of its medieval features. It was

Giant's Causeway, Antrim, Northern Ireland
Photo: Courtesy Northern Ireland Tourist Board

here that Thomas à Becket was murdered. Canterbury was also the destination of the pilgrims in Geoffrey Chaucer's *Canterbury Tales*. Dover and Brighton are on the English Channel coast. Dover is most famous for its white chalk cliffs, whereas nearby Brighton is a crowded summer beach resort. Southampton is a busy commercial and industrial area as well as an important port. The *Queen Elizabeth 2*, which provides the only remaining ship service between New York and England, sails from this port city.

The west country includes interesting attractions in Bristol, Plymouth, and Bath. Bristol is most widely known for the Church of St. Mary Radcliffe, an almost perpendicular style church. In 1497, John Cabot sailed from Bristol on the voyage during which he discovered the North American continent. Plymouth was the port of embarkation for the 1620 sailing of the Pilgrims who settled in New England. Sir Francis Drake began and completed his circumnavigation of the globe in Plymouth.

Bath is named for its thermal baths, which have attracted visitors from the days of Roman settlements in the area. Not far from Bath, near the city of Salisbury, is Stonehenge, site of large monoliths, of unknown origin, believed to date back to 1800 BC.

Oxford and Stratford-upon-Avon are located in central England, a few hours by bus, train, or car from London. Oxford has been an educational center since the 12th century and is the home of Britain's oldest university. Stratford is in the center of "Shakespeare Country" and the site of the famed Globe Theater, in which England's most famous playwright's works are presented in their original form.

Cambridge is located in the East Anglia region of England. Its university, like Oxford, is world famous. King's College Chapel, the Trinity College Library, and the Cloister Court of Queen's College are the most interesting at the university.

The Midlands and north of England combine commercial and industrial cities with areas of rural, scenic beauty. Manchester and Birmingham are primarily industrial. Coventry has been rebuilt since its near destruction from German bombings during World War II. York, dominated by its Cathedral of St. Peter, known as York Minster, has retained much medieval flavor. The cathedral has some of the finest stained glass in all of Europe.

For natural beauty, the Moors and the Lake District are hard to beat. The Moors are windswept, unfenced areas of grass and heather located north of Manchester and York. The Lake District, in the northwest of England, is composed of 900 square miles of unspoiled countryside. Lakes, mountains, and dales are attractive for both driving and hiking.

Scotland is a land of lush, green countryside and sparsely settled areas. Glasgow, Scotland's only truly large industrial city, is served internationally by Prestwick Airport. Thus, visitors can arrive without using London as a gateway.

Edinburgh is the cultural and social capital of Scotland. It is most noted for Edinburgh Castle and the Palace of the Holyroodhouse, the Queen's official residence in Scotland. The Edinburgh International Festival of Music and Drama, held in late August and early September, is world famous. The game of golf originated at St. Andrews. The remote northern parts of Scotland are known as the Highlands. Inverness is their unofficial capital. Loch Ness (of monster fame) and Aberdeen offer areas of stark beauty.

Wales, which lies west of the British Midlands, has been a part of the United Kingdom for more than 700 years. Its people have their own customs and language. Cardiff is the capital of this interesting land of castles and hills.

Northern Ireland's peaceful, rolling, green countryside contrasts with a legacy of more than two decades of political unrest. The fighting has subsided considerably, however, and visitors should be safe if they stay in tourist areas and use common sense even in the cities of Belfast and Londonderry, where fighting was heaviest. The Antrim coast on the north is especially interesting. The Giant's Causeway is a natural volcanic formation that looks as if it were built by man. Because of similar findings off the coast of Scotland, it is widely believed that the "causeway" once connected Ireland and Scotland.

IRELAND

Language: Gaelic, English
Area: 27,137 square miles
Time Zone: GMT
National Airline: Aer Lingus
Capital: Dublin
Currency: Irish pound (IRL)
Population: 3,489,000
Documentation: Passport

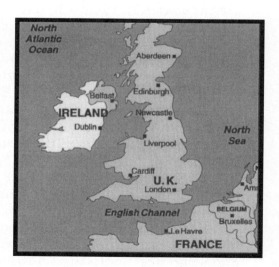

With a wetter climate than Great Britain, Ireland has a green landscape, but the relatively few dry days cause problems in its basically agricultural economy. Blight destroyed the potato crop in the 1840s and resulted in massive Irish emigration, largely to the United States. The farm economy is now shaped around the export of livestock and dairy products to the United Kingdom. More limited emigration continues, with English cities the main destination.

The Irish government has attempted, with limited success, to attract industry to Dublin and other regional centers. However, Ireland remains a relatively poor and underdeveloped member of the European Union. Tourism, largely in the summer season, contributes greatly to the economy. Dublin, on the east coast, is the only large city. Independent only since 1921, Ireland encourages the use of Gaelic, its Celtic language, and strives to preserve Irish culture.

Areas of Touristic Importance. Ireland is a country of mostly rural, picturesque countryside with many small villages and intriguing medieval castles. The total population is less than half of the population of the city of London.

Dromoland Castle, County Clare
Photo: Courtesy Irish Tourist Board

Its capital, Dublin, is its only major city and contrasts sharply with the rest of the nation. Dublin's public buildings house the Irish government and include the historic site of the 1916 uprising that led to Irish independence. Dublin is the cultural center of Ireland, with excellent theater and folkloric entertainment.

Several interesting areas are within short distances of Dublin. Dun Laoghaire, 7 miles down the coast, is the main port for ferry service to England. Several seaside resorts are nearby. Monasterboice, 35 miles north of Dublin, is an early Christian monastic community with ruined medieval churches and high crosses.

A journey along the south coast from Dublin to the west is most interesting. Glendalough, the glen of the two lakes, has unusually beautiful countryside. Kilkenny features a prominent castle and a 13th century cathedral. Waterford has been noted for its fine crystal since the 16th century. Factory tours are popular. Wexford has an interesting harbor with fishing boats.

Killarney, in the southwest, provides a gateway to the mountains and lakes of Ireland. The Ring of Kerry is an intriguing 100-mile circle tour of Ireland's southernmost region. Cork is the gateway for excursions to Blarney and its famous stone.

Shannon, Ireland's largest airport and major international gateway, lies in the west. It has one of the best duty-free shopping complexes of any airport in the world. Bunratty Castle is located between the airport and the town. Medieval banquets with traditional Irish entertainment are served throughout the year. Limerick, at the mouth of the River Shannon, features a prominent, and historically interesting, castle. Dromoland Castle, near Limerick, is now a luxury hotel.

Galway features narrow streets and houses built almost Spanish-style around courtyards. It is said that Columbus stopped here on his way to the New World. Westport attracts hikers and big game fishermen.

Donegal is the most northern Irish county. It has the roughest terrain and its coast is dotted with fishing villages. The poet Yeats was influenced by this land. Sligo is an excellent place to buy Irish tweed.

Ireland is a very popular destination for many American tourists, but especially those of Irish descent who desire a first-hand view of their cultural heritage.

■ THE BENELUX NATIONS

The three Benelux nations of Belgium, The Netherlands, and little Luxembourg, often called the "Low Countries" because of their generally flat topography, lie wedged between France and Germany against the North Sea. Hill country occurs in the southeastern Netherlands and Luxembourg, and low mountains in southeastern Belgium. Small in area (The Netherlands is only 160 miles and Belgium 175 miles east-west), the three nations are among the most densely populated parts of the world.

BELGIUM

Official Name: Kingdom of Belgium
Language: French, Flemish
Area: 11,799 square miles
Time Zone: GMT +1
National Airline: Sabena
Capital: Brussels
Currency: Belgian franc (BFR)
Population: 9,921,000
Documentation: Passport

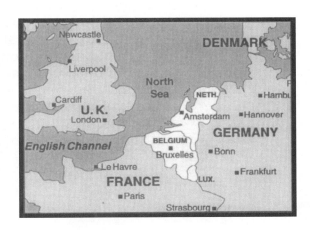

Slightly smaller than The Netherlands, Belgium is triangular in shape and has a narrow seacoast only 40 miles long. Originally a part of The Netherlands, it became independent in 1830 with a population composed of Dutch-speaking Flemish (or Flemings) in the north and French-speaking Walloons in the south. The Flemish are the more numerous, 56 percent of the national population. Since the 1960s, Belgium has been subdivided into two linguistic regions representing the two groups. Brussels, the historic capital and French in language and culture, has been declared bilingual even though it is located in the Flemish-speaking region.

Belgium has a substantial agriculture but is more industrialized than The Netherlands. Heavy industry, which is older and faces economic retrenchment, is found in the southeast; Liege is the main center. New postwar industry has sprung up in the north, in and near the main port city of Antwerp.

Brussels has become one of the most important international administrative cities in Europe. It houses the headquarters of the European Union and the civilian headquarters of the North Atlantic Treaty Organization (NATO), the main Western European military alliance, is based here. Brussels' central location, as well as its accessibility from Europe and the United States, has made it the headquarters of hundreds of international corporation offices.

Areas of Touristic Importance. Brussels houses some of the architectural gems of Europe. The 17th century Grand Place was rebuilt on the original 12th century marketplace site and was considered by Victor Hugo to be the most beautiful square in the world. The 15th century Town Hall, the Maison du Roi, and many guild houses are also on the square. Fine Flemish paintings can be seen at the Musee de l'Art Ancien.

Ostend is the most noted seaside resort town. It features a 5-mile-long, 100-foot-wide, promenade. For entertainment there is the Royal Theater, several casinos, and a fine aquarium.

Antwerp is Belgium's second largest city and its major port. Its Cathedral of Notre Dame contains three of the major works of Rubens, Belgium's most noted artist. Antwerp's Gallery of Fine Arts houses more than a thousand of the works of the Old Masters.

Grand Palace, Brussels
Photo: Courtesy Belgian Tourist Office

Bruges is a quiet town, that has retained much of its original medieval architecture and flavor. Long stretches of its original walls remain intact. Canals wind through the town.

THE NETHERLANDS

Official Name: Kingdom of the Netherlands

Language: Dutch

Area: 15,770 square miles

Time Zone: GMT +1

National Airline: KLM Royal Dutch Airlines

Capital: Amsterdam

Currency: Guilder (DFL)

Population: 15,022,000

Documentation: Passport

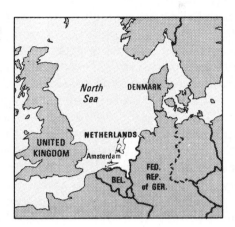

The Netherlands has the largest population and agricultural economy of the three Benelux nations. Yet half of its territory is below sea level. For centuries, the Dutch slowly expanded their land area by reclaiming land from the sea and protecting it with sea walls (dikes). Foods are exported to other western European nations, and the famous Dutch flower bulb industry enjoys a world market.

The Netherlands is often called "Holland," actually the name of the largest Dutch province, which contains the country's three largest and most prosperous cities: Amsterdam, The Hague, and Rotterdam.

A superb location at the mouth of the Rhine River makes Rotterdam one of the world's greatest ports. Thousands of motorized Dutch barges carry imports to and exports from the industrial cores of Germany and France, which are linked by the Rhine. Two other coastal cities are centers of Dutch national life. Amsterdam is the historic royal residence, port, commercial and manufacturing center, whereas The Hague is the seat of government. The three cities together are called the *Randstad,* or "Ring City," where urban and rural land use is carefully planned.

Areas of Touristic Importance. Amsterdam is a well-planned city with four concentric canals and three major squares. Known as the Venice of the North, Amsterdam has more than 1,000 bridges spanning its famous canals. The best way to get an overview of the city is on one of the one and one-half hour canal boat cruises. The Rijksmuseum features the largest collection of paintings by the Dutch masters, including Rembrandt's almost overwhelming *Night Watch.* The Van Gogh Museum houses the works of this eccentric artist. The Anne Frank House, where teenage Anne Frank wrote her diary while seeking refuge from the Nazi occupation, is maintained as a tribute to her courage. Diamond cutting is a major industry and a popular tourist attraction as well. Much of the Netherlands can be seen on excursions from Amsterdam, including the quaint old Dutch fishing villages of Volendam and Marken.

The Hague (also called *Den Haag* or *s'Gravenhague*), while not the official capital of The Netherlands, is the seat of government. In addition to domestic government, The Hague is also home of the United Nations' International Court of Justice. North Sea beaches attract summer tourists as well.

Rotterdam is a very modern city, rebuilt after it was almost totally destroyed by World War II bombings. It is a major port and commercial center. Boat trips through the busy harbor are the best way to view the activity.

The small village of Delft, located between Rotterdam and Amsterdam, has become world famous for its Delftware pottery. Much of the town has been preserved in its 17th century condition.

Dutch cheese is among the best in the world. Near Rotterdam is the village of Gouda, where tourists can visit a cheese factory to learn how the cheese is made.

The nation is also known for tulips and other cultivated flowers. In season, thousands flock to the flower marts. Not far from Amsterdam is the famous flower auction in Aalsmeer.

Although electricity produced by power plants is used throughout The Netherlands, there are still a few picturesque, working windmills dotting the countryside.

LUXEMBOURG

Official Name: Grand Duchy of Luxembourg

Language: French, German

Area: 998 square miles

Time Zone: GMT +1

National Airline: Luxair

Capital: Luxembourg

Currency: Luxembourg franc (LFR)

Population: 388,000

Documentation: Passport

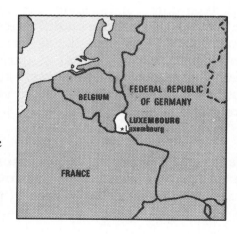

Despite its small size, the Grand Duchy of Luxembourg has managed to maintain its independence since 1866. It is sustained by a thriving industrial economy that has benefited from the Benelux customs union of 1948 and membership in the European Union. Founded in 963, the city of Luxembourg was one of the strongest fortresses in Europe.

Areas of Touristic Importance. Today, visitors can walk through more than 14 miles of underground tunnels cut through solid rock. The Ducal Palace was built in 1580. Fine stained glass windows can be seen in the 15th century cathedral. Luxembourg also has interesting museums including the Museum of History and Art and the National History Museum. Luxembourg is the European gateway for Icelandair, which provides air service from the United States and Iceland.

FRANCE

Official Name: French Republic
Language: French
Area: 220,668 square miles
Time Zone: GMT +1
National Airline: Air France
Capital: Paris
Currency: Franc (FFR)
Population: 56,595,000
Documentation: Passport, visa

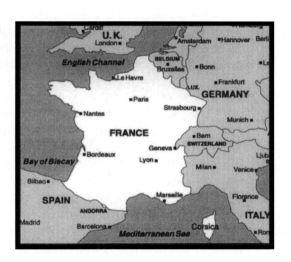

France is one of the great nations of Europe. It has the largest territory and the longest national history of any country in Western Europe. In Paris, it has one of the world's leading cultural and intellectual centers. France has a powerful geopolitical location, with frontage on the Atlantic Ocean, English Channel, North Sea, and the Mediterranean Sea. The nation's rich and complex history is mirrored in its many distinctive regions in dialects, customs, festivals, specialty foods, and economic activities. Its territory includes Corsica, in the Mediterranean Sea, which has a predominantly Italian population.

The Land and Climate. Western France is mainly plains and rolling terrain. In the east, however, France contains part of the Alps and, farther north, the Jura and Vosges Mountains. The south central area is dominated by the plateau known as the Massif Central, and the Pyrenees Mountains form the border with Spain. From the mountainous east, large rivers flow outward. The Seine, on which Paris is located, flows to the English Channel. The Loire and Garonne flow to the Atlantic and the Rhone-Saone system flows southward between the Alps and the Massif Central to the Mediterranean. The Rhone valley is the most used route between Paris and Marseille, the chief city on the Mediterranean coast. Two hilly peninsulas jut westward—larger Brittany and smaller Normandy.

Allowing for many regional climatic variations, winters are milder on the coasts and longer and colder in the interior. The southern, Mediterranean, area has the least rainfall and summers that are generally dry and sunny. The coastal northwest has the largest number of rainy days annually.

The Economy. To a remarkable degree, French national life centers upon Paris, formerly the royal and now the republican seat of government. Paris is France's largest city, far surpassing others in size and importance. It is home to France's greatest assemblage of artistic treasures, best educational institutions and public facilities, and is the country's financial and commercial hub as well as a major industrial center. Paris is also the focus of an excellent transportation network of highways, railways, canals, and air routes. Other major regional cities are Marseille; Lyon, at the head of the Rhone valley; Bordeaux in the southwest; Lille in the north; and Strasbourg in the northeast on the Rhine River, which forms the French-German boundary.

France is Western Europe's largest food producer and exporter. Its products are noted for their quality and variety, and French cuisine is world famous. Gastronomical specialties vary with the region and locality. France is known for its quality wines for domestic use and export. The French fishing industry in the Atlantic Ocean is important.

Large-scale industry came to France relatively late and still is not as large as in the United Kingdom and Germany. The main concentrations of factories and manufacturing cities are in the north and northeast, in and around Lyons in the Rhone valley and its borders, and in and around Paris in the Seine valley. Marseille, on the Mediterranean, and Le Havre, at the mouth of the Seine River, are the main international ports.

Regular ferry service links France with southern England, and the two countries are linked by train transportation that carries automobiles as well as passengers through the Channel Tunnel (the Chunnel). The world's fastest passenger train service (the LGV—La Grande Vitesse) links Paris and Lyon.

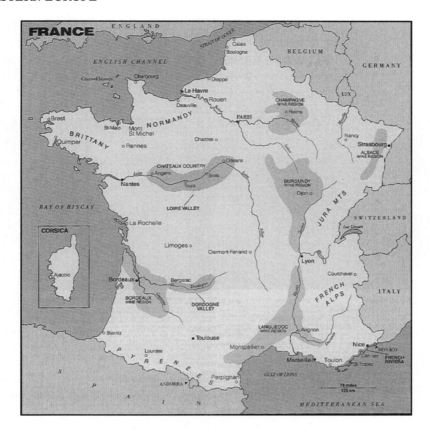

Areas of Touristic Importance. Paris, like London and Rome, is one of the world's great cities. Its most outstanding landmark is the Eiffel Tower. Completed in 1889, it rises more than 1,000 feet. Visitors can see all of Paris from two viewing levels and dine at the tower as well. Another landmark, almost synonymous with Paris, is the Arc de Triomphe, erected by Napoleon. It stands at one end of the broad Champs-Elysees. The Place de la Concorde, where Louis XVI and Marie Antoinette were guillotined during the French Revolution, is at the other end. The broad boulevards of Paris became a model for city planning throughout the world.

A pleasant way to see the city is on the excursion boats (bateaux-mouches) which sail on the Seine River. The boats present excellent views of the famous Left Bank, noted for its artists and poets, and of the Ile de la Cite, home of Notre Dame Cathedral, noted for its prominent flying buttresses.

The Louvre Museum, which houses the Mona Lisa and Venus de Milo, is one of the most important art museums in the world. Other interesting art museums include the Rodin Museum, featuring the artist's world-famous sculpture; the Musee de Cluny, exhibiting medieval tapestries and sculpture; and the Musee du Jeu de Paume, which houses an excellent collection of Impressionist paintings.

The Montmartre district is known for its bohemian cafes. Visit the Sacre Coeur Cathedral by day and the cafes and night-clubs after dark. The Latin Quarter is the home of the Sor-bonne University and the sidewalk cafes of the Boulevards

Eiffel Tower, Paris

Saint Michel and Saint-Germain-des-Pres. This area is the Soho or Greenwich Village of Paris.

Like the rest of France, Paris is known for its food. There is something to please everyone and at prices from the inexpensive to the most expensive. Wines also vary from inexpensive but tasty house table wines to Dom Perignon champagnes.

The palaces of Versailles and Fontainebleau are located within short driving distances of Paris. Versailles was the palace of Louis XIV and is known for its magnificent gardens and opulent living quarters. Louis XIV is said to have employed and boarded 20,000 people at Versailles. During the summer, the fountains and gardens are illuminated for night visitors. Fontainebleau sits in a 42,000-acre forest. Its Renaissance chateau was one of Napoleon's favorite homes.

The provinces of Normandy and Brittany are in Northern France. Rouen is a modernized city that has also retained its historical, medieval character. The old section of town includes the Place du Vieux-Marche, where Joan of Arc was burned at the stake, the Cathedrale de Notre Dame, and the Renaissance Clock. The World War II D-Day beaches are on the English Channel coast. Brittany is where the English Channel and the Atlantic Ocean meet.

The valley of the Loire River is known in France as Chateau country. The abbeys, estates, and fortresses within the area present a microcosm of French history. Tours is the center of the region, and Amboise, Blois, and Chambord all have important historical sites. Tours of prominent wineries are also quite popular.

Alsace-Lorraine is separated from Germany by the Rhine River. Strasbourg is its capital and largest city. The German influence here is great because control of the area has shifted between France and Germany several times in recent centuries.

Lyons is located at the confluence of the Rhone and Saone Rivers. Once the capital of Roman Gaul, it later was a center of the silk trade. Today, it is France's third largest city and a world-famous medical center.

The Alpine region of France stretches from Lake Geneva to the Riviera. The area is exceedingly popular for skiing; chair lifts and cable cars provide access to the ski slopes. Chamonix, Val d'Isere, and Grenoble host thousands each year. In the summer, hiking and camping are increasingly popular.

The Côte d'Azur (Azure Coast), also known as the French Riviera, is an international summer playground. The Mediterranean beaches, cozy harbors, and yacht marinas attract both the middle class and the jet set. The area is large, stretching from Marseilles to the Monaco border. Nice and Cannes have the best resort areas. Marseille is the second largest city in France and its busiest port.

The island of Corsica is a rugged, primarily undeveloped area. It was the birthplace of Napoleon. Corsica has excellent beaches and waters that are ideal for snorkeling and underwater fishing. It is far less crowded than the Riviera and can be reached by air in 40 minutes from Nice.

MONACO

Official Name: Principality of Monaco

Language: French, English, Italian

Area: .6 square miles

Time Zone: GMT +1

Capital: Monaco-Ville

Currency: French franc (FFR)

Population: 29,712

Documentation: Passport

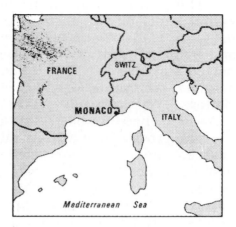

The Principality of Monaco is the second smallest independent state in the world. Only the Vatican City is smaller. Its sovereignty was recognized in 1910 and, since 1918, it has been allied with French political, military, naval, and economic interests. Monaco is a constitutional monarchy. The present leader, Prince Rainier III, was married to former American actress Grace Kelly.

Monaco has been an unrivaled center of tourism for the rich and titled of Europe since its Monte Carlo casino was established in 1856. Today, tourism to that nation has broadened well beyond the rich and famous, and now accounts for more than half of its income. Located just 10 miles from Nice, Monaco is a bridge between the French and Italian Rivieras.

GERMANY

Official Name: Federal Republic of Germany

Language: German

Area: 137,838 square miles

Time Zone: GMT +1

National Airline: Lufthansa

Capital: Berlin

Currency: Deutschemark (DMK)

Population: 79,548,000

Documentation: Passport

History. Germany has the largest population in Europe (excluding Russia) and is Europe's leading economic and industrial power. A federation of 15 states, Germany emerged from World War II defeat under Allied military occupation and from 1949 to 1990 was divided into two separate nations with drastically different political ideologies. West Germany (Federal Republic of Germany) was a democratic nation allied to Western European nations and the United States, while East Germany was under a hard-line Communist government aligned with the former USSR and Communist bloc.

East Germany had within its borders Berlin, the prewar German capital, which was divided into four Allied military sectors. The American, British and French sectors formed West Berlin, with strong West Germany ties, and the Russian sector formed East Berlin, the seat of the East German government. Berlin was divided physically by the Berlin Wall, a fortification built by the East German government in 1961 to prevent the outflow of population to West Berlin and West Germany.

West Berlin remained a free Western outpost in the middle of Communist East Germany. A single road was the only access by land from West Berlin to West Germany. The only other access was by air. With the collapse of the Communist bloc, the two Germanys were formally reunited, on West German terms, in 1990. Reunited Berlin, freed of Allied military control, is once again the official national capital where the parliament meets. However, most administrative offices remain in Bonn, a university town on the Rhine River that served as West Germany's capital. Germany is going through a long, difficult, and expensive period of national integration, during which the former East German portion of the nation makes the shift from public to private ownership.

The Land. German national territory cuts across the east-west topographic grain of Europe. Its southern boundary in the Alps is shared with Switzerland and Austria. Most of southern Germany is hilly to mountainous, and the northern portion is the flat to rolling North European Plain. Although Germany only narrowly fronts on the North and Baltic Seas, which are linked by the Kiel Canal across the base of the Danish Peninsula, it is well-endowed with rivers that are linked by canals.

The Danube River flows eastward into Austria. The Rhine River rises in Switzerland, forms the French-German boundary, becomes a solely German river, is joined by the Moselle River and Main River, and finally passes through The Netherlands to empty into the North Sea. The Elbe rises in Czechoslovakia and crosses Germany to the North Sea. The eastern boundary with Poland follows the Oder River, which flows northward to the Baltic Sea, and its upstream tributary, the

Neisse River. Polish territory was extended westward to this Oder-Neisse Line at the conclusion of World War II.

A major canal linking the Rhine-Main and Danube rivers became a reality in 1992, fulfilling a dream that dates back as far as 793 and Emperor Charlemagne. Most of the Main-Danube Canal has been built since the early 1960s. Along its 106-mile length between Bamberg on the Main River and Kelheim on the Danube River, large locks enable passage through mountainous terrain. Motorized Euro-barges and other craft can now move without interruption between western and southeastern Europe.

The People. Germany's population is predominantly urban, in contrast to the strongly rural character of France. Berlin, the largest city, is followed by Hamburg, the northern port city at the mouth of the Elbe River, and Munich, in the large southern state of Bavaria. Other leading cities are Cologne, Essen, Frankfurt, and Dortmund—all in the west on the Rhine River or its tributaries—Bremen, another northern port, and Dresden and Leipzig in the southeast. Many of these cities were heavily damaged during World War II, but are now restored.

The Economy. Much of the urbanization reflects Germany's prowess in manufacturing. It is Europe's industrial leader. Its main industrial region, the Ruhr, on the Rhine River immediately east of The Netherlands, contains Europe's greatest concentration of heavy industry. Another major industrial complex, based upon local coal and raw materials, is in Saxony in the southeast. Manufacturing plants are concentrated in and around such major cities as Leipzig and Dresden. The lack of pollution safeguards during the Communist era resulted in widespread environmental damage in the former East Germany.

Germany has some of the finest highways (autobahns), trains and air service in Europe. Several major highways cross the Alps to Italy. One of the most historic and heavily used roads leads south from Munich via Innsbruck through the Brenner Pass in Austria; others pass through Switzerland. The Germans are highly mobile people, among the most active in international tourism within Europe.

Areas of Touristic Importance. Berlin is again Germany's capital. Although the Berlin Wall is gone, the open space that it occupied weaves across the city's center. Berlin is one of Europe's greatest tourism magnets and has outstanding cultural, recreational and shopping facilities.

The centrally located Tiergarten is the largest of Berlin's many parks. On its western flank is the Berlin Zoo; Europa-Center, one of Europe's biggest shopping-entertainment complexes; Kaiser Wilhelm Memorial Church, whose bombed-out shell and postwar reconstruction sit side by side; the main concentration of hotels; and stylish Kurfurstendamm (called Ku-damm), Berlin's showcase boulevard. Farther west is Charlottenburg Palace; the Egyptian Museum, containing the famous colored bust of Queen Nefertiti; Olympic Stadium, Botanical Garden; Spandau Citadel; and the wooded lake district of Wannsee.

North and east of Tiergarten is Victory Column; Philharmonic Hall; the battered Reichstag, the Parliament building that was damaged by fire in 1933 and by later wartime bombing; the Soviet War Memorial; and the famed Brandenburg Gate. East of the Gate lies the heart of the old Prussian capital, dominated by elegant old buildings of classical architecture interspersed with concrete and plate glass structures erected by the former East German government. Here is Berlin's former Main Street, Unter den Linden; the State Opera; Humboldt University; Neue Wache War Dead Memorial; the Museum of German History; the Cathedral; and a museum complex centered on the world-famous Pergamon Museum.

Stolzenfils Castle, near Koblenz
Photo: Courtesy German Information Center

Southwest of Berlin is Potsdam, a former royal residence and military garrison town. The Potsdam Conference was held here in 1945 in Cecilienhof Palace. Outside the town center is the magnificent Sans Souci Palace complex built by Frederick II (the Great).

Hamburg, in the north, lies on the Elbe River and has more bridges than Amsterdam and Venice combined. lt is one of the busiest ports in the world. A one-hour boat trip is the best way to view this active city.

Hanover, whose Royal House of Hanover was related to the British throne through the 19th century, and the maritime cities of Bremen and Rostock are also in the northern region of Germany.

Southeast of Hamburg and Hanover is a cluster of three cities—Dusseldorf, Cologne, and Bonn. Dusseldorf and Cologne are industrial and commercial centers. Until 1949, when it became the capital of the new Federal Republic of Germany, Bonn was a quiet university town.

Frankfurt, with its central location, is the major air gateway to Germany. It is a center for international trade, but also has some historic buildings and a world-class zoo. Wiesbaden, not far from Frankfurt, has a major international spa. Fifty miles south is the university city of Heidelberg. A romantic city in the valley of the Neckar River, it features a classic Gothic church and a castle accessed by cable car.

The city of Stuttgart is south of Heidelberg. Although it has some interesting historical areas such as the Schillerplatz and the Altes Schloss (old castle), which serves as a local museum, for most visitors Stuttgart is a gateway to the Black Forest. Called the Black Forest because of dense coniferous growth, the area extends 40 to 60 miles west from Stuttgart to Karlsruhe, Freiburg, and Basel (Switzerland). The region includes many spas and resorts, the most luxurious of which is Baden-Baden.

The Romantic Road, or Romantischestrasse, begins south and east of Frankfurt and continues southward to Augsburg, just outside of Munich, in Bavaria. The road links three small, walled cities, Rothenberg ob der Tauber, Nordlingen and Dinkelsbuhl, which trace their origins to Roman settlements. The largest and most interesting is Rothenburg on the banks of the river Tauber. Many of the buildings along the walls date back to the Middle Ages.

Munich is in the heart of Bavaria. Home of the famous Oktoberfest, which usually takes place in late September, Munich exudes an aura of fun and frivolity. The Rathaus in the Marienplatz features a glockenspiel clock. The square fills at 11:00 AM each day with visitors who come to see the mechanical figures on the clock perform. Just a block away is the Gothic Frauenkirche, with its two prominent black onion-shaped domes. The 100-year-old Hofbrauhaus is the most popular of a number of brewery taverns dating back to 1589. Nymphenburg Palace was the summer palace of "mad" King Ludwig. Outside of Munich, Dachau, a major Nazi concentration camp during Hitler's reign, is maintained as a museum.

Oberammergau, not far from Munich, is the host city of the Passion Play. The play is only performed every 10 years (except for special occasions when it is performed within the decade), but the town attracts hundreds of thousands of visitors during the summers of the play's performance.

South of Munich are the German, or Bavarian, Alps. Garmisch-Partenkirchen is a major Alpine ski resort area. Three of Ludwig's palaces—Linderhof, Herrenchiemsee, and Neuschwanstein—are in this region. Neuschwanstein is a fairy-tale castle and was the model for the castles in Disneyland and Disney World.

In the southeast, Leipzig is an economic and culture center known for its trade fairs. Dresden, known as the Florence on the Elbe, was noted for its classical architecture and art treasures, but it suffered severe wartime bomb damage, some of it still visible. The city's architectural masterpiece is the Zwinger, a restored palace complex built by the rulers of Saxony. Near Dresden is Buchenwald, another of Hitler's infamous concentration camps.

Several southeastern locations closely associated with Martin Luther, leader of the 16th century German (Protestant) Reformation, attract many visitors. He was born and died in the town of Eisleben, west of Halle, and attended the University of Erfurt. It was in Wittenberg that he preached, nailed his demands for reform on the church door in 1517 and publicly burned the papal bull denouncing him in 1520.

Weimar, noted for its ancient buildings and association with some of Germany's greatest literary and artistic figures, was a post-World War I political center. Among many scenic areas noted for their quaint villages and customs are the Harz Mountains in central Germany.

Cruising on the Rhine River has become a popular, relaxing way to enjoy the countryside, visiting castles and other sites along the way.

AUSTRIA

Official Name: Republic of Austria

Language: German

Area: 32,374 square miles

Time Zone: GMT +1

National Airline: Austrian Airlines

Capital: Vienna

Currency: Schilling (AUS)

Population: 7,665,000

Documentation: Passport

Austria is clearly a Western European nation, but it literally sits astride the two parts of Europe. It is overwhelmingly an Alpine nation, like Switzerland, its neighbor on the west. However, it has small plains in the east, part of the Hungarian Plain, and in the north, where the Danube River passes from west to east.

History. German-speaking, Austria is a remnant of the once large and powerful Austro-Hungarian Empire. It inherited the imperial capital of Vienna when the Empire was broken up after World War I, which is why such a small nation has such a large and distinguished capital city. Taken by force by Nazi Germany in 1938, Austria was under an Allied military occupation from 1945 to 1955. During the latter period, central and western Austria received economic assistance through the American Marshall Plan.

Economy. Like Switzerland, Austria's economy relies on a combination of agriculture, manufacturing, and tourism. It is a principal crossroads for people and goods. In its western Alps, the north-south Brenner Pass and the city of Innsbruck provide the easiest overland passage between southern Germany and northern Italy. Vienna is the hub of a web of transportation systems, including Danube River shipping, that link it with both Western and Eastern European nations. Politically free and West oriented, Austria is a politically neutral nation that attempts to remain on good terms with its neighbors regardless of their political complexion.

Areas of Touristic Importance. Austria, like its neighbor, Switzerland, is most famous for its magnificent and breathtaking Alpine beauty.

The name, Vienna, evokes images of the Blue Danube and other Strauss waltzes. The city lives up to its image. With narrow streets and spacious parks, Vienna is both comfortable and attractive. It also has fine museums and excellent world-class shops. St. Stephen's cathedral contains fine carvings and vaults and is easily identified by its single spire. Other interesting buildings include the Augustinerkirche, the Belvedere Palace, designed in a baroque style, and the Hofburg Palace of the Hapsburg dynasty. Vienna is most known for its cultural activities including its Vienna State Opera, the Vienna Boys' Choir, and the famed Spanish Riding School with its performing Lipizzaner horses.

Salzburg, located in a valley and best known for its music, is dominated by the Hohensalzburg Fortress on a mountaintop overlooking the city. The best views of the city are seen from this fortress. The facades of many of the homes in Salzburg date back to the 14th century. Salzburg sponsors a

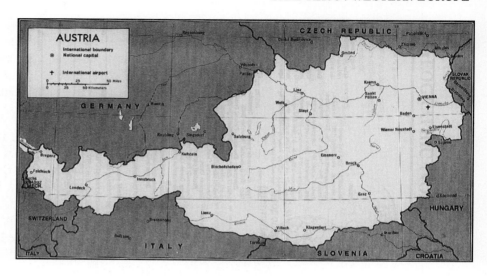

major international music festival each summer featuring the works of Mozart.

Austria is also one of the world's premier skiing locations. Skiing and other sports are popular in winter; camping and hiking attract many during the summer. Innsbruck, provincial capital of the Tyrol, is a most picturesque city. Its Goldenes Dachl (golden roof) is a gilded copper crown which gleams like gold on a three-story Gothic building. Innsbruck is located on the main highway leading from Munich through the Alps into Italy.

LIECHTENSTEIN

Official Name: Principality of Liechtenstein

Language: German

Area: 62 square miles

Time Zone: GMT +1

Capital: Vaduz

Currency: Swiss franc (SFR)

Population: 28,000

Documentation: Passport

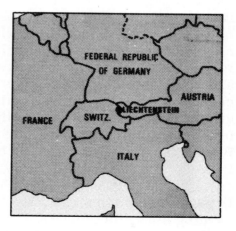

About the size of Washington, DC, the Principality of Liechtenstein is located in the Alps between Austria and Switzerland. One-third of the country is in the upper Rhine Valley, and the rest is mountainous. The population is homogeneous, stemming almost entirely from a Germanic tribe, the Alemanni.

The area became a direct fief of the Holy Roman Empire of the German Nation in 1396. The Principality was established in its present form in 1719. In 1923, a formal customs treaty was signed aligning Liechtenstein economically and politically with Switzerland. Liechtenstein is highly industrialized and produces specialized articles and small machinery.

Areas of Touristic Importance. Although Liechtenstein has some interesting historical sites, primarily in Vaduz, most tourists drive through via car or tour bus. Many take a brief lunch or coffee break and add another country to their trip logs. Those wanting to do more, could visit the Postage Stamp Museum in Vaduz or one of several Roman excavations near Schaan.

SWITZERLAND

Official Name: Swiss Confederation

Language: German, French, Italian

Area: 15,941 square miles

Time Zone: GMT +1

National Airline: Swissair

Capital: Bern

Currency: Swiss franc (SFR)

Population: 6,783,000

Documentation: Passport

The Land. Switzerland is at the crossroads of northern and southern Europe. It is a landlocked nation surrounded by Germany, Austria, France, Liechtenstein, and Italy. The Rhine, Danube, and Rhone Rivers originate in the mountains of Switzerland. The Alps Mountains run from east to west and cover 50 percent of the land. The Jura Mountains stretch from the southwest to northwest and occupy 10 percent of the territory. The remaining 30 percent comprise the lowlands—actually a plateau—where the larger cities and industrial sections of Switzerland are concentrated.

History. So many cultures have influenced Switzerland that it is impossible to define ethnic groups. More than 75 percent of the population live in the central plain between the Alps and the Jura Mountains and from Geneva to the Rhine River. German, French, and Italian are all official languages.

Originally inhabited by the Helvetians, a Celtic tribe, Switzerland was conquered by Julius Caesar during the Gallic period. By the beginning of the 16th century, it consisted of 13 autonomous cantons, which were banded together in a confederation. Except for a 19-year period, during which it was dominated by Napoleon's France (1796-1815), Switzerland has maintained a policy of neutrality. It was able to stay out of both world wars. To preserve its neutrality, Switzerland is not a member of the United Nations. However, the UN's European headquarters is located in Geneva.

The Economy. Switzerland has one of the most stable governments and strongest economies of Europe. Although almost totally lacking in raw materials, it is a well-developed manufacturing country. Its highly skilled and well-educated work force is the backbone of its economy. The Swiss transportation and communications networks are sophisticated and efficient.

Raw materials are imported and high value finished products are exported. Once the undisputed international leader for quality watches, Switzerland has lost its edge to newer techniques in Japan and other countries. However, luxury handmade clocks and other timepieces, and precision instruments are still popular exports, as are special quality products such as chemicals, chocolate, the famous Swiss Army knives, and cheese. Switzerland's negative balance of trade is offset to a great extent by intangible services such as insurance, tourism, and international banking. Swiss banking services are among the best in the world.

Areas of Touristic Importance. Switzerland, like Austria, is a beautiful mountainous nation. Even Zurich, its financial and commercial center, often seems more like a resort than a major modern city. Skyscrapers contrast with the narrow

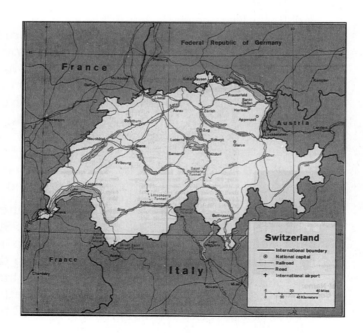

alleyways and quaint squares of its Old Town. A similar contrast can be found in Zurich's Art Museum, which features both medieval and modern works. Zurich is also a cultural center with activities including opera, theater, ballet, and concerts.

Geneva has been Switzerland's most international city for more than 2,000 years. Julius Caesar wrote about it during the Roman occupation. Calvin preached reform from St. Peter's Church in the 16th century. Twenty international organizations are headquartered in Geneva.

Lucerne is the nation's vacation wonderland. Built on one of the world's most scenic lakes, Lucerne has many fine resort hotels. Shopping for watches, cuckoo clocks, and other timepieces is very popular. Its most noted tourist sites are a medieval covered bridge with a painted roof and its large, carved stone lion. Excursions on the lake and into the mountains overlooking the city are quite popular.

Bern, Switzerland's capital, is basically a small quiet city. While somewhat off the beaten path, it does have interesting arcaded medieval streets.

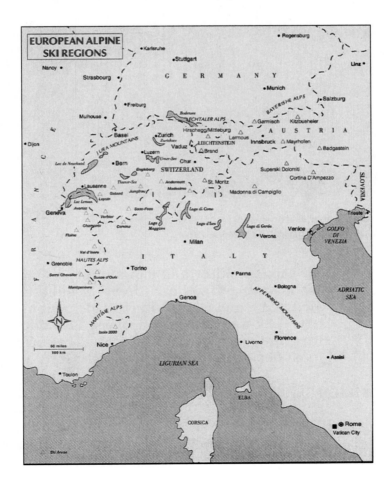

Chapel bridge and water tower, Lake Lucerne
Photo: Courtesy Swiss National Tourist Office

Alpine skiing and mountain climbing are almost synonymous with Switzerland. Resorts such as St. Moritz, Davos, Montreux, and Gstaad were made famous by the wealthy. Today, they welcome all travelers. The Matterhorn is best seen from the resort town of Zermatt. The Interlaken resort area is most beautiful with its view of the lofty Jungfrau peak.

■ THE NORTHERN TIER

The northern tier of nations, popularly called Scandinavia and, more formally, Norden, consists of Norway, Sweden, Denmark, Finland, and Iceland. Finland is often discussed with Eastern Europe because of its politically sensitive location as a neighbor of Russia. Scandinavia is on the northern periphery of Europe. The island nation of Iceland has the greatest relative isolation.

Because these nations are located so far to the north, they experience difficult winters. In addition, Norway, Sweden, and Finland have heavily glaciated uplands, and most of their relatively small populations live in the southernmost part of their territory, where physical conditions are more tolerable and interaction with the rest of Europe is easier.

Except for Finland, the Scandinavian nations are bound by common German-derived languages, Protestant (Lutheran) religion, democratic institutions, trade, and substantial living standards. Yet, politically they are diverse: Norway, Denmark, and Iceland are members of NATO, whereas Sweden and Finland are neutrals in international affairs. Only Denmark was a member of the European Union until Finland and Sweden joined in 1995.

NORWAY

Official Name: Kingdom of Norway

Language: Norwegian

Area: 125,181 square miles

Time Zone: GMT +1 (NKR)

National Airline: SAS

Capital: Oslo

Currency: Norwegian krone (NKR)

Population: 4,273,000

Documentation: Passport

The Land. Norway has austere physical conditions in most of its large territory, which extends north-south for 1,100 miles (including 300 miles north of the Arctic Circle) between the Arctic Ocean and the North Sea. It has a long common border with Sweden and, in the north, shorter borders with Finland and Russia. The western coastline is remarkably long and indented with deep-cut fjords and many offshore islands. In the central and northern areas are heavily glaciated mountains with extensive forests; winters here are long, bitterly cold, and snowy.

The Economy. Most of the small Norwegian population live in the south and southwest where there is level land and small agricultural areas. National life centers on the capital, Oslo, and such smaller regional cities as Bergen, Trondheim, and Stavanger. In the recent past, the Norwegian economy was based upon forest products, some local minerals, and small-scale manufacturing, fishing, and a large merchant marine operating worldwide. However, the discovery of oil and natural gas fields in the North Sea has made Norway an energy exporter and has brought a new prosperity.

Areas of Touristic Importance. Oslo, Norway's capital, offers some unique attractions. The Kon-Tiki Museum houses the famous balsa raft sailed by adventurer Thor Heyerdahl across the Pacific. Oslo's Folkmuseum is a park with 150 buildings depicting Norwegian life from the 12th century. Norway's maritime heritage can also be seen in Oslo's displays of Viking ships and the Arctic polar exploration ship, the *Fram*, sailed by Nansen and Amundsen.

Eagle Pass, Geringer Fjord, Norway

Bergen is the gateway to the fjord country. It is a most colorful city that shows the native Norwegian spirit and heritage. The Norwegian composer, Edvard Grieg, lived and wrote here, and the spirit of the nation can be heard in his music. Fjord excursions and cruises that depart from or stop at Bergen are an excellent way to see the rugged coastline.

This is the famed Land of the Midnight Sun. Cruises as far north as Hammerfest (above the Arctic Circle) are available. Air excursions also take visitors into the region where there is almost no darkness in June and July and almost no sunlight in December and January.

SWEDEN

Official Name: Kingdom of Sweden

Language: Swedish

Area: 173,731 square miles

Time Zone: GMT +1

National Airline: SAS

Capital: Stockholm

Currency: Swedish krona (SEK)

Population: 8,564,000

Documentation: Passport

Prosperous Sweden is hemmed in by Norway on the west and Finland on the north. To the east, it faces on the Gulf of Bothnia, an arm of the Baltic; south on the Baltic Sea proper; and southwest on the narrow straits, the Kattegat, that separate it from Denmark. Physical conditions in the central and northern areas resemble those in Norway, with more lakes and rivers. However, the north does have some of Europe's largest and richest iron ore deposits. Iron ore is exported in quantity to industrial nations of Western Europe. Also in the north, a distinctive ethnic group, the Lapps, who also live in adjacent parts of Norway and Finland, known as Lapland, specialize in the raising of reindeer.

Southern Sweden extends much farther south than Norway. In fact, Sweden lies almost due east of Denmark. There, level topography, better soils, and a longer summer growing season encourage a prosperous agriculture. There, too, are numerous specialized manufacturing towns and cities whose output is consumed at home or exported. These diverse activities support a population twice as large as that of Norway.

Stockholm, on the southeast coast, is the capital and largest city. Goteborg is the major port on the southwest coast. Malmo, which lies only a short water distance east of Copenhagen, Denmark, and Uppsala, north of Stockholm, are the largest regional centers. Sweden has a number of islands along its southeastern coast. The largest are Gotland and Oland.

Areas of Touristic Importance. The Gamla Stan, Stockholm's Old Town, is set in the middle of Lake Malaren. Visit the Royal Palace and the Storkyrkan, the oldest church and home of the Swedish reformation. A boat trip offers views of Stockholm's city islands and its many bridges. Skansen is a unique open-air museum. It features displays and shops with century-old Swedish traditions.

Uppsala was first a Viking religious center and then a Christian one. Today, it is the center of Swedish education with the oldest university in Scandinavia. The Gothic cathedral is built on the site of a gold-sheathed pagan temple. The cathedral houses the tombs of Sir Erik and King Gustav, who founded the Swedish state in the 16th century.

Goteborg, Sweden's second largest city, is its largest seaport. Maritime activities are the central focus of life here. Goteborg has a large fishing fleet and an excellent Maritime Museum with indoor and outdoor exhibits. Its aquarium and botanical garden are excellent as well.

DENMARK

Official Name: Kingdom of Denmark

Language: Danish

Area: 16,633 square miles

Time Zone: GMT +1

National Airline: SAS

Capital: Copenhagen

Currency: Danish kroner (DKR)

Population: 5,134,000

Documentation: Passport

Small Denmark is formed of two distinctive units, the Jutland Peninsula, which borders Germany, and a cluster of large and small islands to the east of the peninsula. Both have flat to rolling topography and a summer climate favorable to agriculture. The strategic location between the North Sea and Baltic Sea has helped Denmark become an important commercial nation.

The national capital, Copenhagen, is located on the large island of Sjaelland in the extreme eastern part, only a short distance from Sweden. Copenhagen is a major Baltic port and trade center. Even though Denmark's population is smaller

The Little Mermaid, Copenhagen Harbor
Photo: Courtesy the Danish Tourist Board, New York

than that of Sweden, Copenhagen is at least as populous as Stockholm.

Danish prosperity has long been based in part upon one of Europe's most productive and best-managed agricultural systems, which permits Denmark to export food to Western European customers. However, manufacturing employs a much larger labor force. Denmark also owns the Faeroe Islands, in the North Atlantic, equidistant from Scotland, Norway, and Iceland. The island of Greenland, off North America, is a self-governing part of Denmark.

Areas of Touristic Importance. The statue of the Little Mermaid, symbol of Copenhagen, stands at the entrance to the harbor. Tivoli Gardens is an amusement park with attractions enjoyed by many who hate amusement parks. Near Tivoli is the Glyptotek, which displays excellent sculpture as well as French Impressionist paintings. Vor Frelser's Kirke (Our Saviour's Church) has an unusual outside spiral staircase, from which there are good views of the city.

The countryside outside of Copenhagen is exactly as described in the fairy tales of Hans Christian Andersen. Odense was his home, and several buildings there have been preserved in his memory. Den Fynske Landsby is an open-air museum where old buildings have been gathered to form a village to preserve the Danish heritage.

The Faeroe Islands are relatively undeveloped. Accessible by air and sea, they attract only the adventurous traveler.

FINLAND

Official Name: Republic of Finland
Language: Finnish
Area: 130,119 square miles
Time Zone: GMT +2
National Airline: Finnair
Capital: Helsinki
Currency: Finnmark (FMK)
Population: 4,991,000
Documentation: Passport

Finland shares the physical conditions of its western neighbors—a cold climate, glaciated topography, poor soil, and extensive forests. The small population is concentrated in the south, where the national capital and largest city, Helsinki, is located, and along the west coast. Among the sparse population in the north are nomadic, reindeer-herding Lapps.

Dominated in earlier centuries by the Swedes and Russians, the Finns remain culturally distinctive and politically independent. Finnish is a distinctive language related to Hungarian. The predominant religion, Protestantism, is shared with other Scandinavian nations. Finland was successful in maintaining positive diplomatic and commercial relations with the former Soviet Union despite its freely elected, non-Communist government and its West-oriented foreign trade. It also has good relations with present Russia. The national economy is shaped around a combination of agriculture, wood and wood products, and small-scale, diversified manufacturing.

Areas of Touristic Importance. For the tourist, Finland offers an unspoiled, rugged forestland dotted with more than 60,000 lakes. Helsinki, although more than 400 years old, is a strikingly modern city with light-colored buildings. It is often called the White City of the North. Helsinki's parks and squares are lined with interesting sculpture.

Outside of Helsinki, Turku, Tampere, Porvoo, and Hameenlinna attract limited numbers of visitors. A visit to Finnish Lapland provides an unusual excursion into the Arc-

Porvoo, Finland
Photo: Courtesy Finnish Tourist Board

tic. Visitors to Rovaniemi, the only town in the region, can learn about the nomadic life style of the Lapps.

ICELAND

Official Name: Republic of Iceland

Language: Icelandic

Area: 39,769 square miles

Time Zone: GMT

National Airline: Icelandair

Capital: Reykjavik

Currency: Kronur

Population: 259,000

Documentation: Passport

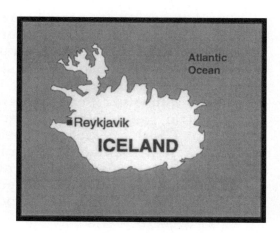

Iceland is a small volcanic island in the North Atlantic Ocean that is noted for its many earthquakes, hot springs, and geysers—all indicative of its subterranean instability—and its glaciers. The small population avoids the mountainous interior and lives along the coast. More than one-third of the entire population lives in the capital and only large city, Reykjavik. Under Danish rule since the 15th century, Iceland became fully independent in 1944. Its economy is based upon farming and commercial fishing. Its location in the North Atlantic makes Iceland an important NATO ally. Important U.S. bases are maintained in Iceland.

Areas of Touristic Importance. Reykjavik is Iceland's main tourist destination. Many of Icelandair's flights between the United States and Europe (Luxembourg, primarily) stop en route at Keflavik Airport. The airline's promotion of 1-, 2-, and 3-day stopover packages has attracted many visitors to this small nation. Because of oceanic influences, the climate in Reykjavik is similar to that of New York, and tourists can be accommodated year-round.

Thingvellir, the site of the world's oldest parliament, the Althing, which first met in 930, is just outside the city.

The major attractions outside of Rekjavik are Gullfoss, a most beautiful waterfall, and the Geysir region, from which the term for periodic sprays of hot springs through the ground was derived. A popular summer excursion is a visit to a whaling station. Hiking and pony trekking are also popular summer activities. Mount Hekla, an active volcano, is the largest mountain in the nation. Akureyri and Lake Myvatn, above the Arctic Circle in the north, attract visitors in the summer months.

■ THE SOUTHERN TIER

The four southern nations of Portugal and Spain, neighbors in the Iberian Peninsula, Italy, and Greece share a number of features. In natural endowment, they are mountainous and have relatively mild winters and dry summers. Except for Greece, they share the common legacy of Roman influence, which is reflected in their languages and culture.

These nations also share a Catholic religious heritage and have predominantly agricultural economies except for some manufacturing in northern Spain and northern Italy. They are poorer and have generally lower living standards than nations to the north. The tiny nations of Andorra, San Marino, Malta, and the Vatican City are also located in this southern tier.

SPAIN

Official Name: Spanish State
Language: Spanish
Area: 194,896 square miles
Time Zone: GMT +1 (except Canary Islands and Melilla)
National Airline: Iberia
Capital: Madrid
Currency: Peseta (PTS)
Population: 39,384,000
Documentation: Passport

The Land and Climate. Occupying the bulk of the Iberian Peninsula, Spain is only slightly smaller than France but has a much smaller population. It is separated from France by the Pyrenees Mountains and has a coastal frontage on both the Atlantic (Bay of Biscay) and the Mediterranean Sea.

Offshore territories include the Balearic Islands, whose main island is Majorca, in the Mediterranean; the Canary Islands off northwest Africa; and two tiny enclaves, Ceuta and Melilla, on the coast of Morocco in northwest Africa. The port of Gibraltar, which commands the narrow Strait of Gibraltar at the western end of the Mediterranean, remains British over Spanish protests.

Spain has very rough topography consisting of numerous mountain ranges and intervening broad plains, forested in the north and more barren in the center and south. Central Spain, the Meseta, gives rise to numerous large rivers. The Ebro in the northeast and the Guadalquivir in the southwest are major ones within Spain, and such rivers as the Douro, Tagus, and Guadiana rise in Spain but flow westward through Portugal.

Variations in climate include the rainier temperate conditions of the Atlantic borders; the dry interior, where winter is longer in the north and shorter in the south; the Mediterranean coast, with short winters and hot summers; and the south and southeast, where warm temperatures prevail throughout the year. The seasonal rainfall varies greatly, more in the north and less in the interior and south, and, for most of Spain, more during the winter.

History. Spain was at least partially under Moslem, or Moorish, control between 711 and 1492, which left Spain with many cultural features that are distinctive in Europe. Castilian Spanish, spoken in the province that led the fight against the Moors and produced the Spanish kingship, became the national language at the expense of older regional languages.

Since the death in 1975 of dictator Francisco Franco, who continued that historical dominance, greater autonomy has been gradually granted to some regions. Galician in Galicia in the northwest, Basque in the north, and Catalan in Catalonia in the northeast, are now officially recognized regional languages on a par with Castilian Spanish.

The Economy. Spain is relatively lightly populated. Most people and cities are found on the periphery and in the large river valleys. Madrid, the national capital and largest city, is an exception, located in the middle of the nation. It happened to be in Castile, the organizing center of Spain, and was not designated the capital until 1607. Other large cities include Barcelona, the flourishing center of relatively prosperous Catalonia in the northeast; Valencia, on the central Mediterranean coast; Seville, inland in the southwest; Zaragoza, inland in the northeast; and Bilbao, the port city serving the Basque country of the north.

Compared to other leading nations of Western Europe, Spain has a relatively low level of overall economic development. Agriculture is still the economic mainstay. It makes limited use of fertilizer, mechanization, and modern techniques, and, therefore, productivity is low. The agricultural land is irrigated wherever possible to offset the poor timing and inadequate amounts of rainfall. Land tenure ranges from the extremes of small farms to huge estates. Wheat, rice, olives, grapes for wine, and citrus fruits are among the main crops, and sheep grazing is widespread.

Spain is relatively well endowed with coal and basic mineral ores in the north, where they form the basis of a variety of heavy and light industries in a number of cities, led by Barcelona. Many raw materials are exported for lack of domestic manufacturing facilities and the low purchasing capacity in the national market. Spain and Portugal finally gained admission to the European Union in 1985. Consequently, the Spanish economy has made great gains and is now well integrated with the broader European economy.

Areas of Touristic Importance. Throughout Spain, numerous cultural and historical sites abound from remains of Roman influence to the Moorish influence on several mosques to a variety of castles and palaces dotting the country.

Madrid is the major gateway for visitors flying into Spain. Its most prominent attraction is the Prado Museum, which is one of the world's finest. The museum features paintings by Goya, El Greco, Rubens, Titian, and many other masters. The Royal Palace has an impressive collection of 15th through 18th century armor, Flemish tapestry, and period furniture. Buen Retiro Park provides a pleasant wooded atmosphere for walking, along with an excellent collection of statuary.

There are several interesting areas within a short distance of Madrid. Toledo is best known for its metalwork, including inlaid gold pieces. The Church of Santo Tome contains paintings by El Greco. Avila, home of Saint Teresa, is a medieval walled city. Segovia is known for its castle and Roman aqueduct.

Seville features the largest Gothic cathedral in the world. Its bell tower is a Moorish minaret. Inside are two of Murillo's most famous paintings and the mausoleum of Christopher Columbus. Seville's Alcazar is an excellent example of Arab-Christian architecture.

Granada's most popular attraction is the spectacular Alhambra. This imposing combination of courtyards, gardens, and fountains was the last stronghold of the Moors. The nearby Royal Chapel, built by Ferdinand and Isabella, celebrates the victory of the Catholic faithful over the Moors. The Alhambra hosts music festivals during the summer season.

Spain is one of the greatest European summer vacation destinations. Its Mediterranean beaches alone attract millions of visitors. The resorts in the Costa del Sol (including the Costa Brava) area on the Mediterranean coast are Spain's playground. Resorts are located near Malaga, Torremelinos, and Marbella. The Marbella area is quieter and more exclusive.

Algeciras is a small city near the British Gibraltar colony. Because the distance across the Mediterranean is relatively short, it serves as a port for regular ferry service to the coast of North Africa (Morocco).

Barcelona, which hosted the Olympic Games of 1992, is considered by many to be the most cosmopolitan city in Spain. As the hub of the Catalonian region, the dominant language is Catalan. Its most interesting area is the Barrio Gotico (Gothic Quarter) featuring a 14th century cathedral. A popular attraction is Gaudi's Church of the Sacred Family, with its intriguing other-worldly architecture. The Palacio de la Diputacion, nearby, housed the ancient Catalonian parliament. Montjuich Park has many attractions including the Palacio National, housing the Museum of Catalan Art, and the fascinating Pueblo Espanol, a folk village where Spanish art is produced and sold and where folkloric presentations are produced during the summer. Barcelona is also the gateway to the Balearic Islands.

Unique entertainment in Spain includes nightclubs with flamenco music, bullfights, and Spanish theater and comic opera. Dining is normally quite late, even for Europeans. A 10:00 or even 11:00 PM dinner is not unusual, especially in Madrid and Barcelona. The best Spanish shopping values are leather goods, embroidered clothing and wall pieces, handmade rugs, handpainted tiles, and Toledo engraved metalwork.

The Balearic Islands. Majorca, Minorca, Ibiza, and Formentera, plus a few other tiny islands comprise the Balearic Islands and are considered part of Spain. Like the Costa del Sol, the Balearic Islands primarily offer sun and fun activities including swimming and boating. However, there are a number of interesting cultural and historical activities.

Palma, on Majorca, is the provincial capital and largest city. Its golden cathedral dates back to 1230. Its intriguing interior includes what is believed to be the original "crown of thorns" above its altar. The hilltop castle of Bellver houses its Municipal Museum. Seaside resorts dot the coastline outside the city.

Minorca was occupied by the British in the 18th century and they left their mark on both life style and architecture. Its main town is Mahon. On this island, archaeologists have found caves, strange monuments, and other artifacts from the Iron and Bronze Ages.

Ibiza is warmer and drier than the other islands. For this reason, it has become a haven for artists, writers, and sun worshipers. Phoenician, Carthaginian, and Roman relics in the Ibiza Archeological Museum show how these nations controlled the Mediterranean in their day.

Canary Islands. The Canary Islands are located in the Atlantic Ocean, off the coast of North Africa. Like the Balearic Islands, the Canaries are considered part of Spain, and in fact form two Spanish provinces. The province of Las Palmas includes the islands of Gran Canaria, Lanzarote, and Fuerteventura. The province of Santa Cruz de Tenerife includes Tenerife, La Palma, Gomera, and Hierro islands. They are primarily resort destinations. Teide, the highest mountain in Spain (12,250 ft.), is on Tenerife.

GIBRALTAR

Language: English, Spanish
Area: 2.25 square miles
Time Zone: GMT +1
Capital: Gibraltar
Currency: Pound sterling
Population: 29,048
Documentation: Passport

Gibraltar is an important strategic dependency of the United Kingdom located at the entrance to the Mediterranean Sea. It is at the southernmost tip of the Iberian Peninsula and serves as a harbor for British ships and was formerly a fortress. Although it is controlled by the United Kingdom, its ownership is contested by Spain. Gibraltar is of increasing importance as a financial and tourist center.

Areas of Touristic Importance. A cable car transports visitors to the top of the Rock for a breathtaking view of the

Mediterranean and to see the colony of famous, wild Barbary apes. The Moorish Castle, Upper Galleries, and St. Michael's Cave are also worth visiting.

PORTUGAL

Official Name: Republic of Portugal

Language: Portuguese

Area: 36,390 square miles

Time Zone: GMT (except Azores and Madeira Islands)

National Airline: Air Portugal

Capital: Lisbon

Currency: Escudo

Population: 10,387,000

Documentation: Passport

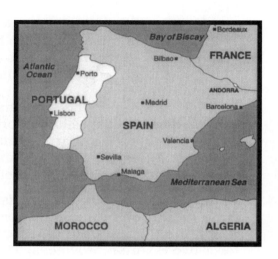

History. Portugal, which occupies western Iberia and faces westward on the Atlantic Ocean, shares much of Spain's history, including the Roman and Moorish periods, but broke away as an independent nation in the mid-12th century. During the 15th and 16th centuries, it fashioned a large overseas trading empire. Macau, on the China coast, is the last remaining of its once extensive colonies and it will revert to China in 1999. The national territory does include the Azores Islands, located in the mid-Atlantic, which are important for their civilian and military airbase, and the Madeira Islands off the northwest Africa coast.

The Land, People, and Economy. Portugal's interior topography is a western continuation of the Spanish Meseta. Mountains occupy northern Portugal as far south as the Douro River. Interior mountains and a coastal plain extend southward to blend with the plains along the Tagus River. In the south, the Algarve has hills and plains. The climate is temperate. The north is cooler and wetter than the Algarve and has drier and hotter summers, much like southern Spain and northwest Africa.

Most Portuguese live in the area north of the Tagus River. The two largest cities are Lisbon, the capital, at the Tagus River mouth, and Oporto, on the lower Douro River. The Algarve is lightly populated. The economy is heavily agricultural with small farms the general rule. Ocean fishing is carried out from coastal ports. Consumer goods and some agricultural specialties are manufactured for export. Portugal remains one of Europe's poorer and more economically underdeveloped nations, yet has improved in recent years as a member of the European Union.

Areas of Touristic Importance. Portugal's capital, Lisbon, is a city built on hills. The oldest monument to the city, Castelo de Sao Jorge, is on top of the highest hill. It dates back to the time of the Visigoths. The old quarter of the city, the Alfama district, is the most charming with narrow cobblestone streets. Much of it survived the earthquake of 1755. The Casa dos Bicos is unusual because of its pointed stones. Sao Vicente is the parthenon of ancient kings and queens. Lisbon's most ornate church is Sao Roque. There are many museums

Thieves' Market, Lisbon
Photo: Courtesy Lisbon National Tourist Office

featuring European masters and many parks and gardens of great beauty.

Portugal's sun coast, the Estoril, is just 15 miles to the west of Lisbon. The Parque do Estoril, at the center of the resort area, is a series of formal gardens from the railway station to the Casino.

Portugal's primary vacation area, the Algarve coast on the south, runs westward from the Spanish border to Cape Saint Vincent. There are many hotels, resorts, villas, and beaches in the region. Monte Gordo, Praia da Rocha, and Faro are among the most prominent towns with good tourist facilities.

Madeira, a beautiful island 600 miles southwest of the mainland, is considered part of Portugal. Primary access, by air, takes less than 2 hours from Lisbon. Home of the famous Madeira wines, the island has great natural beauty. Funchal, the provincial capital, has much old world charm. Although the island has only one beach, most hotels have swimming pools. It is an excellent location for a quiet vacation.

The Azores are a group of nine islands located 800 miles from the mainland. Like Madeira, they are considered part of Portugal. They were important in the days of the early explorers and served as a jumping off point for voyages to the New World. With the development of international air transportation, the islands served as a refueling stop, especially on westbound flights. Some aircraft still make stops when winds are high. There are some small resorts on the larger islands.

ANDORRA

Official Name: Principality of Andorra

Language: Catalan, Spanish, French

Area: 185 square miles

Time Zone: GMT +1

Capital: Andorra la Vella

Currency: Peseta (PTS), franc (FFR)

Population: 53,000

Documentation: Passport

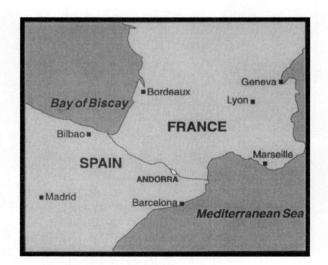

This little nation is located on the Spanish-French border in the Pyrenees Mountains. It offers beautiful scenery and good duty-free shopping. Much of Andorra's rugged terrain consists of gorges, and narrow valleys surrounded by mountain peaks which rise above 9,500 feet in altitude.

Areas of Touristic Importance. A cool, dry summer climate and winter snow attract many tourists. Mountain streams provide good trout fishing.

Because of its remote location, Andorra has existed outside the mainstream of European history. Good roads and a thriving tourist industry, especially for skiing, have propelled it into the 20th century. Vestiges of the past remain, however, in the form of Romanesque churches and bridges.

ITALY

Official Name: Republic of Italy

Language: Italian

Area: 116,303 square miles

Time Zone: GMT +1

National Airline: Alitalia

Capital: Rome

Currency: Lira (LIT)

Population: 57,772,000

Documentation: Passport

Italy is the leading Mediterranean nation in many respects. The widespread diffusion and impact of its earlier Roman culture, its brilliant contributions to the arts over the centuries, and the spiritual leadership of the Roman Catholic religion through the Vatican in Rome have had worldwide impact. Its larger population and more productive agricultural, and larger manufacturing, capacity have given the nation a higher general living standard than the rest of the southern tier.

The Land and Climate. The 700-mile-long Italian peninsula juts far southward into the central Mediterranean and is bordered by the Adriatic Sea on the east and the Tyrrhenian Sea on the west. Italy also includes the large island of Sicily off its southern tip, Sardinia, 125 miles to its west, and other smaller islands off the west coast.

In the north, Italy shares the Alps with France, Switzerland, Austria, and Slovenia. Glaciated lakes (Maggiore, Como, and Garda), in the southern flanks of the Alps in northwest Italy, are among the most scenic in Europe. South of the Alps is the broad Po River Plain, Italy's largest lowland and its economic heart. The Po River flows eastward to the Adriatic Sea, with the plain also increasing in width as it moves east. South of the plain, the Apennine Mountains form the backbone of the peninsula. Volcanic peaks are numerous.

The long north-south extent of Italy results in regional climatic differences. The Alps and the Po River Plain have cold, wet winters. Snowfall in the Alps increases to the east, and is heaviest in the Dolomites. The Italian Riviera on the northwest coast, like its French counterpart farther west, is shielded by the interior mountains and has milder winters. Winter weather moderates and rainfall lessens southward. The southern boot and Sicily have the mildest, clearest winters. Summers are hot and dry. In culture, too, there are many regional variations—in language, folkways, foods, and wines.

The Two Italys. Actually, Italy has two distinct regional personalities, the areas north and south of Rome. Northern Italy is part of the prosperous, industrial Western Europe farther north. The largest industrial operations in the Mediterranean area are found in northwest Italy in and around Milan, the main center, Turin, the port city of Genoa, and a host of smaller northern cities. Steel, autos, textiles, machinery, and a great variety of other products flow into Italian and foreign markets from there. The Po River Plain is Italy's largest food producer.

At the mouth of the Po River at the head of the Adriatic Sea is the famed artistic and port city of Venice. A short distance to the east, another port, Trieste, is administered by Italy through a treaty with the former Yugoslavia. In the northwest Apennines is Florence, another treasure house of Italian art. The historic seat of government and Italy's largest city is Rome, located roughly midway north-south near the west coast.

Southern Italy is the other side of the coin—poorer, less industrial, and based upon a struggling agriculture in spite of continued investment by Italy and the European Union. Naples, the third largest Italian city after Rome and Milan, on the west coast only a short distance south of Rome, is the main center of opportunity for the region. This part of Italy has been the source of large numbers of out-migrants during the past century—to the promise of northwestern Italy, to jobs north of the Alps in other nations, or to the Americas.

The People. As recently as the 1950s, Italy was known in Europe for its relatively large families and high birth rate. However, the 1991 census showed a dramatic change—zero population growth, the lowest birth rate in the world, small families, a rapidly ageing population, and a large influx of migrants from other Mediterranean countries. All six of Italy's largest cities, including Rome and Milan, are declining in population size, although small and medium-size cities are increasing.

Areas of Touristic Importance. Rome, the Eternal City, like London and Paris, is one of the most cosmopolitan and important tourist-attracting cities in Western Europe and the world. Most travelers flying into Italy enter through this, its capital city.

Vestiges of the political and social center of the Roman Empire stand as monuments to its many achievements. Near the Piazza Venezia, with its 19th-century statue dedicated to Victor Emmanuel II, is the Roman Forum, which was the center of the Roman Empire's political, judicial, and business life. Palatine Hill houses the Imperial Forum and the Colosseum. This huge arena which dates to 80 AD was where gladiators, Christians, and beasts fought and died before crowds of 60,000 Romans.

Not far from the Vatican, along Via Appia Antica, are the Catacombs where thousands of early Christians were buried. The fortress, Castel Sant' Angelo, and three impressive basilicas—Santa Maria Maggiore, St. John in Lateran, and St. Paul's Outside-the-Walls—are in the same area. The Villa Borghese houses important paintings and sculptures. It also is surrounded by beautiful gardens and an interesting zoo. The Spanish Steps at the Piazza di Spagna are most beautiful, especially in spring when the azaleas are in bloom.

The Via Veneto with its shops and cafes is the Champs-Elysees of Rome. High-fashion clothing, leather goods including shoes and gloves, and silk are among the most popular items.

The Vatican attracts visitors of all faiths. Because it is a sovereign state, its tourist attractions will be described separately in the "Vatican City" section immediately following.

Beautifully sculpted fountains can be found throughout Rome. Many are illuminated at night. The most frequently visited and remembered is the Trevi Fountain of "Three Coins in the Fountain" fame.

Ostia Antica, near Rome, was a thriving seaport in the 4th century. Also not far is Lido di Roma, Rome's closest beach. In the suburban area on the other side of the city are the beautiful Villa d'Este gardens, including the fountains at Tivoli.

Pisa, in the Tuscany region of Italy, is most famous for its architectural error—the Leaning Tower of Pisa. Currently leaning 14 feet from center, the tower is still slipping. Visitors used to be able to walk to the top and may be able to once again some day when the tower can be made safe.

Florence, the great city of the Renaissance, is 180 miles north of Rome. Ruled by the iron hand of the Medici family, Florence was the clear leader during this period of great art. Michelangelo, Titian, Botticelli, and many more Italian masters of art and architecture are well-represented.

Spanish Steps and Church, Rome
Photo: Courtesy Italian Government Travel Office

The Pitti Palace and the Uffizi Palace have the best collections. Michelangelo's most famous statue, David, stands in the Academia di Belle Arti. Donatello's statue of Saint George is in the Bargello Museum (a prison during the 16th century). The Baptistry of the Cathedral of Santa Maria del Fiore features impressive bronze doors. The cathedral itself is noted for its bell tower of colored marble. The 13th century Church of Santa Croce is the burial place of both Michelangelo and Machiavelli.

Florence is also noted for its leather goods. The Italian Leather School, where the art of leather tooling and gilding is still taught, is located here.

Built on a series of more than 100 islands and served by more than 150 canals, Venice is indeed unique. The Piazza San Marco (St. Mark's Square) is one of the grandest in all of Europe. St. Mark's Cathedral is at one end of the square. Nearby is the 325-foot 14th century bell tower topped by bronze figures which chime the bells. Both this and a 15th century clock tower offer magnificent views of the city. The Palazzo Ducale, where the ruling Doges lived in high style, contains important art treasures. Venice is also a port of call for ships cruising the Adriatic and Mediterranean.

Milan, Italy's second largest city, is a thriving, modern commercial and industrial city. It was once the capital of the kingdom of Italy. Visitors planning to tour only the north often enter Italy by flying to Milan. The city has excellent shopping facilities, including mall-type shopping centers, as well as the famous La Scala Opera House.

The Italian Lake District includes the Lombardy and Piedmont Provinces that border Switzerland and Austria and, like them, is renowned for its superb beauty. The most well-known lakes are Lake Maggiore and Lake Como. Maggiore is shared with Switzerland. Lake Como, 2 miles wide and 40 miles long, is Italy's largest lake. The region features Alpine skiing in winter and lake sailing in summer. Cortina and other parts of the Dolomites, part of the Alps in northeastern Italy, are noted for skiing, bobsledding and other winter sports.

The Italian Riviera is a continuation of the French Riviera, running eastward along the Mediterranean coast from the French border. The most popular and lively resort is San Remo. In addition to beaches and luxury hotels, San Remo features a casino and a funicular railway to the top of Mount Bignone. Genoa, south of the Riviera, was the birthplace of Christopher Columbus and is a cruise and freight port city.

Naples is 140 miles south of Rome. Mount Vesuvius overlooks the city. The Museo Nazionale houses a fine collection of artifacts found at the ruins of Herculaneum and Pompeii. Hydrofoil service to Capri departs from Naples. The city is also a cruise and freight port.

Pompeii, on the slopes of Vesuvius, is only 20 miles from Naples. The city was destroyed and buried by a major eruption of Mount Vesuvius in 79 AD. Excavations of the city have provided much information on life at the time of the Roman Empire. Walking through Pompeii is truly visiting 2,000 years in the past.

Sorrento, south of Naples, has been a vacation paradise since the days of the Roman Empire. It is now a booming beach resort and is world-renowned for inlaid wood furniture, boxes and pictures. The picturesque Amalfi Drive runs along the Mediterranean cliffs from Sorrento. Boat and hydrofoil service to Capri depart from Sorrento. Capri itself is famous for its Blue Grotto. The island has many fine seafood restaurants and several resort hotels.

Except for Sicily, the part of Italy south of Sorrento does not receive many tourists other than those visiting family. The island of Sardinia, in the Mediterranean, south of Corsica, also is not truly developed for tourism. Sardinia does have one resort area—the Costa Smeralda—developed by the Aga Khan as a retreat for the wealthy.

Although part of Italy, Sicily has a primarily Greek heritage. Palermo, its largest city, has a fine Greek temple. The ruins of the Greek city of Syracuse, founded in the 8th century BC, include an amphitheater still used to present Greek plays. Taormina is a year-round resort. Mount Etna's live volcano has erupted several times in recent years.

Italian food is famous all over the world. It should be noted that Italy has two distinctly different cuisines. Northern Italian food is made with cream-based sauces, while Southern Italian food is made with tomato-based sauces. Pizza, too, is from the south.

VATICAN CITY

Official Name: The Holy See
Language: Italian, Latin
Area: 109 acres
Time Zone: GMT +1
Capital: Vatican City
Currency: Italian lira (LIT)
Population: 778
Documentation: Passport

The Vatican City is entirely within the city of Rome. In addition to St. Peter's Basilica, the Sistine Chapel, and the Vatican Apostolic Palace, its museums, archives, and library, the

Vatican City consists of a number of administrative buildings, the Vatican Gardens, and a "village" of apartments. Although the Italian government had passed laws assuring special status for the Vatican, a treaty recognizing its independence and sovereignty was only signed in 1929.

Each Sunday when the Pope is in residence, St. Peter's Square is crowded with those desiring his blessing. Papal audiences can also be made by appointment.

SAN MARINO

Official Name: Most Serene Republic of San Marino

Language: Italian

Area: 24 square miles

Time Zone: GMT +1

Capital: San Marino

Currency: Italian lira (LIT)

Population: 23,000

Documentation: Passport

According to local tradition, San Marino was founded in the 4th century by a Christian stonecutter seeking refuge from religious persecution. Recorded history began in the 9th century when a community developed around a monastery. Since 1862, San Marino has been assured independent status by treaty with Italy.

Areas of Touristic Importance. Located in north central Italy not far from the Adriatic Sea, San Marino's terrain is entirely rugged and mountainous. Its highest point, Mount Titano, is 2,300 feet above sea level and commands a wide view of the Adriatic 12 miles away. The center of the city of San Marino is a well-preserved example of a medieval manufacturing city. Tourism facilities, however, are limited.

MALTA

Language: Maltese, English, Italian

Area: 122 square miles

Time Zone: GMT +1

National Airline: Air Malta

Capital: Valletta

Currency: Maltese pound (MAL)

Population: 354,000

Documentation: Passport

During its recorded history, which dates back before the Christian era, Malta has been under the control of many nations. These include the Phoenicians, Carthaginians, Romans, Byzantines, Arabs, Normans, Aragons, and Spaniards. Many towns, palaces, churches, and gardens were built between 1523 and 1798 when the island was under the control of the Knights of St. John of Jerusalem, the famous Knights of Malta. After brief control by the French, Malta voluntarily became part of the British Empire. It was the headquarters of the British Mediterranean fleet during World War II, and achieved its independence in 1964.

Located in the Mediterranean between Sicily and North Africa, Malta consists of two main islands, Malta and Gozo, and the smaller island, Comino. The terrain consists of low hills with terraced fields. The coast has numerous bays, inlets, rocky coves, and a few sandy beaches. The climate is hot and dry in summer and temperate and rainy for the balance of the year. The islands are densely populated. Its culture has been influenced to varying degrees by Arabs, Italians, and the British. Roman Catholicism is the official state religion.

Areas of Touristic Importance. Valetta is the capital and center of activity. The walls of its bastions were built by the Knights more than 400 years ago. Its museum, palace, and cathedral provide historical background on Maltese culture, especially during the reign of the Knights. Gozo is a fertile island with picturesque towns. Comino is a tiny island (less than 1 square mile), which has small resort hotels and does not permit automobiles.

GREECE

Official Name: Hellenic Republic
Language: Greek
Area: 51,146 square miles
Time Zone: GMT +2
National Airline: Olympic
Capital: Athens
Currency: Drachma (DRA)
Population: 10,042,000
Documentation: Passport

History. Greece, in the eastern Mediterranean, is one of the cradles of civilization. Stone-age humans can be traced to Crete and some of the Aegean islands. Homer chronicled the late history of the Mycenaeans in the Iliad, describing the Trojan War (about 1100 BC). Following the collapse of the Mycenaean civilization, the Greek city-state developed. Despite their differences, the city-states shared the epics of Homer, the Olympics, and the religion, mythology, and language that unified the Greek world. Eventually two city-states, Athens and Sparta, dominated the country.

After the Peloponnesian War weakened all Greece, it was dominated by the Macedonians. Alexander the Great created an empire by conquest. Rome conquered Greece in 146 BC. As Rome's power declined, Emperor Constantine established the Greek-speaking capital at Constantinople (today, Istanbul) in Byzantium in 330 AD. Eventually Rome was overrun and the Latin- and Greek-speaking churches split in the 11th century. The Ottoman Turks ruled from 1453 until Greece's achieved independence in 1827. In 1981, Greece became the tenth member of the European Union, indicative of its strong orientation to Western Europe rather than to Eastern European countries.

The Land and People. Greece is located in southeastern Europe on the southern tip of the Balkan Peninsula. The Greek mainland is bounded on the north by Bulgaria, Macedonia (formerly part of Yugoslavia), and Albania; on the east by the Aegean Sea and Turkey; and on the west and south by the Ionian and Mediterranean seas. The country consists of a large mainland, with the Peloponnesos connected to the mainland by the Isthmus of Corinth, and more than 1,400 islands. Eighty percent of Greece is mountainous or hilly. Much of the country is dry and rocky. Only 28 percent of the land is arable. Greece has mild, wet winters and hot, dry summers.

Greece has a homogeneous population that has retained its national identity. Greece's pride in its Hellenic roots is reflected in its official name, the Hellenic Republic. Greek Orthodox Catholicism is the established religion. The church is self-governing under the spiritual guidance of the ecumenical patriarch, resident in Istanbul. During the centuries of Ottoman domination, the church preserved the Greek language, values, and national identity. Large numbers of Albanians move legally or illegally into northwestern Greece in search of employment.

The Economy. The Greek economy is dominated by the service sector. Manufacturing is growing, but productivity is low. Agriculture contributes more to the economy than in most industrialized Western nations. More than one-half of the labor force is self-employed and 90 percent of Greek firms have fewer than 10 workers. Tourism is a major source of foreign exchange.

Greece's location and maritime tradition have made commerce an important activity since earliest times. Greece has long been a bridge to the Middle East and many companies maintain their Middle Eastern regional offices in Athens. Shipping is a major industry and the Greek fleet is the largest in the European Union, surpassing even that of the United Kingdom.

Areas of Touristic Importance. Athens exemplifies Greece's contrast of modern development combined with ancient ruins. The Acropolis, a hill around which the city has developed, is the site of the Parthenon, one of the most important archeological attractions in the world. This is the sacred temple of Athena, and it is one of the most skillfully crafted buildings of all time. The Acropolis also provides an excellent view of Athens, Piraeus, and the sea. Other points of interest at the

The Parthenon, Athens
Photo: Courtesy Greek National Tourist Office

Acropolis include the small temple of Nike Apteros (also called Winged Victory) and the Propylaea gateway.

The Theater of Dionysus, built in the 5th century BC, and the Theater of Herod Atticus are on the slopes of the Acropolis. The plays of Sophocles were first performed in the Theater of Dionysus. Many other Hellenic ruins including the Arch of Hadrian and the impressive Temple of the Olympian Zeus are but short distances from the Acropolis.

Tours of downtown Athens begin at the Syntagma, or Constitution Square. Colorfully uniformed guards patrol the Parliament with periodic changing of the guard ceremonies. The Plaka area is filled with small native shops.

Short excursions from Athens include the monastery of Delphi, an 11th-century building with superb mosaics, and the monastery and gardens of Kaisariani, which are of Byzantine origin. Marathon, where the Athenians defeated the Persians, is within 28 miles of Athens. The 26.2 mile marathon race was derived from the distance between Marathon and Athens, which was traversed by a military runner bringing the news of the victory to Athens.

Visits to Nauplia, Epidaurus, Corinth, Mycenae, Delphi, and Olympia provide insight into the classical Greek heritage. Nauplia is a former capital of Greece. Epidaurus hosts the vast temple of the Asclepius cult of healing and is the site of the largest and best-preserved ancient Greek theater. Corinth is noted for the remains of the Temple of Apollo. Mycenae has important archeological sites and is the fabled home of Agamemnon. Delphi, home of the Pythian oracle, was the sanctuary of Apollo and the nine muses. Olympia was the site of the first Olympic games in 776 BC.

Thessaloniki, also called Salonika, is the second largest city in Greece. It is also a major commercial seaport. The remains of a once-thriving Byzantine metropolis can be seen in several early basilicas and the Triumphal Arch of the Emperor Galerius.

Piraeus is the main port for Athens. A variety of cruise ships consider this their home port. Cruise lengths vary from a half-day cruise to Aegina to multiday, multi-island cruises visiting islands in the Aegean, Ionian, and Mediterranean Seas. Cruises have become the most popular way to visit the Greek Islands. Cruises are limited from November to April because of rough winter seas.

Rhodes, Corfu, Mykonos, and Crete are among the most visited of the Greek Islands. Rhodes is an island of great natural beauty, ideal for vacations. It also houses major archeological sites of the Hellenic, Roman, and Byzantine periods. Corfu features spectacular scenery and excellent tourist facilities. The former Achilleion Palace is now an ornate casino. Mykonos, an island of winding streets and whitewashed houses, attracts many artists. Crete, the largest of the Greek Islands, features sandy beaches and high mountains.

Many other islands also attract visitors in large numbers. Kos, the birthplace of Hippocrates, features golden beaches and fertile fields. Patmos was the residence of St. John while in exile. It is here that he supposedly wrote Apocalypse. Lesbos contains a petrified forest and large olive groves. Thira, also called Santorini, features cliffs above the crater of a formerly active volcano.

Milos was where the famous statue of Venus (de Milo) was found. Paros is noted for its white marble. The Sporades islands in the northern Aegean also attract many visitors.

■ TYPES OF TOURISM

More Americans visit Western Europe than any other overseas destination. Except for France, which requires a visa, only a passport is required throughout Western Europe. All types of travel are popular. Independent travel includes visits to friends and relatives as well as fly-drive programs and extensive use of the European rail systems. Hosted and escorted programs include budget, moderate, and deluxe tours. The following itineraries are samples of typical tour programs:

- ■ Arctic Circle
- ■ Aegean and Hellenic
- ■ Spain and Portugal
- ■ Best of Italy and Sicily
- ■ Britain and Ireland Panorama
- ■ Great European

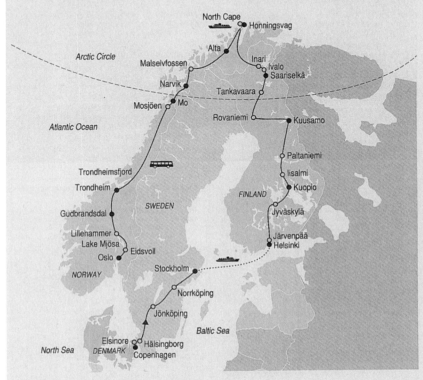

GLOBUS *First Class* ESCORTED

Arctic Circle

Finland and Norway in depth, plus Denmark and Sweden

Tour **ZN** — 18 days incl.air, or 17 days Copenhagen/Oslo

ALL THIS IS INCLUDED

- Scheduled transatlantic flights and airport transfers in Copenhagen and Oslo if Globus issues the tickets; see page 19
- Services of a professional tour director
- Hotels listed below or equivalent; see also 13. Twin-bedded rooms with private bath or shower, hotel taxes, service charges and tips for baggage handling. Accommodations in the Arctic area may not always be of the standard you expect elsewhere
- Welcome drink; 16 full Scandinavian breakfasts (FB); 10 three-course dinners (D)
- Private deluxe motorcoach with extra leg room; see page 11
- First-class two-berth cabins with private facilities on overnight crossing Stockholm-Helsinki; day ferries from Elsinore to Hälsingborg and in Norway

- Sightseeing with local guides in Copenhagen, Stockholm, Helsinki, Maihaugen, Oslo
- Visits to Tivoli Gardens, Kuopio, Paltaniemi, Kuusamo, Rovaniemi, Tankavaara's Gold Museum, Saariselkä, Inari's Open-Air Museum, the North Cape, Alta's Rock Carvings, Narvik's War Museum, Trondheim, Gudbrandsdal Valley, Lillehammer
- Picture stops at Kronborg Castle, Jean Sibelius' Järvenpää, Malselvfossen and Laksfossen waterfalls, the church of Mosjoen, Eidsvoll
- Inside visits as shown in UPPER CASE in the tour description, including admission charges where applicable
- Globus travel bag and travel documents

130 US

Day 1 BOARD YOUR OVERNIGHT TRANSATLANTIC FLIGHT.

Day 2 ARRIVAL IN COPENHAGEN, DENMARK. Time to rest or to start exploring Denmark's fun-loving capital. At 6 p.m. meet your traveling companions for a welcome drink hosted by your tour director.

Day 3 COPENHAGEN. Sightseeing in Scandinavia's largest and liveliest metropolis. See the Church of Our Savior and the Stock Exchange on the way to Christiansborg Palace, where you visit the lavish ROYAL RECEPTION ROOMS (if closed, admire the Danish Crown Jewels at ROSENBORG CASTLE instead). Snap your pictures of Amalienborg Palace and of the wistful Little Mermaid watching the harbor. Afternoon free, and tonight experience TIVOLI GARDENS, the city's colorful amusement park (May through mid-Sept.). (FB)

Day 4 COPENHAGEN-STOCKHOLM, SWEDEN. From Elsinore beneath Hamlet's Kronborg Castle take a ferry to Hälsingborg, and then motor through the Swedish lake district. Pastoral scenes alternate with glimpses of major industrial towns such as Jönköping on Lake Vättern, the world capital of the safety match industry, and Norrköping, a Baltic sea port and important textile manufacturing center. Evening arrival in Stockholm. (FB)

Day 5 STOCKHOLM. NIGHT FERRY TO FINLAND. The Swedish capital's beauty is due to its unique setting on 14 islands between Lake Mälar and the Baltic. Sightseeing features the Royal Palace, Riddarholm Church, and the festive blue and gold chambers in the TOWN HALL. Kungsgatan's smart shops and the skyscrapers and futuristic condominiums on the shores of Lake Mälar form a striking contrast to the Old Town sights. Free time afterwards until, in the late afternoon, you board your luxurious overnight Baltic Sea cruise to Finland. (FB)

Day 6 HELSINKI. After breakfast on board, a local guide explains the sights of Helsinki: City Hall and Parliament House, the Presidential Palace, the monumental railroad station, and the great LUTHERAN CATHEDRAL. Then leave town for an orientation tour to the Olympic Stadium and the Sibelius Monument, and to the showrooms of the HOUSE OF FINNISH HANDICRAFTS. Afternoon at leisure. (FB,D)

Day 7 HELSINKI-KUOPIO. A superbly scenic day in the heart of the Finnish Lake District. Take a morning break in Järvenpää, Jean Sibelius' pretty home town. Proceed past the ski resort of Lahti to Jyväskylä and on to Kuopio. The main attractions here are the sweeping panorama from PUIJO TOWER, and a pretty market square. (FB,D)

Day 8 KUOPIO-KUUSAMO. More sparkling lakes and dark pine forests as you head further north. On the way call at the beer brewing town of Iisalmi, and later near Kajaani to visit the lovely wooden CHURCH OF PALTANIEMI. Overnight in the winter sports and summer hiking resort of Kuusamo. (FB,D)

Day 9 KUUSAMO-ROVANIEMI-SAARISELKÄ. Morning break in Rovaniemi, the "Gateway to Lapland". An orientation tour takes you to ALVAR AALTO'S LAPPIA HOUSE and the modern LUTHERAN CHURCH. You'll know when you cross the Arctic Circle (66°31'N), because Santa Claus in person meets you there. Now you're in incomparable, unspoiled Lapland, land of the reindeer and the midnight sun. On your journey north visit the GOLD MUSEUM at Tankavaara and pan for gold yourself if you wish. Overnight in Saariselkä, at the edge of the virgin wilderness area of Finland's major national park. (FB,D)

Reprinted courtesy of Globus and Cosmos.

Day 10 SAARISELKÄ-HONNINGSVAG, NORWAY. Via Ivalo you drive to Inari for a visit to the fascinating OPEN-AIR MUSEUM giving insight into Lapp life and folk art. On into Norway and across the beautiful Porsangen Fjord to Honningsvag on the island of Mageroya, home to 4,000 people and 5,000 reindeer. Tonight one of the highlights of this tour: drive to the North Cape, Europe's last northern outpost, on a sheer cliff rising 1,000 ft. from the Atlantic Ocean. From May 11 to July 31, if the sky is clear, you'll see the midnight sun rolling over the horizon! (FB,D)

Day 11 HONNINGSVAG-ALTA. By ferry back across the Porsangen Fjord and south through stony, desolate Finnmark. Today's destination is Alta, situated at the mouth of one of the world's richest salmon rivers. See its 6,000-year-old ROCK CARVINGS depicting the life of fishermen, farmers and hunters of a bygone era. (FB,D)

Day 12 ALTA-NARVIK. Continue your unforgettable journey south along the stunning shoreline of Norway. The road meanders along Kvaenangenfjord and Lyngenfjord. You are now in the Troms Province, still way beyond the Arctic

Circle, but with a climate mild enough to allow very successful farming. Stop for pictures at the thundering Malselv waterfall. Hear about fierce World War II battles as you approach Narvik, rebuilt after near total destruction. (FB,D)

Day 13 NARVIK-MO. Visit Narvik's WAR MUSEUM and relive how Norwegian troops, with the help of their allies, showed the world that the Nazi war machine was not invulnerable. Then more soaring mountain peaks, dense forests, countless fjords cutting deep inland. This is Nordland, the narrowest part of Norway. Not far from Mo you cross the Arctic Circle again and are back in a world where the sun rises and sets every day of the year. (FB,D)

Day 14 MO-TRONDHEIM. On the agenda today: the spectacular Laksfossen waterfall; the ancient octagonal church of Mosjöen; the forests and rivers of Namsdalen Valley; finally vistas of Trondheimsfjord, the World War II hideout of the German battleship Tirpitz. (FB,D)

Day 15 TRONDHEIM-GUDBRANDSDAL. Sightseeing in the city where Norway's kings are crowned includes the royal residence

STIFTSGAARD, the magnificent Gothic NIDAROS CATHEDRAL of white marble and blue soapstone, and the famous RINGVE MUSEUM of musical instruments. In the afternoon motor through rugged Trondelag, then enjoy thrilling vistas of the Dovrefjell high plateau and of the Rondane Mountains. Overnight in the Gudbrandsdal Valley, rich agricultural and timber land celebrated in Ibsen's "Peer Gynt". (FB,D)

Day 16 GUDBRANDSDAL-OSLO. Focus on Lillehammer, host of the Winter Olympics 1994. At the fascinating MAIHAUGEN OPEN-AIR MUSEUM (mid-May to mid-Sept.) an expert explains the rich collection of ancient Gudbrandsdal farmhouses, dwellings, workshops, tools and weapons. Proceed along Lake Mjösa to historic Eidsvoll and, after a short visit, on to Oslo, the final destination of your Scandinavian adventure. (FB)

Day 17 OSLO. Norway's capital is a study in farsighted urban planning, seeking growth in harmony with nature. See such landmarks as the National Theater, Parliament and the Royal Palace. Highlight visits: FROGNER PARK with Gustav Vigeland's famous stark sculptures; the RESISTANCE MUSEUM in the lavish grounds of Akershus Fortress; finally the ornate CITY HALL. Later you have a chance to join an optional excursion to the relics of a glorious seafaring past. Tonight your tour director will suggest a venue for an optional farewell dinner. (FB)

Day 18 YOUR HOMEBOUND FLIGHT ARRIVES THE SAME DAY. (FB)

▼ *FLOWERS GROW ON THE ROOFS OF MAIHAUGEN*

▲ *AN OUTNUMBERED VIKING WARRIOR*

▼ *THE MIDNIGHT SUN — AN UNFORGETTABLE SIGHT*

Tour ZN: DATES & PRICES

Tour code	Leave USA or join Copenhagen next day		Return to USA or end Oslo		18 days USA/ USA US$	17 days Copenh./ Oslo US$
ZN0515	Sat	14-May	Tue	31-May	2533	1898
ZN0522	Sat	21-May	Tue	07-Jun	2533	1898
ZN0529	Sat	28-May	Tue	14-Jun	2533	1898
ZN0605	Sat	04-Jun	Tue	21-Jun	2644	1898
ZN0609	Wed	08-Jun	Sat	25-Jun	2644	1898
ZN0612	Sat	11-Jun	Tue	28-Jun	2644	1898
ZN0616	Wed	15-Jun	Sat	02-Jul	2644	1898
ZN0619	Sat	18-Jun	Tue	05-Jul	2644	1898
ZN0623	Wed	22-Jun	Sat	09-Jul	2644	1898
ZN0626	Sat	25-Jun	Tue	12-Jul	2644	1898
ZN0630	Wed	29-Jun	Sat	16-Jul	2644	1898
ZN0703	Sat	02-Jul	Tue	19-Jul	2644	1898
ZN0707	Wed	06-Jul	Sat	23-Jul	2644	1898
ZN0710	Sat	09-Jul	Tue	26-Jul	2644	1898
ZN0714	Wed	13-Jul	Sat	30-Jul	2644	1898
ZN0717	Sat	16-Jul	Tue	02-Aug	2644	1898
ZN0721	Wed	20-Jul	Sat	06-Aug	2644	1898
ZN0724	Sat	23-Jul	Tue	09-Aug	2634	1888
ZN0731	Sat	30-Jul	Tue	16-Aug	2624	1878
ZN0807	Sat	06-Aug	Tue	23-Aug	2614	1868
ZN0814	Sat	13-Aug	Tue	30-Aug	2604	1858
ZN0821	Sat	20-Aug	Tue	06-Sep	2594	1848

For any air fare supplement from your departure city, see list 3 on page 20.

Single room and cabin supplement: $546
Triple room reduction per person: $112

Reduction for joining on day 6 with dinner in Helsinki: $319

APOLLO: TD'GG, **PARS:** G/PTS/GGX, **SABRE:** Y/TUR/QGG

GLOBUS HOTELS

COPENHAGEN Sas Globetrotter (F=First Class), **STOCKHOLM** Reso Anglais (F), **HELSINKI** Arctia Marski (F), **KUOPIO** Arctia Kuopio (F), **KUUSAMO** Kuusamon Tropiikki (F), **SAARISELKA** Saariselaen TunturiHotellit (ST=Superior Tourist), **HONNINGSVAG** Sas Nordkapp (F), **ALTA** Sas Alta (F), **NARVIK** Grand Royal (F), **MO-I-RANA** Meyergarden (F), **TRONDHEIM** Residence (F), **DOMBAS** Dombas Hotell (F), **OSLO** Sas Park Royal (F)

US 131

GLOBUS | *First Class* | ESCORTED

Aegean Hellenic

Greece plus 3-day cruise

Tour RI — 11 days incl.air, or 10 days Athens/Athens

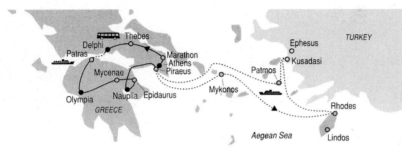

ALL THIS IS INCLUDED

- Scheduled transatlantic flights and airport transfers in Athens if Globus issues the tickets; see page 19
- On land: services of a professional tour director
- Hotels listed below or equivalent; see page 13. Twin-bedded rooms with private bath or shower, hotel taxes, service charges and tips for baggage handling
- Guided sightseeing in Athens, Delphi, Olympia, Mycenae and Epidaurus
- Inside visits as shown in UPPER CASE in the tour description, including admission charges where applicable
- Private deluxe motorcoach featuring full air-conditioning, extra leg room and

emergency washroom; see page 11
- Ferry across the Gulf of Corinth
- Epirotiki cruise in category D inside cabins; supplements for category B outside cabins are listed under DATES & PRICES; all cabins have two lower beds and private shower and toilet; cruise ships are described on page 155
- Welcome drink and buffet breakfasts (BB) in Athens; buffet breakfasts and dinners (D) in Delphi, Olympia and Nauplia; all full à-la-carte breakfasts, lunches and dinners (FB,L,D) while cruising
- Full entertainment program on board
- Globus travel bag and travel documents

Day 1, Sat. BOARD YOUR OVERNIGHT TRANSATLANTIC FLIGHT.

Day 2, Sun. ARRIVAL IN ATHENS, GREECE. Time to rest or to start exploring the Hellenic capital. At 6 p.m. meet your traveling companions at a welcome drink with your tour director.

Day 3, Mon. ATHENS. Enjoy a tour of the classical sights: the Parthenon's crowning beauty atop the ACROPOLIS, the Erechtheum with its Porch of Maidens, the beautifully preserved Theseum, Roman Temple of Zeus, Theater of Dionysus and the Agora where Socrates taught. Vistas of the Royal Palace, government buildings and elegant homes in the modern city provide a striking contrast to the remains of the glorious past. The rest of the day is at leisure. How about a Greek dinner tonight? Your tour director knows exactly where to find a typical taverna with entertainment reminiscent of "Zorba the Greek". (BB)

Day 4, Tue. ATHENS-DELPHI. Two sites along the way to Delphi give your tour director

opportunities to display his knowledge of Greek history and legend: Marathon, where in 490 BC 10,000 Athenians defeated more than twice that number of Persian invaders, and Thebes, the theater of Sophocles' Oedipus Rex. In the afternoon a fascinating tour of the ancient sanctuary of the god Apollo in its dramatic setting on the slopes of Mt.Parnassus. Hear about the Oracle and tour the EXCAVATIONS. Finally visit the ARCHAEOLOGICAL MUSEUM to admire the Charioteer, an extraordinary 5th-century BC bronze statue. (BB,D)

Day 5, Wed. DELPHI-OLYMPIA. Through the picturesque fishing villages along the coast, then by ferry across the Gulf of Corinth to Patras on the Peloponnese. The afternoon is dedicated to OLYMPIA, where the athletes of antiquity performed in honor of the King of Deities. Learn about the history of those original Olympic Games as you walk among the impressive remains of the Gymnasium and the Temples of Hera and Zeus. Also visit the MUSEUM which displays Praxiteles' magnificent statue of Hermes. (BB,D)

Day 6, Thu. OLYMPIA-MYCENAE-EPIDAURUS-NAUPLIA. Spectacular scenery on the way through the Arkadian mountains. Two major features today: MYCENAE, where 19th-century excavations reveal impressions of the splendors so vividly described by Homer. Admire the Beehive Tombs, the Treasury of Atreus, Lion Gate - Europe's oldest known monument, remains of Agamemnon's Royal Palace, and the impressive fortifications of the Citadel. Then a short drive to EPIDAURUS for a tour of its amazingly well-preserved 2,300-year-old open-air theater. Overnight in nearby Nauplia. (BB,D)

Day 7, Fri. NAUPLIA-PIRAEUS-CRUISING: MYKONOS. Head for Piraeus via the bridge spanning the Corinth Canal. Around 11 a.m. sail into the deep-blue waters of the Aegean Sea, easily settling into the cruising routine of sunbathing, sipping cool drinks, splashing in the pool, and reveling in the delights proposed by the ship's expert chefs. Later dock at the mountainous island of Mykonos with its characteristic windmills and dazzling white houses. Time to wander at whim through narrow paved streets lined with trendy boutiques and shady tavernas before returning on board. (BB,L,D)

Day 8, Sat. CRUISING: RHODES. Dock near Rhodes' Mandraki harbor, where two iron deer statues mark the site of the Colossus - one of the seven wonders of the ancient world. All day is dedicated to the island of Rhodes. Explore the sights in the historic Old City with its ramparts and palaces built by the Knights of St.John during the Crusades. Another possibility: join an optional excursion to Lindos and the fabulous Temple of Athena. And if sightseeing is not your thing, Rhodes' sundrenched public beaches and colorful shopping districts are within easy walking distance of the port. (FB,L,D)

Day 9, Sun. CRUISING: KUSADASI, TURKEY & PATMOS, GREECE. Two ports of call today. First the Turkish port of Kusadasi. An optional morning excursion takes you to the fascinating Greek, Roman and Byzantine excavations of Ephesus. Next discover the tiny Greek island of Patmos where St.John the Divine wrote the Revelation. The 11th-century monastery with its valuable manuscript collection is well worth a visit. (FB,L,D)

Day 10, Mon. PIRAEUS-ATHENS. After breakfast on board disembark at Piraeus and return to Athens. The remainder of the day is free to catch up on last-minute shopping. (FB)

Day 11, Tue. YOUR HOMEBOUND FLIGHT ARRIVES THE SAME DAY. (BB)

➤ *Shore excursions can be booked on board. Please allow for a total cost of approximately US$140 per person if you plan to participate in all excursions offered. We also recommend that you plan to spend about US$25 per person for gratuities to the service personnel on board.*

▼ *FIND THOSE CHARMING CORNERS!*

152 US

▲ *MONASTERY OF ST.JOHN ON PATMOS*

▲ *NO RUSH!*

▲ *ANCIENT WINDMILLS IN RHODES* ▼ *SPEND AN EVENING IN TRENDY MYKONOS*

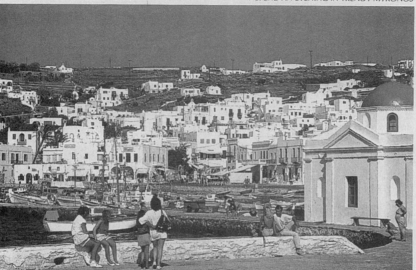

Tour RI: DATES & PRICES

Tour code	Leave USA or join Athens next day		Return to USA or end Athens		11 days USA/ USA US$	10 days Athens/ Athens US$
RI0320	Sat	19-Mar	Tue	29-Mar	1614	968
RI0327	Sat	26-Mar	Tue	05-Apr	1614	968
RI0403	Sat	02-Apr	Tue	12-Apr	1764	968
RI0410	Sat	09-Apr	Tue	19-Apr	1764	968
RI0417	Sat	16-Apr	Tue	26-Apr	1764	968
RI0424	Sat	23-Apr	Tue	03-May	1764	968
RI0501	Sat	30-Apr	Tue	10-May	1824	1028
RI0508	Sat	07-May	Tue	17-May	1824	1028
RI0515	Sat	14-May	Tue	24-May	1824	1028
RI0522	Sat	21-May	Tue	31-May	1824	1028
RI0529	Sat	28-May	Tue	07-Jun	1824	1028
RI0605	Sat	04-Jun	Tue	14-Jun	1985	1028
RI0612	Sat	11-Jun	Tue	21-Jun	1985	1028
RI0619	Sat	18-Jun	Tue	28-Jun	1985	1028
RI0626	Sat	25-Jun	Tue	05-Jul	1985	1028
RI0703	Sat	02-Jul	Tue	12-Jul	1985	1028
RI0710	Sat	09-Jul	Tue	19-Jul	1985	1028
RI0717	Sat	16-Jul	Tue	26-Jul	1985	1028
RI0724	Sat	23-Jul	Tue	02-Aug	1985	1028
RI0731	Sat	30-Jul	Tue	09-Aug	1985	1028
RI0807	Sat	06-Aug	Tue	16-Aug	1985	1028
RI0814	Sat	13-Aug	Tue	23-Aug	1985	1028
RI0821	Sat	20-Aug	Tue	30-Aug	1985	1028
RI0828	Sat	27-Aug	Tue	06-Sep	1985	1028
RI0904	Sat	03-Sep	Tue	13-Sep	2015	1058
RI0911	Sat	10-Sep	Tue	20-Sep	1854	1058
RI0918	Sat	17-Sep	Tue	27-Sep	1854	1058
RI0925	Sat	24-Sep	Tue	04-Oct	1854	1058
RI1002	Sat	01-Oct	Tue	11-Oct	1854	1058
RI1009	Sat	08-Oct	Tue	18-Oct	1854	1058
RI1016	Sat	15-Oct	Tue	25-Oct	1854	1058
RI1023	Sat	22-Oct	Tue	01-Nov	1824	1028
RI1030	Sat	29-Oct	Tue	08-Nov	1764	968
RI1106	Sat	05-Nov	Tue	15-Nov	1614	968
RI1113	Sat	12-Nov	Tue	22-Nov	1614	968
RI1120	Sat	19-Nov	Tue	29-Nov	1614	968

For any air fare supplement from your departure city, see list 8 on page 21.

Our prices are based on twin inside cabins.

Supplement for twin outside cabin per person (tour RIX): $40

Supplement for single room on land and single outside cabin: $281 (single inside cabins not available).

Reduction for triple room on land and triple occupancy of inside or outside cabin: $90

Reduction for leaving on day 10 in Athens (at end of cruise): $35

Cabin assignments and meal seatings are determined during the tour prior to boarding the cruise ship.

APOLLO: TD*GG, **PARS:** G/PTS/GGX, **SABRE:** Y/TUR/QGG

GLOBUS HOTELS

ATHENS Zafolia (F=First Class), **DELPHI** Vouzas (F), **OLYMPIA** Europa (F), **NAUPLIA** Xenia Palace (F)

14 Days (13 Nights) Land Only $2425

Extra Highlights: *Lisbon's Coach Museum* □ *Cabo da Roca* □ *Gibraltar's Barbary Apes* □ *Mezquita-Cathedral* □ *Almagro* □ *Don Quixote's Windmills* — *31 Meals: 14 Breakfasts, 8 Lunches, 9 Dinners*

Spain and Portugal

The Algarve Coast / Costa del Sol / Andalusia / La Mancha / Madrid

Fly to Lisbon... Tauck Tours holds space on TWA departing New York the evening prior to the departure dates listed at the end of this itinerary. Persons using this space will be met by our tour director outside Customs at Lisbon Airport between 8:15 AM and 9:15 AM. Please allow sufficient time to claim luggage and clear Customs. Persons arriving later or the day before can take a taxi to the hotel. Fare is approx. Esc 1,500 (US $10).

1. Arrive Lisbon
Tour departs: Lisbon Airport 9:15 AM.
It is but a short drive to your centrally located hotel. There is time to rest before an afternoon tour of Portugal's capital. Learn about the Period of Great Discoveries when Portuguese explorers ventured into unchartered waters and discovered new continents. See St. Hieronymite Monastery and the Tower of Belem, from where the caravels set off. Drive to St. George's Castle for a panoramic view and experience the Alfama quarter, with it's narrow streets and alleys, and visit the National Coach Museum. This evening enjoy a welcome reception and dinner. MEALS **BD**

2. Sintra / Cascais / Estoril
Today enjoy the colorful and picturesque outskirts of Lisbon. Sintra, one of the oldest Portuguese towns, was the summer retreat of the royal family. Visit their 14th-century

Flowering Balconies on the sidestreets of Granada

palace. Next is Cabo da Roca, located on a windswept promontory at the westernmost point of Europe. Continue to Cascais, a colorful fishing village. Gaily colored boats speckle the bay. Return to Lisbon via Estoril, an international resort on the Portuguese Riviera. The afternoon is free. MEALS **B**

3. Monchique / Algarve Coast
Cross Ponte 25 de Abril, Europe's longest suspension bridge, which links the two sides of the mighty Tagus River. Travel through Portugal's pleasant countryside where eucalyptus, olive trees and cork oak abound. Flocks of sheep and goats are frequently seen by the road side, giving a sense of timelessness to the scene. The narrow, winding roads of the wooded Serra de Monchique come next with splendid mountain views. On a clear day, the vistas extend all the way to the southern coast. Reach the Algarve, Portugal's coastal resort area. Enjoy the facilities and wonderful surroundings of your hotel. MEALS **BLD**

4. Andalusia / Flamenco
Sleep in this morning, shop, take walks along the sea or simply relax by the pool. After lunch it's off for Andalusia, Spain's storied southern province of white-washed villages, tourist resorts, gypsies, flamencos and vast olive groves. Seville, Granada and Cordoba were the pinnacle of civilization some 1000 years ago

44

and have fascinated travelers ever since. Arrive late afternoon in the provincial capital of Seville, a remarkable blend of the old and the new. This evening, prior to dinner, attend a flamenco performance. MEALS **BLD**

5. Sightsee Seville

This morning sightsee Seville. See Maria Luisa Park, site of the 1929 Spanish-American Exhibition; the Tobacco Factory of "Carmen" fame, Murillo Gardens, Macarena district and some exhibition buildings of the 1992 World's Fair. Walk to the cathedral, Seville's unmistakable landmark. The interior offers a wealth of art, architecture and the sarcophagi of kings and cardinals. Here is the grave of Christopher Columbus. Next visit the former Jewish quarter before an afternoon of leisure. MEALS **B**

The Rock of Gibraltar as seen from Algeciras

Andulasian white-washed village

6. Jerez / Sherry Bodega

Drive to Jerez, known as the center for sherry production. Visit a bodega and enjoy a taste before continuing to lunch. En route to Algeciras, catch a glimpse of the Strait of Gibraltar and, weather permitting, view the African continent beyond. MEALS **BLD**

7. Gibraltar / Costa del Sol

While circling the Bay of Algerciras, see the famous silhouette of the Rock of Gibraltar. There are minor border formalities as "The Rock" has been a British territory for nearly 300 years. During both world wars Gibraltar played a strategic role in the Allied defense system. On special mini coaches tour the densely populated town and the nature reserve. Back in Spain, drive to Marbella, a former fishing village that has grown into the most fashionable resort on the Costa del Sol. Your hotel is adjacent to the charming old center of Marbella. Arrive with plenty of time for a dip in the Mediterranean Sea or local shopping. MEALS **BLD**

8. Granada / Alhambra Palace

Leave the coast behind and climb steadily into the mountains. Breathtaking views are everywhere. Enjoy lunch in Granada, located in the foothills of the snow-capped Sierra Nevada. The Alhambra, one of the world's most beautiful palaces is next. It was built by Moorish rulers who governed this part of Spain for more than 800 years. Tour the palace and the lovely terraced Generalife Gardens with its shadowy cypresses, oleander, pavilions and cool fountains. MEALS **BLD**

The Alhambra Palace – The epitome of Moorish imagination and artistry

9. Sightsee Cordoba

This morning enjoy a beautiful drive with olive groves stretching to the horizon. Reach Cordoba, a city which was also influenced by the Moors who came here in the beginning of the 8th century. Then came the golden years of prosperity when Arabs, Jews and Christians lived in great harmony. Cordoba became a meeting place for the world's learned. Enjoy a panoramic tour of the town and walk through the charming former Jewish quarter, the Juderia. It is said that if a traveler to Spain would only see Cordoba's Mezquita-Cathedral the journey would have been more than worth it. You do that today. MEALS **BL**

Monument of the Discoveries, Lisbon

10. Sierra Morena Mountains

Journey to Montoro, a small town whose white-washed houses cling high on the banks of the Guadalquivir. Continue, by yellow roads, to Virgen de la Cabeza, one of Spain's most revered pilgrimage destinations. Cross the remote Sierra Morena mountains, dividing Andalusia from Castilla-La Mancha. Here the scenery offers incredible vistas. Stop in Puertollano, a former mining town before arriving in Almagro for overnight in the historic Parador, once a Franciscan convent. MEALS **BLD**

11. Consuegra / Toledo

Join your tour director for a walk to Almagro's Plaza Mayor, one of Spain's most architecturally unique town squares. Next, drive through the region where Cervante's fearless knight "Don Quixote de la Mancha" jousted with the windmills. Photograph some ancient windmills before driving on to Toledo, the former capital of Spain. The only way to see this great town is on foot. Visit the Church of Santo Tome to see "The Burial of the Count Orgaz," considered by many to be El Greco's finest painting. Also visit a synagogue in the Jewish quarter. Then, on to Madrid, Spain's majestic capital and largest city. MEALS **BLD**

12. Sightsee Madrid

This morning, sightsee Madrid, a city which grew from a 9th-century Arab fortress to this bustling cosmopolitan capital of Spain. See the Royal Palace, great squares, the Neptuno and Cibeles fountains, the major avenues of Gran Via, Castellana and more. The afternoon is free. Your tour director will suggest a host of activities for your free time. MEALS **B**

13. The Prado Museum

Visit the Prado Museum, considered one of the greatest art galleries in the world. Our tour will concentrate on the Spanish School of painters... El Greco, Velazques, Murillo and Goya. Art affecianados may remain to see other exhibits housed nearby such as the private collection of Baron von Thyssen-Bornemisza or Picasso's Guernica, a monumental painting. After an afternoon of leisure, enjoy a farewell dinner. MEALS **BD**

The Windmills of Consuegra

Don Quixote and Sancho Panza, Madrid

14. Return Home

Tour ends: Madrid Airport 11:30 AM. This allows the necessary 2 hours for check-in and clearing security prior to our scheduled TWA flight. Persons departing at other times should secure their own transportation. Taxi approx. Pesetas 2,000 ($15 US). MEALS **B**

Depart Lisbon

Mar 27	Apr 10, 24	May 8, 22
Jun 5, 19	Jul 3, 17, 31	Aug 14, 28
Sep 11	Oct 9, 23	Nov 13

Plan to fly from the U.S. 1 day earlier to meet these dates in Lisbon.

Price Per Person

Twin $2425   Single $2893   Triple $2321

These prices are guaranteed

Price includes everything outlined in General Information, page 66.
31 meals included.
Transatlantic air is additional.

Hotel Itinerary

Night 1,2	**Hotel Tivoli Lisboa** Lisbon, Portugal
Night 3	**Hotel Quinta do Lago** Almansil, Portugal
Night 4,5*	**Hotel Alfonso XIII** Seville, Spain
Night 6	**Hotel Reina Cristina** Algeciras, Spain
Night 7	**Hotel El Fuerte** Marbella, Spain
Night 8	**Hotel Alhambra Palace** Granada, Spain
Night 9	**Hotel Amistad Cordoba** Cordoba, Spain
Night 10	**Parador de Almagro** Almagro, Spain
Night 11,12,13	**Castellana Inter-Continental** Madrid, Spain

* Tour of May 8 will stay at Hotel Tryp Colon.

IT-TAU-IB12
APOLLO ACCESS TD-28029
WORLDSPAN ACCESS .... G/PTS/TTXIB

ESCORTED: 16 DAYS

BEST OF ITALY & SICILY

ROME, PISA, FLORENCE, VENICE, RAVENNA, ASSISI, POMPEII, TAORMINA, AGRIGENTO, PALERMO, NAPLES, CAPRI, SORRENTO

SICILIAN HIGHLIGHTS CONTRAST WITH ITALY'S MAGNIFICENT CITIES.

PLUS THE ENCHANTING ISLE OF CAPRI, THE LEANING TOWER OF PISA AND ANCIENT POMPEII.

NOT TO MENTION SOME OF EUROPE'S MOST FAMED CULINARY DELIGHTS.

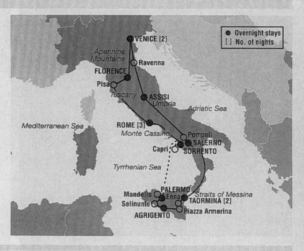

TAORMINA – JOLLY DIODORO HOTEL

COIN-TROWING TREVI FOUNTAIN

TRAFALGAR GIVES YOU MORE

SIGHTSEEING EVERY DAY
Rome Sightseeing including St. Peter's Basilica, the Forum and Colosseum.
Pisa View the Leaning Tower.
Florence Sightseeing features Signoria Square, Santa Croce Basilica and Baptistry. Views from Piazzale Michelangelo.
Venice Canal cruise by private boat. View St. Mark's Square, the Byzantine Basilica, Doges' Palace and the Bridge of Sighs. Visit a glass-blowing factory.
Ravenna Visit the medieval city.
Assisi Orientation tour including St. Francis' Basilica.
Pompeii A guided tour of the excavations.
Enna View the fortress town.
Piazza Armerina Visit the Roman Villa of Casale.
Agrigento Visit the Valley of the Temples.
Selinunte Visit the Dorian Temples and Acropolis.
Palermo Sightseeing including Piazza Bellini, the Cathedral and the Arab-Norman Palentine Chapel.
Monreale Visit the Byzantine Cathedral.
Mondello Visit the typical fishing village.
Capri Visit the picturesque and enchanting isle.
Monte Cassino View the Abbey.

SCENIC DRIVES ON THE WAY
● Along the Tyrrhenian coast ● Across the Apennine Mountains ● Through the Umbrian Hills ● Follow the spectacular Bay of Naples.

DINING & ENTERTAINMENT
● Welcome drink with your Tour Director in Rome.
● Buffet breakfast **(BB)** or Continental breakfast with juice & cereal **(EB)** daily.
● 9 three-course dinners – **(D)** see itinerary.

PIECE OF PISA

FIRST CLASS HOTELS
● Twin-bedded rooms with private facilities; all service charges, local taxes, baggage handling and hotel tips.

TRAVELLING IN EUROPE
● Touring by luxury air-conditioned coach with reclining seats ● Ferry across the Straits of Messina to Sicily ● Overnight cruise from Palermo to Naples ● Cruise to the Isle of Capri ● Rome Airport transfers.

TRAFALGAR ALSO INCLUDES
● Professional, multi-lingual Tour Director on tour ● Specialised local guides in Rome, Florence, Pompeii, Agrigento and Palermo ● Travel bag and wallet containing comprehensive tour documents.

Day 1 Depart USA
Overnight flight to Rome.

Day 2 Arrive Rome (2)
After you are transferred to your hotel, the rest of the day is free for exploration. Tonight, enjoy a **welcome drink** with your Tour Director.

Day 3 Rome sightseeing
The Forum, Colosseum and St. Peter's Basilica are included on morning **sightseeing**. Afterwards, you're at leisure to sightsee further, to window-shop along the elegant Via Condotti, or people-watch from a pavement café on the Via Veneto. **(EB)**

Day 4 Rome – Florence
Leaving the "Eternal City", we follow the Aurelian Way along the Tyrrhenian coast to **Pisa** to view the famed **Leaning Tower**. On to Florence, cradle of the Renaissance and capital of Tuscany. Balance of the day is free. Perhaps take a walk along the River Arno to the Ponte Vecchio and across to the Pitti palace. **(EB)**

Day 5 Florence – Venice (2)
The multi-coloured marble cathedral, Signoria Square, Baptistry and Santa Croce Basilica are featured on our morning **walking tour**. Time also to admire the panoramic view from Piazzale Michelangelo. Later, a short drive to magical Venice where you may choose to take a romantic gondola serenade along the Grand Canal. **(EB D)**

TAORMINA, SICILY – RELIVE THE PAST AT THE ANCIENT GREEK THEATRE

DATES & PRICES

Tour reference ITIS

Tour Ref.	Departs USA		Returns USA	
TOUR $1399			**TOUR+AIR $2089**	
ITIS/026	Fri	6 May	Sat	21 May
ITIS/027	Fri	13 May	Sat	28 May
ITIS/028	Fri	20 May	Sat	4 Jun
ITIS/029	Fri	27 May	Sat	11 Jun
TOUR $1399			**TOUR+AIR $2198**	
ITIS/030	Fri	3 Jun	Sat	18 Jun
ITIS/031	Fri	10 Jun	Sat	25 Jun
ITIS/032	Fri	17 Jun	Sat	2 Jul
ITIS/033	Fri	24 Jun	Sat	9 Jul
ITIS/034	Fri	1 Jul	Sat	16 Jul
ITIS/035	Fri	8 Jul	Sat	23 Jul
ITIS/036	Fri	15 Jul	Sat	30 Jul
ITIS/037	Fri	22 Jul	Sat	6 Aug
ITIS/038	Fri	29 Jul	Sat	13 Aug
ITIS/039	Fri	5 Aug	Sat	20 Aug
ITIS/040	Fri	12 Aug	Sat	27 Aug
ITIS/041	Fri	19 Aug	Sat	3 Sep
ITIS/042	Fri	26 Aug	Sat	10 Sep
ITIS/043	Fri	2 Sep	Sat	17 Sep
ITIS/044	Fri	9 Sep	Sat	24 Sep
TOUR $1399			**TOUR+AIR $2089**	
ITIS/045	Fri	16 Sep	Sat	1 Oct
ITIS/046	Fri	23 Sep	Sat	8 Oct
ITIS/047	Fri	30 Sep	Sat	15 Oct
ITIS/048	Fri	7 Oct	Sat	22 Oct
ITIS/049	Fri	14 Oct	Sat	29 Oct

Single Room Supplement	$275
Triple Room Reduction	10 % of Tour price

SABRE ACCESS Y/TUR/TFG

SKYBARGAIN fares

The above 'TOUR + AIR' prices are from
New York. For details and special low
add-on fares from other US cities,
see page 25.

AIRPORT TRANSFERS

Transfers on arrival will be provided only
for passengers who have booked their
flights on a Trafalgar recommended
airline and advised Trafalgar of their flight
details. Transfers from Rome airport to
your hotel depart at 09.30 and 12.00.
Passengers arriving later should make
their own way to the hotel. See page 28.

HOTELS ON THIS TOUR

Rome: Villa Pamphili
Florence: Holiday Inn
Venice-Grand Canal: Continental
Assisi: Giotto
Salerno: Jolly
Taormina: Jolly
Agrigento: Jolly
Palermo: Jolly
Sorrento: Cesare Augusto
Rome: Jolly Midas

y 6 Venice sightseeing
our the sights and sounds of this
ne city on a *canal cruise* by
ate boat to St. Mark's Square,
ing the *Bridge of Sighs*. Visit a
ss-*blowing factory*, then you are
to shop or sightsee. Why not
the opportunity to discover
ther island in the Venetian Lagoon
urano, and enjoy a colourful
ood lunch? (EB D)

y 7 Venice – Ravenna – Assisi
oss the Apennine Mountains to
ancient city of *Ravenna*, famous
s wonderful mosaics. On to the
stical pink-stoned city of Assisi,
osed by medieval ramparts.
entation highlight is St. Francis'
lica. Time also to visit the Church
t. Clare in this, the 800th
versary year of her birth. (EB D)

y 8 Assisi – Salerno
el south today through Umbria to
peii, the town buried by the
tion of Vesuvius in AD79, for a
ted tour of the excavations. A
rt journey brings us to Salerno,
ing place of the US 5th Army in
3. (EB D)

y 9 Salerno – Taormina (2)
her south to the rustic simplicity
Calabria. Then to the toe of Italy for
ry across the *Straits of Messina*
Sicily. Later we arrive in Taormina
a two-night stay. (BB D)

y 10 Taormina at leisure
ay to relax and mingle with the
-loving Sicilians in this popular

resort – you can swim and sunbathe,
or shop for handmade lace on the
Corso. Perhaps try the local food and
wine for lunch. There's also a chance
to visit the medieval castle of San
Pancrazio, or take an exciting
excursion to the crater of Mount
Etna, Sicily's active volcano. (BB D)

Day 11 Taormina – Agrigento
Journey first to the spectacular
fortress town of *Enna*, then on to the
scenic splendour of *Piazza Armerina*. Here we have an included visit to
see the colourful mosaics of the 4th
century *Roman Villa of Casale*.
Later, down to the vineyards of the
southern slopes for dinner and
overnight in Agrigento. (BB D)

Day 12 Agrigento – Palermo
A local guide shows you the 6th
century BC ruins in the *Valley of
Temples*, which rival even Athens in
their Grecian grandeur. On to more
wonders of ancient Greece at
Selinunte, where we visit the Dorian
Temples and Acropolis on a natural
terrace over the Mediterranean. On to
Palermo for dinner tonight. (BB D)

Day 13 Palermo – At Sea
The ornate Piazza Bellini, the
Cathedral and the Arab-Norman
Palatine Chapel in the Royal Palace
are included in morning *sightseeing*
with a local guide. Stop to admire
the view of the Conca d'Oro from
Monreale, and visit the 12th century
Norman Cathedral with its famous
Byzantine mosaics. We visit
Mondello, a typical fishing village,

then tonight, we board the steamer
back to mainland Italy. (BB)

Day 14 Naples – Capri – Sorrento
Early disembarkation in Naples, then
a cruise across the Bay of Naples to
the *Isle of Capri*. Time to explore
this enchanting island in the bay
where Ulysses resisted the call of the
siren, and where former emperors
made their home. Now white-
washed houses and orange and
lemon groves line the streets. Cruise
back to cliff-top Sorrento. (EB D)

Day 15 Sorrento – Rome
Spectacular morning drive along the
Bay of Naples. Then north to view
the *Abbey of Monte Cassino*.
Returning to Rome later today, why
not finish the tour with dinner in one
of Rome's many restaurants? (EB)

Day 16 Rome – USA
Farewell to Italy and "buon viaggio"
as you embark on your return flight
to America. (BB)

DUBLIN'S FAIR CITY

JAUNTING ROUND KILLARNEY

TRAFALGAR'S CENTRAL HOTELS SEE PAGES 10-17

ESCORTED: 22 DAYS

BRITAIN & IRELAND PANORAMA

LONDON, SALISBURY, STONEHENGE, DEVON, CORNWALL, BATH, WALES, KILLARNEY, LIMERICK, DUBLIN, ENGLISH LAKE DISTRICT, EDINBURGH, SCOTTISH HIGHLANDS, SKYE, GLASGOW, YORK, COVENTRY, STRATFORD

TRAFALGAR'S HIGHLY ACCLAIMED, IN-DEPTH EXPLORATION OF MAINLAND BRITAIN AND THE EMERALD ISLE.

ANCIENT STONEHENGE TO HIGHLAND CASTLES. COTSWOLD COTTAGES TO ROYAL PALACES.

FULL BRITISH BREAKFASTS AND A HOST OF 3-COURSE DINNERS INCLUDED.

TRAFALGAR GIVES YOU MORE

SIGHTSEEING EVERY DAY

London Sightseeing tour.
Hampton Court Admire the Palace.
Salisbury View the Cathedral with the tallest spire in England.
Stonehenge Visit the ancient stone circle.
Cornish Highlights Excursion viewing St. Michael's Mount, Land's End and St. Ives.
Plymouth Sightseeing including the Mayflower Steps.
Tintagel View the 14th century Manor House and Post Office.
Clovelly Visit the picturesque seaside resort.
Glastonbury Visit King Arthur's Abbey.
Wells See the Cathedral.
Bath Sightseeing including the Roman Baths.
Cardiff View the Castle.
Waterford Visit the crystal factory (when open).
Cork Sightseeing including St. Finbar's Cathedral and Blarney Castle .
Ring of Kerry Scenic drive.
Dublin City sightseeing including St. Patrick's Cathedral and Trinity College.
Chester See the "Rows".
Grasmere Visit William Wordsworth's village.
Moffat Visit a Scottish tweed and woollen shop.

Edinburgh City sightseeing, visit the imposing Castle.
St. Andrews See the famous golf course.
Blair Atholl View the Castle.
Culloden Moor See the famous 1746 battle site.
Scottish Highlands Isle of Skye excursion.
Glencoe See the Clan Memorial.
Glasgow Sightseeing including the Burrell Collection.
Gretna Green See a marriage ceremony re-enactment.
Hadrian's Wall See the ancient Roman fortifications.
York Sightseeing including the Minster and the Shambles.
Coventry See the cathedrals.
Stratford Shakespeare's birthplace and see Anne Hathaway's Cottage.
Blenheim View the gardens.
Bladon See the grave of Sir Winston Churchill.
Oxford Orientation tour.
Runnymede See the Kennedy Memorial.

SCENIC DRIVES ON THE WAY

● Salisbury Plain ● Bodmin Moor ● Dartmoor National Park ● Exmoor National Park ● North Devon Coastal Drive ● North Wales Coast ● Snowdonia National Park

● English Lake District
● The Scottish Highlands
● Along Loch Ness & Loch Lomond ● The Scottish Borders
● Northumberland National Park
● Through the Cotswolds.

DINING & ENTERTAINMENT

● Welcome drink with your Tour Director ● Continental breakfast in London **(CB)** and Full British breakfast on tour **(FB)** ● 8 table d'hôte three-course dinners in hotels, plus a highlight restaurant dinner in Glasgow **(D)**. 9 dinners in total.

FIRST CLASS HOTELS

● Twin-bedded rooms with private facilities; all service charges, local taxes, baggage handling and hotel tips.

TRAVELLING IN EUROPE

● Touring by luxury air-ventilated coach with reclining seats ● London Airport transfers – see page 28 ● Pick-up and drop-off at your London hotel.

TRAFALGAR ALSO INCLUDES

● Professional Tour Director on tour ● Specialised local guide in Edinburgh ● Trafalgar representative at your London hotel ● Travel bag and wallet containing comprehensive tour documents.

Day 1 Depart USA
Overnight flight to London.

Day 2 Arrive London (2)
After checking into your Trafalgar hotel, the rest of the day is at leisure.

Day 3 London sightseeing
Many major sights are included on today's *sightseeing tour*. (CB)

Day 4 London – Plymouth (2)
Leaving London on a drive through *Hampton Court* to see Henry VIII's Palace and walk in the ornamental gardens. On through *Salisbury* for a view of the Cathedral, then across the plain to mysterious *Stonehenge*. Continue to *Devon* and the naval city of Plymouth, from where the Pilgrim Fathers sailed. (CB D)

Day 5 Cornish Excursion
Full day included excursion of England's west country and the rugged Cornish coastline. First, across Bodmin Moor to Penzance, viewing *St. Michael's Mount*. On to *Land's End* before returning to Plymouth via the colourful fishing village of *St. Ives*. (FB)

Day 6 Plymouth – Barnstaple
Across the wild beauty of *Dartmoor National Park* to Cornwall's Atlantic coast and *Tintagel*. View the manor house, then on to the fishing village of Boscastle en route to cobbled *Clovelly*. Along the North Devon coast and through *Exmoor National Park* to Barnstaple. (FB D)

Day 7 Barnstaple – Cardiff
Morning drive to King Arthur's *Glastonbury* to visit the remains of the Abbey dissolved by King Henry VIII, and on to *Wells* with its beautiful Cathedral. Historic *Bath* awaits where sightseeing includes a visit to the *Roman Baths*. Finally we cross the Severn Bridge to Cardiff, the Welsh capital. (FB D)

Day 8 Cardiff – Wexford
After viewing majestic *Cardiff Castle*, it's on through South Wales to Fishguard for a *ferry across the Irish Sea*. Landing in Ireland we drive by coach to Wexford. (FB D)

FORGET THE MONSTER, BUT LOCH NESS IS BEAUTIFUL

Day 9 Wexford – Killarney
First to **Waterford**, home of Ireland's renowned crystal. Later at **Blarney Castle**, a chance to kiss the famous stone then in **Cork**, we see City Hall, Shandon Church and St. Finbar's Cathedral. Finally a drive to Killarney, beautifully set on a lake. (FB)

Day 10 Killarney – Ring of Kerry – Limerick
Experience Ireland's most scenic drive – around the 112-mile **"Ring of Kerry"** with its plunging cliffs, lush lakeland, granite mountains and sandy beaches, on the journey round County Kerry's largest peninsula. Also see **Killorglin** (of Puck Fair fame), Daniel O'Connell's Cahirciveen, the fishing village of **Waterville**, the **Black Mountains** and spectacular **Moll's Gap**. On to Limerick, famous for its lace. (FB)

Day 11 Limerick – Dublin (2)
The Emerald Isle's stunning scenery rolls by as we drive to **Galway Bay** for panoramic views. Via Galway City, then through Ballinasloe and Athlone to Dublin. (FB)

Day 12 Dublin sightseeing
Trinity College, St. Patrick's Cathedral, historic Phoenix Park and other notable landmarks are included in morning **city sightseeing**. The rest of the day is free. (FB))

Day 13 Dublin – Chester
Return across the Irish Sea. Then along the **North Wales coast** and through Snowdonia National Park. In **Chester** we admire the Tudor buildings and galleried Rows. (FB D)

Day 14 Chester – Lake District – Edinburgh (2)
North through the beautiful English **Lake District**, a vast area of lake and mountain scenery that inspired the poet Wordsworth. Visit his village of **Grasmere**, then continue over the Scottish border. We visit **Moffat Woollens** en route to Edinburgh, Scotland's elegant capital. (FB)

Day 15 Edinburgh sightseeing
The Castle, Princes Street and the Royal Mile are included on our morning **city sightseeing tour**. Later, view Holyrood House – former home of Mary Queen of Scots. Free time to shop for tartans and tweeds then a chance to enjoy a traditional Scottish night out. (FB)

Day 16 Edinburgh – Strathpeffer (2)
A drive into the Highlands. First stopping at **St. Andrews golf course**. Then via Dundee and Perth to **Blair Atholl**. After viewing the Castle, continue to the Highland town of Strathpeffer. (FB D)

Day 17 Highlands & Skye Excursion
First stop on this spectacular Highland drive is **Culloden**, site of the battle which finally defeated hopes of a Stuart Monarchy. Then through rugged mountains to the **Kyle of Lochalsh** on the West Coast for a ferry **"over the sea to Skye"**. After exploring the isle, return to the mainland for a drive along the banks of **Loch Ness**. (FB D)

Day 18 Strathpeffer – Glasgow
Cross the Grampian Mountains and pass Britain's highest mountain – **Ben Nevis** – en route to **Fort William** and **Glencoe**. Then to the bonnie banks of Loch Lomond on the approach to Glasgow. Included is a visit to the **Burrell Collection of Fine Art**. In the evening a **highlight dinner at the specialty restaurant Harry Ramsdens**. (FB D)

Day 19 Glasgow – York
First stop on the journey south is at **Gretna Green** famous for eloping lovers. On to visit **Hadrian's Wall**, built by the Roman Emperor to keep the Scots at bay, then through the Border Forest and **Northumberland National Park** on a drive to **York**. The city's history is written in its narrow cobbled streets, timbered houses and famous **Minster**. (FB)

Day 20 York – Coventry
A drive through the varied countryside of the Midlands takes us to **Coventry** – home of Lady Godiva. See the awe-inspiring modern **Cathedral** and the old one beside it. Dinner is in our hotel tonight. (FB D)

Day 21 Coventry – Stratford – London
Soak up the Elizabethan atmosphere of Stratford-upon-Avon where we visit **Shakespeare's birthplace** and see Anne Hathaway's Cottage. A scenic drive through the rolling Cotswolds, dotted with gold-stone villages, to view **Blenheim Palace**, birthplace of Sir Winston Churchill. See his grave at Bladon, then to the historic university town of **Oxford**. We drive through Runnymede and Windsor back to London. (FB)

Day 22 London – USA
We transfer you to the airport for your flight to America. (CB)

HOTELS ON THIS TOUR

London: Forte Crest Regents Park
Plymouth: Copthorne
Barnstaple: Park **Cardiff:** Forte Crest
Wexford: Talbot **Killarney:** Ryan
Limerick: Ryan **Dublin:** Gresham
Chester: Plantation Inn
Edinburgh: Royal Scot
Strathpeffer: Highland
Glasgow: Central **York:** Novotel
Coventry: Leofric
London: Forte Crest Regents Park

* On Thursday departures the highlight dinner at Harry Ramsdens will be in Edinburgh instead of Glasgow.

EDINBURGH TATTOO
5-27 August 1994
Tickets can be obtained through your Tour Director
(subject to availability).

SAVE $$$$

For a similar tour featuring excellent tourist class hotels, see page 140 and our 1994 CostSaver brochure.

ESCORTED: 30 DAYS

GREAT EUROPEAN

ENGLAND, FRANCE, SPAIN, MONACO, ITALY, AUSTRIA,
LIECHTENSTEIN, SWITZERLAND, GERMANY, HOLLAND, BELGIUM

THE SCOPE BROADENS TO INCLUDE NEARLY ALL OF WESTERN EUROPE.

WITH THE BONUS OF THREE NIGHTS IN THE ETERNAL CITY OF ROME. PLUS VISITS TO MONACO, VIENNA, CAPRI, MADRID AND BARCELONA.

THE RHINE AND BLACK FOREST, AUSTRIAN TYROL AND SWISS ALPS, THE FRENCH RIVIERA AND VINEYARDS ALL ADD TO THIS GREAT EUROPEAN EXPERIENCE.

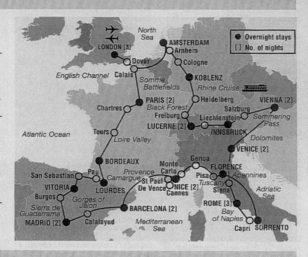

PLAZA MAYOR – MADRID

ISLE OF CAPRI – INCLUDED

TRAFALGAR GIVES YOU MORE

SIGHTSEEING EVERY DAY

Dover See the White Cliffs.
Paris Sightseeing tour including a guided tour of Notre Dame Cathedral.
Chartres Visit the Cathedral.
Lourdes See St. Bernadette's grotto.
Pau Visit this picturesque town of the Pyrenees.
Burgos See the city of El Cid.
Madrid Sightseeing tour including the Royal Palace, Puerta del Sol and Cervantes Memorial.
Calatayud See the ruins of the Moorish castle.
Barcelona Sightseeing including Sagrada Familia Cathedral.
Cannes Visit the resort.
Visit a local perfumery.
St. Paul de Vence Explore the medieval village.
Monaco See the cathedral and palace in the Old Town.
Pisa View the Leaning Tower.
Florence Sightseeing including Signoria Square, Santa Croce Basilica, Baptistry. See Florentine leatherworkers at their craft.
Capri Visit this picturesque isle.
Rome Sightseeing including St. Peter's Basilica, the Forum, and the Colosseum.
Siena Visit the medieval town.
Venice Canal cruise by private boat. See St. Mark's Square, the Byzantine Basilica, Doges' Palace and the Bridge of Sighs.

Visit a glass-blowing factory.
Vienna Sightseeing tour including the Hofburg, Opera, Ring, Belvedere Palace Gardens and St. Stephen's Cathedral.
Salzburg Visit the city of "Sound of Music" fame. Sightseeing includes Mozart's birthplace.
Innsbruck Orientation tour including the Olympic ski jump, the Golden Roof, Wilten Basilica and Hofburg Palace.
Liechtenstein Visit the capital, Vaduz.
Lucerne Orientation tour including the walled Old Town and the Lion Monument.
Freiburg View the Cathedral in the capital of the Black Forest.
Heidelberg View the Castle.
Rhine Valley Cruise past the Lorelei Rock (weather permitting).
Cologne See the Cathedral.
Amsterdam Visit a diamond polishing factory.
London Sightseeing tour.

SCENIC DRIVES ON THE WAY

● Across World War I Battlefields ● Along the Loire Valley ● Across the Sierra de Guadarrama ● Through the Camargue ● French Riviera Drive ● The Sorrento Peninsula ● The Semmering Pass across the Alps ● Through the Black Forest ● Along the Rhine Valley.

DINING & ENTERTAINMENT

● Welcome drink with your Tour Director in Paris.
● Continental breakfast in London (CB); Buffet breakfast (BB) or Continental breakfast with juice & cereal (EB) on tour.
● 11 three-course dinners in hotels, plus 2 highlight restaurant dinners in Nice and Florence (D) and lunch (L) in Salzburg. 14 meals in total.

FIRST CLASS HOTELS

● Twin-bedded rooms with private facilities; all service charges, local taxes, baggage handling and hotel tips.

TRAVELLING IN EUROPE

● Touring by luxury air-conditioned coach with reclining seats and a washroom ● Cross-Channel ferry ● London Airport transfers – see page 28 ● Pick-up and drop-off at your London hotel.

TRAFALGAR ALSO INCLUDES

● Professional, multi-lingual Tour Director on tour ● Specialised local guides in Paris, Madrid, Barcelona, Florence, Rome, Vienna and Salzburg ● Trafalgar representative at your London hotel ● Travel bag and wallet containing comprehensive tour documents.

Day 1 Depart USA
Overnight flight to London.

Day 2 Arrive London
After checking into your Trafalgar hotel, the rest of the day is at leisure.

Day 3 London – Paris (2)
Greetings from your Tour Director, then a drive to the Kent coast for the Channel crossing to Calais in France, with time to admire the famous *White Cliffs of Dover*. Then south across World War I Battlefields to Paris, the 'City of Light'. Tonight, enjoy a *welcome drink* with your Tour Director. (CB)

Day 4 Paris sightseeing
Marvel at famous landmarks on our morning *sightseeing tour*, with views of the Eiffel Tower, the Champs Elysées, Opéra and Louvre. Highlight is a guided *tour of Notre Dame Cathedral*. Rest of the day is at leisure. Perhaps take a Bateau Mouche Seine cruise then tonight, why not hit the bright lights of a typical Parisian cabaret? (EB)

Day 5 Paris – Bordeaux
A short drive to *Chartres*, renowned for its stained glass windows of its cathedral. Then onto the *Loire at Tours* and south to the wine-producing region of Bordeaux. (EB D)

Day 6 Bordeaux – Lourdes
Scenic drive this morning along the valley of the River Garonne through tidy orchards and *vineyards of Sauternes and Graves*. Arriving in the pilgrimage site of Lourdes, we see the beautiful basilica on top of *St. Bernadette's grotto*. (BB D)

Day 7 Lourdes – Vitoria
First stop is the medieval town of *Pau*, where we admire magnificent views from the Boulevard of the Pyrenees. Home of King Henry IV, Pau was a favourite town of 19th

VIENNA – SCHONBRUNN PALACE

century English aristocracy. We then cross into the Basque country of Spain via **San Sebastian**, before continuing to Vitoria. (EB D)

Day 8 Vitoria – Madrid (2)
Follow in the footsteps of El Cid, heading first for **Burgos**, then across the spectacular **Sierra de Guadarrama** to Madrid. Built by Philip II in the 16th century, the city is Europe's highest capital. (BB D)

Day 9 Madrid sightseeing
Morning **sightseeing** includes the Royal Palace. Time later to shop in the city's excellent boutiques. Or stroll through the splendid parks and perhaps take an excursion to the royal city of El Escorial. (BB)

Day 10 Madrid – Barcelona (2)
Across the high plains of the Meseta in Castile and past Guadalajara, scene of Civil War struggles, we drive through the **Gorges of Jalon** and on into the province of Aragon. We see the ruins of the **Castle of Calatayud** en route to Barcelona, recent Olympic host city. (BB D)

Day 11 Barcelona sightseeing
The Gothic wonders of the old Cathedral and fantasies of Gaudi are revealed on morning **sightseeing**. At leisure, perhaps visit the Picasso Museum and stroll along the colourful Ramblas. Maybe enjoy a fiery flamenco show tonight. (BB)

Day 12 Barcelona – Nice (2)
Across the French border to the scenic **Camargue** region, known for its wildlife. Through **Provence** to the sophisticated Nice on the Riviera. Enjoy **Provençal specialities in a local restaurant tonight**. (BB D)

Day 13 Nice – Côte d'Azur Excursion
Along sparkling shores to **Cannes**, scene of the Film Festival, then to the medieval town of **St. Paul de Vence**, a photographer's paradise. We visit a perfumery before returning to Nice. Tonight, perhaps stroll along the Promenade des Anglais. (BB)

Day 14 Nice – Florence
First in Monte Carlo, we visit **Monaco Town** to see the cathedral and palace. Across the Italian border, we pass Genoa, birthplace of Columbus, to **Pisa** to view the **Leaning Tower**. On to **Florence** where our walking tour includes the marble cathedral, Signoria Square, the Baptistry and Santa Croce Basilica. Enjoy **dinner tonight in a Florentine trattoria**. (BB D)

Day 15 Florence – Sorrento
Driving south this morning, we pass the Abbey of **Monte Cassino** and skirt the **Bay of Naples** en route to the lively Sorrento. This favourite Italian resort has a spectacular clifftop setting. Perhaps visit a Tarantella show tonight. (EB D)

Day 16 Sorrento – Capri – Rome (3)
Highlight is a trip to the enchanting **Isle of Capri**, lined with fashionable shops, cafés and beaches. Perhaps visit the Blue Grotto before a ferry back to Naples, then drive on to Rome, the "Eternal City". (EB)

Days 17 & 18 Rome sightseeing & at leisure
St. Peter's Basilica, the Forum and the Colosseum are all included on morning **sightseeing**. Then you're free to shop along the Via Condotti or relax in a café on the Via Veneto. Maybe visit the Sistine Chapel and tour the Catacombs then sit by the fountains on Piazza Navona. (BB)

Day 19 Rome – Venice (2)
Scenic morning drive to medieval **Siena**, heart of Tuscany and scene of the Palio horse race. Then across the **Apennine Mountains** to Bologna and the charms of Venice. Don't miss a gondola serenade on the Grand Canal. (BB D)

Day 20 Venice sightseeing
Savour the atmosphere of this Byzantine jewel on a **canal cruise** by private boat to St. Mark's Square, viewing the **Bridge of Sighs**. Visit a **glass blowing factory**, then you're at leisure to shop or sightsee. Perhaps take a boat ride to the island of Burano for a fantastic seafood lunch. (BB)

Day 21 Venice – Vienna (2)
A day of scenic splendours as the **Dolomites** herald the Austrian border and Lake District. Past forested hillsides studded with ruined castles to the **Semmering Pass** across the Alps. Then, the Danube plains give way to Vienna. (BB)

Day 22 Vienna sightseeing
The highlights of Europe's cultural capital are revealed on morning **sightseeing**: the Opera, Hofburg, Belvedere Palace Gardens, the Ring and St. Stephen's Cathedral. This evening, why not wine and dine at a lively "heurige" inn? (BB)

Day 23 Vienna – Innsbruck
After breakfast drive to the beauties of **Salzburg**, where we explore on foot Mozart's birthplace and scenes from "The Sound of Music". After lunch in a local restaurant, we continue to Innsbruck, winter and summer Tyrolean resort. (BB L D)

Day 24 Innsbruck – Lucerne (2)
Morning **orientation** highlights the Golden Roof and Wilten Basilica. A spectacular drive past the monastery of Stams, through skiing country to **Vaduz**, capital of Liechtenstein. Along the Walensee and Lake Zurich to scenic lakeside Lucerne. (BB D)

Day 25 Lucerne sightseeing
Our orientation of this medieval city includes the Old Town and a visit to the beautiful **Lion Monument**. At leisure, why not ascend Mt. Rigi, and enjoy a Swiss fondue lunch and folklore show. (BB D)

Day 26 Lucerne – Koblenz
Today we head towards the capital of the **Black Forest, Freiburg**, famous for its gothic Cathedral. On to **Heidelberg** castle, heading for picturesque **St. Goar** and our scenic **Rhine Cruise** to Boppard. (BB D)

Day 27 Koblenz – Amsterdam
Along the **Rhine Valley** to **Cologne** where we see the magnificent Gothic **Cathedral**. Over the Dutch border at Arnhem to Amsterdam. (BB)

Day 28 Amsterdam – London
Canals, gabled houses and landmarks are revealed on morning **sightseeing** before a visit to a **diamond polishing factory**. Leaving Amsterdam, journey through **Belgium** on the way to Calais for the ferry to Dover and on to London. (BB)

Day 29 London sightseeing
Many major sights are included on this morning's **sightseeing**. (CB)

Day 30 London – USA
Return flight to America. (CB)

DATES & PRICES

SKYBARGAIN fares

The above 'TOUR + AIR' prices are from New York. For details and special low add-on fares from other US cities, see page 25.

HOTELS ON THIS TOUR

London: Tower
Paris: Cayre
Bordeaux: Holiday Inn Garden Court
Lourdes: Imperial
Vitoria: Canciller Ayala
Madrid: La Habana
Barcelona: Hilton
Nice: Park
Florence: Holiday Inn
Sorrento: Cesare Augusto
Rome: Cicerone
Venice-Grand Canal: Carlton Executive/Principe
Vienna: Scandic Crown
Innsbruck: Scandic Crown
Lucerne: Schiller
Koblenz: Scandic Crown
Amsterdam: Hilton
London: Tower

■ **REVIEW—WESTERN EUROPE**

1. What are the main language families of Western Europe? Where are they spoken? How does English fit in?

2. What are the main religions of Western Europe? Where are they practiced?

3. How do you account for the relatively mild climate in Western Europe despite its far northern location?

4. In what ways is the Mediterranean climate distinctive?

5. What political subunits make up the United Kingdom?

6. What factors contribute to the large size, prosperity, and importance of London?

7. Identify the source, character, and effect on tourism of the "troubles" in Northern Ireland.

8. What factors contribute to the large size and importance of Paris?

9. What countries are located within Scandinavia? What do they have in common?

10. Identify common features shared by the Mediterranean nations.

11. What factors contribute to the large size and importance of Rome?

12. What are the major regional differences between northern and southern Italy?

13. What do Andorra, San Marino, Liechtenstein, and Malta have in common?

14. Compare and contrast Rome, Florence, and Venice.

15. Where is Athens? What is its importance?

16. Which countries share the Iberian Peninsula? Describe their touristic importance.

17. What are the major ski areas of Western Europe? Where are they located?

18. Where are the major beach and resort areas in Western Europe?

19. Describe four areas of scenic beauty in Western Europe.

10

Eastern Europe and the Former Soviet Union

■ EASTERN EUROPE—AN OVERVIEW

Eastern Europe is a dramatic change of pace from Western Europe. It consists of relatively small nations with marked differences in language, religion, and political orientation. As a result, it can be called a "cultural shatter belt." The nations involved are Poland, the Czech Republic, Slovakia, Hungary, Slovenia, Croatia, Bosnia, Yugoslavia, Macedonia, Romania, Bulgaria, and Albania. As shown later in the chapter, some newer nations, created by the dissolution of the former USSR, must also be included.

There is no neat dividing line between Eastern and Western Europe. Although Finland lies within Eastern Europe, it is tied by culture, economy, and tourism to the rest of Scandinavia (Norden) and Western Europe. Another border nation, Austria, is West-oriented politically and touristically, but trades both westward and eastward. Greece, a nation bordering both Eastern Europe and the Middle East, interacts with Western Europe rather than its northern neighbors or its east-

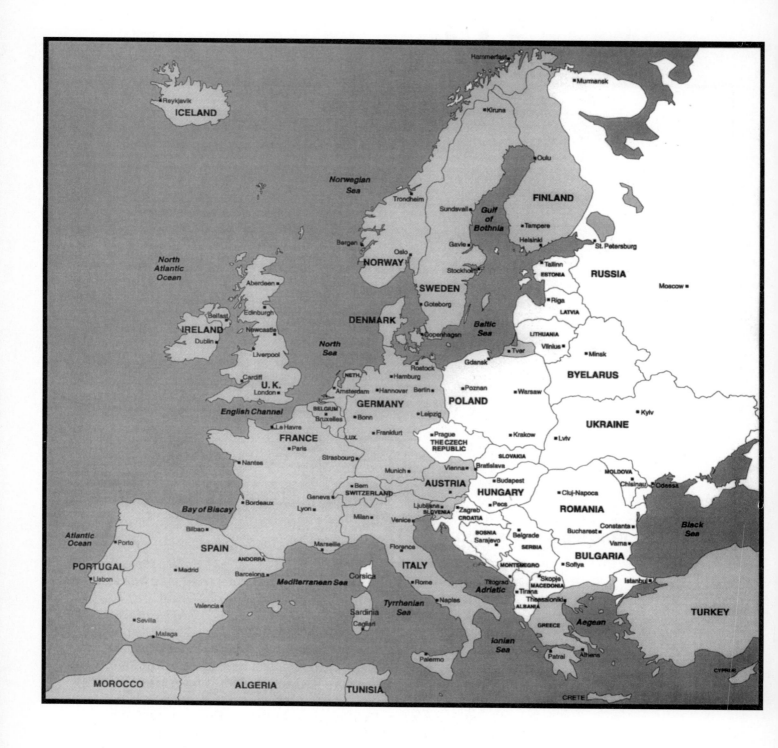

ern rival, Turkey. Therefore, Finland, Austria, and Greece have been covered in Chapter 9 along with Western Europe.

History

The pattern of political units has changed often and drastically over the past several centuries, involving various combinations of territory and culture groups. The greatest changes in this century came after World Wars I and II and during 1989–91 when Communist governments fell from power. After World War I, the largest and strongest Eastern European nation, the Austro-Hungarian Empire, was split up into several new nations, including Czechoslovakia and Yugoslavia, composed of unlike and sometimes warring ethnic groups. Poland, which had been divided among powerful neighbors in the late 18th century, was recreated in 1919, only to be wiped out again by Germans and Russians at the start of World War II. German occupation caused many other boundary changes.

After the war's end in 1945, Poland was recreated, East Germany became a new nation, and most other nations regained their prewar form. From 1945 to 1989–1991, six Eastern European nations had Communist governments and were dominated by the USSR. They were East Germany, Poland, Czechoslovakia, Hungary, Romania and Bulgaria. Yugoslavia and Albania were Communist independents that operated outside the Soviet sphere.

With the collapse of Communism in the USSR in 1989–91, Communist governments in Eastern Europe also were toppled. Long-suppressed ethnic antagonism quickly surfaced, causing the partition of Czechoslovakia (into the Czech Republic and Slovakia) and Yugoslavia (into Slovenia, Croatia, Bosnia, Yugoslavia, and Macedonia). The Czechoslovakian division was peaceful, but that of Yugoslavia has been marred by fierce military action and large losses of property and lives.

The Land and Climate

The historical-cultural fragmentation and frequent boundary changes in Eastern Europe arose from the region's topography and the competition among varied ethnic groups for the most habitable areas. The most dominant physical feature is the North European Plain, which extends eastward through northern Germany to include most of Poland, Belarus, Ukraine, and western Russia.

Created by the retreat of continental ice sheets thousands of years ago, this gently rolling, great plain is crossed by large rivers flowing from the European interior to the North Sea and Baltic Sea. Patches of forest remain. This topography has permitted the easy movement of people throughout history, contributing to the impermanence of Eastern Europe's political units and boundaries. It has been the scene of spirited competition among Germans, Poles, and Russians. Heavily cultivated and populous, it is a leading food producer.

The northern plain is terminated in the south by the high Carpathian Mountains that trend eastward through the Czech Republic, Slovakia, and Poland, and southward into central Romania, where the Transylvanian Alps continue westward in a fishhook shape. South of the Carpathians in the European interior is the second largest plain of Eastern Europe, the Hungarian Plain (Danubian Plain). Most of it lies within Hungary, with its fringes in Slovakia, Austria, Yugoslavia, and Romania. It supports widespread agricultural activity.

The Danube River, Europe's longest, passes through the heart of the plain, flowing from West Germany and Austria to the Black Sea. Farther downstream, the Danube passes Croatia, goes through eastern Yugoslavia and forms the Romania-Bulgaria boundary. Located on the river are several of Eastern Europe's largest cities: Vienna (Austria), Budapest (Hungary), and Belgrade (Yugoslavia). In Romania, broad plains flank the Carpathians to the east and south, where the national capital, Bucharest, lies.

The southern part of Eastern Europe, popularly called the Balkans, is mountainous. The Alps continue eastward into Austria, then bend southward parallel to the Adriatic coast. Other ranges dominate the landscape of Bulgaria and Greece, where people, cities, and economic activities are concentrated in a number of small, scattered plains.

The Eastern European climate is more "continental" than in Western Europe, which means it has longer and colder winters, hot summers, and less rainfall. Snow is common in winter, with deep accumulations in the Carpathian and Alpine ranges.

Languages and Religions

There are many cultural variations from one nation to another, as shown by the geographical distribution of language and religion. Finnish and Hungarian are linguistically related, but are far removed geographically. Polish, Czech, and Slovak are Slavic languages related to Russian. Romanian, as its name suggests, is a Romance language, with strong similarities to Italian. Serbo-Croatian, Slovenian, Macedonian, and Bulgarian compose a south Slavic language cluster. Albanian is a distinctive language. From Hungary and Romania southward, nations also include numerous minority populations that make the linguistic pattern even more complex.

The religious pattern is somewhat simpler. Roman Catholicism extends in a northeast-southwest belt through Poland, the Czech Republic, Slovakia, Hungary, Croatia, Slovenia, and Bosnia. Orthodox Christianity is common in Bosnia, Yugoslavia, Macedonia, Romania, and Bulgaria. A Moslem population that dates from the long period of Turkish domination, prior to the 19th century, is found in Bosnia and southern Yugoslavia, adjacent to Albania. Orthodox Christianity and Islam are reviving in Albania after a long ban by the former Communist government. A once-numerous Jewish population in Eastern Europe was reduced to small numbers by Nazi genocide during World War II and some emigration to Israel since then.

The Economy

Most of Eastern Europe lags behind Western Europe in economic development. Agriculture is important everywhere, especially in the extensive North European Plain and the Hungarian Plain. It is least rewarding in the Mediterranean fringe areas where poor soils and summer drought limit production.

In industrial activities, Poland and the Czech Republic are most advanced, followed by Slovakia and Slovenia. Before 1989–1991, the six-nation Soviet bloc depended on the Soviet Union for energy, raw material and food supplies, and, in turn, shipped most of their surpluses to the Soviet Union under trade agreements. Now, however, they must adjust to broader international supply-demand markets, especially those in Western Europe.

Road and railway networks are extensive in areas other than the Balkans, where the mountainous terrain is partly responsible for simpler and more primitive systems. Horse-drawn carts are still in common use in rural areas. Air service to national capitals and major regional cities is available.

East European nations that had Communist governments face enormous political, social and economic challenges in the 1990s in the transition from public ownership and control to democratic governments and private ownership and operation. Farmland, housing, factories, and businesses are being privatized; unemployment is high; and individual citizens who once enjoyed state protection and patronage must face the realities of an uncertain, competitive world.

Before the fall of communism, these countries each had a central national tourist office that controlled virtually all tourism in the country. This function has also been privatized in many cases and these countries are learning to work in the competitive market-based environment. Tourism is well developed, however, in most Eastern European nations, excluding Albania and is proving a benefit to the economic environment in these countries. Western hotel companies and other western tourism organizations are becoming more involved in the tourism activities of most of these countries.

■ EASTERN EUROPE

POLAND

Official Name: Republic of Poland

Language: Polish

Area: 120,727 square miles

Time Zone: GMT +1

National Airline: LOT Polish

Capital: Warsaw

Currency: Zloty (ZLO)

Population: 37,799,000

Documentation: Passport, visa

Poland is the largest and most populous Eastern European nation. During World War II, it was occupied by the Germans, then liberated by the Red Army advancing westward toward Berlin. At the end of the war, the Soviet Union kept a large eastern slice of former Polish territory and, in return, awarded newly recreated Poland a slice of former German land as far west as the Oder River. These transfers left Poland smaller, with its borders shifted 75 miles farther west than in 1938. Although under a Communist regime, the Polish people remained resolutely independent in politics and staunchly Roman Catholic in religion, proud that the Pope in Rome is one of them. They were leaders in the political movement that brought the Communist era to an end.

Poland is bordered on the north by the Baltic Sea and includes a small section of the Carpathian Mountains in the south. Between these extremes, the rolling North European Plain occupies most of the national territory. Both the rural and urban populations are large.

Among the cities, Warsaw, on the north-flowing Vistula River, is the largest and the national capital. Demolished during the war, it has a restored central historical district and post-war, high-rise public buildings and apartment complexes. The textile center of Lodz, also in central Poland, is the second largest with more than one million people.

The Polish economy is well-balanced between agriculture and manufacturing. Agriculture is practiced everywhere, but is most productive in the southern part of Poland where soils are better. Poland ranks as one of the most industrial nations in Eastern Europe. Industrial activities are heavily concentrated in the south and southwest, making use of major deposits of coal, iron ore, and other raw materials. Here, too, are extensive areas of environmental damage from industrial emissions.

With its long Baltic coastline, Poland is a maritime nation. It has port facilities and shipyards at Gdansk (former Danzig) and Gdynia, near the mouth of the Vistula River, and lesser port facilities at Szczecin, near the mouth of the Oder River. The nation has comprehensive rail, road, and air networks.

Areas of Touristic Importance. Warsaw, capital city of Poland, was one of the most beautiful cities in Europe before World War II. Remarkable restorations were made after the city was devastated by bombings and direct attack during the war. Faithful restorations of the Old Quarter and Market Square greet the visitor.

The city is dominated by the 765-foot-high Palace of Science and Culture that contains theaters, restaurants, scientific organizations, and a congress hall. The top of the hall offers an excellent view of the city. Located below is the Muranow residential district, which replaced the Jewish ghetto made famous by the Jewish uprising during World War II. An impressive monument marks this site.

The Wilanow Palace, which once housed royalty, and the Zelazowa Wola, once Chopin's home, are both located not far from Warsaw and are now museums. South of Warsaw, Czestochowa, with its famous "Black Madonna" icon, is a destination for Catholic pilgrims.

Krakow, 200 miles south of Warsaw, is a beautiful medieval town that escaped damage during World War II. Its old walls, churches, and towers remind the visitor of a time long gone. The Royal Castle, towering above the town, contains a museum with a magnificent collection of medieval tapestries.

Eight miles outside of Krakow is Wieliczka, the oldest salt mine in the world. It has been a working mine since the 10th century. Wieliczka is most famous for underground sculptures and grottos including a chapel and a tennis court.

Forty miles east of Krakow is Auschwitz, (Oswiecim in Polish) where millions of persons from 26 nations perished

Kracow Royal Castle, Kracow
Photo: Courtesy Teodor Hermancyzk

in the years 1940 to 1945. The former Nazi concentration camp is now a museum.

■ THE FORMER CZECHOSLOVAKIA

The Czech Republic and Slovakia were created in 1993 by the partition of the short-lived nation of Czechoslovakia along ethnic lines. Located east of Germany and south of Poland, on territory from the former Austro-Hungarian Empire, Czechoslovakia was created after World War I as a homeland for two related but distinctive Slavic-speaking populations groups, the Czechs in the west and the Slovaks in the east. A model democracy, it had the highest living standards and most prosperous, industrial economy in Eastern Europe. Occupied and divided by the Germans during World War II, Czechoslovakia was reborn at the end of the war. However, a Communist Party victory in national elections in 1948 propelled it into the Soviet political, military, and economic sphere until the collapse of international Communism in 1989–1991. Partition in 1993 resulted from the dominance of the majority Czechs in all aspects of national life and the desire of the minority Slovaks to have their own nation.

CZECH REPUBLIC

Official Name: Czech Republic
Language: Czech, Slovak
Area: 30,448 square miles
Time Zone: GMT +1
National Airline: Czechoslovak Airlines
Capital: Prague
Currency: Czech Crown (CKR)
Population: 10,404,000
Documentation: Passport, visa

The Czechs had a long history of self-government in the Kingdom of Bohemia, with Prague as its capital, before Bohemia was annexed by the expanding Austro-Hungarian Empire in the 17th century. They and their territory later formed the nucleus of Czechoslovakia and now the newly created (1993) Czech Republic.

Low mountains are the rule in the western part of the nation, where they form the boundaries with Germany, Poland and Austria. Roads and rail lines that follow the Elbe River into Germany link Prague with Dresden, Leipzig, and other German cities. The capital, Prague, is located on the Vltava, a tributary of the Elbe River. In the eastern part, plains in the old province of Moravia allow easy links with Poland, Austria, and Slovakia. The Czech industrial economy, noted for its output of consumer goods and military goods, ranks as the best, or one of the best, in Eastern Europe.

Areas of Touristic Importance. Prague is often called the City of a Hundred Spires because of its many churches and castles. Hradcany Castle was the residence of many kings. The National Museum, located in Wenceslaus Square, is most interesting. St. Stephen's Square includes a medieval clock tower with an elaborate animated clock. Prague has a varied nightlife and fine restaurants. The spectacular Karlstein Castle, which was built in the 14th century, is located 20 miles from the city.

Brno, the second largest city in Czechoslovakia, is the capital of Moravia. Its 13th-century Spilberk Castle is known for its torture chambers and dungeons. Slavkov, 13 miles east, was the site of the Battle of Austerlitz in 1805.

The Czech Republic is also well known for its spa towns. It has more than 50 spa resorts. The most noted is Carlsbad. Another popular place is Marienbad, with more than 40 mineral springs.

SLOVAKIA

Official Name: Slovak Republic

Language: Slovak, Czech, Hungarian

Area: 18,923 square miles

Time Zone: GMT +1

National Airline: Czechoslovak Airlines

Capital: Bratislava

Currency: Slovak Crown (CKR)

Population: 5,287,000

Documentation: Passport, visa

Slovakia is a mountainous nation, dominated by the western arm of the Carpathian Mountains and smaller ranges. It also includes a slice of the Hungarian Plain along its southern margin. In the southwest corner, facing on the Danube River, is its capital and largest city, Bratislava, which has easy links with Vienna and Budapest. The population mainly consists of Slavic-speaking Slovaks, but a Hungarian minority resides in the southern plains. The Slovakian economy includes both agriculture and manufacturing, but it is not as advanced as in the Czech Republic.

Areas of Touristic Importance. Bratislava, the capital of Slovakia, was once the capital of Hungary. The Primate's Palace features an ornate Hall of Mirrors and was the place where Napoleon signed the peace treaty after his victory at Austerlitz.

Piestany is the best known of Slovakia's many spa resorts.

HUNGARY

Official Name: Republic of Hungary

Language: Hungarian

Area: 35,919 square miles

Time Zone: GMT +1

National Airline: Malev

Capital: Budapest

Currency: Forint (FOR)

Population: 10,588,000

Documentation: Passport, visa at border

Hungary occupies the heart of the large Hungarian Plain on both sides of the north-south flowing Danube River. Only in the north and west does hilly terrain appear. Lake Balaton, one of the largest lakes of Eastern Europe and a favorite vacationland for the residents of Budapest, is also found in the west. The Hungarian language, of Asian origin and related to Finnish, is distinctive from the neighboring Slavic, Germanic, and Romanian languages. Millions of Hungarians live as minorities in Romania, Yugoslavia, and Slovakia because of the way the Austro-Hungarian Empire was divided after World War I.

The Hungarian population and economy are basically rural. Agriculture yields large surpluses of wheat and other grain for export. The limited industrial activity, like so much of the nation's nonagricultural activities, is centered in Budapest, the capital, by far the largest city and one of the most prosperous cities of Eastern Europe. Budapest's port on the Danube handles a heavy volume of commercial ships, cruise ships and pleasure craft.

Areas of Touristic Importance. Sophisticated Budapest is actually two cities in one. Buda, on one side of the Danube, was once a Roman camp. Pest, on the other side of the river, is the commercial and cultural center of the city. Points of interest include the Royal Castle and the Hungarian National Gallery, which are set within the walls of old Buda. Also worth visiting are the 700-year-old Matthias Church, where Hungarian kings were crowned, and the Fisherman's Bastion. Szentendre, a short distance outside Budapest, is an artists' colony.

There are more than 400 thermal springs in Hungary. Over 120 are in the Budapest area. The ancient Roman camp, Aquincum, was a spa. When the Turks overran Hungary they

built Turkish baths over many of the springs. Today, many of the baths have become health treatment facilities. Most prominent are the National Institute for Rheumatology and Physiology, the Lukacs Baths, the Szechenyi Baths, the Csaszar Baths, and the Rudas Baths.

Danube and Parliament Building, Budapest
Photo: Courtesy IBUSZ Hungarian Travel Bureau

Because Hungary is a small country, many attractions are quite close to Budapest. Lake Balaton, a delightful resort area, is only 65 miles from the capital. Also, the scenic Danube Bend is only an hour's drive from the city.

ROMANIA

Official Name: Romania
Language: Romanian, Hungarian
Area: 91,699 square miles
Time Zone: GMT +2
National Airline: Tarom
Capital: Bucharest
Currency: Lei (LEI)
Population: 23,397,000
Documentation: Passport, visa at border

Romania had a hard-line Communist government until 1989 and is having a difficult transition into a free-enterprise economy and democratic government.

The nation's physical geography is dominated by mountains. The high ranges of the Carpathians and Transylvanian Alps dominate its center. Large plains facing eastward on the Black Sea and south on the Danube River border with Bulgaria contain the bulk of the population and the main cities, including Bucharest, the capital. Western Romania includes a corner of the Hungarian Plain with a large Hungarian population, which is also a politically restive minority. It shares its eastern boundary with Ukraine and Moldova, former parts of the Soviet Union; Bulgaria is to the south; and Yugoslavia and Hungary are to the west.

An important agricultural nation and supplier of agricultural surpluses, Romania has been making strides toward industrialization based upon income derived from the sale abroad of energy from Eastern Europe's largest oil and natural gas fields. Oil and gas production centers on Ploesti, in the southeastern flank of the Transylvanian Alps. From there, pipelines carry energy to the Black Sea port of Constanta for ocean shipment abroad.

Areas of Touristic Importance. Noted for its beautiful parks and gardens in spite of widespread demolition of historic buildings and sites during the Communist era, Bucharest has been called the Paris of the Balkans. Bucharest is home to an excellent Village Museum, which has preserved many forms of folk architecture. The Stavropoleos Church, the Romanian Athenium, and the Mogosoaia Palace, 12 miles outside Bucharest, are also primary attractions.

The Danube River flows from Hungary along Romania into the Black Sea, and it forms the natural border between Romania and Bulgaria.

Constanta, located on the Black Sea, is a major resort area (among many) on the coast. The Danube Delta and the Central Moldavia area also offer many scenic spots.

The Transylvanian section of the Carpathian Mountains brings forth the memory of Count Dracula. Brasov, Romania's second largest city, is located in this area and has good tourist accommodations.

BULGARIA

Official Name: Republic of Bulgaria

Language: Bulgarian, Turkish

Area: 44,365 square miles

Time Zone: GMT +2

Capital: Sofia

Currency: Leva (LEV)

Population: 8,910,000

Documentation: Passport, visa

Like Romania, Bulgaria is a mountainous and Black Sea-facing nation. The Balkan Mountains extend east-west across northern Bulgaria and the Rhodope Mountains are in the west. Habitable lowlands lie among or adjacent to the mountains. One of these, in the northwest, contains Sofia, the capital. Bulgaria remains relatively poor. It is predominantly rural, shaped around an agriculture that produces grains, fruits, and vegetables, many of which are exported.

Slavic in language, Bulgaria's culture differs from that of Romania to the north and of Greece and Turkey to the south.

Areas of Touristic Importance. Sofia is a pleasant city with a heritage more than 2,000 years old. It is one of Europe's oldest cities. Elaborate mosques and Byzantine architecture contrast greatly with modern office buildings. The Church of St. George is the oldest building in the city. Sofia offers outstanding archeological and natural history museums. Several mosques remain from the days of the Turkish occupation.

Varna and Drouzhba are quaint resort towns along the coast of the Black Sea. They offer lovely beaches and good hotels for visitors.

Bulgaria features several fascinating "museum towns" that look like pictures from medieval history. Primary among them are Koprivshtitsa in the Sofia district and Veliko Tumovo, located about halfway between Sofia and Varna.

■ THE DISINTEGRATION OF YUGOSLAVIA—AN OVERVIEW

Official Name: SOCIALIST FEDERAL REPUBLIC OF YUGOSLAVIA

History. Yugoslavia, Land of the South Slavs, was created in 1919 by combining a number of Slavic and other groups, many of them formerly part of the Austro-Hungarian Empire, together with the nation of Serbia and its capital, Belgrade. Occupied and split up by Nazi Germany during World War II, Yugoslavia was recreated by Marshall Tito under a Communist government that broke relations with the Soviet Union in 1948 and operated independently in world politics thereafter.

Yugoslavia was ethnically the most complex part of Eastern Europe. In an attempt to reduce ethnic tensions, the Communist government organized the major ethnic groups in a federal structure of six republics on the Russian model. They were Serbia, Croatia, Slovenia, Bosnia and Herzegovina, Montenegro, and Macedonia. Mounting economic difficulties and ethnic flare-ups from the late 1980s brought civil war and national collapse. In 1991–1992, Slovenia, Croatia, and Bosnia broke away as internationally recognized independent nations, and Macedonia declared independence without international recognition. Serbia and Montenegro now form what is still called Yugoslavia.

The Land. Prepartition Yugoslavia was predominantly mountainous. About two-thirds of the territory contained a southeastern continuation of the Alps that runs parallel to the Adriatic Sea coast. Innermost Yugoslavia had a large segment of the Hungarian Plain, where much of the population, economic life, and cities are concentrated. Belgrade, the capital and largest city, sits astride the Danube River as it passes through the eastern plain.

YUGOSLAVIA

Language: Serbo-Croatian, Slovenian, Macedonian

Area: 39,000 square miles

Time Zone: GMT +1

National Airline: JAT

Capital: Belgrade

Currency: Yugoslav dinar

Population: 10,337,000

Documentation: Passport, visa at border

The People. The Republic of Serbia formed the core of the original Yugoslavia and now occupies most of the greatly reduced territory and population. The large Serbian population speaks Serbo-Croatian, writes it with a Cyrillic (Greek-derived) script, and practices Orthodox Christianity. Serbian military forces have fought for control over territories that are occupied by other Serbian minority populations in neighboring Croatia and Bosnia-Herzegovina. In the southwest, adjacent to Albania, the Yugoslav (Serbian) government must contend with a restless minority of Albanian Moslems in Kosovo. There is also a large Hungarian minority in the north in Vojvodina. Most national life focuses upon the agricultural lands of the interior plain along the Danube River and the capital, Belgrade.

Serbia's remaining partner in Yugoslavia, the small Republic of Montenegro, faces on the Adriatic Sea north of Albania. An independent nation until 1918, it shares the language and religion of Serbia, but does have a Moslem minority. It is mountainous and relatively poor.

Transportation. Transportation links between the interior and the Adriatic coast are few and difficult. They are best and easiest in the northwest via Slovenia to the port city of Trieste, now under Italian administration. At the southern extreme, a road and railway extend from Belgrade southward through the mountains to the Greek port city of Thessaloniki (Salonika).

Areas of Touristic Importance. Belgrade, Yugoslavia's capital, is on the Danube River. Protected by the Kalemegdan Fortress, a relic of Turkish occupation, Belgrade dates back to the days of the Roman Empire. Many fine museums are found in this city, including the National Museum with its collection of Yugoslavian antiquities.

Cruise ships from Belgrade operate downstream on the long, scenic stretch of the Danube River that is impounded behind the Iron Gate dam, built where the river passes through deep gorges in the Transylvanian Alps. Other ships operate upstream to Budapest and Vienna.

SLOVENIA

Official Name: Slovenia

Language: Slovenian, Yugoslavian

Area: 7,819 square miles

Time Zone: GMT +1

Capital: Ljubljana

Currency: Tolar

Population: 1,974,000

Documentation: Passport and visa

Formerly a republic within Yugoslavia, Slovenia lies adjacent to Italy, Austria, and Hungary. Slovenian, a Slavic language, is spoken, and Roman Catholicism is the prevailing religion. The nation has few ethnic problems; Slovenians form 91 percent of the population. With neighboring Croatia, it was the most prosperous and economically advanced portion of prepartition Yugoslavia. It has a balanced agricultural and industrial life. It has primary outside contacts with Austria and with Italy via the port city of Trieste.

Areas of Touristic Importance. Ljubljana, the capital of Slovenia, is located in the Alps, and surrounded by mountain peaks. It was originally built around an old fortress. Parts of the city have been restored to their original 16th-century baroque style.

CROATIA

Official Name: Croatia

Language: Serbo-Croatian

Area: 21,829 square miles

Time Zone: GMT +1

National Airline: Croatia Airways

Capital: Zagreb

Currency: Croatian dinar

Population: 4,763,000

Documentation: Passport and visa

Croatia has a crescent-shaped territory, part in the interior and part along the Adriatic Sea coast. It is bordered by Slovenia and Hungary on the north, and Bosnia, Serbia, and Montenegro (the latter two forming present Yugoslavia) on the east. Its long Adriatic Sea coast, on the west, includes the Istrian Peninsula and the island-studded Dalmatian Coast, except where the latter is interrupted by two tiny prongs of Bosnian territory. The Danube River and its tributary, Save River, pass through the interior plains of Croatia, where the national capital, Zagreb, is located.

Northeastern Croatia (Krajina) and central Croatia have large Serbian populations. Both are under the armed control of Serbian forces whose goal is union with Serbia (Yugoslavia). Bitter fighting between Croatian (Croat) and Serbian forces, which started in 1991, caused widespread death, destruction, and the uprooting of thousands of civilian refugees. This ethnic confrontation has deep historical roots—Croats and Serbs were unfriendly long before Yugoslavia was created. They were opponents during the German military occupation of World War II and Croats chafed under Serbian dominance within Yugoslavia. Both groups speak the same language, Serbo-Croatian, but the Croats are Roman Catholic and use a Roman script in writing, as opposed to the Serbs' Orthodox Christianity and the use of the Cyrillic (Greek-derived) script.

Areas of Touristic Importance. Provided the ethnic and territorial disputes can be resolved, Croatia has an economy that is agricultural with some manufacturing, centered on the interior plains. Its major assets, however, are the coastal resorts of the Adriatic Sea, which accounted for the bulk of Yugoslavia's prepartition income from international tourism. These have been virtually shut down by the civil war. Although coastal, Croatia does not have a first-class port, and, like Slovenia, must rely upon the port facilities of Trieste in Italy.

The beautiful Dalmatian Coast, bordering on the Adriatic Sea, is the most popular tourist area in good times. Dubrovnik was the most popular city and was declared a UNESCO cultural heritage site. In spite of this, it has sustained considerable damage in the civil war. This walled city, however, is a reminder of medieval times and withstood many battles over the centuries—hopefully, it will withstand this one.

Before the war, the capital city of Zagreb was known for its numerous museums and cultural attractions.

The Plitvice Lake area between Zagreb in the interior and Zadar on the coast is one of the most attractive and beautiful places in Europe.

The coastal cities of Split and Zadar offer ancient historic sites as well as resort hotels and fine beaches.

The civil war in Croatia has interrupted the attractiveness of this wonderful area for tourists. We can only hope that soon they can begin to welcome visitors again since the area has so much to offer.

BOSNIA AND HERZEGOVINA

Official Name: Republic of Bosnia and Herzegovina

Language: Serbo-Croatian

Area: 19,741 square miles

Time Zone: GMT +1

Capital: Sarajevo

Currency: Dinar

Population: 4,365,000

Documentation: Passport and visa

Bosnia and Herzegovina (or simply Bosnia) does not have a clear-cut ethnic identity but is a mixture of Croats and Serbs, and, among them, members of the Roman Catholic, Orthodox Christian, and former Yugoslavia's largest Moslem religious communities. Nominally independent, Bosnia is involved in a bloody civil war in which the principal aggressors are Serbian irregular forces who control two-thirds of the territory and are intent upon uniting it with Serbia (Yugoslavia), practicing "ethnic cleansing" by killing or displacing Moslem or other opposition groups, carrying out acts of violence against civilians, and resisting efforts of the United Nations and other outside interests to intercede.

Sarajevo, a heavily Moslem city and the capital, has been severely damaged in the civil war. Under the best of circumstances, Bosnia would have a difficult economic existence—it was one of the poorest and least well developed parts of Yugoslavia, being mountainous and isolated. The question now is whether it can survive as a unit or disappear, partitioned among its two neighbors.

Areas of Touristic Importance. Sarajevo is no stranger to war—its claim to fame rests upon the assassination of Austria's Archduke Ferdinand on June 2, 1914. This infamous deed sparked World War I. Sarajevo has excellent facilities for winter sports and was host to the Winter Olympics in the 1980s.

Another famous tourist attraction is the popular shrine of Medjugorje. Millions of pilgrims have visited this Roman Catholic shrine where people have reported seeing visions of the Virgin Mary.

As with Croatia, we can only hope that this region will soon be able to welcome tourists safely once again.

MACEDONIA

Official Name: Republic of Macedonia

Language: Macedonian

Area: 9,928 square miles

Time Zone: GMT +1

Capital: Skopje

Currency: Macedonian dinar

Population: 2,000,000

Documentation: Passport and visa

Landlocked Macedonia lies among Serbia (Yugoslavia) to the north, Albania to the west, Greece to the south and Bulgaria to the east. Macedonians speak a Slavic language that is closely related to Bulgarian and are predominantly Orthodox Christians. An Albanian minority in the mountainous northwest practices Islam. Poor and undeveloped, the self-proclaimed (1992) independent nation has its capital in Skopje near the Serbian border.

Macedonian populations sprawl across into adjacent western Bulgaria and northern Greece. Those in prepartition Yugoslavia had no formal identity and were a minority within Serbia until after World War II, when they were awarded republic status by the Communist government under President Tito.

Bulgaria has long claimed them and their territory. Greece has opposed the recognition of Macedonia by European nations until it changes its name, claiming that Macedonia is a Greek name and part of Greek heritage. Greece is also fearful that an aggressive Macedonia may attempt to claim some northern Greek territory, even the port of Thessaloniki (Salonika), based upon its present and past ethnicity. However, Bulgaria has recognized independent Macedonia, and it is now a question of when other European nations will follow suit.

In 1993, Macedonia became the last of the former Yugoslav republics to obtain United Nations membership. An awkward compromise ended arguments with Greece over its national name and flag and cleared the way for membership. It has been admitted under the provisional name of "The Former Yugoslav Republic of Macedonia" but cannot fly its flag at any U.N. installations. The compromise, made in response to Greek fears that Macedonia will lay claim to the northeastern province of Greece, also called Macedonia, does not prevent Macedonia from using that name itself.

Areas of Touristic Importance. Skopje, the capital of Macedonia, is a modern town on the Vardar River. There is an old town with well-known Turkish Baths and the newer town, which was rebuilt after an earthquake in the 1960s.

ALBANIA

Official Name: Republic of Albania

Language: Albanian, Greek

Area: 11,100 square miles

Time Zone: GMT +1

Capital: Tirana

Currency: Lek

Population: 3,335,000

Documentation: Passport, visa

Little Albania hugs the Adriatic Sea coast between Yugoslavia (Serbia and Montenegro) and Greece. It was one of the most thoroughly Communist, and one of the most politically isolated, nations in the world until 1992, when a democratic government was installed.

Prior to 1945, Albania was the only European nation with a Moslem majority. Both Islam and Christianity are being revived after decades of governmental suppression.

The nation remains poor and agricultural despite decades of central planning. The former isolationist policy prevented the development of tourism even though the Adriatic Sea coast has resort potential.

With the economy in shambles, some 400,000 Albanians have migrated abroad, mainly to neighboring Greece and smaller numbers to Italy, in search of employment. Their remittances are the key source of funds for otherwise impoverished Albanian families.

Areas of Touristic Importance. Tirana, the capital, is in the central interior. Because of its history since World War II, this city is a long way from being a major tourist destination. At this time, it is for the hardy, educationally oriented traveler who wants to be among the first to go there.

■ THE FORMER SOVIET UNION—AN OVERVIEW

History

The collapse of Communist Party control and the 1991 breakup of the Soviet Union, or the Union of Soviet Socialist Republics (USSR), into 15 independent nations was one of the most significant geopolitical developments of the 20th century. After a relatively short lifespan (1917–1991), its territory is divided among Russia; Estonia, Latvia and Lithuania, all facing the Baltic Sea; Belarus, Moldova and Ukraine in the west; Georgia, Armenia and Azerbaijan in the Caucasus Mountains; and Kazakhstan, Uzbekistan, Turkmenistan, Kyrgyzstan, and Tajikistan in Central Asia. Eleven of the new republics (excluding Georgia, Estonia, Latvia and Lithuania) are joined in a loose political association, the Commonwealth of Independent States (CIS), headquartered in Mensk (formerly Minsk) in Belarus.

At its peak, the Soviet Union was by far the world's largest nation. More than two and one-half times larger than the United States, it contained one-sixth of the world's land area and covered roughly one-half the Eurasian landmass. It measured some 6,000 miles from east to west and incorporated 11 time zones. On the west, the Soviet Union bordered on Scandinavia (Norden) and Eastern Europe; in the southwest, the Middle East; and in the east, Mongolia and China. The eastern coast faced the Pacific Ocean; the northern coast, the permanently frozen Arctic Ocean; and the northwestern coast, the Baltic Sea.

The Land and Climate

Several prominent physical features are useful as present reference. In the southwest are two large inland bodies of water, the Black Sea and the Caspian Sea, between which are the Caucasus Mountains. The Black Sea leads directly into the eastern Mediterranean via the Turkish straits, and is very important for commercial and military ports. In contrast, the Caspian Sea is landlocked. The large volume of water brought to it by the south-flowing Volga River, the longest river of the western Soviet Union, keeps the northern waters relatively fresh, but they become increasingly saline to the south. Northeast of the Caspian Sea, low mountains, the Urals, extend northeast to the Arctic Ocean fringe.

These physical features demarcate three general regions.

- The area between the Caspian Sea and China, where the Soviet territory bulges southward, is Central Asia (formerly Russian Turkestan).

- All other territory east of the Ural Mountains is Siberia. It has three great north-flowing rivers—the westernmost Ob River; the Yenisei River, which rises in Lake Baikal; and the Lena River. A fourth river, the Amur, forms a large segment of the Chinese-Russian border in the east.

- The area west of the Ural Mountains.

Climate conspires with other physical features to reduce the habitability of a large portion of Russian territory. More than three-fourths of the former Soviet Union is farther north than the United States and, as a result, has long and bitterly cold winters and relatively brief summers. Most of Siberia and the northern part of the western former Soviet Union are covered with a vast forest, the taiga, that consists largely of conifers and birches. The Arctic fringe, with its frozen subsoil, supports only grasses and lichens. Central Asia shares the great deserts that extend through the Middle East into western China and Mongolia. Large-scale irrigation systems have made portions of the deserts agriculturally productive.

Between these extremes of taiga and desert is the main inhabited zone, a fertile triangle that extends from the Baltic Sea and Black Sea on the west eastward to southwestern Siberia, around Novosibirsk on the upper Ob River. This triangle has a sufficiently long growing season, good steppe grassland soils, and sufficient warm season rainfall to support agriculture on a large scale. This was the core region of old Russia and the former Soviet Union. It contains the bulk of the population, the major cities, and most food production and manufacturing activity of present Russia, Ukraine, Belarus, and the three Baltic republics.

History

The enormous size of the Soviet Union was the consequence of the growth of the imperial Russian state before 1917. The Russian state traces its origins to the 9th century AD in the west between the Baltic Sea and Black Sea. The first political center was Kiev, on the edge of the steppe grasslands in the southwest. In the 13th century, the Kiev area was overrun by the invading Mongols from the east. Russian leadership from what is now Moscow eventually organized counterattacks against the occupying Mongols and the ruler assumed the title of tsar.

From the mid-1500s, the following one and one-half centuries saw Russian control extended eastward through southern Siberia to the Pacific coast. During the reign of Peter the Great (1682–1725), further territorial gains were made in the west and a new west-facing capital was built at St. Petersburg on an eastern arm of the Baltic Sea. It remained the Russian capital from 1713 to 1918. Under Catherine the Great (1762–1796), Russia acquired the rich steppe farmlands of the Ukraine, north of the Black Sea, from the Turks. The Caucasus Mountains were also taken by military force. Nineteenth-century expansion was eastward, into Central Asia (Russian Turkestan) and the Chinese borderlands, where the Russians demanded and got large territorial awards from a weak Chinese government.

Territorial reverses began with the Russian sale of Alaska to the United States in 1867. Russian expansion into northeastern China (Manchuria) and Korea was checked by military defeat by the Japanese in 1905–1906. World War I brought territorial losses along the western border.

The Soviet Union was born of the defeat of Russian troops in World War 1, unstable domestic conditions, and a 1917 revolution that overthrew the tsarist government and installed a new political system based upon Karl Marx's socialism and modified into communism by the Russian revolutionary leader, V. I. Lenin. Among its goals were social equality and accelerated economic development made possible by state ownership of the means of production and comprehensive long-range economic planning.

The Peoples

The historical expansion of Russian territory added many groups of non-Russians to the national population. By 1923, Lenin had designed a political system that recognized the largest ethnic groups. The Soviet Union eventually consisted of a union of 15 ethnically based Soviet Socialist Republics (SSRs). Within some of the SSRs, smaller political units further recognized lesser ethnic groups. The government allowed the preservation of distinctive cultural features and the use of local languages in the republics. At the same time, it promoted a policy of russification and stressed Russian language use. No political opposition was tolerated, and all control was vested in the central government in Moscow.

This ethnic policy eventually failed. Instead of creating a national unity, it perpetuated ethnic group differences and created political structures shaped around them. Once Moscow's power wavered, 14 of the 15 SSRs split away from the Russian republic and all 15 became independent.

The Economy

The Soviet Union was a world leader in the use of long-term comprehensive economic planning over 5-year periods. It had total control over the economy and did not have to face the complexities and uncertainties of private sector decision-making as in capitalist nations. The greatest achievement resulting from this planning was in manufacturing, where the Soviet Union ranked with the United States and Japan as one of the world leaders. Priority was given to heavy industry (metals, machinery, cement, etc.) partly because it is needed for regional development and partly to supply the Red Army, which was one of the two largest standing military forces in the world. The Soviet Union was the world leader in steel output.

The manufacture of consumer goods, items for everyday use by the general population, including clothing, household appliances, autos, and so forth, had a lower priority. The people generally were adequately fed and dressed, yet the state stores lacked variety, and goods were commonly in short supply. Services such as plumbing, electrical, and auto repair fell far short of need and were met only by illegal but tolerated private enterprise. Because of serious manpower losses during World War II, as well as social policy, women have had a large role in the labor force, including jobs involving heavy manual work.

Soviet agriculture was highly organized into large farming units, either collectives, where the workers shared in the annual profits from selling their output to the government, or state farms, which were operated by wage labor. These units were highly mechanized. However, agriculture remained the most troubled sector of the economy because of both severe climatic obstacles and bureaucratic inefficiency. Food rationing and food imports were the norm.

RUSSIA

Official Name: Russia, (also The Russian Federated Republic)

Language: Russian, many others

Area: 6,592,800 square miles

Time Zone: GMT +3 to +13

National Airline: Aeroflot

Capital: Moscow

Currency: Ruble (ROU)

Population: 148,542,000

Documentation: Passport, visa

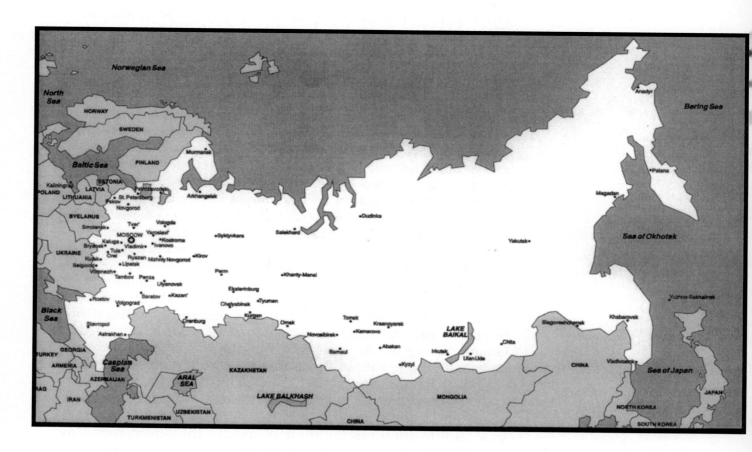

The Land and Peoples. Russia was formerly the Russian Soviet Federative Socialist Republic (RSFSR), the core republic of the USSR, and the historic territory of the Russian people and state. It is still the largest nation in territory in the world, and ranks sixth in population. Russia retains the great west-east sprawl across 11 time zones, the key water bodies, and the climatic zones already described for the former Soviet Union. It incorporates all of Siberia (east of the Ural Mountains) but no longer includes arid areas of Central Asia, the Caucasus Mountains or the extensive steppe areas of Ukraine.

Most of Russia's population is concentrated in the fertile triangle west of the Ural Mountains with a prong eastward through the southern Urals into southwestern Siberia. Beyond Novosibirsk, a thin line of population, cities, and economic activities extends eastward along the southern margins of Siberia to the Pacific coast opposite northern Japan. The vast expanses of northern Siberia, dominated by bitterly cold winter climates, are, for the most part, unpopulated except for isolated areas where some forestry or mining activities are carried on.

Like the Soviet Union before it, Russia faces severe ethnic challenges. Russians form 83 percent of the population, but the remaining 17 percent is composed of some 40 non-Russian groups. Some of these groups, given political-territorial recognition in the Soviet Union, lie on the edge of the Caucasus Mountains, southeast of Moscow along the central Volga River, in northwestern and northern Siberia, and along the Siberian border with Mongolia. There is widespread agitation among them for greater local political and economic control, even outright independence. They will test the federal structure of Russia and its ability to remain in its present territorial form without ethnic secessions. The status in Russia of citizens of the other newly independent nations carved from the Soviet Union, and of the large number of Russians residing in them, is a potential source of international discord.

The Economy. In common with the other 14 newly independent nations, Russia is caught up in the turmoil stemming from the transition from the state-controlled Communist political and economic system to a democracy based upon free enterprise. Job dislocations and unemployment, currency fluctuations, rising costs, the eradication of inefficient older factories, the creation of new enterprises, and the injection of a new spirit of competition have joined the familiar problems of inadequate housing and shortages of affordable food and consumer goods.

Yet the potential for economic recovery is there because Russia inherited the bulk of the natural resources, fuel supplies, and manufacturing capacity of the Soviet Union. Industrial activity is concentrated in clusters in main populated areas, including around Moscow, the capital and largest (10 million) city; St. Petersburg (renamed Leningrad during the Communist era), the main Baltic Sea port and second largest (5 million) city; along the Volga River; the southern Urals; southwestern Siberia in and near Novosibirsk; west of Lake Baikal; and the Amur River (Khabarovsk)-Pacific coast (Vladivostok) area. In some industrial areas, environmental damage is widespread.

Siberia, despite its handicaps of bitter winter weather, small population, huge distances and scattered cities, holds the greatest energy and industrial resources. It has great coal deposits; large hydroelectric output, especially on the upper Yenisey River, where the Bratsk power plant has the world's largest installed capacity; and some of the world's largest oil and gas deposits in the northwest, Ob River valley. Extensive deposits of iron ore, lead and other metallic ores, the vast forests of the taiga and the fish stocks of the Sea of Okhotsk and the Bering Sea are among its assets.

The sale of Siberian oil and gas abroad will be important to the Russian economy. Agriculture and enough food to meet domestic needs remain problems because of farm inefficiency, climatic handicaps, the switch to a new economic system, and the loss of the most productive lands to Ukraine.

Transportation. The populated parts of Russia are linked by a good railway network, densest in the west and shaped around the single Trans-Siberian line that crosses southern Siberia to the port of Vladivostok. The Baikal-Amur Main Line (BAM) was constructed north of Lake Baikal in the 1980s to open that area's rich natural resources to exploitation. Auto ownership is still a luxury and good all-weather surfaced roads and service stations are restricted to main cities and surrounding areas.

The nation has an extensive air network, serving major cities. However, the airline does not stress creature comforts and has erratic schedules in bad weather. Safety is not up to modern standards.

Good ports are at a premium: Murmansk is the only year-round port on the otherwise frozen Arctic Ocean coast. St. Petersburg is on the Baltic Sea, Vladivostok and nearby Nakhodka are on the Pacific coast, and Rostov must replace Odessa, now in Ukraine, as the principal Black Sea port.

Areas of Touristic Importance. Most tourists who visit Russia spend their time on the European side of the Ural Mountains. Moscow, St. Petersburg (formerly Leningrad), and the Black Sea coast are the most frequently visited.

Moscow is both the seat of government and the largest city in Russia. Like many European capitals, it is a contrast of both old and new. Modern buildings such as the skyscraper, Moscow University, are juxtaposed with the old walls of the Kremlin, which date back to the 15th century, and the brilliant onion-shaped domes of St. Basil's Cathedral, built by Ivan the Terrible.

Both the Kremlin and St. Basil's are located in Red Square. Many important palaces, museums, and cathedrals are within the walls of the Kremlin itself. The most prominent include the Armory Museum and the Cathedrals of the Annunciation and Assumption, as well as the Patriarch's Palace, the Church of the Twelve Apostles, and the Cathedral of the Archangel Michael.

The King of Bells and the King of Cannons are in the main square. Both are among the largest in the world—the King of Bells weighs 200 tons and the King of Cannons is 18 feet long and weighs 40 tons. The mausoleum containing Lenin's body is also in the square, although there has been great controversy about whether to move the body, bury it, or leave it in place. Foreign visitors are often ushered around the long lines of Soviet citizens waiting to visit.

The Tretyakov Gallery, near the Kremlin, offers the best collection of Russian paintings, sculpture, and icons. Other fine collections of art and historical items can be found at the Pushkin Museum of Fine Art, Novodyevichi Monastery, and the Andrei Rublyov Museum. Gorky Park and the Moscow Zoo are interesting and attractive.

Moscow is also known for its cultural activities. Prime among them are the Bolshoi Ballet and the Moscow Circus. Some type of drama, opera, or ballet can always be found.

St. Petersburg is located north of Moscow, on the Gulf of Finland. The many bridges over the Neva River lend a romantic atmosphere to the city. It is most beautiful during the "white nights" of late June and July when, because of its northern latitude, it is never really dark.

Known as St. Petersburg during the rule of the tsars and renamed Leningrad under Communist rule, the city has regained its earlier name. St. Petersburg was Russia's capital for more then 200 years until the 1917 revolution. Its development reflects the reverence of Peter the Great for the art and architecture of Western Europe, especially France and Italy. French and Italian artisans designed palaces and residences of the aristocracy. The Fortress of Peter and Paul was designed to withstand attack from Scandinavia. The Hermitage Museum, which houses a fine art collection, also includes the former Winter Palace. Not far from Leningrad is Petrodvorets, the former Summer Palace of the tsars, now a public park, and Pushkin, the site of Catherine the Great's palace.

Another city of interest to visiting tourists is Novgorod, one of Russia's oldest cities, between Moscow and St. Petersburg. More than 1,000 years old, Novgorod is a modern city today. The city has numerous ancient churches and a carefully preserved Kremlin.

Catherine the Great's Palace, Pushkin
Photo: Courtesy of General Tours, Inc.

Murmansk is the largest city found north of the Arctic Circle. For this reason, it is a destination for the most hardy tourists.

The vast Siberian area is mostly bleak and forbidding, but it does have Lake Baikal, the world deepest lake, and large forests. Tourists can travel from Alaska across the Bering Sea to Siberia in the summer. Another popular trip is one on the Trans-Siberian Railroad across much of Russia.

Volgograd (formerly Stalingrad) and Volga River cruises to Zagorsk, Suzdal, or other historical localities are interesting opportunities for the well-traveled tourist.

Russia also has some resorts on the Black Sea.

■ THE BALTIC REPUBLICS—AN OVERVIEW

The new nations of Estonia, Latvia, and Lithuania face the eastern Baltic Sea. Each has a distinctive language and culture, but all have shared earlier control by Russia, brief independence (1919–1940), reannexation as SSRs by the Soviet Union, and a burning desire for independence. Latvia and Lithuania fit most comfortably as part of Eastern Europe, whereas northernmost Estonia matches more closely with Finland and Scandinavia. All are relatively small in size and population, look westward to Western Europe and North America for their primary external political and economic associations, and have shown no interest in membership in the Commonwealth of Independent States. However, they do have

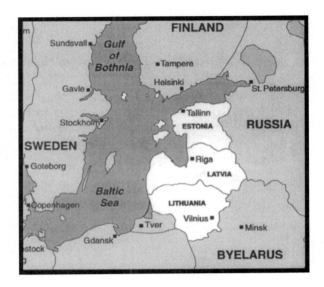

large Russian populations as the result of postwar immigration, and their economies are still linked with that of Russia.

LITHUANIA

Official Name: Republic of Lithuania

Language: Lithuanian

Area: 25,170 square miles

Time Zone: GMT +3

Capital: Vilnius

Currency: Ruble

Population: 3,754,000

Documentation: Passport and visa

Lithuania, the southernmost of the three Baltic republics, is bordered by Latvia on the north and Belarus and Poland on the south. Snuggled between Lithuania and Poland on the coast is Kaliningrad, formerly part of Germany's East Prussia and under Russian administration since 1945. The Russians maintain a naval base at the port city of Kaliningrad (former Konigsberg) even though the small territory is awkwardly separated from Russia.

Lithuanians, 80 percent of the population, are Roman Catholic, as in neighboring Poland, and have their own language. There is a relatively small (10 percent) Russian population. The capital Vilnius, is in the southeast, near Belarus. Baltic Sea trade is handled through the small coastal port of Klaipeda. The national economy, based upon agriculture and some manufacturing, is not as strong or as developed as in Latvia and Estonia.

Areas of Touristic Importance. The capital city of Vilnius is dominated by the Guediminas Castle, from which there is a beautiful view of the city. There is also the Church of St. Casimir, the patron saint of Lithuania. Vingio Park has been the scene of many protest meetings during the Soviet occupation and serves as an open-air theater as well.

LATVIA

Official Name: Latvia

Language: Latvian

Area: 24,900 square miles

Time Zone: GMT +3

Capital: Riga

Currency: Ruble

Population: 2,680,000

Documentation: Passport and
visa

Latvia, the middle Baltic republic, borders Russia and Belarus on the east. Latvians, who have their own language and are predominantly Lutheran, are 55 percent of the population. Unlike Lithuania, Latvia's economy and living standards benefited from Russian industrial development programs. The price is continuing dependence upon Russian fuel and raw materials and a large (35 percent) Russian population. The capital, Riga, ranks as one of the best eastern Baltic Sea ports.

Areas of Touristic Importance. Riga, the capital, includes an old town with gilded roofs and a prominent cathedral, and is the most beautiful of the Baltic republic capitals. With its Lutheran background, Latvia almost has a Germanic feeling. The Freedom Monument, which was erected in 1935 to commemorate the country's freedom and was allowed to stand during the Russian occupation, again stands for freedom.

ESTONIA

Official Name: Estonia

Language: Estonian, Russian

Area: 17,413 square miles

Time Zone: GMT +3

Capital: Tallin

Currency: Ruble

Population: 1,581,000

Documentation: Passport and
visa

Northernmost Estonia borders Russia on the east, Latvia on the south, and faces northward toward Finland across the Gulf of Finland. Much of the Estonia-Russia boundary passes through large Lake Peipus. Russia's St. Petersburg is only a short distance to the east. The Estonian language is related to Finnish, and Lutheranism is the main faith. A large (25 percent) Russian minority consists mainly of migrants who came during the long period of Communist Russian control. The industrial economy is strong, living standards were among the highest in the USSR, and Baltic summer resorts are well patronized.

Areas of Touristic Importance. The Estonian capital city, Tallin, serves as a major port for the region. It features Gothic buildings, tall towers and the massive Toompea Castle. Estonia was perhaps the most patriotic of the three Baltic republics and worked tirelessly for independence. In spite of some difficult economic times now, there is a great spirit among the people.

■ FORMER SOVIET UNION EUROPEAN REPUBLICS

UKRAINE

Official Name: Ukraine
Language: Ukrainian
Area: 233,100 square miles
Time Zone: GMT +3
Capital: Kiev
Currency: Hryvnia
Population: 51,994,000
Documentation: Passport and
  visa

Among the 15 new nations, Ukraine is second only to Russia in territory, population, and economic importance. In European terms, it has more territory and a population as large as France, Italy, and the United Kingdom. Kiev, its capital on the upper Dnieper River, is its largest city and was formerly the third largest city in the Soviet Union.

Ukraine boasts a strong, balanced economy. Lying within the fertile triangle of historical Russia, it has fine grassland (steppe) soils, rolling topography and large output of wheat, corn, rye, sunflowers, and other crops. Its eastern portion is heavily industrialized, especially in the coal-producing Donetz Basin. Control over much of the northern Black Sea coast, including the Crimean Peninsula, gives it important ports, led by Odessa, naval facilities and summer resorts.

Ukraine has achieved its long-sought freedom from Russian control, but it faces serious internal problems in addition to those associated with political and economic change. One major problem is regional ethnic differences. Overall, Ukrainians are 78 percent and Russians 21 percent of the population. Western Ukraine is more rural, agricultural, more solidly Ukrainian and Roman Catholic, whereas Eastern Ukraine is heavily urbanized, industrial, Orthodox Catholic and with heavy Russian minorities there and in the Crimean Peninsula. A second major problem facing Ukraine is that it has inherited the widespread effects of the 1986 nuclear power plant explosion of Chernobyl, north of Kiev.

Along with Moldova, Belarus, Latvia, and Lithuania, Ukraine must be considered as a new addition to Eastern Europe. It shares a western boundary with Moldova, Romania, Hungary, Slovakia, Poland, and Belarus. The expectation is that it will build its trading, diplomatic and other relationships with these neighbors even while maintaining normal international relations with Russia to the east. Russia needs foodstuffs from Ukraine in exchange for Russian oil, natural gas, and selected industrial resources.

Areas of Touristic Importance. Ukraine's capital city of Kiev features new white buildings that replaced those destroyed during World War II, and lush green parks. The gilded, multi-domed Cathedral of St. Sophia is its most magnificent structure. The Kievo-Percherski State History and Cultural Reservation, near the city, includes the cave dwellings of the first Percherski Monastery, catacombs, and 10th- and 11th-century churches. The Shevchenko Opera House is the home of Russian and Ukrainian opera, drama, and ballet.

The Black Sea coast was the playground of the former Soviet Union and is still a primary vacation destination for many East Europeans. The former palaces of the aristocracy are now vacation resorts for workers. Yalta, on the tip of Crimean Peninsula, is Eastern Europe's Riviera and has year-round sun and fun activities. The industrial port city of Odessa is worth a visit for travelers in the area. The Potemkin steps, leading down to the harbor, the Opera House and the Archaeological Museum are all worthwhile attractions.

The varied cultural history of Lvov makes it attractive to visitors. Known as the Paris of Ukraine, the city presents a wide display of various architectural styles. It boasts an open-air museum of wooden buildings from barns to churches to palaces.

Plans are being made to take tourists to Chernobyl, the site of the world's worst nuclear power plant disaster. Tours of the area would show the ghost towns left from the tragedy and the plant itself.

MOLDOVA

Official Name: Republic of Moldova

Language: Romanian, Ukrainian

Area: 13,012 square miles

Time Zone: GMT +3

Capital: Kishinev

Currency: Ruble

Population: 4,300,000

Documentation: Passport and visa

Moldova lies between Ukraine to the east and Romania to the west, and historically it has been pulled in one of those directions. The Moldovan people are of Romanian ancestry but their homeland, Bessarabia, was long under Turkish control before it was ceded to Russia in 1812. During 1919–1940, it was awarded to Romania, only to have the Russians retake it during World War II and establish it as the Moldavan SSR. To obliterate the Romanian heritage, the Russian government imposed Russian culture, including use of the Cyrillic alphabet. This move only heightened nationalist feelings, however, and the Russian overlay was quickly shed after independence. The capital, Kishinev, is the only large city.

Landlocked Moldova faces a difficult future because of its small territory and population and limited agricultural economy. A logical move will be interaction with Ukraine, giving it access to the international shipping facilities of Odessa. Earlier sentiment favoring union with Romania has cooled because of the unattractive economic and political circumstances there. Some domestic ethnic problems loom—only two thirds of the population is Moldovan, and there are large Russian, Ukrainian and other minority groups that must be accommodated in national life.

Areas of Touristic Importance. Travel to Moldova is not a major factor for Americans at the present time. The capital city of Kishinev is on the Bik River and boasts a love of Romanian and Moldavan writers. Pushkin Park, named after a writer who was exiled to Kishinev, has Writers' Walk, which has statues of a number of authors.

BELARUS

Official Name: Belarus

Language: Belorussian, Russian

Area: 80,134 square miles

Time Zone: GMT +3

Capital: Mensk

Currency: Ruble

Population: 10,200,000

Documentation: Passport and visa

Formerly Belorussia, or Belorussian SSR, landlocked Belarus lies between Poland to the west and Russia to the east, with Ukraine to the south and Latvia and Lithuania to the north. There it occupies a transition zone between historically strong neighbors. In fact, western Belarus was part of Russia until World War I, fell under Polish control and then reverted to the Soviet Union after World War II. Most of the Polish population was transferred to western Poland and settled on lands taken from Germany. Belarussians, or so-called White Russians, are Slavs who are related to Poles and Slovaks. They are 80 percent of the population, whereas Russians are 12 percent.

German and Russian armies that fought across Belarussian territory during World War II left terrible destruction that took two postwar decades to repair. The country remains largely agricultural except for some industry built in the postwar era. As might be expected, its primary economic ties and transportation links are eastward with Russia. Its capital, Mensk (formerly Minsk), is also the administrative seat for the 11-member Commonwealth of Independent States (CIS).

Areas of Touristic Importance. The capital city of Mensk, like so many cities in this part of the world, was largely destroyed in World War II and has been rebuilt. Therefore, there is little left from earlier times. The city has a number of attractive parks.

■ TRANSCAUCASIAN REPUBLICS— AN OVERVIEW

Three so-called transcaucasian nations—Georgia, Armenia, and Azerbaijan—lie in the narrow lands dominated by the Caucasus Mountains between the Black Sea and Caspian Sea. They are a cultural transition zone between Russia and the Middle East marked by highly fragmented culture groups, keen ethnic rivalries, and complex histories of outside control. All three nations have relatively small territories and populations and relatively weak national economies to sustain them in independence.

GEORGIA

Official Name: Republic of Georgia

Language: Georgian, Russian

Area: 26,911 square miles

Time Zone: GMT +3

Capital: Tbilisi

Currency: Ruble

Population: 5,500,000

Documentation: Passport and visa

Georgia, the northernmost transcaucasion nation, sits between Russia to the north and Turkey to the south. Internally, it faces in two directions. The capital, Tblisi, is in the mountainous interior, while western Georgia and its port of Batumi face on the Black Sea. Georgia's Mediterranean climate promotes summer coastal resorts and the production of tea, citrus fruits, flowers and other agricultural specialties within a diversified economy. Georgians have a reputation as astute businessmen and place a premium upon education. There is still local pride in Georgian Josef Stalin, the Russian dictator, despite his vicious extremes and his failure to bestow favors upon his homeland.

Within the national population, Georgians are 70 percent and the rest are Russians, Armenians, Azeris, and other minorities. Three minority groups have their own political territory, a holdover from political structuring in the Soviet Union. One of them, the Ossetians, spill across the boundary into Russia and are politically restless.

Areas of Touristic Importance. Georgia includes the area from the shores of the Black Sea into the Caucasus Mountains. Tblisi, its capital, was founded in the 5th century and was once a stopover point on the trade routes founded by Marco Polo in the 13th century. It is an industrial city that enjoys a mild climate.

The Black Sea coast is known for its warm weather and fine beaches. The port city of Batumi, with its Turkish influence, is a popular resort.

ARMENIA

Official Name: Republic of Armenia

Language: Armenian

Area: 11,306 square miles

Time Zone: GMT +5

Capital: Yerevan

Currency: Ruble

Population: 3,300,000

Documentation: Passport and visa

Landlocked Armenia is hemmed in by Georgia on the north, Azerbaijan on the east, Turkey on the west and Iran on the south. The Armenians were an early Christian group that had a long and difficult struggle to survive in Islamic Turkey. The large-scale slaughter of Armenians by Turkish military forces in 1915 prompted an international dispersal of Armenians, especially to Western Europe, North America, and across the boundary into Russia.

After World War I, present Armenia declared its independence, but it was quickly taken over by Communist Russia and later was designated an SSR. Armenia and its Christian church received relatively favored treatment by Moscow in order to strengthen the Armenian strategic border position and hostile attitudes against the Turks, an adversarial neighbor. The capital, Yerevan, is very near the Turkish border.

Armenians form 90 percent of the small population. An isolated large group of Christian Armenians, who reside in the territory of Nagorno-Karabakh (or simply Nagorno) in adjacent Azerbaijan, claim mistreatment by Islamic Azeris and desire union with Armenia. Azerbaijan has resisted such a move with force. The ethnic conflict is marked by sporadic fighting, loss of life and property, and strained relations between the two nations. Although Armenia does benefit from some mineral and agricultural assets, it also suffers from periodic, highly destructive earthquakes.

Areas of Touristic Importance. For a number of years this area has not been a safe destination because of periodic internal fighting, especially between Armenia and Azerbaijan, and the poverty and shortages that accompany this instability. In Yerevan, one of the most attractive Eastern European cities, there are museums with exhibits describing the history of the region and a memorial to the Ottoman massacre of many in the area in the early 1900s.

AZERBAIJAN

Official Name: Republic of Azerbaijan

Language: Azeri, Turkish, Russian

Area: 33,400 square miles

Time Zone: GMT +5

Capital: Baku

Currency: Ruble

Population: 7,000,000

Documentation: Passport and visa

Azerbaijan faces eastward on the Caspian Sea, with Russia and Georgia to the north, Armenia to the west, and Iran to the south. A small detached segment lies between Armenia and Iran. It is the most populous of the three Transcaucasian nations, and a related large Azeri group lives across the international border in northwestern Iran. Azeris speak a Turkic language, related to Turkish and other Central Asian languages, and are Moslems. Their culture is a compound of Middle Eastern traits with a strong Russian overlay.

Baku, the capital, largest city and Caspian Sea port, is the site of an important oil and natural gas industry. As noted earlier, Azerbaijan is at odds with Armenia over the political status of their Nagorno territory, occupied by Christian Armenians.

Areas of Touristic Importance. The seaside city of Baku is known for its beaches and spas. The Caspian Sea, on which Baku is located, is the world's largest inland body of water.

■ FORMER SOVIET UNION ASIAN REPUBLICS—
AN OVERVIEW

Between the Caspian Sea and China are five new Central Asian nations—Kazakhstan, Uzbekistan, Turkmenistan, Kyrgyzstan, and Tajikistan. They are historically Islamic (Moslem) in religion, speak either Turkic or Iranic languages, have high birth rates, minority problems, and such severe environmental constraints as deserts, towering mountains, and isolation in the heart of Asia. Pastoral nomadism, once prevalent, has been reduced by urbanization and varying degrees of economic development by Moscow.

KAZAKHSTAN

Official Name: Republic of Kazakhstan

Language: Kazakh, Russian

Area: 1,049,200 square miles

Time Zone: GMT +5 and +6

Capital: Alma-Ata

Currency: Ruble

Population: 16,500,000

Documentation: Passport and visa

Kazakhstan is larger than the other four nations combined. It lies south of Russia and west of China. Turkmenistan and Kyrgyzstan border it on the south and it shares part of the Caspian Sea coast on the west. Sufficient rainfall supports grasslands in the north, but the climate is arid in the south. Rivers that form in the north flow northward as part of the Ob River system of western Siberia in Russia. Two major salt lakes, the Aral

Sea (shared with Uzbekistan) and Lake Balkhash, and numerous smaller ones are fed by freshwater streams.

The Kazakhs, Turkic speakers, are outnumbered in their own nation. They are only 36 percent of the population, whereas Russians drawn by administrative and economic development jobs in earlier years are 41 percent, and numerous minorities form the rest. Most of the population, cities and economic activities are in the north, yet the capital, Alma-Ata, is in the mountainous southeast.

The Russian government invested heavily in a number of large-scale development projects in Kazakhstan, more than in any other Central Asian SSR. During the 1950s, unplowed grasslands were opened for wheat and other dry grain cultivation despite erratic and undependable rainfall. Periodic droughts make grain output highly variable and have led to widespread wind erosion of surface soils. Other undertakings included a heavy industrial complex at Karaganda; the Soviet outer space station at Baykonur; and atomic bomb testing grounds at Seminpalatinsk. Oil and natural gas potential along the Caspian Sea coast and varied mineral wealth in the northeast are important to future economic development. The political climate is volatile, marked by anti-Russian sentiments and ethnic clashes on a small scale.

Areas of Touristic Importance. The capital, Alma-Ata, is the main city and is known for its enormous apples. It is also the home of several movie studios. The area is also good for skating and skiing.

UZBEKISTAN

Official Name: Republic of Uzbekistan
Language: Uzbek, Russian
Time Zone: GMT +5 and +6
Capital: Tashkent
Currency: Ruble
Population: 19,900,000
Documentation: Passport and visa

Uzbekistan is nestled among its four Central Asian neighbors and has a short border stretch with Afghanistan to the south. Its population is the largest in Central Asia and was formerly third largest among the Soviet Union's republics. A Turkic language is spoken and fundamentalist Islam is strong.

Before their conquest by Russia, Uzbek rulers operating from such cities as Samarkand and Bukhara controlled most of Central Asia. In today's nation, the majority Uzbeks (71 percent) must interact with numerous minorities, including Russians (8 percent). Ethnic conflict flares intermittently. Uzbek minorities are found in neighboring nations.

Tashkent, the capital and largest city of Central Asia, is in the extreme northeast. Severely damaged by an earthquake in 1966, it has been rebuilt in high-rise western style rather than the original low, sun-dried brick style.

The main Soviet economic thrust was to expand irrigated agriculture, using fresh water drawn from two rivers that flow from high Central Asian mountains into the Aral Sea—the Amu Darya in Turkmenistan and Uzbekistan, and the Syr Darya in Kazakhstan. As a result, the Uzbek SSR became a leading world producer of cotton, and independent Uzbekistan continues to base its economy on cotton growing and cotton textiles. However, there has been a price—the Aral Sea is an ecological disaster on a grand scale. Overuse of its fresh water source for irrigation has reduced the lake size by more than one half, and the remaining water resource is severely polluted by pesticides, which have caused widespread public health problems.

Areas of Touristic Importance. Tashkent, the capital and largest city of Uzbekistan, is a blend of a variety of cultures—Islamic, Russian and Persian. It was at the crossing of caravans from Europe to Asia in the Middle Ages. Although much of the city was destroyed in the 1966 earthquake, there are some fascinating buildings left—especially the Kukeldash and the Barak Khan's Madrasa.

Bukhara rises from an oasis in the Kara Kum Desert and is an ancient city filled with many important religious monuments and mosques, including the famous Djuma Mosque.

The city of Samarkand, which was destroyed by both Alexander the Great and Genghis Khan, contains numerous ruins from early times.

KYRGYZSTAN

Official Name: Republic of Kyrgyzstan

Language: Turkic, Russian

Area: 76,642 square miles

Time Zone: GMT +6

Capital: Bishkek

Currency: Ruble

Population: 4,300,000

Documentation: Passport and visa

Kyrgyzstan is bordered by Kazakhstan, Uzbekistan, and Tajikistan on three sides and China on the east. Its topographic heart is the towering peaks of the Tian Shan, the great mountain range that continues eastward into China's northwest Xinjiang Province. External transportation links are either north into Kazakhstan or southwest into Uzbekistan. The capital, Bishkek, is in the north near Kazakhstan.

The Turkic-speaking Kyrgyz make up only 52 percent of the population; Russians are 22 percent and other minorities the rest. Large numbers of Kyrgyz also live in northwestern China. Remote and poorly integrated by transportation, Kyrgyzstan has a primarily pastoral economy and some irrigated agriculture.

Areas of Touristic Importance. Even in the capital city of Bishkek, there is really not much for a tourist to see or do. There is also occasional fighting and safety is not assured.

TAJIKISTAN

Official Name: Republic of Tajikistan

Language: Tadzhik, Russian

Area: 54,019 square miles

Time Zone: GMT +6

Capital: Dushanbe

Currency: Ruble

Population: 5,100,000

Little Tajikistan lies on the flanks of the towering Pamir Mountains in the southeastern corner of Central Asia. Two of its peaks, at more than 23,000 feet, were the highest elevations in the Soviet Union. Dushambe, the capital, and most of the small population are in lower elevations in the west.

The Tajik, who speak a Turkic language, constitute 60 percent of the population. The rest is a compound of minorities. Ethnic strife and old clan rivalries have flared since independence, but the most serious fighting has been between fundamentalist Islamic agitators, who support a nation based upon Koranic principles, and Communist loyalists. The economy is based on irrigated agriculture and mining and manufacturing started during the Soviet era.

Areas of Touristic Importance. This area, like its neighbors in Central Asia, is not a meaningful tourist area. The capital city of Dushanbe is a mediocre, relatively modern city.

TURKMENISTAN

Official Name: Republic of Turkmenistan

Language: Turkmen, Russian

Area: 188,417 square miles

Time Zone: GMT +6

Capital: Ashkhabad

Currency: Ruble

Population: 3,500,000

Documentation: Passport and visa

Turkmenistan faces Kazakhstan and Uzbekistan on the north, Iran and Afghanistan on the south, and the Caspian Sea on the west. Largely desert, it has a small population consisting of 72 percent Turkmen, who are Iranic-speaking; 10 percent Russians, and various minorities.

The capital, Ashkhabad, lies in the south near Iran on the only east-west rail line. A large-scale Soviet project, the Karakum Canal, brings Amu Darya fresh water into the interior to irrigate expanded farmland. Traditional nomadic herding is still practiced in this little-visited part of central Asia. Krasnovodsk, the main seaport in Turkmenistan, has ferry service westward across the Caspian Sea to Baku in Azerbaijan.

Areas of Touristic Importance. The capital city of Ashkhabad is in an oasis in the Kara Kum desert. Its history museum is the site for many excellent exhibitions. However, this area is not a major destination for Americans.

■ TYPES OF TOURISM

Most tourists participate in preplanned escorted tour programs. The following itineraries are examples of tour programs available in the area.

- ■ Grand Capitals of Eastern Europe
- ■ The Bolshoi Express
- ■ Russia and the Baltic States

GRAND CAPITALS OF EASTERN EUROPE

WARSAW, CRACOW, BUDAPEST, PRAGUE, DRESDEN AND BERLIN

15 DAYS FROM $2,199 TO $2,499 INCLUDING AIRFARE

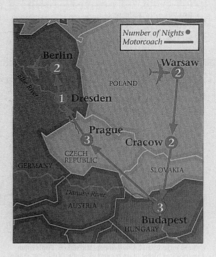

An intriguing blend of Central and Eastern Europe's liveliest cities is featured on this delightful tour. Geography has linked the fortunes of Poland, Hungary, the Czech Republic, Slovakia and Germany for centuries; their contemporary societies are intertwined as well. Architecture, music, politics, religion and royalty all play a part in this journey to the heart of Central and Eastern Europe — don't miss a moment!

Day 1 – Depart USA
Our vacation begins with an overnight Delta flight bound for Warsaw.

Day 2 – Arrive Warsaw, Poland
Arrive in Warsaw and transfer to the hotel. The afternoon is free to get acquainted with the city. Tonight we gather with fellow tour members for a Welcome Dinner. (D)

Day 3 – Warsaw
Today's tour takes us along the Royal Route to Lazienki Palace, summer residence of the last Polish royals. We pay respects at the Monument to Heroes of the Warsaw Ghetto. Amidst the cobbled streets of 14th-century Old Town, we admire the restored baroque buildings of Market Square. Following a free afternoon we attend a Chopin piano recital in historic Warsaw. (BB)

Day 4 – Warsaw / Cracow
We travel today via the village of Czestochowa to visit Jasna Gora, a Paulite Monastery which houses Poland's holiest object, the famed painting of the Black Madonna. Our next stop is in Oswiecim, where we have the option to visit the somber memorial at Auschwitz. We continue to a city that was once the seat of Polish kings, Cracow. We enjoy dinner at the hotel and a free evening. (BB,D)

YOUR DELTA **DREAM VACATION** INCLUDES

TRANSPORTATION
▲ Roundtrip trans-Atlantic airfare via Delta Air Lines
▲ Deluxe air conditioned motorcoach
▲ All transfers and luggage handling

ACCOMMODATIONS
▲ 13 nights in First Class and Deluxe hotels with private bath or shower
▲ All hotel taxes and service charges

MEALS
▲ Buffet breakfast (BB) daily
▲ 7 Dinners (D) including festive Welcome and Farewell Dinners

TOUR HIGHLIGHTS
▲ Fully-escorted by a professional Tour Manager
▲ Enjoy city tours of Warsaw, Cracow, Budapest, Prague, Dresden and Berlin
▲ Attend a Chopin piano recital in Warsaw

▲ Walk the cobbled streets of Warsaw's 14th-century Old Town
▲ See Poland's holiest shrine with the famed painting of the Black Madonna
▲ Tour Wawel Royal Castle in Cracow
▲ Explore the delights of Budapest on a free afternoon
▲ Stroll the statue-lined Charles Bridge and Wenceslas Square in Prague
▲ Visit Dresden's Zwinger Palace, home to a fabulous medieval art collection
▲ Pause at the remains of the Berlin Wall
▲ Celebrate with fellow tour members at a festive Farewell Dinner in Berlin
▲ Dream Vacations travel bag, document folder, luggage tags, personal road map of the itinerary
▲ Plus you'll receive the benefits of the TravelAssist Network. Travel information and emergency on-tour assistance available 24 hours-a-day.

Lively folklore is a cultural highlight of travel to Eastern Europe.

Reprinted courtesy of Globetrotters and Delta Dream Vacations.

This Budapest cafe on Fishermen's Bastion has an excellent view across the Danube.

Day 5 – Cracow

On today's tour we discover Cracow's architectural riches that date back to the 10th-century. Our first stop is the 16th-century Wawel Royal Castle, followed by the Armory, Treasury and Wawel Cathedral, where generations of Polish kings are buried. A walking tour of the Old Town shows us the Main Market Square, Cloth Hall and St. Mary's Church. Enjoy the afternoon on your own in Cracow. (BB)

Day 6 – Cracow / Budapest, Hungary

We travel through the High Tatras mountains whose jagged granite and limestone peaks create a stunning backdrop to the many lakes and forests of the region. We continue across Slovakia to Hungary's twin capital cities, Buda and Pest, for dinner and the night. (BB,D)

Days 7 and 8 – Budapest

Our stay in Budapest includes a panoramic sightseeing tour of the city. We see the Opera House, Heroes' Square, cross the Elizabeth Bridge to visit the Citadel atop Gellert Hill, Fishermen's Bastion, and the great Coronation Church. Lovely views of the Hungarian Parliament building, on the Pest side, are easily seen from Buda. The rest of the stay in Budapest is free to spend as you please. Be sure to visit with local residents in one of the many cafes that dot the city. On one of the evenings in Budapest we enjoy a festive dinner in a traditional Hungarian Czarda restaurant. (BB, D)

Day 9 – Budapest / Bratislava, Slovakia / Prague, Czech Republic

Today's drive takes us through the historic towns and picturesque villages of the Hungarian countryside to Bratislava, the capital of Slovakia. After a short stop we continue through Slavkov and Brno to Prague. The evening is at leisure for us to spend as we wish. (BB,D)

Days 10 and 11 – Prague

The whole of Prague is filled with gothic and baroque buildings and cobblestone streets that wind over seven hills. A sightseeing tour takes us by the 14th-century Charles Bridge and on to Wenceslas Square. We also see the Tyl Theater where the first performance of Mozart's Don Giovanni took place in 1787. Visit Hradcany Castle before stepping into Old Town on a walking tour that includes the Loretto Church Treasury, St. George's Church and the Astronomical Clock. The tour ends at the Jewish Quarter, a place that was a lively, ancient community before the Nazi Holocaust. The rest of your time in Prague is free to do as you wish. (BB)

Day 12 – Prague / Dresden, Germany

Today's drive brings us to Dresden, a beautiful city built of sandstone. An afternoon tour includes visits to the Semper Opera House, where Wagner once conducted, and the Zwinger Palace, home to a fabulous medieval art collection. (BB,D)

Day 13 – Dresden / Berlin

Upon arrival in Berlin, a city with a tumultuous past, we enjoy the sights including the Memorial Church, the Rathaus Schöneberg where John F. Kennedy delivered his famous *Ich bin ein Berliner* speech, KaDeWe Department store, Europa Center and the glittering shopping street, Kurfürstendamm. The evening is free to enjoy this dynamic city on your own. (BB)

Day 14 – Berlin

This morning we continue our sightseeing passing by the Victory Column, Brandenburg Gate, and travel down Unter den Linden Boulevard to visit the Pergamon Museum. There's time for reflection during a stop at the sparse remains of the Berlin Wall and the Checkpoint Charlie Museum. The rest of the day and evening are free to explore this vibrant city on our own. Tonight, gather with fellow tour members at a local restaurant for a festive Farewell Dinner. (BB,D)

Day 15 – Return to USA

We bid farewell to all the *Grand Capitals* and return home the same day aboard Delta. (BB)

15 DAYS

ROUNDTRIP
TRANS-ATLANTIC
AIRFARE INCLUDED

DEPART *Saturday*	RETURN *Saturday*	
APR 23	MAY 07	$2199
MAY 07	MAY 21	$2299
MAY 21	JUN 04	
JUN 11	JUN 25	$2499
JUN 25	JUL 09	
JUL 02	JUL 16	
JUL 23	AUG 06	
AUG 06	AUG 20	
AUG 20	SEP 03	
SEP 03	SEP 17	$2399
SEP 17	OCT 01	
OCT 01	OCT 15	
OCT 15	OCT 29	
Single Supplement		$550
Land Only from	$1699 to $1799	

Half twin rates are per person, based on double occupancy. Rates include land arrangements and airfare. Triple room rates are available upon request. A charge of $38 per person is included for Security Surcharge, U.S Departure Tax, Custom Fees, and Federal Inspection Fees. To compute prices from your Delta departure city, add the above prices to the rates listed in the supplemental rate chart shown on page 59.

✓ Ask your Travel Agent to check for guaranteed departures as the season progresses.

SPECIALLY SELECTED HOTELS

Warsaw - Forum
First Class hotel close to the city center, shopping and major attractions.

Cracow - Forum
Modern First Class hotel close to town's major attractions.

Budapest - Helia
A new First Class hotel set on the Danube embankment of the Pest side.

Prague - Diplomat
Excellent First Class hotel convenient to the city center.

Dresden - Astron
New First Class hotel convenient to the city center.

Berlin - Hilton
Deluxe hotel with excellent central location on Friedrichstrasse near Brandenburg Gate.

THE BOLSHOI EXPRESS–THREE JOURNEYS THROUGH

MOSCOW, ST. PETERSBURG, ASTRAKHAN, BUKHARA, TASHKENT, SAMARKAND, TALLINN, RIGA, VILNIUS

11, 12 OR 16 DAYS FROM $2,899 TO $4,899 INCLUDING AIRFARE

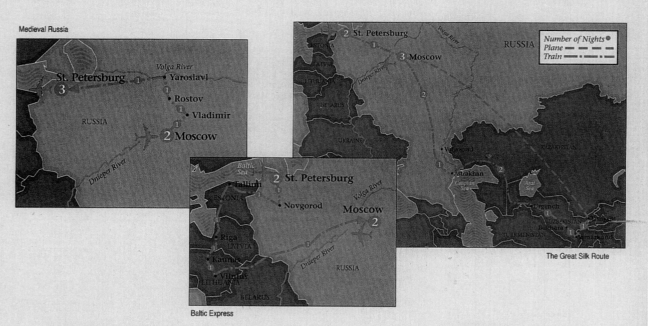

Three Deluxe Journeys By Rail: *Medieval Russia, The Great Silk Route* and *Baltic Express*

Recall An Era of Grandeur

The Bolshoi Express recalls an era when every journey was one of exploration and discovery and when time was not of the essence. Through the train window Russian life unfolds before you in an ever-changing kaleidoscope of color; the bustle and activity of the station platform; lively villages, sleepy hamlets and open stretches of exquisite natural beauty.

Rail Travel - A Russian Tradition

Rail has long been the favored transport for tsars, Soviet presidents and senior government officials - it was with the exacting standards of these types of passengers that the Bolshoi Express was originally designed. This elegant train was built in Russian workshops in the 1930's and restored in 1990; it now travels some of the most spectacular and remote routes of the longest railway system in the world.

Today's Bolshoi Express

The Bolshoi Express comprises 16 carriages including six sleeping cars, three restaurant cars and a saloon car, and is pulled much of the time by magnificent steam locomotives.

Each sleeping carriage has eight compartments that are elegantly furnished with mahogany interiors, brass fittings, a comfortable armchair, writing table and sofa. For night use, two beds are lowered from the wall. Bathrooms are

Journey with the elegance and style of the golden age of rail travel aboard the Bolshoi Express carriages.

shared between two compartments; each has a washbasin and shower, hot and cold water, and complimentary bathrobes and toiletries. Lavatories and extra showers are positioned at either end of each carriage.

The three dining cars of the Bolshoi Express are furnished in traditional Baltic, Ukrainian and Georgian styles. A delightful mixture of Russian and European cuisines are served, with regional specialties prepared to highlight the areas visited. Food and drink are imported from Europe; first-quality ingredients are complemented by Russian specialties such as caviar and vodka. Fresh fruit and vegetables are selected as the Bolshoi Express stops on its journeys. French wine and champagne are offered along with a selection of local Moldavian and Georgian wines. Each table is offered a complimentary bottle of wine, mineral water, tea and coffee at all meals. At dinner, gentlemen are requested to wear jacket and tie.

With its parquet floor, the saloon car is reminiscent of the 1920's. It's an elegant, comfortable gathering place used for a lounge, library and lecture room during the day; as a social bar complete with live music during the evening.

54

TIME

YOUR DELTA DREAM VACATION INCLUDES

TRANSPORTATION
▲ Roundtrip trans-Atlantic airfare via Delta Air Lines
▲ Deluxe Bolshoi Express train on *Medieval Russia, The Great Silk Route* or *Baltic Express*
▲ Airfare from Tashkent to Moscow on *The Great Silk Route*

HOTEL ACCOMMODATIONS
▲ Deluxe Moscow Palace
▲ St. Petersburg's Deluxe Nevsky Palace
▲ All taxes and service charges

MEALS
▲ Buffet breakfast daily
▲ All meals while on the Bolshoi Express
▲ Celebrate in imperial style with fellow tour members in St. Petersburg's Shuvalov Palace at a private reception and dinner

TOUR HIGHLIGHTS
▲ Services of our own professional local hosts in Moscow and St. Petersburg
▲ Services of local guides
▲ All transfers and luggage handling
▲ Enjoy city tours of Moscow and St. Petersburg
▲ Tour Moscow's Kremlin grounds
▲ Visit St. Petersburg's Hermitage Museum

MEDIEVAL RUSSIA HIGHLIGHTS
▲ Tour the best of Russia's Golden Ring: Vladimir, Suzdal, Rostov, Yaroslavl
▲ See Vladimir's impressive Golden Gate
▲ Marvel at Suzdal's 18th-century skyline
▲ Tour 1,000 year-old Yaroslavl

THE GREAT SILK ROUTE HIGHLIGHTS
▲ Enjoy tours of Volgograd, Astrakhan, Khiva, Bukhara, Samarkand, and Tashkent
▲ Learn about the Battle of Stalingrad, in modern Volgograd
▲ Travel the ancient Silk Route to Bukhara
▲ Tour Samarkand's magnificent mosques and the lively Registan, or town square

BALTIC EXPRESS HIGHLIGHTS
▲ See Tallinn's ancient Toompea Castle
▲ Walk Old Riga's winding, narrow streets
▲ Tour Lithuania's baroque capital, Vilnius
▲ Dream Vacations travel bag, document folder and map of the itinerary
▲ Plus you'll receive the benefits of the TravelAssist Network. Travel information and emergency on-tour assistance available 24 hours-a-day

MEDIEVAL RUSSIA
11 Days from $2,899 to $3,199
ROUNDTRIP TRANS-ATLANTIC AIRFARE INCLUDED

This deluxe journey by rail takes you on the route of the Tsars, in imperial style. On your travels between Moscow and St. Petersburg, visit Russia's ancient Golden Ring towns of Vladimir, Suzdal, Rostov, and Yaroslavl; each unique, each filled with churches, frescoes, icons and classic Russian architecture.

DEPART	RETURN	
MAY 06	MAY 16	$2949
MAY 13	MAY 23 *	
MAY 24	JUN 03 *	
JUN 04	JUN 14 *	$3199
JUN 10	JUN 20	
JUN 25	JUL 05 *	
JUL 08	JUL 18	
JUL 23	AUG 02 *	
JUL 29	AUG 08	
AUG 19	AUG 29	
AUG 26	SEP 05 *	
NOV 01	NOV 11	$2899
NOV 12	NOV 22	
NOV 15	NOV 25 *	
Single Supplement		$750
Land Only from		$2229 to $2329

* Reversed itinerary

Steam engines are used for part of every deluxe Bolshoi Express journey.

THE GREAT SILK ROUTE
16 Days from $4,599 to $4,899
ROUNDTRIP TRANS-ATLANTIC AIRFARE INCLUDED

Travel by luxurious rail from Russia's capitals of Moscow and St. Petersburg through dramatic deserts, past the Caspian Sea and along the Silk Route to Central Asia while being cradled in the comfort of the Bolshoi Express. Volgograd (formerly Stalingrad), Astrakhan at the mouth of the Volga, Urgench, Samarkand, Bukhara and Tashkent are the treasures you discover on this grand journey.

DEPART	RETURN	
MAR 12	MAR 27	$4599
APR 09	APR 24	
SEP 14	SEP 29	$4899
SEP 26	OCT 11 *	$4699
OCT 12	OCT 27	
Single Supplement		$1000
Land Only from		$3999 to $4199

* Reversed itinerary

BALTIC EXPRESS
12 Days for $3,799
ROUNDTRIP TRANS-ATLANTIC AIRFARE INCLUDED

Trace the Amber Way along the shore of the Baltic Sea with the deluxe comfort and services of the Bolshoi Express train. See Russia's medieval Novgorod and the Baltic capitals, Tallinn, Riga and Vilnius. On the way, explore the Lithuanian fortress of Trakai and Kaunas. Your elegant journey by rail is framed by the Russian capitals, Moscow and St. Petersburg.

DEPART	RETURN	
AUG 11	AUG 22	$3799
Single Supplement		$900
Land Only		$2999

All rates are per person, based on double occupancy. Rates include land arrangements and airfare. Triple room rates are available upon request. A charge of $38 per person is included for Security Surcharge, U.S Departure Tax, Custom Fees, and Federal Inspection Fees. To compute prices from your Delta departure city, add the above prices to the rates listed in the supplemental rate chart on page 59.

✓ Ask your Travel Agent to check for guaranteed departures as the season progresses.

SPECIALLY SELECTED HOTELS

Moscow - Moscow Palace
Deluxe hotel in downtown Moscow, just minutes from Red Square.

St. Petersburg - Nevsky Palace
Deluxe hotel in the heart of the historic city.

GLOBUS   *First Class*   ESCORTED

Russia and the Baltic States

Tour RP
— 16 days incl.air,
or 15 days Helsinki/Helsinki

ALL THIS IS INCLUDED

- Scheduled transatlantic flights and airport transfers in Helsinki if Globus issues the tickets; see page 19
- Services of a professional tour director
- Hotels listed below or equivalent; see also page 13. Twin-bedded rooms with private bath or shower, hotel taxes, service charges and tips for baggage handling
- Welcome drink; 14 full breakfasts (FB); 14 three-course dinners (D); 12 lunches (L)
- Private deluxe motorcoach featuring forced air ventilation, extra leg room and

emergency washroom; see page 11
- Day ferry Tallinn-Helsinki
- Sightseeing with local guides in Helsinki, St.Petersburg, Moscow, Smolensk, Vilnius, Riga, Tallinn
- Visits to Vyborg, Novgorod, Minsk, Pärnu
- Theater or folklore performance in Moscow
- Inside visits as shown in UPPER CASE in the tour description, including admission charges where applicable
- Globus travel bag and travel documents

Day 1, Sat. BOARD YOUR OVERNIGHT TRANSATLANTIC FLIGHT.

Day 2, Sun. ARRIVAL IN HELSINKI, FINLAND. Time to rest or to start exploring the Finnish capital. At 6 p.m. meet your traveling companions at a pre-dinner welcome drink hosted by your tour director. (D)

Day 3, Mon. HELSINKI. Morning sightseeing with a local guide features City Hall and Parliament House, the Presidential Palace, the monumental railroad station, and the great LUTHERAN CATHEDRAL. Then leave town for an orientation tour to the Olympic Stadium and the Sibelius Monument, and to the showrooms of the HOUSE OF FINNISH HANDICRAFTS. Afternoon at leisure. (FB,D)

Day 4, Tue. HELSINKI-ST.PETERSBURG, RUSSIA. East along the coastline to the timber port of Kotka and on to the Russian border. After completing frontier formalities, stop at the city of Vyborg for lunch. In the afternoon cross the Karelian Isthmus, the land bridge between the Gulf of Finland and Lake Ladoga, on the way to St. Petersburg. (FB,L,D)

Day 5, Wed. ST.PETERSBURG. Few cities in the world match the grace of St.Petersburg, founded by Peter the Great. Construction began in 1703, and the city eventually spread over 100 islands linked by 700 bridges. It suffered severe damage during the revolution of 1917 and later during World War II, when a cruel 900-day siege claimed more than half a million victims. See today how

the city has been restored to its former splendor. Drive along elegant Nevsky Prospect, then admire ST.ISAAC'S CATHEDRAL with its gilded dome and marble columns. Afternoon excursion to Pushkin, the home of Russia's last Czar, for a visit to the magnificent CATHERINE PALACE. A gala dinner tonight features Russian specialties and vodka. (FB,L,D)

Day 6, Thu. ST.PETERSBURG-NOVGOROD. Highlight of the day is a visit to the Winter Palace complex, formerly the residence of the Czars and now home of the world famous HERMITAGE MUSEUM. Among the exhibits are celebrated works by Rembrandt, Leonardo da Vinci, and the major French impressionists. Afterwards a drive through timeless Russian landscapes to Novgorod. (FB,L,D)

Day 7, Fri. NOVGOROD-MOSCOW. Novgorod has preserved a large part of its medieval heritage. View the restored castle and venerable churches dating as far back as the 11th century. Then to Tver for lunch, and on to the sprawling capital of Russia. (FB,L,D)

Day 8, Sat. MOSCOW. Red Square is the center of this 800-year-old city. At its core: the Lenin Mausoleum and St.Basil's Cathedral. Walk across the square to the KREMLIN, a city-within-a-city adorned with medieval towers, cathedrals and palaces. At the ARMORY MUSEUM see treasures such as Ivan the Terrible's throne and Peter the Great's sword. Other sights include the Bolshoi Theater and Novodevichy Convent, from where you enjoy a sweeping panoramic view. Tonight

attend an unforgettable theater or folklore performance especially selected for you. (FB,L,D)

Day 9, Sun. MOSCOW-SMOLENSK. Travel westward, tracing the road taken by the retreating Grande Armée in the cruel winter of 1812. Afternoon in ancient Smolensk on the Dnieper River, coveted and much fought over by regional powers because of its key position on the medieval Amber Road from the Baltic to the Black Sea. The city was rebuilt according to original plans after suffering massive destruction in World War II. See the impressive fortified walls from the time of the struggle between Lithuania and Moscow, 17th-century USPENSKY CATHEDRAL, and a monument to Kutuzov, the old general whose patience and strategic cunning defeated Napoleon's military genius. (FB,L,D)

Day 10, Mon. SMOLENSK-MINSK-VILNIUS, LITHUANIA. Journey through the White Russian plains to historic Minsk, where you have time for lunch and for an orientation drive to Victoria Square. Next focus on the Baltic States, three small countries which recently regained their independence. Each has its own language and distinct culture. First visit Lithuania, the largest and southernmost of the three. You spend the night in its capital, Vilnius. (FB,L,D)

Day 11, Tue. VILNIUS. See the sights in what was once the splendid center of the mighty Grand Duchy of Lithuania. Vilnius' picturesque historic nucleus is clustered around the remains of a castle built by Prince Gediminas in 1323. Stroll from Kutuzov Square through narrow, winding lanes to the OLD UNIVERSITY founded by Jesuits in 1569. Afternoon at leisure. (FB,L,D)

Day 12, Wed. VILNIUS-RIGA, LATVIA. A scenic traveling day from the River Neris to the Baltic port of Riga. Enjoy vistas of a landscape alternating dark forests, swamps, fertile black earth fields, and lush pastures with iron red cattle. (FB,L,D)

Day 13, Thu. RIGA. All day in the Latvian capital, the northern terminus of the ancient Amber Road about which you heard in Smolensk. See today why Riga is considered one of the loveliest towns on the Baltic Sea. Tour the historic center on the right bank of the Daugava River, and visit the Lutheran DOMA CATHEDRAL with its colorful stained-glass panels and amazing 7,000-pipe organ. For glimpses of the old way of life visit the open-air ETHNOGRAPHICAL MUSEUM on the shores of nearby Lake Jugla. A Latvian village, complete with smithy, taverns, tar-works, pottery, church and peasants huts has been reconstructed in a suggestive pine-forest setting. (FB,L,D)

Day 14, Fri. RIGA-TALLINN, ESTONIA. Trace the coastline of the Gulf of Riga to the Estonian health resort of Pärnu, a site inhabited since the early Stone Age. After a leisurely lunch break head through boulder-strewn lowlands for Tallinn, the capital of the smallest of the Baltic States. (FB,L,D)

Day 15, Sat. TALLINN-HELSINKI, FINLAND. Situated right opposite Helsinki, Tallinn has a strong Scandinavian flavor. The local language resembles Finnish and Hungarian. Admire the beautifully preserved Hanseatic Old Town with its 15th-century Lühike Jalg Gate and remains of the old battlements. Visit the OLD TALLINN EXHIBITION in the Town Hall, and the onion-domed ALEXANDER NEVSKY CATHEDRAL. Time to wander at whim before you board your ferry for the 4-hour crossing of the Gulf of Finland. Aboard ship enjoy a last dinner with the friends made on this fascinating tour. Late evening arrival at your Helsinki hotel. (FB,L,D)

Day 16, Sun. YOUR HOMEBOUND FLIGHT ARRIVES THE SAME DAY. (FB)

138 US

▲ A WHOLE DAY TO ENJOY HISTORIC RIGA   ▼ THE HANSEATIC OLD TOWN OF TALLINN

▲ LITHUANIAN FOLKLORE IS ALIVE AND WELL

➤ Arrangements in Russia are under the management of Intourist. Slight changes to the day-by-day itinerary cannot be excluded. Accommodation in Eastern Europe may not always be of the standard you expect elsewhere.

▲ ST.ISAAC'S CATHEDRAL IN ST.PETERSBURG   ▼ ONION-DOMED ORTHODOX CATHEDRALS IN THE KREMLIN

Tour RP: DATES & PRICES

Tour code	Leave USA or join Helsinki next day		Return to USA or end Helsinki		16 days USA/ USA US$	15 days Helsinki/ Helsinki US$
RP0501	Sat	30-Apr	Sun	15-May	2547	1778
RP0508	Sat	07-May	Sun	22-May	2567	1798
RP0515	Sat	14-May	Sun	29-May	2567	1798
RP0522	Sat	21-May	Sun	05-Jun	2567	1798
RP0529	Sat	28-May	Sun	12-Jun	2567	1798
RP0605	Sat	04-Jun	Sun	19-Jun	2689	1798
RP0612	Sat	11-Jun	Sun	26-Jun	2689	1798
RP0619	Sat	18-Jun	Sun	03-Jul	2689	1798
RP0626	Sat	25-Jun	Sun	10-Jul	2689	1798
RP0703	Sat	02-Jul	Sun	17-Jul	2689	1798
RP0710	Sat	09-Jul	Sun	24-Jul	2689	1798
RP0717	Sat	16-Jul	Sun	31-Jul	2689	1798
RP0724	Sat	23-Jul	Sun	07-Aug	2689	1798
RP0731	Sat	30-Jul	Sun	.14-Aug	2689	1798
RP0807	Sat	06-Aug	Sun	21-Aug	2689	1798
RP0814	Sat	13-Aug	Sun	28-Aug	2689	1798
RP0821	Sat	20-Aug	Sun	04-Sep	2689	1798
RP0828	Sat	27-Aug	Sun	11-Sep	2689	1798
RP0904	Sat	03-Sep	Sun	18-Sep	2567	1798
RP0911	Sat	10-Sep	Sun	25-Sep	2567	1798
RP0918	Sat	17-Sep	Sun	02-Oct	2567	1798
RP0925	Sat	24-Sep	Sun	09-Oct	2567	1798
RP1002	Sat	01-Oct	Sun	16-Oct	2567	1798
RP1009	Sat	08-Oct	Sun	23-Oct	2547	1778

For any air fare supplement from your departure city, see list 3 on page 20.

Single room supplement: $413
Triple room reduction per person: $13
APOLLO: TD*GG, **PARS:** G/PTS/GGX, **SABRE:** Y/TUR/QGG

GLOBUS HOTELS

HELSINKI Sas Royal (F=First Class), **ST.PETERSBURG** Pulkovskaya (F), **NOVGOROD** Intourist (F) **MOSCOW** Cosmos (F), **SMOLENSK** Phoenix (F), **VILNIUS** Lietuva (F), **RIGA** Latvia (F), **TALLINN** Viru (F)

■ REVIEW—EASTERN EUROPE AND THE FORMER SOVIET UNION

1. What are some of the ways that Eastern Europe differs from Western Europe?

2. What are the principal languages and religions of Eastern Europe?

3. Describe the changes that have occurred in Germany since its reunification. Discuss three primary areas attractive to tourists.

4. Discuss the current status, from a touristic viewpoint, of what was Yugoslavia. Name the countries and describe the tourism available and safe at the present time.

5. What are the main climatic features of Russia?

6. Where is most of the Russian population concentrated? Where are the largest areas of little or no population? Why?

7. Compare and contrast St. Petersburg, Moscow, and Kiev in terms of their background and present character. Name the correct country for each of these cities.

8. Where are the major beach and resort areas of Eastern Europe?

9. Describe four areas of scenic beauty in Eastern Europe.

10. From current newspapers or magazines, discuss current happenings in Eastern European countries and how events might affect tourism in the area.

11

The Middle East and North Africa

Four factors—a dry climate, Islam as the major religion, Arab language and culture, and oil wealth—combine to give the Middle East a distinctive regional identity. Throughout history, the Middle East has been a crossroads where armies have marched and empires waxed and waned, where different cultures have met and interblended, and where great religions have developed and spread. This dynamism continues. In recent years, the region's enormous oil wealth and unsettled international conditions, often involving open warfare, have placed it in a central position in world affairs.

To European explorers, cartographers, and travelers of earlier centuries who looked eastward toward China and Japan (formerly called the Far East), this sprawling territory, especially the part from Egypt eastward, was the Middle East or Near East.

The region may be identified more accurately by its two geographical components, Southwest Asia and North Africa, which cut across and involve the continents of Eurasia and Africa. It extends in a broad sweep for some 5,000 miles south of Europe and the former Soviet Union, terminated in the east by the Indian culture area (Pakistan) and in the west by the Atlantic Ocean. In the northwest, it borders the Mediterranean Sea, and in the southeast, on two arms of the Indian Ocean that flank the Arabian Peninsula—the Red Sea and the Persian Gulf.

A rather large number of nations lie in the Middle East. On the Eurasian mainland, a northern tier of nations consists of Turkey, Iran, and Afghanistan. South of Turkey is the cluster of Syria and Iraq and the small nations of Lebanon, Israel, and Jordan. The island nation of Cyprus is also south of Turkey in the eastern Mediterranean Sea. Most of the enormous Arabian Peninsula is administered by Saudi Arabia, but small coastal nations fringe it on the east (Kuwait, Bahrain, Qatar, and United Arab Emirates) and south (Oman and Yemen). West of the Red Sea in North Africa are Egypt, Sudan, Libya, Tunisia, Algeria, and Morocco.

There is sufficient rainfall for agriculture and city development on the seacoasts—a narrow zone in North Africa and the fringes of the Arabian Peninsula—and in the lands bordering on and extending eastward from the Mediterranean Sea where the same prevailing westerly winds that cross southern Europe bring winter rains. In addition to these rainfall zones, population also crowds into the plains along the region's two major rivers. The Nile River of Egypt and the Tigris-Euphrates River of Iraq—where irrigated agriculture can be carried on. Most of the Sahara Desert, the interior Arabian Peninsula, and eastern Iran are devoid of population. Summers are hot everywhere, with winters chilly in the southern, and cold in the northern, areas.

The Middle East was the source of three of the world's major religions—Judaism, Christianity, and Islam. Islam is now the prevalent faith, and Mecca, in Saudi Arabia, is the focus of religious devotion during daily prayers and the holy place to which all Moslems hope to make at least one pilgrimage in a lifetime. The mosques (some of them among the world's architectural jewels), religious and social practices, and food preferences are visible manifestations of a unifying set of regional values and way of life.

Other faiths are also represented. Nearly half of the population of Lebanon is Christian; Cyprus has a Christian majority and a Moslem minority; Egypt has a large Coptic Christian population; and Israel is a Jewish state with a growing Moslem minority. Christianity is also practiced among the black population of southern Sudan.

The Middle East is often called the Arab world because the Arabic language and culture predominates in the region in a band extending through North Africa and eastward through the Arabian Peninsula to Iraq. But non-Arab languages and

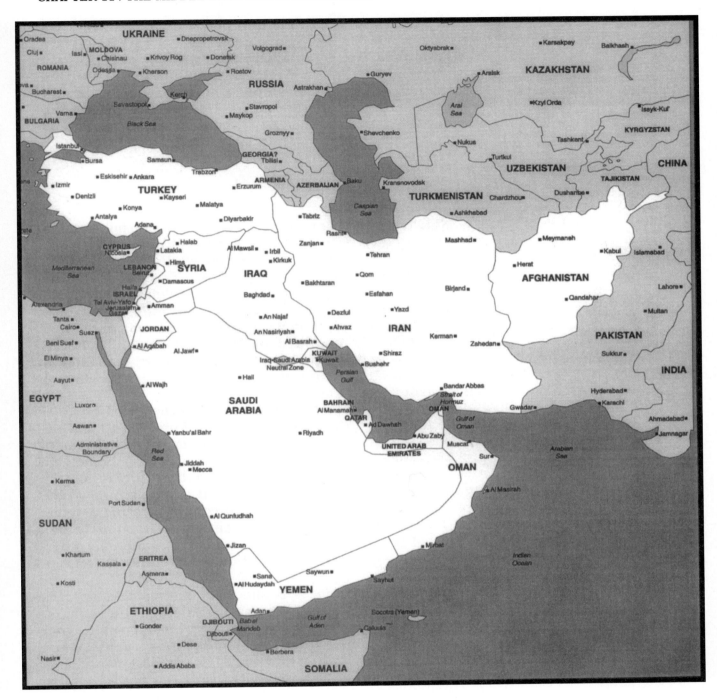

cultures are also common. The Turkish spoken by the Turks
is of Central Asian origin, not a Semitic language like Arabic.
The Turks also have adopted a Latin alphabet instead of the
flowing calligraphy of Arabic. They are Moslems, however, and
like other adherents of the faith follow the Koran, the holy
book that is written in Arabic.

In Iran, Farsi is an Indo-European language related historically to the languages of Europe, the Soviet Union, and northern India. Greek is the majority language of Cyprus and is written in the Cyrillic, Greek-derived, alphabet. Other languages are spoken by the Kurds of northeastern Iraq, northwestern Iran, and southeastern Turkey; the Berbers of northwestern Africa, especially in Morocco and Algeria; and the black tribal groups of southern Sudan.

■ HISTORY

The Middle East has long been subject to outside political and military controls. Most areas east of Egypt were under Turkish control or influence for centuries, while in North Africa, Turkish decline was followed by British, French, and Italian colonialism. Following World War I and the defeat of the Turks and their Austro-Hungarian and German allies, League of Nations mandates or "temporary" territorial responsibilities were awarded to France (present Syria and Lebanon) and Great Britain (present Israel and Jordan). Also, the British held Iraq as a protectorate, and Iran was within the Russian (north) and British (south) spheres of power.

Most Arab groups became masters of their own territory for the first time in recent history after World War II and the collapse of colonialism. Faced with common development problems and the creation of Israel as a Jewish homeland, Arab leaders created the Arab League to try to weld the Arab nations together into an international action group. President Nasser of Egypt pursued the dream of creating a single Arab federation centering on his nation. Neither move has succeeded because the Arab nations have numerous differences that are greater than their linguistic, cultural, and religious bonds.

Among the differences is sheer population size. Egypt is by far the most populous Arab nation, although third to non-Arab Turkey and Iran in the Middle East. This large manpower supply has been an important element in Egypt's political and military leadership during much of the post-World War II era.

The Middle East also abounds in historical rivalries between Arab groups and nations that make movement toward uniform, coordinated policies impossible. For example, Syria and Iraq, despite being Arab neighbors and under similar political systems, are bitter rivals. Iraq's army invaded Kuwait and had to be ousted by an international army during the Gulf War of 1990–1991. Egypt and Libya are sometimes at odds with each other; more generally, Libya has a tendency to meddle wherever opportunity arises within the Islamic world. In North Africa, Morocco and Algeria face each other across a border of tension and distrust. The Arab nation of Lebanon has been ripped apart by warring Christian and Moslem factions.

Arab nations are also pulled into discord, even conflict, with their non-Arab neighbors. The war between Iraq and Iran and the poor relations between Turkey and adjacent Arab nations are cases in point. All Arab nations have opposed the existence of Israel, and only Egypt and Jordan have opened formal diplomatic relations with Israel. Yet, no specific anti-Israeli policy has been adopted and put into effect, leaving the hostility to be shown by individual Arab nations in different ways, ranging from angry words to warfare.

In governmental form, most Arab nations can be placed into one of two broad categories, each distrustful of the other. These are the traditional monarchies, exemplified by Saudi Arabia, Jordan, and Kuwait, and the more radical governments, such as those in Algeria, Egypt, Iraq, Syria, and Yemen, who aspire to modernization under Socialist principles.

The United States, with its strong pro-Israel stance, has managed to hold the friendship of such Arab nations as Morocco, Egypt, Jordan, Saudi Arabia, and the Persian Gulf states. The United States also strongly supports Turkey and favors stabilized internal conditions in Cyprus and Lebanon. American military forces are stationed in Turkey under North Atlantic Treaty Organization (NATO) agreements, and the American Sixth Fleet patrols the Mediterranean.

The vast oil and natural gas resources of the Middle East, the degree of world dependency upon them, and the prodigious wealth that the export of oil generates make Middle Eastern affairs the concern of the world community. A few statistics tell the importance of the Middle East in the world energy picture: it is the source of more than 60 percent of the oil that enters international trade, and it has 55 percent of the world's known petroleum reserves. Its primary markets are western Europe and Japan, secondary ones are in North America, and then the rest of the oil-importing world. Vast natural gas deposits are as yet little exploited and can be the source of additional future income when moved in liquid form in special tankers.

Oil is found in two broad zones; the larger and more important one is in the form of an arc around the borders of the Persian Gulf and the adjacent Tigris-Euphrates plains. Within this region are the wells of the major oil producers—Iran, Iraq, Kuwait, Saudi Arabia, and the United Arab Emirates. The lesser belt extends east-west across the northern Sahara in North Africa, where it is tapped by two major producers, Algeria and Libya, and a smaller producer, Egypt.

The ideal route for shipping Persian Gulf oil to western markets is via the Suez Canal, the man-made, sea-level (no locks) waterway that links the Red Sea and the Mediterranean

Sea. However, the size of the canal limits its use to small and medium-sized tankers; the supertankers that are in general use must sail around the southern tip of Africa to their western destinations. Small amounts of oil, principally from Iraq and Saudi Arabia, move by pipeline from the oil fields to Mediterranean ports, thus avoiding the Suez Canal bottleneck. North African producers have a geographical advantage—their oil moves shorter distances and more directly to western customers.

The oil business in the Middle East has passed through several development stages since the first oil strike in southwestern Iran in 1908. Initially, western oil companies held concession areas, awarded them by local rulers, where they had exclusive rights to explore for and pump oil. In return, a share of oil profits was paid to the local government. American oil companies were the most active, followed by British, Dutch, French, and other companies. Following World War II, local governments demanded and received a growing share of oil profits and finally, in the 1960s, took over full control by nationalizing of the western oil companies.

The sale of oil abroad has brought super wealth to major oil exporters. Large sums are being spent on modernization—in raising the national levels of education, public health, housing, employment, and living standards. Saudi Arabia and Kuwait have been pacesetters in such investment in social and economic improvement. At the same time, however, most oil-rich nations have also invested heavily in military equipment purchased from foreign suppliers. Other than for status purposes, this armament build-up is in response to existing rivalries and perceived threats to national security within the region.

Two major oil producers, Iran and Iraq, were involved in a costly war in 1980–1988 that resulted in heavy casualties and property damage, a sharp reduction in both nations' oil income, and a diversion of income from pressing social and economic needs to immediate military needs. Kuwait and Iraq suffered great damage during the Gulf War of 1990–1991.

No single issue has so profoundly affected international conditions within the Middle East in recent times as the creation of the new nation of Israel by the United Nations in 1948 as a Jewish homeland. As brief background, Israel is the culmination of a Jewish hope that dates from the 1st century AD, when the Jews were evicted from their home in Palestine (the area around Jerusalem) by the Romans. Over the following centuries, they became widely dispersed with concentrations in parts of Europe, Russia, the Middle East, and, eventually, the United States. Often treated as an alien group, they maintained their religious and ethnic identity.

In the 19th century, a formal Zionist "return to the homeland" movement was organized in Europe and eventually gained the promise of support by the British government. Once the British were awarded the Palestinian Mandate by the League of Nations after World War I, Jewish immigration into Palestine greatly increased. It was prompted further by the anti-Jewish actions of the Nazi German government in the 1930s. However, local Arabs became resentful of the immigration and soon armed hostilities between resident Arabs, Jewish settlers, and British troops trying to keep peace became the norm.

The United Nations decision to create Israel was prompted in part by the termination of the British mandate and world sympathy for the wartime genocide of Jews and other ethnic groups by the Nazis. Once Israel was created, fighting between Arab and Israeli forces broke out, the original Israeli territory was expanded, and more than one million Arabs resident in Palestine were displaced into adjacent Arab nations. Since then, unremitting Arab opposition to Israel has resulted in three wars (1956, 1967, and 1973) and anti-Israeli guerrilla attacks by the Palestinian Liberation Organization (PLO), whose ultimate goal is the reestablishment of a Palestinian Arab homeland. Even with strong American backing and the establishment of formal diplomatic ties with Egypt, its chief adversary in the three wars, Israel continues to face Arab hostility and must keep armed and militarily alert to survive. A 1993 peace agreement signed by Israel and the PLO offers much promise for the area.

■ TURKEY, IRAN, AND AFGHANISTAN

These three nations are Moslem but non-Arab. They form the northern tier of Middle Eastern nations.

TURKEY

Official Name: Republic of Turkey

Language: Turkish

Area: 301,381 square miles

Time Zone: GMT +2

National Airline: Turkish Airlines

Capital: Ankara

Currency: Turkish lira (TUL)

Population: 58,580,000

Documentation: Passport

The Land. Turkey is formed by a large peninsula that juts westward between the Black Sea and eastern Mediterranean Sea and a linking narrow water passageway, the Straits, consisting of the Dardanelles (west), Sea of Marmara (center), and the Bosporus (east). A small Turkish territory also lies on the European side of the Straits, placing the strategic waterway under Turkish control. The peninsular position has a mountainous core, the Anatolian Plateau, and narrow coastal plains. The latter have good rainfall, the best agricultural land, and the densest population. By contrast, the interior is dry and, in winter, cold.

History. The Turks came originally from Central Asia, gained control of Turkey by the 15th century, and expanded their empire into southeastern Europe and the Middle East, including North Africa. A gradual territorial decline was completed by the end of World War I, when Turkey was reduced to its present size. Among other national reforms of the 1920s, a Latin alphabet was adopted to replace Arabic script, and the national capital was shifted from Istanbul (formerly Constantinople) to Ankara in the north central Anatolian Plateau.

People and Politics. Turkey is the second most populous Middle Eastern nation, slightly smaller than Iran. Turks make up 90 percent; Kurds, in the southeast, are the largest minority (7 percent); and there are smaller Arab, Greek, Armenian, and Georgian minorities, either in peripheral areas or Istanbul. Located on the Bosporus, Istanbul is the largest city and main manufacturing and commercial center. The country's economy is basically agricultural, producing typical Mediterranean crops in the coastal plains and dry grains in the interior. Tobacco is an important cash crop. Manufacturing has developed in pockets, especially in Istanbul and the north coast.

Turkey's main international involvements are outside the Middle East. It has long taken an anti-Russian stance, is a member of the North Atlantic Treaty Organization (NATO), and is strongly allied with the United States in military, political, and economic matters. The Straits are a highly strategic asset because they potentially control all shipping between Black Sea ports and the Mediterranean Sea. Turkey does not have cordial relations with its Arab neighbors and is embroiled with neighboring Greece in a conflict over Cyprus.

Areas of Touristic Importance. Istanbul is one of the most intriguing cities in the world. With its long history as a crossroads for travelers, it has carried many names over the years. In ancient times, it was Byzantium, headquarters for a huge empire. To Marco Polo, it was Constantinople, a major port in the development of East-West trade. Today's Istanbul shows both old and new to the visitor.

The city straddles the Bosporus and, thus, belongs to two continents. The western part of the city is on the European continent, and the eastern sector is part of Asia. They are linked by two bridges and ferry service.

Over 400 mosques can be found in Istanbul. The most famous is the Blue Mosque, unique with its six minarets. Sound and light shows are shown in the summer. The rambling Topkapi Palace, home of the Ottoman sultans, is also a must. Shopping in the Turkish bazaars provides excellent

The Blue Mosque, Istanbul
Photo: Courtesy Office of the Culture and Information Attaché, Turkey

values in jewelry, handmade metal goods, and woodwork. Naturally, Turkish baths are also in abundance.

Izmir, a busy port city, is a major port for Eastern Mediterranean and Greek Island (Aegean) cruises. It is an excellent base for excursions to nearby ruins. Most important is Ephesus, once home of the Temple of Diana. The ruins of the cities of Troy and Aphrodisia are also within a day's travel of Izmir.

Ankara, the capital, located near the center of the country, features both modern buildings and old, decaying fortresses. Monuments to the foundation of the Turkish Republic and ancient Roman baths can be seen in the same half-day. The Valley of Goreme, south of the city, has strange rock formations sculpted by winds and rains of thousands of years.

Seaside resort towns dot the Mediterranean coast, offering sun and fun to the traveler. Tourism along the scenic northern Black Sea coast has greatly increased.

IRAN

Official Name: Islamic Republic of Iran

Language: Farsi, Turkish, Kurdish, Arabic

Area: 636,293 square miles

Time Zone: GMT +3.30

National Airline: Iranair

Capital: Tehran

Currency: Rial (IRI)

Population: 59,051,000

Documentation: Passport, visa

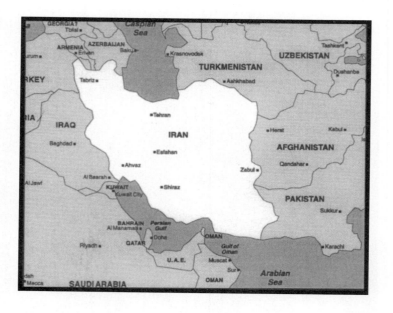

The Land. Deserts and mountains dominate the large territory of Iran, Turkey's eastern neighbor. The central and eastern parts are dominated by the Plateau of Iran, which is high, desert, and almost devoid of population. The bulk of the population and human activity is in the west, where light winter rains and irrigation water from the Zagros Mountains of the southwest and Elburz Mountains, which lie along the southern edge of the Caspian Sea, the largest inland lake in the world, provide a basis for agriculture and city life. Desert conditions also persist along the long Persian Gulf and Arabian Sea coastline except in the southwest, where Iran and Iraq, its other western neighbor, share the combined lower course of the Tigris-Euphrates river system.

People and Religion. Iran has the largest population in the Middle East. The Iranians, who make up only two-thirds of the population, are descended from Indo-European peoples, related to the early Aryans of India, who appeared in the second millennium, BC. The Iranian language thus springs from a different source than Semitic Arabic. The numerous minorities include Kurds in the northwest and Turkish (Turkic)-language groups in the north.

The national religion is Islam, but more than 90 percent are members of the minority Shiite branch of Islam, known for its religious fundamentalism. The dominant, more conservative Sunni branch predominates in the Islamic nations of the region except in Iran and Iraq. Iran's historic mosques are among the most famous in the Middle East.

History. Formerly named Persia, Iran was the seat of great empires in antiquity. In more recent times, British and Russian influence prevailed in the 19th century; in 1857, the British, operating out of British India, created present Afghanistan from Persian territory. In the 1950s and 1960s, the ruling shah used the nation's growing oil wealth to accelerate economic and social modernization. In 1979, conservative religious interests opposed to western innovations overthrew the shah, who was anti-Russian, West-oriented, and militarily allied with the United States. They established a clergy-dominated Islamic republic. In 1980–1988, Iran and Iraq engaged in a costly and bloody war.

Economy and Politics. The Iranian economy is based on the production and export of oil in the southwestern area, where the massive Abadan oil refinery and Persian Gulf tanker facilities are located. The other focal point in Iranian life is the capital, Tehran, located on the southern edge of the Elburz Mountains. As in Turkey, the capital is linked by roads to major towns, cities, and regions.

Before the 1979 proclamation of the Islamic Republic, Tehran was an oasis of westernization in the Islamic world. Broad avenues and chic shops reminded the traveler of Paris. Persian marketplaces added to the city's flavor. International trade flourished and the city attracted both commercial and cultural travelers.

At this time, the United States does not maintain official diplomatic relations with Iran, and few westerners visit. Hopefully, the tiled mosques, white stone houses, Persian palaces and many museums and the Caspian Sea resorts will be available to our tourists in the future.

AFGHANISTAN

Official Name: Democratic Republic of Afghanistan

Language: Pushtu, Dari

Area: 251,773 square miles

Time Zone: GMT +4:30

National Airline: Air Afghanistan

Capital: Kabul

Currency: Afghani (AFG)

Population: 16,450,000

Documentation: Passport, visa

Afghanistan is a landlocked nation northeast of Iran; its principal outside links are with Central Asian nations (formerly part of the Soviet Union) to the north and Pakistan on the east. Desert and mountainous conditions prevail, yet there is a relatively large population of over 16 million, mainly on the northern and eastern fringes. The population is diverse and is broken down into many regional tribal groups. Pushtu, an Iranian-related language, is spoken by the majority Pushtuns (Pathans). Other Iranian and Turkic languages, the latter related to languages spoken across the borders to the north and in Western China, are also spoken by large groups. Islam is the prevailing religion. Kabul, in the east, is the largest city and capital.

Afghanistan was within the British Indian sphere of influence until World War II. After the war, it received extensive economic assistance from the Soviet Union and the United States. A pro-Soviet government took power in 1978 and in the following year had the support of invading Russian military forces who became engaged in a long war against opposing guerrilla forces. Several million refugees from the war who sought sanctuary in Pakistan are gradually returning to a homeland where tribal warfare continues.

Afghanistan has always been a destination only for the adventurous traveler. Kabul, the capital, offers the opportunity to see (and even participate in) nomadic caravanserai. Because of unsettled political conditions, few westerners now visit this rugged nation.

■ CYPRUS AND LEBANON

These two nations are distinctive because of their large Christian populations and the degree to which they have been embroiled in domestic ethnic strife.

CYPRUS

Official Name: Republic of
  Cyprus

Language: Greek, Turkish

Area: 3,572 square miles

Time Zone: GMT +2

Capital: Nicosia

Currency: Cyprus pound
  (CYL)

Population: 708,000

Documentation: Passport

Cyprus is a small, mountainous island nation in the eastern Mediterranean south of Turkey. Seventy-five percent of the 660,000 population are of Greek origin and Christian; the remainder are Turkish Moslems. Held by the British between the two world wars, Cyprus became independent in 1960 even though the Greek majority preferred union with Greece. Civil war between the two ethnic groups erupted in 1973, and Turkish armed forces intervened to protect the Turkish minority.

Most Turkish Cypriots are now concentrated in the northern third of the island, which is a self-declared Turkish Federated State of Cyprus. Administered from the small capital city of Nicosia, Cyprus does not recognize the Turkish zone but is faced with the reality of a culturally and politically divided island. The struggling economy is shaped around tourism and poor agriculture.

Areas of Touristic Importance. The ethnic warfare within the country makes travel between Greek and Turkish areas difficult. Most international visitors arrive by air at Larnaca. Archeological sites are among the most interesting attractions for the tourist. Examples of the neolithic, Hellenic, Macedonian, Roman, Crusader, and Turkish periods are abundant. Mediterranean cruise passengers visit Cyprus through the port of Limassol as well as Larnaca.

Gymnasium at Salamis, Cyprus
Photo: Courtesy Public Information Office, Republic of Cyprus

LEBANON

Official Name: Republic of
Lebanon

Language: Arabic, French,
English

Area: 4,015 square miles

Time Zone: GMT +2

National Airline: Middle East
Airlines

Capital: Beirut

Currency: Lebanese pound

Population: 3,384,000

Documentation: Passport,
visa

Lebanon, once a political success, is the Middle East's most
tragic example of the extremes of ethnic conflict. Located on
the eastern Mediterranean coast, it was carved out of former
Turkish-controlled territory and was under French mandate
control from 1923 to 1943. Initially, Lebanon flourished; all
public positions were shared by the religious communities,
with Christians in a majority position. The coastal capital city
of Beirut became the main international banking and educational center in the Middle East.

As the Moslem population increased to majority status
in the 1970s, it demanded greater political and economic
representation and pressed for aggressive action against
neighboring Israel. Christian-Moslem relations gradually de-

generated into civil war in 1975, with the two sides split into many factions, each controlling parts of the nation. Partisan foreign forces also edged into the fray—Israeli military units fighting a hostile PLO force in southern Lebanon; Syrian army units to support the Moslems in the northeast; and American and other foreign troops as part of a United Nations peacekeeping action.

The ancient Roman and Arabic ruins at Baalbek including the Temples of Venus and Jupiter await future visitors when political tensions ease and security issues are solved.

■ SYRIA, IRAQ, AND JORDAN

South of Turkey is a block of three Moslem Arab nations. Syria, Iraq, and Jordan have cultural similarities but often unfriendly relations.

SYRIA

Official Name: Syrian Arab Republic

Language: Arabic, Kurdish

Area: 71,498 square miles

Time Zone: GMT +2

National Airline: Syrian Arab

Capital: Damascus

Currency: Syrian pound (SYL)

Population: 12,965,000

Documentation: Passport, visa

Syria fronts on the Mediterranean Sea, but most of its land is in the interior, sharing an eastern boundary with Iraq. The population is concentrated in the western one-third, where winter rainfall and irrigation water support agriculture. The eastern portion is desert with irrigated tracts using water from the Euphrates River, which flows southward out of Turkey en route to Iraq and the Persian Gulf.

The capital, Damascus, an ancient commercial center in the extreme southwest, is only a short distance from Beirut in Lebanon, Amman in Jordan, and Jerusalem in Israel. This proximity has intensified relations between them, usually for the worse. Syria has a radical government that is ardently pro-Arab and anti-lsrael. Although non-Communist, it formerly received wholesale economic and military aid from the Soviet Union and has one of the Middle East's larger armies, fully equipped with Russian weaponry. It is Israel's principal armed opponent; is unfriendly toward Turkey, Iraq, and Jordan; and has been involved militarily in Lebanon.

Areas of Touristic Importance. Damascus is built on 4,000 years of history. It is believed to be the oldest continually inhabited city in the world. The city is a blend of Biblical history and Arabic culture. The House of Ananias, mentioned in the Bible, as well as the Tomb of Saladin, St. Paul's Church, and the street called Straight are found here. Crusader fortresses are nearby. Copper inlays, brass, wood, and spices abound in the souks (marketplaces). Political conditions, however, keep tourism to a minimum.

IRAQ

Official Name: Republic of Iraq

Language: Arabic

Area: 167,924 square miles

Time Zone: GMT +3

Capital: Baghdad

Currency: Iraqi dinar (IRD)

Population: 19,524,000

Documentation: Passport, visa

Iraq is similar to Syria in some ways. It has a radical government that has few international friends and is anti-Israel. Important differences are that its Moslem population is predominantly of the Shiite sect, as in Iran, and that it has a large oil income.

Larger in size than Syria, Iraq borders Turkey on the north, Syria and Jordan on the west, Iran on the east, Saudi Arabia on the south, and has a narrow frontage on the Persian Gulf between Kuwait and Iran. Iraq is traversed by one of the Middle East's two largest river systems—the Tigris River coming from the north is joined by the Euphrates River coming from the west and they flow as one river, the Shatt-al-Arab, into the Persian Gulf. Baghdad, the historic capital, is located on the central Tigris River.

Western Iraq is desert, but winter rains in the north support a flourishing agriculture based upon wheat and other dry grains. The river system is tapped for irrigation water in its central and lower courses. Some 5,000 years ago, the land between and around the rivers was Mesopotamia, the cultural center in which Western civilization took form and from which it spread into the Mediterranean borderlands.

In recent decades, Iraq was a pacesetter in modernization in the 1960s and 1970s, using its large oil revenues to improve and diversify the economy. The main oil fields are in the northeast. However, development was set back seriously by the 1980-1988 war with Iran, the heavy purchase of military goods from the Soviet Union, and the sharp reduction in oil exports resulting from Iranian military activity. Iraq received material support from other Arab nations, including conservative Saudi Arabia, who were fearful of an expansion of Iran's religious fundamentalism. Crushed in the Gulf War following its invasion of Kuwait in 1990, Iraq has faced reduced oil income, United Nations sanctions, reparations to Kuwait, restoration of wartime damage, and a restless Kurdish minority in the northeast.

Iraq will always be remembered as the cradle of civilization, home of one of the Seven Wonders of the Ancient World, the Biblical Hanging Gardens of Babylon, and the birthplace of codified law, the wheel, and the plow. Hopefully, it will be fit for tourism in the future.

JORDAN

Official Name: Hashemite Kingdom of Jordan

Language: Arabic

Area: 37,737 square miles

Time Zone: GMT +2

National Airline: Alia Royal Jordanian

Capital: Amman

Currency: Jordan dinar (JOD)

Population: 3,412,000

Documentation: Passport, visa

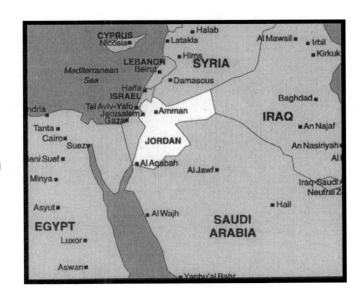

Little Jordan has most of its population and its capital, Amman, crammed into the western edge close to Israel, where its border is formed in part by the Jordan River and the Dead Sea. Eastern Jordan is empty desert, but a tiny coastal frontage on an arm of the Red Sea enables Jordan to maintain international shipping contacts through its port of Aqaba, which is also a key outlet for Iraq.

Under a British mandate between the world wars, Jordan is now ruled by a hereditary king. Jordan's lack of wealth compels it to depend upon American and other foreign economic and military assistance. Jordan's queen, the wife of ruling King Hussein, is an American. A majority of its population consists of displaced Palestinians and their families.

Areas of Touristic Importance. Amman, Jordan's capital, is a city of old and new limestone buildings. Traces of Biblical days and Roman rule can still be found. Amman has a fine archeological museum with tools dating to earliest civilization. The Roman Theater of Amman and the ruins of the Temple of Hercules are most interesting.

Petra, south of Amman, was carved out of red cliffs more than 2,500 years ago. Intricately sculpted cave entrances can be seen throughout the valley. The ruins of a Crusader fortress complex can be visited at Kerak on the road between Petra and Amman. Excavations of Greco-Roman architectural treasures can be seen at Jerash.

ISRAEL

Official Name: State of Israel
Language: Hebrew, Arabic
Area: 7,847 square miles
Time Zone: GMT +2
National Airline: El Al Israel
Capital: Jerusalem
Currency: Israeli shekel (ILS)
Population: 4,477,000
Documentation: Passport

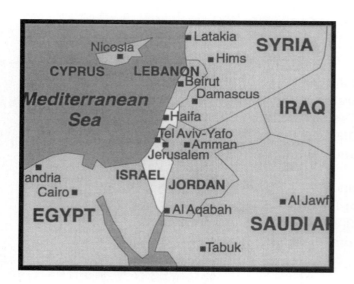

Israel is the most modern nation in the Middle East, a remarkable achievement considering the economic, military, and other adversities that it has faced during its short existence. It lies among Arab neighbors: Lebanon to the north, Jordan and Syria to the east, and Egypt to the west. The northwestern half of the small territory borders the Mediterranean and, on the east, the Jordan River and its ultimate destination, the saline Dead Sea. Southward, the territory, the Negev, narrows to a point on an arm of the Red Sea, where the Israeli port of Elat has been developed.

After the Israeli-Arab War of 1967, Israel retained territories that had served as bases for hostile guerrilla operations. The area west of the Jordan River (Jordan West Bank), containing a large Arab population and the older section of Jerusalem where the major shrines holy to Christians, Jews, and Arabs are found, was gained from Jordan. Israel has formally annexed East Jerusalem despite Jordanian protest, thus placing the entire capital city under Israeli administration. The Golan Heights, on the north-eastern border, was gained from Syria, and that, too, has been annexed.

Recently, the Gaza Strip and the West Bank city of Jericho have been transferred to Palestinian control. Negotiations

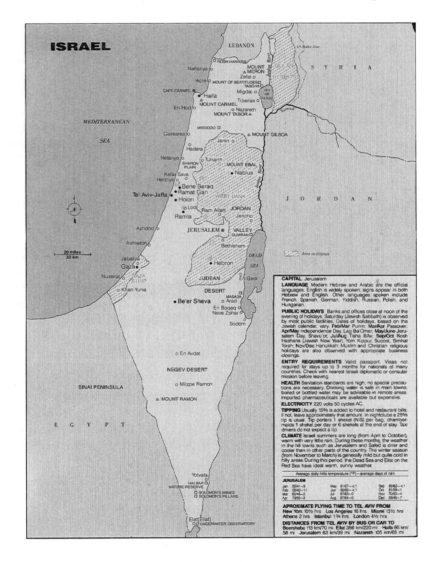

with Syria may result in the return of some or all of the Golan Heights to Syria.

The Climate and the People. Northern Israel has winter rainfall and irrigation water for agriculture; the south is desert. Jordan River water is piped southward to irrigate farming areas in the northern Negev. Most Israelis live in the north, three-fourths of them in cities, such as Tel Aviv, Jaffa, and Haifa on the coast; and Jerusalem in the interior.

Although Israel is nominally a Jewish nation, it has a sizeable and fast-growing Palestinian Arab minority that holds citizenship. Jewish immigration from abroad had virtually stopped until a large-scale influx of Russian Jews in 1989–1993 after the collapse of the Soviet Union.

The Economy. In its economic life, Israel has a flourishing agriculture that produces domestic food and citrus fruit for export. However, farming is too small-scale and faces severe water shortages, hence food imports are necessary. Industrialization, spurred by domestic, military, and export needs, is important, especially in and around Haifa. Energy and raw materials must be imported. The nation continues to be heavily supported by aid from foreign governments, especially the United States, and investments and contributions from the international Jewish community. National problems include continued Arab hostility, military costs, and a slender economic base.

Moves toward Coexistence. In a dramatic 1993 move that could change the geopolitics of the Middle East, the government of Israel recognized the Palestinian Liberation Organization as the legitimate representative of the Palestinian people, and the PLO recognized the right of Israel to exist in peace and security, and renounced the use of terrorism and other acts of violence. An accord signed in Washington, DC, on October 13, 1993, built upon this mutual recognition, called for a shift of authority from Israel to Palestinians in Gaza and the West Bank in such matters as police, culture, health, social welfare, direct taxation, and tourism.

Areas of Touristic Importance. Few places mean as much to as many people as Israel. As the Holy Land for three major religions—Judaism, Christianity, and Islam—religious pilgrims visit from all over the world. Jerusalem is the site of the Wailing Wall (Western Wall of the Temple of King Solomon), sacred to the Jews; the Church of the Holy Sepulchre, sacred to the Christians; and the Dome of the Rock (Mosque of Omar) where Mohammed ascended to heaven, making this a most holy city. Visiting Israel is like walking through the pages of the Bible and the Koran.

In addition to being the seat of government, Jerusalem has many historical sites and museums. The famous Chagall

The Dead Sea, Israel
Photo: Courtesy the Israel Government Tourist Office

windows can be seen and a relatively new attraction is the Museum of the Holocaust. The Israel Museum contains the famed Dead Sea Scrolls.

Jerusalem's Old City features eight-gated walls and Arab, Christian, and Jewish quarters and markets. A visit to Mount Zion will take the tourist to the Tomb of David and the Chamber of the Last Supper.

Christians can trace the life of Jesus in Israel, including his birth in Bethlehem, experiences in Nazareth and along the Sea of Galilee, and final walk to crucifixion along the Via Dolorosa in Jerusalem.

Tel Aviv is the leading commercial city and stands beside the ancient city of Jaffa. Modern hotels, shops, and office buildings dominate this largest city served by Ben Gurion International Airport.

Haifa, to the north, is Israel's second largest city and primary seaport. Haifa is the port of call for Mediterranean cruises visiting Israel.

Netanya, located on the Mediterranean between Haifa and Tel Aviv, hosts deluxe beachfront resorts for rest and relaxation.

South of Jerusalem lies the Dead Sea, approximately 1,300 feet below sea level. The water has a high salt content, like Utah's Great Salt Lake. Masada, site of a long siege by the Romans, is nearby.

The Negev Desert occupies the southern half of the nation. Reclamation has enabled the Israelis to make desert land grow food. Elat, on the Gulf of Aqaba, provides access to the Red Sea and has developed beach resort.

Tourists desiring to understand how the people have brought life to the earth should visit a kibbutz or moshav, the collective farms in Israel. Several throughout the country have small hotels and guest houses and encourage international visitors.

■ ARABIAN PENINSULA NATIONS

SAUDI ARABIA

Official Name: Kingdom of Saudi Arabia

Language: Arabic

Area: 839,996 square miles

Time Zone: GMT +3

National Airline: Saudi Airlines

Capital: Riyadh

Currency: Saudi riyal (ARI)

Population: 17,869,000

Documentation: Passport, visa

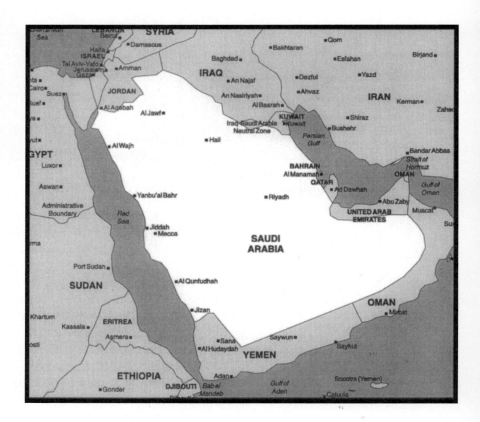

Saudi Arabia occupies most of the Arabian Peninsula. Three-fourths of its 10 million people live in the western part of this dry to arid territory. There are three urban concentrations. On the Red Sea coast is the port city of Jidda, which handles the import trade, and, 45 miles inland, Mecca, the holy city of Islam that attracts millions of pilgrims each year. Near the center of the nation is the capital, Riyadh, a modern, planned, air-conditioned city with all conveniences.

On the east coast is Dhahran, the service center for the main Saudi Arabian oil fields, which were developed by an American oil company, Aramco, before nationalization. Saudi Arabia produces more oil and has more oil income than any other Middle Eastern nation.

Saudi Arabia was created by a tribal leader, Ibn Saud, who pieced together regional tribes and territory during and after Turkish control. The nation was formalized in 1932 under Saud's kingship, and his descendants continue in power. The enormous annual oil income is used in part for the most ambitious economic modernization program in the Middle East, employing hundreds of thousands of foreign contractors, technicians, and laborers.

Politically conservative and religiously orthodox Islamic, Saudi Arabia is a strong ally of the United States, from whom it purchases military equipment and advanced technology. It is a key stabilizing force in the Middle East and in the international oil business, a counterbalance to radical Arab nations and violent Islamic fundamentalism.

Historically, the Arabian Peninsula's east and south coast was dotted with petty sheikdoms. Grouped together, usually under British or other outside influence, these loose territorial arrangements have evolved into independent nations. Typically, their populations are small and live along the coast, while their interiors are unpopulated desert and have poorly demarcated boundaries. Those on the east coast benefit from oil income and, like Saudi Arabia, are conservative Islamic kingdoms.

KUWAIT, BAHRAIN, QATAR, UNITED ARAB EMIRATES, OMAN

The population of oil-rich Kuwait, at the head of the Persian Gulf between Iraq and Saudi Arabia, has the highest per capita income and living standards in the region. Housing, health care, education, and a broad range of services are provided free of charge by the government.

East of the main Saudi Arabian oil fields are the island nation of Bahrain and peninsular Qatar, both with some oil income. Bahrain is the main international business center in the Persian Gulf area and has an American naval base and headquarters. Farther east is the United Arab Emirates, which is a federation of seven former sheikdoms. Abu Dhabi has the greatest oil income and serves as the federation's administrative center.

Occupying a curved territory on the peninsula's eastern corner, Oman has a small oil income. Most of its population is in or around the capital of Muscat, due east of the strategic Strait of Hormuz that marks the entrance of the Persian Gulf from the Indian Ocean.

YEMEN

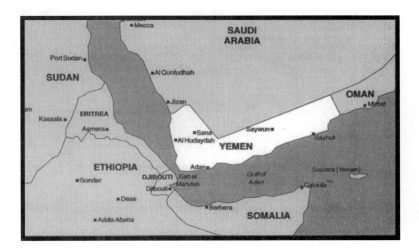

Yemen, the large nation in the southwestern peninsula, was formed in 1990 by the union of two very different economic and political units. South Yemen (People's Democratic Republic of Yemen) was a revolutionary Socialist government that had cast its lot with the Soviet bloc. Its major asset is the port city of Aden, which was developed by the British as the control point on the southern approach to the Red Sea and Suez Canal. The port was used by Russian naval and commercial shipping, and the Aden airport was an important refueling point for Russian aircraft prior to the demise of the former Soviet Union.

Tourism on the Arabian Peninsula. Travel to the nations of the Arabian Peninsula is limited to two primary types—business travel associated with the petroleum industry and construction in the oil-rich nations, and religious pilgrimages by followers of Islam, primarily to Mecca and Medina. Pleasure travel by non-Moslems is discouraged and applications for visas are closely scrutinized.

Excellent international airports can be found at Riyadh, Abu Dhabi, Muscat, and Kuwait. These cities often serve as refueling stops for international flights between Europe and Asia and the South Pacific.

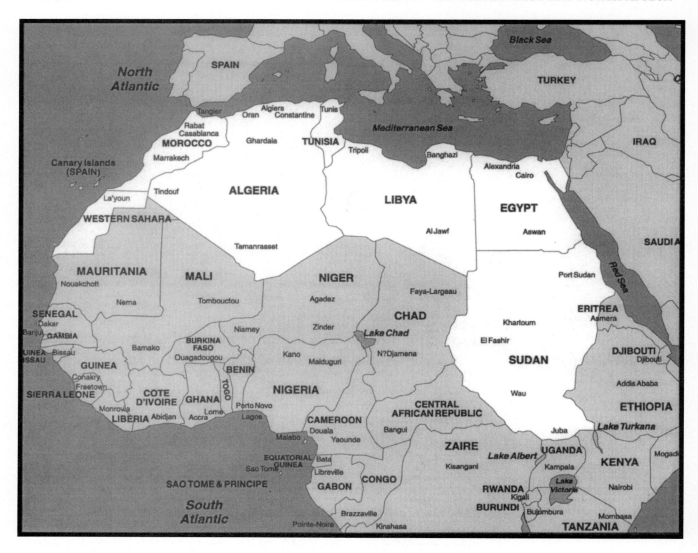

■ EGYPT, SUDAN, AND LIBYA

EGYPT

Official Name: Arab Republic of Egypt

Language: Arabic, English, French

Currency: Egyptian pound

Area: 386,650 square miles

Time Zone: GMT +2

National Airline: Egyptair

Capital: Cairo

Currency: Egyptian pound (EGL)

Population: 54,451,000

Documentation: Passport

The River and the People. Egypt has the largest population in the Middle East and has played a key leadership role among Arab states in recent decades. Located in northeastern Africa, it faces on the Mediterranean Sea and the Red Sea; on the east the Suez Canal artificially separates the main territory from the Sinai Peninsula. In the predominantly desert environment, Egyptian national life is remarkably concentrated along the course of the Nile River as it flows from south to north through eastern Egypt. All but 5 percent of the Egyptian people live near the river; the rest live in scattered oases in western Egypt.

The Nile River is formed by two branches—the White Nile, issuing from Lake Victoria in East Africa, and the Blue Nile, from the Ethiopian highlands. These branches unite in Sudan and flow northward as one river into Egypt. Irrigation, using the seasonal rise and fall in water level and fertile mud left in fields after the flood stage had passed, was practiced along the river for centuries. However, the high Aswan Dam built in upper (southern) Egypt in 1971 now impounds the river water in Lake Nasser, one of the world's largest artificial lakes, which extends 300 miles upstream into Sudan. As the now man-managed Nile approaches the Mediterranean coast, it fans out into a 100-mile-wide delta that is home to Egypt's best agricultural land and half the total population.

Agriculture is still the main livelihood, and the Aswan Dam has made it possible to expand the cultivated acreage along the Nile and in its delta. Yet rapid, unchecked population increases have resulted in per capita decline in acreage, increased food imports, and continued poverty for a major segment of the farm population. Urban centers are also growing in size, in part from rural-urban migration.

History. Egyptian culture took form in the central Nile valley some 5,000 years ago, at about the same time as Mesopotamia, as one of the leading centers of the ancient world. The massive pyramids and monuments produced in later centuries remain among the world's architectural marvels. Egypt was eventually overrun by a succession of outside forces. One of the last, the Arabs, introduced their language and religion, Islam. The British controlled Egypt from 1914 to 1951.

Shortly after independence, the kingship was replaced by a revolutionary Socialist government. One of its actions was the nationalization of the Suez Canal in 1956. Egypt fought Israel in three wars, but in 1979 it was the first Arab nation to establish diplomatic relations with Israel. In return, Israel returned the Sinai Peninsula, lost in 1967. Following a period of military and economic assistance from the former Soviet Union, Egypt reoriented itself to the West and since the late 1970s has been closely aligned with the United States.

Economy. Cairo, located at the head of the Nile delta, is the capital and largest city; its population of 10 million ranks

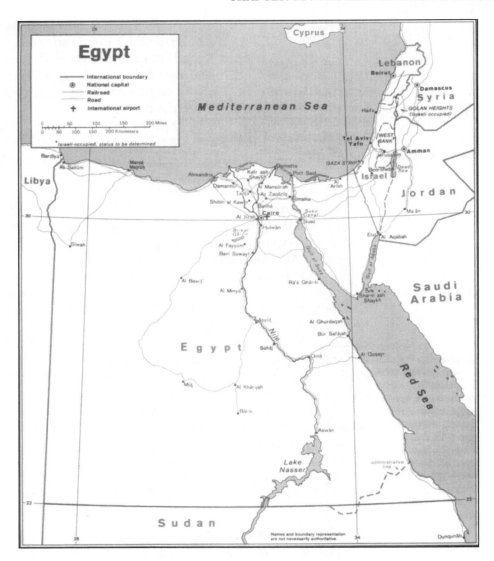

it among the 15 largest metropolises in the world. It is a study in contrasts: a modern urban core, scores of handsome mosques and minarets, and fine public buildings on the one hand, and extensive slums and grinding poverty on the other. Cairo has a growing manufacturing activity carried out in enterprise units ranging from handicrafts to large, modern factories.

Egypt's second-largest city, Alexandria, is situated on the Mediterranean coast west of the Nile delta. The nation's leading seaport and naval base, manufacturing center, and seaside resort, it has a population of nearly three million persons. On the eastern edge of the delta, Port Said serves Suez Canal traffic. These three cities are linked by good transportation services, and Cairo and major upstream locations along the Nile

Al Azhar Mosque, Cairo
Photo: Courtesy Ministry of Tourism/by Sobhi Affi

River have road, railway, river boat, and air linkages. Roads extend to the western desert oases and along the seacoasts.

Areas of Touristic Importance. Egypt is a fascinating country with something for everyone. From its ancient treasures to the Red Sea beach and diving resorts, Egypt is an exciting destination.

Most tourists fly into Cairo, whose sprawling mass is an attraction in itself. The many contrasts of the capital city have already been described.

Near Cairo, the three Pyramids of Giza and the Sphinx are the main attractions. The Step Pyramid of King Zoser at Sakara, 1 hour from Cairo, is the oldest stone building in the world, dating before 2500 BC. Also near Cairo is the ancient capital city of Memphis. The Egyptian Museum in Cairo holds many of the artifacts of ancient Egypt including the King Tut collection and a number of royal mummies. At the fascinating Khan-el-Khalili Bazaar, visitors can bargain for a wide variety of items.

Luxor is 316 miles upriver on the Nile (south of Cairo). It is part of the ancient city of Thebes, one of the mightiest empires of ancient times. In ancient Egypt, the east bank was for the living and the west bank for the dead because the sun rises in the east and sets in the west. The impressive temples of Luxor and Karnak are on the east bank of the Nile. Ferries take visitors to the west bank to the City of the Dead and the Valley of the Kings where King Tut's tomb was discovered in 1922.

Cruises are available from Cairo to Luxor (and beyond to Aswan), but many tourists with limited time take a short one-hour flight.

Farther upriver is Aswan, site of one of the largest and tallest dams in the world. Building of the dam created Lake Nasser, the largest man-made lake in the world. The Island of Elephantine and the Necropolis of the Sacred Rams are primary attractions. Cruising on the Nile between Luxor and Aswan provides views of steep cliffs as well as ancient temples and statues created at the time of Cleopatra. From Aswan, tourists can take a 1-day excursion to the Great Temple of Abu Simbel.

Alexandria, 140 miles north of Cairo, is the port of call for cruises visiting Egypt. Ruins of Greek and Roman civilizations are open to view. Seaside resorts on the Mediterranean offer opportunities for sun and swimming.

Resorts on the Sinai on the Red Sea, such as Sharm El Sheikh and Taba are excellent diving destinations. Also on the Sinai is Mt. Sinai of biblical fame and the famous St. Catherine's Monastery.

SUDAN

Official Name: Democratic Republic of Sudan

Language: Arabic, English

Area: 966,757 square miles

Time Zone: GMT +2

Capital: Khartoum

Currency: Sudanese pound (SUL)

Population: 27,220,000

Documentation: Passport, visa

Physically the largest nation in Africa, Sudan stands astride the Sahara Desert to the north and the well-watered equatorial lands of central Africa, and the Arab-Islamic Middle East and black Africa to the south. On the north, it borders Egypt and Libya; on the east, the Red Sea and Ethiopia; and on the south and west, five African nations. As in Egypt, national life is centered around the Nile River and its two branches. The White Nile spreads into a vast, reed-covered marshland in southern Sudan, regains its river form, and, at Khartoum, joins the Blue Nile. Much of western Sudan and a smaller area between the Nile valley and the Red Sea are desert.

Sudan was under joint British-Egyptian control during 1898–1956. In 1959, after independence, a radical government took power. Arabs, who number more than one-half the population, are concentrated in the north and dominate the government, army, and economy. There are more than two dozen languages other than Arabic, including those spoken by the black tribes in the south. Seventy percent of the people practice Islam. Most of the 25 percent who practice traditional, or animistic, religions and the 5 percent who are Christians live in the south. Black minorities in the south, culturally distinctive from the Arabs in the north, press for greater recognition and regional improvement, often in the form of antigovernment guerrilla action. The southern ethnic problems are compounded by the influx of refugees as a result of unrest in Ethiopia and Uganda.

The economy is essentially agricultural and based upon Nile River irrigation water. Cotton is an important export crop. Roads lead from Khartoum to regional cities, and Port Sudan on the Red Sea handles the nation's import-export trade.

Although there are museums and an interesting zoo in Khartoum, Sudan has little to offer the tourist.

LIBYA

Official Name: Socialist People's Libyan Arab Jamahiriya

Language: Arabic, English, Italian

Area: 679,359 square miles

Time Zone: GMT +1

National Airline: Libyan Arab

Capital: Tripoli

Currency: Libyan dinar (LBD)

Population: 4,350,000

Documentation: Off limits to United States tourists

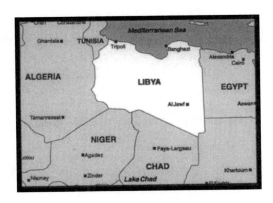

Although larger than Egypt, its eastern neighbor, Libya has only 3 million people living in a narrow zone along the Mediterranean coast. The driest part of the Sahara Desert dominates the rest of the territory. Since the 1960s, Libya has been oil rich; oil from interior fields moves by pipeline to the coast for export. Three-fourths of the Arab-Moslem population live in and around Tripoli, the capital, on the northwestern coast. Benghazi, on the northeastern coast, is the second largest city. In these and smaller cities, modern facilities have been provided with oil revenues. Agriculture remains locally important.

Long under Turkish control, Libya became an Italian colony in 1912, was administered briefly by France and Great Britain after World War II, then gained independence under a hereditary kingship in 1952. A revolutionary Socialist government took over in 1969. Non-Communist, Libya had cordial political ties with, and bought advanced military equipment from, the former Soviet Union. The Libyan leadership has been a turbulent force internationally—it has had unfriendly relations with Egypt and Chad, and has meddled in Uganda, Lebanon, and various unstable situations within the Islamic world. It is strongly anti-Israel and anti-United States of America.

The United States does not have direct diplomatic relations with Libya and has asked its citizens to avoid the country. Some Western petroleum industry personnel do travel in the area.

■ MOROCCO, ALGERIA, AND TUNISIA— AN OVERVIEW

The Land

West of Libya are three North African nations—Morocco, Algeria, and Tunisia—known collectively as the Maghreb, the western anchor of the Arab world. As with Egypt and Libya, their interiors are dominated by the desert wastes of the Sahara. However, in their northern portion, the high Atlas Mountains extend in an arc roughly parallel to the Mediterranean coast. Between the mountains and the seacoast are well-watered plains that support agriculture and contain most of the region's population.

History

These nations were once called the Barbary States, a name derived from their pre-Arab inhabitants, the Berbers, who still retain their ancient language and distinctive customs and live in and around the Atlas Mountains. The 19th century brought colonial control from France and, in several coastal locations, Spain. More than one million French settlers moved into the colonies, especially Algeria, where they stimulated the growth of coastal cities, commercial agriculture, roads, and railways. As a result, the three nations have a more substantial European stamp and orientation than most other Arab nations. Predominantly Arab and Islamic, they operate under different economic and political systems.

MOROCCO

Official Name: Kingdom of Morocco

Language: Arabic, Berber, French, Spanish

Area: 172,413 square miles

Time Zone: GMT

National Airline: Royal Air Maroc

Capital: Rabat

Currency: Dirham (MDH)

Population: 26,181,000

Documentation: Passport

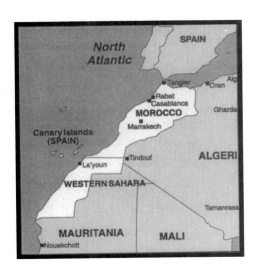

Morocco faces seaward in two directions—westward on the Atlantic Ocean and northward on the Mediterranean Sea—around a prominent peninsula that juts northward to form the African flank of the Strait of Gibraltar. Most of its people are found in habitable plains in the northwest, whereas the desert south and northeast have few inhabitants. The population is composed of an Arab majority, about two-thirds of the total, and a Berber minority, the latter concentrated in the interior mountains. Both groups are Islamic.

There is a thriving urban life: Casablanca, on the northwestern coast, has more than 1 million people; farther northeast along the coast, Rabat, the capital, has 500,000; Marrakesh and Fez are leading interior cities; and the formerly internationalized city of Tangier has shipping links with Gibraltar on the opposite side of the Strait of Gibraltar.

After Morocco became independent in 1956, it gained Ifni and Spanish Sahara (now known as Western Sahara), two adjacent Spanish colonial holdings. However, the two Mediterranean port cities of Ceuta and Melilla remain under Spanish control. A monarchy, Morocco is politically conservative. It has received American military and economic aid, and is both Western- and Arab-world oriented. It has tense, unfriendly relations with Algeria. In Western Sahara, on the south Atlantic coast, it must contend with a sporadic Algerian-supplied guerrilla movement that has independence as its goal.

The national economy includes a thriving commercial agriculture with exports of food (wheat, oranges) to Western Europe. Mineral products, especially iron ore and phosphates used in chemical fertilizer, are also exported in quantity. In fact, Morocco is the world's largest exporter of phosphates. As in other Maghreb nations, per capita income remains low.

Areas of Touristic Importance. Morocco is a land of contrasts—in development, in architecture, and in nature. Major cities like Rabat and Casablanca are modern and bustling, whereas old ways of life continue in Fez and Marrakesh. Inland farmers till the soil with their camels as they have done for centuries. Skyscrapers contrast with the minarets of ancient mosques. The fertile Mediterranean lowlands, hilly Er Rif, and the snowcapped Atlas Mountains offer the visitor widely differing sights.

Casablanca, served by Morocco's prime international airport, is the industrial and commercial center. Differing perspectives can be gained by visiting the Sacre Coeur Cathedral, the modern Notre Dame de Lourdes with stained-

Casbah, Morocco
Photo: Courtesy Moroccan National Tourist Office

glass windows and walls, and the Grand Mosque and Royal Palace. Many fine beaches can be found along the coast, north of the city.

Rabat, although a modern capital, was, along with Fez, Marrakesh, and Meknes, one of the four imperial cities of Moroccan dynasties. The ancient walls and gateways remain. Visit the Royal Palace, still the residence of the king.

Tangier is the European gateway to Morocco, with ferry service across the Strait of Gibraltar. It was an international city from 1920 to 1956. A must for visitors is the Sultan's Palace in the Casbah. Nearby beaches attract visitors from all over the world.

Fez, south of Tangier, is the oldest city in Morocco and served as its capital from the 8th to the 14th centuries. It was the intellectual center of Islam. The Medina contains some interesting souks (marketplaces), monuments, and alleyways.

Marrakesh, an oasis city, serves as the gateway to the Sahara. It is famous for its perfect twilight and red-ochre color. Snows in the nearby Atlas Mountains make this colorful city popular as a winter resort.

The souk is characteristic of almost all Moslem lands, but the finest are in Morocco and North Africa. Colorful native crafts, clothing, and foodstuffs are sold at individual stalls throughout the market area. Goods and sellers can change daily. Buyers are expected to bargain; the price first asked is not the price one should pay.

ALGERIA

Official Name: Democratic and Popular Republic of Algeria

Language: Arabic, French

Area: 918,497 square miles

Time Zone: GMT +1

Capital: Algiers

Currency: Algerian dinar (ALD)

Population: 26,022,000

Documentation: Passport, visa

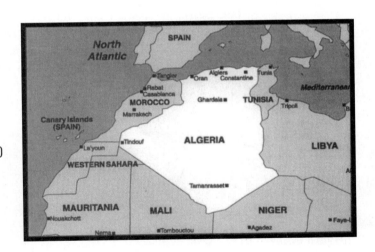

Algeria is by far the largest North African nation facing on the Mediterranean Sea, but more than three-fourths of it lies in the Sahara Desert. Its population is slightly smaller than that of Morocco; Islam is the prevailing religion; and Arabs form the majority (three-fourths) and Berbers the minority (one-fourth).

Algeria attracted most of the French settlers who moved into North Africa during the colonial period. An independence movement after World War II precipitated a bitter armed struggle between the French army and Algerian guerrilla forces that lasted from 1954 to 1962. The achievement of independence of 1962 saw the flight to France of most of the French-descended population, putting the economy in chaos. Bitter feelings toward France, the installation of a revolutionary Socialist government, and military and economic aid from the Soviet Union resulted. Relations with Morocco have remained unfriendly. Algeria is among the more radical Arab nations.

Algeria has the good fortune to have a substantial income from oil fields opened in the Sahara south of the Atlas Mountains. Oil moves to coastal ports by pipeline. Oil revenues are badly needed to bolster the sagging agriculture, which produces such exports as wine, citrus, and dates; to expand the mining of iron ore, phosphates, and other metallic ores for export; and to stimulate some manufacturing. Living standards remain low.

Cities have grown rapidly since independence, in part because of rural-urban migration. Algiers, the capital and port, has more than 2 million inhabitants; Oran is another major port; and Constantine and Annaba are smaller coastal centers.

Areas of Touristic Importance. Algiers is the most visited of Algerian cities. It is home of the infamous Casbah where Barbary pirates sold their loot. Many museums offer glimpses of the past.

Constantine, west of Algiers, is filled with history dating to Biblical times. A deep moat surrounds the city. The Palace of Almond Bey once housed a harem of 300 women.

TUNISIA

Official Name: Republic of Tunisia

Language: Arabic, French

Area: 63,170 square miles

Time Zone: GMT +1

Capital: Tunis

Currency: Tunisian dinar (TUD)

Population: 8,276,000

Documentation: Passport

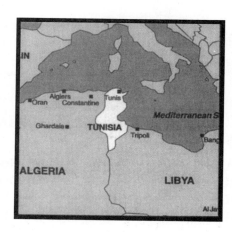

Tunisia had a glorious past as the site of ancient Carthage and as the granary of the Roman Empire, but later fell under Turkish, then French, control. Independent in 1956, it adopted a parliamentary-type government headed by a president. Although ardently Arab and Islamic, it has one of the more moderate political stances in the Arab world.

One million of the nearly 7 million population live in Tunis, the capital. Other important regional cities include Sfax, Sousse, and Bizerte. Tunisia is relatively poor and lacks the large-scale natural resources of its Maghreb neighbors. It has some agriculture (olive oil) and small mining product exports.

Areas of Touristic Importance. Tunis, with its broad boulevards and good restaurants, is a most comfortable city. The ruins of Carthage and its Roman conquerers are a prime attraction. The museums and remains of temples and public buildings remind visitors that this was once the world's richest city.

Huge flocks of flamingos can be seen in the Lake of Tunis and the Lake of Rades. The nearby village of Sidi Bon Said with its bright homes with iron balconies and sky-blue doors have made it a gathering place for artists.

The perfect climate on the Mediterranean coast makes Tunisia ideal for sun and fun vacationing.

■ TYPES OF TOURISM

The types of tours and travel throughout the Mideast region vary greatly with the specific country or grouping of countries. Few westerners, if any, visit Afghanistan, Iran, Iraq, Lebanon, Syria, Yemen, Libya, and Sudan—primarily because of political and/or safety problems. Travel to Algeria and Tunisia is also somewhat limited.

Travel to the Arabian Peninsula is generally limited to Moslem pilgrimages and business travel associated with the oil and construction industries.

Turkey is visited as an independent destination, although visitors often combine it with visits to Greece and other European nations. Turkey is also part of many Greek Island cruises, especially 1-week cruises. It is also visited on many Mediterranean cruises.

Israel is often a destination in itself, with many independent (for example fly/drive), hosted, and escorted tours. Many programs are designed specifically for Jewish or Christian travelers. Israel is also included with Egypt on tour programs, sometimes combined with European destinations, and is a stop on Mediterranean cruises.

Egypt is most often a destination in itself. Although independent travel is possible, most Americans visit the country on a hosted or escorted tour. Egypt is also sometimes combined with Israel or Europe and is a Mediterranean cruise destination.

Morocco, because of its proximity to Spain, is often on the itineraries of Iberian tour programs. It is also a single country destination.

The following tour itineraries give a picture of tourism in the region:

- Egyptian Splendor
- Grand Tour of Israel and Sinai
- Treasures of Turkey
- Spain, Morocco and Portugal

GLOBUS. *First Class*   ESCORTED

Egyptian Splendor

Mediterranean Sea

Giza Cairo
Sakkara
Memphis

Nile

Valley
of Kings Karnak
Luxor
Esna
Edfu

EGYPT

Kom Ombo

Aswan
Philae

High Dam

Abu Simbel (optional) Lake Nasser

Tour QE
— 10 days incl.air,
or 9 days Cairo/Cairo

ALL THIS IS INCLUDED

- Scheduled transatlantic flights and airport transfers in Cairo if Globus issues the tickets; see page 19
- Services of a licensed Egyptian guide
- Hotels listed below or equivalent; see page 13. Twin-bedded rooms with private bath or shower, hotel taxes, service charges and tips for baggage handling
- Nile cruise accommodation in luxury two-berth outside cabins with private facilities on one of the great Hilton, Oberoi or Sheraton hotel boats; all shore excursions are included
- Flights Cairo-Aswan and Luxor-Cairo, including airport transfers

- Welcome drink; 4 buffet breakfasts (BB); 4 full breakfasts (FB); 5 dinners (D); 4 lunches (L)
- Transportation on land by private deluxe air-conditioned motorcoach
- Complete sightseeing program: Cairo, the Pyramids, Aswan, Philae, Kom Ombo, Edfu, Esna, Valley of Kings and Valley of Queens, Luxor, Karnak
- Inside visits as shown in UPPER CASE in the tour description, including admission charges where applicable
- Globus travel bag and travel documents

Day 1, Fri. BOARD YOUR OVERNIGHT TRANSATLANTIC FLIGHT.

Day 2, Sat. ARRIVAL IN CAIRO, EGYPT. Settle into your hotel and start soaking up the atmosphere of this exciting city. At 7 p.m. meet your traveling companions at a welcome drink with your Egyptian guide.

▼ *THE ALABASTER SPHINX AT MEMPHIS*

Day 3, Sun. CAIRO AND THE PYRAMIDS. All-day sightseeing in and around Africa's largest metropolis starts at the EGYPTIAN MUSEUM with Tutankhamon's fabulous treasures, an exciting first encounter with the splendor of 3 millennia of Egyptian civilization. Then leave for ancient MEMPHIS to admire the 40-ft. statue of Ramses II and the Alabaster Sphinx. On to SAKARA'S "stairway to the sky", the oldest of all Pyramids. Finally, at GIZA, a close-up look at the enigmatic SPHINX and the daunting Great Pyramids. Cheops, with an original height of 756 ft., is the most colossal ever built. A suggestion for tonight: return to Giza to enjoy the optional Sound and Light show. (BB)

Day 4, Mon. CAIRO-ASWAN. Time this morning for independent activities or to join an optional excursion to walled Old Cairo. Saladin's 12th-century Citadel, the Alabaster Mosque and the labyrinthine bazaar are well worth a visit. In the afternoon fly 500 miles up the Nile Valley to the lovely resort town of Aswan. (BB,D)

164 US

Day 5, Tue. IN ASWAN. BOARD HOTEL BOAT. A special treat today: board a felucca and sail right across the blue waters of the river. En route see the ancient "nilometer" on Elephantine Island, Kitchener Island's lush BOTANICAL GARDENS, and the splendid AGA KHAN MAUSOLEUM on the left bank. Board your elegant hotel boat in time for lunch. During your stay in Aswan you should take advantage of the opportunity (weather permitting; approximately US$130) to join an optional flight to the huge sandstone temples of Abu Simbel. (BB,L,D)

Day 6, Wed. CRUISING: ASWAN, KOM OMBO. Morning excursion to the turn-of-the-century Old Dam, to this day the widest dam in the world, and the gigantic Aswan High Dam completed in 1970. Board a motor launch to the island of Agilka between the two dams and visit the TEMPLE OF ISIS transplanted from the submerged island of Philae. Also stop at the ancient GRANITE QUARRIES to see the famous unfinished obelisk. In the afternoon start your leisurely cruise down Egypt's river of destiny. Dock at KOM OMBO for a short walk to its bluff-top temple dedicated to the crocodile and falcon gods. Time to haggle for bargains in the local market before returning to the boat. (FB,L,D)

Day 7, Thu. CRUISING: EDFU, ESNA. Board a horse-drawn carriage for the drive through Edfu to the TEMPLE OF HORUS with its menacing black stone statue of the falcon god. Built in the time of Cleopatra about 2,000 years ago, it is recent by Old Egyptian standards, and beautifully preserved. During the hot part of the day sip a drink on the sun deck of your cruise boat and savor the panorama. See white clad farmers with their donkeys, camels and water buffaloes work their lush green fields; and ever present on the horizon, beyond the palm trees, the desert. Late afternoon visit to Esna's colorful market and the "SUNKEN TEMPLE" devoted to the ram-headed deity Khnum. (FB,L,D)

Day 8, Fri. CRUISING: LUXOR. Focus on the VALLEY OF KINGS and VALLEY OF QUEENS on the west bank of the Nile, where generations of pharaohs and nobles were buried in great splendor in crypts cut into the cliffs. 62 royal tombs have so far been uncovered, of which one, the tomb of Tutankhamon, was nearly inviolate when discovered in 1922. Visit DEIR EL-BAHARI, Queen Hatshepsut's monumental rock temple. Also stop for pictures at the two COLOSSI OF MEMNON guarding the valleys. After dinner tonight you may want to take in the optional Sound and Light show at Karnak. (FB,L,D)

Day 9, Sat. LUXOR-CAIRO. A grand finale to your sightseeing in the Nile Valley. See the stunning monuments of LUXOR and KARNAK, the greatest cities of ancient Egypt with, in their heyday, a combined population of more than one million. To walk among the pillars of the colossal TEMPLE OF AMON RA and along the AVENUE OF THE SPHINXES is an experience which you will treasure for the rest of your life. In the afternoon fly from Luxor back to Cairo. (FB)

Day 10, Sun. HOMEBOUND FLIGHT. (BB)

➤ *All arrangements in Egypt are under the management of the official Government Tourist Organization Misr Travel. As traffic conditions and the water level of the Nile are not always predictable, slight changes to the day-by-day itinerary cannot be excluded.*

➤ *We recommend that you plan to spend about US$20 per person for gratuities to service personnel of the Nile cruise ship.*

Reprinted courtesy of Globus and Cosmos.

▲ FELUCCAS ON THE NILE NEAR ASWAN

▼ WALK AMONG THE COLOSSAL PILLARS OF KARNAK

▲ LUXOR'S AVENUE OF THE SPHINXES

▼ INSCRUTABLE FACES OF EGYPT

Tour QE: DATES & PRICES

Tour code	Leave USA or join Cairo next day		Return to USA or end Cairo		10 days USA/ USA US$	9 days Cairo/ Cairo US$
QE0108	Fri	07-Jan	Sun	16-Jan	2360	1164
QE0115	Fri	14-Jan	Sun	23-Jan	2263	1164
QE0122	Fri	21-Jan	Sun	30-Jan	2263	1164
QE0129	Fri	28-Jan	Sun	06-Feb	2263	1164
QE0205	Fri	04-Feb	Sun	13-Feb	2263	1164
QE0212	Fri	11-Feb	Sun	20-Feb	2263	1164
QE0219	Fri	18-Feb	Sun	27-Feb	2263	1164
QE0226	Fri	25-Feb	Sun	06-Mar	2263	1164
QE0305	Fri	04-Mar	Sun	13-Mar	2263	1164
QE0312	Fri	11-Mar	Sun	20-Mar	2263	1164
QE0319	Fri	18-Mar	Sun	27-Mar	2263	1164
QE0326	Fri	25-Mar	Sun	03-Apr	2398	1299
QE0402	Fri	01-Apr	Sun	10-Apr	2503	1216
QE0409	Fri	08-Apr	Sun	17-Apr	2451	1164
QE0416	Fri	15-Apr	Sun	24-Apr	2451	1164
QE0423	Fri	22-Apr	Sun	01-May	2451	1164
QE0430	Fri	29-Apr	Sun	08-May	2451	1164
QE0507	Fri	06-May	Sun	15-May	2243	956
QE0514	Fri	13-May	Sun	22-May	2243	956
QE0521	Fri	20-May	Sun	29-May	2335	956
QE0528	Fri	27-May	Sun	05-Jun	2335	956
QE0604	Fri	03-Jun	Sun	12-Jun	2335	956
QE0611	Fri	10-Jun	Sun	19-Jun	2335	956
QE0618	Fri	17-Jun	Sun	26-Jun	2335	956
QE0625	Fri	24-Jun	Sun	03-Jul	2335	956
QE0702	Fri	01-Jul	Sun	10-Jul	2335	956
QE0709	Fri	08-Jul	Sun	17-Jul	2335	956
QE0716	Fri	15-Jul	Sun	24-Jul	2335	956
QE0723	Fri	22-Jul	Sun	31-Jul	2335	956
QE0730	Fri	29-Jul	Sun	07-Aug	2335	956
QE0806	Fri	05-Aug	Sun	14-Aug	2335	956
QE0813	Fri	12-Aug	Sun	21-Aug	2335	956
QE0820	Fri	19-Aug	Sun	28-Aug	2335	956
QE0827	Fri	26-Aug	Sun	04-Sep	2335	956
QE0903	Fri	02-Sep	Sun	11-Sep	2335	956
QE0910	Fri	09-Sep	Sun	18-Sep	2335	956
QE0917	Fri	16-Sep	Sun	25-Sep	2335	956
QE0924	Fri	23-Sep	Sun	02-Oct	2335	956
QE1001	Fri	30-Sep	Sun	09-Oct	2582	1203
QE1008	Fri	07-Oct	Sun	16-Oct	2490	1203
QE1015	Fri	14-Oct	Sun	23-Oct	2490	1203
QE1022	Fri	21-Oct	Sun	30-Oct	2490	1203
QE1029	Fri	28-Oct	Sun	06-Nov	2490	1203
QE1105	Fri	04-Nov	Sun	13-Nov	2302	1203
QE1112	Fri	11-Nov	Sun	20-Nov	2302	1203
QE1119	Fri	18-Nov	Sun	27-Nov	2302	1203
QE1126	Fri	25-Nov	Sun	04-Dec	2302	1203
QE1203	Fri	02-Dec	Sun	11-Dec	2302	1203
QE1210	Fri	09-Dec	Sun	18-Dec	2399	1203
QE1217	Fri	16-Dec	Sun	25-Dec	2544	1348
QE1224	Fri	23-Dec	Sun	01-Jan	2544	1348
QE1231	Fri	30-Dec	Sun	08-Jan	2472	1276
				1995		
QE0107	Fri	06-Jan	Sun	15-Jan	2399	1203
QE0114	Fri	13-Jan	Sun	22-Jan	2302	1203
QE0121	Fri	20-Jan	Sun	29-Jan	2302	1203
QE0128	Fri	27-Jan	Sun	05-Feb	2302	1203
QE0204	Fri	03-Feb	Sun	12-Feb	2302	1203
QE0211	Fri	10-Feb	Sun	19-Feb	2302	1203
QE0218	Fri	17-Feb	Sun	26-Feb	2302	1203
QE0225	Fri	24-Feb	Sun	05-Mar	2302	1203
QE0304	Fri	03-Mar	Sun	12-Mar	2302	1203
QE0311	Fri	10-Mar	Sun	19-Mar	2302	1203
QE0318	Fri	17-Mar	Sun	26-Mar	2302	1203

For any air fare supplement from your departure city, see list 5 on page 21.

Supplement for single room on land and single occupancy of cabin on cruise: $278 (QE0507-0924); $373 (QE0108-0430) and (QE1001-0318)

Triple rooms and cabins are not available.

1995 departures are subject to itinerary and price modification. Details will be available in Nov.'94.

GLOBUS HOTELS

CAIRO Cairo Ramses Hilton (SF=Superior First), **ASWAN** Oberoi Aswan (SF)

GRAND TOUR OF ISRAEL & SINAI

15 DAYS

VISITING: TEL AVIV, JAFFA, CAESAREA, NAZARETH, GALILEE, HAIFA, GOLAN HEIGHTS, DEAD SEA, MASADA, ST. CATHERINE'S, MOUNT SINAI, EILAT, JERUSALEM, BETHLEHEM, QUMRAN

EXTRA LEISURE

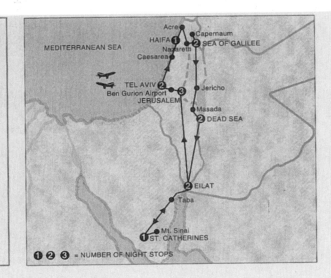

① ② ③ = NUMBER OF NIGHT STOPS

INSIGHT HOTELS

All Insight hotels are first class or better and mainly centrally located. The Insight Money-Back Guarantee applies to the following cities on this itinerary - **Jerusalem and Tel Aviv.** See page 6 for details

YOUR TOUR INCLUDES

- Centrally located hotels guarantee (see pages 6/7)
- Deluxe, air conditioned coach
- Services of a professional multi-lingual Tour Manager
- Included highlights - extensive sightseeing, guided tours, scenic drives and visits to special attractions all included in the price. Refer to our highlights list.
- 13 Breakfasts, 1 Lunch and 8 Dinners including local speciality dishes and 1 Highlight Evening of Dinner and Entertainment
- Hotel taxes and porterage
- Elegant travel bag, wallet and information pack
- A transfer on arrival in Tel Aviv and on departure from Jerusalem between the airport and your tour hotel

FEATURING 2 OR 3 NIGHTS IN

■ Tel Aviv ■ Galilee ■ Dead Sea
■ Eilat ■ Jerusalem

Save 5% Early Payment Discount

(see page 11)

18

DAY 1 - DEPART USA. Overnight flight to Tel Aviv.

DAY 2 - ARRIVE TEL AVIV. After arriving at Ben Gurion Airport, you are met and **transferred to your Tel Aviv hotel.** Our tour gets off to a grand start this evening with *'Welcome to Israel'* drinks and dinner. (D)

DAY 3 - TEL AVIV - JAFFA EXCURSION. Today our sightseeing is focused on the highlights of this lively city, including the *Museum of the Diaspora* - which chronicles the history of Jewish people outside Israel. Later we visit the 5,000 year old port of *Jaffa,* where our guided walk takes us through the colorful artists' quarter. (BB)

DAY 4 - TEL AVIV - CAESAREA - HAIFA. Today we visit *Caesarea* where we see the Roman ruins and amphitheater. From here we go on to *Haifa,* enjoying the panoramic view from Mount Carmel before touring the sights of the city, including the *Bahai Temple* with its great golden dome. (BB,D)

DAY 5 - HAIFA - ACRE - NAZARETH - GALILEE. From Haifa we drive to ancient *Acre* with its harbor, fortress and Crusader crypt. During our tour of the town, we walk through the busy market to the modern marina, before continuing to *Nazareth* where we visit the *Church of the Annunciation.* Tonight we stay in Tiberias on the Shores of the *Sea of Galilee.* (BB,D)

DAY 6 - GALILEE - GOLAN HEIGHTS - CAPERNAUM AND KIBBUTZ EXCURSION. This morning we climb to the *Golan Heights* and see *Mount Hermon,* Israel's only ski resort. Then we stop for a swim near *Banias,* one of the sources of the river Jordan, continuing afterwards to the 'Good Fence', the northernmost point of Israel. We also see the *Nimrod Fortress,* a fine Crusader castle. From here we drive to Capernaum to visit the ancient synagogue, center of Christ's ministry, before visiting the *Mount of Beatitudes,* where Jesus preached his Sermon on the Mount. We end the day by visiting a Kibbutz. (BB)

DAY 7 - GALILEE - MASADA - DEAD SEA. Today we travel south towards the *Dead Sea.* On our route through the Jordan Valley we stop at the ruins of *Jericho,* the oldest known city in the world. We continue to *Masada,* where we ascend by cable car to this awe- inspiring fortress, defended by Jewish zealots against the Roman Legions for three years around 70 AD. We continue now to the *Dead Sea,* where we can have a dip tonight in its buoyant waters. (BB,D)

DAY 8 - DEAD SEA - LAHAV - QUMRAN EXCURSION. Our morning starts with a visit to a *Bedouin market* at Beersheba, where we have a chance to see and maybe buy the works of local craftsmen. Then we go to *Lahav* to visit the *Bedouin Folk Museum,* followed by a stop for coffee in a Bedouin tent. On our way back, we pass the caves at *Qumran*

Drive through the spectacular Sinai Desert (Day 9)

CHOOSE INSIGHT

Reprinted courtesy of Insight International Tours.

The magnificent Western Wall (Day 13)

Visit the remote Monastery of St. Catherine's (Day 10)

where the Dead Sea Scrolls were discovered. (BB,D)

DAY 9 - DEAD SEA - ST. CATHERINE'S (EGYPT). We start early this morning for our drive south across the Egyptian border into *Sinai* and down to *St. Catherine's* village, built in the local style. Here we spend the night. (BB,D)

DAY 10 - ST. CATHERINE'S - MOUNT SINAI - EILAT. Unless we prefer to stay in bed, we are called at 2 am for the 3-hour ascent to the summit of *Mt. Sinai*. Those joining the climb will be rewarded by an unforgettable view and the cave where Moses is believed to have hidden himself after coming face to face with God. We descend for breakfast and a visit to the famous *Monastery of St. Catherine* before departing for Eilat. (BB,D)

DAY 11 - EILAT AT LEISURE. A day to relax and enjoy the facilities of Israel's premier seaside resort. You can bask on the sands - or if you feel more adventurous you can scuba dive over the coral reef, water ski, or even parasail behind a speedboat. (BB)

DAY 12 - EILAT - BETHLEHEM - JERUSALEM. We drive north today through the Negev Desert to *Jerusalem*, via the 'little town of *Bethlehem*' where we visit *Manger Square* and the *Church of the Nativity*. Approaching Jerusalem, one of the world's most beautiful cities, our first breathtaking view is from *Mount Scopus*. Tonight, enjoy a *Highlight Dinner with Entertainment*. (BB,D)

DAY 13 - JERUSALEM - SIGHTSEEING. Our sightseeing today includes *King David's tomb* on Mt. Zion, the Room of the Last

Supper and the *Western Wall*, Judaism's most sacred monument. Next we tour the *Holocaust Museum* and visit the *Shrine of the Book*, home of the *Dead Sea Scrolls*, before seeing Chagall's celebrated stained glass windows. (BB)

DAY 14 - JERUSALEM - SIGHTSEEING. After visiting the *Garden of Gethsemene*, we walk along the cobbled ways of the Old City to the *Dome of the Rock* and *El Aqsa Mosque*, before following in the footsteps of Jesus along the *Via Dolorosa*, with its Stations of the Cross, to the Church of the Holy Sepulchre - purported to be the site of Calvary. Later, time to explore Jerusalem's bustling bazaars. (BB)

DAY 15 - RETURN TO USA. Your tour ends today after breakfast. You will be **transferred to Ben Gurion airport** for your onward flight - or perhaps you'd like to join another Insight tour? For extra nights in Jerusalem, see page 13. (BB)

MORE INCLUDED HIGHLIGHTS IN YOUR TOUR PRICE

◆ **Highlight Evening of Dinner and Entertainment**
◆ **Full sightseeing tours by professionally qualified local guides in** • Tel Aviv • Jaffa • Acre • Nazareth • Bethlehem • Jerusalem
◆ **Orientation tours in** • Caesarea • Haifa

    All these attractions, including entrance fees for inside visits

ISRAEL
• Welcome Drinks and Dinner, Tel Aviv • *Highlight Evening of Dinner and Entertainment, Jerusalem* • Visit Tel Aviv's Diaspora museum • Visit the Dome of the Rock • See Chagall's magnificent windows • Ascend Masada by cable car and view the excavations • Visit the Bedouin museum and drink coffee in a Bedouin tent • Tour the Roman remains at Caesarea • See the excavations of ancient Jericho • See the Shrine of the Book, home of the Dead Sea Scrolls • Visit the Holocaust Museum • Visit the Garden Tomb • Visit old Jaffa's artist colony • Visit the Western Wall • Walk along Via Dolorosa • Visit the Church of the Holy Sepulchre • Tour the Golan Heights • Visit to a Kibbutz • Visit the Mount of Beatitudes and Capernaum • Visit Manger Square and the Church of Nativity, Bethlehem • Float in the Dead Sea • Visit the Church of the Annunciation, Nazareth • Visit the Crusader port of Acre • Visit the Garden of Gethsemene • Visit King David's tomb, Room of the Last Supper • Panoramic view of Mount of Olives • Drive along the Jordan Valley

EGYPT
• Visit St. Catherine's Monastery • Ascend Mount Sinai with Bedouin guide • See crusader fortress • Magnificent Sinai Desert drive

Relax in Eilat (Day 11)

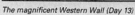

TREASURES OF TURKEY

11 DAYS

VISITING: ISTANBUL, ANKARA, CAPPADOCIA, KONYA, PAMUKKALE, KUSADASI, EPHESUS, TROY, PERGAMON & GALLIPOLI

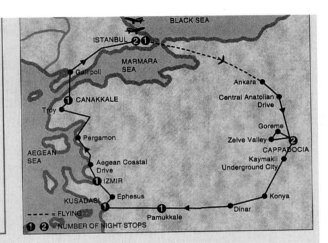

INSIGHT HOTELS

 All Insight hotels are first class or better and mainly centrally located. The Insight Money-Back Guarantee applies to the following city on this itinerary - **Istanbul**. See page 6 for details.

YOUR TOUR INCLUDES

- Centrally located hotels guarantee (see pages 6/7)
- Deluxe, air conditioned coach
- Economy airfare Istanbul - Ankara
- Services of a professional multi-lingual Tour Manager
- Included Highlights - extensive sightseeing, guided tours, scenic drives and visits to special attractions all included in the price. Refer to our highlights list
- 9 Breakfasts, 7 Dinners - including local speciality dishes and 1 Highlight Evening of Dinner and Entertainment
- Hotel taxes and porterage
- Elegant travel bag, wallet and information pack
- A transfer on arrival and departure in Istanbul between the airport and your tour hotel

FEATURING 2 OR 3 NIGHTS IN

- Cappadocia ■ Istanbul

GRAND TOUR OF GREECE & TURKEY

Combine the Glories of Greece and Treasures of Turkey. Take the Glories of Greece, then fly to Istanbul on Day 8 to join the Treasures of Turkey on Day 2. See price panel.

DAY 1 (FRI) - DEPART USA. Overnight flight to Istanbul.

DAY 2 (SAT) - ARRIVE ISTANBUL. Transfer to your hotel. *Welcome drinks* tonight.

DAY 3 (SUN) - ISTANBUL - ANKARA - CAPPODOCIA. We fly to Ankara to visit the *Hittite Museum* and Ataturk's mausoleum. On to the caravanserai of *Agzikara Han* and the citadel of *Uchisar*. (BB,D)

DAY 4 (MON) - CAPPADOCIA - EXCURSION TO GOREME. Tour the unique landscape in the valleys of *Goreme* and *Zelve*. Then we tour the tunnels of *Kaymakli* underground city. Tonight a special dinner and *Turkish show*. (BB,D)

DAY 5 (TUE) - CAPPADOCIA - KONYA - DINAR - PAMUKKALE. We start with a visit to *Konya*, center of the mysterious Whirling Dervishes. Next the *tomb* of the mystic *Mevlana*, then to Pamukkale. (BB,D)

DAY 6 (WED) - PAMUKKALE - KUSADASI. The white terraces of *Pamukkale* and a visit to

ruined *Hieropolis*. Finally to *Kusadasi*. (BB,D)

DAY 7 (THU) - KUSADASI - EPHESUS - IZMIR. We visit the last home of the Virgin Mary and the *archaeological museum*. We continue to Ephesus and then to the port of Izmir. (BB,D)

DAY 8 (FRI) - IZMIR - PERGAMON - TROY - CANAKKALE. A visit to Pergamon's *Asklepeion Hospital* and *Temple of Apollo*, then to ancient Troy to see the *Trojan Horse*. Now to Canakkale. (BB,D)

DAY 9 (SAT) - CANAKKALE - GALLIPOLI - ISTANBUL. Across to the *Gallipoli peninsula* to see *Anzac Cove* and visit *Lone Pine cemetery* of poignant memory. Then to Istanbul. (BB,D)

DAY 10 (SUN) - ISTANBUL SIGHTSEEING. A full day visiting the *Roman aqueduct*, the *Blue Mosque* and Hippodrome. *St. Sophia*, *Topkapi* Palace and finally a *highlight cruise*. (BB)

DAY 11 (MON) - RETURN TO USA. Your tour ends after breakfast and you are *transferred to the airport*. (BB)

MORE INCLUDED HIGHLIGHTS IN YOUR TOUR PRICE

- ◆ Highlight Evening of Dinner and Entertainment
- ◆ Full sightseeing tour by professionally qualified local guides in • Ephesus • Pergamon • Troy • Istanbul
- ◆ Orientation tours in • Ankara • Konya

All these attractions, including entrance fees for inside visits.

- Welcome Drinks • *Turkish show* and Dinner • Visit the Blue Mosque • Bosphorus cruise • Tour Topkapi Palace • Visit the Tomb of Mevlana • Visit Ankara's Hittite Museum and Ataturk's mausoleum • Tour Kaymakli underground city • Tour Ephesus and

Hieropolis • See the 'Trojan Horse' • Visit Asklepeion & Citadel • Visit Lone Pine cemetery Anzac Cove • Visit Pamukkale terraces • Tour Cappadocia • Visit Virgin Mary's House and Archaeological Museum • Visit Agzikara Han caravanserai

COSTS & DEPARTURES

Tour	Starts USA	Ends USA	Land Only	Air & Land
1049/91	Apr 08 '94	Apr 18 '94	$1070	$1770
1049/92	Apr 15 Fri	Apr 25 Mon	$1070	$1770
1049/93	Apr 22 Fri	May 02 Mon	$1070	$1770
1049/94	Apr 29 Fri	May 09 Mon	$1090	$1790
1049/95	May 06 Fri	May 16 Mon	$1090	$1790
1049/96	May 13 Fri	May 23 Mon	$1090	$1790
1049/98	May 27 Fri	Jun 06 Mon	$1090	$1790
1049/99	Jun 03 Fri	Jun 13 Mon	$1090	$1955
1049/01	Jun 10 Fri	Jun 20 Mon	$1090	$1955
1049/03	Jun 24 Fri	Jul 04 Mon	$1090	$1955
1049/04	Jul 01 Fri	Jul 11 Mon	$1090	$1955
1049/05	Jul 08 Fri	Jul 18 Mon	$1090	$1955
1049/07	Jul 22 Fri	Aug 01 Mon	$1090	$1955
1049/09	Aug 05 Fri	Aug 15 Mon	$1090	$1955
1049/11	Aug 19 Fri	Aug 29 Mon	$1090	$1955
1049/13	Sep 02 Fri	Sep 12 Mon	$1090	$1790
1049/14	Sep 09 Fri	Sep 19 Mon	$1090	$1790
1049/15	Sep 16 Fri	Sep 26 Mon	$1090	$1790
1049/16	Sep 23 Fri	Oct 03 Mon	$1090	$1790
1049/17	Sep 30 Fri	Oct 10 Mon	$1090	$1790
1049/18	Oct 07 Fri	Oct 17 Mon	$1090	$1770
1049/19	Oct 14 Fri	Oct 24 Mon	$1090	$1770
1049/20	Oct 21 Fri	Oct 31 Mon	$1070	$1750
1049/21	Oct 28 Fri	Nov 07 Mon	$1070	$1750

SUPPLEMENTS:
Single room supplement $294

Athens - Istanbul, one way flight $213
(Available to passengers taking Grand Tour of Turkey and Greece combination only)

AIR & LAND PRICES

Air & Land prices include economy class transatlantic roundtrip air travel from New York. For supplements from other U.S. gateways, see page 10. Airport and departure taxes, security, agricultural and customs fees are not included.

EXTRA SAVINGS

If you're traveling alone, SAVE $294 by using our twin share program.

FOR FURTHER VALUABLE SAVINGS AND DISCOUNTS SEE PAGE 11

Reprinted courtesy of Insight International Tours.

ESCORTED: 17 DAYS

SPAIN, MOROCCO & PORTUGAL

MADRID, CORDOBA, GRANADA, TORREMOLINOS, TANGIER, FEZ, MARRAKESH, CASABLANCA, RABAT, SEVILLE, LISBON, SALAMANCA

THE TRAFALGAR IBERIAN EXPERIENCE REACHES INTO NORTH AFRICA AND FEATURES MOROCCO'S IMPERIAL CITIES.

PLUS THE BEAUTY OF ANDALUSIA AND VISITS TO MADRID AND LISBON.

THE SHRINE AT FATIMA AND THE ALHAMBRA IN GRANADA ARE ALL INCLUDED.

SALAMANCA • Sierra de Guadarrama
Serra d'Aire Mountains • MADRID [2]
Fatima • Toledo
LISBON [2] • Elvas
Forests of Alentejo
SEVILLE [2] • CORDOBA
Sierra Nevada
GRANADA • Mediterranean Sea
Jerez Vineyards • TORREMOLINOS
Algeciras • Gibraltar
Cape Spartel • TANGIER
Atlantic Ocean • FEZ
RABAT
Casablanca • Atlas Mountains
MARRAKESH [2]

● Overnight stays
[ ] No. of nights

PORTUGUESE FAVOURITE

GRAN HOTEL – SALAMANCA

TRAFALGAR GIVES YOU MORE

SIGHTSEEING EVERY DAY

Toledo Sightseeing including the Gothic Cathedral.
Cordoba Sightseeing tour including the Mosque of the Caliphs.
Granada Sightseeing tour including a visit to the Moorish Alhambra Palace.
Tangier Orientation including the King's Palace.
Fez Sightseeing including a walking tour of the Medina.
Marrakesh Sightseeing tour including the Bahia Palace and Djemma el F'na Square.
Casablanca View El Hank Lighthouse.
Rabat Orientation tour including the Royal Palace, Mausoleum and Royal Mosque.
Gibraltar See the famous Rock.
Seville Sightseeing tour including Columbus' tomb.
Lisbon Sightseeing tour including the Hieronymite Monastery.
Fatima Visit the celebrated religious shrine.
Madrid Sightseeing tour including the Royal Palace.

SCENIC DRIVES ON THE WAY

● The Sierra Nevada Mountains ● The foothills of the Atlas Mountains ● Costa del Sol coastal drive ● Drive to Cape Spartel where the Atlantic and the Mediterranean meet ● North African coastal drive ● The Serra d'Aire Mountains ● Across the Sierra de Guadarrama.

MOSQUE OF THE CALIPHS, CORDOBA

DINING & ENTERTAINMENT

● Welcome drink with your Tour Director in Madrid.
● Buffet breakfast **(BB)** daily.
● 10 three-course dinners **(D)** – see itinerary.

FIRST CLASS HOTELS

● Twin-bedded rooms with private facilities; all service charges, local taxes, baggage handling and hotel tips.

TRAVELLING IN EUROPE

● Touring by luxury air-conditioned coach with reclining seats
● First class ferry crossings between Spain and Morocco
● Madrid Airport transfers.

TRAFALGAR ALSO INCLUDES

● Professional, multi-lingual Tour Director on tour ● Specialised local guides in Toledo, Cordoba, Fez, Granada, Tangier, Marrakesh, Seville, Lisbon and Madrid ● Travel bag and wallet with comprehensive tour documents.

Day 1 Depart USA
Overnight flight to Madrid.

Day 2 Arrive Madrid
Trafalgar greets you and accompanies you to your hotel. Then a chance to unwind and relax before exploring the lively Spanish capital. Stroll through the beautiful parks and gardens before a **welcome drink** with your Tour Director tonight – a chance to get to know your travelling companions. Later, perhaps try the traditional dish of paella in one of the many restaurants lining the Plaza Mayor.

Day 3 Madrid – Cordoba
After breakfast we travel south to **Toledo**, capital of Castile. Included **sightseeing** highlights the Gothic Cathedral. Then to the Andalusian city of Cordoba for dinner and overnight. **(BB D)**

Day 4 Cordoba – Granada
The magnificent 8th century **Mosque of the Caliphs** is included in this morning's **sightseeing tour**. There is time to shop for famed Cordoban leather. Then through Andalusia to Moorish hill-top Granada with spectacular views of the Sierra Nevada Mountains en route. Overnight stay and dinner in your hotel. **(BB D)**

Day 5 Granada – Torremolinos
Our morning **sightseeing tour** visits the exquisite Alhambra Palace, Spain's most beautiful Moorish building and former residence of the Moorish kings. Then on to the centre of the **Costa del Sol** – Torremolinos,

MOROCCO – OVERLOOKING THE OLD CITY OF FEZ

evening, perhaps take a stroll or sample the nightlife of this lively resort. (BB)

Day 6 Torremolinos – Tangier
Excellent start to the day with a Mediterranean coastal drive to Algeciras for the ferry to North Africa. Drive via *Cape Spartel*, where the Atlantic meets the Mediterranean, to a different world in the gateway city of Tangier. You may have time to savour the exotic sights and sounds of the city on a visit to the *Casbah* – a maze of twisted streets and alleys; stalls of spices, beaten brass and famous Moroccan leather. This evening, you have a chance to see Moroccan belly dancing. (BB D)

Day 7 Tangier – Fez
The elaborate King's Palace is included in our morning *orientation tour*. Then continue on a drive to the imperial city of Fez where this afternoon's *sightseeing tour* includes the fascinating labyrinthine Medina. (BB D)

Day 8 Fez – Marrakesh (2)
A breathtaking drive through the foothills of the *Atlas Mountains* to the intriguing city of Marrakesh, North Africa's most popular year-round sun resort. It faces south towards the Sahara and was once the favourite resort of Winston Churchill where he came to relax and paint. (BB D)

Day 9 Marrakesh sightseeing
Morning guided *sightseeing tour* includes the *Bahia Palace* and the vast Djemma el F'na Square with its palm-readers, acrobats, camels, markets and more! Then free time for

bargain hunting in the many colourful souks and bazaars, or perhaps take an excursion to a nearby Berber village in the Ourika Valley. (BB D)

Day 10 Marrakesh – Casablanca – Rabat
North to cosmopolitan Casablanca, scene of Bogart's most magical moments. You'll also find some of North Africa's best beaches and coastline here. Then continue on along the Atlantic to the imperial city of Rabat where our fascinating *orientation tour* includes the Royal Mosque. (BB D)

Day 11 Rabat – Seville (2)
Morning drive to Tangier, then by ferry to Algeciras. Enjoy views of the *Rock of Gibraltar* before a drive through the vineyards of *Jerez*, home of sherry, leading to Andalusia's most beautiful city – Seville for a two-night stay. (BB D)

Day 12 Seville sightseeing
This romantic city was deeply influenced by the Moors, who dwelt in this area for 700 years. Hence the distinctive Moorish architecture of Giralda Tower, included on morning *sightseeing* along with the Palace of Alcazar, the pools and fountains of Maria Luisa Park, Murillo's house and the tomb of Christopher Columbus. Tonight, why not enjoy a fiery flamenco show in one of the many lively night spots? (BB D)

Day 13 Seville – Lisbon (2)
Through the arid country of Estremadura to the Portuguese border, stopping at *Elvas* with its 16th century aqueduct. On to the

capital of Portugal – Lisbon. Why not spend the evening dining on fresh seafood and young wines and listening to haunting Fado melodies along the Bairro Alto? (BB)

Day 14 Lisbon sightseeing
The picturesque medieval quarter and Vasco da Gama's tomb inside the Hieronymite Monastery, as well as spectacular views from the *Belem Tower* are included on morning *sightseeing*. Rest of the day at leisure with time to shop for pottery, cork and fishermen's sweaters in cobbled Rossio Square. Later, perhaps an excursion to Sintra and the casino at Estoril. (BB)

Day 15 Lisbon – Salamanca
Continue through Portugal on a scenic morning drive through the *Serra d'Aire Mountains*, en route to the *Shrine at Fatima*, scene of celebrated religious miracles. Then cross the border back into Spain and continue to Salamanca. (BB D)

Day 16 Salamanca – Madrid
A scenic route past the *Sierra de Guadarrama* back to Madrid for a *sightseeing tour* of the Royal Palace, Puerta del Sol and Cervantes Memorial. This evening, why not try the varied nightlife and one of the many restaurants? (BB)

Day 17 Madrid – USA
Transfer to the airport for our return flight to America. (BB)

SKYBARGAIN fares

The above 'TOUR + AIR' prices are from New York. For details and special low add-on fares from other US cities, see page 25.

AIRPORT TRANSFERS

Transfers on arrival will be provided only for passengers who have booked their flights on a Trafalgar recommended airline and advised Trafalgar of their flight details. Transfers from Madrid airport to your hotel depart at 08.30 and 12.00. Passengers arriving later should make their own way to the hotel. See page 28.

HOTELS ON THIS TOUR

Madrid: Principe Vergara **Cordoba:** Alfaros **Granada:** Corona **Torremolinos:** Melia Costa del Sol **Tangier:** Solazur **Fez:** Merinides **Marrakesh:** Nassim **Rabat:** Safir **Seville:** Ciudad de Sevilla **Lisbon:** VIP Zurique **Salamanca:** Gran Hotel **Madrid:** Principe Vergara

■ **REVIEW—THE MIDDLE EAST
AND NORTH AFRICA**

1. What physical and cultural factors give the Middle East a distinctive regional character?
2. Which Middle Eastern nations have friendly relations with the United States? With the Soviet Union?
3. Where are the main oil fields in the Middle East and North Africa?
4. Which bodies of water are linked by the Suez Canal? What is its importance to tourism?
5. Define OPEC and state its goal.
6. Why and how was Israel created?
7. Why are most Arab nations opposed to Israel?
8. Linguistically and culturally, who are the Turks?
9. Which straits does Turkey control and what is their importance? Where is Mecca and what isits importance?
10. Where is the Aswan Dam and what is its importance?
11. Which areas are of touristic importance in Egypt? Describe their attractions.
12. Where are the major beach and resort areas of the Middle East and North Africa?
13. What countries within the region are having major internal or external problems? How have these problems affected tourism?
14. Why could this region be called the "archeology treasure house" of the world?
15. What would you include in the following specialized tours within the region:
    a. Christian Heritage Tour
    b. Moslem Heritage Tour
    c. Jewish Heritage Tour

12

Sub-Saharan Africa

■ A CHANGING WORLD VIEW

From the standpoint of the more developed nations of the Northern Hemisphere, sub-Saharan Africa is on the periphery of the world's main economic and political currents. As a result, it is widely viewed as primarily a source of energy and industrial raw materials.

However, what were once local African problems have grown to such magnitude that they attract increasing world attention and involvement. The widespread droughts and famines of the past two decades have made headlines around the world. Guerrilla actions and tribal fighting threaten political stability. The general problems of poverty that can be tackled only with concerted international assistance appear to almost defy solution. The few politically stable and economically advanced and prosperous African nations are clear exceptions to the general condition.

Africa is a huge continent containing one-fifth of the world's land surface and close to one-third of its nations. In reality, however, most African populations and nations are found

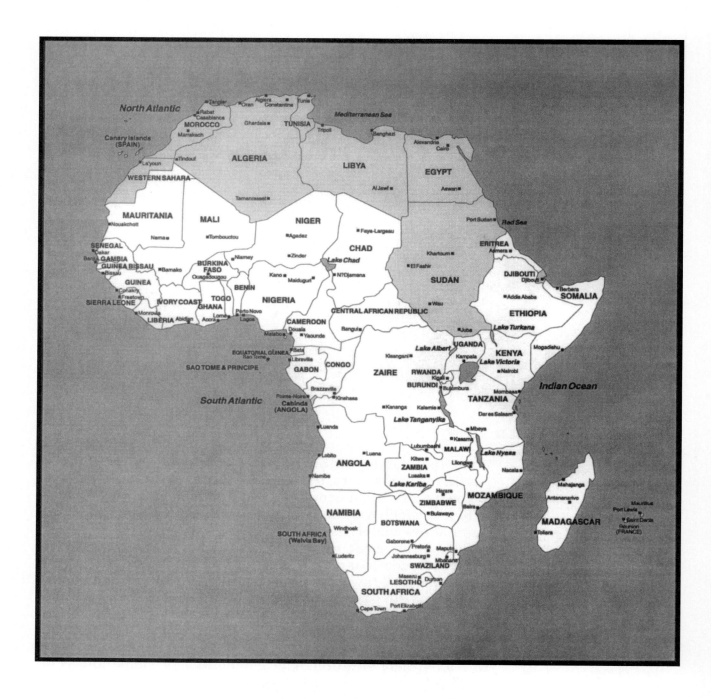

in sub-Saharan Africa, or the three-fourths of the continent south of the Sahara Desert, which extends in a broad east-west band across northern Africa. Most sub-Saharan nations are still young politically, having emerged from colonialism only since the 1950s. They are culturally complex, consisting of the numerous tribal groups that were arbitrarily combined by the colonial powers. Vestiges of European languages, culture, and social systems add to the diversity and problems. Economically, most are typical Third World nations; that is, they are undeveloped, relatively poor with low living standards, low literacy levels, and have severe problems of health and housing.

■ THE LAND

Africa lies astride the Equator, 4,800 miles from north to south. It has a much broader northern half (4,400 miles from east to west) and a narrower southern half (1,800 miles from east to west). Clearly, it is a continent of great distances.

In the north, Africa borders on the Mediterranean Sea. In the northwest it is separated from Spain by the narrow Strait of Gibraltar and, in the northeast, it is linked to the Arabian Peninsula by the small Sinai Peninsula, whose flank is traversed by the manmade Suez Canal. The long, narrow Red Sea separates Africa from the Arabian Peninsula. The African east coast, facing the Indian Ocean, features a prominent horn-like projection in the northeast and, farther south, the large offshore island of Madagascar. The west coast faces the Atlantic Ocean.

One of the most striking aspects of Africa's topography is the absence of great, continuous mountain systems like the Himalayas of Asia, the Andes of South America, or the Rockies of North America. Overall, Africa is an older, worn-down land surface of irregular plateaus, river basins, and smaller mountains. The Atlas Mountains are in the extreme northwest, part of the Mediterranean fringe, and the primary sub-Saharan highlands extend from north to south along the eastern margin of the continent. The crustal instability of the latter is shown in their volcanic peaks and rocks and a series of deep north-south trenches, or rift valleys, that hold Africa's largest lakes—among them Lake Victoria, Lake Tanganyika, and Lake Malawi. The coastal lowlands are narrow because the higher elevations of the interior continue almost to the ocean borders.

River systems, however, are on a grand scale. The Nile flows into the Mediterranean Sea. The Niger describes a great bend northward in western Africa before moving southward to join the Atlantic Ocean. The Zaire (Congo), along with its tributaries, drains much of central Africa and, like the Orange River farther south, flows into the Atlantic. The Zambezi enters the Indian Ocean opposite Madagascar. Sub-Saharan rivers typically have falls and rapids along their courses, limiting their usefulness as transportation to local boat movements.

■ CLIMATE

Climatic conditions make large segments of Africa uninhabitable or only marginally habitable. There is a general problem of either too little water supply or rainfall that is very seasonal and erratic in amount. Climatic conditions can be broadly described as tropical or subtropical in temperature range, but there are sharply different regional and local differences.

At one extreme is the equatorial climate found in a narrow band north and south of the equator, where temperatures remain moderately high, with heavy rainfall and dense forest cover. At the other, drier, extreme are desert conditions, as in the enormous Sahara, the Kalahari of the southwest, and part of the horn of northeast Africa. Semiarid steppes are found on the desert margins.

Between these two extremes, savanna, or tropical grassland, climates prevail. Grasslands have much less rainfall than the equatorial area, and experience a rainy season in summer and a dry season in winter. Seasons are reversed north and south of the Equator. As average rainfall decreases, the vegetation of an area changes from trees and tall grass to short grass and scattered, hardy shrubs.

During the rainy season, the landscape is green, and during the dry season, it is brown. If the dry season is prolonged, or if rains are minimal during the rainy season over several years, severe droughts occur over wide areas, wiping out farms and herds, and killing, weakening, and displacing large numbers of people who are at the mercy of nature. Temperate climate in sub-Saharan Africa is found along the southern and southeastern coastal margin and in eastern and southern mountains and high plateaus, where temperature and rainfall are modified by elevation.

Africa has the most spectacular and varied animal life of any continent, highlighted by the large-hoofed animals—elephants, zebras, rhinoceroses, many varieties of antelope, giraffes, hippopotamuses, buffalo, and others. Once found in great numbers, mainly in the savannas of eastern and southern Africa, the animals are rapidly decreasing in number because of the opening of farmland that limits their habitat, and the grazing competition of domestic cattle. Even in the few large national parks where remaining native animals are protected, poaching by local hunters for ivory, skins, and meat poses a serious threat to their survival.

■ THE PEOPLE AND THEIR LANGUAGES

Predominantly Negroid, the peoples of sub-Saharan Africa are subdivided into a remarkably large number of different ethnic groups, each with its own language, dialect, customs, or identity. As many as 1,000 different languages are spoken. Most are loosely grouped in a broad language family, Niger-Congo, whose variants occur not only in the region around and between those two river systems but in southern Africa as well.

There are several other distinctive language groups. The Khoisan of southwestern Africa includes the Bushmen and Hottentots, two of Africa's oldest peoples. The Malayo-Polynesian languages of Madagascar were presumably introduced there by seafaring migrants from Southeast Asia. The languages of the northeastern horn are linked to those of the Middle East. There are also great variations in the physical build of the population.

■ HISTORY

Little is known of the sub-Saharan past because written records are lacking. Clearly, however, the primary center of cultural development before the 15th century was in the savannas of western Africa. There, empires flourished, trade was carried on with other parts of the continent, and high levels of artistic creativity, especially in the casting of bronze, were achieved.

European interest in Africa was kindled by the historic explorations of the 15th and 16th centuries, when European ships sailed along African shores and around the southern tip, the Cape of Good Hope, to reach the Indian Ocean and the "spice islands" of Southeast Asia. Coastal trading and control points were established along the way. Encouraged by the growing demand for labor in the Americas, especially Brazil and the Caribbean, a widespread slave trade grew to a peak in the 17th and 18th centuries before being terminated in the 19th century. Although estimates vary, it seems that as many as 10 million black Africans were torn from their homes and shipped across the sea in bondage.

Growth of Colonialism

The rise of nationalism in the 19th century brought a mad scramble by European nations to formalize and expand their control over huge chunks of the still unexplored African interior, the dark continent. Little concern was shown for ethnic realities. Colonies lumped diverse tribal groups together or split single groups asunder.

France and Great Britain staked out the largest territory. French holdings were in a massive bloc in western and equatorial Africa, and the island of Madagascar. The British controlled a north-south swath, "Cape to Cairo," the entire length of eastern Africa, and four holdings in western Africa. Portugal gained two large colonies in southern Africa and smaller west coast units. The Belgians had only one large colony, but it encompassed almost the entire Zaire (Congo) River drainage basin in central Africa. Italy had small holdings in the northeast and Spain in the northwest. Four German colonies were lost to France and Great Britain at the end of World War I.

As in other world areas that experienced colonialism, the main European goal was economic exploitation—the development of cash crops and the opening of mines and forest stands for exports. Typically, each colony had one European-founded primary city, the nerve center where administration, commerce, and transportation facilities were concentrated. Links with the more remote "bush" areas were minimal.

A two-tiered culture consisting of European language, legal, educational, and behavioral systems was placed on top of the languages and traditional cultural practices of the local populations. In most instances, a small number of whites administered the colonies. In four colonies, however (present South Africa, Zimbabwe, Kenya, and Angola), large numbers of white immigrants took up permanent residence and carried out white-controlled development. To further intensify the colonial ethnic mix, Indians (both Hindu and Moslem) came as laborers from India and remained permanently in South Africa, Kenya, and Uganda.

Independence and Its Aftermath

After World War II, the collapse of colonialism was dramatic. Within a period of 25 years, most colonies became independent nations. Most have problems resulting from the colonial period. A westernized capital city contrasts vividly, and often is in cultural conflict, with the relatively isolated rural villages that house the predominantly farming population. A raw material export economy has little or no manufacturing and an over-abundance of poor farmers working at or near the subsistence level.

Depressed socioeconomic conditions and friction between tribal groups pose unresolved problems to unstable governments. Health conditions are among the worst in the world. Africa has more than its share of debilitating diseases, such as malaria, and a host of more regional ones, such as river blindness and sleeping sickness. Health care facilities tend to be in limited supply in the main city or larger regional cities; few are found elsewhere where the need is even greater.

Within these generally difficult conditions, however, there are some success stories. Ghana, Cote d'Ivoire, Kenya, and Zimbabwe have achieved some degree of prosperity from agricultural exports. Nigeria and Gabon have substantial oil income. Gabon, Zaire, and Zambia benefit from minerals export. The one nation that stands apart is South Africa, which has the most comprehensive, modern economy in Africa, but also has severe social and political problems, due in part to a long-standing and only recently (1991) abandoned official policy of racial segregation. Many nations have friendly economic and political ties with their former European colonial nations, and most retain the use of the European colonial language as their official national language.

North Africa, the area north of the Sahara, was covered in Chapter 11 because it is related more closely to those countries because of the domination of Arab culture and the Islamic religion.

Because of the tropical climate and limited health facilities throughout much of sub-Saharan Africa, vaccinations for cholera and yellow fever are recommended for tourists visiting many areas. Visitors should check requirements at the time of travel to the area.

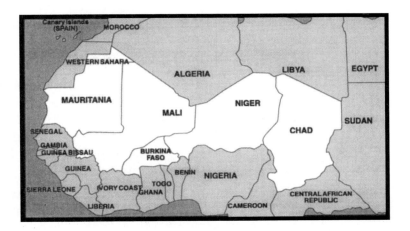

■ WEST AFRICA—AN OVERVIEW

The nations of West Africa fall into two adjacent broad west to east bands, one in the interior and the other along the coast. They have the largest combined population of any African region and one of them, Nigeria, has the largest population in Africa. The interior units have large uninhabited tracts of the Sahara Desert in their northern portions and their populations are concentrated in the savannas and near water sources in the south.

A wide zone of very dry (steppe) grasslands on the southern borders of the Sahara, known as the Sahel, experienced severe drought conditions in the 1970s and 1980s. The Sahelian nations, formerly French colonies, still use French as their official language. Islam, which has penetrated south of the Sahara, is the dominant religion, followed by Christian and animist groups of varying size. Subsistence foods, such as millet, sorghum, and corn are grown; peanuts and cattle hides are chief sources of income.

MAURITANIA

Official Name: Islamic Republic of Mauritania
Language: French, Arabic
Area: 397,954 square miles
Time Zone: GMT
Capital: Nouakchott
Currency: Ouguiya
Population: 1,995,000
Documentation: Passport, visa

Westernmost Mauritania faces on the Atlantic Ocean. Its capital, Nouakchott, and the bulk of the population are in the southwest, where there is sufficient water supply for agriculture. Herding and the mining of iron ore and copper for export support some population in the northwest. The interior is largely unoccupied desert.

Areas of Touristic Importance. A truly underdeveloped nation, Mauritania possesses some excellent, unspoiled Atlantic Ocean beaches that could be developed in the future. The Moslem influence from centuries of Moorish control as well as the French atmosphere from colonial control in the 19th and 20th centuries remains. Nouakchott was one of the first French settlements in Africa. Chinguetti, in the interior, is the seventh holy city of Islam, and 13th-century homes and mosques may be seen there.

MALI

Official Name: Republic of Mali

Language: French, Bambara

Area: 478,764 square miles

Time Zone: GMT

National Airline: Air Mali

Capital: Bamako

Currency: Mali franc

Population: 8,338,000

Documentation: Passport, visa

The inhabited southern part of Mali, to the east, is shaped around the upper and central course of the Niger River, which sweeps northward in a great arc. Near the tip of the arc on the margin of the Sahara is the historic city of Timbuktu, the major center that handled trans-Saharan trade in the precolonial era. However, the capital of Bamako and the agricultural life of the nation are in the south. Like other landlocked African nations, Mali depends on a combination of roads and single railways to reach port facilities in neighboring friendly states.

Areas of Touristic Importance. The best time to travel to Mali is during the cool season from November to March when trips up the Niger River are possible. The photographic opportunities are excellent, but travel is considered quite difficult. Caravans through the Sahara still go through Timbuktu. Air Mali provides service within the country and to neighboring African states.

NIGER

Official Name: Republic of Niger

Language: French, Hausa, Djerma

Area: 489,189 square miles

Time Zone: GMT + 1

Capital: Niamey

Currency: CFA franc

Population: 8,154,000

Documentation: Passport, visa

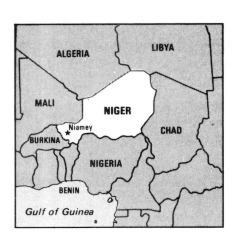

The geographic pattern in Niger is similar to that in Mali. The interior is about two-thirds desert, and most of the population and agriculture are found in the south. Its capital is Niamey, through which the Niger River passes.

Areas of Touristic Importance. There are wildlife parks at the Paul W. Boubon Island recreation area in the Niger River near Niamey, and Dia on Lake Chad. Historic sites include Tahoua, a 16th-century mosque at Agadez, and the ruins of the Sokoto Empire at Maradi and Konni. Travel is difficult, however, and tourism is limited.

BURKINA FASO

Language: French, tribal
Area: 105,869 square miles
Time Zone: GMT
Capital: Ouagadougou
Currency: CFA franc
Population: 9,359,000
Documentation: Passport, visa

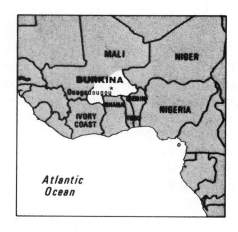

Small and poor Burkina Faso (named Upper Volta until 1984) abuts on southern Mali and Niger. Ouagadougou, its capital, is centrally located. Islam is a minor religion; half or more of the large population are animist. This landlocked country of rolling savannas obtained independence from France in 1960.

Areas of Touristic Importance. Although its facilities are limited by international standards, Burkina Faso provides interesting opportunities for the adventurous tourist. The Arly and Park W game preserves and the pool of the sacred crocodiles in Sabou attract photographers. Examples of ancient cave art are also found here.

CHAD

Official Name: Republic of Chad

Language: French, tribal, Arabic

Area: 495,755 square miles

Time Zone: GMT +1

Capital: N'Djamena

Currency: CFA franc

Population: 5,122,000

Documentation: Passport, visa

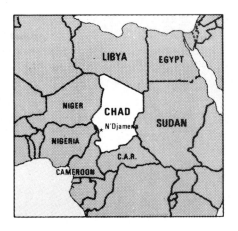

East of Niger is Chad, whose capital, N'Djamena, and national life are in the southwest. Lake Chad, fed by rivers flowing northward from the equatorial region, supports Africa's largest freshwater fishery even though most of the country is in a dry environment.

From old Arab manuscripts, it is known that developed societies flourished around Lake Chad in ancient times. From then until the present, Chad has served as a crossroads for Moslem peoples of the desert. Chad was involved in the 1980s in sporadic warfare with its northern neighbor, Libya. Few westerners visit this nation.

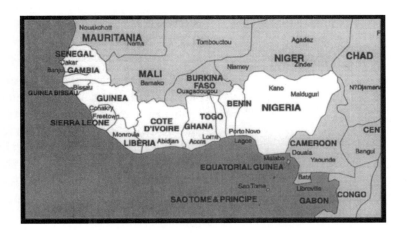

■ THE WEST AFRICAN COAST—AN OVERVIEW

Coastal West African nations have diverse colonial backgrounds. Four were British, one was Portuguese, five were French, and one, Liberia, was not a colony but evolved under

American influence. Extending inland from the Atlantic coast, most of the nations have well-watered and forested coastal areas and drier interiors. All capitals are of colonial origin and are situated on the coast. Another facet of colonialism, Christianity, is important in the capitals and among coastal tribes, but animism and Islam are stronger in the interior. In contrast to the poverty of the interior nations, several coastal nations have flourishing tropical plantation enterprises or minerals and oil for export.

SENEGAL

Official Name: Republic of Senegal

Language: French, tribal

Area: 75,750 square miles

Time Zone: GMT

Capital: Dakar

Currency: CFA franc

Population: 7,952,000

Documentation: Passport, visa

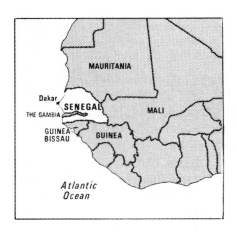

Senegal's capital, Dakar, was the chief colonial administrative center of France's African empire. With a population of more than 1 million persons, Dakar ranks as the fourth largest city in West Africa. Its importance as a port and commercial center is enhanced by a French-built railway that extends eastward through Senegal to Bamako in Mali.

Areas of Touristic Importance. Dakar is a cosmopolitan city with broad avenues and boulevards patterned after Paris. Theater, ballet, and other cultural attractions flourish here. A comprehensive exhibit of African crafts can be seen at the IFAN Museum. The juxtaposition of French and African cultures is apparent throughout the city. Colorful native markets vie with Paris fashion shops for the traveler's attention. Just outside of Dakar is Cape Almadies, the westernmost point in Africa.

Beaches along the Atlantic coast are excellent. The coastal town of Saint Louis, 160 miles north of Dakar, is the former capital of colonial Senegal and Mauritania. Hundreds of boats leave its fishing quarter each morning.

Wildlife preserves also attract the visitor. Niokolo-Koba National Park in the southeast corner of the country features lions, hippos, elephants, water buffalo, and the Derby eland, the largest antelope in the world. In the south, below the Gambia River, is Basse Casamance National Park, a forest park rich with monkeys and exotic birds.

CAPE VERDE

Official Name: Republic of Cape Verde

Language: Portuguese, Crioulo

Area: 1,557 square miles

Time Zone: GMT −1

Capital: Praia

Currency: Cape Verdian escudo

Population: 386,000

Documentation: Passport, visa

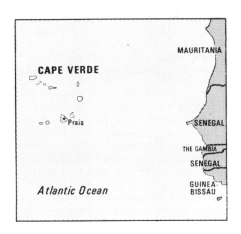

Cape Verde is an archipelago of ten islands and five islets located 385 miles off the coast of Senegal. The islands were controlled by Portugal from the 1600s until independence in 1975, and are divided into two groups—Barlavento and Sotavento. There are few resources and almost no tourism.

THE GAMBIA

Official Name: Republic of The Gambia

Language: English, tribal

Area: 4,127 square miles

Time Zone: GMT

Capital: Banjul

Currency: Gambian dalasi

Population: 874,000

Documentation: Passport

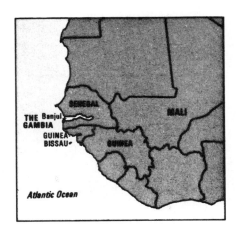

The Gambia, a small, formerly British colony, lies astride the Gambia River and is engulfed by Senegal. It has strong economic and political ties with Senegal, despite the differences in British and French colonial backgrounds.

Areas of Touristic Importance. More than 400 different species of birds can be found in this small nation. The story in Alex Haley's historical novel, *Roots,* began in Gambia. Like surrounding Senegal, the Atlantic Ocean beaches are a mecca for sun lovers.

GUINEA BISSAU

Official Name: Republic of
  Guinea-Bissau
Language: Portuguese, tribal
Area: 13,948 square miles
Time Zone: GMT
Capital: Bissau
Currency: Guinea-Bissau peso
Population: 1,023,000
Documentation: Passport,
  visa

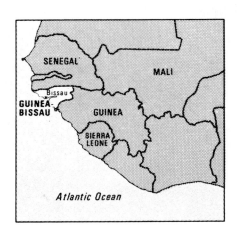

Guinea-Bissau is a small, former Portuguese holding. Bissau is the capital and is added to the national name to differentiate it from neighboring Guinea. The country became independent in 1975. Essentially an agricultural economy, mineral deposits, especially bauxite, are thought to be present. There is virtually no tourism.

GUINEA

Official Name: Republic of
  Guinea
Language: French, tribal
Area: 94,964 square miles
Time Zone: GMT
Capital: Conakry
Currency: Syli
Population: 7,455,000
Documentation: Passport,
  visa

Guinea, like Senegal, was French and is overwhelmingly Moslem. For a long time, it was one of the staunchest Socialist (non-Communist) nations in West Africa, but is now trying to move toward democratization in the face of political discord. Its raw material and crop exporting economy centers on the capital, Conakry. Development of bauxite mining has revitalized its economy.

Areas of Touristic Importance. The visitor will find beautiful scenery in the mountains and valleys as well as sea bathing, hunting, and fishing. However, tourism is not encouraged and facilities are quite limited.

SIERRA LEONE

Official Name: **Republic of Sierra Leone**

Language: **English, tribal**

Area: **27,925 square miles**

Time Zone: **GMT**

Capital: **Freetown**

Currency: **Leone**

Population: **4,274,000**

Documentation: **Passport, visa**

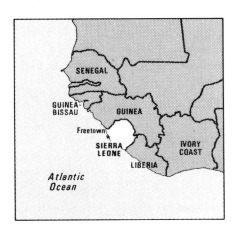

The history of Sierra Leone and Liberia is closely allied to the former slave trade. Sierra Leone was used in part as a homeland for freed slaves by the British. In fact, about 25 percent of the population of its capital, appropriately named Freetown, is descended from freed slaves from the West Indies. A much larger number of slaves landed from intercepted slave ships after the abolition of slavery by the British in 1807. Their descendants are the nation's elite. Freetown houses one of West Africa's oldest and best universities.

Areas of Touristic Importance. Freetown is attractively situated on a lush, green series of hillsides where the Sierra Leone River meets the Atlantic Ocean. Nearby is Lumley Beach, perhaps the finest in West Africa. An interesting National Museum is located at the foot of the famous Cotton Tree in the heart of the city. The Heddle Farm, outside of the city, attracts bird hunters.

LIBERIA

Official Name: Republic of
Liberia
Language: English, tribal
Area: 38,250 square miles
Time Zone: GMT
Capital: Monrovia
Currency: Liberian dollar
Population: 2,730,000
Documentation: Passport,
visa

Liberia was founded in 1822 by an American Christian missionary group to settle freed American slaves, most of whom took up residence in or near the capital, Monrovia, which was named in honor of United States President James Monroe. It became an independent republic in 1847. Even today, descendants of these slaves dominate political life although most of the population belong to 28 tribes. English is the official national language and the economy is buoyed by American corporate investments in rubber plantations and iron ore mining. Since 1990, however, national life has been seriously disrupted by armed rivalries among tribal and political groups.

Areas of Touristic Importance. Tourism facilities are limited, especially in the interior of the country. An unspoiled coastline and inviting beaches are available for visitors.

COTE D'IVOIRE

Official Name: Republic of
Cote d'Ivoire
Language: French, tribal
Area: 124,503 square miles
Time Zone: GMT
Capital: Yamoussoukro
Currency: CFA franc
Population: 12,977,000
Documentation: Passport,
visa

Cote d'Ivoire (formerly Ivory Coast) has one of the most prosperous tropical plantation economies and stablest governments in West Africa. Its former coastal capital, Abidjan, with a population of more than 1.5 million persons, is one of the largest cities in West Africa.

Areas of Touristic Importance. Tourism is better developed in the Ivory Coast than in many West African nations. The wide beaches and beautiful lagoons of the coast have been attracting European tourists for many years. Luxury resorts can be found at Grand-Bassam and Sassandra. The government has built a number of tourist villages to attract visitors.

Abidjan is a large, modern city with many skyscrapers, especially in the central plateau area. It is called the pearl of the lagoon, has an excellent zoo, and several fine botanical gardens. It has one of the world's largest Roman Catholic cathedrals. Game reserves can be found at Grand Lahou and Bouna.

GHANA

Official Name: Republic of Ghana

Language: English, tribal

Area: 92,098 square miles

Time Zone: GMT

National Airline: Ghana Airways

Capital: Accra

Currency: New cedi

Population: 15,616,000

Documentation: Passport, visa

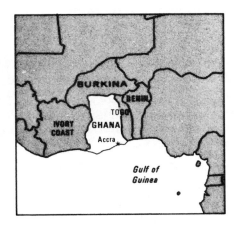

Located between Cote d'Ivoire and Togo, Ghana, the former British Gold Coast colony, resembles the Cote d'Ivoire in its plantation crop exports, especially cocoa, its prosperity, and the large size of its capital, Accra. In 1957, Ghana was the first African colony to receive independence.

Areas of Touristic Importance. Ghana has 350 miles of tropical coast with palm trees, great beaches, and excellent swimming and fishing. Accra, the capital, combines a modern city with native tribal customs. Dancing and ceremony are important to Ghanaians, who are proud of their heritage.

Points of interest in and around Accra include the National Museum, Aburi Botanical Gardens, Black Star Square, and modern government buildings. Christianborg Castle is the burial place of American civil rights leader and author, W.E.B. Du Bois.

Kumasi, is the capital of the Ashanti Region where the British fought against the Ashantis in the 19th century. The area is rich in traditional crafts such as weaving, wood carving, and bronze work. Other places of interest in the area include the National Cultural Center, the zoo, and the Manhyia Palace, the home of the Ashanti chiefs.

TOGO

Official Name: Republic of Togo

Language: French, tribal

Area: 21,622 square miles

Time Zone: GMT

Capital: Lome

Currency: CFA franc

Population: 3,810,000

Documentation: Passport, visa

Togo was a German colony from 1884 until the end of World War I. It was then administered by the British and French until it became independent in 1960. The British portion is now part of neighboring Ghana. Subsistence agriculture is the primary economic activity. It is troubled by periodic political disturbances.

Areas of Touristic Importance. Tourism activities are limited, although the government is actively seeking to increase them. There are beaches on the Gulf of Guinea coast and wildlife in the Tchanga Game Reserve.

BENIN

Official Name: The People's Republic of Benin

Language: French

Area: 43,483 square miles

Time Zone: GMT +1

Capital: Cotonou

Currency: CFA franc

Population: 4,831,000

Documentation: Passport, visa

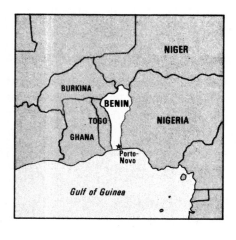

Like neighboring Togo, Benin (formerly Dahomey) is less well developed than other West African states. First Portugal and then France controlled the kingdom of Dahomey until independence in 1960. In 1975, the Republic of Dahomey became Benin and installed a Marxist-Leninist government, which lasted until the shift to a market economy in 1990 with accompanying political and economic upset.

Areas of Touristic Importance. Benin offers some of the finest national parks and game reserves in Africa. Tourists enjoy bamboo villages and beautiful beaches. Cotonou has surprisingly good restaurants and interesting nightlife. Ouidah, not far from Cotonou, features a restored fortress dating back to the days of the Portuguese explorers, and the Temple of the Serpents in which pythons are kept.

NIGERIA

Official Name: Federal Republic of Nigeria

Language: English, tribal

Area: 356,667 square miles

Time Zone: GMT +1

National Airline: Nigerian Airways

Capital: Lagos

Currency: Naira

Population: 88,500,000

Documentation: Passport, visa

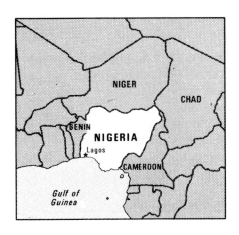

The Land and People. Nigeria, with a population of nearly 100 million, is by far the most populous nation in all of Africa. A large territory located in the inner big bend of the West African coast, it is bisected by the Niger River and its major tributary from the east, the Benue. The Niger flows southward and forms a delta as it enters the Gulf of Guinea. With a population of four million persons, the capital of Lagos is the largest city of sub-Saharan Africa, second only to Cairo in all of Africa. A new federal capital is being built at Abuja, 450 miles from Lagos on a plateau north of the confluence of the Niger and Benue Rivers. Another southwestern city, Ibadan, has almost one million persons.

Economy. The most important of the British West Africa colonies, Nigeria had an exceptionally good preparation for independence. Nigeria has a prosperous agriculture and a western educational system, including one of Africa's best universities, as well as a good national road and railway system and experience with administration and democratic processes. The discovery of oil in the Niger delta after independence made Nigeria one of the world's leading oil exporters and dramatically increased its revenues.

Factions and Conflicts. However, competition among some 250 ethnic groups has brought periodic political instability. Among the major groups involved are the Yoruba in the southwest, who are urbanized, well-educated, Christian, and prominent in the civil service; the Ibo in the southeast, who like the Yoruba include many Christians; and Moslem groups of the north, among whom the Hausa-Fulani are the largest. In fact, Moslems compose more than one half of the national population.

The most serious ethnic disputes occurred in 1967–1970, when the Ibo attempted secession as the independent state of Biafra. After a bitter civil war, the Ibo were defeated and reincorporated into the federal structure. Military leaders have remained dominant in national affairs since then.

Areas of Touristic Importance. Connected by bridges and overpasses, the city of Lagos is a modern capital built on a series of islands. The Museum of Nigerian Antiquities features the full range of Nigerian art. Tarqua Bay, near Lagos, is a popular beach resort area.

Ibadan, 90 miles northeast of Lagos, literally means "between the forest and the savanna." It is the headquarters of the Yoruba tribe and is most noted for its university. Museums at Ife and Benin City exhibit bronze objects illustrating the beginning of bronze casting.

The Museum at Jos, Nigeria's mining center, houses terra cotta pieces discovered at Nok and thought to be over 4,000 years old. Jos also has a fine zoo.

Kano, a 500-year-old city founded by Moslems, still welcomes visitors with silver trumpets. This city, 600 miles northeast of Lagos, was once the center of a thriving caravan trade.

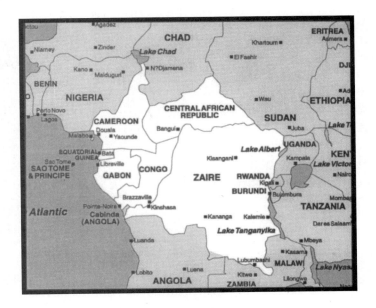

■ EQUATORIAL AFRICA—AN OVERVIEW

Zaire is, by far, the largest nation in Equatorial Africa. Four former French colonies lie on the northern and western flanks of Zaire: the landlocked Central African Republic and the coastal Congo, Cameroon, and Gabon. Both the Central African Republic and the Congo are poorly developed. The Cameroon economy is based on tropical plantation exports. Gabon has oil and mineral resources that stoke a growing prosperity. Equatorial Guinea consists of two tiny former Spanish units, Rio Muni on the coast between Gabon and Cameroon and several offshore islands, including Bioko (former Fernando Po), where the capital, Malabo, is located. West of Africa in the South Atlantic Ocean are the small island nation of Sao Tome and Principe and two British island dependencies, Ascension and St. Helena.

ZAIRE

Official Name: Republic of
   Zaire
Language: French, tribal
Area: 905,563 square miles
Time Zone: GMT +1 and +2
Capital: Kinshasa
Currency: Zaire
Population: 37,832,000
Documentation: Passport, visa

Located in the heart of the continent, Zaire is the centerpiece of Equatorial Africa. Formerly the Belgian Congo, its vast territory is shaped by the Zaire (Congo) River system. In the east, it borders on Lake Tanganyika. Its population, the second largest of any sub-Saharan nation, is composed of more than 200 ethnic groups. French is the formal language of government. As in Nigeria, tribal rivalries and political agitation are common.

The economy is based on mineral wealth in the extreme southeastern corner, the so-called Copperbelt that is shared with neighboring Zambia. The capital, Kinshasa, on the lower Zaire River has 3 million persons, making it second in size only to Lagos in sub-Saharan Africa. Near the mouth of the Zaire River and Zaire's tiny bit of Atlantic coastline is the port of Matadi.

Other regional cities are Kisangani in the north, Kananga in the center, and Lubumbashi in the mineral-rich province of Shaba in the southeast. For such a large territory and diverse population, Zaire has only a skeleton transportation network of railways, roads, riverboats, and air service.

Areas of Touristic Importance. Kinshasa, the capital, has fine Presidential Gardens and an excellent zoo. Its Academie des Beaux Arts features an ethnological museum and an African art salesroom. At Kisantu, 75 miles along the Zaire River from Kinshasa, tourists can enjoy the rapids, Zongo Falls, and the Kisantu Botanical Gardens.

The Kivu district in the east centers on scenically beautiful Lake Kivu, bordered by snowcapped mountains. National parks in the north and east feature hippos, gorillas, white rhinos, and buffalo.

CONGO

Official Name: People's Republic of the Congo
Language: French
Area: 132,046 square miles
Time Zone: GMT +1
Capital: Brazzaville
Currency: CFA franc
Population: 2,411,000
Documentation: Passport, visa

The Congo was ruled by tribal kings before becoming part of French Equatorial Africa. It became an independent state in 1960. The South Atlantic beaches and Bouenza Falls are places of natural beauty. Tourism facilities are very limited.

EQUATORIAL GUINEA

Official Name: Republic of Equatorial Guinea
Language: Spanish, tribal
Area: 10,832 square miles
Time Zone: GMT + 1
Capital: Malabo
Currency: CFA franc
Population: 360,000
Documentation: Passport, visa

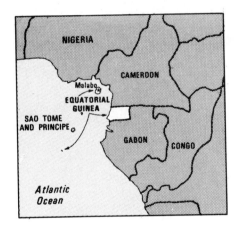

Formerly Spanish Guinea, Equatorial Guinea became an independent nation in 1968. It consists of a small section of the mainland bordered by Cameroon, Gabon, and the Atlantic Ocean along with several islands in the Gulf of Guinea. There is little tourism.

GABON

Official Name: Gabonese
  Republic
Language: French, tribal
Area: 103,346 square miles
Time Zone: GMT +1
Capital: Libreville
Currency: CFA franc
Population: 1,079,000
Documentation: Passport,
  visa

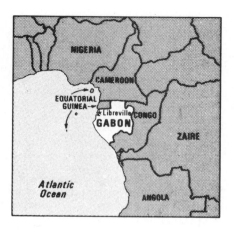

Gabon is underpopulated but prosperous, based on its oil and mineral resources. Lambarene is the location of the Albert Schweitzer hospital where the famous missionary worked.

Areas of Touristic Importance. The adventurous can take guided canoe trips on the Ogooue River. The capital, Libreville, was founded by freed slaves and has colorful open air markets and botanical gardens.

CENTRAL AFRICAN REPUBLIC

Language: French, tribal
Area: 240,534 square miles
Time Zone: GMT +1
Capital: Bangui
Currency: CFA franc
Population: 2.7 million
Documentation: Passport,
  visa

The southwestern portion of the Central African Republic is rain forest and jungle; the extreme north is mountainous and desert. The French established an outpost at Bangui in the 19th century; the area was part of the massive French holdings in Africa until independence in 1960. The country has endured extreme internal turmoil in recent years.

Areas of Touristic Importance. The Ubangi River flows through the Central African Republic and adventurous travelers can take canoe trips past pygmy villages and game preserves.

CAMEROON

Official Name: Republic of Cameroon

Language: French, English

Area: 179,714 square miles

Time Zone: GMT +1

Capital: Yaounde

Currency: CFA franc

Population: 11,390,000

Documentation: Passport, visa

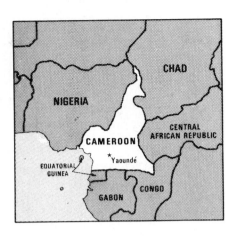

Cameroon is another of the African states that achieved independence in 1960. It was controlled by the Germans before World War I and by the French and British afterwards. Economic development is low.

Areas of Touristic Importance. The beaches at Kribi and the Waza Forest Game Reserve are of interest to the few visitors who come here. Mount Cameroon, at 13,353 feet, is the highest peak in sub-Saharan West Africa.

SAO TOME AND PRINCIPE

Official Name: Democratic Republic of Sao Tome and Principe

Language: Portuguese

Area: 372 square miles

Time Zone: GMT

Capital: Sao Tome

Currency: Escudo

Population: 128,000

Documentation: Passport, visa

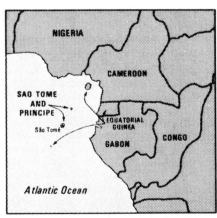

This nation is composed of a cluster of small volcanic islands located 180 miles off the coast of West Africa. Formerly a Portuguese dependency, Sao Tome and Principe became independent in 1975. There is little touristic activity.

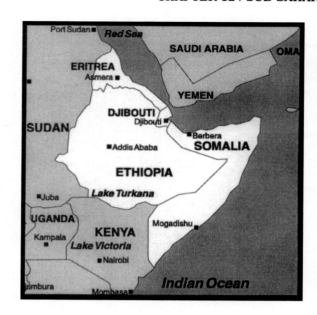

■ NORTHEAST AFRICA—AN OVERVIEW

The horn of northeast Africa, occupied by Ethiopia, Eritrea, Somalia, and tiny Djibouti, is a peripheral part of sub-Saharan Africa. Its people are dark-skinned, non-Negroid groups whose ancestors entered the region from Arabia. Most of their languages are related to those of the Middle East/North Africa.

ETHIOPIA

Official Name: People's Democratic Republic of Ethiopia

Language: Amharic, English, tribal

Area: 471,776

Time Zone: GMT +3

National Airline: Ethiopian Air

Capital: Addis Ababa

Currency: Birr

Population: 53,131,000

Documentation: Passport, visa

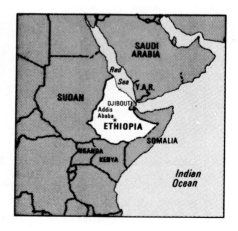

The Land and People. A physically and culturally complex nation, Ethiopia occupies the largest portion of the region. It is shaped around a large plateau that has some of Africa's higher elevations and is broken into many parts by spectacular valleys. Many of the highlands are habitable, but the lower flanks of the nation are desert or semidesert (steppe).

The peoples of the highlands are Coptic Christians, speak Amharic, the national language, and constitute almost two-thirds of the national population. A highlands city of more than 1 million persons, Addis Ababa, is the national capital. The eastern lowlands are inhabited by groups related to the people of neighboring Somalia, Moslems, who make up almost one-third of Ethiopia's population. A few African tribal units live within Ethiopia's southwestern boundary, thus making it transitional to sub-Saharan Africa.

History. Ethiopian history is replete with tribal rivalries between groups in the highlands and between Christians and Moslems. One of the few African areas to remain free during the 19th century, Ethiopia was finally occupied by Italian military forces from 1936 to 1941. Primarily agricultural on a subsistence level, Ethiopia has had limited commercial interaction with other nations. The history of Ethiopia dates back more than 3,000 years. Aksum was a powerful kingdom from 300 to 600 AD.

Until 1990, Ethiopia had a Communist government that was bolstered by Russian economic aid and Cuban military forces. It faces severe domestic problems, including widespread drought, crop failure, and famine, and the hostility of Somalia.

In 1993, the northern coastal province of Eritrea gained independence from Ethiopia. This means that Ethiopia no longer has direct access to the sea.

Areas of Touristic Importance. A railway links Addis Ababa to the port in the tiny nation of Djibouti. A single road network radiates from Addis Ababa to other parts of the nation.

Museums house many pre-Christian antiquities that are well worth seeing. However, travel to Ethiopia is not recommended because of internal economic and political instability.

ERITREA

Official Name: State of Eritrea

Language: Several native languages

Area: 36,170 square miles

Time Zone: GMT +3

Capital: Asmara

Population: 3,467,087

Documentation: Passport and visa

Eritrea, formerly the northernmost province of Ethiopia facing on the Red Sea, achieved independence in 1993, after 17 years of bitter antigovernment warfare. A former Italian colony, it was placed in federation with Ethiopia by the United Nations in 1954 and was annexed by Ethiopia 10 years later.

Massawa is its largest city and main seaport. Bitterly poor, badly damaged by war and food shortages, Eritrea depends heavily on international economic aid. Tourism is not currently a major factor in Eritrea.

DJIBOUTI

Official Name: Republic of Djibouti

Language: Arabic, French

Area: 8,950 square miles

Time Zone: GMT +3

Capital: Djibouti

Currency: Djibouti franc

Population: 541,000

Documentation: Passport, visa

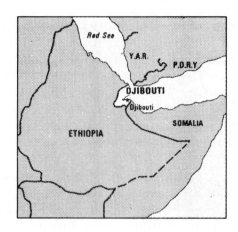

Tiny Djibouti was a French colony whose port and railhead served the Ethiopian highlands. Its Moslem population is closely related to groups in Somalia, which would like to annex it.

Lake Asal, 80 miles west of the city of Djibouti, is the lowest point in Africa and the second lowest point in the world. Many consider travel in Djibouti to be quite difficult.

SOMALIA

Official Name: Somali Democratic Republic

Language: Somali, Arabic

Area: 246,300 square miles

Time Zone: GMT +3

Capital: Mogadishu

Currency: Somali shilling

Population: 6,709,000

Documentation: Passport, visa

Independent Somalia was created by combining two former British and Italian colonies. Somali language and Islamic religion are the rule everywhere. As noted, Somali people spill over into Ethiopia and Djibouti. They are also found in Kenya to the south. The greater part of the population and the capital of Mogadishu are in the south where more rainfall and river water are available. Elsewhere, migratory herding is common.

International peace-keeping military forces, including Americans, were dispatched in 1993 to Somalia to guarantee the circulation of relief supplies from donor nations and to disarm feuding local military groups. There is a strong separatist movement in the northwest, in former British Somaliland. Its headquarters are in Hargeisa, the main town, which is inland from the small port city of Berbera on the Gulf of Aden. Tourism is essentially undeveloped.

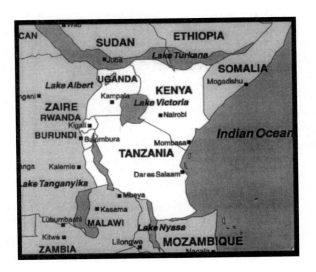

■ EAST AFRICA—AN OVERVIEW

The Land

East Africa is formed of three large nations—Kenya, Uganda, and Tanzania—situated around Lake Victoria, the source of the White Nile, and two small western units—Rwanda and Burundi. Although this area lies due east of Equatorial Africa, its physical conditions are very different. Higher in elevation, it is also so much drier (savanna, with even drier steppe along the coast) that great stretches of land are unusable or only marginally useful for herding or farming. The highest elevations are in the west along a series of rift valleys and lakes, and in the east, where mountains and towering volcanic peaks prevail.

The People

Considering the environmental limitations, populations are relatively large and fast-growing. Tanzania ranks fifth, Kenya sixth, and Uganda seventh in size in sub-Saharan Africa. Collectively, they are one of Africa's largest population concentrations. The main grouping of people is in the interior, especially around Lake Victoria, where rainfall is heavier.

Despite their common British colonial experience as part of British East Africa, each of the three large nations is distinctive.

KENYA

Official Name: Republic of Kenya

Language: Swahili, English

Area: 224,960 square miles

Time Zone: GMT +3

National Airline: Kenya Airways

Capital: Nairobi

Currency: Kenya shilling

Population: 25,241,000

Documentation: Passport, visa

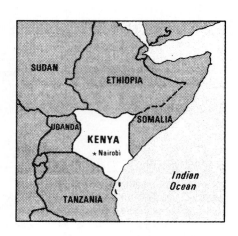

Kenya's core is in the better-watered highlands of the southwest. The northern and coastal areas are arid. Among the numerous tribal groups, the Kikuyu are dominant in numbers and politics. The Masai are important cattle herders. Swahili is the official language, although English remains widely used in government and higher education.

Three non-African minorities add further complexity to the ethnic mix. Most of the 70,000 whites are descended from earlier settlers, who opened the southwestern highlands to commercial plantations and built up Nairobi (the capital), now a modern, western city of more than 1 million. The 200,000 Asians (Hindu and Moslem Indians), descended from laborers brought from India for rail construction, now dominate small business. Thirty thousand Arabs live on the coast. Ethnic relations have been relatively peaceful since independence. About half the population is Christian. The rest, except for a small Moslem group, are animists.

The private enterprise national economy is based on agriculture, herding, and tourism. Tourists are attracted in large numbers by some of Africa's most spectacular wildlife parks and such volcanic peaks as Mt. Kenya, north of Nairobi. A rail line from Mombasa, on the coast, extends through Nairobi and western Kenya into Uganda. A good road system links Nairobi with the principal regional towns and smaller cities.

Areas of Touristic Importance. Nairobi is a modern city. The Kenyatta Conference Center is an excellent example of modern architecture within a relatively short distance of wilderness. The Nairobi National Museum contains thousands of African artifacts. Just 5 miles from the center of the city is Nairobi National Park with wildlife in its natural habitat. The park is filled with cheetah, giraffes, lions, buffalo, rhinos, and hippos.

The national park system was created to protect wildlife. Tourists from all over the world flock to Kenya to visit these parks. Some of the most prominent are the Masai Mara Game Reserve, Amboseli National Park, Tsavo National Park, and Amberdare National Park. Lake Nakuru is a bird sanctuary.

Mt. Kenya, at an elevation of 17,058 feet, is Africa's second highest mountain. The central highlands area extends westward to include the Amberdare Mountains and park.

Marsabit National Park, Kenya
Photo: Courtesy Kenya Tourist Office

Here, too, is the famous Tree Tops Hotel from which guests can watch elephants, buffalo, rhinos, and other animals drink from a large watering hole.

Nakuru and Thompson's Falls provide amazing views of the Great Rift Valley. This geological fracture stretches from Turkey to Tanzania. Created millions of years ago when sections of the earth broke off and sank, the rift is as much as 80 miles wide.

Mombasa, on the Indian Ocean, presents a totally different atmosphere from Nairobi. Nearly 50 mosques dot the city. The population is over 40 percent Moslem. The small shops of Arab craftsmen have much to offer.

UGANDA

Official Name: Republic of Uganda

Language: English, Swahili

Area: 93,354 square miles

Time Zone: GMT +3

Capital: Kampala

Currency: Ugandan shilling

Population: 18,690,000

Documentation: Passport, visa

Landlocked Uganda had the potential to become the best developed East African nation. Flourishing agriculture, industrial raw materials, hydroelectric power, and small amounts of manufacturing were started by the British. However, internal order was shattered in the 1970s by tribal armed warfare and a dictatorship that ousted the 75,000 Asians who controlled business life. Small numbers of Indians are returning to regain their lost properties and businesses and to resume their lives as Ugandan citizens.

English is the official language, and the seat of government is Kampala, inland from Lake Victoria. The rail line from Kenya continues in two branches to the western borders.

Areas of Touristic Importance. Uganda's attractions are generally similar to Kenya's natural wilderness, mountains, and exotic wildlife. Seasoned travelers considered it to be the most beautiful country in Africa. However, tourism was all but eliminated during earlier unrest, and it has not yet been reborn.

Several areas are attractive for tourism. The Lake Victoria shoreline is picturesque. The Ruwenzori Mountains in the west straddle the equator yet are covered with snow. Kabalega (formerly Murchison) Falls drops 130 feet to the beginning of the Nile River.

TANZANIA

Official Name: United Republic of Tanzania

Language: Swahili, English

Area: 364,886 square miles

Time Zone: GMT +3

Capital: Dodoma

Currency: Tanzania shilling

Population: 26,869,000

Documentation: Passport, visa

Tanzania is physically larger than Kenya and Uganda combined, but it remains poor and undeveloped. The territory includes several offshore islands, including Zanzibar which contributes the second syllable to the national name.

The population contains two conspicuous groupings. One is on the coast, centered on the former capital, Dar es Salaam ("Dar"), and offshore Zanzibar. The other is south of Lake Victoria in the interior. Nearly half the population is Christian and a third is Moslem.

Some of the factors bearing on Tanzania's underdevelopment are insufficient rainfall over wide areas, the widespread occurrence of sleeping sickness, and severe problems with malaria. The population is fragmented into many tribal groups, none providing national leadership. The country had an unstable history that saw it a German colony until acquired by the British after World War I. As in Kenya, international tourists are attracted to the wildlife preserves and volcanic peaks, including Mount Kilimanjaro near the Kenya border.

Zanzibar was a British protectorate from 1890 to 1963, then became part of the new nation of Tanzania in 1964. The traditional trade in cloves has declined and has been replaced in part by expanded international tourism, financial aid programs by Oman, an Islamic patron, and the smuggling of goods from Middle Eastern sources into the national mainland.

The capital has been moved to Dodoma, some 425 miles inland from Dar es Salaam, the former capital and still the largest city with a population of one million. A rail line links Dar es Salaam with the shores of Lake Tanganyika in the west and Lake Victoria in the north. In 1975, the Tan-zam Railway was opened linking Dar es Salaam with the mining district of central Zambia to the southwest.

Areas of Touristic Importance. Mount Kilimanjaro, at 19,340 feet, is the highest peak in Africa. It is not, however, inaccessible and its peak can be reached by the serious climber in 5 days.

Dar es Salaam is the commercial center of Tanzania. It is a bustling port as well as the major arrival point for visitors. Its National Museum contains the skull of "Nutcracker Man," estimated to be more than 1.75 million years old.

The Selous Game Reserve covers over 15,500 square miles, and is home to the largest number of elephants in the world. Serengeti National Park has the largest concentration of migratory animals on the continent.

The island of Zanzibar is a short distance off the mainland not far from Dar es Salaam. It was a Persian and Arab trading center. It is the "isle of cloves" and is the world's leading producer of this spice. Most interesting is Zanzibar's Stone Town, featuring ornate Arab homes.

■ RWANDA AND BURUNDI

RWANDA

Official Name: Republic of Rwanda

Language: French, Kinyarwandu

Area: 10,169 square miles

Time Zone: GMT +2

Capital: Kigali

Currency: Rwanda franc

Population: 7,902,000

Documentation: Passport, visa

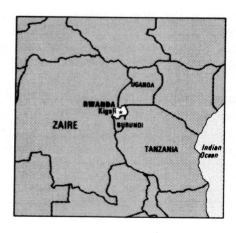

BURUNDI

Official Name: Republic of
 Burundi
Language: Kirundi, French
Area: 10,759 square miles
Time Zone: GMT + 2
Capital: Bujumbura
Currency: Burundi franc
Population: 5,831,000
Documentation: Passport,
 visa

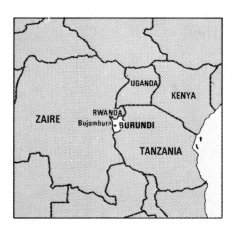

Little Rwanda and Burundi were held by Germany until passing to Belgian administration in 1919 and independent in 1962. Mountainous and well-watered, they are densely populated. Located in one of Africa's most inaccessible interior areas, they are poor and overpopulated and suffer from the acute rivalries between two of the dominant tribes, the pastoral Tutsi (Watusi) and the majority, farming Hutu (Bahutu). Most of the population is Roman Catholic. Administration is located in two small cities, Kigali, near the center of Rwanda, and Bujumbura, on Lake Tanganyika in Burundi.

The massacres resulting from tribal warfare in 1994 will keep Rwanda off limits for tourists for some time to come.

Areas of Touristic Importance. Rwanda is best known for gorilla trekking in the Park of the Virungas. It also has excellent game preserves. Lake Kivu, at 4,790 feet, is the highest lake in Africa. Burundi's lush mountains also provide a habitat for gorillas.

Because of the hostilities described above, the future survival of the gorillas is uncertain.

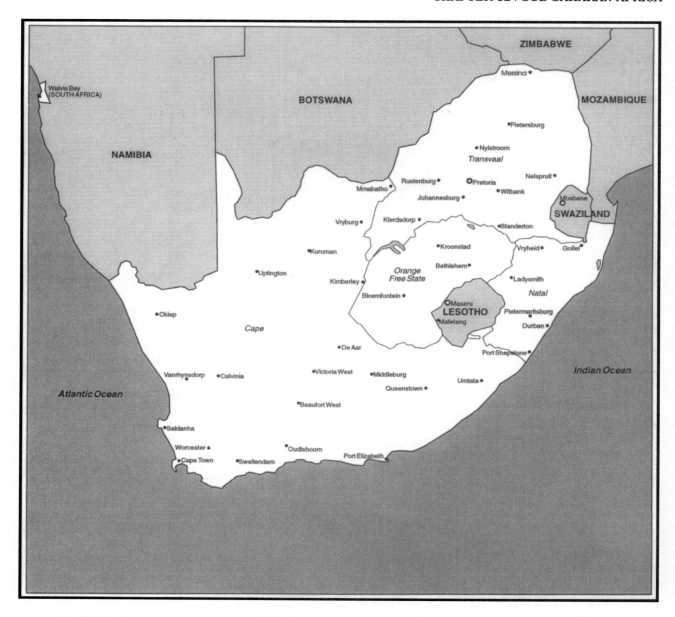

■ SOUTHERN AFRICA—AN OVERVIEW

The nations of Southern Africa can be placed into three sub-groups. One consists of South Africa, the three adjacent nations of Lesotho, Swaziland, and Botswana (once British colonies), and Namibia (former South-West Africa). The second, Zambia, Zimbabwe (former Rhodesia), and Malawi, also are former British colonies. The third, Angola and Mozambique, are former Portuguese holdings.

This part of Africa is marked by economic and political extremes. On the one hand, it has in South Africa the continent's most advanced national economy and, spread across several nations, great mineral wealth. On the other hand, it has fierce intertribal stresses, the commonplace African problems of rural and urban poverty, and, until recently, formal racial discrimination (South Africa), extreme leftist governments (Angola and Mozambique), and armed guerrilla action within and across national boundaries.

SOUTH AFRICA

Official Name: Republic of South Africa

Language: English, Afrikaans, Bantu

Area: 472,359 square miles

Time Zone: GMT +2

National Airline: South African Airways

Capital: Pretoria

Currency: Rand

Population: 40,600,000

Documentation: Passport, visa

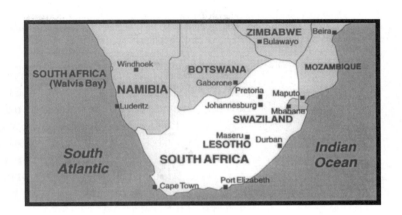

The Land. By any measure, South Africa is the most modern, westernized, and prosperous nation in sub-Saharan Africa, but its system of legal racial segregation (1948–1990) prevented it from having greater interaction with, and impact upon, most other African nations. Internally, topography and climate have posed limitations on the use of the national territory. The eastern and southern half is most habitable and contains most of the population.

Coastal hills and mountains rise sharply to an interior plateau, the high veld, whose eastern edge is marked by the Drakensberg Mountains. The plateau is drained by the west-flowing Orange River system. The southern coast has a temperate Mediterranean-type climate. The eastern coastal areas receive even better rainfall. The savanna of the interior dries out to desert conditions in the west.

The Peoples. The diverse population consists predominantly of Africans of many tribal affiliations; 4.5 million whites, the largest group of permanent white inhabitants in sub-Saharan Africa; and 2.5 million "coloured" people of mixed ancestry, resident in the south, especially in Cape Town. In addition, there are one million Asians, descendants of Hindu and Moslem laborers from India, who were brought to South Africa during the colonial period as plantation labor. The Asians are now very active in small businesses and heavily concentrated in the port city of Durban, on the Indian Ocean.

Ethnic relations have been dominated by three confrontations: One is between the black majority that is in a subordinate position and the numerical minority, but otherwise dominant, white group. The second is between black ethnic groups and political parties. The third is between English-speakers and Afrikaans-speakers (Afrikaaners or, formerly, Boers) of Dutch extraction. The latter problem dates from the early 19th century when the original Dutch settlement at Cape Town fell to the British.

History. A growing British presence in the area prompted thousands of Boers in the 1830s to move into the interior where they formed two independent Dutch republics, Transvaal and Orange Free State. In the course of this expansion, the large tribal groups of the east and northeast were subdued by force and placed under white control.

The discovery of gold at present Johannesburg and diamonds at Kimberley brought in waves of British and other outsiders. The resultant tensions and heightened British colonial interest in the Dutch-held areas led to the Boer War of 1899–1902. Defeated, the Boers and their territory were joined with the British Cape and Natal Provinces in 1910 to form the self-governing unit of the Union of South Africa. The last British ties were cut in 1961.

The legislative capital of the republic is Cape Town, while the administrative offices of the government are in Pretoria in the northeast. English and Afrikaans are both official languages.

The Afrikaaners outnumber the English-speakers and since 1948 have controlled the government. One of their main policies was racial segregation, apartheid, or separation of the four population groups. Each group had to live in its own area. Priority has been given to consolidating much of the black population into tribally defined "homelands," known as "Bantustans." Ten such homelands were organized, most in isolated, unproductive rural areas, and four (Bophuthatswana, Transkei, Ciskei, and Venda) have been designated as self-governing by South Africa, although no other nation has formally recognized them.

In response to internal turmoil and international pressure, the South African government dismantled the formal legal basis of apartheid in 1990–1991, but profound racial and ethnic problems remain. Movement toward a new constitution that is acceptable to the many societal groups has been difficult. The end of apartheid eased South Africa's international isolation, and it has restored working relations with most African and other nations.

In September 1993, in an historic shift in policy, the White government of South Africa agreed to share broad powers with a multiracial political transition committee, which was followed by South Africa's first universal elections in 1994. South Africa's first black president was elected. In addition to giving the predominantly black population a share of governmental power, the move cleared the way for ending the international economic sanctions against South Africa because of its former apartheid policies.

Economy. The South African economy is diversified and advanced. A flourishing agriculture provides surpluses for export. Citrus fruit, grapes for wine, and other cash crops are grown in the south. Sugar cane is an east coast specialty, and wheat and cattle are raised in the drier interior. The mining industry in the northeast is the world leader in gold and diamond production. Large supplies of coal, electric power, and industrial minerals contribute to the largest manufacturing operation in all of Africa. Important fisheries operate from Cape Town and other ports.

Internationally, South Africa is the largest national and international labor market in Africa, and its mines attract black contract workers from Lesotho, Swaziland, Botswana, Malawi, and Mozambique. The economy is a study in contrasts; progressive westernized cities have black slums and depressed rural areas are inhabited by black populations. Johannesburg has nearly two million persons and both Cape Town and Durban have more than one million persons.

Areas of Touristic Importance. Johannesburg, called the Golden City because of the area's mines which produce nearly half of the world's gold supply, has evolved from a small mining town to a large modern metropolis in less than 100 years. The Gold Museum depicts the mining of this precious metal since the turn of the century. Southwest of Johannesburg is Kimberley, known for diamond mining. Tours of gold and diamond mines can be arranged.

Pretoria, 36 miles from Johannesburg, is the administrative center of the nation. It is a quiet city with 300 miles of streets lined with jacaranda trees. When the trees bloom in October, the city takes on a purplish glow. Pretoria is one of the oldest cities in the country and the Paul Kruger House and other museums trace the connections with the Transvaal Republic.

The most southern point in Africa is Cape Agulhas where the Indian and Atlantic Oceans meet. Cape Town, on the Cape of Good Hope, slightly to the northwest of the most southern point, was the site of the first Dutch settlement in the 17th century. The Castle of Good Hope, built in 1666, is the oldest building in South Africa, and the visitor may view its fine collection of furniture and art and the Military Museum, which it also houses. Cape Town is also noted for its Cape Dutch-style architecture and several buildings are open to tourists. Nearby Table Mountain can be reached by a cable car that climbs 4,000 feet to an observation point. Cape Town Province is full of scenic contrasts with valleys, beaches, high mountains, and harbors. These can be viewed from the comfort of the famous Blue Train that operates between Cape Town and Johannesburg.

Durban, on the Indian Ocean, is a year-round Riviera. Its beaches have some of the world's finest surfing waves. Its Centenary Aquarium contains more than 1,000 fish that are fed twice daily by a scuba diver. Resort hotels, restaurants, and nightlife can provide a restful vacation or a brief respite on a longer tour.

Kruger National Park, on the northeast border with Mozambique, is one of the largest game reserves in Africa. It covers nearly 7,500 square miles, stretching 200 miles from the Crocodile River to the Limpopo River, and is almost 40

Harbor and Table Mountain, Cape Town, South Africa
Courtesy South African Tourist board

miles wide. Winter and spring (June through October), when the grass is low, are the best times to visit. Giraffes, zebras, elephants, cheetah, lions, wildebeests, and impala are common. There are more than 450 species of birds in the park.

Zululand has five separate game parks. For the mountain climber, the Drakensberg Mountains rise to an elevation of 11,000 feet and are snowcapped in winter. Many mountain chalets and resorts cater to visitors.

NAMIBIA

Official Name: Namibia (South-West Africa)

Language: Afrikaans, English

Area: 317,818 square miles

Time Zone: GMT +2

Capital: Windhoek

Currency: Rand

Population: 1,520,000

Documentation: Passport, visa

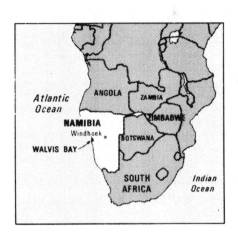

Namibia, a former German colony, was placed under South African administration after World War I. Largely desert, it has a basically rural African population and some 70,000 whites. It is governed from the small coastal city of Windhoek. South Africa claimed Namibia and applied the apartheid system there, while the United Nations claimed jurisdiction and favored self-determination. Until 1990, South African troops used it as a base for operations against leftist, Cuban-backed forces in neighboring Angola. Namibia became independent in 1990. Its economy is still tied to South Africa and its main port, Walvis Bay, claimed by South Africa, is administered jointly while the South African government remains in transition toward a new constitution.

Areas of Touristic Importance. Etosha National Park contains a large game preserve.

■ LESOTHO, SWAZILAND, AND BOTSWANA

The black republics of Lesotho, Swaziland, and Botswana depend heavily on employment of their men in the mines of South Africa.

LESOTHO

Official Name: Kingdom of
    Lesotho
Language: English, Sesotho
Area: 11,716 square miles
Time Zone: GMT +2
Capital: Maseru
Currency: Rand
Population: 1,801,000
Documentation: Passport,
    visa

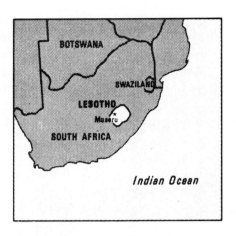

Lesotho is wholly surrounded by the nation of South Africa.
The tiny country was granted independence by Great Britain
in 1965.

Areas of Touristic Importance. A spectacular national
park is located at Sehlabathebe. There are hotels and casinos
in Maseru and skiing facilities are available in the Maluti
Mountains.

SWAZILAND

Official Name: Kingdom of
    Swaziland
Language: English, siSwati
Area: 6,704 square miles
Time Zone: GMT +2
Capital: Mbabane
Currency: Rand
Population: 859,000
Documentation: Passport

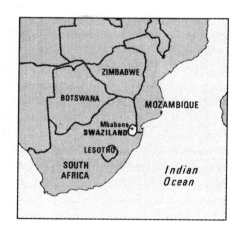

A former British protectorate, Swaziland was granted inde-
pendence in 1968. Surrounded by the Transvaal and Natal
Provinces of South Africa, it has a short, 70-mile border with
Mozambique.

Areas of Touristic Importance. Touristic features include
casinos, game reserves, and mountain scenery.

BOTSWANA

Official Name: Republic of Botswana
Language: English, Setswana
Area: 231,804 square miles
Time Zone: GMT +2
Capital: Gaborone
Currency: Pula
Population: 1,300,000
Documentation: Passport

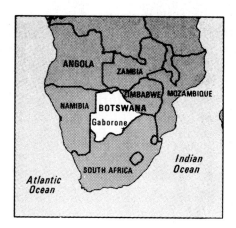

Most of Botswana is arid. The bulk of its population and its capital, Gaborone, are in the southeast adjacent to South Africa. Nearly 20 percent of the land has been designated as game preserves. The national economy is based on herding and the mining of gold and diamonds.

Areas of Touristic Importance. Chobe National Park and Moremi Wildlife Reserve are considered superb in terms of animal life and natural beauty.

■ ZIMBABWE, ZAMBIA, AND MALAWI—AN OVERVIEW

Historically, British colonial interests pressed northward from South Africa into the interior and gained control of present Zambia, Zimbabwe, and Malawi. After World War II, a federation of the three was attempted (1953–1964), but broke apart. English remains the official language in all three countries.

ZIMBABWE

Language: English, tribal
Area: 150,803 square miles
Time Zone: GMT +2
Capital: Harare
Currency: Zimbabwe dollar
Population: 10,720,000
Documentation: Passport

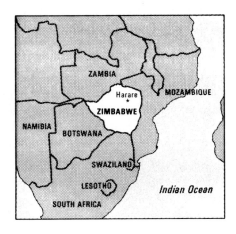

The Land. Zimbabwe, formerly called Rhodesia, is comparatively well-developed, but is ethnically and politically troubled. Physically, it is a northeastern continuation of the high veld of interior South Africa. Its savanna climate is drier in the north and very dry in the west. Part of the southern boundary is formed by the Limpopo River, which drains through Mozambique into the Indian Ocean. Most of its northern boundary with Zambia is along the Zambezi River. The latter river course features Victoria Falls, Africa's mightiest waterfall, and man-made Kariba Dam and Lake Kariba.

The Peoples. Although only 3 percent of the total population, the white residents of Zimbabwe were in control from the start of the colonial period. They owned the best-watered farmlands, promoted agricultural and industrial development, opened the mines, and ran the government in Salisbury, now renamed Harare. The white-run government declared independence from Britain in 1965; thereafter, it was subject to United Nations sanctions and faced increasingly heavy attacks by black guerrilla groups for more than a decade. A new constitution in 1979 ended the white political domination and transferred power to the black majority.

About 100,000 whites remain in Zimbabwe and, although less than 2 percent of the population, they continue to dominate the mines, mills, banks and farms. They enjoy a high standard of living that contrasts vividly with the low standard of the typical black citizen. Some uneasiness remains over the feasibility of further government expropriation of white farms for redistribution to black farmers.

The nation remains disrupted by numerous armed clashes between rival tribal groups, especially the Mashona of the east and northeast, the Ndebele (Matabele) of the west and southwest, and other political action groups. Under more peaceful conditions, Zimbabwe ranks second to South Africa in overall economic development in sub-Saharan Africa.

Economy. In contrast with the usual subsistence farming of the black population, white-owned holdings are large and concentrate on cash crops for export. Tobacco is the most valuable crop. Zimbabwe shares the mineral-rich geology of northeastern South Africa and is a major source of copper, asbestos, chrome, and other minerals that are shipped to overseas markets. Manufacturing centers dot the rail line between Harare and the second largest city, Bulawayo, in the southwest. Landlocked, Zimbabwe relies upon rail lines through neighboring nations for shipment of its imports and exports—eastward through Mozambique and southward through Botswana and South Africa.

Areas of Touristic Importance. In the north, high plains and velds provide game reserves. Famed Victoria Falls and the Hwenge (Wanhe) Game Reserve are located in the northwest of the country. The ruins of an ancient Zimbabwean civilization are near Masvingo, formerly Fort Victoria, in southeast Zimbabwe. As is true in many other African nations, real or perceived political unrest has greatly limited the development of tourism.

ZAMBIA

Official Name: Republic of Zambia

Language: English, tribal

Area: 290,586 square miles

Time Zone: GMT +2

Capital: Lusaka

Currency: Kwacha

Population: 8,445,000

Documentation: Passport, visa

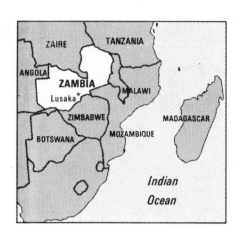

Zambia is a gently rolling plateau with a savanna climate in the area between the Zambezi and Zaire (Congo) River systems. Low mountains rise in the northeast. It shares the Zambezi River, Victoria Falls, and Lake Kariba with Zimbabwe on its southern boundary.

In the 1920s, white financial interests opened rich copper deposits in what is known as the Copperbelt, near the north central border with Zaire. Copper remains the backbone of the economy, and its main export. The agriculture that supports the bulk of the population is low-producing and subsistence in nature. Zambia has few whites and little tribal infighting.

Its major problem has been how to get its copper to market from its landlocked position. Shipments moved by rail through Angola; Mozambique, where internal conditions remain unstable; and white-dominated South Africa. An alternative now is the Tan-zam Railway, a line that runs from the Copperbelt to the Tanzanian port of Dar es Salaam, that was built by China as a foreign aid project. Lusaka, in central Zambia, is the capital and main city.

Areas of Touristic Importance. Zambia is on a high plateau which climbs to 7,000 feet near the Malawi border. It offers spectacular scenery at Kalambo Falls, Lake Tanganyika, and

Victoria Falls. Victoria Falls has become the center of a modern resort area with good tourist facilities. Weekend tours from Lusaka are popular.

Kafue and Luangwa Valley National Parks are among the largest in Africa. Both are well inhabited by wildlife and have ample facilities for visitors.

MALAWI

Language: English, Chichewa
Area: 45,747 square miles
Time Zone: GMT +2
Capital: Lilongwe
Currency: Kwacha
Population: 9,438,000
Documentation: Passport

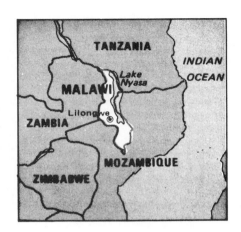

Malawi, a narrow state that faces eastward on Lake Malawi, has sufficient rainfall and good soils for a thriving agriculture. The north is mountainous, so the population is concentrated on the border of Lake Malawi, formerly Lake Nyasa, and on the plains in the central and southern regions. Tea, cotton, peanuts, and other cash crops are grown. Male workers move to mining jobs in Zaire and South Africa. Relations with the latter remain relatively cordial in spite of South Africa's former apartheid policy. Malawi's largest city, Blantyre, is in the south. The capital is Lilongwe in the central region.

Areas of Touristic Importance. Malawi offers an abundance of game reserves in the Rift Valley. There are three major game parks. Lengwe, noted for its antelope, is in southern Malawi, one and one-half hours by car from Blantyre. Kasungu, in central Malawi, is famous for elephant, hippos, buck, zebra, and an occasional lion and leopard. Nyika, in the north, is, at more than 6,000 feet, one of the highest game areas of the world.

Lake Malawi has lovely beaches and a large variety of tropical fish. Snorkeling is popular. The Dedza, Mulanje, and Zomba Mountains are popular for hunting and fishing.

■ ANGOLA AND MOZAMBIQUE—AN OVERVIEW

The early history of Portugal's colonial control of the two large units of Angola and Mozambique was marked by exploitation of local labor and resources, limited economic improvement, and the installation of only small numbers of permanent white settlers. However, after World War II, at the very time when other colonial powers were withdrawing from Africa, the Portuguese dictatorship decided to accelerate development to encourage white immigration into the colonies and to consolidate its hold on the region.

Only in 1975, with the end of the dictatorship and with armed resistance against the Portuguese colonial government, did the two nations achieve independence. Physical damage, continued regional tribal rivalries, and warfare are legacies of the preindependence period.

ANGOLA

Official Name: People's Republic of Angola

Language: Portuguese, tribal

Area: 481,353 square miles

Time Zone: GMT +1

Capital: Luanda

Currency: Kwanza

Population: 8,668,000

Documentation: Passport, visa

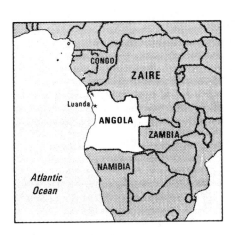

The Land. Angola, closer to Portugal in location, had greater economic promise and attracted more Portuguese investment than Mozambique. It has a 1,000-mile Atlantic frontage, including the small, detached portion of Cabinda, located to the north of a thin strip of Zaire along the lower Zaire (Congo) River, and extends almost as far into the interior. Mostly savanna in climate, it blends into the Kalahari Desert in the south and equatorial rain forest along the Zaire border. Because of the offshore cold Benguela Current, coastal districts are dry and foggy. A number of rivers flow outward from higher topography in the center.

Its natural resources endowment is among the best in Africa. Portuguese exploitation concentrated on cash crops, led by coffee and cotton, and minerals, including iron ore and oil. The north and central regions were the main centers of economic activity.

The Peoples. By the time of independence, about 500,000 white settlers, the second largest white group in sub-Saharan Africa (after South Africa), had moved to Angola. More than half resided in the northwest in and near the capital, Luanda.

The rest were found in regional towns and cities and in large agricultural settlements laid out by the government. Today, only about 30,000 whites remain. The main railway from Zambia and Zaire, used for some copper shipments, crosses central Angola to the twin ports of Benguela-Lobito. The latter has one of the best natural harbors in Africa as well as some manufacturing. Two shorter rail lines link the northern and southern coasts with interior towns and resources.

Civil War. Angola has been seriously damaged and torn by civil war involving long-standing tribal rivals. In the area around Luanda, the Mbunda are the dominant group and support a leftist government that was bolstered by Soviet aid and as many as 40,000 Cuban troops. The Bakongo, in the east, are antigovernment and receive some outside support. The Ovambo, in the south, are militantly antigovernment and were backed by South Africa. An uneasy peace was achieved in 1991 through the joint agreement of the internal forces, the United States, the former Soviet Union and the United Nations. Some 300,000 people died during the long civil war, which left the economy in shambles.

The civil war also brought tourism to a halt, despite many natural features that would attract visitors.

MOZAMBIQUE

Official Name: People's Republic of Mozambique
Language: Portuguese, tribal
Area: 303,769 square miles
Time Zone: GMT +2
Capital: Maputo
Currency: Metical
Population: 15,113,000
Documentation: Passport, visa

The Land. Situated on the Indian Ocean coast, Mozambique, like Angola, is large and even more populous, but it was overshadowed by Angola in Portugal's development programs. The southern part is coastal plain, unusually broad by African standards but narrower to the north; the northern interior is mountainous. Mozambique is divided roughly in half by the Zambezi River; the Limpopo River flows through its southern plain. There are strong cultural differences between the northern and southern tribes.

Economy. Mozambique remained stagnant economically except where it benefited from developments in adjacent British territories. Lourenco Marques, now renamed Maputo, flourished as a railhead and port serving the South African mining centers and as a coastal resort for vacationing South Africans. In addition it was the colonial capital, which helped offset the geographic disadvantage of being at the southern extreme of a political unit that stretched 1,200 miles northward.

Farther north on the coast, Beira served as a railhead and port for Zambia, Zimbabwe, and, by a separate rail line, Malawi. South African ties were strengthened further by the movement of Mozambique men to the South African mining districts as contract labor.

Last-ditch Portuguese efforts to improve the economy in the 1970s included the Cabora Bassa Dam project on the Zambezi River. Commercial crop production was increased in the south, but the north remained poor and remote. There was little mining or manufacturing.

In addition to its inherited problems, Mozambique has continuing problems with armed clashes among ethnic and political factions, a shattered economy, and widespread food shortages and suffering. The white population had increased to about 100,000 persons by the early 1970s, but has dropped sharply since independence. The government of Mozambique does not encourage international tourism.

■ MADAGASCAR AND INDIAN OCEAN UNITS— AN OVERVIEW

A number of islands off the east coast of Africa are of interest. Madagascar is the largest and best known. Tourism is a developing force in the Seychelles. Comoros and the other islands receive few visitors, but some general information can complete the picture of this part of sub-Saharan Africa.

MADAGASCAR

Official Name: Democratic Republic of Madagascar

Language: Malagasy, French

Area: 226,657 square miles

Time Zone: GMT +3

Capital: Antananarivo

Currency: Malagasy franc

Population: 12,185,000

Documentation: Passport, visa

The Land and Climate. The island and nation of Madagascar, also known as Malagasy, lies off the southern African coast in the Indian Ocean. The world's fourth largest island, it measures 1,000 miles north to south and 350 miles east to west. Its mountainous spine runs north to south, with lower elevations on its flanks and a straight eastern coastline. Mount Maromokotro, at 9,450 feet, is the highest in the country. Most of the interior is savanna.

Very dry conditions prevail in the southwest, and the well-watered east coast lies in the path of hurricanes coming from the Indian Ocean. Temperate conditions prevail in the central highlands where the capital and largest city, Antananarivo (formerly Tananarive) is located.

The Peoples. Madagascar sits apart from the African mainland culturally as well as physically. Its numerous tribes speak variations of a language, Malagasy, that is related to Indonesian. The population is believed to be descended from migrants who crossed the Indian Ocean by boat from Southeast Asia in prehistoric times. The use of rice as the main food and hillside terracing may stem from that heritage.

Economy. In 1885, Madagascar became a French protectorate, which it remained until 1958. It achieved full independence in 1960. Limited economic development during the French colonial period has left Madagascar primarily agricultural. Coffee, cloves, and vanilla are the main exports. The herding of cattle, sheep, and goats is widespread. A small mining industry is currently being developed.

Transportation on the island is limited to a simple road network and several short rail lines. There are few good natural harbors. Tamatave (or Toamasina), the best one on the east coast, serves the capital. The best harbor is at Diego Suarez (Antsiranana), at the northern tip of the island, isolated from the main population groupings.

French influences remain strong. The French language is still used in government, business, and education along with Malagasy. French technicians aid the government, and there are friendly diplomatic and commercial ties with France. However, at present, a leftist government is working toward nationalization of selected facets of the economy in the face of public strikes and political party crises. Small numbers of Chinese, Indians, and migrants from the Comoros Islands are active in business in the main towns and cities. Christians form one-half of the population.

Areas of Touristic Importance. Although Madagascar is not a popular tourist destination, the country does offer an unusual blend of African, Malay, Polynesian, and French people and culture. Its unspoiled beaches and lush forests offer outdoor recreation activities and distinctive fauna highlighted by rare lemurs. Unfortunately, Madagascar has suffered from deforestation and the rare lemurs are endangered as well.

COMOROS

Official Name: Comoros Federal Islamic Republic

Language: French

Area: 838 square miles

Time Zone: GMT +3

Capital: Moroni

Currency: CFA franc

Population: 476,000

Documentation: Passport, visa

Between Madagascar and the African mainland are the four volcanic Comoros Islands. Three of them form a separate nation, Comoros, with the capital, Moroni, on Grande Comore, the largest of the archipelago. A fourth island, Mahore (formerly Mayotte), retains its affiliation with France as a dependency. Its people are Christians, whereas those of Comoros are mainly Moslem. Many islanders have migrated to Madagascar in search of better economic opportunity. Tourism has not yet developed on the Comoros Islands.

SEYCHELLES

Official Name: Republic of Seychelles

Language: Creole, English, French

Area: 171 square miles

Time Zone: GMT +4

Capital: Victoria

Currency: Rupee

Population: 68,000

Documentation: Passport

Northeast of Madagascar are the Seychelles, a group of almost 100 islands, only one-third of them inhabited. The four major islands are Mahe, Praslin, La Digue, and Silhouette Island. The Seychelles are located 1,000 miles due east of Mombasa, Kenya and 500 miles northeast of Madagascar.

The Seychelles received their independence from Britain in 1976. The small population of 70,000 is composed of blacks, descended from former slaves, Chinese, and Indians. French-derived Creole is the main language.

Areas of Touristic Importance. Tourism is a major factor in the economy of this small nation. Beaches and water sports are the main attractions of this tropical paradise. Mahe is surrounded by coral reefs and its coastline is among the most beautiful in the world. The islands feature a Marine National Park and a variety of tropical bird life. A high level of tourism promotion by the government has made this isolated island group popular with European visitors. It is growing in popularity with United States tourists, but travel from the United States will continue to be limited by the cost and time required to reach it.

Other Islands

In the Indian Ocean east of Madagascar, the island of Reunion remains under French control.

Still farther eastward, Mauritius got its independence from the British in 1968. It has a mixed population of 1 million persons, mostly Africans descended from slaves and Indians imported as farm laborers. Both groups work on sugar plantations. The Roman Catholic blacks speak French, a holdover from earlier French ownership of the island. The Hindu and Moslem Indians speak English, the official language.

South of the Maldive Islands off India in the middle of the Indian Ocean, are scattered islands that form the British Indian Ocean Territory. One of the islands, Diego Garcia, has been leased to the United States by the British for use as a naval facility.

■ TYPES OF TOURISM

Sub-Saharan Africa receives the fewest visitors from the United States of any populated continent. Travel costs are high, and, except for a few areas, facilities are limited. In addition, few cultural ties exist for nearly 90 percent of the population. Although the west coast of Africa from Senegal to Cameroon attracts sun-seeking Europeans during the winter, travel costs and distances limit the number of visitors from the United States.

The major attraction, and what makes this region unique, is wildlife. Game parks, preserves and reserves (different titles for the same type of facility) contain animal life not found elsewhere other than in zoos. The most popular form of travel is the small, escorted group. The following itineraries are typical examples.

■ Uganda, Tanzania, Kenya.

The President's Tour

Come on our fully escorted tour to South Africa! Your Tour Leader will be Gilbert Zalman, the President and owner of Safariworld. South Africa holds a very special place in Gil's heart and he is looking forward to showing this magnificent country to you. Just contemplate how pleasant it would be to let someone else worry about those myriad travel details... especially if that "someone" was the President of Safariworld! So, relax and come with us to explore this extraordinary "world in one country"!

Friday, Day 1: Depart U.S.A. Depart this evening on your flight to South Africa.

Saturday, Day 2: Arrive Johannesburg. Upon arrival at Jan Smuts Airport in Johannesburg, you will be met and transferred to your hotel. An informal welcome cocktail and dinner at the hotel this evening.
Overnight: SANDTON SUN HOTEL/CARLTON HOTEL.   (D)

Sunday, Day 3: Johannesburg/Durban. Morning tour of Johannesburg, the financial and commercial center of South Africa. Your tour will include a visit to Gold Reef City. Afternoon flight to Durban where you will be met and transferred to the hotel. Time to relax before going to the home of a South African family for dinner this evening. Return to the hotel after dinner.
Overnight: MAHARANI HOTEL.   (B,D)

Monday, Day 4: Durban. After breakfast, set out on a sightseeing excursion of Durban beginning along the Victoria Embankment and including the colorful Indian spice market and the Botanical Gardens. Then, continue north through the sugar cane fields to Shakaland for an informative visit back into the history of the proud Zulu people. Return to Durban in the late afternoon. Overnight: MAHARANI HOTEL.   (B,L)

Tuesday, Day 5: Durban/The Garden Route. Morning flight to Port Elizabeth, the starting point for your trip along the glorious Garden Route. From here it is an easy drive through the rural landscape of the Eastern Cape to the forests of the spectacular Tsitsikamma Coastal Park and on to Storms River and the resort town of Knysna. Overnight: KNYSNA PROTEA HOTEL.   (B,L)

Wednesday, Day 6: The Garden Route. Today's visit to Oudtshoorn will include a guided tour of a working ostrich farm where you will learn some of the intricacies and ingenious by-products of this unusual business. After lunch, continue on to the Cango Caves, a spectacular series of pre-historic, subterranean caves. Return to your hotel in the late afternoon.
Overnight: KNYSNA PROTEA HOTEL.   (B,L)

Thursday, Day 7: The Garden Route/Cape Town. Explore the highlights of the scenic lake district today, including Plettenberg Bay and the Knysna Lagoon. Late afternoon flight from George to Cape Town, where you will be met and transferred to the hotel.
Overnight: CAPE SUN HOTEL.   (B,L)

Friday, Day 8: Cape Town. Cape Town, South Africa's "Mother City", lies nestled between Table Mountain and Table Bay. It is truly one of the world's most gracious and lovely cities. A morning sightseeing excursion of the city includes Table Mountain and Signal Hill, the rejuvenated waterfront area and the South African Museum. Afternoon at leisure. Overnight: CAPE SUN HOTEL.   (B,L)

Saturday, Day 9: Cape Town/The Winelands. Today's itinerary to the Winelands area outside of Cape Town is a delight for all your senses! The lime washed Cape Dutch architecture stands out against the lush green of the vineyards and the lavender hue of the distant mountains. You will visit one of the premier vineyards of the area for a brief education in South

4   Winelands region outside of Cape Town.

Ostriches

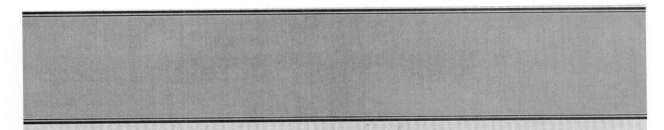

African wines. Then on to Stellenbosch for lunch and tour of this historic and charming town. Return to Cape Town in the afternoon. Overnight: CAPE SUN HOTEL. (B,L)

Sunday, Day 10: Cape Town/Cape of Good Hope. Full day excursion along the spectacular coastal Marine Drive to the Cape of Good Hope, the dramatic meeting point of the Atlantic and Indian Oceans. As you approach Cape Point, you will pass through the Cape of Good Hope Nature Reserve, which was created specifically to preserve the varied flora of the Cape region. Overnight: CAPE SUN HOTEL. (B,L)

Monday, Day 11: Cape Town/Blue Train. Board the world famous Blue Train this morning as it departs Cape Town bound for Pretoria. The Blue Train is justly famous for its 5 star service, food and elegant furnishings. Accommodations in a Category "D" cabin (Luxury accommodations with communal facilities) Overnight: THE BLUE TRAIN. (B,L,D)

Tuesday, Day 12: Pretoria. The Blue Train arrives at the Pretoria Station at 11:00 a.m. You will be met and taken for a sightseeing excursion of Pretoria, the charming Administrative Capital of South Africa. Overnight: BURGERSPARK HOTEL. (B,L)

Wednesday, Day 13: Pretoria/Kruger National Park/ Private Reserve. Morning flight to the famed Kruger National Park where you will be met and transferred to Ngala, a private game reserve adjoining the Kruger Park. Afternoon/evening game drive in open 4-wheel drive vehicles, followed by a traditional dinner in the "Boma" back at the Lodge. Overnight: NGALA LODGE. (B,L,D)

Thursday, Day 14: Kruger National Park/Private Reserve. Begin your day with an early morning game drive. Return to the Lodge for a hearty breakfast and time to engage in some bird-watching or join a walking safari or just relax around the pool. In the late afternoon, set out again with your ranger and tracker to scout the area in search of The Big Five. Your Farewell Dinner will be under the stars tonight in a setting you will long remember. Overnight: NGALA LODGE. (B,L,D)

Friday, Day 15: Kruger National Park/Johannesburg/ Depart. A final morning game drive, then return to the airport for the flight back to Johannesburg. Day room at the Airport Sun Hotel until time to return to Johannesburg Airport for your flight back to the U.S.A.

Saturday, Day 16. Arrive U.S.A. Morning arrival in the U.S.

The President's Trip includes:
- Accommodations as per itinerary
- Breakfast daily, other meals as per itinerary
- All sightseeing as per itinerary
- Blue Train Category "D" accommodations with communal facilities. Upgrade is available.
- All hotel taxes and entrance fees
- Tour is escorted by Gilbert Zalman, President of Safariworld.

1993 Departure Dates and Prices
IT3SA1N016

Land Arrangements:
Price per person based on double occupancy:
March 12; April 23, October 29 .... $4,550
Single Supplement: $775

International Airfare:
New York/Johannesburg/New York .... from $1,699

1994 Departure Dates
January 28; March 11; October 28; November 11.

The Blue Train

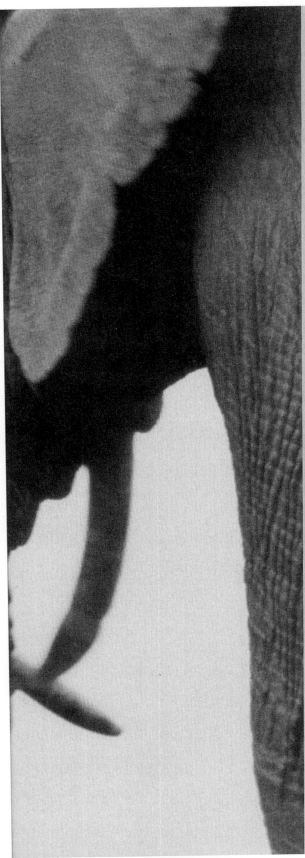

Irving Berner

KENYA AND TANZANIA

17 DAYS

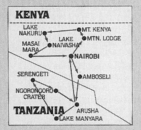

The opportunity of a lifetime. The luxury of Kenya coupled with the spectacular game reserves of Tanzania...from the lush ground forest of Manyara to the basin of the largest unbroken crater on earth ...from the snows of Kilimanjaro to the depths of the Great Rift Valley...from the vast plains of the Serengeti to the rich highlands of Mt. Kenya. Join us on this great combination of two fascinating countries.

THE KENYA AND TANZANIA ITINERARY

Friday, Day 1: U.S.A. Depart U.S.A. on your scheduled flight to Kenya with a brief stop-over in Europe.

Saturday, Day 2: En route/Nairobi. Arrive Europe in the morning and connect to your non-stop flight to Nairobi, arriving there in the evening. The resident Safariworld representative will greet and escort you to the hotel where your room has been pre-registered for immediate check-in.
Overnight: SAFARI PARK HOTEL.

Sunday, Day 3: Nairobi. Awake to the sounds of Africa! At the morning briefing meeting your Safariworld host will outline the Kenya portion of your safari and will answer any questions you might have. Then, board your safari vehicle for a unique sight-seeing excursion of Nairobi and its environs. First stop will be the National Museum, then on to Karen Blixen's home in the Ngong Hills; and the new Artisans' Center in Langata. Back to the hotel in the afternoon. Welcome cocktails and dinner at the home of a prominent Kenyan. Overnight: SAFARI PARK HOTEL.

Monday, Day 4: Amboseli. Your safari begins! Drive south across the Athi Plains to the Masai Amboseli Game Reserve and your first game drive. The mighty, snow-capped Mt. Kilimanjaro looms above the plains and provides a spectacular backdrop to the herds of plains game that abound here.
Overnight: AMBOSELI SERENA LODGE.

Tuesday, Day 5: Tanzania/Lake Manyara. The predators (lions, cheetah, leopard, hyena) are on the move in the early morning, so a pre-breakfast game drive provides an excellent time to view and photograph the wildlife. Later this morning, cross the border and enter into Tanzania. Your first stop is the

Mt. Meru Hotel in Arusha for a luncheon briefing. Continue on to the Lake Manyara Hotel, located on the rim of the Great Rift Wall. Overnight: LAKE MANYARA HOTEL.

Wednesday, Day 6: Serengeti. A morning game drive in Lake Manyara National Park, famous for its spectacular bird life and the indigenous tree-climbing lions. Afternoon drive to the vast Serengeti National Park, viewing game en route. The legendary Serengeti is synonymous with "AFRICA".
Overnight: SERONERA WILDLIFE LODGE.

Thursday, Day 7: Serengeti. Within the 5700 square miles of this reserve are enormous herds of wildebeest, zebra and gazelle grazing on the wide open plains. Here too, are the cats - lion, cheetah and leopard - as well as a multitude of other animal and bird life. Overnight: SERONERA WILDLIFE LODGE.

Friday, Day 8: Olduvai Gorge/Ngorongoro Crater. First stop this morning is Olduvai Gorge, the site of the Leakey team's discovery of Homo habilis, the 1.75 million-year old remains of early man. From here, we ascend the top rim of Ngorongoro Crater. Millions of years ago, Ngorongoro was the largest mountain in the world. It erupted and collapsed into itself, becoming a caldera, or collapsed volcano. The resulting crater is in excess of 100 square miles with steep rim sides that create a unique, self contained ecosystem. The floor of the crater is home to a multitude of wildlife - huge herds of plains game, rhino, hippo, leopard, lion and even elephant. Arrive at

the Lodge in time to enjoy the sight of the sun setting over the crater. Overnight: NGORONGORO WILDLIFE LODGE.

Saturday, Day 9: Ngorongoro Crater. Your 4-wheel drive vehicle will descend 2000 feet to the floor of the crater for a full day game drive with picnic lunch. In the late afternoon return to the lodge. Overnight: NGORONGORO WILDLIFE LODGE.

Sunday, Day 10: Mountain Village Plantation. The last visit in Tanzania is Mountain Village, a charming lodge located amid the coffee plantations on Lake Duluti. Afternoon at leisure. Overnight: MOUNTAIN VILLAGE PLANTATION.

Monday, Day 11: Mountain Lodge. Board your chartered aircraft this morning for the flight to Nairobi, and from there, continue north by safari van to Mountain Lodge Tree Hotel on the slopes of Mt. Kenya. Your room with its private balcony overlooks the night lit water hole. Overnight: MOUNTAIN LODGE.

Tuesday, Day 12: Mount Kenya Safari Club. A short drive takes you across the Equator (be sure to have your picture taken while straddling the line!) and on to the luxurious Mt. Kenya Safari Club. This mid-safari break is a perfect opportunity to make use of the numerous sports, excercise and beauty facilities of the Club. Overnight: MT. KENYA SAFARI CLUB.

Wednesday, Day 13: Lake Nakuru/Lake Naivasha. Continue South into the Great Rift Valley and on to the Lake Nakuru

Bob Burch

National Park. Lake Nakuru is a fresh water lake that supports a huge population of flamingos, pelicans and storks. In addition, a sanctuary for the endangered Black Rhino has recently been established here. Continue to Lake Naivasha, perhaps the most beautiful of the numerous lakes of the Great Rift Valley, for a relaxing evening.
Overnight: LAKE NAIVASHA CLUB.

Thursday, Day 14 and Friday, Day 15: Masai Mara. The topography changes as you enter the vast grassy plains of the Masai Mara Game Reserve - the northern section of the great Serengeti Plains. This is the home of the Big Five... elephant, lion, leopard, buffalo and rhino, as well as thousands of the greater and lesser plains game. It is not uncommon here to encounter a pride of as many as 30 lions, dominated by magnificent, black-maned males or, to come upon a huge gathering of hippo lazing away the day in the Mara River. Everything seems to be magnified here! Two overnights: MARA SERENA LODGE.

Saturday, Day 16: Nairobi. The morning game run heads northeast across the reserve and on to Nairobi. A dayroom is reserved at the Safari Park Hotel until time for dinner and transfer to the airport for your departing flight to Europe.

Sunday, Day 17: Arrive USA. Arrive in Europe in the morning and connect with your flight back to the USA.

The Kenya and Tanzania safari includes:

- Best accommodations as per itinerary
- All meals while on safari and in Nairobi
- Welcome cocktails and dinner
- Safari briefing by Safariworld staff in Nairobi and Arusha
- Chartered flight from Arusha to Nairobi
- Transfers and Game Drives via safari vans which are personally chauffeured by your own guide through the game reserves of Kenya and Tanzania as per the itinerary
- The full day game drive in the crater is operated by the crater guides in 4-wheel drive vehicles
- Olduvai Gorge and Museum visit
- Night game viewing at Mountain Lodge Tree Hotel
- All entrance fees to National Parks and Game Reserves
- Exclusive sightseeing tour in Nairobi including Karen Blixen's House, The National Museum, and the Utamaduni Craft Center
- Flying Doctor Service
- All airport Transfers and baggage handling
- And Safariworld's *Safari Savvy* kit

KENYA AND TANZANIA
1993 DATES & PRICES

Departure Dates from the U.S.	Land Only Cost per person	Land & Air From New York Cost per person
January 8, 15, 22 February 5, 12, 19, 26 March 5, 12, 19, 26	$3,295	$5,085
April 2, 9 May 28	$2,995	$4,785
June 4, 11	$2,995	$4,980
June 18, 25; July 2, 9, 16, 23, 30 August 6, 13, 20, 27	$3,495	$5,480
September 3, 10, 17, 24 October 1, 15, 29 November 5, 19	$3,495	$5,285
December 3, 17, 24	$3,495	$5,480

(Air taxes not included)

All tour prices are based on two persons sharing a room.

Single Supplement: $595 (March 26 - June 11: $435)

* Holiday Surcharge: $150 per person. On these dates the Aberdare Country Club may replace the Mt. Kenya Safari Club.

• **Special rates available from other KLM / NORTHWEST gateway cities.**

1994 DEPARTURE DATES
January 7, 21; **February** 4, 11, 25; **March** 4, 11, 18, 25; **April** 8; **May** 27; **June** 3, 10, 17, 24; **July** 1, 8, 15, 22, 29; **August** 5, 12, 19, 26; **September** 2, 9, 23, 30; **October** 7, 21; **November** 4, 18; **December** 2, 16*, 23*.

Extensions
SEASIDE RESORTS

A perfect beginning or ending to any of our safaris! Relax and enjoy the long stretches of palm fringed white, coral sand beaches that form Kenya's superb coastline.

MOMBASA

An exotic culture, an intriguing history and fabulous beaches are the draws to Mombasa, a port town visited by Arab traders for over 2,000 years. The blend of African, Arab, Indian and European people has created a fascinating atmosphere, best appreciated in the Old Town, fringing the Dhow harbor.

Sample Itinerary: 4 Days.
Depart from Nairobi on the evening train bound for Mombasa, arriving there the next morning. Transfer to the Serena Beach Hotel, your home for the next two nights. Sightseeing excursion of Mombasa. Meals on a "half board" basis. Return to Nairobi by air and connect with your flight back to the U.S.A.
Cost per person: $595   **Single Supplement: $135**

LAMU

The Lamu archipelago is located 150 miles off the Kenya Coast. It was founded by Arab traders around the 9th Century and gained notority as a trading port in the 18th and 19th Centuries. Outwardly, little has changed since then, and Lamu's appeal is in its unspoiled character and nearly deserted white sand beaches.

Sample Itinerary: 4 Days.
Depart Nairobi via scheduled aircraft for Manda Island and transfer by dhow to the Peponi Hotel on Lamu. This quaint hotel will be your home for the next 3 nights. Meals on "half board" basis. Return to Nairobi by air and connect with your flight back to the U.S.A.
Cost per person: $865   **Single Supplement: $180**

THE SEYCHELLES

Comprised of more than 100 islands, the Seychelles are scattered like pearls in the Indian Ocean, 1000 miles off the Kenya Coast. Millions of years of isolation enabled a unique amalgam of flora and fauna to develope here. The people are just as fascinating, originating from Europe, Africa, India and China.

Sample Itinerary: 8 Days.
Depart from Nairobi on your scheduled flight for Mahe, Seychelles. Relax for three nights at the Fisherman's Cove Hotel on Mahe and then take the short flight to Praslin for four nights at La Reserve Hotel. All meals on "half board" basis. Return to Nairobi via Mahe and connect with your flight back to the U.S.A.
Cost per person: $1895   **Single Supplement: $595**
Nairobi/Mahe/Nairobi: $390

MT. KILIMANJARO CLIMB

At 19,340 feet above sea level, the "roof-top of Africa" is an apt name for the mighty Kilimanjaro. The climb itself is not a technically hard climb and requires no special equipment or skills. It is, however, a rigorous climb which demands excellent health, stamina and a high degree of personal determination.

MT. KILIMANJARO CLIMB ITINERARY

Day 1: Namanga/Marangu: Arrival at Kenya/Tanzania border town of Namanga. You will be met and transferred to the Kibo Hotel for overnight on the lower slopes of Mount Kilimanjaro.
Overnight: KIBO HOTEL

Day 2: Mt. Kilimanjaro: Meet your guide and porters in the morning and begin your walk through several different landscapes that bring you to the Mandara Hut.
Overnight: MANDARA HUT

Day 3: Mt. Kilimanjaro: Continue following the ten mile trail to Horombo Hut. Like all huts, Horombo is clean, well-maintained and in radio contact with Park Headquarters.
Overnight: HOROMBO HUT

Day 4: Mt. Kilimanjaro: Vegetation gradually disappears as you near the saddle, a sort of high altitude desert between the peaks of Mawenzi and Kibo. Climbers turn in early to rest before the final ascent that begins early in the morning.
Overnight: KIBO HUT

Day 5: Mt. Kilimanjaro: Arise early to begin the steep, final ascent to the top of Kibo. Reach Gillman's Point, which is considered the summit of Kilimanjaro. Time, weather, and stamina permitting, continue onto Uhuru Peak. Descend to Kibo Hut and on to Horombo Hut for your overnight.
Overnight: HOROMBO HUT

Day 6: Marangu: A long walk today from Horombo Hut to Park Headquarters, but the official climbing certificate makes it all worthwhile. Continue down to the Kibo Hotel, where you collect your non-climbing gear and transfer to the MOUNTAIN VILLAGE PLANTATION for dinner and overnight.

Day 7: Marangu/Namanga: Morning transfer to the Kenya/Tanzania border town of Namanga.

Mt. Kilimanjaro Climb includes:
- Roundtrip transfers Namanga/Marangu/Namanga.
- Accommodations per itinerary. Please note: there are no private bath facilities at mountain huts.
- Meals as follows: 1 night at Kibo Hotel on half-board basis; 4 nights in huts on Kilimanjaro on full board basis.
- Services of guide and porter on climbing portion.
- All hotel taxes and service charges.
- Kilimanjaro park entry fees and mountain rescue fees.

PRICE PER PERSON
BASED ON DOUBLE OCCUPANCY

Group of 6 people: $1,285   Group of 4 people: $1,485
Group of 2 people: $1,685   Single Supplement: $205
Prices are based on two persons sharing a room.

GORILLA TREKKING in RWANDA

The prospect of watching Rwanda's rare and magnificent high mountain gorillas at close range in their natural habitat is terribly exciting ... but gorilla trekking is not for everyone. If you are prepared to climb through the forest (some days, hiking up to four hours) over steep terrain at high altitudes to view these gentle giants, then gorilla trekking is for you. The reward is worth the effort!

GORILLA TREKKING ITINERARY

Day 1: Kigali/Ruhengeri. Upon arrival in Kigali, you will be met and transferred directly to Ruhengeri. Dinner and overnight: MUHABURA HOTEL. (D)

Day 2: Gorilla Trekking. Your adventure begins! After breakfast, drive to the Parc du Volcans, where you will meet with your guide and trackers, and begin the trek through the bamboo forest in search of the elusive gorilla families. The location of the gorillas that morning determines the length of your hike. When contact is made with a family group, you will spend time observing their extraordinarily human antics. Return to the hotel for dinner and overnight: MUHABURA HOTEL. (B,L,D)

Day 3: Gorilla Trekking. Return to the Parc today to trek up the mountain trail again in search of these magnificent and powerful giants. After the excursion today, drive to Gisenyi for dinner and overnight: IZUBA MERIDIEN HOTEL. (B,L,D)

Day 4: Gisenyi/Kigali. After breakfast, drive to Kigali and transfer to the airport for your departure flight.

Please note: The above four-day tour departs from Nairobi on Tuesday and returns back to Nairobi on Friday. If that sequence does not match up with your safari, there is also a five day tour which departs from Nairobi on Friday and returns on the following Tuesday.

The Gorilla Trekking extension includes:
- 2 nights at the Muhabura Hotel in Ruhengeri
- 1 night at the Izuba Meridien Hotel in Gisenyi
- All meals
- 2 Gorilla tracking permits
- All transfers.

PRICES PER PERSON
BASED ON DOUBLE OCCUPANCY

Group of 6 people: $1,295   Group of 4 people: $1,495
Group of 2 people: $1,695   Single Supplement: $195

The current round trip air fare Nairobi/Kigali/Nairobi is $294 per person.

VICTORIA FALLS

Day 1: Nairobi/Harare. Leave Nairobi for arrival in Harare. You will be met and transferred to the MONOMATAPA HOTEL for dinner and overnight. (D)

Day 2: Harare/Victoria Falls. Morning transfer to the airport for the flight to Victoria Falls, where you will be met and transferred to the hotel. More than a mile wide and over 350 feet deep, "Vic Falls" and bigger by half than Niagara! You will fully explore this natural wonder by bus and on foot, viewing the 8 cataracts and the rain forest caused by the enormous spray. In the evening, you will see the "African Spectacular" presentation. Dinner and overnight: VICTORIA FALLS HOTEL. (B,D)

Day 3: Victoria Falls/Harare. Morning at leisure to explore the Falls. Afternoon transfer to the airport for the flight back to Harare. Transfer to the MONOMATAPA HOTEL for dinner and overnight. (B,D)

Day 4: Harare/Nairobi. Depart Harare for Nairobi. (B)

Please note: The above three-day tour departs from Nairobi on Monday. If a Monday departure does not match up with your safari, there is also a four day extension that departs from Nairobi on Friday and returns back to Harare on Monday.

The Victoria Falls extension includes:
- 2 overnights at the Monomatapa Hotel in Harare
- One overnight at the Victoria Falls Hotel in Victoria Falls
- Breakfast and dinner daily
- Sightseeing tour of Victoria Falls
- The African Spectacular performance
- Local transfers

Price per person, based on double occupancy: $685
Single supplement: $138

The current round trip air fare Nairobi/Victoria Falls/Nairobi is $721 per person.

Balloon Safari

An exhilarating experience! Ascend over the vast plains at dawn and drift with the air currents over herds of wildlife below you. A champagne breakfast on the savannah at the end of the flight.
Price per person with confirmed reservations:
From the Masai Mara: Approximately $325 per person
From the Serengeti: Approximately $325 per person

■ REVIEW—SUB-SAHARAN AFRICA

1. Identify the general character of Africa's topography and its main river systems.

2. What are the main climatic conditions encountered over wide areas of Africa?

3. Why did Europeans establish colonies in Africa? Which former colonies are currently most successful in attracting tourism?

4. What are the major characteristics of the nations that line the western coast of Africa?

5. What characteristics and conditions set South Africa apart from other African nations?

6. Name the major African game preserves. Where are they located?

7. Describe the touristic importance of Rwanda.

8. Describe the touristic attractions of Zimbabwe. Discuss the nation's problems.

9. Where are the major beach and resort areas of sub-Saharan Africa?

10. Describe four areas of major scenic beauty in the region.

13

South Asia

The huge continent of Asia contains three major cultural worlds other than the Middle East and Russia, already discussed. These are South Asia, East Asia, and Southeast Asia.

South Asia, called the Indian subcontinent by the British, lies on the southern flank of Eurasia between the Middle East and Southeast Asia. Its nations include India, Pakistan, Bangladesh, Nepal, Bhutan, and Sri Lanka (formerly Ceylon). Both the physical region and its human patterns are on a vast scale. India is the cultural heart of the region, much as China is of East Asia, and has one of the world's most distinctive assemblages of people, languages, and religions. Here, too, is the largest grouping of people anywhere in the world except East Asia, and the problem of how to provide better living standards for the growing numbers is baffling.

■ THE LAND

The entire subcontinent measures some 2,000 miles east-west and north-south, and the bulk of it juts southward as a giant

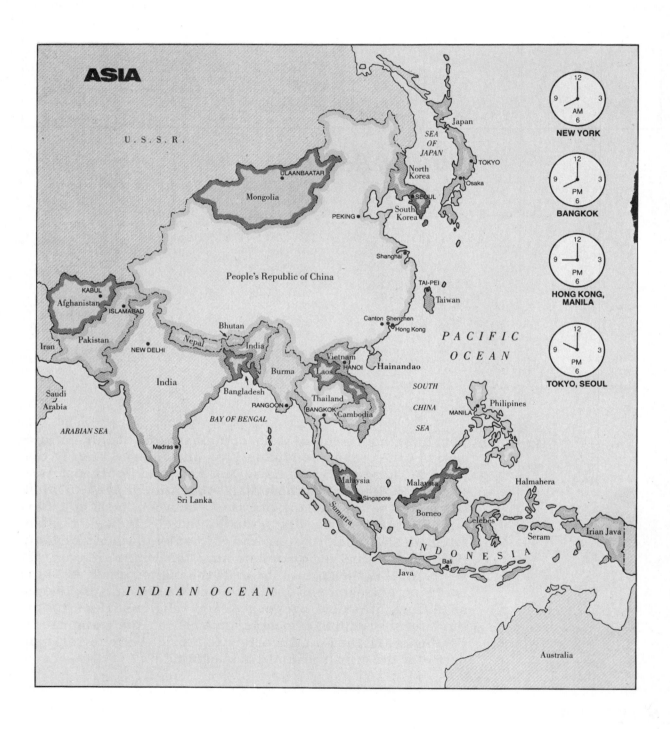

peninsula into the Indian Ocean, with the Bay of Bengal to the east and the Arabian Sea to the west. Physically, it is cast in three grand units: the Himalaya Mountains, the Indus-Ganges Plain (called the Indo-Gangetic Plain by the British), and the Deccan Plateau.

The Himalayas, the highest mountain range in the world, extend in a giant arc along the northern edge of the subcontinent. Among the numerous peaks over 20,000 feet high is Mount Everest (29,028), the world's tallest. Combined with the high, cold, and dry Tibetan Plateau to the north, other mountains and deserts on the west in Afghanistan and eastern Iran, and mountains in western Burma, the Himalayas have been the chief barrier isolating the subcontinent from China and the Middle East. They are also an important climatic agent. Their south slopes intercept moisture-bearing winds in summer and cause unusually heavy seasonal precipitation in the region from Delhi to Bangladesh.

South of the Himalayas and western mountains, an almost continuous lowland runs east-west for about 1,500 miles. It is crossed by two great river systems originating in the Himalayas. In the west, the Indus River and its tributaries flow from the mountains to the Arabian Sea, and in the east, the Ganges River and its tributaries flow eastward to the Bay of Bengal. Before reaching the ocean, the lower reaches of the Ganges blend with those of the Brahmaputra River, another major river that rises in Tibet, in a compound delta.

Since prehistoric times, this giant Indus-Ganges Plain has been the heartland of Indian culture, the largest producer of foodstuffs, and has supported the major concentration of people.

The peninsular portion, which juts southward into the tropics, consists of several plateaus having hilly and mountainous surfaces and fringing coastal plains. The central and southern portions are called the Deccan. Elevations are highest in the west in the West Ghats, which run north-south parallel to the coast, causing most of the large Deccan rivers to flow eastward to the Bay of Bengal.

■ CLIMATE

The subcontinent has a classic monsoon climate marked by well-defined wet and dry seasons. The rains begin dramatically with torrential downpours in May and June, slacken during the summer, and taper off in early fall. The heaviest rainfalls, in excess of 100 inches per year, occur along the Deccan coasts and the Ganges lower valley and delta; the Deccan interior is much drier, as a result of its topography, and is subject to drought.

The Indus valley is dry to desert, but comprehensive irrigation systems using river water have been developed. The dry season prevails during late fall, winter, and spring. Summers are hot, sultry, and oppressive; winters are generally sunny and warm during the day and, in northern India, chilly at night. Premonsoon temperatures during the spring months are very high; everything is dry, dusty, and stifling before the rains once again bring relief. Hill stations at higher elevations, built in the last century by the British to provide relief from the intense heat, are still well-patronized by the middle class—Darjeeling, Simla, and Poona are well-known examples.

■ PEOPLE, RELIGIONS, AND HISTORY

Population distribution matches that of the availability of water for agriculture. It is heaviest in the Ganges Plain, upper Indus Plain (the Punjab), and along the coasts; lighter in the Deccan; and least in the deserts of the west and northwest except where irrigation is available.

As in China and the Middle East, the archeological record goes back some 5,000 years, when an advanced agriculture and urban life has been identified in the central and upper Indus River Plain. It was from these beginnings that Indic (Indian) civilization developed and expanded.

About 4,000 years ago, new people, collectively called the Aryans, gradually infiltrated from central Asia and Afghanistan and took over the earlier Indus Plain settlements. The Aryans brought with them folk beliefs that eventually were formalized into Hinduism, and a social-economic organization that became the caste system.

Their languages, part of the Indo-European language tree that rises from the root language of Sanskrit, became the main tongues of the northern and central subcontinent. In the south, however, the pre-Aryan Dravidian languages spoken by the earlier inhabitants are still used.

Buddhism, an offshoot of Hinduism, developed in northeastern India in the 6th century BC, then spread northward into the Chinese culture realm, southward to Ceylon, and eastward to the Southeast Asian mainland. Ironically, Buddhism has not been a principal religion in its land of origin.

Beginning in the 10th century AD, invasions from Persia brought Islam into the continent, adding another religion and cultural overlay. Conversions to Islam were heaviest in the northwest and the northeast, lighter in the overwhelmingly Hindu Ganges Plain and its borders, and least in the south. The Moslem invasions also modified the political make-up, creating various combinations of Hindu or Moslem rulers who ruled in the numerous princely states that operated under a national Moslem dynasty.

European interest in trade in India began in the 16th century with intense rivalry between Portuguese and Dutch, and later the French and British, over control of both trade and territory. By 1763, the British, operating through the East India Company, were in command. The Indian Mutiny of 1857 brought East India Company control to an end. India then became a colony under the direct administration of the British government and remained so until 1947.

During this long period, the most important populated and productive areas had British administrators, while hundreds of territories, large and small, remained under hereditary local rulers who were subject to British law. Among the many other British-induced changes was the emergence of three port cities—Calcutta, Bombay, and Madras—as the main centers of commerce. Calcutta served as the capital until 1925, when the government was moved inland to a new planned location adjacent to Delhi, which had once been a ruling seat of Indian dynasties.

A comprehensive railway network was built, linking the port cities and all parts of the subcontinent, and the dry areas of the upper Indus Plain were made productive by the world's largest irrigation system, created by British engineers. English became the official language and British law, education, military organization, and government the norm.

Independence

An Indian independence movement, started early in the 20th century, gained momentum before it was sidetracked temporarily by World War II. Independence moved to successful conclusion after the war. Then, however, Moslem leaders demanded and secured the partition of India in order to create a separate Moslem nation, Pakistan.

Pakistan consisted of two units or "wings"—West Pakistan, shaped around the Indus Plain, and East Pakistan, shaped around the Ganges-Brahmaputra delta—separated by 1,000 miles of unfriendly Indian territory and based solely on a majority Moslem population. Partition set in motion an enormous population exchange between the two new nations in an atmosphere of distrust and ill-feeling that still persists. Hastily fashioned on the uncertain basis of a common Moslem faith, Pakistan had a troubled existence until 1971, when East Pakistan seceded and became independent Bangladesh. Pakistan was thus reduced in size to the unit formerly called West Pakistan.

Much of Jammu and Kashmir, a princely state in the western Himalayas with a Moslem majority, remains under Indian control and is a continuing source of conflict. Partition also dominantly Hindu population. Ceylon (now Sri Lanka), Nepal, Bhutan, and Sikkim also achieved self-rule; Sikkim was later absorbed by India.

■ INDIA, PAKISTAN, AND BANGLADESH— AN OVERVIEW

India (Republic of India) is the world's second most populous nation after China. Attempts to slow the population's growth rate, currently at 2.2 percent per year, have not been successful primarily because of widespread cultural opposition. Population densities in rural areas, where 80 percent of the people live, are among the highest in the world. Although India occupies only 2.4 percent of the world's land area, it supports nearly 15 percent of the world's population.

INDIA

Official Name: Republic of India

Languages: Hindi, English

Area: 1,266,595 square miles

Time Zone: GMT +5:30

National Airline: Air India

Capital: New Delhi

Currency: Indian rupee (INR)

Population: 866,000,000

Documentation: Passport, visa

Religions and Languages. As a result of its historical evolution, India has as much cultural diversity as any nation, but, because of its size, on an unmatched scale. Hinduism, the dominant religion, is practiced by 83 percent of the people. Hindu temples, religious festivals and holidays, tenets and practices, arts, pilgrimages, and political action groups are central features of Indian life everywhere and a key source of national social cohesion. Moslems make up 11 percent of the population, with a much larger presence in cities and the rural areas of the Ganges Plain. In fact, India qualifies as one of the world's largest Moslem-populated nations. Moslem-Hindu civil tensions flare frequently to the point of street fighting and bloodshed.

Numerous other minority religions include the Sikhs of the northwest, whose religion is an offshoot of Hinduism; Buddhists, including refugee Tibetans living in northern India; Jains, whose religion also is an offshoot of Hinduism, Christians, in the south, cities, and northeastern areas; and northeast tribesmen who practice animism.

Many languages, representing at least four language families, are spoken in India. About three-fourths of the population speak some Indo-European language. Hindi, the prevailing tongue of north central India, is spoken by several hundred million persons and has been declared the national language. Among related Indo-European languages, the Bengali spoken in and around Calcutta in the east and the Marathi spoken in the west around Bombay rival Hindi in their rich literary tradition.

In the southern Deccan, one-fourth of the national population speak one of four main Dravidian languages. Tamil, used in and around Madras, is the most important. Dravidian-speakers have resisted the imposition of Hindi, which is very different in words, structure, and pronunciation, as the national language.

Because of these regional linguistic conflicts and the lingering British tradition, English remains the language of government, higher education, and international business. Tribal units in the remote northeast speak a variety of Tibeto-Burmese languages. Scattered in a southwest to northeast band through peninsular India, usually in remote areas, are "tribals," some of whom still speak ancient pre-Aryan languages unrelated to any others in India.

Language has also been used as a basis for the territories of the 22 Indian states. The political units inherited from the British period have been reworked since independence and are now based on historical precedent, or, more commonly, the local majority language. Thus, three large states, each with a population larger than any European nation, represent Hindi-speakers; West Bengal represents Bengali-speakers; and Maharashtra represents Marathi-speakers.

In the south, each of four states represents the dominant local Dravidian language, and a cluster of small states in the northeast recognize major Tibeto-Burmese languages. These are not clearcut linguistic units. Each also contains varying numbers of minority languages or dialects. In one state, Punjab, the Sikhs are trying to blend their religion with the Punjabi language as the basis for a separate state, a move strongly resisted by the Indian government, which has the recent history of partition and continuing Moslem-Hindu problems before it.

The Peoples. More than three-fourths of the Indian population live in rural towns and villages spread across the nation's habitable areas, yet cities are growing quickly as the result of immigration. The four largest cities remain those of the colonial period: Calcutta, Bombay, Madras, and Delhi.

Calcutta, with 12 million persons, and Bombay, with 11 million, are among the world's twelve largest metropolitan areas. Calcutta is the chief port, manufacturing, and commercial center for northeastern India. Bombay has India's finest deep-water port and is the economic center for western India. It also has an important manufacturing function, specializing in cotton textiles based upon local cotton supplies.

Although smaller than Calcutta and Bombay, Madras is the principal urban service center of the more agricultural southeast. Delhi has two distinct urban personalities; the older city with its time-worn buildings and monuments to the imperial past, and the modern, planned government complex of New Delhi, that is laid out on a sweeping scale. Delhi also provides the usual range of urban services for India's northwest.

In addition to the four major metropolises, there are numerous large and fast-growing regional cities that combine pre-British, British, and modern features. As might be expected, they occur in the largest number in the densely settled Ganges Plain. Varanasi (Benares), Patna, Allahabad, Cawnpore, Lucknow, and Agra are among them. Hyderabad, the main city of the southern central Deccan, has more than 2 million inhabitants.

Economy. These cities typically reflect the socioeconomic classes of Indian society—on the one hand, they have lovely residential areas, historic cores, and splendid old and new buildings; and on the other, decaying districts and some of the world's worst slums. Government housing cannot be erected fast enough to accommodate the human wave of migrants sweeping cityward from the crowded countryside in search of jobs and a better life.

An important factor in the life of the Indian peoples is the caste system, comprising the classes of Indian society. This system is based theoretically on employment-related categories ranked on a defined hierarchy. Traditionally, four classes were identified, plus a class of outcastes or untouchables. Despite economic development, modernization, and laws prohibiting discrimination against the lower classes, the caste system remains an important factor in Indian society, especially in rural areas.

India's economy is underdeveloped and still relies on a slowly improving agriculture. One fundamental problem is that land tenure is lopsided. Five percent of the farm families own the bulk of the farmland; about one-half have only tiny holdings of 1 to 2 acres or less; and some own none at all. Also, the supply of farmland, which is large by world standards, simply is insufficient for the enormous numbers of rural people desiring their own holdings.

The bulk of the peasantry remains poor, underemployed, or works for minute wages as farm laborers, with no hope of improvement. These conditions prompt movement to the cities. Traditional, inefficient farming techniques continue in use and, when combined with the limited use of fertilizer and insecticides, result in very low yields. Except for some simpler equipment, such as pumps for irrigation, farm machinery is scarce but is increasing as the government's policy of rural electrification gradually brings electricity to the farm villages.

On the brighter side, some advanced agricultural areas, marked by the application of modern operating techniques, high yields, and a more prosperous peasantry, can be found in the dry, irrigated northwest, where the Sikhs are good farmers, and in the well-watered, irrigated southeast. Both areas have benefited from the "green revolution," the use of new hybrid grain strains, wheat in the northwest and rice in the southeast, to get much higher yields.

Major Indian crops are rice in the areas of heavy rainfall on the coasts and in the northeast; wheat in the dry or irrigated croplands of the west and northwest; and millets and sorghums, crops that tolerate a limited and variable moisture supply, in the Deccan and dry northern interior. Maize, peanuts, peas, and a great variety of vegetables and fruits are also raised.

Emphasis is usually upon subsistence, enough to feed the farm family; and only then is some attention given, where possible, to surpluses for sale of such cash crops as cotton, sugar cane, and coconuts. Commercial tea production, started during the colonial period, is found on large estates in the northeastern Himalaya forefront and in the hills of the southern Deccan. Year-round cultivation of crops is possible in many parts of India.

In its economic modernization attempts, India lacks oil but is fortunate to have plentiful supplies of coal, iron ore, and other industrial raw materials. The best single concentration of these assets and heavy industry utilizing them is west of Calcutta, in the Chota Nagpur region. There, the landscape includes steel mills, busy machinery works, and railways carrying raw material or manufactured goods.

Overall, India has made good progress in industrialization and has one of the world's largest industrial labor forces. Textile and consumer goods manufacture is widespread. Manufacturing growth is slowed by shortages of development capital, limited domestic purchasing power, and government policies that limit foreign investment. Some coal and iron ore are exported. One major accomplishment of the government since independence has been the construction of numerous large dams on major rivers to boost the electric power supply, control floods, and store irrigation water for the dry season. The nation is crisscrossed with excellent rail, road, and air transportation systems.

Areas of Touristic Importance. India has been exciting travelers from the world over for centuries. Its complex cultures have created a mystique that must be experienced to be appreciated.

Agra is home of the Taj Mahal, the most celebrated and beautiful attraction in India and one of the greatest attractions in the world. Edward Lear said: "Henceforth let the inhabitants of the world be divided into two classes: those who have seen the Taj Mahal and those who have not." Agra is 125 miles from New Delhi. The Taj can be visited on a 1-day excursion from New Delhi.

New Delhi (which includes the old city, Delhi, and the new city developed by the British as well as the post-British leaders) itself has many magnificent monuments as well as a most modern government cluster. The Jama Masjid is a remarkable mosque made of red and white marble. Inside the Red Fort, built in 1647, is the Imperial Palace of Shah Jahan, builder of the Taj Mahal. The Qutb Minar is a 234-foot fluted, sandstone minaret built by Moslems in the 13th century. Modern New Delhi contains the remnants of at least seven royal cities and hundreds of interesting historical monuments.

Bombay, like New Delhi, is a major gateway to India. It is India's main port city and it reflects both British and Indian history. Bombay is a cosmopolitan city and a major industrial center. Elephanta Island, 6 miles across the harbor, provides an unequaled view of the Bombay skyline and contains cave-temples dating to the 6th century.

Varanasi, also known as Benares, stands on the banks of the Ganges River, halfway between New Delhi and Calcutta. Varanasi is one of the oldest cities in the world and the spiritual center of the Hindu religion. For thousands of years pil-

Taj Mahal, Agra
Photo: Courtesy Government of India Tourist Office

grims have come to Varanasi to cleanse themselves of their sins in the holy (now polluted) waters of the Ganges. Just south is Sarnath, the center of the Buddhist world.

Jaipur is a walled city that is called the "pink city" because of the shade of marble used in the maharajah's palace and other buildings. It is surrounded on all sides by rugged hills crowded with forts.

Srinagar, in the Vale of Kashmir at the north of India, is a natural masterpiece. The very name, Kashmir, evokes thoughts of natural beauty. It is a land of rivers, misty lakes, and flower meadows. Tourists can choose to spend several nights living on a houseboat on Dall Lake instead of in a hotel. The lake has a life of its own, with its floating markets and families living on boats. Taking a boat ride on the lake provides an inside view of the lifestyle of the families living on the lake. Moguls, maharajahs, and British rajs all found Srinagar to be a relaxing retreat. Unfortunately, since the late 1980s, political unrest and sporadic fighting has made this a destination only for the adventurous.

Udaipur is, perhaps, the most romantic city in India. Elegant marble palaces appear to be floating on blue lakes. The city was built to fulfill the visions of Indian princesses.

Madras, in the south, features classical art. It was the home of Fort St. George, Britain's first settlement in India. Nearby, Mahabalipuram is the site of 7th century monolithic shrines carved from solid rock.

Aurangabad is the site of the Ajanta and Ellora caves, which rank with Egypt's pyramids as some of the ancient world's most impressive remains.

Goa, a former Portuguese colony, adds another element to the mystique of India. Fine Jesuit and Renaissance architecture attest to its heritage. Excellent beaches on the Indian Ocean provide an opportunity for rest and relaxation.

Calcutta, just a village in the 17th century, is today one of the world's largest and most crowded cities. It is a large port and the commercial hub of eastern India. Important sights include the Eden Gardens, New Secretariat, New Market, and the Victoria Memorial. Calcutta also has some of the worst slums and highest levels of poverty in the world.

Sanitation is a problem throughout this region, and travelers are advised to use only bottled water.

PAKISTAN

Official Name: Islamic Republic of Pakistan

Language: Urdu, English

Area: 310,403 square miles

Time Zone: GMT +5

National Airline: Pakistan International Airlines

Capital: Islamabad

Currency: Pakistan rupee (PAR)

Population: 117,490,000

Documentation: Passport, visa

The Islamic nation of Pakistan resulted from the partition of India in 1947. It was reduced to its present size by the secession of East Pakistan, now Bangladesh. Like neighboring India, it faces the stern challenges of a large, fast-growing population living in a difficult physical environment and an underdeveloped economy.

The Land and Economy. Pakistan is shaped physically by the plains of the Indus River and its tributaries, which emerge from the western Himalayas and flow through the broad Punjab plains before joining to become a single river. The Punjab gets light winter rains, but most of the national territory is dry to arid. However, the seasonal availability of a large amount of water from the western Himalayas enabled British engineers, in the 19th century, to create the world's largest irrigation system and the subcontinent's greatest food surplus area.

The Pakistani economy is based upon this agricultural resource. Its output of wheat, cotton, and local specialties meets domestic needs and leaves surpluses for export. As in India, agricultural efficiency is low, there is limited use of fertilizers, and water-using techniques remain traditional. The irrigated land resource supports a large population that is increasing at the rate of 3 percent each year.

The People. The population is almost entirely Moslem and the main language is Urdu, an Indo-European tongue related to Hindi but with many Persian influences. There are also numerous regional dialects and languages. Most of the population resides in the Punjab and in a narrow band following the lower course of the Indus River. In the west, Baluchistan and the rugged hills and mountains of the Pakistan-Afghanistan borderland have a desert climate.

Lahore, with nearly 3 million inhabitants and located in the east central Punjab, has long been the main Moslem cultural center in this part of the subcontinent and the source of practical services to the Punjab population. At the time of partition in 1947, however, it was too disrupted by population transfers to and from India and too close to the new, troubled border with India, so the national capital was placed in Karachi, a British-developed port on the western flank of the Indus River delta. Still the largest city (4 million persons) in Pakistan, Karachi proved too isolated from the rest of the nation and its climate too hot and unpleasant.

Starting in the 1960s, a new planned capital city, Islamabad, was built in a more pleasant location in the hills of the northern Punjab, near the older city of Rawalpindi (Pindi). A short distance west is the important military garrison city of Peshawar, which guards the eastern approaches to the Khyber Pass and the main overland route leading through the mountains to Kabul in Afghanistan.

The Pakistani government has been trying to use both hydroelectric power, generated at dams on the Indus River system, and natural gas to power industrial expansion. Unfortunately, there are few industrial raw materials other than those of agricultural origin. The textile industry flourishes because cotton is locally available, and many consumer goods also are produced.

In sum, however, Pakistan remains a relatively poor, struggling nation with a heavy burden of Islamic and rural traditionalism. It has militarily tense relations with India that date back to partition, causing both nations to depend too heavily on military budgets. Pakistan occupies the western part of Jammu and Kashmir in the western Himalayas, and has demanded, unsuccessfully, that India cede the rest of the territory and its predominantly Moslem population.

Its difficulties in controlling the fierce hill tribes of the Afghan border were complicated in the 1980s by the influx of several million refugees from Afghanistan and the Soviet military occupation there. Pakistan has strong external ties. The United States is one of its strongest allies.

Areas of Touristic Importance. Karachi, on the Arabian Sea, is the main port of Pakistan. Main attractions include the Mausoleum of Quaid-i-Azam, the founder of the nation, the Defence Housing Society Mosque, Frere Hall in the Jinnah Gardens, and the National Museum. Close to Karachi are the hot sulphur springs at Manghopir and the ancient town of Thatta.

Lahore is known as the City of Gardens. It is the educational and cultural (Moslem) center of the country. Many priceless Mogul monuments including the Shalimar Gardens and the Tomb of Emperor Jahangir can be found in Lahore, as well as Badshahi, the world's largest mosque.

Peshawar is known for its bazaars. The most famous is the Quissi Khawani Bazaar, also known as the Street of the Storytellers. The nearby Khyber Pass is critical to the defense of Pakistan and India.

The cities of Rawalpindi and Islamabad in the northern hills are near many summer resorts. There are also many archeological sites dating to the 6th century BC in the area. The best are at Gir, Jaulain, and Taxila. The new, planned city of Islamabad is Pakistan's governmental center.

BANGLADESH

Official Name: People's Republic of Bangladesh

Language: Bengali, English

Area: 55,813 square miles

Time Zone: GMT +6

Capital: Dacca (Dhaka)

Currency: Taka

Population: 116,601,000

Documentation: Passport

The Islamic nation of Bangladesh has had a difficult existence since seceding from Pakistan in 1972. Only one fifth the size of present Pakistan, it has about as many people and is growing at the rate of 2.4 percent each year. The majority language is Bengali, much as it is across the border in India. In addition to Moslems, who comprise 85 percent of the population, there is a Hindu minority in the west near India. Scattered hill tribes are in more remote areas of the northeast and southeast.

The large and essentially agricultural population is crowded into the well-watered lands of the Ganges-Brahmaputra delta, where the farming economy is based on rice, jute, sugar cane, and wheat. Jute, a strong fiber used in heavy-duty commercial sacking, and tea, grown on plantations in northern hilly locations, are the main export crops and income earners. Bangladesh is depends heavily on economic assistance from many other nations.

Areas of Touristic Importance. Dacca, the centrally located, river-fronting capital, is the only large city. A few modern industrial enterprises have been built in the port city of Chittagong on the southeast coast. Bangladesh remains bitterly poor, burdened with too many people and too few means of support.

Like northern India, there are many areas of natural beauty in Bangladesh. Dacca also has hundreds of mosques; the most interesting are the Star Mosque and the Baitul-Mukarram Mosque. Bangladesh does not attract many western visitors.

■ NEPAL, BHUTAN, AND TIBET

Two independent kingdoms, Nepal and Bhutan, lie on the southern flanks of the Himalayas between India and Chinese Tibet. Nepal is, by far, the larger of the two. Tibet, actually part of China, is often part of an itinerary to Nepal and/or Bhutan.

NEPAL

Official Name: Kingdom of
   Nepal
Language: Nepali
Area: 56,136 square miles
Time Zone: GMT +5:45
Capital: Kathmandu
Currency: Nepal rupee (NER)
Population: 19,611,000
Documentation: Passport

Nepal has a northern zone of high mountains, including Mount Everest, astride the Nepal-China border, and a southern zone of hills and low mountains. The former area is the source of several tributaries of India's Ganges River.

The bulk of the population, which is increasing at a rapid rate, is crowded into the more habitable lands of the south. They are of Mongoloid stock. Nepali, an Indo-European language, is the main tongue; and the main religion is Hinduism, with a Buddhist minority. Two groups are well known outside Nepal: the Gurkhas, who have served for generations in the British army, and the Sherpas, who serve as bearers on international mountain-climbing expeditions.

The residence of the Hindu king and his capital are in Kathmandu, the only large city, which is located in an eastern valley. Very poor, Nepal has attracted a host of foreign aid missions. It is a mecca for foreign climbers eager to tackle Mount

Everest and other towering Himalayan peaks. Kathmandu is reached from India by road and air, but internal transportation is primitive.

Areas of Touristic Importance. Trekking is the best way to see Nepal. Porters may be hired for treks ranging from spartan to luxurious. Guides and equipment are secured in Kathmandu. Hunting is strictly controlled and quite expensive.

Hindu and royal shrines and monuments also attract the tourist. Most interesting are the Temple of the Living Goddess and the Temple of Katha Mandap, said to have been built from the timber of a single tree.

Bhaktapur (formerly called Bhadgaon), a short distance from Kathmandu, is the center of Nepalese medieval art. Stone sculptures, wood carvings, temples, and palaces abound.

Meghanli, the Royal Chitwan National Park, is a 1,000-square-mile wildlife preserve. Tigertops, a modern "Treetops" type hotel, offers visitors excellent opportunities to view tigers and other native animals.

BHUTAN

Official Name: Kingdom of Bhutan

Language: Dzongkha

Area: 18,147 square miles

Time Zone: GMT +6

Capital: Thimphu

Currency: Ngultrum

Population: 1,598,000

Documentation: Passport, visa

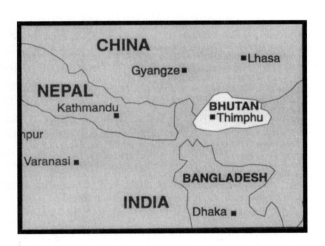

Farther east, little Bhutan has a population of 1.9 million persons, most of whom are related to Tibetans and are Buddhist. Traditional agriculture is the main means of support. Long isolated and oriented northward toward Tibet, Bhutan now has improved air and road links with India. Nominally independent under a kingship with its capital at Thimphu, Bhutan has been drawn increasingly into the Indian commercial and political sphere.

Areas of Touristic Importance. Bhutan opened its borders to tourists only a few years ago. Its natural beauty and Buddhist shrines provide interesting sights. The Simtokha Dzong in Thimphu is situated on a lofty mountain perch. It is one of the oldest fortresses of its kind. Punakha, Bhutan's former is carried on with rainwater stored in thousands of small earthen reservoirs, or tanks. Rice must also be imported to meet the needs of the large population, which grows by 1.5 percent each year. There is little nonagricultural economic activity.

Three-fourths of Sri Lanka's people speak Sinhala, an ancient language, and are Buddhist. The minority population is composed of Hindus whose forebears came from the Dravidian-speaking area of southern India. Tamil is their main language. They are concentrated in the north, where contacts with India are easiest, and have spread southward into the plantation country to work as farm labor. Strife flares intermittently between Sinhalese and Tamils, the latter seeking more security as well as cultural and religious recognition.

Areas of Touristic Importance. Sri Lanka is a tropical island with both palm-fringed beaches and lush, green mountains. It is as close to the equator as Aruba and other lower Caribbean islands, and is thus an excellent location for sun and relaxation.

Colombo is a gracious city with gardens and parks. Its British heritage is seen easily in its Victorian homes and administrative buildings. The National Museum features a large collection of stone and bronze sculptures and other artifacts of ancient Sri Lanka. The Zoological Gardens are among the best in the world with their walk-in aviary and elephant circus.

Kandy, located 72 miles from Colombo, is a beautiful mountain city. It was the capital of ancient Sri Lanka and is the site of the sacred Buddhist Temple of the Tooth, which houses the Sacred Tooth Relic of the Buddha. Outside Kandy, the Royal Botanical Gardens house 150 acres of tropical plants including a fine orchid collection.

MALDIVES

Official Name: Republic of Maldives

Language: Divehi

Area: 115 square miles

Time Zone: GMT +5

National Airline: Air Maldives

Capital: Male

Currency: Maldivian rupee

Population: 226,000

Documentation: Passport

capital, is the religious center of the country. Beautiful temples and intriguing fortresses can be found in Paro, a city set in a magnificent valley dominated by Mount Chomolhari.

TIBET

Because Tibet is now part of China, its geographic features are covered in the chapter on East Asia. From the tourist's standpoint, however, it is part of South Asia itineraries.

Areas of Touristic Importance. Unknown to most westerners, Tibet is a primitive land, almost entirely surrounded by high mountains. Lhasa, its capital and cultural center, was, until its takeover by China, home of the Dalai Lama. It has flourished as a religious center since the 7th century. Xigaze is the location of the Tashilumpo Monastery. It is the seat of the Panchen Lama and a center of the Buddhist religion.

■ SRI LANKA AND THE MALDIVES

SRI LANKA

Official Name: Democratic Socialist Republic of Sri Lanka

Language: Sinhala, Tamil, English

Area: 25,332 square miles

Time Zone: GMT +5:30

National Airline: Air Lanka

Capital: Colombo

Currency: Sri Lanka rupee (CER)

Population: 17,423,000

Documentation: Passport

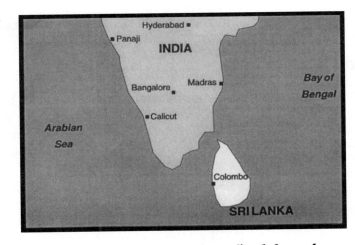

Formerly Ceylon, Sri Lanka benefited from heavy British investment in tropical plantations, and commercial crop exports remain the main source of national revenue. Lying a short distance off the southeast Indian coast, it is a relatively small island, measuring 120 miles east-west and 230 miles north-south. The southern portion contains forested, well-watered mountains, and the northern and eastern plains have more erratic seasonal rainfall.

The plains and mountains in the southwestern corner of the island are the core of the country. This area has coconut, rubber, and tea plantations and, on the coast, the capital and port of Colombo. In the drier areas elsewhere, rice cultivation

The Maldives lie in the Indian Ocean southwest of India. Of the 1,201 islands in the Maldives, only about 200 are inhabited. The population is scattered throughout the chain, with the largest concentration on the capital island, Male.

Over the years, Arab and strong Sinhalese ethnic strains have been added to the original Aryan and Dravidian population, the first of which arrived as early as the fourth century BC Maldivian ethnic consciousness is strong and is reinforced by the almost 100 percent Moslem affiliation.

The Maldives were briefly under the rule of Portugal and then, for a longer period of time, Britain. Commercial ties were primarily with Sri Lanka. The Maldives became an independent republic in 1965.

In 1971 the United Nations included the Maldives on a list of the 25 least-developed nations. Fishing is the major occupation of the islanders.

Areas of Touristic Importance. The Maldives began developing tourism in 1972. Development is based on a major natural resource—some of the most beautiful beaches in the world. Air service is generally through India and Sri Lanka and more than 4,000 beds have been added over the last 10 years. Because of distances and routings, the Maldives have not yet gained general popularity as a tourist destination.

■ TYPES OF TOURISM

Ethnic travelers visiting their homelands represent a major source of travel to this region. Westerners visiting here usually participate in escorted tour programs. Although some of these programs visit only India, most include at least one or two of the other nations. The sample tour that follows explores the area in depth:

■ Grand India
■ The Himalayan Shangri-la

GRAND INDIA WITH NEPAL AND TIGER TOPS

30 days

visiting
Hong Kong / Bangkok
or London, Madras, Kanchipuram,
Mahabalipuram, Mysore, Belur,
Halebid, Bangalore, Cochin,
Goa, Bombay, Aurangabad,
Udaipur, Jaipur, Delhi, Agra,
Khajuraho, Varanasi
INDIA
Kathmandu, Patan,
Bhadgaon, Tiger Tops
NEPAL

*I*ndia's allure has long beckoned travellers to this vast and mysterious world bordered to the north by the mighty Himalayas and surrounded elsewhere by the sea. Offering the traveller an unparalleled cultural experience, SITA's GRAND INDIA highlights the best of this amazing land and offers an unbeatable sampling of India's cultural treasures, from it's magnificent architectural accomplishments to it's living arts — Indian music and dance, recitals of astonishing diversity.

SOUTH INDIA home to elaborate temples, rock-cut monoliths and edifices beyond compare; picturesque harbors, islands, and backwaters coinciding with the rich cultural history of its coastal cities.

WESTERN INDIA, former Portugese stronghold, famed for resplendent white churches and golden beaches; hillsides carved into huge temples and sculptures; and 5th century cave paintings.

NORTH INDIA, illusive and fabled land of the Royal retreats of Rajputs; romantic Taj Mahal; the madcap juxtaposition of old and modern Delhi; and Khajuraho's temple structures depicting Hindus in celebration of life and love. Finally, no visit to this subcontinent would be complete without the vision of paradise that is NEPAL: Shangri-La of the East, home of Gurkha soldiers, a primitive yet captivating culture, and the extensive game reserve and treetop lodge of TIGER TOPS — a fascinating experience to top off a truly enchanting trip.

Revel in the grandeur that is SITA's GRAND INDIA, for a fascinating travel adventure to last a lifetime.

Special Exclusive SITA Features:

- Deluxe & First Class Hotels with private bath/shower.
- Three a-la-carte meals daily including room service.
- Dine Out Plan with reimbursement from Tour Manager on presentation of restaurant bill.
- Welcome & Farewell Dinners with cultural dance and music presentation.
- Kathakali Dance Drama & Backwaters Boat Ride, Cochin.
- Sound & Light Show at Red Fort.
- Mount Everest Flightseeing tour.
- Tharu tribal dancing in Nepal.
- Services of accompanying SITA Tour Manager.
- Touring by private motorcoach, automobile with English speaking guide.

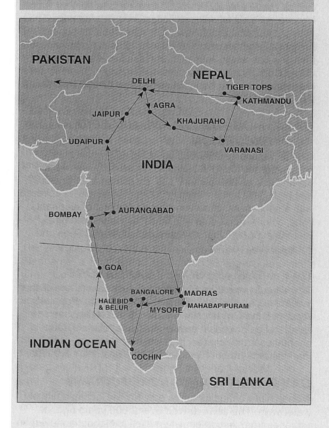

TOUR PRICE:	1993	1994
Land Arrangements	5,695.00	6,180.00
Single Supplement	1,495.00	1,690.00

AIRFARES:		
East Coast		2,310.00
West Coast		2,212.00

NOTE: Airfares are based on Low Season and include flying within India and Nepal as per tour itinerary. Please check for High Season fares and applicable add-on fares from your home city. Airfares are subject to change without notice.

Departure Dates   IT3AI11203

1993

Tour No.	Depart	Return
SGI 244	*Jan 12	Feb 10
SGI 245	Jan 26	Feb 24
SGI 246	Feb 9	Mar 10
SGI 247	Feb 23	Mar 24
SGI 248	Mar 9	Apr 7
SGI 249	Mar 30	Apr 28
SGI 250	Apr 27	May 26
SGI 251	Jun 15	Jul 14
SGI 252	Jun 29	Jul 21
SGI 253	Aug 3	Sep 1
SGI 254	Aug 31	Sep 22
SGI 255	Sep 7	Oct 6
SGI 256	Sep 28	Oct 27
SGI 257	**Oct 5	Nov 3
SGI 258	**Oct 12	Nov 10
SGI 259	***Oct 26	Nov 24
SGI 260	Nov 16	Dec 15
SGI 261	Nov 30	Dec 22
SGI 262	****Dec 7	Jan 5, 94
SGI 263	****Dec 14	Jan 12, 94

1994

Tour No.	Depart	Return
SGI 264	*Jan 18	Feb 16
SGI 265	Jan 25	Feb 23
SGI 266	Feb 8	Mar 9
SGI 267	Feb 22	Mar 23
SGI 268	Mar 8	Apr 6
SGI 269	Mar 29	Apr 27
SGI 270	Apr 26	May 25
SGI 271	Jun 14	Jul 13
SGI 272	Jun 21	Jul 20
SGI 273	Jul 12	Aug 10
SGI 274	Aug 2	Aug 31
SGI 275	Aug 30	Sep 28
SGI 276	Sep 13	Oct 12
SGI 277	Sep 27	Oct 26
SGI 278	Oct 4	Nov 2
SGI 279	Oct 11	Nov 9
SGI 280	Oct 18	Nov 16
SGI 281	Nov 1	Nov 30
SGI 282	Nov 8	Dec 7
SGI 283	****Dec 6	Jan 4, 95
SGI 284	****Dec 13	Jan 11, 95

*REPUBLIC DAY PARADE, ** DUSSEHRA FESTIVAL, *** DIWALI, **** CHRISTMAS & NEW YEAR

OUR JOURNEY BEGINS:

DAY 1: TUE - WEST COAST / HONG KONG OR BANGKOK EAST COAST /LONDON

Cathay Pacific Airways and **Air India** welcome you aboard a 747 jet for your journey to the mysterious and exotic India and Nepal.

DAY 2: WED - HONG KONG / BANGKOK OR LONDON

West coast members will have a choice to spend a restful overnight stay in Hong Kong or Bangkok; East Coast tour members will stay in London. **HOTEL SHANGRI LA / HOTEL FORTE CREST**

DAY 3: THU - ARRIVE MADRAS

After a day at leisure both East and West Coast Tour members arrive in Madras, gateway to Southern India. Madras traces its origin to 1639 A.D. when the British East India Company built a trading post, Fort St. George, near the fishing village of Madraspatnam. The city of Madras is the fourth largest city of India and capital of Tamil Nadu. This evening your Tour Manager will host a get-together Cocktail and Dinner party giving everyone a chance to become better acquainted. **TAJ COROMANDEL HOTEL**

DAY 4: FRI - KANCHIPURAM AND MAHABALIPURAM EXCURSION

Kanchipuram, one of South India's most ancient cities, dates back to 2nd century B.C. This former capital of Chola and Pallava kings is one of the seven great holy cities of Hindus, boasting 126 temples of breathtaking beauty. The pick of them for architectural and artistic excellence are the "Kailasanathar Temple, the Ekambareswarar Temple, the Kamakshi Temple, the Vaikunta Perumal Temple and Varadarajaswamy Temple". Festivals are celebrated throughout the year with rich pageantry, elaborately carved chariots & sounds of vedic chants and traditional melodies. Enjoy lunch at a lovely seaside resort in Mahabalipuram, city of seven pagodas noted for its monolithic monuments and marvelous stone sculptures. The world's largest bas-relief "Penance of Bhagiratha" and the tall, lovely shore temples are haunting treasures of the Pallava Empire. Return to Madras in the evening after spending time at the beach.

DAY 5: SAT - MADRAS

Today's tour of Madras includes Fort St. George, England's powerful Bastion and entrance to Southern India. Memorabilia of British rule is preserved here. The oldest Anglican Church in India, the Church of St. Mary, which was consecrated in 1680, and the museum with records of the old church are interesting sights. The 16th century Portuguese colony of San Thomas and its old Cathedral are closely associated with the legend of St. Thomas, one of the apostles of Christ. Visit the Marina, a splendid esplanade by the sea, Mylapore Temple and People's Park. The afternoon is free.

20

Indian Wedding Ceremony

DAY 6: SUN - MADRAS / MYSORE

This morning we fly to Bangalore and drive to Mysore, wending along through a verdant and hilly countryside. Enroute we stop at Srirangapatna where the legendary warrior Tipu Sultan built the island fortress and summer Palace made entirely of wood with exquisite painted walls. Mysore, a beautiful palace-filled town is rich in crafts. The 19th century Maharajas earned a reputation for superb hospitality and spectacle. Brindavan Gardens sprawl, amid beautiful cascading fountains besides the Krishnaraja Sagar Dam. The City Palace and Brindavan Gardens are illuminated today in honor of our arrival. **LALITHA MAHAL PALACE HOTEL**

DAY 7: MON - BELUR AND HALEBID EXCURSION

One of the supreme examples of Indian temple architecture is found in Halebid. Hoysaleshwara temple, dating back to 12th century A.D. stands on a terrace six feet high. The entire height —700 feet in length, is covered with a succession of eleven running friezes: of elephants, lions, scrolls, horsemen and celestial beasts and birds. Belur is over 800 years old and depicts in paintings and sculpture the ancient civilization of the South.

DAY 8: TUE - MYSORE / BANGALORE

Travelling by road, we head back to Bangalore, one of the most beautiful and well planned cities of India. Popularly known as the Garden city, situated 3,000 feet above sea level, Bangalore has a bracing, pleasant climate. Our orientation tour includes the botanical Gardens, colorful markets and the bull Temple. **TAJ RESIDENCY HOTEL**

DAY 9: WED - BANGALORE / COCHIN

A short flight brings us to the port city of Cochin, a city of waterways. The Jews arrived over 2,000 years ago, as refugees from Jerusalem when it fell to Nebuchadnezzar in 587 B.C., and have been a strong community in Cochin for last 1,000 years. Hungry for spices, Dutch, Portuguese and the British followed, all leaving their mark in this scenic city. Visit the Portuguese church built by St. Francis in 1562, the Jewish Synagogue of 1567 and the famed Mattancherry Palace built by the Portuguese. This evening we are treated to a special presentation of Kathakali Dance drama. **MALABAR HOTEL**

DAY 10: THU - THE BACKWATERS

Cochin is linked with Ernakulum and rest of the state of Kerala through the "backwaters", a series of canals and lagoons snaking their way through several tiny villages and tropical vegetation. Stop on tiny Gundu island to see the Coir factory, Chinese fishing nets and the Bolghatty Palace a beautiful Dutch Palace.

DAY 11: FRI - COCHIN / GOA

Goa's history stretches back to the Mauryan Empire of 3rd century B.C. Then followed a string of distant rulers such as the Chalukyas, Vijaynagars, Bahmanis and the Adilshahis of Bijapur. The character of the city we see today was forged by Portuguese rule from 1510 to 1961. At **FORT AGUADA BEACH RESORT,** built around a Portuguese fort, relax and enjoy some of the most beautiful palm-fringed beaches in the world.

DAY 12: SAT - OLD GOA

Our exploration of old Goa takes us to the Patriarch's Palace; Dona Paula beach, to view India's largest natural harbor; Old Goa's Se Cathedral, the Basilica of Bom Jesus where the body of St. Francis Xavier is enshrined and the Church of St. Francis of Assisi, which has beautiful murals and an excellent museum.

DAY 13: SUN - GOA / BOMBAY

Today we fly to Bombay, the gateway city of India. An ancient port and trading center, this palm-fringed shore of the Arabian Sea was the British Empire's entrance to its proudest "crown jewel". This evening we are treated to a special Indian Cuisine Dinner accompanied by classical Indian Dances and music. **TAJ MAHAL HOTEL**

DAY 14: MON - ELEPHANTA CAVES EXCURSION AND CITY TOUR

This morning we take a motor launch across the harbor to Elephanta, a small island also called "Gharpuri," to visit the Great Cave Temple. Believed now to date from 550 A.D. during the flowering of Gupta art, Elephanta's most striking figure represents the three aspects of Shiva — the creator, preserver and destroyer. This afternoon we tour Bombay, a blend of East and West. A survey of the city will include the British-built Arch "Gateway of India," Bombay's landmark, built in commemoration of the visit of King George V in 1911; the Hanging Gardens; Malabar Hills and the stately domed Prince of Wales Museum. The museum is among the best in India and has a particularly rich collection of miniature paintings, ancient sculptures and jade.

DAY 15: TUE - BOMBAY / AURANGABAD

Our exploration continues as we fly to Aurangabad to see the world famous rock-cut temples of Ajanta and Ellora. Here the most spectacular example of a rock-cut temple was hewn in the 8th century during the reign of a Rashtrakuta king. The three distinct groups of temples relate the story of the evolution of Hinduism, Jainism and Buddhism. These 2000 year old colossal temples, carved out of living rock, have sculptures intricate as ivory miniatures. **RAMA INTERNATIONAL HOTEL**

DAY 16: WED - AJANTA CAVES EXCURSION

Ajanta, one of India's most impressive archaeological sites, is today's excursion. Here Buddhist art attained the peak of its development, revealing a lifestyle and society amazing to the modern eye. There are 29 rock-hewn caves where both the facade and interior chambers are decorated with sculptures. The inside walls are covered with frescoes and the chapels are so constructed that a flood of natural light pours into them at various times during the day.

DAY 17: THU - AURANGABAD / UDAIPUR

Today we fly to Udaipur, famous as the "City of Lakes." It is one of the most picturesque and beautiful cities of India. Situated in a delightful natural setting, its many absorbing attractions include lovely lakes, marble palaces, luxurious gardens and old temples. It is considered one of the most romantic places in India. We will check-in at the world-famous **LAKE PALACE HOTEL.** Once a royal island retreat, it is now a luxurious hotel which seems to float upon the waters of Lake Pichola. Sunset is an especially beautiful hour when, across the lake, a splendid view of the City Palace can be enjoyed. We will visit City Palace with its scalloped arches, fretted balconies and cupolas; Saheliyon ki Bari or Garden of Maids; and folklore museum where we will enjoy a presentation of the string puppet show typical to this area.

Colorful Garb is a Tradition among Indian Women

DAY 18: FRI - UDAIPUR / JAIPUR

This morning our flight takes us to Jaipur, known as the "Pink City," the first city of Rajasthan. This uniquely planned city is girdled by a massive wall pierced by magnificent doorways. Jaipur is called the "Pink City" since a great deal of the older part of it was painted pink to commemorate the visit of Prince Albert in 1876. Our tour of the city will include visits to the Observatory; City Palace characterized by balconies, tiny windows, cupolas, courtyards and arched entrances. It houses an excellent collection of Rajasthani costumes, miniatures and an armory of Rajput weapons. The Hawa Mahal faces the main street of the old city. Called the "Wind Palace," it is a high and intricately carved wall behind which women of the court stood while watching processions. **RAMBAGH PALACE HOTEL**

DAY 19: SAT - AMBER FORT EXCURSION

We are transported back in time today as we ride like royalty, on elegantly draped and painted elephants, high into the mountain fortress of Amber. A complex of palaces, temples, exquisite marble and mirror-inlaid halls and apartments were once protected by this spectacular fortress-palace, home to the royals. There are taks (niches) for gold and silver ornaments; walls painted with floral dadoes, floor borders and cornices; distemper wall-paintings of hunting and battle scenes. To make the walls shine, powdered marble, egg shells and even pearls were added to the last coat of paint.

DAY 20: SUN - JAIPUR / DELHI

We fly this morning to Delhi, India's bustling capital, from where Hindu, Muslim and Mughal dynasties, as well as the British, ruled India. Old and New Delhi are a stunning juxtaposition of sights and sounds — the ancient city built by Emperor Shah Jehan (builder of Taj Mahal), and the new garden city built by the British in 1931. This evening we witness a spectacular Sound and Light Historical Performance at the Red Fort, a fortified palace also built by Shah Jehan. **TAJ MAHAL HOTEL**

DAY 21: MON - OLD AND NEW DELHI TOUR

Our sightseeing includes both Old and New Delhi. We will explore the Red Fort with its Pearl Mosque and exquisite audience halls; see the marble domes and slender minarets of Jama Masjid Mosque; Raj Ghat, the Mahatma Ghandi memorial; the Ashoka Pillar and the mile-long Chandni Chowk bazaars where craftsmen sell their wares; drive along Rajpath, New Delhi's broadest avenue for a look at the Houses of Parliament, the Diplomatic Enclave, the President's house, and India Gate (memorial to India's soldiers); and visit Birla Mandir, a colorful and modern Hindu temple.

DAY 22: TUE - DELHI / AGRA

Today we travel by one of the fastest trains in India, "Shatabadi Express," to Agra. This morning includes a visit to the abandoned city of Fatehpur Sikri. This nearly intact

Tantric Temple , Khajuraho

Mughal city is a master-piece of Muslim architecture unique in India. The Buland Darwaza or "Sublime Gate" flanked by colossal statues of elephants served as principal entrance to this ancient capital city . This afternoon we tour Agra, the last capital of the Mughal Empire in India, visit the 16th century Agra Fort, and end at the fabled Taj Mahal, the sublime monument to the memory of love. Sure to captivate us, its perfect structure and delicate beauty are enhanced by the romance of viewing this magnificent edifice at sunset. **TAJ VIEW HOTEL**

DAY 23: WED - AGRA / KHAJURAHO

Today's short flight brings us to Khajuraho, the religious and political capital of the Chandela Dynasty during the 9th to 13th centuries. Khajuraho is known for its Tantric temples with erotic sculptures, the only one of its kind in the world. We'll visit the principal temples noted for their exquisite and erotic sculptures. The shrines are buff colored sandstone and stand on high terraces. Every square inch of the temple is covered with sculptures depicting human and divine celestials in every aspect of life. **CHANDELA HOTEL**

DAY 24: THU - KHAJURAHO / VARANASI

Today we take a short flight to Varanasi (Benares), the holy city of India located on the sacred Ganges River. On arrival we drive to Sarnath, scene of Buddha's first sermon, some eight miles from the center of Varanasi. Here we will see the museum, one of the most important in India. We will also see the many stupas, ruins and Mulagandhakuti Vihara, containing relics found during the early excavations of this buried city. **TAJ GANGES HOTEL**

DAY 25: FRI - VARANASI / KATHMANDU

Early this morning a boat ride takes us past incredible scenes of the multitudes coming to pay homage to the Sun God. As we pass the bathing ghats, we will witness thousands of pilgrims taking a dip in the holy water of the Ganges River. We also see the burning ghats where cremations are conducted. This afternoon we fly to Kathmandu, ancient capital of the mountain kingdom of Nepal, an isolated world where people live much as they have for 1200 years. On approach, we see a breathtaking view of terraced hilltops set against the dramatic backdrop of the mighty Himalayas. This afternoon we explore the Durbar Square with its pagoda-shaped temples, bazaars and the Royal Residential Palace, and the temple of the Living Goddess — a young girl worshipped as a deity by all Nepalese. We then continue to Bodhnath, the largest Buddhist stupa in the world, and Pashupatinath, the sacred temple dedicated to Lord Shiva located near the holy river Bagmati. **HOTEL SOALTEE OBEROI**

DAY 26: SAT - PATAN / BHADGAON

Our morning's excursion brings us to Patan, the "city of beauty," with it's many palaces and temples embellished with intricately carved gods and goddesses in erotic poses. The art and architecture reflect an interesting mixture of Hindu and Buddhist influence. A visit to the Tibetan refugee camp presents an opportunity to see the deft hands of Tibetans weaving carpets and other handicrafts. This afternoon we drive to the primitive city of Bhadgaon, the "city of devotees," where more examples of Nepalese architecture can be studied.

DAY 27: SUN - KATHMANDU / TIGER TOPS

A one-hour sightseeing flight (weather permitting) over the "roof of the world" provides us with spectacular close-up views of the vast granite and snow ridges of the Himalayas and the Shangri-la of green valleys and meandering streams below them. See the highest peak on earth — 29,029 foot Mt. Everest, straddling the Tibet-Nepal border. Later, we fly to Meghauly from where we will be transferred to our **TIGER TOPS LODGE** by way of elephant or jeep. Our treetop hotel is situated in the heart of the Royal Chitwan National Park, one of Nepal's largest jungle and forest regions. Tiger Tops' treehouses and bungalows are built with materials of the forest itself. Trained elephants, each driven by an expert mahout, will take us on thrilling game runs to "shoot" — with camera — the rhino and tiger inhabiting the tall grasses and deep forests of Nepal. Dinner awaits us, by candlelight, in the Nepalese style dining room with its huge domed roof and central open hearth. Night around the fireside offers a relaxing and peaceful setting, yet one charged with an excitement, as tiger or leopard are often sighted in evening.

Fruit Vendor, Kathmandu

Wildlife Viewing , Tiger Tops

DAY 28: MON - THARU VILLAGE

We continue viewing the wildlife of Chitwan this morning. We will view nearly 400 species of birds, a variety of deer, leopard, wild boar, one-horned rhinoceros, crocodile, and the now endangered and exclusive Royal Bengal Tiger. One of the day's highlights, upon return from our jungle excursion, is the bathing and feeding of the elephants at the elephant camp. We then proceed to Tharu Village, where we have a chance to mingle with the tribal village people. This evening we are treated to a lively dance presentation by the Tharu Village tribesmen and women in their traditional costumes. **THARU VILLAGE**

DAY 29: TUE - TIGER TOPS / DELHI OR HONG KONG

Early this morning we take a short hike into the jungle and tour the Hill Tribe Village. Later, East Coast passengers will fly to Delhi. **VASANT CONTINENTAL HOTEL.** West Coast passengers fly to Hong Kong. **SHANGRI-LA HOTEL**

DAY 30: WED - HONG KONG / DELHI / HOME

We reluctantly say goodbye to India . . . remembering that in India they never say "Goodbye" but "we shall return."

THE HIMALAYAN SHANGRI-LA
PAKISTAN, INDIA, SIKKIM & NEPAL

visiting

Islamabad, Gilgit, Hunza, Chilas,
Swat Valley, Peshawar, Lahore

PAKISTAN

Delhi, Sikkim, Darjeeling

INDIA

Kathmandu, Patan,
Bhadgaon, Dhulikhel

NEPAL

The name Pakistan was coined from Persian and used to designate a spiritual or religious realm meaning 'land of the pure'. Ever since James Hilton wrote 'Lost Horizons', man has been searching for the mystical lands of Shangri-La. The valley of Swat, Chitral and Hunza could well be this.

Around 1500 B.C. Aryans established themselves in the Ganges valley influencing the Hinduism. Persians occupied the Northern region in 5th century B.C. Greeks came in 327 B.C. under Alexander of Macedonia, commonly known as Alexander the Great. The influences left by these great races are even visible today. The Himalayan Shangri-La tour gives you an opportunity to get the first hand experience.

Come face to face with the mighty Himalayas ... The HIMALAYAN SHANGRI-LA offers the best of these fabled lands. Pakistan, combined with Lahore and Delhi where the Mughal dynasties left admirable forts, mosques, palaces, gardens and tombs, followed by the treasures of Nepal, Darjeeling and Sikkim, the last Shangri-La, this SITA tour offers a holiday equaling few anywhere in the world.

28

Special Exclusive SITA Features:

- Deluxe & First class Hotels (Best available in each place) with private bath/shower.
- Three meals daily. A-la-carte where available.
- Services of professional SITA Tour Manager.
- Baggage handling and porterage.
- Touring by private motor coach, automobile with English speaking guide.
- Welcome and Farewell Dinner with cultural dance and music presentation.
- Sound & Light show at Red Fort.
- Dhulikhel excursion to view sunset over Himalayas.
- Ghoom excursion to view sunrise over Himalayas.

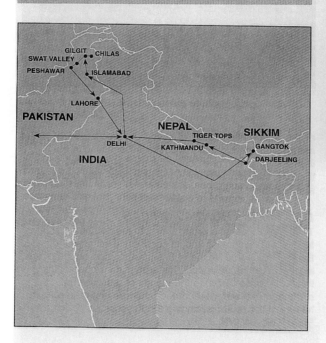

TOUR PRICE:	1993	1994
Land Arrangements	4,490.00	4,990.00
Single Supplement	1,290.00	1,495.00

AIRFARES:	
East Coast	2,100.00
West Coast	1,990.00

NOTE: Airfares are based on Low Season and include flying within Pakistan, India and Nepal as per tour itinerary. Please check for High Season fares and applicable add-on fares from your home city. Airfares are subject to change without notice.

Departure Dates

1993

Tour No.	Depart	Return
SHS 320	Apr 9	May 2
SHS 321	Apr 23	May 16
SHS 322	May 7	May 30
SHS 323	May 21	Jun 13
SHS 324	May 28	Jun 20
SHS 325	Jun 4	Jun 27
SHS 326	Jun 25	Jul 18
SHS 327	Sep 3	Sep 26
SHS 328	Sep 17	Oct 10
SHS 329	Oct 1	Oct 24
SHS 330	Oct 15	Nov 7

IT3AI11204

1994

Tour No.	Depart	Return
SHS 331	Apr 15	May 8
SHS 332	Apr 29	May 22
SHS 333	May 6	May 29
SHS 334	May 13	Jun 5
SHS 335	May 20	Jun 12
SHS 336	Jun 3	Jun 26
SHS 337	Jun 24	Jul 17
SHS 338	Sep 9	Oct 2
SHS 339	Sep 23	Oct 16
SHS 340	Oct 7	Oct 30
SHS 341	Oct 14	Nov 6

OUR JOURNEY BEGINS:

DAY 1: FRI - WEST COAST / BANGKOK OR EAST COAST / DELHI

Depart Los Angeles or New York on our **Cathay Pacific** or **Air India** jet flight.

DAY 2: SAT - BANGKOK OR DELHI

Rest at our deluxe accommodations in Delhi or Bangkok before leaving tomorrow for Pakistan. **VASANT CONTINENTAL / SHANGRI-LA HOTEL**

DAY 3: SUN - ISLAMABAD

We arrive at Islamabad, the capital of Pakistan and are escorted to **THE PEARL CONTINENTAL HOTEL.** Our evening is highlighted by a welcoming party to meet fellow tour members and learn about the adventures ahead in Pakistan, India and Nepal.

DAY 4: MON - TAXILA EXCURSION

Our excursion to Taxila is a multi-dimensional experience. Center of ancient Gandhara, the origins of which date back to Cyrus the great, Darius and Alexander the great. It's time of highest glory came during the Kushan rule when it was the cultural center of the region. The pilgrims created a school of Gandharan art which endured for five centuries and influenced the arts of central Asia, China and South Asia. We will visit several of the sites including Jaulian Monastery, Sirkap, Museum with its treasure of Buddhist remains.

DAY 5: TUE - ISLAMABAD / GILGIT

Our early morning flight (weather permitting) soars above some of the world's highest mountain peaks to Gilgit, the administrative center of Northern Pakistan. Our tour of Gilgit includes a visit to local school, the home of a city market and nearby Kargha, where a huge Buddha is carved from a cliff face. **SERENA LODGE**

DAY 6: WED - GILGIT / HUNZA

Today's drive along the Karakorum highway takes us to the Hunza Valley, long renowned as the original Shangri-La. In spring its terraced fields are redolent with the fragrance of apple, plum and apricot blossoms. The Hunza residents are famous for their longevity and simple, uncomplicated life. After settling in, we will tour the Altit and Baltit forts. **RAKAPOSHI PALACE HOTEL**

DAY 7: THU - KHUNJERAB PASS OR NAGAR VALLEY EXCURSION

Continue our travel thru upper Hunza Valley with fantastic views of Rakaposhi and other giant mountains along the Karakorum highway as it snakes its way upwards to the Khunjerab pass. International Herald Tribune mentioned "to stand at the pinnacle of this pass is to stand in wonder

Tribal Man Smoking A Hookha

at the accomplishments of man." At an altitude of 4,594 meters, it is the highest paved border crossing in the world. Alternately, one could visit the Nagar Valley to meet the local villagers and enjoy the beauty of their orchards and mountain flowers.

DAY 8: FRI - HUNZA / CHILAS

The highway takes a broad swing to the southeast as it follows the Gilgit river and its confluence with the Indus River. The river is lifeline of Pakistan, source of one of the largest irrigation systems. This area is an archeological treasure house because thousands of petroglyphs scratched into water-smoothed boulders proved a running history of the region spanning 2,500 years. **SHANGRI-LA INN**

DAY 9: SAT - CHILAS / SWAT VALLEY

Our drive brings us to Saidu Sharif, capital of the Swat Valley, land of gentle summers, golden autumns and flower-laden springs. **SWAT SERENA LODGE**

DAY 10: SUN - SWAT VALLEY

Today we tour Swat valley, the northern terminus of the Gandharan Kingdom. The ancient Buddhist stupa at Butkara is comprised of five stupa shells, one inside the other as the shrine was enlarged five times over the years. Visit the local market at Mingora and continue to the old palace of Mir at Marghazar. Wander along the main street of Bahrain, home of wood carvers and a unique wire bridge. This is an exciting place to buy the local fabrics or traditional Swati vest and hat.

DAY 11: MON - SWAT VALLEY / PESHAWAR

Continue to Peshawar, the city of flowers and gateway to Central Asia. A frontier town in every sense of the word, Aryans, Scythians, Persians, Greeks, Bactrians, Kushans, Huns, Turks and Mughals have trod the streets of Peshawar for conquest, migration, pilgrimage or commerce. The most romantically interesting part of the city is old Peshawar, a true picture of what it was almost 500 years ago. Pathan tribesmen of nearby villages in their native dresses throng the narrow paths bargaining for a good price. We visit the Mosque of Mahabat Khan, built in 1670's; Peshawar museum; and Qissa Khawani bazaar of story tellers, **PEARL CONTINENTAL HOTEL**

DAY 12: TUE - KHYBER PASS EXCURSION / LAHORE

This morning we will visit the historic Khyber Pass. Mughal emperor Babur the Great marched through Khyber Pass to conquer Southern Asia. We will also visit a tribal gun factory at Darra. Later we will take a short flight to Lahore. The 2,000 years old city is the second largest in Pakistan. Lahore flourished during the Mughal empire from 1525 to 1724. Some of the finest masterpieces of Mughal architecture still stand, preserved in their original grandeur, a testimony to the artistic genius of the Empire. **PEARL CONTINENTAL HOTEL**

DAY 13: WED - LAHORE

We spend a full day exploring historic Lahore. The Lahore Fort is a complicated mix of the several phases of development. Many rulers contributed money and talent to complete this fort. Visit the Palace of Mirrors, Shah Jehan's Quadrangle and the Pearl Mosque; Badshahi Mosque, the world's largest mosque of Islamic worship Aurangzeb, the last Mughal emperor; The imposing minar-e-Pakistan commemorating the historic resolution creating the country of Pakistan in 1940; and Shalimar Gardens, built by the Mughals but still much appreciated and enjoyed by Lahore residents.

Sound and Light Show

Qutab Minar, Delhi

DAY 14: THU - LAHORE / DELHI

Our time is at leisure before we fly to another former mughal capital Delhi, India. This evening see a Sound and Light Historical Performance highlighting the main events of Mughal and British rule in India. **HOTEL TAJ MAHAL**

DAY 15: FRI - OLD AND NEW DELHI

Old and New Delhi are a stunning juxtaposition — the ancient city built by Emperor Shah Jehan and the new garden city built by British. Explore the Red Fort with its Pearl Mosque and exquisite audience halls; see the Jama Masjid Mosque with its marble domes and slender minarets; Raj Ghat, where Mahatma Gandhi was cremated; the Ashoka pillar and the mile long Chandani chowk bazaars where craftsmen sell their wares. Drive along Rajpath, New Delhi's broadest avenue to see the houses of Parliament, the Diplomatic enclave, the President's House, India Gate and Birla Mandir, a colorful modern temple, and Humayun's tomb which served as a prelude to Taj Mahal. Our final stop is Qutab Minar.

Note: Alternately a day trip to Agra can be arranged for those interested. Day trip will include round trip train ride by Shatabadi express and sightseeing of Fatehpur -Sikri, Agra Fort and Taj Mahal. Additional cost $95.00 per person.

DAY 16: SAT - DELHI / SIKKIM (Gangtok)

Head for Gangtok, capital of the tiny state of Sikkim. Its captivating beauty radiates with Pagoda-like wooden houses, painted turquoise roofs and busy bazaars. Gentle swaying and elegant costumes of the Sikkimese people, their smiling faces, the unhurried pace of their life-style and the towering beauty of Kanchenjunga, all cast a magic spell on this delightful location in the foothills of the grand Himalayas. **NORKHILL HOTEL**

DAY 17: SUN - RUMTEK MONASTERY

Sikkim's 194 monasteries or gompas, belonging to the Nyingma and Kagyu order, have not only been influencing the cultural heritage and lifestyle of the people but also demonstrate the ancient rituals in practice. The Rumtek Monastery was built in 1960's by His Holiness the late 16th Gyala Karmapa when he took refuge in Sikkim after the Chinese attack. It is an excellent replica of original Kagyu headquarters in Tibet. Devoted Lamas robed in red, chant ancient mantras to the rhythm of drums and trumpets while soft lights flicker from decorative lamps. On return, visit the Namgyal Research institute of Tibetology with a collection of almost 30,000 volumes on diverse subjects like astrology, philosophy, magic and religion etc. The orchid sanctuary below the Institute houses over 300 species of temperate and intermediate orchids.

DAY 18: MON - SIKKIM / DARJEELING

Our next destination is Darjeeling, a premier hill resort. The drive to this 7,000 foot high city is made over roads winding through the lush, green terrain of the Indian countryside. Often called the queen of the Himalayas, it affords unparalleled views of majestic mountains. The snow-clad Kanchenjunga ranges turn orange-gold in the early morning sun, providing an unforgettable sight. **WINDAMERE HOTEL**

DAY 19: TUE - DARJEELING

Early this morning (weather permitting) we drive to glimpse rays of the morning sun dancing against some of the world's tallest peaks, Mount Kanchenjunga and Mount Everest. Also visit Ghoom Monastery; Lebong Valley with world's highest racetrack; Mountaineering Institute of India and a Darjeeling tea estate. Darjeeling tea is considered to be the best due to its favorable growing conditions.

DAY 20: WED - DARJEELING / KATHMANDU

Fly to Kathmandu, capital of Nepal where people live as they have for 1,200 years. On our approach to Kathmandu Valley we see a breathtaking view of terraced hilltops set against the backdrop of the Himalayas. Nestled in the cradle of the highest mountains on earth, this mountain kingdom is said to be where deities mingle with mortals. **HOTEL SOALTEE OBEROI**

Nepalese Women Plant Rice On Terraces

Tribal Women are Known by their Silver Jewelry

DAY 21: THU - KATHMANDU AND PATAN

Explore the Durbar Square with pagoda-shaped temples, Royal residential Palace, bazaars and temples, including the Temple of the living Goddess, a young girl worshipped as a deity by all Nepalese. Continue to Bodhnath, the largest stupa in the world and Pashupatinath temple. After lunch travel to Patan, the 'city of beauty' with its many palaces and temples embellished with intricately carved gods and goddesses in erotic poses. The art and architecture shows an interesting mixture of Hindu and Buddhist influence. Continue on to the Tibetan refugee camp and see the deft hands of the Tibetans weaving carpets and other handicrafts.

DAY 22: FRI - BHADGAON AND DHULIKHEL

This morning visit the primitive city of Bhadgaon where more examples of Nepalese architecture can be studied. The tiny cobbled streets are lined with beautifully carved old black and white houses and temples. Continue by road up to the fabulous mountain retreat of Dhulikhel. Delight in a complete panoramic view of the snowy ranges from Makalu in the east to Himalchuli and Manasulu to the west.

DAY 23: SAT - KATHMANDU / HONG KONG OR DELHI

After a day at leisure, West Coast tour members will board their flight to Hong Kong and East Coast members to Delhi. **VASANT CONTINENTAL/SHANGRI-LA HOTEL**

DAY 24: SUN - HONG KONG / DELHI / HOME

Our exploration of Himalayan Shangri-La comes to an end as we board our flight for home taking with us memories of a vacation to last a lifetime.

■ REVIEW—SOUTH ASIA

1. When does the summer monsoon, the rainy season, generally start in the region? When is the dry season?

2. Where did Hinduism originate? Buddhism? From what source did Islam enter the subcontinent?

3. Why was Pakistan created? Bangladesh?

4. Name the main religions of India. Name some of the large religious minorities in India.

5. Why is English still so important in India?

6. Point out the distinctive characteristics and touristic role of Bombay, Calcutta, Madras, and Delhi in Indian life.

7. Describe the caste system.

8. What is the importance of Kashmir?

9. Where is Mount Everest? Who are the Sherpas?

10. What two ethnic groups are in conflict in Sri Lanka? Why?

11. Where are the major beach and resort areas in South Asia?

12. Describe four major areas of scenic beauty in South Asia.

14

East Asia

East Asia includes the mainland political units of the People's Republic of China (PRC); the British colony of Hong Kong; and the Portuguese colony of Macau on the southeast China coast; the Mongolian People's Republic; and the two Koreas (People's Republic of Korea, or North Korea, and the Republic of Korea, or South Korea). Not far offshore are the island nations of the Republic of China (Taiwan) and Japan. The names Far East, used interchangeably with East Asia, and the Orient, which includes East Asia and often all or parts of Southeast Asia, persist in travel promotion literature although they are considered outdated.

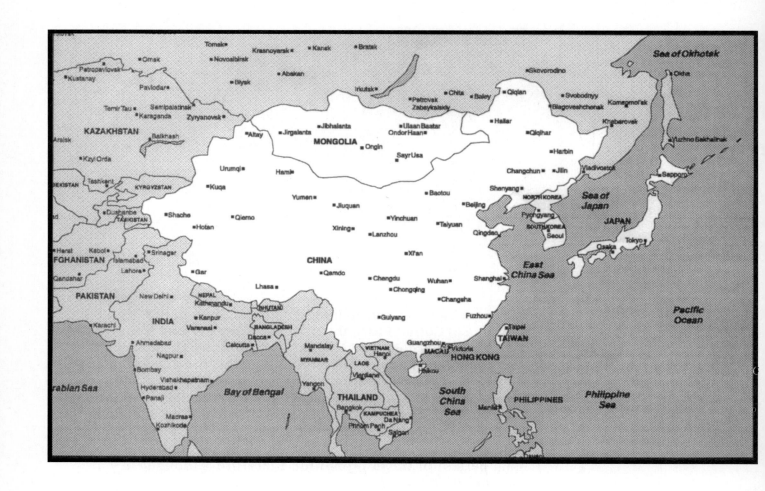

CHINA

Official Name: People's Republic of China

Language: Mandarin, Cantonese, many local Chinese dialects

Area: 3,696,100 million square miles

Time Zone: GMT +8

National Airline: CAAC

Capital: Beijing

Currency: Yuan (RMB)

Population: 1,151,486,000

Documentation: Passport, visa

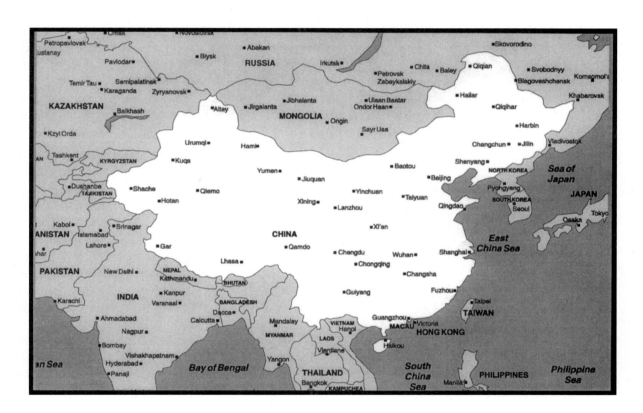

China occupies the central position in East Asia in location, physical and population size, and historical importance. In fact, East Asia is commonly referred to as the Chinese (Sinic) culture world because of the distinctiveness and high level of its culture over the past 5,000 years and the powerful influence it had upon its neighbors until the mid-19th century, when a large-scale influx of westerners began to influence the culture of East Asia.

Climate. China is a large block of territory roughly the size of the United States. Consequently, travel in China involves long distances. However, most of the Chinese population, cities, and economic activities are concentrated in the eastern half of the country where there is enough rainfall for sustained agriculture. Most rainfall in eastern China occurs during the summer, whereas winter is usually dry (a monsoon-type climate). Typhoons, violent storms identical to the hurricanes of North America, are a feature of the southeastern coastal districts during late summer and early fall. The rainfall is most plentiful in the southeast and decreases to the north and northeast. Summers are hot, but winter climates range from mild in the southeast (like Florida) and the central area (like the Carolinas) to bitterly cold with some snow in the north and northeast.

Western China contains much of the climatically dry heart of Asia. It is dominated by desert and semidesert, high plateaus, and towering mountain ranges. Like the American West, it has great open expanses with few or no people. Small pockets of population occur only where there is sufficient rainfall (in southern Tibet around Lhasa) or meltwater from snowfields (in the northwestern province of Xinjiang, including Urumqui and smaller oasis cities).

The Peoples. The 1990 census showed China to have more than 1 billion people, making it the most populous nation by far. Ninety-five percent of this vast number live in the eastern half of China in densely settled rural and urban areas—people are an overwhelming fact there! Strict governmental restrictions on family size are in effect to slow the rate of population growth. About 94 percent of the population is Han Chinese, the dominant group. Although a standard spoken language, Mandarin, and a written language using ideographs (characters) are used in formal education everywhere, local languages and dialects abound.

Around China's inner borders minorities are important: Koreans in southeastern Manchuria; Mongols near Mongolia; various peoples who speak Turkic (Turkish) languages and practice Islam in Xinjiang in the northwest; Buddhist Tibetans in Tibet; and in the hill country of south China, millions of people related to the Burmans, Thai, Vietnamese, and other peoples of Southeast Asia.

History. Known Chinese history dates back about 5,000 years, and can be traced to its starting point near the Yellow River just west of the North China Plain, around the present city of Xian. At an early date, the Chinese developed advanced agriculture, had an imperial ruling system, a written language, city life, and advanced military weapons and skills.

Expansion was gradual into the North China Plain, then southward and westward. Buddhism, imported from India via Central Asia more than 2,000 years ago, was adopted and had a great religious and artistic impact. Chinese culture spread outward to Korea, Japan, and present Vietnam, profoundly influencing life there. Within China such public works as the Great Wall, designed to protect against raiders from the north, and the Grand Canal, to ship rice and other foods from the Yangtze Plains to the North China Plain, were completed after centuries of labor.

China attempted to remain aloof from trade with Western nations as the wave of Western colonialism swept into India and Southeast Asia. After 1842, however, China was forced by Western powers to open its ports to commerce, and Western influences flowed in. The imperial system was overthrown in 1912; most of eastern China was united under Nationalist China in the mid-1930s, with Manchuria under Japanese control. From 1937–1945, most of eastern China was held by the invading Japanese army.

Soon after World War II, the domestic Communist forces seized control (1949), and the Nationalist government was driven into refuge on Taiwan. The Beijing government exercises tight control over all aspects of national life. There is great emphasis on raising the living standard in what is still a relatively poor nation and on making China economically advanced and militarily strong. Although economic liberalism is encouraged, political dissent is not tolerated.

Key Economic Regions. Within eastern China, five key economic regions, or dense concentrations of people and activities, can be singled out. The first is South Manchuria. (Manchuria is a Western name; it is the Northeast to the Chinese.) This is a leading industrial region and producer of food surpluses. Its main cities include Shenyang and the port of Dalian. The second is the North China Plain, which lies astride the Yellow River, one of China's two great rivers. This is the historical core in the development of China as a culture and nation. Measuring some 500 miles north-south and east-west, it supports about one fourth of the Chinese population, is heavily cultivated, and has many industrial cities. The river is of limited use for irrigation or transportation and has a serious flooding problem that is checked only by huge man-made embankments. On the northern edge of the plain is Beijing, the national capital, and to the east on the coast the major port of Tianjin.

The great Yangtze River (Ch'angjiang in Chinese) passes through two more of these key economic regions. Third is the plains strung along the central and lower course of the river.

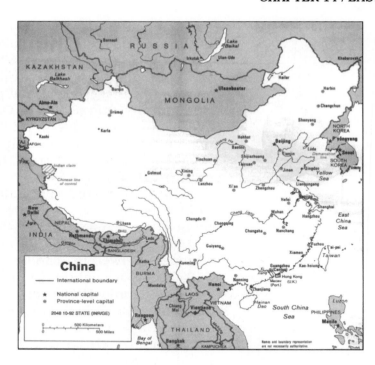

They have a dense rural population and such major cities as Shanghai, near the river mouth, and Nanjing, and the tri-city Wu-han farther upstream. Shanghai is China's largest city. In the interior, some 1,000 miles upstream, is a fourth great population cluster in the Sichuan Basin and its main cities, Chongqing and Chengdu. Southern China is fragmented by hills and mountains into many small pockets of habitable plains. The fifth and largest key economic region is the Canton Plain, on the southeast coast inland from British Hong Kong. Its urban hub is Guangzhou (Canton).

Economy. Some 80 percent of the Chinese are involved in agriculture, and all land and property is owned by the state. However, most farmland is leased to farm families who operate on a profit-making basis. Many families have become relatively prosperous. There is great regional variety in agriculture. In the North China Plain, for example, agriculture produces around wheat and dry grains, depends on natural rainfall, and involves only one cropping cycle per year. Northern cuisine is distinctive, too, featuring dough-based dishes.

The productive areas of the well-watered Yangtze Plains, Sichuan, and Southern China utilize the system most Americans associate with China—year-round cultivation. Rice, under irrigation, is the main crop; a great variety of vegetables, fruit, and meats, especially pork are also produced. With one of the world's greatest productions of foodstuffs, China is able to produce most of the food needed by its large and growing population.

Rice Planting, Central China
Photo: Courtesy Japan Airlines

The Chinese government is attempting to industrialize as quickly as possible, and industrial cities are increasingly part of the Chinese landscape. Heavy manufacturing, owned by the government, is concentrated in South Manchuria, Shanghai, and other major cities of northern and central eastern China. Newer, privately owned small-scale factories using advanced technology and producing export goods are especially concentrated in "enterprise zones" around Shanghai and Guangzhou, in the south, near Hong Kong. These are currently the fastest-growing and most prosperous industrial areas in China. Cities and regions are linked by simple but adequate transportation, especially rail and air service. Road systems are poor, the private ownership of automobiles is small but growing, and the bicycle is the general public's usual conveyance for short distances.

Areas of Touristic Importance. China is a huge nation. Totally closed to western tourists for almost 30 years after the Communist take-over, it is now developing over 100 tourist destinations within its borders. As in the United States, a visitor could travel for months and not see everything.

Like all facets of Chinese life, tourism is tightly controlled. Although independent travel is possible, it is difficult. The vast majority of tourists travel in groups on itineraries ranging from 2 or 3 days to 2 or 3 weeks. Travel in China is expensive and comfort levels, food, and accommodation quality are often lower than what is provided for similar costs in other parts of Asia and the world.

Beijing (formerly Peking) has been the capital of China through much of its stormy history. Each of the dynasties from Zhou to Qin to Ming has left its imprint on the city. Today, Beijing is the economic and political seat of power of China.

Any list of Beijing's attractions can only scratch the surface. The most prominent include the Imperial Palace, also known as the Forbidden City, a major architectural masterpiece. Also on the must-visit list are the Great Wall, the Ming Tombs, The Summer Palace, the Beijing Zoo, and Tian An Men (Heavenly Peace Square).

Xian was once the world's largest city, and it was the capital for eleven dynasties. It is now the most important archeological center in China. Thousands of life-size, terra-cotta warriors guard the entrance to one of the imperial tombs.

Shanghai is one of the world's largest cities. It is China's most populous urban center, as well as its largest port city and most important commercial center. The Temple of the Jade Buddha attracts many tourists with its famous white statues. The garden of the Mandarin Yu provides a welcome respite from the city traffic. The Museum of Art and History contains one of the best art collections in Asia.

Suzhou is an ancient city on the Grand Canal. It has been called the Venice of the Orient because of its canals and it claims the most beautiful gardens in Asia. Its portion of the Grand Canal is fronted on both sides with statues and pagodas. Important places to visit include Tiger Hill with its leaning pagoda, the Surging Wave Pool, and the Tarrying Gardens.

Guilin is a city of vast natural beauty. Mountain peaks rise sharply from a green landscape. Located on the west bank of the Li River, Guilin may be the most beautiful area in all China. A short journey down the Li reveals exceptional rock formations, bamboo groves, and peaceful valleys. Beautiful caves also attract visitors.

Guangzhou, previously known as Canton, is an industrial and commercial city just 80 miles by rail from Hong Kong. This city's lifestyle and commerce have been strongly influenced by Hong Kong, and it was the first Chinese city to trade with the west.

The city of Nanjing is one of the most attractive cities in China. The city has a history dating back more than 2,000 years and the Yangtze River Bridge, considered impossible by many engineers at the time was completed in 1968 and provided the first overland link between Beijing and Shanghai.

The Yangtze River is China's longest river and the third longest in the world, running 3,430 miles from west to east. A cruise on its waters covers only a small portion of its full length but includes some breathtaking scenery of striking gorges. Wall-sided mountains plunge almost perpendicular from the sky to the water, forming spectacular narrow canyons that virtually shut out the sun. A huge dam, currently under construction, will flood the famous Three Gorges area, eliminating much of its scenic beauty. The dam is not scheduled for completion until well into the 21st century.

Attractions in Tibet are discussed along with South Asia in Chapter 13 because visitors to Tibet usually visit Nepal and India as well.

■ HONG KONG AND MACAU

HONG KONG

Language: Cantonese Chinese, English

Area: 409 square miles

Time Zone: GMT +8

National Airline: Cathay Pacific

Capital: Hong Kong

Currency: Hong Kong dollar (HKD)

Population: 5,700,000

Documentation: Passport

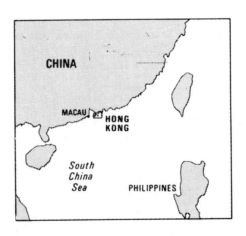

Hong Kong has been developed under British colonial control as one of Asia's greatest ports and centers of commerce and manufacturing. The Crown Colony consists of Hong Kong Island (the city of Victoria is on its northern coast) and, northward, across the natural harbor, the Kowloon Peninsula. Both were formally ceded to Great Britain by China. Most of the colony's land area is in the New Territories, inland from Kowloon, which were leased from China on a 99-year lease that expires in 1997. Because Hong Kong would not be viable without the New Territories, the British have agreed to cede all of Hong Kong back to China in 1997. China, in return, has promised to continue the capitalist economic system for a minimum of 50 years.

The colony's population is overwhelmingly Chinese in composition. Its atmosphere is very cosmopolitan and it has superb public and private facilities. Hong Kong relies on the world trading network, and, in turn, it is a focal point for ocean and air transportation in the western Pacific and a major portal for entering China via Guangzhou, where it has had a tremendous impact through investment in industrial development in recent years.

Areas of Touristic Importance. Hong Kong harbor is one of the world's busiest and presents an ever-changing sight. It is best viewed from Victoria Peak on Hong Kong Island. The junks still seen in the harbor are no longer under sail but use motor power instead. They and the freighters, container ships, and midharbor loading and unloading by barge/lighters are a fascinating sight. A rail tram provides the fastest transportation to the peak.

Aberdeen, on the south side of Hong Kong Island, is one of the last sampan villages, with thousands of inhabitants living on junks, sampans, and other floating vessels. Bedecked in Oriental splendor, three floating restaurants, accessible only by motorized sampan, attract many visitors.

A ride on the Star ferry between Hong Kong Island and Kowloon costs only a few pennies and is an experience not to

Jumbo Floating Restaurant, Hong Kong
Photo: Courtesy Hong Kong Tourist Association

be missed. It is the primary transportation for pedestrians between the island and the mainland; vehicular traffic moves through tunnels beneath the harbor.

The entire colony is a shopper's delight with thousands of stores selling everything from electronics to antiques. Mainland Chinese goods are featured in many stores. Excellent tailors offer made-to-measure men's and women's clothing sewn within a few days. Although there are shopping districts on Hong Kong Island, the greatest variety are in Kowloon. World-class hotels and restaurants on both Hong Kong Island and in Kowloon cater to the traveler's every need.

A visit to the New Territories reveals large industrial areas and housing developments. A major viewing point is the border between the New Territories and the People's Republic of China.

Hong Kong is an especially popular destination for those who want to see it before the colony is returned to China.

MACAU

Language: Cantonese, Portuguese

Area: 6 square miles

Time Zone: GMT +8

Capital: Macau

Currency: Pataca

Population: 399,000

Documentation: Passport

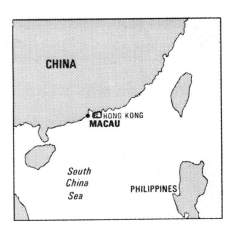

Macau, in contrast with Hong Kong, is a small, quiet Portuguese colony dating from an original lease in 1557.

Areas of Touristic Importance. Macau has experienced little modernization and is best known as a gambling center patronized by tourists coming by hydrofoil from Hong Kong. Although there are a few first-class hotels, most visitors do not stay overnight. A new airport and new hotels are in the planning stages and should improve the tourism capabilities of Macau.

Macau's very existence, not to mention its economic situation, depends on Hong Kong. The Portuguese will cede Macau to China in 1999.

■ MONGOLIA AND TAIWAN

MONGOLIA

Official Name: Mongolian People's Republic

Language: Khalkha, Mongolian

Area: 604,247 square miles

Time Zone: GMT +7 through +9

Capital: Ulan Bator

Currency: Tugrik

Population: 2,247,000

Documentation: Passport, visa

Lying between Russian Siberia and China, the Mongolian People's Republic (MPR) has a large territory but a small population. An even larger group of Mongols live in China and a smaller group lives in adjacent Siberia. Southern Mongolia is occupied by one of Asia's largest and driest deserts, the Gobi. In contrast, the north has sufficient rainfall to support grasslands, forests, and a permanent river system, the Selenga, which drains northward into Lake Baikal. Within the northern portion, one-fourth of the population live in Ulan Bator, the capital and only large city.

Most Mongols depend on herding, which is organized into large, state-owned collectives. The traditional yurt (or ger), a tent-like dwelling consisting of a wooden frame and felt covering, can be dismantled easily and transported and is still used by the seasonally mobile herders. The Mongolian government was closely allied to the Soviet Union ideologically, economically, diplomatically, and militarily prior to 1990. It is now in an uneasy period of non-Communist political and economic change. The formerly suppressed Buddhist religion is slowly being revived.

Ulan Bator is most easily reached from Russia by rail or air. The Trans-Mongol Railway, which runs from Ulan Bator across the Gobi Desert to the Chinese border, provides a link with China, but train service is infrequent.

Areas of Touristic Importance. Because of the inferior infrastructure and accommodations, few western visitors travel to Mongolia, but foreign tourism is now being encouraged by the Mongolian government. However, at this time it is a destination only for the adventurous, experienced traveler.

TAIWAN

Official Name: Republic of China

Language: Mandarin Chinese

Area: 13,885 square miles

Time Zone: GMT +8

National Airline: China Airlines

Capital: Taipei

Currency: New Taiwan dollar (NTD)

Population: 20,658,000

Documentation: Passport, visa

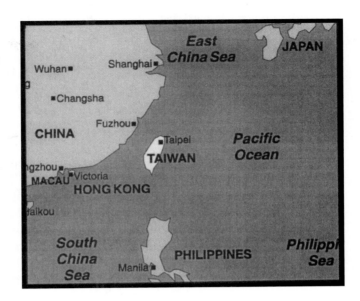

History. Taiwan (formerly Formosa) has had a checkered history. Lying 120 miles off the coast of China, it was peopled originally by Malayo-Polynesian tribes. Migrants from southeastern China gradually took over after the 16th century. From 1895 to 1945, Taiwan was under Japanese colonial control and was developed as a source of food and raw material. With the Communist victory in China in 1949, the island became the final refuge of the Nationalist government, supported by the United States.

During the period of "two Chinas," Taiwan was the Republic of China, and was formally recognized by the United Nations until 1971, when it was replaced by the mainland People's Republic (Beijing). American recognition and support ended in 1979. Taiwan is now in political limbo, claimed by China but carrying on an independent existence without international recognition. Yet it has developed one of the most dynamic and successful economies of East Asia.

The Land, People, and Economy. Taiwan is small (about 250 miles north-south and 75 miles east-west) but densely populated. The central and eastern portions are forested mountains and narrow northern and western plains. The latter, facing the Taiwan Strait, supports the large population, which includes more than two million "mainlanders" who fled to the island with the Nationalist government and their descendants.

The island still has a prosperous and intensive agriculture featuring rice, sugar cane, tea, bananas, and other export crops. Production is aided by a relatively mild year-round climate and advanced technology. It is in manufacturing that Taiwan now excels. It has a Japanese-style import (energy, raw materials)-export (manufactured goods) economy that has created relatively high living standards and incomes and makes Taiwan an important member of the world commercial community.

Factories are clustered in the northern cities of Taipei (the nation's capital and its largest city with more than 2 million inhabitants) and Chilung (Keelung), the main northern port; Kaohsiung, the main port and manufacturing center of the south; and a host of regional cities between Taipei and Kaohsiung. All are linked by excellent rail, highway, and/or air service.

Areas of Touristic Importance. Taipei is the major city frequented most by visitors. The National Palace Museum features a stunning collection of Imperial Chinese arts. The Chiang Kai-shek Memorial is of special importance to the Taiwanese because it honors their first leader. The Martyr's Shrine is modeled after Beijing's Forbidden City. The busy and colorful Lungshan Temple, built in 1776, is the oldest temple in Taiwan. Another temple in Taipei is the Confucian Temple, where the front gates are opened only on Confucius's birthday. The adventurous tourist shouldn't miss the opportunity to visit "Snake Alley." Taipei is a cosmopolitan city with excellent restaurants and good shopping opportunities.

The beautiful city of Taichung also attracts many visitors. Its location near Sun Moon Lake makes it one of Taiwan's most scenic and popular spots. Visitors can take a train from Taipei to Taichung to visit Sun Moon Lake.

Another spectacular attraction is Taroko Gorge, which can be visited on a very full day's trip out of Taipei.

Taiwan also has a number of beach areas, but most visitors from the United States don't go to Taiwan for beach vacations.

JAPAN

Language: Japanese
Area: 145,856 square miles
Time Zone: GMT +9
National Airline: Japan Airlines, All Nippon Airways
Capital: Tokyo
Currency: Yen (YEN)
Population: 124,017,000
Documentation: Passport, visa

Japan was the first Asian nation to modernize along Western lines and now ranks with the United States and the European Union (former European Community) as the third most powerful economic unit in the world. It is the model for development efforts in other East Asian nations, such as the Republic of Korea, Taiwan, and Singapore, and the British crown colony of Hong Kong.

The Islands. The Japanese success has been achieved in a relatively small land area, only about the size of California. There are four main islands. Honshu is the largest and has most of the population and economic ability. Kyushu and small Shikoku are in the southwest, separated from each other and Honshu by the Inland Sea. Northernmost is Hokkaido, which was developed only in the past century and still has a relatively small population.

The islands extend in a bow-shape for more than 1,000 miles off the northeast Asian coast; the southwestern tip is only 125 miles from the Korean Peninsula and the northern tip is near Russian Siberia and Sakhalin Island. The long, mountainous spine of the islands is studded with volcanoes, of which the celebrated Mount Fuji is the tallest at over 12,000 feet.

The long latitudinal stretch of Japan gives it many south-to-north climatic conditions, similar to the Florida to New England corridor on the eastern United States coast, with some moderating influences from the surrounding Pacific Ocean. Summers are hot and sultry. Winter temperatures range from chilly to cold in the southwest to bitter cold in the north. A permanent snow cover is on much of the western (Sea of Japan) coast and northern Honshu and Hokkaido from October to April.

The People. Most Japanese are densely clustered on a succession of small coastal plains. The Kanto Plain on the central Pacific coast of Honshu is the largest plain; the fact that it is only 50 miles wide speaks to the small scale and compactness of Japanese life.

The Japanese are a homogeneous people—they speak the same language and adhere to the same general behavioral system. Most practice Buddhism and Shintoism, the latter a domestic religion whose best-known symbol is the torii entrance gate to a Shinto shrine. Only 1 percent of the Japanese are Christians. There are some Ainu, an older and distinctive ethnic stock in Hokkaido, and 500,000 permanent residents of Korean stock.

History. The ancestors of the present Japanese probably migrated, in a series of waves, to southwestern Japan from the mainland more than 2,000 years ago. As numbers increased

and expanded around the plains facing the Inland Sea, a clan organization developed. The importation of Buddhism from China and Korea in the 6th century brought with it strong Chinese influences that affected all aspects of Japanese life. An imperial system of rule was adopted and the first permanent capital, Nara, was built on the Chinese urban model in 710 AD. It was moved a short distance to Kyoto in 794, and remained there until 1869 when the imperial residence was formally moved eastward to what is now Tokyo.

The Japanese borrowed and modified the Chinese written system, which uses ideographs, but spoken Japanese is not related to Chinese and lacks its use of tones to create new meanings.

After centuries of regional strife involving warriors serving under local lords, Japan enjoyed internal peace and prosperity under the rule of the Tokugawa shoguns, a military family that actually ruled Japan from its castle in Edo, present Tokyo, from 1600 to 1868. Trying to avoid the threat of western commercial inroads, Japan remained in isolation during much of this period until, in 1854, it was compelled to sign trade agreements by an American naval squadron under Admiral Perry.

Modern Japan began in 1868 with the overthrow of the Tokugawa feudal regime and the restoration of the Emperor to actual rule. Attempting to strengthen itself quickly to prevent the Western domination it saw in China, the Japanese government imported and adopted Western government, military, educational, and economic systems. Successful in wars with China (1895) and Russia (1904–1905), Japan grew stronger militarily and economically.

Colonies such as Taiwan (1895) and Korea (1910) were added, and Manchuria, now part of China, was controlled through a puppet government after 1931. The invasion of China in 1937 was followed by World War II, during which Japan's military conquered most of eastern China and all of Southeast Asia. Eventually defeated, Japan was occupied by the Allied powers (1945–1952). After the occupation, Japan embarked upon an extraordinary economic development unequalled in the postwar world. The Japanese formula was to import most of the needed oil and raw materials, utilize advanced domestic technical skills, and export high-quality goods to world markets.

Economy. The core area of Japan is a relatively narrow zone extending westward from the Kanto Plain along the Pacific coast of Honshu and through the Inland Sea to northern Kyushu. Within this 600-mile-long belt are more than two-thirds of the population, the largest cities and international ports, and the bulk of the commercial and manufacturing activity. Three great urban clusters dominate the belt.

The largest centers on Tokyo and extends from the shores of Tokyo Bay across the southern Kanto Plain. One of every five Japanese lives here, making Tokyo and its environs the world's largest metropolitan area. Tokyo dominates all phases of Japanese national life. For example, it houses the headquarters of most major companies and financial organizations, has the most educational institutions, publishing houses, artistic groups and facilities, leisure activities, restaurants, and large and small manufacturing plants. Nearby is the companion port city of Yokohama, now Japan's second largest city.

The second-ranking urban cluster is at the eastern end of the Inland Sea and includes three large cities—Osaka and Kobe on the coast and Kyoto, a short distance inland and just west of Lake Biwa. Osaka, formerly the second and now the third largest city, is a bustling commercial and manufacturing center, whereas neighboring Kobe is a great port city with a strong international atmosphere. Kobe is hemmed in by mountains and has turned to extensive land reclamation to expand its coastal land area. Kyoto, known as the center of Japanese art, is also an industrial area with industries producing electrical equipment, chemicals, and textiles.

The third cluster lies on the Pacific coast between the two other clusters and centers on the manufacturing city of Nagoya. Among these three major clusters, hundreds of small cities are expanding outward, filling in farmlands to create a continuous, high-density urbanized area. Many cities are found throughout Japan and an urban lifestyle exists everywhere.

Once the national backbone, agriculture now employs only one of every 12 workers. Agriculture is carried out on a tiny scale; the average farm is several acres per family in central and southwestern Japan. Most farmers depend on nonfarming income from other jobs held by family members. Production is highly commercial, intensive, and mechanized. Although rice, bolstered by government subsidies, is in surplus supply, Japan must import one-fourth of its total food needs, including wheat, meat, and even some fresh fish.

Manufacturing employs one of every four workers; some work in large export-oriented factories, but most are employed in small factories producing consumer goods for domestic use or parts for larger firms. As in the United States and Western Europe, the larger share of the labor force works in white-collar jobs in offices and laboratories—in wholesale and retail trade, banking and insurance, and education and specialized services, to mention a few. Education is universal and of high quality at all levels.

Several characteristics of Japanese life stand out. One is the easy blending of things old and new, Japanese and Western, in the cities and rural areas. Second, even though Japan has one of the lowest population growth rates among advanced nations, it is crowded. Distances are short and everything is compact—homes and other buildings on tiny lots, high-rise office buildings in the city centers, high-rise apartments, crowded public transportation, and spirited competition for space at public events.

Third, the Japanese people are overwhelmingly middle-class. Generally prosperous, they have access to a full range of modern consumer goods, opportunity for leisure and travel, and generally high rates of employment. Finally, there is the diversity of landscapes, both natural and artificial. Excellent modern transportation of all kinds makes swift movement possible, and modern communications contribute to the operation of a carefully structured and well-ordered national life.

Areas of Touristic Importance. Like China, it is possible to spend weeks in Japan without seeing everything. Because distances are relatively short, Japan's rail transportation system is the prime method of intercity transportation. The famous high speed Bullet trains travel between major urban clusters.

Tokyo is where East meets West in a blend of both the contemporary and the traditional. The Imperial Palace Plaza, containing the Emperor's residence, is a reminder of imperial Japan. The Meiji Shrine contains forests and gardens that are the sacred ground of the Shinto religion. Explore the fabled Ginza—Tokyo's "Broadway" and "Fifth Avenue." A spectacular view of the city is available from the Tokyo Tower. The highest skyscrapers are clustered in Shinjuku, a major shopping and business sub-center.

For Disney lovers, a visit to Tokyo Disneyland is a must. It is quite similar to Disneyland in California, but seeing it in Japan is an experience.

A short excursion to Nikko provides the grandeur of a 200,000-acre national park with Shogun shrines and pagodas. The setting is breathtaking.

Kamakura/Hakone is not far from Tokyo. It is best known for the Daibutsu, a giant Buddha more than 730 years old. Hakone also features a hot springs resort. Many tourists enjoy cruising excursions on Lake Hakone.

Kyoto remains Japan's best preserved historical city; its famous buildings, folk art tradition, and seasonal festivals make it the mecca of mass tourism in Japan. Mount Fuji is visible on a clear day when traveling from Tokyo. For the adventurous, Mt. Fuji can be climbed best in the summer. Kyoto is

Kinkakuji, Kyoto
Photo: Courtesy Japan National Tourist Organization

home to more than 1,600 temples and 200 shrines. Nearby Nara is home of the Todaiji Temple, the largest wooden structure on earth, housing a giant bronze Buddha.

The northern island of Hokkaido offers a respite from the hustle and bustle of most of Japan. Akan National Park with its lakes and hot springs, Lake Toya, and Sapporo offer pleasant resort areas. Sapporo was the site of the 1972 Winter Olympics and is a fascinating place to visit in winter, especially at the time of their Snow Festival with its giant ice carvings.

Yokohama is Japan's leading seaport and the gateway for cruise and steamship passengers. It also has many temples, shrines, and attractions of its own.

A visit to the industrial city of Osaka provides an opportunity to enjoy their puppet theater, the Osaka Castle and one of the world's largest aquariums.

The city of Nagoya, which was greatly damaged in World War II, has become a major business center. Visitors to Nagoya can tour the Noritake China Factory and visit the Atsuta Shrine. The Toyota auto assembly factories are nearby.

Hiroshima and Nagasaki, the two cities that were destroyed by atomic bombs during World War II each have memorials to the devastation of that experience and a Peace Park to remind us of what can result from war. Both cities have been fully rebuilt.

■ THE KOREAS—AN OVERVIEW

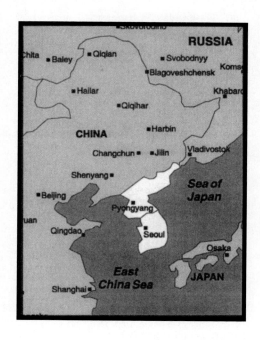

Jutting from the Chinese mainland toward Japan is the long Korean Peninsula, which is divided between the People's Republic of Korea (North Korea) and the Republic of Korea (ROK, South Korea). A mountainous spine leaves most habitable plains on the west (Yellow Sea) and south coasts and only narrow plains on the east (Sea of Japan) coast.

Caught historically between strong neighbors, the Korean people, who are related linguistically to the Japanese, Mongols, and other Central Asian peoples, have been subject to outside influences. They were under the control of China for many centuries and, like Japan, were profoundly affected by Chinese Buddhism, arts, and political, social, and economic forms. In the late 1800s, Russia replaced China as the emergent power in the area. Korea eventually became a Japanese colony (1910–1945), and was administered with a heavy military hand while Japanese government and private interests promoted agricultural and industrial development.

In 1945, the 38th parallel, which divides the peninsula roughly into halves, was selected as a "temporary" dividing line for two zones in which the victorious Soviet and American armed forces could complete the Japanese military surrender. Within a short period, two new Korean nations emerged—in the south with American military and economic support and in the north with support from the Soviet Union and, later, China. War between the two Korean nations (1950–1953), with the United States and other United Nations forces fighting with South Korea and Chinese forces aiding North Korea, resulted in a ceasefire along a demilitarized zone (DMZ) that now forms the international border. Military tension between the Koreas remains high and necessitates the continued presence of American troops in South Korea.

Both Koreas have made remarkable economic advances but under very different political systems.

NORTH KOREA

Official Name: Democratic People's Republic of Korea

Language: Korean

Area: 46,540 square miles

Time Zone: GMT +9

Capital: Pyongyang

Currency: Won

Population: 21,814,000

Documentation: Passport, visa

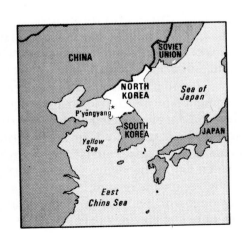

North Korea, with a larger land area but smaller population, is a highly centralized Communist dictatorship that gives priority to heavy industry and military build-up. It is virtually closed to non-Communist visitors. Very few westerners visit North Korea, and their visits are restricted to the capital, Pyongyang, or a few large-scale showpiece public works.

SOUTH KOREA

Official Name: Republic of Korea

Language: Korean

Area: 38,025 square miles

Time Zone: GMT +9

National Airline: Korean Air Lines

Capital: Seoul

Currency: Won (WON)

Population: 43,134,000

Documentation: Passport

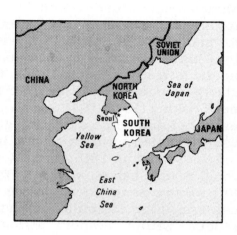

South Korea has a popularly elected national assembly and strong central government and gives a large share of the responsibility for economic development to private enterprise. Its agriculture provides sufficient food for its 44 million people. South Korea has a rapidly advancing industrial economy based upon the Japanese model of importing oil and raw materials and exporting manufactured goods. It has the second lowest labor costs in East Asia, after those of mainland China.

Buddhism is still the major religion in South Korea, but Christianity is widely practiced and growing fast. The Korean language is now written in Hangul, a native alphabet, instead of the Chinese and Japanese ideographs used earlier.

The urban and rural populations are densely packed into the western and southern plains, with massive concentrations in the northwest and southeast.

The urban concentration centers on Seoul, the national capital of more than 9 million persons. Like Tokyo in Japan, Seoul dominates South Korean life and has the best facilities and opportunities. The metropolitan area includes Inchon, a leading port and industrial center on the Yellow Sea.

In the southeast, Pusan is the central city. It is South Korea's second largest city and is a leading commercial and fishing port and industrial center with easy links with Ulsan and other nearby concentrations of modern industry.

Areas of Touristic Importance. Seoul is Korea's major tourist attraction. It is a blend of old and new; ancient temples sit side-by-side with modern hotels and office buildings. The Yi Dynasty palaces show how life used to be. The National Museum houses a collection of over 72,000 items. Numerous museums, palaces and temples throughout the city are attractive to visitors.

Ready-to-wear and made-to-measure clothing is available at bargain prices. Korean tailors can produce a well-made suit within 36 hours. Itaewon is the major shopping district for western visitors.

The Korean Folk Village, located at Suwon, just an hour's drive from Seoul, is an excellent example of a living museum with authentically dressed staff presenting folk history in an authentic setting.

The highly indented southern coast, Sorok Mountain, and offshore Cheju Island offer fascinating scenery and relaxing resorts. Pusan, in the south, is an example of a modern port and industrial city. The southeastern city of Kyongju has many fine antiquities.

The Demilitarized Zone (DMZ) in Panmunjom separates South Korea from North Korea and is still patrolled by the military at full alert. There continue to be periodic confrontations

Shopping at Itaewon, Seoul
Photo: Courtesy Korea National Tourism Corporation

in this area. A visit to the DMZ can be arranged as a full-day tour from Seoul and helps visitors gain an understanding of the tensions in this country.

For skiing enthusiasts wanting a new experience, Korea has several major ski resort areas within just a few hours of Seoul.

Visitors from all over the world to South Korea have increased in great numbers since Seoul hosted the Pan Asian Games in 1986 and the 1988 Olympics.

■ TYPES OF TOURISM

Escorted and hosted tours are the main types of programs used by most leisure travelers to East Asia. City packages and independent travel are becoming increasingly popular with sophisticated travelers.

Independent travel is difficult in China, where prepaid arrangements are required of most visitors. Tourists visit China as a single destination, as well as in conjunction with travel to other Asian nations, especially Japan and Hong Kong, its primary gateways.

Japan is also popular as both a single destination and combined with other countries in Asia. Hong Kong, South Korea, Taiwan, and Macau are rarely visited as single destinations. However, 1-week shopping trips to both Hong Kong and Seoul attract some visitors. The following itineraries are samples of the types of tour programs available for the region:

- Highlights of the Orient
- Yangtze River Experience
- Orient Escapade
- Imperial Japan
- Korea

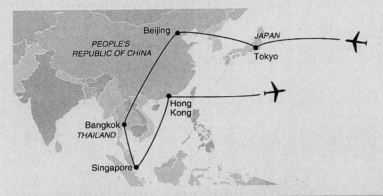

GLOBUS *First Class* ESCORTED

Highlights of the Orient

Japan, People's Republic of China, Thailand, Singapore and Hong Kong

Tour OTA – 16 days

ALL THIS IS INCLUDED

- All flights if Globus issues the tickets
- Transfers, including baggage handling, to and from airports
- Services of a professional tour director
- First-class hotels listed below or equivalent (see page 7). Twin-bedded rooms with private bath or shower, hotel taxes, service charges and tips for baggage handling
- In-flight meals as indicated in the itinerary; 14 American breakfasts (B); 4 lunches (L); 3 dinners (D), with a special farewell dinner in Hong Kong

- Cruise on Bangkok's Chao Phraya River with dinner
- Guided sightseeing in Tokyo, Beijing, Bangkok, Singapore, Hong Kong
- Visits to Beijing's Tian An Men Square, The Great Wall of China, The Ming Tombs, Singapore's Botanical Gardens, a jewelry workshop in Hong Kong
- Inside visits as shown in UPPER-CASE LETTERS in the tour description, including admission charges where applicable
- Globus travel bag and travel documents

▼ *JAPANESE SCHOOL CHILDREN AT A TRAIN STATION*

Day 1, Fri. LOS ANGELES. The tour begins aboard a luxurious wide-bodied jet. Relax and enjoy the excellent cabin service and in-flight movies. (In-flight meals)

Day 2, Sat. TOKYO, JAPAN. Arrival time is late afternoon because a day is "lost" crossing the International Date Line. After clearing customs, meet your tour director and transfer to the hotel.

Day 3, Sun. TOKYO. A full free day for independent activities. Highly recommended is the optional excursion to the historic city of Kamakura with its spectacular Daibutsu, a 700-year-old Buddha 42 feet high and weighing 94 tons. A cruise on Lake Hakone and a cable-car ride up 4354-foot Mt. Komagatake complete the day before a thrilling ride on the famous bullet train back to Tokyo. Lunch is included. (B)

Day 4, Mon. TOKYO-BEIJING, CHINA. For a rare combination of old and new Japan, the local guide takes you through the Asakusa district's alleys and covered passageways on the sightseeing tour this morning. Visit the MEIJI SHRINE, a magnificent 20th-century Shinto monument set in elaborate gardens and expressing the classic beauty associated with Japan. Lunch today is a delicious Japanese-style barbecue served with "sake". The flight to Beijing is in the late afternoon. Upon arrival in China's political and cultural capital, transfer to the hotel. (B,L,in-flight meal)

Day 5, Tue. BEIJING. Today's sightseeing includes a visit to the IMPERIAL PALACE, once sacred home to China's Great Emperors and the focal point of power of this mighty dynasty. The now infamous Tian An Men Square stands adjacent. It was in this vast public square, the largest in the world, that the Republic of China was proclaimed in 1949. A short drive out of the city leads to the former imperial SUMMER PALACE, a complex of pavilions, temples and galleries situated around an immense lake. The whole structure was rebuilt by the Dowager Empress Ci Xi in 1888 after having been burnt down by British and French troops. (Time permitting, the tour ends with a visit to Beijing Zoo to see the pandas). (B,L)

Day 6, Wed. BEIJING. The GREAT WALL OF CHINA once stretched for over 3,000 miles across northern China's most barren terrain. The part that has been best preserved and restored lies 40 miles north of Beijing in the village of Badaling. A walk along the wall affords unforgettable vistas of this mammoth fortress spanning the countryside as far as the eye can see. Returning to Beijing, visit the MING TOMBS, underground burial sites for 13 of the Ming emperors, and whose approach is lined with magnificently-carved marble animals, real and mythical. (B,L,D)

Day 7, Thu. BEIJING-BANGKOK, THAILAND. Time still for last-minute shopping today. Perhaps visit the Friendship Store, which most visitors have found to be the best in China with its wide range of silks. A late afternoon transfer for the flight to exotic Bangkok. (B, in-flight meal)

Day 8, Fri. BANGKOK. WAT ARUN, the Temple of the Dawn, is first on today's sightseeing agenda. Its magnificent spires, inlaid with millions of pieces of chinese porcelain, are a dazzling sight in the early morning sunshine. Next is the GRAND PALACE, the truly grand seat of the court of old Siam, and the adjoining royal temple, WAT PHRA KEO, housing the Emerald Buddha. The 31-inch statue sits high on a golden altar. Dinner this evening is aboard a luxurious teak barge, the Tassaneeya Nava. Cruise along the broad Chao Phraya River, past Bangkok's splendid temples and palaces and the landing stage from which the gilded royal barge departs on the king's ceremonial visits. (B,D)

36 US

Reprinted courtesy of Globus and Cosmos.

Day 9, Sat. BANGKOK. At one time the main streets of Bangkok were canals (klongs in Thai) and a good deal of life today is still waterborne. As the day is at leisure, why not join our recommended optional full-day trip to the floating market at Damneon Saduak? En route, the excursion stops at Nakorn Pathom Chedi, then the Rose Gardens for a delightful lunch; and lastly, a visit to the Thai Cultural Village to see a performance of a typical Thai folk dance as well as a demonstration of elephants at work. (B)

Day 10, Sun. BANGKOK-SINGAPORE. A late morning flight means a mid-afternoon arrival in Singapore, the international crossroads that is the world's second busiest seaport. After checking in at the hotel, the remainder of the day is free. Perhaps enjoy a leisurely walk around this clean, compact city, whose mixture of Oriental peoples has caused it to be nicknamed "Instant Asia". (B,in-flight meal)

Day 11, Mon. SINGAPORE. East and West blend neatly in this island republic, and a city tour shows off its varied sights: Queen Elizabeth Walk overlooking the harbor, the statue of Sir Stamford Raffles, Mount Faber with its sweeping view of the city and waterfront and the BOTANICAL GARDENS, noted for its hybrid orchids. The remainder of the day is free. Take a ride in a trishaw, a combination of rickshaw and tricycle, through the bustling city roads with a stop at the famous Raffles Hotel for a "Singapore Sling". (B)

Day 12, Tue. SINGAPORE-HONG KONG, B.C.C. This morning board your flight to Hong Kong, one of the last bastions of British commerce in Asia. Flying into this British Crown Colony is a memorable experience; view the sweeping expanses of sandy beaches and countless islands dotting the South China Sea, and then Hong Kong's teeming harbor sparkling in the sun. (B,in-flight meal)

Day 13, Wed. HONG KONG. Take the cable car up to Victoria Peak for a panoramic view of the harbor and city. The morning sightseeing continues with a drive to Repulse Bay, a popular beach with the locals. Stanley Market is next, a narrow street jammed with inexpensive clothing, arts and crafts stalls. Last stop on the tour is at a JEWELRY FACTORY that designs and makes fine jewelry – each piece by hand. Lunch today is at La Ronda – 30 floors up – overlooking the bustling harbor of Hong Kong's Central District. With the evening free, we recommend an optional sunset cruise on Hong Kong harbor. (B,L)

Days 14 & 15, Thu. & Fri. HONG KONG. Two full days to explore the city's many other attractions. Perhaps spend a day visiting exotic Macau, the gambling resort and Portuguese colony that is the oldest European settlement in the Far East. Your tour director can arrange the excursion and provide suggestions on where to get the best buys and best meals at reasonable prices. For the last evening together on tour, your tour director hosts a farewell dinner, a festive finale to a great touring adventure. (B daily,D)

Day 16, Sat. HONG KONG-LOS ANGELES. A late-morning transfer to the airport to board your flight home. Cross the International Date Line and arrive back in the U.S. on the same day. (B,in-flight meals)

▼ HONG KONG HARBOUR   ▲ SENTRY AT THE GREAT WALL OF CHINA

One of the HAWAII ADD-ONS may be booked in conjunction with this tour. See page 49.

Tour OTA: DATES & PRICES

Tour Code	Leave USA		Return USA		Air/land incl. US$	Land only US$
OTA0408	Fri	08-Apr	Sat	23-Apr	3732	2108
OTA0422	Fri	22-Apr	Sat	07-May	3732	2108
OTA0506	Fri	06-May	Sat	21-May	3732	2108
OTA0520	Fri	20-May	Sat	04-Jun	3732	2108
OTA0603	Fri	03-Jun	Sat	18-Jun	3854	2108
OTA0617	Fri	17-Jun	Sat	02-Jul	3854	2108
OTA0708	Fri	08-Jul	Sat	23-Jul	3854	2108
OTA0722	Fri	22-Jul	Sat	06-Aug	3854	2108
OTA0812	Fri	12-Aug	Sat	27-Aug	3854	2108
OTA0826	Fri	26-Aug	Sat	10-Sep	3854	2108
OTA0909	Fri	09-Sep	Sat	24-Sep	3732	2108
OTA0916	Fri	16-Sep	Sat	01-Oct	3851	2228
OTA0923	Fri	23-Sep	Sat	08-Oct	3851	2228
OTA0930	Fri	30-Sep	Sat	15-Oct	3851	2228
OTA1007	Fri	07-Oct	Sat	22-Oct	3851	2228
OTA1014	Fri	14-Oct	Sat	29-Oct	3851	2228
OTA1021	Fri	21-Oct	Sat	05-Nov	3851	2228
OTA1104	Fri	04-Nov	Sat	19-Nov	3732	2108
OTA1118	Fri	18-Nov	Sat	03-Dec	3732	2108
OTA1216	Fri	16-Dec	Sat	31-Dec	3746	2108

Air/land inclusive price includes all flights from/to Los Angeles.
Land only price covers land arrangements from Tokyo (day 2) to Hong Kong (day 16).
Single room supplement: $975
Triple room reduction per person: $89

APOLLO: TD*GG, **PARS:** G/PTS/GGX, **SABRE:** Y/TUR/QGG

ADD-ON AIR FARES

From	Add	From	Add
Chicago	$250	New Orleans	$250
Dallas/Ft. Worth	$230	New York	$250
Denver	$230	Phoenix	$100
Miami	$250	Seattle	$100

All air fares are subject to change without notice. For travel from one of the cities listed above, add the roundtrip per person amount to the 'air/land' inclusive price. If your hometown is not listed, please check with your travel agent for the applicable add-on fare.

GLOBUS HOTELS

TOKYO Hilton International, **BEIJING** The Kempinsky, **BANGKOK** Le Meridien President, **SINGAPORE** Hilton International, **HONG KONG** The Nikko Hotel

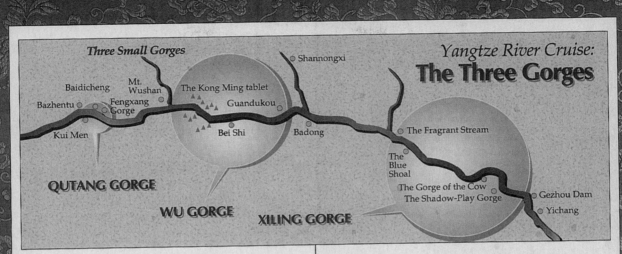

Yangtze River Experience
Tour A and Tour B Cruise Itinerary
Aboard the
MV *Yangtze Paradise*

UPSTREAM ITINERARY (Wuhan/Chongqing)

DAY 01 YANGTZE RIVER CRUISE:
DEPART WUHAN (B,L,D)
Board your luxurious cruise ship. Spend the rest of the day relaxing aboard, perhaps at the pool, as you sail upstream. Appetizing meals are served aboard..

DAY 02 YANGTZE RIVER CRUISE:
SHASHI/JINGZHOU (B,L,D)
Early morning arrival in Shashi. Go ashore to visit ancient Jingzhou, where the Jingzhou Museum displays relics including a well-preserved 2000-year-old mummy. Continue to sail in the afternoon and through the night..

DAY 03 YANGTZE RIVER CRUISE:
XILING GORGE/WU GORGE/WUSHAN
(THREE SMALL GORGES) (B,L,D)
Early morning sail through the Lock of Gezhouba Dam and into the peerless magnificence of Xiling, longest of the Three Gorges. Cruise through the splendor of Wu Gorge, surrounded by the beautiful Twelve Peaks. Upon arrival at Wushan, where you're transferred to a motorboat to cruise the Daning River's splendidly scenic Dragon Gate Gorge, Misty Gorge and Emerald Gorge, known as the Three Small Gorges.

DAY 04 YANGTZE RIVER CRUISE:
WUSHAN/QUTANG GORGE/WANXIAN (B,L,D)
Depart this morning. Cruise through the grandeur of Qutang Gorge, walled by the moss-covered precipices limed starkly against the sky, is a thrilling sight. Arrive in Wanxian in the late afternoon and enjoy a shore excursion before sailing in the late evening bound for Fengdu and on to Chongqing.

DAY 05 YANGTZE RIVER CRUISE:
WANXIAN/FENGDU/CHONGQING (B,L,D)
Early morning arrival at legend-rich Fengdu, where a shore excursion shows Mingshan Hill's temples, filled with statuary. Leave Fengdu this morning for Chongqing. Morning cruising past terraced fields and farming villages brings you to Chongqing, where you disembark this evening.

Yangtze River Experience
Tour C Cruise Itinerary
Aboard the
MV *Yangtze Paradise*

DOWNSTREAM ITINERARY (Chongqing/Wuhan)

DAY 01 YANGTZE RIVER CRUISE:
DEPART CHONGQING/FENGDU/WANXIAN (B,L,D)
Board your deluxe cruise ship for a memorable journey and relax as you cruise downstream. Depart Chongqing at 8:00 am. Appetizing meals are served aboard. Afternoon arrival at legend-rich Fengdu, where a shore excursion shows Mingshan Hill's temples, filled with statuary. Leave Fengdu in the evening for Wanxian.

DAY 02 YANGTZE RIVER CRUISE:
WANXIAN/QUTANG GORGE/WU GORGE/BADONG/
SHENNONG STREAM/BADONG/ZIGUI (B,L,D)
Up on deck early this morning, for ahead lies the unforgettable experience of cruising through the first of the fabled Three Gorges: Qutang Gorge, walled by the moss-covered precipices limned starkly against the sky, is a thrilling sight. Sailing continues, and you will pass through the second of the major gorges, spectacular Wu Gorge, celebrated for its towering peaks which blot out the sun. Late morning arrival in Badong, where you board a 'pea-shaped' boat for an exciting excursion on the Shennong Stream, cruising through its spectacularly scenic Parrot Gorge and Dragonboat Gorge. Marvel at remnants of the ancient plank road and precariously suspended emperor's coffins visible amidst the towering cliffs. Rejoin the mighty Yangtze to return to Badong. Arrival early evening in Zigui.

DAY 03 YANGTZE RIVER CRUISE:
ZIGUI/XILING GORGE/YICHANG (B,L,D)
Enjoy a leisurely breakfast this morning before sailing from Zigui. Cruise through the last and most scenic of the Three Gorges, Xiling Gorge, then pass through the Lock of Gezhouba Dam to arrive at Yichang. Afternoon excursion here visits the Gezhouba Water Conservative Project and the Research Institute of Chinese Sturgeon. Sail from Yichang tonight.

DAY 04 YANGTZE RIVER CRUISE:
YICHANG/YUEYANG/WUHAN (B,L,D)
Morning arrival at Yueyang, a 4000-year-old city in northern Hunan Province located where the Yangtze River and Donging Lake merge, for a shore excursion. As well as Yueyang Tower, overlooking the expansive lake with its Junshan Island — inspiration for artists and weavers of fairytales through the ages — the city's historical and cultural relics include Yueyang Mansion, famed as one of China's most beautiful, the Cishi Pagoda and the Quzi and Wen Temples. Sail from Yueyang at about noon, heading for Wuhan, where you disembark this evening.

** Sailings that will not anchor in Fengdu, will sail on and anchor in Wanxian.

Yangtze River Experience

TOUR A: 21 DAYS • *FULLY ESCORTED BY AN AMERICAN TOUR MANAGER FROM SAN FRANCISCO*

17 DAYS in CHINA visiting 13 cities : Beijing, Xi'an, Shanghai, Suzhou, Wuhan, Shashi, Jingzhou, Wushan, Wanxian, Fengdu, Chongqing, Guilin and Guangzhou, plus Hong Kong

COST   IT3UA1YRA4

	MAR 11	APR 01 NOV 18	APR 22 OCT 28	MAY 13 JUN 03	JUN 24 JUL 15 AUG 05	AUG 26	SEP 16 OCT 07
TOUR FARE (WC)	$3540	$3870	$4060	$4120	$3950	$4170	$4220
TOUR FARE (EC)	$3680	$4090	$4280	$4340	$4170	$4390	$4440
Single Supplement	$ 850	$ 950	$1120	$1130	$ 950	$1130	$1280

Land fare is available upon request.
For domestic Add-On airfares from interior U.S. cities to West Coast, please refer to Add-On Fare Chart on Page 55.

DEPARTURES: FRIDAYS

1994:

MAR 11	APR 01	MAY 13	JUN 03	JUL 15
	APR 22		JUN 24	

AUG 05	SEP 16	OCT 07	NOV 18
AUG 26		OCT 28	

DAY	CITY/ITINERARY

01 SAN FRANCISCO/BEIJING
FRI   Your tour manager will meet you at the airport and accompany you on board United Airlines' 747 jetliner for your transpacific flight bound for China. Cross the International Date Line.

02 ARRIVE BEIJING
SAT   Arrive in Beijing. Your Tour Manager will assist you through Immigration & Customs for your entry into China. You will then be escorted to the prestigious Great Wall Sheraton Hotel. Enjoy a delicious breakfast, lunch and dinner each day in China.

03 BEIJING (AB,L,DS)
SUN   Sightsee imposing Tian An Men Square; the Imperial Palace in the once Forbidden City; the Summer Palace, where you cruise Lake Kunming. Tonight, you're our guest at a delicious Beijing Duck dinner party with delightful entertainment.

04 BEIJING (AB,L,WD)
MON   Day-long excursion lets you mount the Great Wall and descend into the Ming Tombs. Later, admire the exquisite Temple of Heaven. Enjoy a western dinner this evening.

05 BEIJING/XI'AN (AB,L,WD)
TUE   Fly to Xi'an, site of amazing archaeological discoveries. Check into the Sheraton Xi'an Hotel or the Hyatt Regency Hotel. Today's tour takes you to the ancient Forest of Steles stone tablets and the Big Wild Goose Pagoda if time permits. Tonight, a western dinner is served in the hotel.

06 XI'AN (AB,L,DS)
WED   View the terra-cotta legion buried with the first emperor. Later, visit the Banpo Neolithic Museum and Huaqing Hot Spring. Tonight brings a memorable

dinner show at the Tang Dynasty Theatre Restaurant.

07 XI'AN/SHANGHAI (AB,L,D)
THU   Wing on to Shanghai and transfer to the deluxe Hua Ting Sheraton Hotel.

08 SHANGHAI (AB,L,DP)
FRI   Sightsee Nanjing Road's shopping district, Yu Yuan Garden, the famous Nanjing Road, the Bund, the Jade Buddha Temple and visit the Children's Palace. A Chinese Banquet is planned for you this evening and later, a very entertaining acrobatic show.

09 SHANGHAI/SUZHOU/
SAT **SHANGHAI (AB,L,WD)**
Today, enjoy an excursion to Suzhou, a beguiling canal-laced city which harbors centuries-old gardens. Enjoy a Grand Canal cruise. Visit Silk Reeling Factory, Pan Men City Gate, Garden of the Master of Fishing Net and the Embroidery Research Institute. Enjoy a western dinner tonight

10 SHANGHAI/WUHAN (AB,L,D)
SUN   Fly to Wuhan, a fusion of three cities spanning the Yangtze River. Stay at the Asia Hotel or the Yangtze Hotel. Visit the Hubei Province Museum and East Lake Park.

11 YANGTZE RIVER CRUISE:
MON **DEP WUHAN (B,L,D)**
Begin your thrilling five-day cruise
to   aboard a deluxe cruiser, the MV
14 *Yangtze Paradise*. Enjoy three delicious
THU   meals each day. (Please refer to page 20 for a detailed daily itinerary of your upstream cruise.)

15 ARRIVE CHONGQING (B,L,D)
FRI   Morning cruising past terraced fields and farming villages brings you to

Chongqing where you disembark. Check into the Holiday Inn Yangtze.

16 CHONGQING/GUILIN (B,L,D)
SAT   Scenic splendors await you in Guilin, center of a magnificent karst landscape. Transfer to the Sheraton Guilin Hotel. Dinner is served in the hotel.

17 GUILIN (AB,L,WD)
SUN   Spend a tranquil day cruising the serene Li River on a deluxe boat bound for Yangshuo, set against the hauntingly beautiful karst landscape. Enjoy a western dinner in the hotel.

18 GUILIN/GUANGZHOU/
MON **HONG KONG (AB,L)**
Wing on to Guangzhou today and enjoy a city tour. After lunch, you take a train to scintillating Hong Kong. Check into the super deluxe Nikko Hotel or the luxurious Sheraton Hong Kong Hotel & Towers.

19 HONG KONG (AB)
TUE   Breakfast in your hotel. Today's sightseeing circuit of Hong Kong Island shows you the cosmopolitan Central District, scenic Repulse Bay with beautiful sandy beach, Stanley Market, the waterborne community at Aberdeen and a cable car ride up to Victoria Peak for a panoramic view of the spectacular view of the famous Hong Kong Harbor.

20 HONG KONG (AB)
WED   Breakfast in your hotel. Spend this day at your leisure for individual activities.

21 HONG KONG/LOS ANGELES (AB)
THU   Breakfast in your hotel. Today you fly homeward aboard United Airlines wide-cabin 747 jetliner. Cross the International Date Line and arrive home the same day.

WC=from West Coast   EC=from East Coast

B=Breakfast AB=American Breakfast L=Lunch D=Dinner
WD=Western Dinner DP=Dinner Party DS=Dinner Show

21

Orient Escapade

TOUR A: 16 DAYS • *ESCORTED*

Visiting Japan including Osaka, Kyoto, Hakone, Kamakura, Tokyo plus Bangkok, Singapore and Hong Kong

IT3UA1OEA4

COST

	JAN 01-MAR 31	APR 01-MAY 31 SEP 01-SEP 15	JUN 01-AUG 31	SEP 16-NOV 16
TOUR FARE (WC)	$3240	$3340	$3460	$3440
TOUR FARE (EC)	$3380	$3560	$3680	$3660
Single Supplement	$ 920	$ 910	$ 890	$1010

Please add additional tour fare for the following departures:
Aug 24, add $30.

Land fare is available upon request.

DEPARTURES: WEDNESDAYS

1994:

JAN 26	FEB 23	MAR 23	APR 13	MAY 11	JUN 15	JUL 13	AUG 10	SEP 07	OCT 05	NOV 02
		MAR 30	APR 27	MAY 25	JUN 29	JUL 27	AUG 24	SEP 14	OCT 12	NOV 09
								SEP 21	OCT 19	NOV 16
								SEP 28	OCT 26	

1995:

FEB 22   MAR 22

Tour fares for 1995 departures are subject to change.

For domestic Add-On airfares from interior U.S. cities to West Coast, please refer to Add-On Fare Chart on Page 55.
Optional Dine-Around Plan: 1 Dinner Kyoto, 2 Dinners Tokyo = Total 3 Dinners in Japan $199.

DAY	CITY/ITINERARY	DAY	CITY/ITINERARY	DAY	CITY/ITINERARY

01 SAN FRANCISCO/OSAKA
WED Start your exciting adventure as you board your luxurious United Airlines' wide-cabin jetliner for your transpacific flight. Cross the International Date Line.

02 ARRIVE OSAKA/KYOTO
THU Upon arrival in Osaka, motorcoach on to Kyoto nestled among the surrounding mountains and your impressive Kyoto Grand Hotel. You will enjoy your stay in this fascinating city.

03 KYOTO (AB,ODA)
FRI Breakfast in the hotel. Morning sightseeing shows the vermilion-coated Heian Shrine with its lovely gardens, Kinkakuji Temple (Golden Pavilion), Nijo Castle

and Handicraft Center. The rest of the day at your leisure. [Optional Japan Dine-Around Dinner Plan]

04 KYOTO/HAKONE/KAMAKURA/ TOKYO (AB,ODA)
SAT Breakfast in the hotel. Bullet train to Atami traveling at the speed of lightning in complete comfort and enjoyment. Later, motorcoach to the Hakone National Park via the scenic Jukkoku (Ten Province) Pass. From the Hakone Bypass you will enjoy the breathtaking panoramas of surrounding mountains and view the awe-inspiring Mt. Fuji. Continue to drive to Kamakura where you'll view the legendary Daibutsu, a

700-year-old bronze image of the great Buddha. Proceed to Tokyo, where you check into the luxurious Akasaka Prince Hotel. [Optional Japan Dine-Around Dinner Plan]

05 TOKYO (AB,ODA)
SUN Breakfast in the hotel. Sightseeing includes a city tour of Tokyo visiting the Imperial Palace plaza, an oasis of serenity in the heart of this bustling metropolis. A visit to the Outer Garden of the Meiji Shrine is followed by a comprehensive look at Asakusa Kannon Temple and its animated Nakamise Arcade. [Optional Japan Dine-Around Dinner Plan]

WC=from West Coast   EC=from East Coast

AB=American Breakfast   DP=Dinner Party
DA=Dine-Around Dinner   ODA=Japan Optional Dine-Around Plan

06 TOKYO/BANGKOK (AB)
MON Breakfast in the hotel. Morning is at your leisure. In the late afternoon, fly on to Bangkok. This is a fascinating city of glorious temples and stone figures. Accommodations are at the new super deluxe Royal Orchid Sheraton or Royal Garden Riverside.

07 BANGKOK (AB,DP)
TUE Enjoy breakfast in the hotel. Today you tour the Royal Grand Palace which reveals exquisite pavilions of the palace complex and Thailand's most sacred object, the Emerald Buddha within Wat Phra Keo. Tonight features an exotic Thai dinner party with entertainment by Thai classical dancers.

08 BANGKOK (AB,DA)
WED Free day after breakfast to explore. You could elect to join our optional tour of Bangkok's klongs (canals) to the Floating Market. Also, see the ancient gold leafed Temple of Dawn with its porcelain cloaked tower and ornate royal barges etched against the rising sun. You will also watch housewives bargaining for fresh fruits and vegetables from bobbing sampans filling the klong. Tonight features a Dine-Around dinner in a selective restaurant.

09 BANGKOK/SINGAPORE (AB,DA)
THU Breakfast in the hotel. Take your morning flight to Singapore, tiny island-state off the tip of the Malay Peninsula. Enjoy your stay in your harbor view room at the luxurious Marina Mandarin Hotel. This evening Dine-Around in a selective restaurant for dinner.

10 SINGAPORE (AB,DA)
FRI Breakfast in the hotel, then tour Singapore and its temples, pavilions, Botanic Gardens with its magnificent display of orchids, skyscrapered malls and ethnic districts. Here, you will be acquainted with this multi-racial city renowned for its lush foliage and cleanliness. From atop Mt. Faber we enjoy a panoramic view of the city's southern islands. Tonight, enjoy a Dine-Around dinner in a selective restaurant.

11 SINGAPORE (AB,DA)
SAT Breakfast in the hotel. Spend the day at your leisure to shop and explore this fascinating multi-cultural city. Enjoy a Dine-Around dinner in a selective restaurant.

12 SINGAPORE/HONG KONG (AB)
SUN After breakfast in the hotel, fly on to scintillating Hong Kong and check into the deluxe Hyatt Regency Hotel, the luxurious Sheraton Hotel and Towers, or the Ramada Renaissance Hotel.

13 HONG KONG (AB,DA)
MON After breakfast in the hotel, come discover this intriguing city. Our tour will take you to bargain-filled stalls of Stanley Market, a shoppers haven, the crowded Aberdeen floating community, the beautiful beaches of Repulse Bay and a cable car ride up to Victoria Peak for a panoramic view of the harbor. A delicious Dine-Around dinner will be served at a selective restaurant tonight.

14 HONG KONG (AB,DA)
TUE Breakfast in the hotel. Enjoy this free day to discover the hundreds of malls and boutiques in the city of perpetual motion where shopping abounds. This evening features a Dine-Around dinner in a selective restaurant.

15 HONG KONG (AB,DP)
WED After breakfast in the hotel, the day is at your leisure. By now, your interests will encourage you to explore some places on your own and satisfy your spirit of adventure. Perhaps take an optional excursion via jetfoil to Portuguese Macau and visit Zhongshan of the People's Republic of China. A farewell dinner party is arranged for you on your final night in Hong Kong.

16 HONG KONG/LOS ANGELES (AB)
THU After breakfast in the hotel, board your United Airlines' jetliner homeward bound. Cross the International Date Line and arrive home the same day.

AB=American Breakfast DP=Dinner Party
DA=Dine-Around Dinner ODA=Japan Optional Dine-Around Plan

Imperial Japan A

11 days visiting Tokyo, Hakone, Matsumoto, Takayama, Kanazawa, Ama-no-hashidate and Kyoto

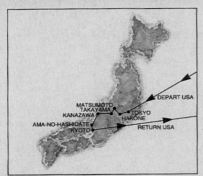

Gassho-zukuri (joined-hands farmhouses), Ogimachi

ITINERARY

1
Wed **USA/Tokyo** ✈
Depart the USA. Cross the International Date Line en route.

2
Thu **Arrive Tokyo**
After completion of customs formalities, transfer to the **Keio Plaza Inter-Continental Hotel.**

3
Fri **Tokyo**
Morning sightseeing of Tokyo visits the Imperial Palace Plaza, Asakusa Kannon Temple and Nakamise Arcade and Meiji Shrine.

4
Sat **Tokyo/Kamakura/Hakone**
Motorcoach to Kamakura, home of the enormous Daibutsu Buddha. Then, on to Hakone, where you will enjoy a cruise on the lake (weather permitting). Stay at the **Hotel Kowaki-en**.

5
Sun **Hakone/Lake Yamanaka/Mt. Fuji/Matsumoto**
Drive to the fifth station of Mt. Fuji via Lake Yamanaka. Travel on to Matsumoto, gateway to the Japanese Alps. Afternoon sightseeing of Matsumoto Castle and Ukiyoe (woodblock print) Museum. Stay at the **Matsumoto Tokyu Inn**.

6
Mon **Matsumoto/Takayama (HD)**
Morning drive over winding roads to Takayama. Overnight at **Hida Hotel Plaza** with dinner in the hotel.

7
Tue **Takayama/Kanazawa (B)**
After a Japanese breakfast, enjoy the scenic ride to Kanazawa via Ogimachi. Stay at the **Kanazawa Tokyu Hotel**.

8
Wed **Kanazawa**
Tour Kutan-yaki Shop and Kenrokuen Park. Afternoon at leisure.

9
Thu **Kanazawa/Tsuruga Bay/Mikata Five Lakes/Ama-no-hashidate (HD)**
Pass the rugged cliffs of Tsuruga Bay and the charming, mountainous Mikata Five Lakes District. Japanese dinner and overnight at the **Genmyoan Inn**, a ryokan in Ama-no-hashidate.

10
Fri **Ama-no-hashidate/Kyoto (B)**
After Japanese breakfast at the inn, depart for Kyoto. Afternoon sightseeing of Heian Shrine, Kinkakuji Temple (Golden Pavilion) and Sanjusangendo's 1,001 images of Buddha. Stay at the **International Hotel Kyoto**. Or, experience a traditional Japanese inn, the **Ryokan Yoshi-ima**, with breakfast, Japanese dinner and a tea ceremony. You'll feel you're in old Japan.

11
Sat **Kyoto/Osaka/Tokyo-Narita/USA** ✈
Transfer to the airport for your flight to the USA. Cross the International Date Line and arrive home the same day.

Why not add Hong Kong to your tour?
See page 8 for details.

TOUR DATES & PRICES			IT3JL1PAIJA
	FROM HONOLULU	FROM NEW YORK OR CHICAGO	FROM WEST COAST
MAR 23–APR 2 MAR 30–APR 9	$3140	$3395	$3225
APR 6–16 MAY 4–14 MAY 11–21 MAY 25–JUN 4	$3190	$3475	$3295
JUN 1–11 JUN 15–25 JUN 29–JUL 9 JUL 13–23 JUL 20–30 AUG 17–27 AUG 31–SEP 10	$3290	$3570	$3390
SEP 7–17 SEP 21–OCT 1 SEP 28–OCT 8 OCT 5–15 OCT 12–22 OCT 26–NOV 5	$3190	$3475	$3295
NOV 2–12 NOV 23–DEC 3	$3140	$3395	$3225

Land only: $2670   Single extra: $530.
Yoshi-ima Ryokan surcharge: $130 per person double, $110 single.
Optional daily American breakfast (7): $135
Optional Breakfast/Dinner Plan (7 American breakfasts, 6 dinners): $510

Add-on airfares available from many cities. See page 6.

Land only cost does not include any flights nor arrival and departure transfers in Japan. Tour fares do not include $18 US transportation taxes and fees or foreign airport departure taxes ($20, payable locally).

Reprinted courtesy of TBI Tours.

Imperial Japan B

17 days visiting Tokyo, Hakone, Matsumoto, Takayama, Kanazawa, Ama-no-hashidate, Kyoto, Takamatsu, Kurashiki, Hiroshima and Osaka

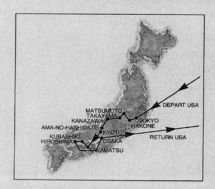

ITINERARY

Days 1–10 follow the itinerary of Imperial Japan A; then the itinerary continues as follows:

11
Sat **Kyoto**
Explore Kyoto on your own today. An optional tour to Nara or to Ise and Pearl Island is recommended.

12
Sun **Kyoto/Kobe/Awaji Island/Naruto/Takamatsu** 🚆 🚢
Drive to Kobe, gateway to the Inland Sea National Park. Hydrofoil to Awaji Island. Enjoy the Awaji Ningyo-jyoruri puppet show. Pass over the whirlpools of Naruto Straits on the scenic drive to Takamatsu. Overnight at the **Takamatsu Kokusai Hotel**.

13
Mon **Takamatsu/Uno/Kurashiki** 🚆
Morning sightseeing of Takamatsu visits beautiful Ritsurin Park. Then, cross the Seto Ohashi Bridge over the Inland Sea to Honshu Island and drive on to Kurashiki, where you will stay at the **Hotel Kurashiki**.

14
Tue **Kurashiki/Hiroshima** 🚆
Morning walking tour takes you through Kurashiki's old streets to Ohara Art Museum, Kurashiki Folk Museum and Ivy Square. Afternoon bullet train to Hiroshima. Stay at the **Hiroshima Grand Hotel**.

15
Wed **Hiroshima/Miyajima/Hiroshima** 🚆 🚢
Tour Peace Memorial Park and its museum in Hiroshima. Cross the channel to Miyajima to visit beautiful Itsukushima Jingu Shrine and Torii Gate rising from the sea.

16
Thu **Hiroshima/Osaka** 🚆
Morning bullet train to Osaka. Balance of day at leisure. Stay at the **Osaka Terminal Hotel**.

17
Fri **Osaka/Tokyo-Narita/USA** ✈
Transfer to the airport for your flight to the USA. Cross the International Date Line and arrive home the same day.

Affordable Choices, Choices, Choices

A Spring Wedding

Why not add Hong Kong to your tour? See page 8 for details.

TOUR DATES & PRICES			IT3JL1PAIJB
	FROM HONOLULU	**FROM NEW YORK OR CHICAGO**	**FROM WEST COAST**
MAR 23–APR 8 **MAR 30–APR 15**	$4375	$4650	$4480
APR 6–22 **MAY 4–20** **MAY 11–27** **MAY 25–JUN 10**	$4430	$4710	$4540
JUN 1–17 **JUN 15–JUL 1** **JUN 29–JUL 15** **JUL 13–29** **JUL 20–AUG 5** **AUG 17–SEP 2** **AUG 31–SEP 16**	$4550	$4840	$4660
SEP 7–23 **SEP 21–OCT 7** **SEP 28–OCT 14** **OCT 5–21** **OCT 12–28** **OCT 26–NOV 11**	$4430	$4710	$4540
NOV 2–18 **NOV 23–DEC 9**	$4375	$4650	$4480

Land only: $3875 Single extra: $750.
Optional daily American breakfast (13): $230
Optional Breakfast/Dinner Plan (13 American breakfasts, 12 dinners): $965

Add-on airfares available from many cities. See page 6.

Land only cost does not include any flights nor arrival and departure transfers in Japan. Tour fares do not include $18 US transportation taxes and fees or foreign airport departure taxes ($20, payable locally).

11

Korea

Korea, more than Seoul. In mountainous national parks ancient temples stand. The historic city, Kyongju, is known as the "museum without walls". On Cheju Island, "stone grandfathers" were once venerated as village guardian deities. Vibrant markets and fish markets reveal a way of life still thriving.

VISIT KOREA YEAR 1994

Traditional Korean Drum

Seoul

3 Days/2 Nights   CSEL

1   Arrival and transfer to your hotel.

2   Half day sightseeing includes a visit to Kyongbok Palace, National Museum, Folklore Museum and Bukak Skyway. The afternoon is at leisure.

3   Transfer to the airport for your onward flight.

	Package		Extra Night	
	Double	Single	Double	Single
Westin Chosun	$340/375*	$540/595*	$114/135*	$228/269*
Hilton	$285/345*	$440/550*	$ 83/115*	$167/229*
Lotte	$250/320*	$380/525*	$ 74/105*	$147/209*
Lotte World	$250/295*	$380/490*	$ 74/105*	$147/209*
Sheraton Walker Hill	$270/290*	$420/470*	$85/99*	$169/197*
Ramada Olympia	$215/265*	$310/410*	$54/83*	$108/166*

*High Season: March 15 - June 30, Sept-Nov.

Korean Totem Poles

Cheju Island

3 Days/2 Nights   CCHJ
Includes breakfast daily.

1   Transfer to Kimpo Airport for a morning flight to Cheju Island. Afternoon tour to Dragon Head Rock, Samsonghyol, Moksokwon and the Folkcraft Museum. Transfer to your hotel.

2   Breakfast. Full day tour to Sungsan Peak, Sungup Folk Village, Tangerine Farm, Sanbanggulsa Temple, Chungbang and Chonjeyon Waterfall.

3   Breakfast. Transfer to the airport for your flight to Seoul. Transfer to your hotel.

	Package	
	Double	Single
Cheju Oriental	$625	$920

Citipak Holiday
Kyongju/Pusan

3 Days/2 Nights   CHO9
Includes breakfast daily.

1   **Seoul/Kyongju**
    Pick–up from your hotel; Express Train to Kyongju. In Kyongju, visit the National Park, tour Sukkuram Grotto and Bulkuksa Temple. Transfer to the **Kyongju Chosun Hotel**.

2   **Kyongju/Pusan (B)**
    Breakfast. Tour of Pusan visits Yongdusan Park, Taejongdae Sea Park and Chagalch'i Fishery Market. Continue to Pusan by Express Bus and transfer to the **Pusan Tourist Hotel**.

3   **Pusan (B)**
    Breakfast. Day at leisure or depart for another tour.

	Package	
	Double	Single
Package	$495	$750

Seoul/Mt. Songnisan/Haeinsa Temple/ Kyongju/Pusan

6 Days/5 Nights   CHO8
Departures Daily. Includes Breakfast Daily.

1   **Arrive Seoul**
    Arrive in Seoul. Transfer to the **Ramada Olympia Hotel** or similar.

2   **Seoul (B)**
    Full day tour to Kyongbok Palace, Bukak Skyway, East Gate Open Market, Changduk Palace, Secret Garden and the National Museum.

3   **Seoul/Songnisan (B)**
    Coach to Mt. Songnisan and tour Popchusa Temple and Haeinsa Temple. Stay at the **Songnisan Tourist Hotel**.

4   **Songnisan/Kyongju (B)**
    Breakfast. Transfer to Kyongju, "Museum without Walls". Stay at the

Kyongju Chosun Hotel. Visit Kyongju Pulkuksa Temple and Sukkuram Grotto.

5   **Kyongju/Pusan (B)**
    Continue to Pusan. Stay at the **Pusan Tourist Hotel**. Tour Taejongdae Sea Park and the Fishery Market.

6   **Depart Pusan (B)**
    Breakfast. Transfer to Pusan Kimhae International Airport for your flight.

	Package	
	Double	Single
Package	$1095	$1695

■ **REVIEW—EAST ASIA**

1. What was the original function of the Great Wall? Of the Grand Canal?

2. What is the relative importance of Shanghai and Beijing? Where are they located?

3. What is the current political status of Hong Kong and Macau? How does it affect their touristic importance?

4. How has Taiwan developed its prosperity? What is its current political status?

5. What are the four main islands of Japan? How are they important touristically?

6. How and why were North and South Korea created? What is the DMZ?

7. What are the primary features and activities for the traveler to Taiwan and South Korea?

8. Where are the primary ski areas in East Asia?

9. Where are the primary beach and resort areas in East Asia?

10. Describe four major areas of scenic beauty in East Asia.

15

Southeast Asia

Lying between China and India, Southeast Asia is a mosaic of many different physical and human units. There are numerous ethnic groups with different languages, religions, and lifestyles in each nation. An overlay of European colonialism prior to World War II left varying degrees and kinds of imported cultural influence, and independence has created varied degrees of political stability and economic development.

■ THE LAND

The region consists of two distinctive physical units. One is a mainland portion, a southern projection of the Asian landmass that terminates in the long, narrow Malay Peninsula, between the Indian Ocean and the Pacific Ocean. The nations of Myanmar, Thailand, Vietnam, Laos, Cambodia (Kampuchea), and Singapore are located here. Here, too, is West Malaysia, the western component of the nation of Malaysia, whose eastern portion, East Malaysia, is on the island of Borneo.

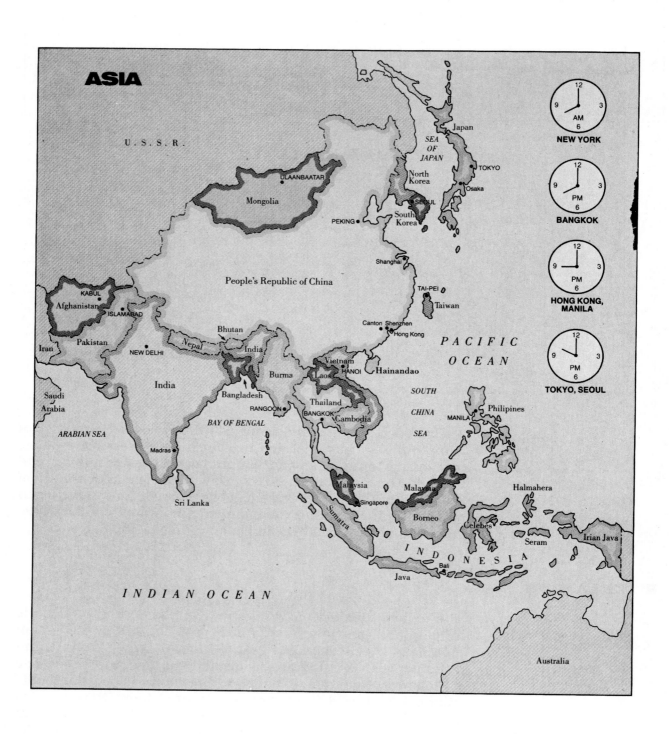

Two large island groups, or archipelagos, to the east and south of the mainland form the nations of Indonesia and the Philippine Islands. The little nation of Brunei occupies a coastal position in western Borneo surrounded by East Malaysia.

The topography of the mainland is dominated by high mountains and plateaus that run north-south. Between them flow great rivers: the Irrawaddy and Salween of Myanmar; the Chao Phraya of central Thailand; the Mekong, the longest of them all, in Laos-Thailand-Cambodia-Vietnam; and the Red of northern Vietnam. The river plains and deltas are the most habitable areas, offer the best opportunity for agriculture by large numbers of people, and have become the core areas around which the mainland nations are shaped.

The islands of Indonesia and the Philippines generally have mountainous cores and fringing coastal or interior plains where the bulk of the population is concentrated. A volcanic zone that extends eastward through Indonesia and then northward in a massive arc through the Philippines and the western Pacific is evident in the large number of volcanic peaks (occasionally active or dormant) and the long regional history of earthquakes and eruptions.

■ THE CLIMATE

The Equator passes through Indonesia, and maritime Southeast Asia is tropical in climate with a well-distributed rainfall and dense natural forests, now partially cleared for agriculture. On the mainland, however, a monsoon climatic pattern prevails, with a rainy season during the summer and a dry season during the winter. Winter days there are warm but winter nights are cool to chilly, depending upon elevation and latitude. There are dense forests in the mountains including valuable commercial species, such as teak.

■ THE PEOPLES

Numerous ethnic groups in Southeast Asia are descendants of people who gradually migrated southward over the past several thousand years out of what is now China. Groups farthest south, like the Malays of Malaysia and Indonesia, migrated earlier, whereas the Thai of Thailand and Burmese of Myanmar and others have infiltrated their areas within the past 1,000 years. Even today, residual ethnic groups related to the peoples of Southeast Asia remain as important minorities in the mountains of southern China.

Group movements southward involved a competition for space, leaving the larger, more dominant groups in the choice lowlands and smaller, more subordinate groups in the hill and mountain country. This process has resulted in a highly fragmented pattern of ethnic groups.

■ RELIGIONS

The principal cultural influences on these peoples in the precolonial era came eastward from India in the company of new religions. As early as 2,000 years ago, Indian traders, Buddhist monks, and Hindu Brahmins introduced Hinduism and Buddhism and, along with them, the full range of Indian fine arts, writing systems, and political forms. Kingdoms incorporating these influences arose in Myanmar, Thailand, Cambodia, and western Indonesia, especially on the islands of Java and Sumatra. Their richness may be seen in the surviving temple complexes of Pagan in Myanmar, Angkor Wat in Cambodia, and Borobudur in Indonesia that rank among the artistic marvels of Asia.

Buddhism remains today the dominant religion among the major ethnic groups of Myanmar, Thailand, Laos, Cambodia, and Vietnam. Vietnam is distinctive because it was pulled into the political and cultural sphere of China. Vietnamese Buddhism is of the northern, Chinese, variety and the society is strongly conditioned by Confucian ethics.

In the 14th and 15th centuries, Indian traders brought a new religion, Islam, to the Malay Peninsula and from there it quickly spread and became the major faith in present Malaysia, Indonesia, Brunei, and the southern Philippines (the island of Mindanao). Within the nations where Buddhism or Islam predominates, hill tribes still practice animistic, or natural spirit oriented, beliefs.

■ COLONIALISM

Southeast Asia gradually came under European commercial influences and eventual colonial control from the 16th century, when the first Portuguese ships reached Malacca, a trading center on the western Malay Peninsula. The Portuguese, Dutch, and Spanish competed for the lucrative spice trade of the "East Indies." The Philippines was especially affected because the Spanish introduced Christianity to their culture on a broad scale.

In the 19th century, European commercial interest focused on China, and because Southeast Asia was on the most direct shipping route between the Indian Ocean and the western Pacific Ocean it, too, attracted European expansionist interest. The net result was that the region was gradually carved up into colonial holdings.

The British controlled present-day Myanmar, Malaysia, Singapore, and Brunei; the French had Vietnam, Laos, and Cambodia; and the Dutch had Indonesia. The Spanish held the Philippines until 1899, when it passed to American control. Only Siam, present Thailand, remained independent, but even it lost peripheral territory to the French and British. Colonialism continued until the Japanese invasions of World War II and postwar independence.

By superimposing European political, economic, and social systems upon those already existing, colonialism brought profound changes that differed from one colony to another. Several are of geographical pertinence.

First, in creating their colonies, the Europeans combined ethnic groups that otherwise probably never would have joined in voluntary association. Second, peace, stability, new jobs, and better public health services in the colonies prompted large annual population increases and greater pressure on the land resources. Third, European-created port cities developed as the nerve centers for administration and commerce. These cities typically had a European-style core and peripheral indigenous housing areas, reflecting the two culture groups involved. Examples are Yangon (formerly Rangoon) in Myanmar, Manila in the Philippines, Jakarta in Indonesia, and Ho Chi Minh City (formerly Saigon) in Vietnam.

A fourth change was the commercialization of agriculture. Cash crops were introduced into what was previously a subsistence economy. This was one aspect of the imposition of a cash economy. Rice became so commercialized and produced in such large amounts in Myanmar and Cambodia, as well as independent Thailand, that they became leading rice exporters, primarily to other Asian nations.

Large-scale commercial plantations designed to produce export materials sprang up with foreign investment. The largest and most successful were in West Malaysia, Java, and Sumatra in Indonesia. In the Philippines, large Spanish-held land grants were used to grow such cash crops as sugar cane, tobacco, and coconuts. Commercialization made the least headway in the hill and mountain country, where even today hill tribes practice slash and burn cultivation. Forest is cleared by slashing and burning, the cleared land is tilled for several seasons until soil fertility is exhausted, then the fields are abandoned for forest regrowth, and newly cleared fields take their place.

The relative prosperity of some colonies and the need for a dependable supply of plantation workers attracted aliens from India and China. As a result, Indians became an important minority in Myanmar and West Malaysia, and even larger numbers of ethnic Chinese came to West Malaysia and most other parts of Southeast Asia, where they eventually settled in towns and cities in business occupations. Singapore's population, for example, is predominantly of Chinese origin.

A sixth impact of colonialism was the exploitation of raw materials in a continuing search for exports. Tin mining took place in West Malaysia and Indonesia. Oil production began in Myanmar, Indonesia, and Brunei, and widespread cutting of selected forest species was also practiced. Finally, colonial governments built transportation systems linking the port cities with principal population clusters and raw material areas.

Whether railways, roads, or river shipping, these networks were usually of limited geographical coverage and left many colonial areas relatively isolated and bypassed. Manufacturing was given little or no encouragement. The purpose of a colony, after all, was to serve as a source of raw materials as well as a market for the manufactured surpluses of the colonial power.

■ INDEPENDENCE

Moving into independence, the nations of Southeast Asia have faced a number of challenges that derive in part from their colonial heritage. Population growth rates continue to be relatively high, commonly about 2 percent or more each year, leading to even greater crowding in the most favored agricultural areas. Rural to urban migration from these crowded rural districts pours masses of newcomers into the region's main cities, creating vast slums and deplorable housing and sanitary conditions.

The uneasy relations among ethnic groups that were thrown together arbitrarily by the colonial powers in each colony have degenerated into guerrilla warfare by numerous groups since independence. Armed uprisings have been of serious dimension in recent years in the southern Philippines, Cambodia, Myanmar, and eastern Indonesia. On a national scale, Vietnam invaded and set up friendly Communist governments in Laos and Cambodia. Refugees from these nations have moved abroad, into Southeast Asian or more distant nations, seeking sanctuary. Tension between indigenous people and residents of Chinese descent flares up periodically in the form of riots and mass killings.

On the brighter side, modernization programs are under way in most Southeast Asian nations. Singapore, now the most modern nation of the region, leads the way. Tiny Brunei thrives on its oil income rather than balanced development.

Thailand, Malaysia, and Indonesia still rely upon foodstuffs and raw materials export, but are rapidly building up their manufacturing capabilities. Myanmar lags far behind as the result of decades of self-isolation. Laos, Cambodia, and Vietnam suffer from the destruction caused during the Vietnam War and domestic military and economic problems, with food and consumer goods in short supply. Vietnam is now hungry for foreign investment, tourism and economic development.

Alignments with powerful nations outside the region, including the United States, are important means of getting development and military assistance. Funds disbursed by the Asia Development Bank and other international agencies also help foster economic improvement. Although relatively new, cooperation among the non-Communist nations of the region is growing through membership in the Association of Southeast Asian Nations (ASEAN).

SINGAPORE

Official Name: Republic of Singapore

Language: Malay, Chinese, English, Tamil

Area: 224 square miles

Time Zone: GMT +8

National Airline: Singapore Airlines

Capital: Singapore

Currency: Singapore dollar (SID)

Population: 2,756,000

Documentation: Passport

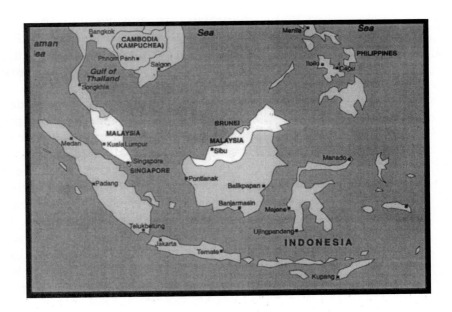

Singapore is the most modern, urban, and industrial nation of Southeast Asia. Its progress and prosperity resembles that of the other rising export economies of Taiwan, Hong Kong and South Korea. It has a superb strategic location on the Strait of Malacca, the main route for ocean vessels moving between the Indian Ocean and the western Pacific Ocean. Consequently, it is one of the world's busiest ports.

The residents of Singapore live on a small, crowded island at the southern tip of the Malay Peninsula. A narrow body of water separates it from the West Malaysian mainland. More than three-fourths of the population are of Chinese descent. However, a long history of British colonial administration, when Singapore was part of British Malaya, has left English the formal language of education, government, and business.

The city-nation is blessed with a stable government, public security, high levels of education and technical skills among the labor force, and outstanding business facilities. The main business center adjacent to the port on the island's south shore is studded with high-rise office buildings that are fast displacing the older colonial period buildings. High-rise apartments, the main means of coping with the public demand for housing, loom everywhere above the urban horizon.

Singapore is far south of the east-west air trunk line that passes through Bangkok in Thailand. Yet it is a major air hub for easy contacts with Malaysia and Indonesia as well as points farther west and northeast.

The very stability of its government and its intense desire for modernization have resulted in what is perhaps too much of a good thing. The very high degree of cleanliness and new construction achieved in the 1970–1985 period has almost obliterated ethnic markets and neighborhoods once part of Singapore's charm. The government has now recognized this problem and is protecting remaining historic areas.

Areas of Touristic Importance. The many cultures represented in Singapore make it an international shopping and eating delight. The cosmopolitan city boasts world-class restaurants and exciting nightlife. Malaysian satays and Indian curries as well as all styles of Chinese cuisine are most popular.

The primary tourist attraction in Singapore is shopping, where values include electronics, jewelry, luggage, and clothing. Books, records and tapes, and computer programs are very inexpensive. Many are bootlegged, because Singapore does not adequately enforce international copyright laws. Thus, these items could be confiscated by United States customs authorities when the visitor returns home. Singapore's many shopping centers are 4- and 5-story buildings crammed with a wide variety of entrepreneurial vendors. Raffles Hotel, modernized with air-conditioned guest rooms, retains its English colonial charm. The famous Singapore Sling cocktail was invented here.

Other points of interest include excellent zoological and botanical gardens and Jungle Bird Park, teaming with a variety of tropical Asian birds. Haw Par Villa, also known as Tiger Balm Gardens, overlooks the sea and houses a priceless collection of jade. Although now much smaller than in earlier years, Arab Street and Chinatown offer the visitor interesting ethnic experiences.

Chinese Garden, Singapore
Photo: Courtesy Singapore Tourist Promotion Board

MYANMAR

Official Name: Union of
Myanmar

Language: Burmese, tribal
languages

Area: 261,789 square miles

Time Zone: GMT +6:30

Capital: Yangon (formerly
Rangoon)

Currency: Ktat

Population: 42,112,000

Documentation: Passport,
visa

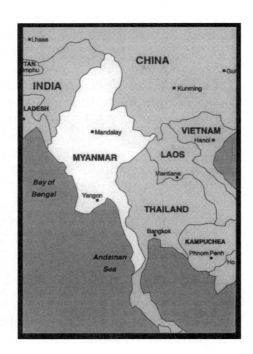

Myanmar (formerly Burma) is among the least developed economically, and has probably the most complex ethnic friction, of the nations in the region. A former British colony, it has experimented with Socialism and self-isolation under a strongman government most of the time since independence, with depressing results.

The Land. Myanmar has a long north-south extent. Its main body borders on India and Bangladesh on the west, and China, Laos, and Thailand on the east. A long tail carries the national territory southward into the Malay Peninsula.

Physically, Myanmar is enclosed within an arc of forested mountains on the west, north, and east. Among the uplands is the habitable Shan Plateau in the northeast, which is crossed by the Salween River, flowing southward out of China. Within the arc of mountains, extensive plains lie along the course of the navigable Irrawaddy River. The central plain, around the historic Myanmar city of Mandalay, and the river delta, served by the British-built capital and principal city of Yangon, form the core of the nation. This area is the homeland of the Burmese (or Burmans), the dominant and most numerous ethnic group, who run national affairs.

The Peoples. The Burmese moved southward from the borderlands of Tibet and China from about the 10th century and gradually conquered or pushed aside other ethnic groups. Mandalay eventually became their royal capital. Captured by British forces from India in several stages during the 19th century, Burma experienced little of the commercial development that occurred in British Malaya. The main emphasis was on encouraging rice production for export by farmers in the Irrawaddy delta. By the 1930s, Burma had become the world's largest rice exporter.

Yangon flourished as the main rice exporting port and replaced Mandalay as the colony's administrative and commercial nerve center. Alien Indians became important in small business and landowning. Terrible destruction in the final stages of the Japanese retreat in 1944–1945 left the national economy in shambles. Yet, to avoid involvement with big powers, especially neighboring China, Burma went into seclusion after independence, depriving itself of foreign aid and any economic improvement of consequence during the 1960s and 1970s. In 1989, Burma adopted the new name of Myanmar.

Minorities with nominal political representation are the Chin in the west, Kachin in the north, Shan in the northeast, and Karen in the southeast. These and numerous other smaller ethnic groups maintain their own languages and customs even though Burmese is the official national language. Antigovernment guerrilla activity is so widespread in peripheral, usually hilly or mountainous, areas that government control there is minimal or nonexistent. Because of this chronic armed unrest, foreign visitors are restricted to a few secure areas under government control.

Economy. The economy has been improving gradually as Myanmar resumes its outside contacts. It is based on an expansion of rice growing in the delta, still much less than before the war; the export of teak from the northern forests; and small amounts of tin, rubber, and copra from the south. There is one north-south railway with local spurs and riverboat traffic on the Irrawaddy. Land transportation is poor. Yangon is rundown, without significant new construction since independence.

Areas of Touristic Importance. Although Myanmar's accommodations and other physical facilities are limited, there are several areas of interest to the adventurous traveler. The very effects of its isolation provide a contrast to other nations in the region.

Mandalay is the second largest city and the last capital of the Burmese kings. It offers many cultural and historic sights. Most prominent is the Kuthodaw Pagoda with 729 miniature pagodas, each housing the text of a Buddhist canon.

Yangon, although rundown, retains much of its British colonial heritage. It is home for one of the most revered Buddhist shrines, the 2,500-year-old Shwe Dagon Pagoda and the most interesting and colorful Shwe Dagon Pagoda Bazaar. Also worth visiting are the Sule Pagoda, the Kaba Aye (World Peace Pagoda), and the National Museum.

Pagan, the ancient capital during the golden age of Burmese history, offers 16 square miles of ruins of more than 5,000 pagodas. The Pagan Dynasty flourished from the 11th through the 13th centuries. Sacked by the mighty Kubla Khan, the area was also devastated by a 1975 earthquake. The government is now restoring 30 of the most significant temples.

THAILAND

Official Name: Kingdom of Thailand
Language: Thai
Area: 198,456 square miles
Time Zone: GMT +7
National Airline: Thai Airways
Capital: Bangkok
Currency: Baht (BHT)
Population: 56,814,000
Documentation: Passport

Formerly called Siam, Thailand's size and shape resemble Myanmar's. Its main body is bordered by Myanmar on the west and Laos and Cambodia on the east; a long tail extends southward in the Malay Peninsula as far as West Malaysia. Although Thailand did not become a European colony, it did experience strong Western influences in the 19th and 20th centuries.

The Land and Climate. The northern, western, and northeastern borderlands are mountainous, but a large central plain drained by the Chao Phraya River, flowing southward into the Gulf of Thailand, is the nation's habitable heartland. Here is Bangkok, the national capital, the biggest population cluster, and most productive agricultural lands. The northeast, sometimes called the Korat Plateau, is next in regional importance.

Thailand is a tropical land, with high temperatures and humidity. The climate of much of the country is dominated by monsoons. In most regions there are three seasons: rainy (June–October), cool (November–February), and hot and dry (March–May). Rainfall varies throughout the country but is usually heaviest in the south.

The People. The Thai people originally lived in China, pressed southward against the Cambodians (Khmer), and gained control of their present territory by the 16th century. Buddhism was adopted as the main religion. Under astute royal leadership in the late 19th century, the Siamese government imported Western political and military systems, built rail lines, and encouraged rice production for export. Little damaged during World War II, Thailand later aligned itself with Western powers. As an important ally of the United States and its allies during the Vietnamese War, it received extensive economic and military benefits.

Economy. Thailand's economy has been dominated by the export of rice, tin, plantation crops (rubber and copra) from the south, and teak from the northern forests. However, it now has a booming industrial sector, centered on Bangkok. Export oriented manufacturing is strongly supported by foreign, especially Japanese, investments. The government places emphasis upon irrigation and river control works, including dams to impound monsoon rains for flood control, irrigation, and hydroelectric generation and energy development.

Bangkok, a fast-growing city of more than 5 million, with high-rise buildings and traffic jams, dominates all phases of national life. Its large Chinese population is very active in wholesale and retail businesses. There has also been considerable Thai-Chinese intermarriage. The second largest city of Chiang Mai, in the north, is only one-twentieth the size of Bangkok.

Rail lines radiate from Bangkok to the borders in four directions, and there is an excellent network of modern roads built during and since the Vietnamese War with foreign assistance. These facilities extend the government's authority into distant regions where disruption is sporadic. Restless hill tribes are in the north, Cambodian and Laotian refugees in the east and southeast, and antigovernment Moslem and Communist guerrillas in the south. All are kept in check only by the well-trained and well-armed Thai army.

Areas of Touristic Importance. Bangkok is home to almost 300 Buddhist temples. Most noted are the Temple of the Emerald Buddha on the grounds of the Grand Palace, the Temple of the Reclining Buddha (which houses the largest Buddha in Asia), and the Temple of the Golden Buddha. The Marble Temple, which houses a fine collection of Buddhas, is an excellent example of Thai architecture. Patpong, the red-light district of Bangkok, is a popular walking area for tourists and is relatively safe.

The Damnern Saduak, 65 miles from Bangkok, is an authentic and unspoiled floating market, far nicer than Bangkok's own floating market. The canals are filled with small boats selling food and consumer goods.

Chiang Mai, 90 minutes from Bangkok by air, is in the far north country, known as The Golden Triangle, where they

Bridge on the River Kwai, Kanchanaburi
Photo: Courtesy Tourism Authority of Thailand

grow much of the opium consumed throughout the world. Life in the hills is in sharp contrast to the seaport capital. The Pu Ping Palace with its lovely gardens is still the summer home of the royal family. From Chiang Mai, trekking excursions are available to see the hill tribes who still use working elephants.

Pattaya Beach, on the Gulf of Thailand, is one of the best seaside resort areas in Asia. Ideal for swimming, snorkeling, and sailing, Pattaya has many good hotels with excellent meeting and convention facilities. New resort facilities have been built on Phuket Island in the Andaman Sea. This area has become very popular.

■ VIETNAM, LAOS, AND CAMBODIA—
AN OVERVIEW

No other part of Southeast Asia has been so disrupted by warfare in recent times as the three neighboring nations of Vietnam, Laos, and Cambodia (Kampuchea), formerly parts of French Indochina under French colonial control. Vietnam militarily occupied and supported Communist governments in Laos and Cambodia, but the latter is now under United Nations transitional management.

Vietnam occupies an S-shaped coastal portion of the mainland facing the South China Sea. It has a forested, mountainous spine and large plains in the north around the Red River, centering on Hanoi, the national capital, and in the south in the Mekong River delta, centering on Ho Chi Minh City (formerly Saigon).

The Cambodians (Khmer) are among the oldest ethnic groups. They were pushed aside by both the southward advancing Thai and the Vietnamese. The latter were also originally from China and for centuries were under Chinese control, which left them with a strong Confucian social structure. The Lao, or Laotians, are related to the Thai in language and culture. All three groups are Buddhist, although the Vietnamese type is of Chinese, not southern, origin.

Unsuccessful in their attempt to penetrate the southern Chinese market via north Vietnam, the French made limited investment in and improvement to their colony, except in the Mekong delta, where rice culture was stressed and Saigon was developed.

French attempts to retain the colony after World War II in the face of guerrilla resistance from Vietnamese forces under Ho Chi Minh failed. In 1954, an armistice divided Vietnam at the 17th degree parallel into Communist North Vietnam, supported by the the former Soviet Union and China, and anti-Communist South Vietnam, supported by the United States and its allies. After a long and bloody war, fought mainly in the south but with extensive bombing of the north, the American and other allied troops evacuated. In 1975, North Vietnamese troops overran the south and in 1976 the two units were re-united as the Socialist Republic of Vietnam.

Current political conditions severely restrict western visitors to Laos and Cambodia. In 1994 trade sanctions were lifted and travel to Vietnam directly from the United States was allowed.

VIETNAM

Official Name: Socialist Republic of Vietnam

Language: Vietnamese, French

Area: 127,330 square miles

Time Zone: GMT +7

Capital: Hanoi

Currency: Dong

Population: 67,568,000

Documentation: Passport, visa

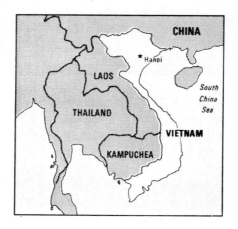

Vietnam is the second most populous Southeast Asian nation. The north is densely crowded. It has an intensive agriculture yet is food-deficient. The north also has some industry, built with aid from the Communist bloc and operated with local coal and raw materials. Hanoi, in the north, is the administrative center of Vietnam. The south is agricultural, has food surpluses, and is generally more prosperous. It centers upon Ho Chi Minh City (the former Saigon).

As a whole, the nation remains relatively poor, beset with the problems of a growing population, lack of development, and the costs of a large military operation. Vietnam faces an unfriendly China across its northern border and, with the collapse of the Soviet Union, has lost its main source of international support. It is now eager for tourism and foreign investment.

Areas of Touristic Importance. Ho Chi Minh City (formerly Saigon) and Hanoi both have sufficient accommodations for limited numbers of American tourists.

The Floating Hotel in Ho Chi Minh City is quite popular. Area attractions include Thong Nhat Conference Hall and excursions to the Chu Chi Tunnels, the Cao Dai Temple at Tay Ninh and boat trips into the Mekong Delta. Hanoi's major sites include Ho Chi Minh's Mausoleum, the One Pillar Pagoda, Sword Lake, and the Temple of Literature.

LAOS

Official Name: Lao People's Democratic Republic

Language: Laotian, French

Area: 91,428 square miles

Time Zone: GMT +7

Capital: Vientiane

Currency: Liberation Kip (KIP)

Population: 4,113,000

Documentation: Passport, visa

West of the Vietnam mountains, Laos is shaped around a series of small plains along the Mekong River. One contains Vientiane, the capital. About half the population are Laos, and the remainder are of tribal Thai, Meo, and Yao extraction. The economy is weak as a result of prolonged warfare and the fact that 85 percent of the population is engaged in subsistence agriculture.

Areas of Touristic Importance. Vientiane and Luang Prabang offer interesting activities for tourists. Vientiane's Monument de Mars bears a striking resemblance to Paris' Arc de Triumphe. Attractions in Luang Prabang include the former Royal Palace and cruises along the Mekong River.

CAMBODIA (KAMPUCHEA)

Official Name: State of Cambodia

Language: Khmer

Area: 70,238 square miles

Time Zone: GMT +7

Capital: Phnom Penh

Currency: Riel

Population: 7,146,000

Documentation: Passport, visa

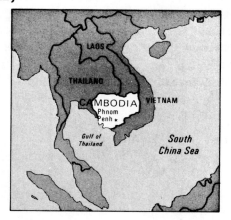

Cambodia (Kampuchea) shares the lower Mekong River plains and delta with Vietnam. Its capital, Phnom Penh, is on the river. Sporadic anti-government guerrilla attacks make the countryside dangerous.

Areas of Touristic Importance. The Grand Lake, noted for its freshwater fisheries, and the ruins of nearby Angkor Wat, one of the world's most magnificent archaeological sites, are in the west.

The wondrous temples of Angkor Wat and Angkor Thom are once again open to western tourists. Cambodia's capital, Phnom Penh, features a National Museum filled with Khmer artwork from the 4th through the 15th centuries.

■ MALAYSIA, INDONESIA, AND BRUNEI

MALAYSIA

Language: Bahasa, Malay, English

Area: 127,316 square miles

Time Zone: GMT +8

National Airline: Malaysian Air System

Capital: Kuala Lumpur

Currency: Malay dollar (MAD)

Population: 17,981,000

Documentation: Passport

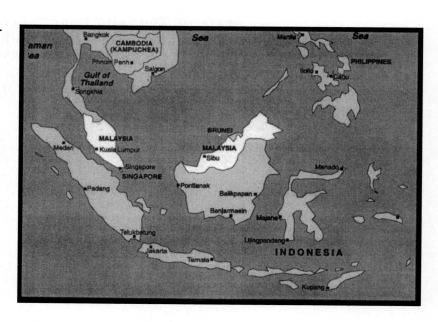

Malaysia (Federation of Malaysia) is one of the most prosperous and stable nations of the region. Unfortunately, it has serious ethnic tensions between the numerically and politically dominant Malays and the economically powerful Chinese minority.

History. The former British Malaya, on the Malay Peninsula, achieved independence in 1957, but without Singapore because of the latter's large Chinese population. In 1963, Malaya and Singapore, along with two former British units in north Borneo, Sabah and Sarawak (the present East Malaysia), formed the larger compound nation of Malaysia. However, Singapore withdrew 2 years later in favor of an independent existence. Malaysia thus remains in two separated units with Kuala Lumpur in the west as capital.

The Land, Peoples, and Languages. West Malaysia is the core unit. It has forested mountains in its interior and fringing coastal plains. Those on the west have most of the population, cities, and economic activity. The Malay segment of the population is Moslem in religion and is predominantly rural. The largest Malay majorities are in the northwest and northeast. The typical Malay is a small-scale farmer and/or fisherman.

Malay is the national language, although English is still important in higher education, government, and business. The government follows the British model, including a royal representative of the traditional Moslem local rulers who still serve as state administrators in West Malaysia.

Indian and Chinese labor flocked to Malaya in the 19th century to work in a developing plantation economy. The Chinese also moved into tin mining and small business, all the while retaining their cultural identity. Their energy, ambition, and group organization enabled them to gain control of such activities as rice milling, tin mining, lumbering, trucking, coastal shipping, and retail and wholesale trade. They stress education and chafe under a Malay-dominated government that clearly favors Malays in university administration and government jobs.

The Indians, like the Chinese, have thrived in the urban economy as shopkeepers, doctors, and engineers, as well as on the plantations. They have maintained their Hinduism and many Indian cultural practices.

East Malaysia, more of a frontier zone, has a mixture of Malays and Chinese too, as well as a large Dayak population, an older local stock, who live either on the coast or in the forested interior. The city of Kota Kinabalu is the administrative seat for Sabah, in the north, and Kuching for Sarawak, in the south.

Chinese shop-houses, Penang
Photo: Courtesy Malaysian Tourist Information Center

Economy. The Malaysian economy remains geared to the export of rubber, palm oil, copra (dried coconut meat), and tin. Large plantations are typical of the west coast of West Malaysia and Sabah. The government is striving to develop the west coast ports of Port Swettenham and Penang Island (city of Georgetown) in West Malaysia to replace their former reliance upon Singapore. West Malaysia has an excellent road network and shares a railway line that runs from Singapore northward to Bangkok in Thailand. Transportation in East Malaysia is less well developed.

Kuala Lumpur is a large, fast-growing, planned capital that grew up in the western plain amidst tin-mining activities. Between it and Port Swettenham a modern industrial district has emerged. Heavy industry is also found in the northwest opposite Penang Island. Malaysia ranks with Thailand as one of the fastest-growing industrial nations in Southeast Asia. Government development programs are gradually spreading Malay agricultural settlements and expanding tourism into the east and southeast. The Cameron Highlands, in the interior, are used for hydroelectric generation and resorts with cooler climates.

Areas of Touristic Importance. Kuala Lumpur shows its Moslem heritage in a skyline of domes and minarets. The Moorish style of architecture is most apparent in the railroad station and the National Mosque. The National Museum features local antiquities and the National Art Museum hosts a collection of Malay artists.

Penang Island off the northwest coast of Malaysia is ringed with beaches and has many resort facilities. It is a frequent port of call for cruises in the area. Some of the finest and lowest cost shopping in Asia can be found in Penang.

Malacca, halfway between Kuala Lumpur and Singapore, was founded as a Malay kingdom and is the oldest city in the nation. It is home to the oldest Chinese temple in Malaysia as well as to Portuguese churches and Moslem mosques.

East Malaysia offers only limited tourist attractions and facilities. Kota Kinabalu, capital of Sabah, is a good base for exploring the lifestyles of little known native tribes in the area. Kuching, capital of Sarawak, is situated in an area occupied by former headhunters. It was the home of a Britisher who started his own dynasty—the White Rajah. Kuching houses many Chinese temples, Moslem mosques, and a picturesque bazaar.

INDONESIA

Official Name: Republic of
  Indonesia
Language: Bahasa, Indonesian
Area: 736,000 square miles
Time Zone: GMT +7 through
  +9
National Airline: Garuda
  Indonesian
Capital: Jakarta
Currency: Rupiah (RPA)
Population: 193,000,000
Documentation: Passport

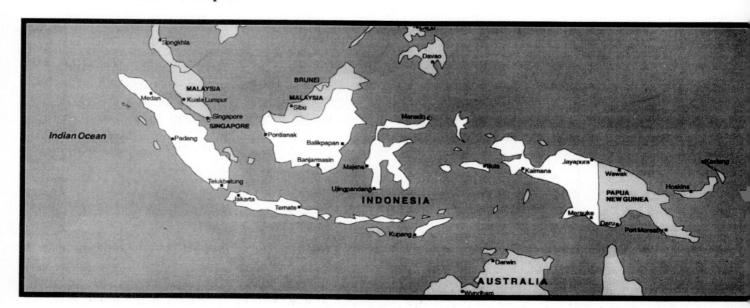

The Islands. Indonesia is highly fragmented. It is composed of more than 3,000 islands strung along the equator for 2,000 miles, and has some 300 distinctive ethnic groups. The largest islands are Sumatra, Java, Kalimantan (Borneo), and Sulawesi (Celebes) in the west, and West Irian (western New Guinea) in the east. Of these, Java and Sumatra dominate national affairs. Jakarta (Djakarta), on the northwest coast of Java, is the national capital.

The Peoples and Languages. Indonesia has the largest population in Southeast Asia and it is growing at about 1.7 percent each year. More remarkably, two-thirds of the people live on Java, making it one of the most densely inhabited places on earth. Malay-speakers are the dominant ethnic group, and Bahasa, a major form of Malay, is the nation's official language. Islam is the major religion.

However, the islands are studded with different language groups. In West Irian, the nation extends into Melanesia, where the people are black and related to the aborigines of Australia. There are many different religious clusters as well. Bali is noted for its Hindu culture, and Christianity is practiced in localities in the central and eastern archipelago.

History. The Dutch penetrated the islands from the mid-17th century, stimulating commercial farming by the local population, and introducing large-scale plantations, especially in Java and Sumatra. Chinese immigrants came in large numbers to the expanding rural economy. The colony, formerly the Dutch East Indies, got its independence in 1949 following occupation by the Japanese during the war. A small Portuguese colony on Timor passed to Indonesia in 1976.

Economy. Long suffering from political and economic drift, Indonesia is now under a strong central government that stresses long-range planning and growth in both agriculture and manufacturing. The industrial sector is expanding rapidly, especially on Java and in some localities in Sumatra. Although plantation exports (rubber, palm oil, copra, tobacco), tin, and timber remain important, oil and natural gas from fields in Sumatra and southeastern Kalimantan are the great income earners. Air and shipping networks link Jakarta with cities on other major islands.

Java is the national core in every respect. It has the capital, more than one-half of the national population, rich volcanic soils, the largest rice and other food output, the best rail and road networks, and the largest number of urban facilities and manufacturing firms. Jakarta's 7 million people make it the biggest city in Southeast Asia; it also rivals Manila for the most extensive slums. Bandung, Jogyakarta, and other highland cities are also fast-growing.

Sumatra is also alive with development activities. Urban growth is notable at Palembang, near major oil fields, and at Medan, in the northern plantation zone, just west of Singapore and West Malaysia.

Areas of Touristic Importance. Bali is the most visited place in Indonesia. It is an island of unusual beauty, one of the most beautiful in the world. Its colorful temples and ceremonies appear to resist the modern age. Considered true paradise by many, the island is crowned by the 10,000-foot peak of Bali. Tourists fly into Denpasar in the center of Bali, but generally stay at tourist-oriented beach resorts. The Bali Museum presents the best of native Balinese arts and crafts.

Java attracts tourists, primarily to the western part of the island. Jakarta, the capital of the nation, is its major commercial center. The tourist will see many examples of its

Dutch colonial period. The Botanical Gardens of Bogor, 40 miles outside of Jakarta, houses more than 10,000 varieties of tropical plants on a 275-acre site.

Jogyakarta, in central Java, is the cultural center of Indonesia. It features the finest Indonesian batik as well as silverware and leather goods. A day trip is possible from here to the 1,000-year-old great Hindu-Buddhist temple complex, supposedly the largest in the world, at Borobudur.

East Java is a land of volcanoes and tropical jungle. Attractions include Surabaya, the provincial capital, and the 12th century Singosari Temple.

Sumatra is a land of wild animals. Visitors can see elephants, rhinos, gabon, and the famous Sumatran tiger.

Conditions are primitive in most other locations, including Kalimantan, Sulawesi, and Irian Jaya. The adventurous will find an abundance of natural flora and fauna and ethnic distinctiveness.

BRUNEI

Official Name: Brunei Darussalam

Language: Malay, Chinese, English

Area: 2,226 square miles

Time Zone: GMT +8

Capital: Bandar Seri Begawan

Currency: Brunei dollar (BRD)

Population: 397,000

Documentation: Passport, visa

Tiny Brunei is an independent oil-rich nation on the northwest coast of Borneo. Its small population is Malay with a Chinese minority, primarily Moslem, and ruled by an hereditary sultan. British influence is strong. It was a British protectorate until 1983. Wealth from its oil field has been used to erect modern government buildings, a national mosque, and basic urban facilities. Per capita income is among the highest in the world. Tourism is not encouraged.

THE PHILIPPINES

Official Name: Republic of the
  Philippines

Language: Tagalog, English

Area: 115,831 square miles

Time Zone: GMT +8

National Airline: Philippine
  Airlines

Capital: Quezon City (located
  within Manila)

Currency: Peso (PHP)

Population: 65,758,000

Documentation: Passport

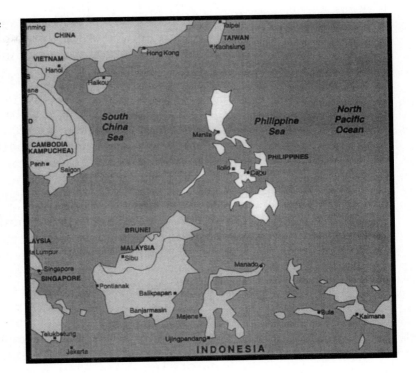

Historical Influences. The island nation of the Philippines, lying north of Indonesia and east of Vietnam, has been strongly westernized through long contacts with Spanish and American cultures under colonialism. Made a Spanish colony in the 16th century, it was ceded to the United States as a war prize in 1898. Following the Japanese occupation and defeat in World War II, the islands gained their independence in 1946.

The Spanish language has virtually disappeared, but the Spanish imprint remains, in place-names and in the prevailing Roman Catholic faith, which makes the Philippines the region's most Christian nation. In addition, the large estates that dominate the rural economy and Filipino formal attire are of Spanish origin.

American influences are evident in the education and government systems, urban architecture, roads, hotels, and other modern facilities.

The Islands. The Philippines consist of some 7,000 islands, of which only 11 figure prominently in national life. Luzon, the largest and northernmost, houses the capital, Manila, the largest population cluster, and the largest agricultural area. Mindanao, the second largest, is the southern anchor. Between these two, nine larger islands are collectively called the Visayans. The most important one is Cebu. The islands typically have interior highlands, often of volcanic origin, and thick forest cover as well as habitable coastal plains and a tropical climate. Destructive typhoons move across the islands in late summer and early fall.

The People and Languages. The population of the Philippines is the third largest and one of the fastest growing in Southeast Asia. The typical Filipino is of Malay ancestry and may have some Chinese or Spanish blood. More than 80 Malay-related languages are spoken among the islands, but Tagalog, the principal Luzon tongue, has been declared the national language. English is the second language, important in business, education, and government.

Economy. Luzon dominates national life. Manila, its chief city, is the capital, main port, and manufacturing center as well as the transportation center of Luzon and the nation. It is also where the largest concentration of wealth and influence can be found, side by side with extensive slums.

The rural economy is based on large estates and their cash crops for export. Sugar cane, copra, and hemp are the leaders. Rice and corn are the main subsistence foods, along with root crops, fruits, and vegetables. A large, landless, rural population that suffers from unemployment or low wages is the source of cityward population movements on a large scale. There has been some growth in manufacturing, but most manufactured goods are still imported.

Political Unrest. Internal discord between the government and dissident groups increased during the 1970s and 1980s. A large Moslem (Moro) population in southern Mindanao opposed the army in sporadic guerrilla operations. Smaller scale armed actions by Communist guerrillas and other groups flare occasionally, especially in more isolated areas. There is widespread disenchantment with the government and its inability to move toward remedying the nation's fundamental economic and social ills.

Areas of Touristic Importance. Manila maintains some of its Spanish heritage, although many areas were destroyed during World War II. Fort Santiago was used for political prisoners both by the Spanish and, later, the Japanese during its World War II occupation. The Church of St. Augustin is the oldest church in the city. Spanish colonial architecture with iron grillwork and balconies can be found throughout the city.

Manila and much of the Philippines is a shopper's paradise. Clothing, including the Spanish-influenced barong worn by men even for formal dinners, silver and gold filigree, and fine embroidery abound. Expect to bargain at Manila's Pistang Pilipino and other bazaar-type markets throughout the country.

The modern Philippine Convention Center in Manila is one of the largest in the region. It is well-supported by first-class and deluxe hotels in the downtown and Makati sections of the city.

Fifty miles across Manila Bay is Corregidor, an island fortress during World War II. Accessible by hydrofoil, the island attracts many visitors wanting to view General MacArthur's wartime headquarters and scene of the United States army's last stand before total Japanese occupation.

Outside of Manila, Lake Taal in a dormant volcano attracts many to its resort atmosphere. At Pagsanjan, visitors can travel through a beautiful river gorge in dugout canoes manned by expert boatmen.

Baguio, 150 miles north, offers a cooler climate and is a haven for summer vacationers. Parks and gardens abound. Baguio is an excellent base for excursions into the Benaue Rice Terraces, literally carved into the mountainside by local tribesmen.

The Philippines' second largest city, Cebu City on the island of Cebu, is full of history, including the landing and the death of Ferdinand Magellan. Cebu is best known for seaside resort hotels.

Zamboanga, a busy port of the tip of Mindanao, is known as the "Gateway to Moroland," the Moslem center of the Philippines. In addition to the traditional domes and minarets of the mosques, Zamboanga is noted for its beautiful hanging gardens and parks and brightly striped, broad-sailed fishing boats called Moro vintas.

■ TYPES OF TOURISM

Most leisure travelers visiting Southeast Asian nations participate in a hosted or escorted tour program, although independent travel and city packages are becoming popular. Most of the destinations are part of multicountry itineraries, often combined with visits to East Asian nations. Southeast Asia is also developing as a cruise destination.

The following sample itineraries are good examples of travel in this region:

- Enticing Southeast Asia
- Enticing Indonesia and Malaysia
- Philippines Taiwan
- Vietnam, Cambodia, and Laos

Enticing Southeast Asia

15 days visiting Bangkok, Chiang Rai, Chiang Mai, Singapore and Hong Kong

★**DEPARTURES GUARANTEED with minimum 2 passengers**★

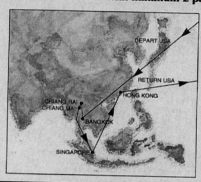

Bangkok's Floating Market

ITINERARY

1 Thu USA/Tokyo ✈
Depart the USA. Cross the International Date Line en route.

2 Fri Arrive Tokyo
After clearing customs formalities, proceed to the **Hotel Nikko Narita** for an overnight stay.

3 Sat Tokyo/Bangkok (B) ✈
Fly to Bangkok, where you will stay at the **Bel-Aire Princess Hotel**.

4 Sun Bangkok (B)
This morning tour the Grand Palace, once the seat of the court of old Siam. See the celebrated Wat Phra Keo (the Temple of the Emerald Buddha), the Pantheon of Kings and Coronation Hall. Free afternoon for exploring on your own.

5 Mon Bangkok (B)
Entire day at leisure. Perhaps take an optional tour of the Floating Market and Temple of Dawn, or of Ayuthaya, Thailand's former capital.

6 Tue Bangkok/Chiang Rai (B) ✈
Fly to Chiang Rai; stay at the **Dusit Island Resort**. Afternoon visit to hilltribe villages and the Golden Triangle.

7 Wed Chiang Rai/Chiang Mai (B, L, SD) 🚌
Scenic drive to Chiang Mai with lunch en route. Stay at the **Royal Princess Hotel**. Khantoke dinner tonight features the cuisine and dances of northern Thailand.

8 Thu Chiang Mai (B)
This morning, venture into the jungle to see the elephants at work. You will realize just how important these beasts are in the heavy labor of the jungle. Visit the lovely Mae Sa Waterfall, and the famous kilns of Celadon. Afternoon at leisure, or take an optional tour to Doi Suthep and the Meo Village. (Full-day elephant safari can be substituted—see notes.)

9 Fri Chiang Mai/Singapore (B) ✈
Fly to Singapore, a city with an exotic blend of Chinese, Malay and Indian cultures. Stay at the **Omni Marco Polo Hotel**.

10 Sat Singapore (B)
Morning sightseeing tour of the attractions of Singapore takes you to Mt. Faber, Sri Mariamman Hindu Temple and Little India, Chinatown and the Botanical Gardens. Afternoon at leisure.

11 Sun Singapore (B)
Entire day at leisure to explore Singapore on your own.

12 Mon Singapore/Hong Kong (B) ✈
Fly to Hong Kong. Stay at the **Royal Pacific Hotel, Tower Wing**.

13 Tue Hong Kong (B)
Explore Hong Kong Island by coach today, visiting Aberdeen Fishing Village, Stanley Market, Repulse Bay and Victoria Peak. Balance of day free for shopping and exploring on your own.

14 Wed Hong Kong (B)
Full day at leisure. Consider an optional excursion to the Portuguese colony of Macau, or to Zhongshan on the Chinese mainland.

15 Thu Hong Kong/USA (B) ✈
Fly back to the USA today. Cross the International Date Line and arrive home the same day.

TOUR DATES & PRICES

IT3JL1PAESA

	FROM HONOLULU	FROM NEW YORK OR CHICAGO	FROM WEST COAST
MAR 17–31			
MAR 31–APR 14			
APR 7–21	$2060	$2270	$2080
MAY 5–19			
MAY 19–JUN 2			
JUN 2–16			
JUN 16–30			
JUL 7–21	$2170	$2380	$2190
JUL 21–AUG 4			
AUG 18–SEP 1			
SEP 1–15			
SEP 22–OCT 6			
OCT 6–20	$2105	$2315	$2125
OCT 20–NOV 3			
NOV 3–17			
NOV 17–DEC 1			
DEC 1–15			
JAN 26–FEB 9 '95	$1970	$2175	$1990
FEB 16–MAR 2 '95			
MAR 2–16 '95	$2060	$2270	$2080

Land only: $925 Single extra: $598.
Full day elephant safari supplement: $59

Add-on airfares available from many cities. See page 6.

Land only cost does not include any flights nor arrival and departure transfers in the Orient. Tour fares do not include $18 US transportation taxes and fees or foreign airport departure taxes ($40, payable locally). Departures guaranteed upon written confirmation from TBI Tours. Due to current Japan Airlines schedules, passengers returning to New York or Chicago will overnight in Tokyo on Day 15, returning to the US on Day 16 (Friday). Overnight accommodations and breakfast provided by Japan Airlines.

26

Reprinted courtesy of TBI Tours.

Enticing Indonesia and Malaysia

16 days visiting Kuala Lumpur, Kota Kinabalu, Singapore, Yogyakarta and Bali

★DEPARTURES GUARANTEED with minimum 2 passengers★

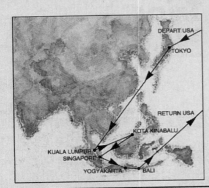

In Balinese Fields

ITINERARY

1
Sat
USA/Tokyo ✈
Depart the USA. Cross the International Date Line en route.

2
Sun
Arrive Tokyo
After clearing customs, proceed to the **Narita Nikko Hotel**.

3
Mon
Tokyo/Kuala Lumpur (B) ✈
Fly to Kuala Lumpur where you will stay at the lovely **Hotel Istana**.

4
Tue
Kuala Lumpur (B)
Morning sightseeing of Kuala Lumpur takes you through Chinatown and to the War Memorial, King's Palace and National Museum.

5
Wed
Kuala Lumpur/Kota Kinabalu (B) ✈
Fly to Kota Kinabalu on the northern end of Borneo, where you will stay at the lovely **Shangri-la Tanjung Aru Beach Hotel**. Afternoon at leisure.

6
Thu
Kota Kinabalu (B, L) ✈
Morning flight to Sandakan to visit the Sepilok Orang Utan Sanctuary. The Orang Utan (Wild Men of Borneo) were on the verge of extinction before the sanctuary was established. Return to Kota Kinabalu this evening.

7
Fri
Kota Kinabalu (B)
Day at leisure for exploring on your own or relaxing on the beach. Perhaps take an optional tour to Kinabalu National Park.

8
Sat
Kota Kinabalu/Singapore (B) ✈
Fly to Singapore, a city with an exotic blend of Chinese, Malay and Indian cultures. Stay at the **Omni Marco Polo Hotel**.

9
Sun
Singapore (B)
Morning sightseeing tour of the attractions of Singapore takes you to Mt. Faber, Sri Mariamman Hindu Temple and Little India, Chinatown and the Botanical Gardens. Afternoon at leisure.

10
Mon
Singapore/Yogyakarta (B) ✈
Fly to Yogyakarta, where you will stay at the **Ambarrukmo Palace Hotel**.

11
Tue
Yogyakarta (B)
Excursion to the magnificent temple at Borobudur. Built in the 8th century but covered in jungle until the 19th, the temple boasts the world's largest collection of Buddhist relief sculptures. Afternoon at leisure.

12
Wed
Yogyakarta/Bali (B) ✈
Fly to sensuous, romantic Bali, where traditional cultures and arts continue to flourish. Stay at the **Bali Dynasty Hotel**.

13
Thu
Bali (B)
Explore this exotic island on your morning sightseeing tour. Visit Mas and Ubud, centers of woodcarving and painting, and the sacred spring at Tampaksiring. Afternoon at leisure.

14
Fri
Bali (B)
A full day at leisure to enjoy the beautiful beaches or explore as you wish. Or, take an optional tour to Sangeh, Mengwi and Tanah Lot.

15
Sat
Bali/Jakarta/Tokyo (B) ✈
Morning at leisure. Evening flight to Jakarta, where you connect to your overnight flight to Tokyo.

16
Sun
Tokyo/USA ✈
Connect in Tokyo for your flight to the USA. Cross the International Date Line and arrive home the same day.

TOUR DATES & PRICES			IT3JL1PAEIM
	FROM HONOLULU	FROM NEW YORK OR CHICAGO	FROM WEST COAST
MAR 19–APR 3 APR 9–24 APR 23–MAY 8 MAY 21–JUN 5	$2915	$3165	$2975
JUN 11–26 JUL 9–24 AUG 13–28	$3030	$3280	$3090
SEP 10–25 OCT 1–16 OCT 22–NOV 6 NOV 12–27	$2915	$3165	$2975
DEC 3–18 JAN 28–FEB 12 '95 FEB 18–MAR 5 '95	$2860	$3110	$2920
MAR 4–MAR 19 '95	$2915	$3165	$2975

Land only: $1350 Single extra: $690.

Add-on airfares available from many cities. See page 6.

27

Philippines

Friendly, welcoming people, beautiful, natural scenery, wide, sandy beaches, out-of-the-ordinary shopping. An undiscovered jewel of the Orient.

San Agustin Church, Manila

Taiwan

An intriguing mix of the traditional and the modern world, great food, treasures from ancient China in the wonderful National Museum.

Manila

4 Days/3 Nights   CMNL

1   Arrival and transfer to your hotel.

2   Half day of sightseeing in Manila includes the Intramuros Walled City, San Agustin Church and Fort Santiago.

3   Full day at leisure.

4   Transfer to the airport for your flight onward.

	Package		Extra Night	
	Double	Single	Double	Single
Mandarin Oriental	$325	$575	$77	$154
Edsa Shangri-La	$315	$560	$75	$149
Shangri-La Manila	$350	$625	$87	$173
Hyatt Regency	$250	$395	$49	$ 92

Boracay

3 Days/2 Nights   CKLO

Includes breakfast daily.

1   Transfer to the Domestic Airport and fly to Kalibo. Transfer to Caticlan wharf for the "pumpboat" to Boracay. Transfer to your beach hotel.

2   Breakfast in the hotel. Day at leisure to relax on beautiful Boracay, the white sand beaches and sparkling water some have called "the world's best."

3   After breakfast in the hotel, return by boat to Caticlan Wharf, then transfer to Kalibo Airport for your flight to Manila. Transfer to your hotel.

	Package		Extra Night	
	Double	Single	Double	Single
Friday's Beach Resort	$370/390*	$480/520*	$92/105*	$124/151*

*High Season: Jan-Mar. Call for rates after October, 1994.

Chiang Kai-Shek Memorial Hall

Citipak Holiday
Manila/Pagsanjan/Village Escudero/Tagaytay Ridge/Manila

2 Days/1 Nights   CH10
Breakfast daily. lunch as indicated. Daily departures.

1   **Manila/Village Escudero (L, D)**
Depart by coach for the quaint town of Pagsanjan. There, board a native dugout canoe for the trip upriver through lush tropical vegetation, steep gorges and towering canyons to picturesque Pagsanjan Falls. Shoot the rapids through huge boulders on the return trip downriver.

Proceed to historic Village Escudero. Tour the Village by carabao (horsedrawn cart). Lunch and overnight at the lovely **Villa Escudero**, set in a grove of coconut palms amidst lush green fields. Dinner. Evening at leisure.

2   **Village Escudero/Manila (B)**
After breakfast, coach through the countryside, past native villages, tropical fruit orchards and coconut plantations to the volcanic crater at Tagaytay Ridge. On the return to Manila visit the "jeepney" factory and stop to listen to the Bamboo Organ at Las Pinas.

	Package	
	Double	Single
Package	$450	$675

Taipei
3 Days/2 Nights   CTPE

1   Arrival and transfer to your hotel.

2   Half day sightseeing tour includes a visit to the Chiang Kai-Shek Memorial Hall, Presidential Square, National Palace Museum and a view of the changing of the guards.

3   Transfer to airport for your departure flight.

	Package		Extra Night	
	Double	Single	Double	Single
Grand	$325	$445	$ 83	$152
President	$295	$420	$ 77	$147
Fortuna	$280	$400	$ 73	$141
Imperial	$275	$390	$ 71	$136

Vietnam, Cambodia & Laos

One of Asia's last untouched, untouristed regions. Beautiful, lush Vietnam, the wonders of Angkor in Cambodia, and the last true shangri-la, Laos, are perfect destinations for the adventurer.

Ho Chi Minh City (Saigon)
4 Days/3 Nights   CSGN
Three meals daily. Departures daily.

1. Arrive and transfer to your hotel. Dinner at a local restaurant.
2. Visit Thong Nhat Conference Hall. After lunch, balance of day at leisure for exploring on your own. Dinner.
3. Full day excursion to Cu Chi Tunnels and the Cao Dai Temple at Tay Ninh.
4. Transfer to the airport for departure.

	Package	
	Double	Single
Omni Saigon	$850	$1090
Floating Hotel	$795	$1070
Century Saigon	$815	$ 990
Rex or similar	$645	$ 750

One passenger traveling alone: add $161.

Hanoi
3 Days/2 Nights   CHAN
Three meals daily. Departures daily.

1. Transfer to your hotel. Afternoon city tour. Dinner.
2. After breakfast, visit Ho Chi Minh's Mausoleum, One Pillar Pagoda, Sword Lake, and The Temple of Literature. Evening variety show.
3. Transfer to the airport for your flight.

	Package	
	Double	Single
Pullman Metropole	$595	$775
Thang Loi	$450	$515

One passenger traveling alone: add $130.

Phnom Penh & Angkor Wat
4 Days/3 Nights   CPNH
Three meals daily.
Departures daily.

1. Transfer to the **Cambodiana Hotel.** Explore the National Museum, filled with Khmer artwork from the 4th to 15th centuries.
2. Transfer to the airport for your flight to Siem Reap. Visit the wonders of Angkor Wat and Angkor Thom. Overnight at the **Ta Prohm Hotel** or similar.
3. Return flight to Phnom Penh. Visit the Russian and Wholesale Markets.
4. Transfer to the airport for departure.

	Package	
	Double	Single
Package	$1050	$1280

One passenger traveling alone: add $121.

FOR INDOCHINA CITIPAKS AND CITIPAK HOLIDAYS
1. ALL ARRANGEMENTS IN INDOCHINA SUBJECT TO CHANGE AT THE DISCRETION LOCAL TOURISM AUTHORITIES.
2. TBI will process visas for Indochina, to be issued in Bangkok.
3. Meals provided according to flight schedules.
4. **MINIMUM TWO PERSONS.**

Vientiane & Luang Prabang
5 Days/4 Nights   CVTE
Three meals daily. Departures daily.

1. Arrival and transfer to the **Lane Xang Hotel** or similar. After lunch, enjoy a city tour.
2. Transfer and fly to Luang Prabang. Full day city tour with lunch. Stay at the **Luang Prabang Hotel (Phuo Vao)** or similar.
3. Cruise on the Mekong River to the caves at Pak-Ou, with a picnic lunch en route.
4. Visit the former Royal Palace before your return flight to Vientiane. Afternoon Central Market tour.
5. Transfer to the airport for your flight onward.

	Package	
	Double	Single
Package	$845	$970

One passenger traveling alone: add $109.

Photos courtesy A. Schoch

In the mountains of Laos

Citipak Holiday
Hanoi/Ho Chi Minh/Phnom Penh & Angkor   8 Days/7 Nights
                                                           CHO4
Three meals daily in Indochina. Departures daily.

1. **Bangkok/Hanoi**
Fly to Hanoi and transfer to the **Pullman Metropole (DLX)** or **Thang Loi Hotel (FIR).**
2. **Hanoi (B, L, D)**
After breakfast, visit Ho Chi Minh's Mausoleum, One Pillar Pagoda, Sword Lake, and The Temple of Literature. Evening variety show.
3. **Hanoi/Ho Chi Minh City (B, L, D)**
Transfer to the airport and fly to Ho Chi Minh City (Saigon). Afternoon sightseeing. Stay at the **Saigon Floating Hotel (DLX)** or the **Rex Hotel (FIR).**
4. **Ho Chi Minh City (B, L, D)**
Full day excursion to Cu Chi Tunnels and the Cao Dai Temple at Tay Ninh.
5. **Ho Chi Minh City/Phnom Penh (B, L, D)**
Transfer and fly to Phnom Penh. Explore the National Museum, filled with Khmer artwork from the 4th to 15th centuries. **Cambodiana Hotel** or similar.
6. **Phnom Penh/Siem Reap (B, L, D)**
Transfer to the airport for your flight to Siem Reap. Visit the wonders of Angkor Wat and Angkor Thom. Overnight at the **Ta Prohm Hotel** or similar.
7. **Siem Reap/Phnom Penh (B, L, D)**
Return flight to Phnom Penh. Visit the Russian and Wholesale Markets.
8. **Phnom Penh/Bangkok (B)**
Transfer to the airport for your flight to Bangkok. Transfer to your hotel.

	Package	
	Double	Single
Deluxe	$2720	$3325
First Class	$2470	$2870

One passenger traveling alone: add $315.

Reprinted courtesy of TBI Tours.

■ REVIEW—SOUTHEAST ASIA

1. What are the two principal physical units of Southeast Asia? What nations are found in each?

2. How did Buddhism and Islam come to Southeast Asia? In which nations are they important today?

3. What colonial powers held colonies in Southeast Asia before World War II? What sorts of changes have been made in these countries since 1945?

4. What are some of the problems faced by these newly independent (postwar) nations? Where does tourism fit in?

5. What is the distinctive character and role of Singapore?

6. What are the important tourism features of Bangkok?

7. What are the major problems faced by the Philippines? How have they affected tourism?

8. Where are the major beaches and resort areas in Southeast Asia?

9. Describe three areas of scenic beauty in Southeast Asia.

16

Oceania: The South Pacific

Between the Americas and Asia stretches the Pacific Ocean, the world's largest and deepest body of water. It occupies one-third of the earth's surface and stretches almost half way around the world near the equator. On its southern flank are its three largest landmasses, the island nations of Australia and New Zealand; and north of Australia, New Guinea, whose western half is part of Indonesia and whose eastern half is the independent nation of Papua New Guinea. Elsewhere there are hundreds of scattered islands and island groups of varying sizes, mostly small. Three regional island groupings are recognized: Micronesia in the northwest; Melanesia in the southwest; and Polynesia in the center and southeast.

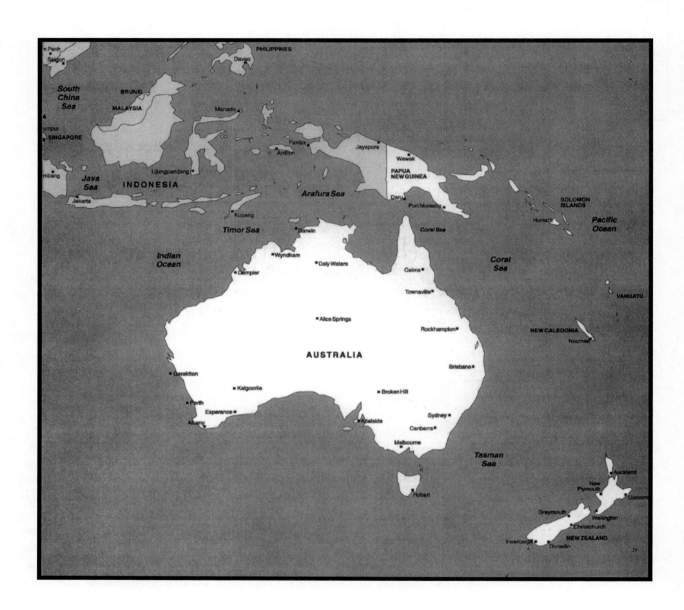

■ AUSTRALIA AND NEW ZEALAND

AUSTRALIA

Official Name: Commonwealth of Australia

Language: English

Area: 2,966,200 square miles

Time Zone: GMT +8 through +10

National Airline: Qantas

Capital: Canberra

Currency: Australian Dollar (AUD)

Population: 16,849,496

Documentation: Passport, visa

The Land and Climate. Australia is the largest body of land in the Pacific and designated a continent based on its size. About the size of the United States, it measures a maximum 1,700 miles north-south and 2,500 miles east-west. It is bordered on the west and south by the Indian Ocean. The island of Tasmania lies off the southeast coast, and the Great Barrier Reef, a massive coral formation, extends for 1,200 miles along the northeast coast. Australia has a very distinctive flora and fauna; kangaroos, koalas, and other pouched mammals are among its best-known animals. Most of the continent's surface consists of interior plateaus on a grand scale; the only major mountain system, the Great Dividing Range, runs north-south along the east coast.

The principal climatic characteristic and drawback is aridity—the center is desert bordered by vast areas of dry grass and scrublands, the Australian outback. The best watered and most habitable areas are along the east, southeast, and southwest coasts, and Tasmania. Consequently, 90 percent of the Australians live, and most towns and cities have developed, in these districts.

Organization and History. Politically, Australia consists of six states: Western Australia and South Australia in the center; Queensland in the northeast; New South Wales and Victoria in the southeast; Tasmania; and Northern Territory in a federation. The federal capital, Canberra, is inland in New South Wales. State capitals are the leading cities: Brisbane and Sydney on the east coast; Melbourne and Adelaide on the south coast; and Perth on the southwest coast. Sydney and Melbourne are the largest; Sydney (3 million people) alone has 20 percent of the national population. Darwin is the main city of the northern coast, and Hobart is the capital of Tasmania.

Developed as a British colony (many of the earliest settlers were prisoners), Australia still has a population of predominantly British extraction, although modified by the immigration of other Europeans and small numbers of Asians since 1945. A small minority of black Aborigines, the pre-European population, remain. They are a depressed socioeconomic group, adjusting poorly to the lifestyle that has replaced their simpler hunting and gathering existence.

Economy. Australia is a modern, urban nation with a broad-based, developed economy. Agriculture and grazing have always been important, and wheat, wool, and meat are still important exports. In recent decades, Australia has become a world leader in the mining and export of industrial raw materials, including iron ore, bauxite, uranium, and copper. The semiprecious gemstone, opal, is mined heavily in Australia. Australia's principal overseas customer is Japan. The domestic resources, combined with local supplies of coal, hydro-electric power, and some oil and natural gas in eastern Australia, have sustained good growth in manufacturing despite the small domestic market.

Both Australia and neighboring New Zealand are handicapped in international exchanges of goods and people by the great distances separating them from the main centers of North America, Europe, and Asia. London is 12,500 miles from Sydney. Los Angeles is 6,000 miles; and Tokyo is 4,300 miles.

Areas of Touristic Importance. Australia is the only country that occupies an entire continent. Because of its position in the Southern Hemisphere, it is often referred to as "the land down under." Most tourists first arrive at Sydney, New South Wales, Australia's oldest and largest city. Sydney's most popular landmark is the Opera House, a modern structure visible to all visitors to the city's harbor.

To the south of Sydney lies Canberra, the nation's capital. Victoria is the state on the southeast coast and its capital, Melbourne, is perhaps the most beautiful city in the country with many parks, gardens, and government buildings.

Judging Australia by visiting only Sydney, Melbourne, and Canberra is like judging the United States by visiting only Boston, New York, and Washington. Yet, most of the shorter South Pacific tours only visit these three cities.

The Great Barrier Reef in Queensland is reached from Brisbane, Queensland's capital and largest city, and from Cairns in the northeast. The reef is a chain of coral islands running for more than 1,000 miles. Australia's "gold coast" resort area has developed along the ocean north from Brisbane with the finest beaches in the South Pacific. The coral formations of the reef create waves for surfing that rival Hawaii's Bonzai Pipeline and attract scuba divers and snorkelers from all over the world.

Alice Springs in Australia's outback or interior is more than one thousand miles from Sydney. Although it is quite small, Alice Springs hosts many tourists desiring to see the aborigines, most of whom lead a nomadic life in the dry areas of the country. Alice Springs is also the gateway to Ayers Rock, the world's largest monolith, which stands 1,000 feet above the plains and is 5.5 miles in circumference. Visitors to this region can also experience life on a sheep ranch, or station as it is called in Australia, or visit opal mines.

Ayers Rock, Australia
Photo: Courtesy Australian Tourist Commission

Perth, capital of Western Australia, located on the Indian Ocean, is newly developing as a major tourist destination. It was the site of the 1987 America's Cup yacht race that attracted entries from all over the world. While most visitors fly to Perth, the Perth-Sydney Railway is a 2,461-mile journey for the rail enthusiast. It includes the world's longest, dead-straight stretch—287 miles without a turn or curve.

Kangaroos and koalas are also on the must list for tourists. They can be seen in their natural environment or in the zoos of the major cities.

NEW ZEALAND

Language: English

Area: 103,736 square miles

Time Zone: GMT +12

National Airline: Air New Zealand

Capital: Wellington

Currency: N. Z. dollar (NZD)

Population: 3,308,000

Documentation: Passport

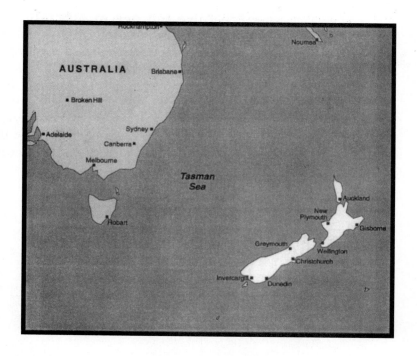

The Land. The main island nation of New Zealand, only one-twenty-eighth the size of Australia, lies 1,250 miles southeast of that continent. It consists of two narrow main islands, each about 500 miles in north-south extent, and many smaller islands. Both main islands have magnificent mountain scenery. North Island has a high volcanic core, hot springs, and geysers. To the south across Cook Strait, South Island is dominated by a high, snowcapped mountain range, the Southern Alps, that runs the length of the west coast. In sharp contrast to Australia in climate as well as topography, New Zealand is well-watered and forested.

The Peoples. British settlers displaced the original dark-skinned Maori people during the colonial period. Today, Maori constitute 10 percent of the small national population. The rest of the population is overwhelmingly of British origin. The population is 85 percent urban. About three-fourths live on North Island, heavily concentrated in the two largest cities, Auckland in the north and Wellington on the south coast.

Christchurch, the largest city of South Island, is on its east coast. Most Maoris live on North Island and have been joined in recent years by an influx of other dark-skinned Polynesians from Pacific island dependencies of New Zealand, forming a more sizable urban minority presence.

Economy. Partly because of the uneven topography and the excellent planted pastures, grazing has been the backbone of the economy. New Zealand is the world's largest exporter of lamb, mutton, and dairy products, and ranks second in wool production. The main farming area is on the Canterbury Plain on the east coast of South Island. New Zealand does not have the mineral or energy wealth of Australia, has less manufacturing, and depends on imports. There is strong commercial and general interaction with Australia, the nearest major neighbor.

Areas of Touristic Importance. Most visitors begin their tour of New Zealand at its international gateway, Auckland, its

Lake Hayes, South Island, New Zealand
Photo: Courtesy Air New Zealand

major commercial and industrial center. The Maori center of Rotorua is a 5-hour car or bus ride away. Rotorua is also known for its thermal springs. Excursions to Rotorua usually include a visit to the Glowworm Grotto at Waitomo.

Wellington, the capital, lies at the southern tip of North Island. It has an excellent harbor with a view of the Cook

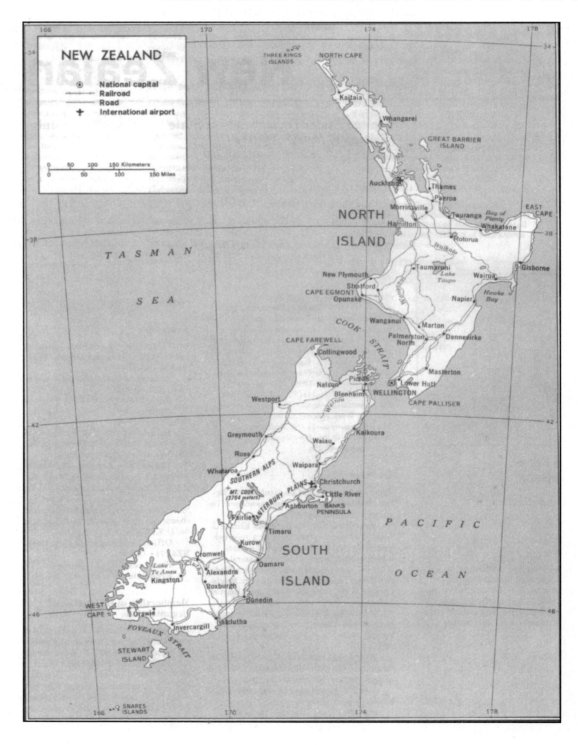

Strait, which separates the two islands. Ferries connect Wellington to Picton, on the South Island.

The Southern Alps run the length of South Island and give the impression of Colorado or Switzerland. Mount Cook is the highest peak and provides excellent winter skiing (June–August) and great views of the glaciers throughout the year. The southwest coast includes both cool rain forests and fjordland, with sheer cliffs towering thousands of feet above the water. Milford Sound is the most popular attraction in this area, both for cruises in the fjords and for tramping tours in the forests.

Christchurch, founded by the Canterbury Pilgrims who came from England more than 100 years ago, is the largest city on South Island and is a picture of old England. The Christchurch area is known as the Canterbury Plain, and contains more than 3 million acres of rich, fertile grain and grazing lands. Dunedin, south of Christchurch, was settled by Scottish emigrants. The nearby Otago Peninsula houses breeding grounds for the rare Royal albatross, and is an attraction for birdwatchers.

■ MELANESIA—AN OVERVIEW

The islands north of Australia are named Melanesia, a name that refers to the black color of their populations, some of whom may be related to the Aborigines of Australia. The main island is New Guinea; its eastern half is the nation of Papua New Guinea (PNG), and its western half is part of Indonesia and classified as part of Southeast Asia even though it has a large black population.

PAPUA NEW GUINEA

Official Name: Independent State of Papua New Guinea

Language: English, Pidgin English

Area: 178,260 square miles

Time Zone: GMT +10

National Airline: Airnuguini

Capital: Port Moresby

Currency: Kina (NGK)

Population: 3,913,000

Documentation: Passport

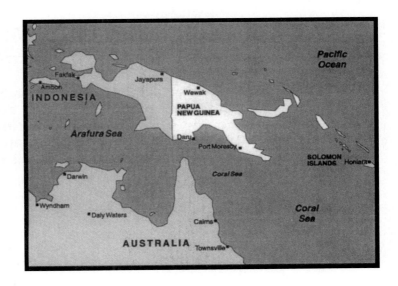

The PNG population, the biggest in Melanesia, is subdivided into hundreds of tribal groups, many of whom live in small villages in the remote, forested mountains of the island interior. The heaviest population density is on the northern and eastern coasts, where tropical temperatures and rainfall conditions prevail, but the capital, Port Moresby, a fast-growing city of 400,000, is on the southern coast. English is the official language, but a pidgin version is more generally used.

Still undeveloped, PNG receives assistance from Australia and New Zealand to supplement income earned from exporting foods, wood, and raw materials. Islands of PNG off the northeast coast include Bougainville, where copper mines produced PNG's main export until closed by civil war in 1989.

Areas of Touristic Importance. PNG is truly off the beaten path and, thus, is visited only by the adventurous. Throughout history it has been isolated from the surrounding countries and civilizations. For this reason, it is an anthropologist's dream with stone-age cultures living in dense jungles. The tribes living in PNG are, perhaps, the most primitive that most tourists will ever see.

SOLOMON ISLANDS

Language: Pidgin English, English

Area: 10,640 square miles

Time Zone: GMT +11

Capital: Honiara, Guadalcanal

Currency: Solomon Island dollar (SBD)

Population: 347,000

Documentation: Passport

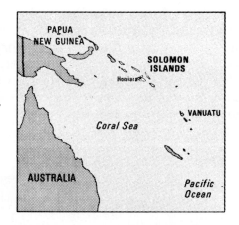

A group of islands east of Papua New Guinea, the Solomon Islands are a relatively isolated and poorly developed nation. The seat of administration is Honiara on the main island of Guadalcanal, where American and Japanese forces engaged in bitter combat in the early stages of World War II.

VANUATU

Official Name: Republic of Vanuatu

Language: French, English

Area: 5,700 square miles

Time Zone: GMT +11

Capital: Vila

Currency: Australian dollar (AUD); Vanuatu franc (VUV)

Population: 170,000

Documentation: Passport

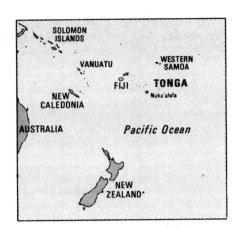

Vanuatu, formerly the colonial unit of New Hebrides, is an island cluster southeast of the Solomon Islands. Its capital is Vila, a small city on the largest island, Espiritu Santo. The former colony was administered jointly by the British and French, and both influences remain. The population is primarily Melanesian, but contains mixtures of Vietnamese, who came as plantation workers in the 1920s, and Europeans. Vanuatu was the setting for the well-known musical *South Pacific,* based on a book by James Michener.

NEW CALEDONIA

Language: French

Area: 8,548 square miles

Time Zone: GMT +11

Capital: Noumea

Currency: French Pacific franc (PFR)

Population: 172,000

Documentation: Passport, visa

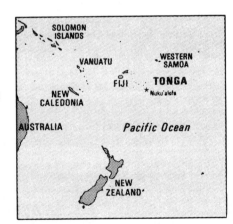

New Caledonia, the southernmost Melanesian unit, remains a French dependency. One-third of the population lives in Noumea, the capital. About one-third of the people are European, mostly French; one-fifth are Vietnamese or Indonesian; and the rest are Melanesian. Nickel mining and coffee plantations are the main sources of export income. Demands by the non-French portion of the population for independence from

France has resulted in political turmoil and public disturbances in recent years. Very few tourists visit New Caledonia.

FIJI

Official Name: Republic of Fiji

Language: English, Hindustani, Fijian

Area: 7,056 square miles

Time Zone: GMT +12

National Airline: Air Pacific

Capital: Suva

Currency: Fiji dollar (FID)

Population: 744,000

Documentation: Passport

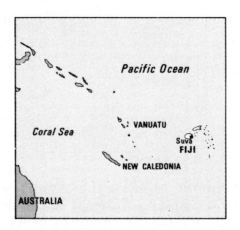

The easternmost nation of Melanesia is Fiji, a former British colony that abuts, and has strong racial and cultural influences from, Polynesia. It is composed of two large islands and hundreds of small islands; the capital, Suva, is on the coast of Viti Levu, the largest and most densely settled island. Among the population, half are Indians descended from laborers brought from India to work in sugar plantations in the 1880s. The Melanesian population is Christian; the Indians are mainly Hindu, with a small Moslem minority.

There is a relatively high literacy rate; English remains the main, official language, but Fijian and Hindustani are widely used. Fiji's main exports are sugar and copra (dried coconut meat). A main external contact point, Sydney, Australia, is 2,000 miles away.

Areas of Touristic Importance. Fiji is a popular stopover destination on many South Pacific itineraries. Swimming, boating, and fishing are among the more popular activities. A stop in Suva is a restful break after the long transpacific flight en route to Australia and New Zealand. It is also an excellent place to relax after intense touring throughout the Pacific. Its hotel and other tourism facilities are well developed.

■ MICRONESIA

The islands of Micronesia and Polynesia are either high islands of volcanic origin with higher interior elevations or low islands, low-lying coral atolls. The former have a better agricultural base, while in the more restricted environments of the latter, fishing and coconuts figure most prominently in the traditional economy.

Both Micronesians and Polynesians are dark-skinned peoples but their language and culture differ sharply; both groups, in turn, are subdivided into many local language groups. Both share an important seafaring tradition and have felt the impact of colonial rule imposed by outside powers.

Colonialism and Independence. Micronesia consists of the island groups stretching westward between Hawaii and the Philippine Islands. Most have been held as colonies by the Spanish, Germans, and Japanese, and were placed under American custody by the United Nations after World War II as the United States Trust Territory of the Pacific Islands.

The trusteeship was terminated in favor of independent governments in the easternmost group: the Marshall Islands (capital, Majuro); and the Federated States of Micronesia, formerly called the Caroline Islands, composed of Pohnpei (formerly Ponape) (capital, Palikir), Chuuk (formerly Truk) (capital, Moen), Kosrae (formerly Kusaie) (capital, Lelu), and Yap (capital, Colonia). Palau (capital, Koror) in the southeast remained under United Nations auspices until the terms of independence were agreed upon in 1994.

The northwesternmost group, the Northern Mariana Islands (capital, Saipan), has opted for status as an American Commonwealth, much like Puerto Rico in the Caribbean Sea.

With a total population of 350,000, the Micronesian units have received large appropriations from the United States government to build up government and public facilities in the main city (capital) of each unit. These centers dominate island life, are increasing in size, are partly Western in character, and depend on continued outside financing. English is the language of government and education.

Areas of Touristic Importance. Each unit has some outstanding features. The Marshall Islands have a major American military facility on Kwajalein Island. At Nan Madol, Pohnpei has at Nan Madol some of the largest and most important archeological ruins in the Pacific. Chuuk has an enormous lagoon that contains dozens of Japanese ships sunk by American bombing during World War 11. Yap is noted for its more traditional lifestyle and its giant stone money, quarried and used in precolonial times.

Palau has, on its small southern island of Peleliu, the site of one of the most fiercely contested American-Japanese battlegrounds of World War II, as does Saipan, where Japanese forces were overwhelmed by the victorious American landing forces. Saipan has the best paved roads, hotels, general ser-

Tumon Bay, Guam
Photo: Courtesy Guam Visitors Bureau

vices, and tourist flows (mostly from Japan). It was the former official headquarters of the Trust Territory Administration.

GUAM

Language: English, Chamorro
Area: 209 square miles
Time Zone: GMT +10
Capital: Agana
Currency: US dollar (USD)
Population: 133,152
Documentation: Identification

Guam, the largest, most populated, and southernmost island of the Mariana Islands, is not included in the Micronesian trusteeship. It was acquired from Spain at the end of the Spanish-American War in 1898 and is now an American self-governing unit with its capital at Agana. Guam is proud of its location "where America's day begins." The island is thoroughly Americanized. Its economy is based on United States government spending, and Guam imports all its goods. There is a large American military presence; much of the island is used for American air and naval bases.

Apart from American military and civilian personnel, the island's population is basically Chamorro, a precolonial people blended with Spanish and Filipino strains. There are also Micronesian and Filipino minorities in and near Agana.

Areas of Touristic Importance. The modern coastal resort at Tumon Bay, which benefits from investments by American and Japanese hotel chains and streams of Japanese tourists arriving by air, has the best hotel facilities in Micronesia. The Tumon Bay resorts are Japan's Caribbean and are most popular with Japanese newlyweds. Americans returning from Guam are given additional duty-free customs allowances.

NAURU

Official Name: Republic of Nauru

Language: Nauruan, English

Area: 8 square miles

Time Zone: GMT +12

Capital: No capital city

Currency: Australian dollar (AUD)

Population: 9,333

Documentation: Passport, visa

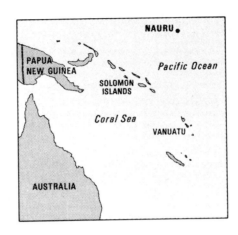

The young nations of Nauru and Kiribati are also part of Micronesia. Nauru is a single small island with fewer than 10,000 people, but it has valuable phosphate deposits and exports. The government of Nauru invests some of its export earnings in hotels, office buildings, airline facilities, and other money-making enterprises in several other Pacific political units. However, the phosphate resource is nearing depletion and mining has damaged the environment on this tiny island.

KIRIBATI

Official Name: Republic of Kiribati

Language: English

Area: 266 square miles

Time Zone: GMT +12

Capital: Bairiki, Tarawa

Currency: Australian dollar (AUD)

Population: 71,000

Documentation: Passport

Kiribati, formerly the British Gilbert Islands, consists of three widely separated groups of islands. The capital is Bairiki on Tarawa Atoll, where a bloody battle was fought by invading American forces against entrenched Japanese forces during World War II. Phosphates from Banaba (Ocean Island) were the government's main source of income, but mining has ceased. The large segment of ocean under Kiribati administration has potentially valuable fish resources. As in Nauru, English is the official language.

■ POLYNESIA—AN OVERVIEW

The thousands of islands of Polynesia are scattered across a vast expanse of the central and southern Pacific Ocean. Only three island groups—Tuvalu, Western Samoa, and Tonga—have achieved independence, leaving the rest under colonial administrations. French Polynesia, especially Tahiti and the Society Islands, attracts the majority of American tourists visiting this area.

TUVALU

Language: Samoan, Gilbertese

Area: 10 square miles

Time Zone: GMT +12

Capital: Funafuti

Currency: Australian dollar (AUD)

Population: 9,317

Documentation: Passport, visa

Tuvalu, formerly the British Ellice Islands, has a small population, of whom 2,500 live in the capital, Funafuti. Tuvalu lies due south of Kiribati.

WESTERN SAMOA

Official Name: Independent
 State of Western Samoa
Language: Samoan, English
Area: 1,133 square miles
Time Zone: GMT +11
Capital: Apia
Currency: Tala (SAT)
Population: 190,000
Documentation: Passport

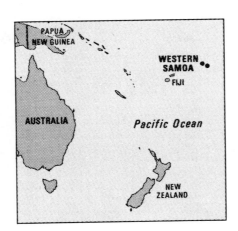

Located roughly midway between Hawaii and Sydney, Australia, Western Samoa was formerly administered by New Zealand. Of the total population, 35,000 live in the capital, Apia. The islands are volcanic in nature and characterized by exceptional beauty and climate. Robert Louis Stevenson had a home in Valima on the picturesque coastline.

AMERICAN SAMOA

Language: English, Samoan
Area: 77 square miles
Time Zone: GMT +11
Capital: Fagotogo
Currency: US dollar
Population: 46,773
Documentation: Identification

East of Western Samoa is American Samoa, a non-self-governing territory of the United States. Its capital, Fagotogo, (formerly Pago Pago) is on Tutuila Island, where most of the population live.

Areas of Touristic Importance. Swimming and boating are major activities. The Samoans have a distinct culture of their own, most often reflected in specific types of Polynesian dancing. As with Guam, Americans returning from American Samoa are given additional duty-free customs allowances.

Adjacent to American Samoa, three island groups—Tokelau Islands, Niue, and Cook Islands—are self-governing units under New Zealand.

Aoa Camping Grounds, Fagotogo, American Samoa
Photo: Courtesy Office of Tourism, American Samoa Government

TONGA

Official Name: Kingdom of
 Tonga
Language: Tongan, English
Area: 270 square miles
Time Zone: GMT +13
Capital: Nuku'alofa
Currency: Pa'anga (TOP)
Population: 102,000
Documentation: Passport

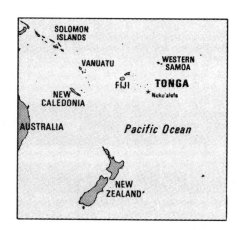

Tonga, located east and southeast of Fiji at the same latitude as northern Australia, was formerly a British protectorate. The capital, Nuku'alofa, has a fifth of the national population. The island's primary outside links are with Australia and New Zealand. The Tonga Islands are often called the "Friendly Islands" because of their carefree inhabitants.

FRENCH POLYNESIA

Language: French

Area: 1,544 square miles

Time Zone: GMT +10

National Airline: UTA, Air France

Capital: Papeete

Currency: French Pacific franc (PFR)

Population: 195,000

Documentation: Passport, visa

Southeastern Polynesia is largely occupied by sprawling French Polynesia, which includes the well-known island of Tahiti in the Society Islands. This overseas territory of France is administered from Papeete, a city of 25,000 on Tahiti. The fourteen Society Islands have belonged to France since 1843.

Areas of Touristic Importance. The four most important islands in the group are Tahiti, Moorea, Bora Bora, and Raiatea. All are volcanic in nature. Their beautiful blue lagoons and lush green mountains as well as prolific tropical vegetation make them dreams come true for the tourist imagining paradise.

Papeete, Tahiti is only 8 hours flying time from Los Angeles and is the gateway for international visitors. Tahiti is a destination in its own right, both for rest and relaxation and for those interested in the French culture and the spiritual source of Gauguin's paintings. Several cruise lines offer 1-week cruises through the islands with air/sea packages from most United States cities. A shorter stay in the islands is also part of many South Pacific tours.

Visitors can travel to Bora Bora, Moorea, and Raiatea by water launch, flying boat, and commuter-type aircraft. The Bora Bora airstrip is a coral reef in the lagoon. Bora Bora and Moorea feature native bungalows and small beachfront hotels. The island of Raiatea with its ancient Polynesian temples remains even more unchanged by the modern world.

Life in French Polynesia is relaxed and informal. The islands are subtropical with day temperatures averaging 85° and evenings in the 70°s on a year-round basis.

French Polynesia and both Western Samoa and American Samoa are located east of the International Date Line. As a result, the date in these locations is one day earlier than the Oceania destinations to their west. Many travelers are surprised to find that Tahiti and most of French Polynesia are actually located at a longitude east of Hawaii.

Tahiti
Photo: Courtesy Service du Tourisme de la Polynésia Française

■ ANTARCTICA

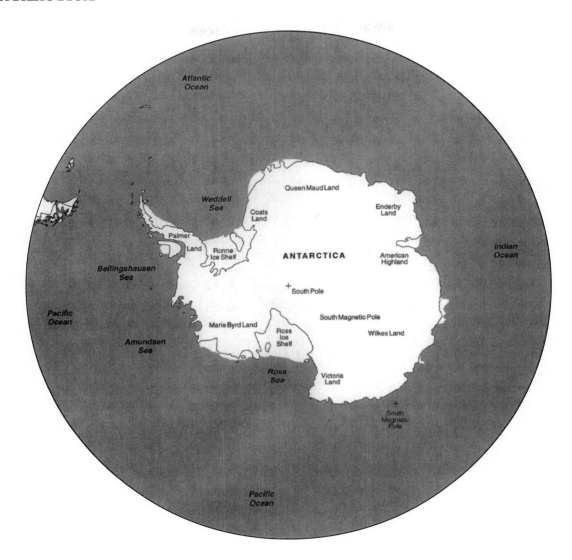

The Antarctic continent, where the South Pole is located, is covered by a huge, thick ice sheet; some high mountains and active volcanoes are exposed. The continent is divided politically into pie-shaped segments centered on the South Pole, which represent the national claims, based upon exploration records, of Australia, New Zealand, France, Norway, the United Kingdom, Chile, and Argentina. One segment, Marie Byrd Land, remains unclaimed.

A 1961 international treaty has put aside temporarily the questions of ownership and conflicting claims and stressed international cooperation in studying the continent's geology, climate, marine life, environment, distinctive fauna, and other features. A number of research stations and ships operate to study local conditions as well as broader global processes. The United States group operates from a base at the edge of the Ross Ice Shelf facing the Ross Sea in the New Zealand segment.

Tourism has not yet reached Antarctica. However, flight-seeing from New Zealand and Australia is available and there are a few exploration cruises offered during the year for adventurous travelers. There is also a worldwide attempt to protect the ecology of the area so tourism will most likely always be quite limited.

■ TYPES OF TOURISM

Individual and group tour programs are available throughout this region. Many group itineraries, with both escorted and hosted tour programs, are offered throughout the South Pacific. Australia, New Zealand, Tahiti, and Fiji are the most popular and have the most programs.

The following programs are examples of primary products on the market.

- ■ The Complete South Pacific
- ■ Papua New Guinea and Sepik Cruise
- ■ Pacific World Circle
- ■ Australia and New Zealand

GLOBUS *First Class* ESCORTED

The Complete South Pacific

Fiji, New Zealand, Australia and Tahiti

Tour **PSH** – 30 days

ALL THIS IS INCLUDED

■ All flights if Globus issues the tickets
■ Transfers, including baggage handling, to and from airports
■ Services of a professional tour director
■ First-class hotels listed below or equivalent (see page 7). Twin-bedded rooms with private bath or shower, hotel taxes, service charges and tips for baggage handling
■ In-flight meals as indicated in the itinerary; 28 American breakfasts (B); 7 lunches (L); and 5 dinners (D), with a special "hangi" dinner and a Maori concert in Rotorua and a farewell Tahitian dinner in Papeete
■ Private air-conditioned motorcoach when touring
■ Cruise to Mana Island, cruise on spectacular Milford Sound, Sydney Harbour cruise with lunch on board, full-day excursion to the Outer Barrier Reef

by catamaran with sub-sea coral viewing
■ Sightseeing tours of Auckland, Christchurch, Port Arthur Penal Settlement, Sydney, Melbourne and Papeete plus the Lagoonarium
■ Visits to Kelly Tarlton's Underwater World in Auckland, the Waitomo glow-worm caves, Rotorua's Thermal Reserve, Launceston's Cataract Gorge, Ayers Rock, the Olgas and the renowned Yulara tourist resort, a Camel Farm for a camel ride, Sydney's Opera House with an included performance
■ Scenic highlights: Mount Cook National Park, Fjordland National Park and the Tasman Peninsula
■ Inside visits as shown in UPPER-CASE LETTERS in the tour description, including admission charges where applicable
■ Globus travel bag and travel documents

Day 1, Sat. LOS ANGELES. The tour begins aboard a wide-bodied jet with an evening flight to Fiji. (In-flight meals)

Day 2, Sun. EN ROUTE. A day is "lost" crossing the International Date Line.

Day 3, Mon. NADI, FIJI. After an early morning arrival, meet your tour director and transfer to your beautiful resort hotel on Nadi Bay. The remainder of the day is free to relax. This evening attend a "Meke", a traditional Fijian-style dinner. (B,D)

Day 4, Tue. NADI-CRUISE TO MANA ISLAND. This morning a full day cruise to Mana Island. Spend the day swimming and snorkeling in the lagoon or just strolling along the white sand beaches. Lunch is included. (B,L)

Day 5, Wed. NADI-AUCKLAND, NEW ZEALAND. Transfer to the airport to board the

flight to New Zealand. (B,in-flight meal)

Day 6, Thu. AUCKLAND. Today's sightseeing of the beautiful "City of Sails" visits the Auckland Domain – an expanse of parkland leading to the WAR MEMORIAL MUSEUM with its large collection of Maori artifacts. View the panorama of Auckland and surrounding harbors from the summit of Mt. Eden's extinct volcano. The morning's highlight is a visit to KELLY TARLTON'S UNDERWATER WORLD, a journey through a unique underwater complex where visitors see native ocean life, sharks and stingrays. After lunch at the Rose Gardens, the remainder of the day is at leisure. (B,L)

Day 7, Fri. AUCKLAND-WAITOMO-ROTORUA. The morning drive is through the lush farmlands of the Waikato, en route to the famous WAITOMO GLOW-WORM CAVES and their eerie limestone

formations. The cavern is studded with the lights of a million glow-worms which are reflected in the still surface of the underground river. In the afternoon, continue over the Mamaku ranges to Rotorua to see some of nature's marvels. (B)

Day 8, Sat. ROTORUA. First on our agenda today, a visit to WHAKAREWAREWA, Rotorua's most famous thermal area with New Zealand's largest geyser, boiling pools, mud pools and silica terraces. With the afternoon at leisure, maybe join our optional excursion to Rainbow Springs and the Agrodome. Included at the hotel this evening a traditional "hangi" dinner followed by a memorable Maori concert. (B,D)

Day 9, Sun. ROTORUA-MOUNT COOK. In the morning fly to the magnificent MT. COOK NATIONAL PARK, named after New Zealand's highest peak. Weather permitting, why not do some "flightseeing"? Take an optional ski plane that actually lands on the 18-mile long Tasman Glacier or perhaps you would prefer a thrilling helicopter ride? (B,D)

Day 10, Mon. MOUNT COOK-QUEENSTOWN. Leave this alpine wonderland, ringed by 17 permanently snow-capped peaks and travel by coach through the delightful village of Cromwell to the stunning resort-area of Queenstown, nestled on the shores of Lake Wakatipu. Our optional for this evening: a New Zealand family will invite you into their home and host you to a delightful 3-course dinner. (B)

Day 11, Tue QUEENSTOWN. A full day at leisure to explore this beautiful resort town. A jet-boating ride down the Shot-over River provides quite a thrill; or cruise on Lake Wakatipu and visit a sheep station. Your tour director can help with suggestions for shopping and sightseeing. (B)

Day 12, Wed. QUEENSTOWN-MILFORD SOUND-TE ANAU. Today journey into FIORDLAND NATIONAL PARK, through the Homer Tunnel and to Milford Sound, set amongst some of the most breathtaking scenery in the world. This southern region of New Zealand has the elite status of belonging to the "World Heritage Parks". After lunch, cruise on the fjord amidst sheer rock walls rising thousands of feet from the water's great depths. The majestic Mitre Peak dominates at 5,560 ft. Overnight in Te Anau. (B,L)

Day 13, Thu. TE ANAU-DUNEDIN. Travel across the island to the Pacific coastline and reach Dunedin in the afternoon. The city is built round an octagon in place of the usual square and was originally renowned for its Victorian and turn-of-the-century grand buildings. This evening, why not join in the fun of the optional Haggis Ceremony dinner at the hotel. (B)

Day 14, Fri. DUNEDIN-CHRISTCHURCH. After breakfast depart for the airport to board the flight to Christchurch. Upon arrival, drive to the Cashmere Hills for a delicious lunch at the "Sign of the Takahe" restaurant. Sightseeing this afternoon commences with a drive up the winding Summit Road for views of Lyttleton Harbour, then past many of Christchurch's old stone buildings, the charming Avon River and acres of beautiful parks. (B,L)

Day 15, Sat. CHRISTCHURCH-HOBART, AUSTRALIA. This morning transfer to Christchurch airport for your flight across the Tasman Sea to the island of Tasmania. A short drive to your hotel in Hobart, with the balance of the evening free. (B,in-flight meal)

Day 16, Sun. HOBART. Today's tour takes you into the splendid Tasman Peninsula to visit the Blow-hole, Devil's Kitchen and the Tasman Arch – all natural features of the island's rocky coastline. On to BUSH MILL PIONEER SETTLEMENT before

28 US

arriving at Port Arthur, where the first convicts arrived in the 1830s. A guided tour of the PENAL SETTLEMENT shows you the ruins of the 4-story penitentiary, the commandant's house and the model prison... all grim reminders of Australia's days as a penal colony. (B,D)

Day 17, Mon. HOBART-LAUNCESTON-MELBOURNE. An early departure by coach north to the historic township of Ross. Continue to Launceston's CATARACT GORGE for a thrilling ride over on the world's longest single span chairlift in the world. On to the airport for the flight to Melbourne. (B)

Day 18, Tue. MELBOURNE. A morning tour focuses on the city's most famous landmarks: Melbourne University, Parliament House and the state government offices. Visit CAPTAIN COOK'S HISTORIC COTTAGE in Fitzroy Gardens, drive through Toorak and the Royal Botanical Gardens. Other sights include the Shrine of Remembrance and the Arts Centre of Victoria and a stop at the VICTORIA MARKETS. The afternoon is at leisure and, we highly recommend an optional excursion to Philip Island for the Fairy Penguin Parade. (B)

Day 19, Wed. MELBOURNE-AYERS ROCK. In the morning, fly to the center of Australia, Ayers Rock. The afternoon tour takes in ULURU NATIONAL PARK, THE ROCK and THE OLGAS, a magnificent jungle of some 30 brilliant monoliths scattered across the plains. There is time for a walk through OLGA GORGE before returning to "SUNSET STRIP" to see the unbelievable changing colors on Ayers Rock at sunset. (B)

Day 20, Thu. AYERS ROCK-ALICE SPRINGS. An opportunity this morning to climb to the top of AYERS ROCK, or for the less energetic, the optional light aircraft flight over the rock. Tour around the BASE OF THE ROCK, which is actually the tip of an underground sandstone mountain. Leave Ayers Rock and travel through the rugged Outback via Erlunda and Finke Rivers to "The Alice". (B)

Day 21, Fri. ALICE SPRINGS. For the early risers, start the day with an optional hot-air balloon ride over the township as the sun rises. Quite a thrill! Major attractions on the mid-morning tour include PANORAMA GUTH, the ROYAL FLYING DOCTOR BASE, a visit to Anzac Hill, the OVERLAND TELEGRAPH STATION and the CAMEL FARM for a long-to-be-remembered camel ride and see a display of Australian reptiles. Tonight there is a rare opportunity for an Aussie bush experience: the optional "night out" provides a meal typical of campfire fare, tales of the outback and aboriginal folklore. (B)

Day 22, Sat. ALICE SPRINGS-CAIRNS. Later this morning depart by air for Cairns, gateway to the Great Barrier Reef. (B)

Day 23, Sun. CAIRNS-BARRIER REEF EXCURSION. Today – a highlight of the trip! North along spectacular coastline to Port Douglas and then by fast catamaran to the outer edge of the famous Great Barrier Reef. View the coral and, for the more adventurous, snorkeling gear is available. A lavish smorgasbord lunch is included. (B,L)

Day 24, Mon. CAIRNS. Our suggestion for this morning is the optional rail/road tour to Kuranda. This unique excursion shows magnificent scenery, lush rain forests and tropical waterways all from the comfort of a restored, historical mountain railway. When in Kuranda, why not see "The Tjapukai Aboriginal Dance Theatre," with its mystical sounds and dances performed corroboree-style. The afternoon is at leisure. (B)

Day 25, Tue. CAIRNS-SYDNEY. An early flight south to Sydney – the "Harbour City." The afternoon is at leisure. This evening we recommend the optional outing to "The Jolly Swagman Show" in the famous Rocks area. (B)

Day 26, Wed. SYDNEY. A morning city tour packed with variety. Highlights include the Domain, Mrs. Macquarie's Chair, Kings Cross, Bondi Beach, Paddington, the ultra-modern Darling Harbour development and the Rocks area. End at the splendid OPERA HOUSE for a guided tour. At the Opera House wharf, board a luxury launch for a luncheon cruise on beautiful Sydney Harbour. In the afternoon there is an optional coach tour to Sydney's northern beaches with a visit to a wildlife sanctuary for close-ups of koalas, kangaroos, emus and colorful Australian birds. (B,L)

Day 27, Thu. SYDNEY. A day at leisure for shopping or individual sightseeing. Also available is an optional tour to the Blue Mountains. Special treat this evening: a performance at the famous Sydney Opera House with a complimentary glass of champagne and chocolates provided during the intermission. (B)

Day 28, Fri. SYDNEY-PAPEETE, TAHITI. Plenty of free time still today until the evening flight to Tahiti. Cross the International Date Line and arrive Papeete in the early morning of the same day. Transfer to the hotel and the remainder of the day is at leisure. Perhaps take our optional excursion to the magical island of Moorea. (B, in-flight meal)

Day 29, Sat. PAPEETE. A full-day Circle Island tour includes a stop at Point Venus, the historic landing place of Captain Cook. Then, it's on through the districts of Papenoo, Hitiaa and Faaone to the GAUGUIN MUSEUM. After lunch,

visit the cool FERN GROTTO OF MARAA. At the end of the day explore the LAGOONARIUM, a large natural underwater observatory that has myriad species of sea life. For the last evening together on tour – a farewell "Tahitian" dinner to celebrate the success of our South Pacific adventure. (B,L,D)

Day 30, Sun. PAPEETE-LOS ANGELES. This morning transfer to the airport to board the flight home. (B, in-flight meals)

One of the HAWAII ADD-ONS may be booked in conjunction with this tour. See page 49.

Tour PSH: DATES & PRICES

Tour Code	Leave USA		Return USA		Air/land incl. US$	Land only US$
PSH0115	Sat	15-Jan	Sun	13-Feb	5876	3842
PSH0129	Sat	29-Jan	Sun	27-Feb	5876	3842
PSH0205	Sat	05-Feb	Sun	06-Mar	5876	3842
PSH0219	Sat	19-Feb	Sun	20-Mar	5876	3842
PSH0305	Sat	05-Mar	Sun	03-Apr	5762	3842
PSH0319	Sat	19-Mar	Sun	17-Apr	5762	3842
PSH0326	Sat	26-Mar	Sun	24-Apr	5762	3842
PSH0416	Sat	16-Apr	Sun	15-May	5660	3842
PSH0514	Sat	14-May	Sun	12-Jun	5566	3748
PSH0618	Sat	18-Jun	Sun	17-Jul	5566	3748
PSH0716	Sat	16-Jul	Sun	14-Aug	5566	3748
PSH0813	Sat	13-Aug	Sun	11-Sep	5566	3748
PSH0903	Sat	03-Sep	Sun	02-Oct	5918	3998
PSH0917	Sat	17-Sep	Sun	16-Oct	5918	3998
PSH1001	Sat	01-Oct	Sun	30-Oct	5918	3998
PSH1008	Sat	08-Oct	Sun	06-Nov	5918	3998
PSH1015	Sat	15-Oct	Sun	13-Nov	5918	3998
PSH1022	Sat	22-Oct	Sun	20-Nov	5918	3998
PSH1105	Sat	05-Nov	Sun	04-Dec	5668	3748
PSH1119	Sat	19-Nov	Sun	18-Dec	5668	3748
PSH1217	Sat	17-Dec	Sun	15-Jan	5782	3748
1995						
PSH0114	Sat	14-Jan	Sun	12-Feb	5782	3748
PSH0128	Sat	28-Jan	Sun	26-Feb	5782	3748
PSH0211	Sat	11-Feb	Sun	12-Mar	5782	3748
PSH0225	Sat	25-Feb	Sun	26-Mar	5782	3748

Air/land inclusive price includes all flights from/to Los Angeles.

Land only price covers land arrangements from Nadi (day 3) to Papeete (day 30), including domestic air fares in New Zealand (Rotorua-Mount Cook and Dunedin-Christchurch).

Single room supplement: $1593

Triple room reduction per person: $220

1995 departures are subject to itinerary and price modifications. Details will be available in August '94.

APOLLO: TD*GG, **PARS:** G/PTS/GGX, **SABRE:** Y/TUR/QGG

ADD-ON AIR FARES

From	Add	From	Add
Chicago	$300	New Orleans	$300
Dallas/Ft. Worth	$290	New York	$330
Denver	$290	Phoenix	$100
Miami	$330	Seattle	$200

All air fares are subject to change without notice. For travel from one of the cities listed above, add the roundtrip per person amount to the 'air/land' inclusive price. If your hometown is not listed, please check with your travel agent for the applicable add-on fare.

GLOBUS HOTELS

NADI Sheraton Hotel, **AUCKLAND** Sheraton Hotel, **ROTORUA** Sheraton Hotel, **MOUNT COOK** The Hermitage, **QUEENSTOWN** Gardens Parkroyal, **TE ANAU** The Village Inn, **DUNEDIN** Southern Cross Hotel, **CHRISTCHURCH** The Chateau, **HOBART** Westside Hotel, **MELBOURNE** Southern Corss Hotel, **AYERS ROCK** Sails in the Desert, **ALICE SPRINGS** Alice Springs Pacific Resort, **CAIRNS** Matson Plaza, **SYDNEY** Hilton International, **PAPEETE** Hyatt Regency

▼ *LAWN BOWLING IN NEW ZEALAND*

GLOBUS   *First Class*   ESCORTED

Papua New Guinea and Sepik Cruise

Tour PSK – 18 days

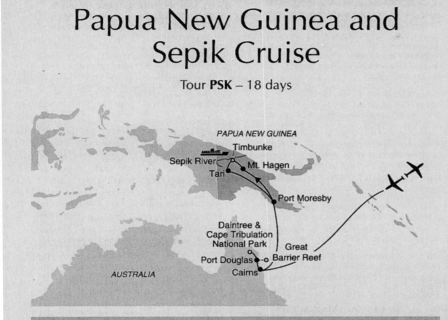

ALL THIS IS INCLUDED

- All flights if Globus issues the tickets
- Transfers, including baggage handling, to and from airports
- Services of a professional tour director
- First-class hotels listed below or equivalent (see page 7). Twin-bedded rooms with private bath or shower, hotel taxes, service charges and tips for baggage handling
- Cruise accommodations on the *Melanesian Discoverer* in cabins with two lower berths and private shower and toilet
- In-flight meals as indicated in the itinerary; 15 American breakfasts (B); 8 lunches plus 1 boxed lunch (L); 7 dinners (D), with a special farewell dinner in Cairns
- Private air-conditioned motorcoach when touring
- Full day excursion to the Outer Barrier Reef by catamaran with sub-sea coral viewing; ferry cruise on the Daintree River; 4-night Sepik River cruise on the splendid *Melanesian Discoverer*
- Visits to Daintree and Cape Tribulation World Heritage Parks, Wahgi Valley of the Western Highlands, famous "Mudmen" performance, the McCarthy Museum in Mt Hagen, a native village to attend a "Sing Sing", home of the Huli Clans
- Other scenic highlights: the Blackwater and Middle Sepik River region
- Inside visits as shown in UPPER-CASE LETTERS in the tour description, including admission charges where applicable
- Globus travel bag and travel documents

Day 1, Thu. LOS ANGELES. The tour begins aboard a wide-bodied jet with an evening flight to Australia. (In-flight meals)

Day 2, Fri. EN ROUTE. A day is "lost" crossing the International Date Line.

Day 3, Sat. CAIRNS-PORT DOUGLAS, AUSTRALIA. After a morning arrival, meet your tour director and depart Cairns for the drive north along spectacular coastline to Port Douglas on Trinity Bay. The remainder of the day is free to relax.

Day 4, Sun. BARRIER REEF EXCURSION. Today, the first of many exciting highlights! Travel by fast catamaran, the MV Quicksilver, to Agincourt Reef, on the outer edge of Australia's famous Great Barrier Reef. Enjoy coral viewing from the UNDERWATER OBSERVATORY or cruise among the coral gardens in a modern SUB-SEA VIEWER. Snorkeling gear is available for the more

adventurous and an informative talk by a marine biologist enhances this "reef experience". A lavish smorgasbord lunch is included. (B,L)

Day 5, Mon. DAINTREE AND CAPE TRIBULATION EXCURSION. Start the day with a drive through Mossman, a major sugar-cane center, then cross the crocodile-infested waters of the Daintree River by cable-driven ferry. The track narrows as you travel through CAPE TRIBULATION WORLD HERITAGE NATIONAL PARK, a rare and well-preserved tropical ecosystem. This unique mist-covered forest is an important natural site embracing some of the best undeveloped coastal scenery and rain forests of Australia. A stop is made amongst the silica sands to see the remarkable "bouncing stones", stones possessing an extraordinary bouncing characteristic. Before returning to Port Douglas, take an exploratory cruise on the Daintree River,

through tropical mangroves and primeval forest wilderness. (B)

Day 6, Tue. PORT DOUGLAS-CAIRNS. Retrace the route back to Cairns, with the balance of the day at leisure. Our suggestion for today is the optional coach and rail tour to Kuranda. First see the a fascinating portrayal of Aboriginal culture and traditions at the Tjapukai Dance Theatre, then return to Cairns via a restored mountain railway. (B)

Day 7, Wed. CAIRNS-PORT MORESBY, PAPUA NEW GUINEA. A morning transfer to the airport for the flight to Port Moresby, where you will be met and taken to your hotel. The afternoon and evening is at leisure. (B,in-flight meal)

Day 8, Thu. PORT MORESBY-MT HAGEN. This morning's tour provides an introduction to a unique adventure through the vast island-nation of "PNG". A land of 1,000 ethnic groups... over 700 distinct languages... a landscape comprising fabulous beaches, rain forests and volcanoes... a flora that is a botanist's dream, with myriad varieties of orchids and rhododendrons. Start with an educational hour at the NATIONAL MUSEUM with its fine collection of exhibits and artifacts, then PARLIAMENT HOUSE, and a colorful local market. An early afternoon flight to Mount Hagen, the provincial capital of the Western Highlands. (B)

Day 9, Fri. MT. HAGEN. Today's full-day tour includes a visit to the Mt. Hagen market, with displays of local artifacts. Continue by coach through the extensive pre-historic Wahgi Valley – a patchwork of native gardens, huge tea and coffee plantations and many elongated bush homesteads. At one of the various villages visited, take in a fascinating performance by the MUDMEN, a ghostly ceremonial dance that re-enacts an important battle won by tribal ancestors. Before returning to your hotel, a stop at the J.K.McCARTHY MUSEUM to learn more about the history and culture of the highland tribes. (B,boxed lunch).

Day 10, Sat. MT. HAGEN-SEPIK RIVER. A short flight from Mt. Hagen to Timbunke, on the mighty Sepik River. Board your ship, the *Melanesian Discoverer*, to begin the expeditionary cruise of the Blackwater Region and Middle Sepik River. Life along this remote and mysterious river is virtually untouched by western ways – the village women dutifully process their food staple, the sago palm and weave colorful baskets; men return from their fishing trips, with the daily catch and feathers, skins, animal bones for headdresses and body adornments; and laughing children splash about at the river banks. Later, dock at Mindimbit on the Karawari River to see a fascinating and unique display of local artworks. (B,L,D)

Day 11, Sun. SEPIK RIVER CRUISE. After morning tea on board, drop anchor and step ashore at the villages of Sangriman and Yesimbit. Both villages have interesting "Haus Tambarans" – spirit houses. Next a stop at Kraimbit to tour the ceremonial grounds and visit its superb Haus Tambaran with soaring finial figures and gable masks on the facade. While navigating the narrow "barats" (canals) in the Blackwater, numerous birds can be seen including hornbills, cockatoos, parrots, herons, egrets and cormorants. A good chance to spot a sleepy "pukpuk" (crocodile) on the sandy bends of the river! (B,L,D)

Day 12, Mon. SEPIK RIVER CRUISE. The expedition continues. A morning stop at Numeri Village for a "Sing Sing", the noted traditional ceremonial dance. Continue down the Korosmeri and Karawari Rivers to re-enter the Sepik. After lunch, head out by speedboat skimming beneath a canopy of junglegrowth, to visit the Chambri Lakes area, and the Womrun Village, with its attractive "Haus Tambaran"; then Aibom Village, noted for its fine pottery and learn about the legend of the ubiquitous face seen on the pots. (B,L,D)

Day 13, Tue. SEPIK RIVER CRUISE. Sail upstream this morning to visit Kamindimbit and explore the marketplace, with the villagers selling their assortment of artifacts. Later today take the speedboat again to reach Tambanum, one of the largest villages on the Sepik and where Margaret Mead, the renowned anthropologist, spent much of her time. Stroll along the decorated houses lining the river bank and watch the women weaving their baskets or fashioning the string bags from the roots of the pandanus palm. (B,L,D)

Day 14, Wed. SEPIK RIVER-TARI. Leave the *Melanesian Discoverer* this morning and by charter plane fly to Tari. This afternoon, the local guide takes you on an exploratory walk through the splendid forest of the Ambua Lodge grounds. Visit the lodge's Orchid House, with its magnificent vine bridges and waterfalls. Follow the trail to Tari Gap (at 9,000 feet), where the scenery changes from moss forest to alpine grasslands. The area is home to the colorful bowerbird, a relative of the bird-of-paradise. (B,L,D)

Day 15, Thu. TARI EXCURSION. When the first white men made their way through the mist-covered Tari Basin in 1935, they came across a remarkably distinct culture from any previously known in Papua. They found a population of light-skinned, stocky warrior farmers – the Huli. A very male-dominated society, where the men take great pride in their appearance, cultivating flowers to decorate their magnificent wigs, along with the colorful feathers of the revered native bird-of-paradise and the flightless cassowary. Today, you will have the opportunity to meet these proud people and learn of their traditions and way of life, which are still governed by their fervent belief in ancestral spirits and sorcery. (B,L,D)

Day 16, Fri. TARI-MENDI-PORT MORESBY. The morning is at leisure at Ambua Lodge, with time to relax, or take a stroll through the grounds. Early this afternoon transfer to the airport for the flight to Port Moresby. (B,L)

Day 17, Sat. PORT MORESBY-CAIRNS. An early morning flight back to Cairns. On arrival, transfer to your hotel with the remainder of the day free. This evening your tour director hosts a festive farewell dinner, a perfect finale to a truly memorable adventure in the South Pacific. (B,in-flight meal,D)

Day 18, Sun. CAIRNS-LOS ANGELES. After breakfast, transfer to the airport for the flight home. Once again, cross the International Date Line and arrive in Los Angeles on the same day. (B,in-flight meals)

➤ *Papua New Guinea lies just south of the Equator to the north of Australia. Its climate is generally hot and wet, with rain mainly falling in the evening. Temperatures in the coastal areas are stable, ranging between the 70s to 80s F; but inland – in the Highlands – it is cooler. Pack comfortable summer clothes, a sweater, a sunhat and sunglasses. It is advisable to take anti-malaria pills as prescribed by your doctor. Check with your travel agent for the most up-to-date visa and health requirements.*

YOUR CRUISE SHIP

The *Melanesian Discoverer* was designed and built to suit the special needs of navigating the remote parts of the mighty Sepik River. All cabins have lower berths, private facilites and large picture windows; a dining room and cocktail lounge; library; laundry; zodiacs and speedboats for a variety of excursions.

One of the HAWAII ADD-ONS may be booked in conjunction with this tour. See page 49.

Tour PSK: DATES & PRICES

Tour Code	Leave USA		Return USA		Air/land incl. US$	Land only US$
PSK0317	Thu	17-Mar	Sun	03-Apr	4988	3548
PSK0721	Thu	21-Jul	Sun	07-Aug	4892	3548
PSK0818	Thu	18-Aug	Sun	04-Sep	4892	3548
PSK0915	Thu	15-Sep	Sun	02-Oct	4988	3548
PSK1013	Thu	13-Oct	Sun	30-Oct	4988	3548

Air/land inclusive price includes all flights from/to Los Angeles.

Land only price covers land arrangements from Cairns (day 3) to Cairns (day 18), including charter flights to/from Timbunke.

Single room supplement: $1235

Triple room reduction per person: $33

APOLLO: TD*GG, **PARS:** G/PTS/GGX, **SABRE:** Y/TUR/QGG

ADD-ON AIR FARES

From	Add	From	Add
Chicago	$300	New Orleans	$300
Dallas/Ft. Worth	$290	New York	$330
Denver	$290	Phoenix	$100
Miami	$330	Seattle	$200

All air fares are subject to change without notice. For travel from one of the cities listed above, add the roundtrip per person amount to the 'air/land' inclusive price. If your hometown is not listed, please check with your travel agent for the applicable add-on fare.

GLOBUS HOTELS

PORT DOUGLAS Radison Royal Palms, **CAIRNS** Hilton International, **PORT MORESBY** Travelodge, **MOUNT HAGEN** Highlander Hotel, **TARI** Ambua Lodge, **CAIRNS** Hilton International

▼ *TYPICAL VILLAGE ALONG THE SEPIK RIVER*   ▲ *NATIVES OF PAPUA NEW GUINEA*

GLOBUS *First Class* ESCORTED

Pacific World Circle

Fiji, New Zealand, Australia, Singapore, Malaysia, Thailand and Hong Kong

Tour PSU – 26 days

ALL THIS IS INCLUDED

- All flights if Globus issues the tickets
- Transfers, including baggage handling, to and from airports
- Services of a professional tour director
- First-class hotels listed below or equivalent (see page 5). Twin-bedded rooms with private bath or shower, hotel taxes, service charges and tips for baggage handling
- In-flight meals as indicated in the itinerary; 24 American breakfasts (B); 5 lunches (L); 5 dinners (D) with a special "hangi" dinner and Maori concert in Rotorua and farewell dinner in Hong Kong
- Private air-conditioned motorcoach when touring
- Sightseeing tours in Auckland,

Melbourne, Sydney, Singapore, Bangkok, and Hong Kong
- Cruise to Mana Island; dinner cruise on Auckland's harbor; Sydney Harbour cruise with lunch on board; full day catamaran tour to the Outer Barrier Reef; cruise with dinner on Bangkok's Chao Phraya River
- Visits to Kelly Tarlton's Underwater World, the Waitomo glow-worm caves, Whakarewarewa Thermal Reserve, Kiwi Fruit Orchard at Te Puke, the famous Sydney Opera House with an included performance, and Johore in Malaysia
- Inside visits as shown in UPPER-CASE LETTERS in the tour description, including admission charges where applicable
- Globus travel bag and travel documents

Day 1, Sat. SAN FRANCISCO. The tour begins aboard a wide-bodied jet with an evening flight to Fiji. (In-flight meals)

Day 2, Sun. EN ROUTE. A day is "lost" crossing the International Date Line.

Day 3, Mon. NADI, FIJI. After an early morning arrival transfer to your beautiful resort hotel on Nadi Bay. After a restful day attend a "Meke" dinner at the hotel. (B,D)

Day 4, Tue. NADI-CRUISE TO MANA ISLAND. This morning a full day cruise to Mana Island. Spend the day swimming and snorkeling in the lagoon or just strolling along the white sand beaches. Lunch is included. (B,L)

Day 5, Wed. NADI-AUCKLAND, NEW ZEALAND. Transfer to the airport to board the

flight to New Zealand. (B,in-flight meal)

Day 6, Thu. AUCKLAND. Today's sightseeing of the beautiful "City of Sails" visits the Auckland Domain – an expanse of parkland leading to the WAR MEMORIAL MUSEUM with its large collection of Maori artifacts. View the panorama of Auckland and surrounding harbors from the summit of Mt. Eden's extinct volcano. The morning's highlight is a visit to KELLY TARLTON'S UNDERWATER WORLD, a journey through a unique underwater complex where visitors see native ocean life, sharks and stingrays. After lunch at the Rose Gardens, the remainder of the day is at leisure. (B,L)

Day 7, Fri. AUCKLAND-WAITOMO-ROTORUA. This morning's drive is through the lush farmlands of the Waikato, en route to the famous WAITOMO

GLOW-WORM CAVES and their eerie limestone formations. The cavern is studded with the lights of a million glow-worms which are reflected in the still surface of the underground river. In the afternoon, continue over the Mamaku ranges to Rotorua. Our optional this evening: a New Zealand family will invite you into their home for a delicious three-course dinner. (B)

Day 8, Sat. ROTORUA. First on the agenda today, a visit to WHAKAREWAREWA, Rotorua's most thermal area, with New Zealand's largest geyser, boiling pools, mud pools and silica terraces. As the afternoon is at leisure, perhaps join the optional excursion to Rainbow Springs and the Agrodome. Included at the hotel this evening, is a traditional "hangi" dinner followed by an enjoyable and memorable Maori concert. (B,D)

Day 9, Sun. ROTORUA-TE PUKE-AUCKLAND. First stop today is Te Puke – "Kiwifruit capital of the world" for a guided tour through an extensive KIWIFRUIT ORCHARD. Then continue on to Auckland for this evening's exciting dinner cruise aboard a spectacular yacht on the harbor (B,D)

Day 10, Mon. AUCKLAND-MELBOURNE, AUSTRALIA. Early morning departure from Auckland for the flight to Melbourne. (B,in-flight meal)

Day 11, Tue. MELBOURNE. A morning tour focuses on the city's most famous landmarks: Melbourne University, Parliament House and the state government offices. Visit CAPTAIN COOK'S HISTORIC COTTAGE in the Fitzroy Gardens, and then drive through the exclusive residential section of Toorak and the Royal Botanical Gardens. Other sights include: the National Trust's historic Como House, the Shrine of Remembrance and the Arts Centre of Victoria and the QUEEN VICTORIA MARKETS. The afternoon is at leisure and, we highly recommend an optional excursion to Philip Island for the Fairy Penguin Parade. (B)

Day 12, Wed. MELBOURNE-SYDNEY. Fly to Sydney late morning and the afternoon is free in the harbor city. Special treat this evening: a performance at the famous Sydney Opera House with a complimentary glass of champagne and chocolates provided during the intermission. (B)

Day 13, Thu. SYDNEY. A morning tour packed with variety. Travel via Sydney's commercial centre and along Macquarie Street to the Domain and Mrs. Macquarie's Chair. Stop for magnificent views of the Opera House and Harbour Bridge before continuing to Kings Cross, hub of local entertainment. On through elite harbor suburbs to famous Bondi Beach and then back through trendy Paddington, and finally the ultra-modern Darling Harbour development, and the famous Rocks area and end at the OPERA HOUSE for a guided tour. At the Opera House wharf board a luxury launch for a luncheon cruise on beautiful Sydney Harbour. The afternoon is free and we suggest to make the most of it by joining an optional coach tour to Sydney's northern beaches with a visit to a wildlife sanctuary for close-ups of koalas, kangaroos, emus and colorful Australian birds. (B,L)

Day 14, Fri. SYDNEY. A day at leisure for shopping or perhaps an optional excursion to Canberra, the capital city, with its War Memorial, diplomatic embassies and the new Parliament House. (B)

Day 15, Sat. SYDNEY-CAIRNS. All day at leisure in Sydney and then an evening flight to Cairns, capital of the "Tropic Wonderland". Recommended today is our optional by train and launch, to visit an historic homestead on the Hawkesbury River, the wheat and grain area of the early settlers. (B)

Day 16, Sun. CAIRNS. A day at leisure and our suggestion is the optional rail/road tour to

46 US

Reprinted courtesy of Globus and Cosmos.

Kuranda. This unique excursion features magnificent scenery, lush rain forests and tropical waterways all from the comfort of a restored, mountain railway. When in Kuranda, why not take time to see "The Tjapukai Aboriginal Dance Theatre" with its mystical sounds and dances performed corroboree-style. (B)

Day 17, Mon. CAIRNS. BARRIER REEF EXCURSION. After a scenic coach drive along tropical coastline to the resort town of Port Douglas, travel on the fast catamaran, the MV Quicksilver, to Agincourt Reef, on the outer edge of Australia's famous Great Barrier Reef. Enjoy coral viewing from the UNDERWATER OBSERVATORY or cruise among the coral gardens in a modern SUB-SEA VIEWER. Snorkeling gear is available for the more adventurous and an informative talk by a marine biologist enhances this "reef experience". A lavish smorgasbord lunch is included. (B,L)

Day 18, Tue. CAIRNS-SINGAPORE. A final chance to shop in Australia this morning before boarding the flight to Singapore. Arrive in the island republic late in the day. (B,in-flight meal)

Day 19, Wed. SINGAPORE. A tour of the city includes QUEEN ELIZABETH WALK overlooking the harbor, ST. ANDREW'S CATHEDRAL, MOUNT FABER with its sweeping view of the city and waterfront – and the BOTANICAL GARDENS, noted for its hybrid orchids. The afternoon is at leisure. An optional ride in a trishaw – a combination of rickshaw and tricycle – can be arranged. (B)

Day 20, Thu. SINGAPORE. EXCURSION TO JOHORE, MALAYSIA-BANGKOK, THAILAND. A morning tour to visit the state of Johore in Malaysia. Take the causeway bridge that separates

the island of Singapore from the Malay Peninsula. See the ABU BAKA MOSQUE renowned for its Moorish-style architecture. Stops will be made along the way at a village to meet some local people, a handicraft center and a rubber plantation. Before returning to Singapore visit the Central Market. Free time still in the afternoon, then transfer to the airport for your evening flight to Bangkok. (B,in-flight meal)

Day 21, Fri. BANGKOK. Sightseeing begins early with WAT ARUN – THE TEMPLE OF THE DAWN, its magnificent spires inlaid with millions of pieces of Chinese porcelain, a dazzling sight in the early morning sunshine. Next is the GRAND PALACE, the truly grand seat of the court of old Siam, and the adjoining royal temple, WAT PHRA KEO, housing the EMERALD BUDDHA. The 31-inch statue sits high on a golden altar. Dinner this evening is aboard a luxurious teak barge, the Tassaneeya Nava, as it cruises the broad Chao Phraya River, winding through Bangkok past splendid temples and palaces and the landing stage from which the gilded royal barge departs on the king's ceremonial visits. (B,D)

Day 22, Sat. BANGKOK. At one time the main streets of Bangkok were canals ("klongs" in Thai) and a good deal of life today is still waterborne. As the day is at leisure, why not join our recommended optional full-day trip to the floating market of Damneon Saduak, including a stop at Nakorn Pathom Chedi, the Rose Gardens and a visit to the Thai Cultural Village. This evening, perhaps take the optional outing for dinner at a typical Thai restaurant with entertainment of classical Thai dancing. (B)

Day 23, Sun. BANGKOK-HONG KONG, B.C.C. A morning flight to Hong Kong. Flying into Hong

Kong is an exciting experience with splendid views of its teeming harbour sparkling in the sun and its 235 islands! (B,in-flight meal)

Day 24, Mon. HONG KONG. Take the cable car up to Victoria Peak for a panoramic view of the harbor and city. The morning sightseeing continues with a drive to Repulse Bay, a popular beach with the locals. Stanley Market is next, a narrow street jammed with inexpensive clothing, arts and crafts. Last stop on the tour is at a JEWELRY FACTORY that designs and makes fine jewelry – each piece by hand. Lunch today is at La Ronda – 30 floors up – overlooking the bustling harbor of Hong Kong's Central District. With the evening free, we recommend an optional sunset cruise on Hong Kong harbor. (B,L)

Day 25, Tue. HONG KONG. A full day to explore the city's many other attractions. Perhaps spend the day visiting the People's Republic of China and exotic Macau, the gambling resort and Portuguese colony that is the oldest European settlement in the Far East. This evening, your tour director hosts a farewell dinner, a festive finale to a great touring adventure. (B,D)

Day 26, Wed. HONG KONG-SAN FRANCISCO. An hour or so free for last-minute shopping before the transfer to the airport for the midday flight home. Cross the International Date Line and arrive in San Francisco on the same day. (B,in-flight meal)

The JAPAN ADD-ON and one of the HAWAII ADD-ONS may be booked in conjunction with this tour. See pages 48 and 49.

▼ *YOUNG MONKS IN BANGKOK*

▼ *MAORI WOMAN*

▼ *ISLAND IN THE GREAT BARRIER REEF*

▼ *REPULSE BAY, HONG KONG*

Tour PSU: DATES & PRICES

Tour Code	Leave USA		Return USA		Air/land incl. US$	Land only US$
PSU0115	Sat	15-Jan	Wed	09-Feb	5374	3046
PSU0212	Sat	12-Feb	Wed	09-Mar	5374	3046
PSU0312	Sat	12-Mar	Wed	06-Apr	5374	3046
PSU0416	Sat	16-Apr	Wed	11-May	5374	3046
PSU0514	Sat	14-May	Wed	08-Jun	5281	2953
PSU0618	Sat	18-Jun	Wed	13-Jul	5281	2953
PSU0716	Sat	16-Jul	Wed	10-Aug	5281	2953
PSU0813	Sat	13-Aug	Wed	07-Sep	5281	2953
PSU0910	Sat	10-Sep	Wed	05-Oct	5596	3268
PSU0924	Sat	24-Sep	Wed	19-Oct	5596	3268
PSU1001	Sat	01-Oct	Wed	26-Oct	5596	3268
PSU1015	Sat	15-Oct	Wed	09-Nov	5596	3268
PSU1029	Sat	29-Oct	Wed	23-Nov	5596	3268
PSU1112	Sat	12-Nov	Wed	07-Dec	5596	3268
PSU1217	Sat	17-Dec	Wed	11-Jan	5281	2953
			1995			
PSU0114	Sat	14-Jan	Wed	08-Feb	5281	2953
PSU0211	Sat	11-Feb	Wed	08-Mar	5281	2953

Air/land inclusive price includes all flights from/to San Francisco.

Land only price covers land arrangements from Nadi (day 3) to Hong Kong (day 26).

Single room supplement: $1588

Triple room reduction per person: $207

1995 departures are subject to itinerary and price modifications. Details will be available in August '94

APOLLO: TD*GG, **PARS:** G/PTS/GGX, **SABRE:** Y/TUR/QGG

GLOBUS HOTELS

NADI Regent of Fiji, **AUCKLAND** The Sheraton, **ROTORUA** Kingsgate Rotorua, **MELBOURNE** Regent Hotel, **SYDNEY** Ramada Renaissance, **CAIRNS** Hilton International, **SINGAPORE** Le Meridien, **BANGKOK** Le Meridien President, **HONG KONG** The Nikko Hotel

TWENTY-ONE DAYS
Australia & New Zealand

*The best of both countries... plus The Australian Outback,
The Gold Coast and New Zealand's spectacular Mount Cook*

Fly To Sydney . . . Tauck Tours holds reserved space on Qantas Airways departing Los Angeles Fridays, in the late evening. Upon booking, Tauck Tours will advise flight schedule (subject to change). Persons choosing this flight will be met by our Tour Director at Sydney Airport on Sunday morning. (Although approximately a 15-hour flight, you lose a day when you cross the International Date Line.) Persons arriving earlier may wait for this transfer; those arriving later may take a taxi to the hotel at approximately AU$26 (US$20).

1. Arrive Sydney

Tour departs Sydney Airport Int'l Arrivals area one hour after the arrival of our Qantas flight, (usually 7AM–9AM).
Cosmopolitan Sydney is set around one of the world's most splendid harbors. After clearing Customs, you are met by your Tauck Tour Director at Door B and escorted to your hotel, located just minutes from the harbor and the center of activity. Enjoy a leisurely luncheon in the gracious surroundings of this hotel. The Inter-Continental is one of Sydney's most notable hotels and encompasses the 1849 Treasury Building. Tonight, we welcome you with a Sunset Cocktail Cruise on the harbor, after which you dock at the Rocks, where a dinner of Australian specialties awaits in a popular waterfront restaurant. MEALS **LD**

2. Sydney/Koala Park

Head out of the city this morning, bound for the Koala Park Sanctuary, where you meet some of Australia's unique wildlife. Enroute back to Sydney you will see the old and new; the Harbor Bridge, Sydney's famous beaches and "The Rocks," built by convicts for Australia's first settlers. The afternoon is yours to do as you wish . . . shop for opals, visit the Opera House or stroll along the Harbor. Your hotel is ideally located a few blocks from the harbor. Tonight you dine out at a prestigious Sydney restaurant with splendid vistas of the harbor. MEALS **BD**

3. Fly to Melbourne

Today, fly south from Sydney to the Victorian capital of Melbourne, a gracious city with stately, 19th-century architecture. This is the "other Australian city." It is different from Sydney, but every bit as alluring. You'll have time this afternoon to explore on your own. This evening, we've arranged a special dinner and theater performance that will introduce you to the renown cultural activities of Melbourne. MEALS **BD**

4. Melbourne Sightseeing

Melbourne is known as the "Garden City." Its parks, its gardens and its culture are beautiful. Join us this morning for a tour of the city that includes Fitzroy Gardens, the impressive Parliament House, St. Patrick's Cathedral and the modern business center. The afternoon is at leisure. MEALS **B**

5. Alice Springs/Ross River Homestead

This morning take an early flight from cosmopolitan Melbourne to Alice Springs, also known as Australia's Red Center and the heart of the Outback. Alice Springs was forged in gold, cattle and thirst. The town was built from supplies that were ferried north on camels. Hundreds of these animals still roam the Outback. This afternoon tour the Alice and visit the symbol of the pioneer spirit – the Royal Flying Doctor quarters. Mid-afternoon travel northeast to Ross River Homestead for a real Outback experience. Originally a working cattle station, the Homestead is one of the oldest establishments in the territory, dating from the late 1800's. This evening experience an authentic bushman's barbeque dinner under the stars. Enjoy bush tucker (food) and listen to ancient Aboriginal legends. Then retire in the simple accommodations of the Homestead. Although primitive by modern

7

Ayers Rock...a massive formation revered by the Aboriginals

hotel standards, the Ross River overnight will give you a feel for the traditional lifestyle of the Outback. MEALS **BLD**

6. Ayers Rock

Australian Aboriginals revered Ayers Rock as the holy place from where all life emanated... a lone, massive sentinel looming high above the desolate flat outback at the geographic center of their world. It remains hallowed ground today for the Aboriginal. Fly here today from Alice Springs. Enjoy lunch at your nearby hotel. This afternoon, meander around the Rock's base and explore the numerous caves with ancient Aboriginal wall paintings. Later, watch the sunset

paint the Rock with an ever-changing spectrum of colors. Return to your hotel for dinner, and perhaps a refreshing dip in the pool. MEALS **BLD**

7. Fly to Daintree Nat'l Park

Today, fly from the arid desert to the lush wilderness of Northern Queensland. Arrive in tropical Cairns, gateway to the Great Barrier Reef. Drive up the coast to Silky Oaks, a unique hideaway near Daintree National Park. Secluded within 80 acres of splendid rainforest, the private cabins and public buildings are built in the style of tree houses! Dine in the open-air Rainforest Restaurant. MEALS **BD**

8. Great Barrier Reef

The sounds of birdsong and cascading waterfalls greet you as you wake this morning. Enjoy a leisurely breakfast, then you're off on an excursion of a lifetime! Travel by motorcoach to Port Douglas, where you board the "Quicksilver" catamaran bound for the Great Barrier Reef. After docking at a private viewing platform, there is time to swim, snorkel or view this underwater wonderland from a semi-submersible. Enjoy a buffet lunch aboard Quicksilver before returning to the tranquility of Silky Oaks. Later this afternoon you may explore nature trails, swim in one of the natural pools or just relax before dinner. MEALS **BLD**

9. Kuranda Train/Cairns

Motor through the mountains to the small village of Kuranda for a performance of the award winning Tjapukai Aboriginal Dance Troupe. Next board a Victorian-era railroad car for a journey back through the lush mountain jungle, one of Australia's more scenic treks. It took hundreds of men four years to cut through the dense underbrush, bridge the deep streamlined gorges and finally tunnel through the mountains to create the railroad. Arrive at Freshwater Station for lunch before returning to Cairns mid-afternoon where the remainder of the day is free to explore this tropical city. MEALS **BLD**

10. Cairns/The Gold Coast

Today you'll fly along the Eastern Seaboard from Cairns to Brisbane. From Brisbane, drive south to the heart

Venture out to the Great Barrier Reef to explore the world's largest living reef.

A kaleidoscope of brightly colored tropical fish and living coral

of Australia's vacation land, the Gold Coast. This area has mountains and rainforests to the west and wide beautiful beaches with sophisticated resorts along the coast. Along its 20 miles of white sand beaches and inland waterways are the homes of many of Australia's "rich and famous." Your hotel for the next two nights is the Sheraton Mirage Gold Coast. MEALS **BD**

11. Gold Coast Leisure

Start the day with a leisurely breakfast followed by a mid-morning cruise along the inland waterways of the Gold Coast. Along the shores of the canals are the homes of some of the area's more prominent residents. Return to the Marina Mirage Wharf mid-day to enjoy the surroundings of the resort. The Marina Mirage complex includes famous name boutiques, specialty stores and tantalizing restaurants and eateries. The hotel has direct access to the beachfront, a 2-acre lagoon and 35 acres of lushly landscaped, tropical gardens. Adjacent to the property is Sports Mirage, an exceptional health and fitness center where tennis, swimming, saunas and massage are available. MEALS **B**

12. Fly to Auckland

Today, bid farewell to Australia and fly across the Tasman Sea to the lovely island nation of New Zealand. Touch down in Auckland, the North Island's "City of Sails." Your flight arrives this evening. After a long

It's hard to resist the cuddly koala!

day of travel, relax in the luxury of the Regent of Auckland, your hotel located in the heart of the business and shopping districts. MEALS **BD**

13. Auckland Sightseeing

Join us for a tour of this attractive city set on two harbors between the Tasman Sea and the Pacific Ocean. From atop Mount Eden you have a stunning view of Auckland as well as Rangitoto Island, a dormant volcano which broods over Waitemata Harbour. Visit Kelly Tarlton's Underwater World, a unique aquarium built of plexiglass tubes, which offers a close-up look at the marine life. Next, see the splendid War Memorial Museum, situated in the Domain, one of Auckland's finest parks. The museum houses one of the finest displays of Maori and Polynesian culture in the world. The balance of the afternoon and evening is yours to follow your own interests. MEALS **BL**

The Outback   *Australian Aboriginals*   *Try a camel ride at Ross River Homestead*

9

Flightseeing over Mount Cook National Park

16. Fly to Mount Cook

Today you fly to the South Island and Mount Cook National Park in the heart of New Zealand's Southern Alps. Your hotel is at the mountain's base in the rustic Hermitage Lodge. After lunch at the lodge, take a flight-seeing excursion over the spectacular alpine scenery of mountains and glaciers (weather permitting). MEALS **BLD**

17. Milford Sound/Fiords

Board an early morning flight to Te Anau, "Gateway to New Zealand's Fiordland National Park." After lunch, you're off to Milford Sound where you board our private launch to explore the grandeur of the Sound. Far from the bustle of any city, you cruise the quiet waters, admiring the beauty of waterfalls cascading down sheer cliffs, glacier carved inlets and the occasional basking seal. This evening, relax over dinner before retiring for a quiet night. MEALS **BLD**

18. Queenstown

This morning, after a leisurely breakfast, ride through the ruggedly picturesque countryside to Queenstown, New Zealand's premier resort town. With The Remarkables mountain range as a backdrop, Queenstown is situated on the shores of beautiful Lake Wakatipu. MEALS **BLD**

19. Jet Boat/Private Homes

Embark on a fun day of sightseeing and activities. First, shoot the rapids through narrow gorges on the Shotover River aboard a "Shotover Jet Boat." Then take a gondola ride to the top of Bob's Peak for a panoramic vista. The remainder of

14. Waitomo/Rotorua

Depart early this morning for a drive through the scenic heart of the North Island. Your first stop is in the rugged hills south of Otorohanga, to visit the famous Glow Worm Caves. You glide silently in a flat-bottomed boat along an underground river through the caves, to enter a cavern alive with the radiance of thousands of tiny glow worms clinging to the ceiling. After lunch in the Waitomo area, continue on to Rotorua, where your accommodations are on the shores of lovely Lake Rotoiti. MEALS **BLD**

15. Geysers/Agrodome

Enjoy breakfast viewing the peaceful lake shore before setting off to explore the Rotorua area. Learn about New Zealand's vital sheep industry at the Agrodome. Continue to Rainbow & Fairy Springs to see the shy, nocturnal, kiwi bird, as well as many varieties of trout. Walk through the Whakarewarewa Thermal Reserve to view bubbling mud pools and geysers. You will also see exhibits showing the village life and crafts of the native Maori people. Tonight, enjoy a special Maori "Hangi" dinner with authentic Maori entertainment. MEALS **BLD**

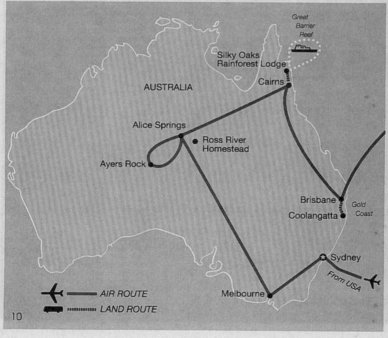

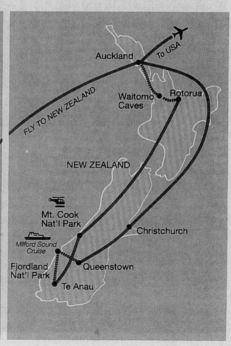

the day is yours to explore Queenstown and perhaps seek out special New Zealand woolen articles. This evening you will be picked up at the hotel and driven to dinner at the home of a local Queenstown resident. Here you will enjoy home-cooked food and learn more about life on the South Island. Ask about local politics, schools, shopping, etc. After dinner, return to your hotel. MEALS **BD**

20. Fly to Christchurch

This morning fly up the South Island to Christchurch, "the most English city outside England." You understand why when you see swans gliding along the willow edged Avon River. Your Tour Director introduces you to this lovely city; then the afternoon is yours for further exploration. This evening bid adieu to New Zealand and your traveling companions at a special farewell dinner party. MEALS **BD**

21. Depart New Zealand

Fly to Auckland mid-day to connect with your flight back to Los Angeles. **Tour ends: Auckland Int'l Airport, late afternoon.** Flying back over the Pacific, you recross the International Date Line, regaining a day. You'll arrive in the United States the same day. (Those extending their tour to Fiji will depart Christchurch earlier to connect to a mid-day flight from Auckland to Fiji, see page 15.) MEALS **B**

Queenstown, New Zealand...a favorite place to visit

Departs Sydney:

SUNDAYS – Jan. 2 to Dec. 25, 1994
Jan. 1 to Aug. 13, 1995
Additional departures as demand dictates

Plan to fly from the U.S. the Friday before to meet these dates in Sydney.

Price Per Person:

Twin $4875   Single $6135   Triple $4575
Prices are guaranteed through 8/13/95

Price Includes everything outlined in General Information, back cover, plus 48 meals – 20 breakfasts, 11 lunches and 17 dinners. Also included is the Mt. Cook flightseeing and the air fare for 8 flights on days 5, 6, 7, 10, 16, 17, 20, 21... a $1780 value as of 9/30/93. Departure taxes (approx. $25 US) are not included.

Additional Air Costs – Transpacific air is additional. Tauck holds roundtrip space from Los Angeles via Qantas Airways in a fare class that allows stopover privileges. At this printing (Sept. 1993) this fare ranged from $1416 to $2124 and is subject to change. If using this space, the Sydney/Melbourne flight (day 3) and the Brisbane/Auckland flight (day 12) are part of the air fare, and therefore not included

in the tour price. Persons not flying Qantas, or flying a fare class that does not permit stopovers must pay additional for these two flights (approximately US $450). Check with your booking agent. While Tauck holds space, your booking agent must ticket these flights. Your Tauck Tour director will have all other airline tickets.

Australia Only:

Persons wishing to take only the Australia portion of this tour will join in Sydney and end after breakfast on Day 12 in the Gold Coast.

Price Per Person: (12 Days)
Twin $2950   Single $3687   Triple $2774

New Zealand Only:

Persons wishing to take only the New Zealand portion of this tour should arrive in Auckland on day 12 and proceed to the hotel on their own. (A taxi will cost approximately NZ $32, or US $19.) Tour will arrive from Australia later that evening.

Join Auckland:

THURSDAYS – Jan. 13 to Dec. 29, 1994
Jan. 12 to Aug. 25, 1995
(Fly from the U.S. the Tuesday before.)
Additional departures as demand dictates.

Price Per Person: (10 Days)
Twin $2290   Single $2803   Triple $2182

Hotel Itinerary

Nights 1, 2	**Hotel Inter-Continental** Sydney, Australia
Night 3,4	**Regent of Melbourne** Melbourne, Australia
Night 5	**Ross River Homestead** Alice Springs, Australia
Night 6	**Sails in The Desert** Ayers Rock, Australia
Night 7,8	**Silky Oaks Lodge** Mossman Gorge, Australia
Night 9	**Cairns Hilton** Cairns, Australia
Night 10,11	**Sheraton Mirage Gold Coast** Gold Coast, Australia
Night 12,13	**Regent of Auckland** Auckland, NZ
Night 14,15*	**Okawa Bay Resort** Rotorua, NZ
Night 16	**Hermitage Lodge** Mount Cook, NZ
Night 17	**Te Anau Travelodge** Te Anau, NZ
Night 18,19	**Parkroyal Hotel** Queenstown, NZ
Night 20	**Parkroyal Hotel** Christchurch, NZ

* Tour of Feb. 3, 1994, stays at Sheraton Rotorua.
Tours of Feb. 10, 13, 1994 stay at Kingsgate Hotel.

APOLLO ACCESS TD*28050
WORLDSPAN .... G/PTS/TTX/NA

11

■ **REVIEW—OCEANIA: THE SOUTH PACIFIC**

1. What is the Great Barrier Reef? Where is it located?

2. Who are the Australian aborigines?

3. Name Australia's largest cities. Where are they located?

4. How does New Zealand differ in landform and climate from Australia? What do the two nations share historically and culturally?

5. What does the regional name Melanesia mean? Why is it used? Which nations are in the region?

6. Where is Guadalcanal? Why is it well known to Americans?

7. Define Polynesia and Micronesia.

8. Where is Tahiti located? What is its touristic importance?

9. Where is the International Date Line? What time difference prevails east and west of the line?

10. Where are the major beach and resort areas in Oceania?

11. Describe three major areas of scenic beauty in the region.

17

Documentation, Customs, Immigration and Health Information

"Know before you go" should be the philosophy of all travelers leaving the United States. Travel agents and others who advise travelers must have a basic understanding of the documentation, customs, immigration, and health regulations that affect travelers leaving from and returning to the United States. All requirements described in this book are for United States citizens. If the traveler is not a United States citizen, the embassy or consulate of the country to be visited should be consulted for appropriate requirements.

■ DOCUMENTATION

The term *documentation* refers to the type of identification and, if required, level of governmental permission that is required of travelers visiting a specific country. The following levels of documentation were used in the country description headings throughout this book:

647

- Proof of identity
- Proof of citizenship
- Tourist card
- Passport
- Passport, visa

Because countries have the right to change required documentation at any time, the information about documentation in this book is current at the time of printing. A more up-to-date source, such as a country's embassy or consulate, a computer reservation system database, or the appropriate area *Air Travel Planner* should be checked before advising a traveler abaout specific requirements.

Proof of identity should be carried by travelers at all times, even when traveling within the United States. A driver's license is the most common form of proof of identity. A proof of identity document must contain a photograph of the individual.

Bermuda, the Bahamas, and many Caribbean islands require visiting United States citizens to present proof of citizenship upon entering their nations. A birth certificate or naturalization certificate is the most acceptable form of proof of citizenship. A currently valid passport is always acceptable. Expired passports are generally acceptable. Military service documents, such as discharge papers, are also usually acceptable. Although a voter registration card is accepted by many nations requiring proof of citizenship, some will not accept it. The acceptability of this documentation should be verified before recommending its use.

A few Latin American nations require visiting United States citizens to secure a tourist card. Tourist cards are usually issued by airlines that fly to countries requiring them. Sometimes pictures and/or small fees are required along with the application. Travel agents can issue Mexican tourist cards. Often, the proof of citizenship required for issuance of the tourist card must also be presented when entering the country requiring the tourist card.

A passport is the document most often required to enter a foreign nation. Passports are travel documents issued by the country of citizenship of the traveler. United States passports are currently valid for 10 years for citizens 18 years of age or older. Passports for persons under eighteen are valid for 5 years.

A traveler's first passport must be applied for in person at one of the regional passport offices, specific court clerk's offices, or at many United States post offices. The traveler must present a completed application, show a birth certificate with raised official seal or naturalization certificate, pay a required fee, provide two photographs, and personally pledge allegiance to the United States. Subsequent passports may be applied for by mail (the expiring passport acts as proof of citizenship and allegiance). Although emergency passports can be secured quickly, normally at least 1 month should be allowed for processing.

A visa is a document issued by the country to be visited that grants permission for the traveler to enter the country. When a visa is required, the traveler must already possess a valid passport. The passport, along with the visa application and any required fees and/or photographs, is given by the traveler to the embassy or consulate of the country to be visited for processing. Factors such as length of stay and/or purpose of trip (business, student or vacation, for example) can affect whether a visa is required. Some visas are for a single trip to the country only while others may permit multiple reentries.

Processing time is often overnight, but can be as long as several weeks, depending on the country to be visited and the reason for the trip. A few countries requiring visas will process them on the spot at the border when entering the country. The visa, itself, is usually a stamp or sticker affixed to one page of the passport permitting the traveler to enter the country one or more times over a specific period of time. The United States requires visitors from many countries to secure visas before traveling here.

■ IMMIGRATION AND CUSTOMS REGULATIONS

Upon returning from abroad, travelers must establish their identity with officials of the United States Immigration and Naturalization Service (INS) and declare all articles acquired abroad to officials of the US Customs Service. In most instances, travelers complete immigration and customs formalities at their first port of reentry into the United States. Occasionally, clearance may take place at the final destination of the airplane and traveler, after an earlier stop within the United States. Travelers returning from some nearby destinations such as Canada, Bermuda, and the Bahamas clear immigration and customs after checking in, but before boarding, their return flight home.

Upon arrival in the United States, travelers must clear immigration. Often, returning United States citizens are permitted to bypass immigration or go through special express lines directly to the customs clearance area. One official may check both proof of United States citizenship and customs declaration after baggage is claimed. If a passport was required by the country visited by the traveler, it must be shown upon returning to the United States. If no passport was required for the visit, none is required for the return.

Travelers receive a customs declaration form on board the plane or vessel on which they are returning. The forms should be prepared in advance for presentation to immigration and customs officials. The identification portion of the declaration form must be completed by all arriving travelers. If duty-free exemptions have not been exceeded, travelers may make an oral declaration to the customs inspector. A written declaration is required only when exemptions have been exceeded.

The head of a family may make a joint declaration for all members residing in the same household and returning together to the United States. Family members making a joint declaration may combine their personal exemptions even if the articles acquired by one member of the family exceeds the personal exemption allowed. Infants and children returning to the United States are entitled to the same exemptions as adults, except for alcoholic beverages.

Travelers must declare articles acquired abroad and in their possession at the time of return. These include:

- Articles purchased
- Gifts received
- Items being brought back for another person
- Repairs to articles taken abroad and returned to the United States
- Articles intended to be used or sold in business

The wearing of an article purchased abroad does not exempt it from duty. The price paid for an item must be stated in the declaration. Estimates may be used for gifts.

Exemptions

Articles acquired abroad and brought into the United States are subject to applicable duty and internal revenue tax, but returning residents are allowed certain exemptions from paying duty on items obtained while abroad.

Articles totaling $400 ($600 from most Caribbean or Central American countries), based on the fair retail value of each item in the country where acquired, may be brought into the United States free of duty, subject to limitations on alcohol, cigarettes, and cigars, if

1. The articles were acquired on the trip for personal or household use.
2. The traveler brings the articles with him or her at the time of reentry into the country.

3. The traveler has been out of the United States for at least 48 hours, except when returning from the United States Virgin Islands or Mexico.

4. The traveler has not used the $400 (or $600) exemption or any part of it within the preceding 30-day period.

5. The articles are not prohibited or restricted.

Not more than 100 cigars and 200 cigarettes (one carton) may be included in a traveler's exemption. Cigarettes may, however, be subject to state or local taxation. One liter (33.8 fluid ounces) of alcoholic beverages may be included by a traveler in the exemption if the traveler is 21 or older, the alcohol is for personal or gift use, and its importation does not violate the laws of the state where the traveler is arriving.

Travelers who have included the United States Virgin Islands, American Samoa, or Guam on their trips may receive a customs exemption of $1200. Not more than $400 ($600 from most Caribbean and Central American countries) of the exemption may be applied to merchandise obtained in locations other than those islands. The countries eligible for the $600 exemption can change, so it is important to verify with the United States Customs Department if you have questions for a specific trip.

Travelers who are 21 or older may bring in 5 liters (169 fl. oz.) of alcoholic beverages. At least 4 liters must have been purchased in these islands, and at least 1 liter of the 5 must have been produced there. Articles acquired in these islands may be shipped to the United States and claimed under this personal exemption.

If travelers cannot claim the $400, $600 or $1,200 exemption because of the 30-day or 48-hour minimum limitations, they may bring in articles for personal or household use free of duty and tax if the total fair retail value does not exceed $25 per person. This is an individual exemption and may not be grouped with other members of a family on one declaration. The total may include 50 cigarettes, 10 cigars, 4 ounces of alcoholic beverages, and 4 ounces of alcoholic perfume.

Bona fide gifts of not more than $50 in fair retail value where purchased may be shipped to friends or relatives in the United States free of duty and tax if the same person does not receive more than $50 in gift shipments in one day. Perfume containing alcohol valued at more than $5 retail, tobacco products, and alcoholic beverages are excluded from this gift provision. Travelers cannot send gifts to themselves or to others in the traveling party.

Foreign made articles purchased in the United States or previously brought into the country and taken by travelers on a trip abroad are subject to additional duty unless the travelers can prove purchase or previous entry. Cameras and other items with serial numbers can be registered with the Customs Service, but the registration application must be made in person before taking the item out of the country.

Articles bought in duty-free shops in foreign countries are free of the duty of the host country and are subject to United States customs duty and restrictions, but may be included in a traveler's personal exemption. Articles purchased in a United States duty-free shop will be subject to duty if brought back into the United States.

Duty Preferences

The Generalized System of Preferences (GSP) is a system used by many developed countries including the United States to help developing countries improve their financial or economic condition through export trade. In effect, it provides for the duty-free importation from certain countries of a wide variety of products that would otherwise be subject to customs duty. Returning travelers may bring GSP items into the United States without duty in addition to articles declared as part of their applicable personal exemptions.

More than 140 nations and territories have been designated "Beneficiary Countries" for GSP preferences. Types of articles covered vary from country to country, but generally include handicrafts, art, and unset precious or semiprecious stones. All covered goods must be produced and purchased in the covered country. Articles of clothing are never covered. These listings change frequently. More specific information may be obtained from the United States Customs Service.

Articles imported in excess of customs exemptions will be subject to duty unless entitled to free entry or confiscated because they are prohibited. The customs inspector will place items having the highest rates of duty under the allowed personal exemption and will assess the duty based upon the lower rated items. A flat 10 percent duty will be assessed upon the first $1,000 fair retail value of imported articles that are not covered by GSP and are in addition to the allowed personal exemption. The flat rate is 5 percent for items purchased in the United States Virgin Islands, American Samoa, and Guam. If the $1,000 is exceeded, a written declaration is required and items above the $1,000 will be taxed at the applicable customs duty rate. Duty must be paid in United States currency (personal, government, or travelers checks are accepted).

Prohibited and Restricted Articles

In addition to collecting duty, one of the major responsibilities of the United States Customs Service is to keep prohibited articles from entering the country. Certain articles such as controlled drugs and fireworks are considered injurious to the general welfare and are totally prohibited. Other items such as automobiles and many food items must meet certain requirements and can only be imported if appropriate permits are issued.

Articles that are trademarked within the United States may be subject to import quantity limitations. Counterfeit items manufactured abroad are also controlled. However, travelers can be granted an exemption and allowed to bring in one article of a type protected by trademark, even if the item is counterfeit. Books, records, and computer programs produced in violation of copyright laws are subject to confiscation.

Import licenses are required for merchandise originating in Cuba and a few other nations. In addition, a license is required to import any item containing Cuban components. These licenses are strictly controlled and unavailable to tourists. Visitors to Cuba have a general license for a $100 exemption for personal use.

There is no limitation on the amount of money and monetary instruments that may be taken out of or brought into the country. However, if a traveler causes more than $10,000 to be brought into or taken out of the United States, the transactions must be reported to Customs.

Endangered species of wildlife and products made from them may not be brought into the country (for example, tortoise shell or ivory jewelry and leopard skin coats are prohibited). Specific rules are issued by the Department of the Interior, Fish and Wildlife Service.

■ HEALTH DOCUMENTS

Not too many years ago, most international travelers had to carry documents certifying inoculations. Today, thanks mainly to the efforts of the World Health Organization, a United Nations agency, smallpox has been officially eradicated from the world and cholera and yellow fever areas have been substantially reduced.

Proof of vaccination for yellow fever and cholera is required when entering an infested area and when returning from an infested area to the United States and many other nations. The United States Public Health Service maintains a list of countries where visitors are required to have proof of vaccination. Currently, the certifications are only required when visiting certain tropical areas in Asia, Africa, and the Pacific. No vaccinations are required to visit countries within Europe, North America, the Caribbean, or Australia. Updated information can be secured from the Public Health Service, a computer reservation system database, or appropriate editions of the OAG *Travel Planner.*

International travelers should be advised to carry copies of prescription for needed medicines, showing the generic names. In addition, if glasses are necessary for normal activities, the traveler should carry a spare pair and a copy of the prescription should also be available. A vacation can be ruined when the traveler can no longer enjoy the sights or read the menus.

The State Department periodically puts out advisories warning Americans of health, political, or other potential problems within a particular country. It is important to be aware of these advisories, but read them carefully. They frequently pertain to only a small area that the tourist will not be visiting, but they are put out on the country as a whole.

■ REVIEW—DOCUMENTATION, CUSTOMS, IMMIGRATION, AND HEALTH INFORMATION

1. Identify three documents that can be used to prove United States citizenship.

2. How is a United States passport obtained?

3. What is a visa?

4. Describe the basic customs rules for returning United States citizens.

5. Describe the concept and types of provisions contained in the GSP.

6. Identify three types of items that may not be brought into the United States. Why?

Glossary

Acculturation. The adoption by the people of one culture of aspects of another culture; in effect, cultural transfer.

Adiabatic rate. The decrease in temperature as altitude increases, approximately 3.3° per 1,000 feet.

Air mass. A large area of relatively homogeneous air.

Antarctic. The zone of characteristic bleak and cold weather around and south of the Antarctic Circle. The Antarctic Circle is the parallel 66½° south of the Equator that defines this zone.

Apartheid. The official policy of racial segregation practiced in South Africa until 1994.

Archipelago. A group or chain of islands.

Arctic. The zone of characteristic bleak and cold weather around and north of the Arctic Circle. The Arctic Circle is the parallel 66½° north of the Equator that defines this zone.

Atoll. A low-lying coral island that has a generally circular shape enclosing a lagoon.

Basin. A hollow, or relatively low-lying area, on the earth's surface.

Bauxite. The ore from which aluminum is derived.

Birthrate. The ratio between the number of births and a total population in a given place and time period; also known as fertility rate.

Black Current. *See* Japan Current.

Cartogram. A map whose dimensions are purposely distorted to give an impression of relative magnitudes of data, such as population size or volume of trade.

Cartography. The science and art of mapmaking.

Central business district (CBD). The "downtown," or the main concentration of business activities, of a city.

Climate. The statistically derived average of weather conditions that prevail in a specified part of the world.

Collective. A large agricultural unit, characteristic of Communist economies, that is operated cooperatively by its resident labor force.

Colonial dependency. A territory directly under the control of another state. The same as colony, although a colony may also mean a group of people who migrate to another land but keep ties with their homeland.

Colonialism. The extension and maintenance of control by a country over a dependent territory and people.

Continental drift. The slow, imperceptible movements of large landmasses, including continents, as a result of the interaction of tectonic plates and earth rotation.

Culture. The total behavioral system and material artifacts of a people.

Cultural landscape. The total identifiable impress of a society, or culture group, on its physical environment.

Death rate. The ratio between the number of deaths and a total population in a given place and time period; also known as mortality rate.

Delta. A generally flat area near the mouth of a river, crossed by diverging branches (distributaries) of the river, and formed of soil (alluvium) deposited by the river.

Demography. The science of population, especially its vital and social statistics.

Desert. An area where there is little precipitation or vegetation.

Diffusion. The spread of culture elements from a point of origin over a wider area.

Dual economy. An economy composed of both a traditional, often agricultural or pastoral, sector and a modern sector geared to export.

Earth grid. The network formed of lines of latitude and longitude that makes it possible to determine the exact location of any point on the earth's surface.

Easterlies. *See* Trade wind.

Ecology. The science of the relationships between organisms and their environment.

Ecosystem. A distinctive community consisting of plants and animals and their environment.

Elevation.   The height of a point relative to sea level.

Environment.   The surrounding conditions in which organisms and communities live.

Environmental perception.   The mental image of the environment that is held by individuals and groups.

Equator.   A great circle drawn around the earth equidistant from the poles (0° latitude).

Equatorial.   Pertaining to the zone at or near the equator or the climatic conditions that prevail there.

Estuary.   The mouth or lower part of a river, often an inlet, where river water meets seawater and tidal action.

Faulting.   The fracturing of the earth's crust along lines of stress; an important element in mountain formation.

Fertility rate.   *See* Birthrate.

Fjord.   A long, narrow coastal inlet formed by glaciation, such as those found in Norway, Alaska, and Chile.

Floodplain.   A low-lying area bordering a river that is subject to seasonal or periodic flooding by the river.

Glacier.   A large mass, or river, of ice.

Glacial landscape.   A landscape produced or modified by masses of ice.

Green revolution.   Agricultural advances achieved by the introduction of improved, high-yielding crop varieties and related cultivation methods, resulting in increased food production. Secondary definition is protection of the earth through recycling efforts.

Greenwich Mean Time (GMT).   The time at 0° longitude (measured in Greenwich, England).

Ground water.   Water found beneath the earth's surface.

Growing season.   The number of frost-free days when crops can be grown.

Gulf Stream.   A major warm-water ocean current that moves from the Gulf of Mexico in an arc northward into the North Atlantic Ocean, where it becomes the North Atlantic Drift.

Hacienda.   A large estate, or working farm, in Latin America.

Hinterland.   The service area around a city or smaller central place.

Human ecology.   The science that studies the mutual relationships between human groups and their environment.

Humidity.   The amount of water vapor in the air. Relative humidity is the amount present at a given temperature relative to what it can potentially hold at the same temperature. Absolute humidity is the amount actually present, as measured by the weight of the water vapor in a given volume of air.

Hurricane.   *See* Typhoon.

Interior drainage.   A drainage system in which streams do not reach the ocean but terminate in salt lakes or salt flats.

International Date Line. A north-south line in the Pacific Ocean coinciding with 180° meridian in general, but bent in places for political reasons. Regions on either side of the line differ by one day in their calendar dates.

Isthmus. A narrow stretch of land between two water bodies that links two larger land units.

Japan Current. A major warm-water ocean current of the Pacific Ocean corresponding to the Gulf Stream of the Atlantic Ocean. Also known as the Black Current (Kuro-shio), it originates over waters east of the Philippine Islands and arcs northward off the Asian coast and past Japan into the North Pacific.

Jet stream. Fast-moving air currents in the upper atmosphere in the midlatitudes.

Landscape. The complex of natural and manmade features in any part of the earth's surface.

Latitude. A location north or south of the equator, as identified by a parallel of latitude or its subdivisions (minutes and seconds).

Leeward. Facing the direction toward which the wind is blowing; side of a mountain protected from the wind.

Llanos. A tropical savanna grassland found on the northern margins of the Amazon Basin in northern South America.

Longitude. A location east or west of the Prime Meridian as identified by a meridian of longitude or its subdivisions (minutes and seconds).

Map. A representation of all or any part of the earth on a flat surface.

Map legend. Information included with a map that identifies the meaning of symbols, colors, and other ways in which data is presented.

Map projection. Any one of a number of systems by which the curved earth's surface is projected onto a flat plane, creating a map. Every projection has some distortion in size, shape, distance, or direction.

Map scale. The ratio of distance on the earth's surface to the same distance shown on a map.

Maritime climate. A climate usually found along a seacoast and influenced by air coming off the ocean. It is characterized by moderate seasonal temperatures, relatively high humidity, and moderate to heavy rainfall.

Megalopolis. A very large continuous zone of urbanization involving many cities.

Meridian. A line of longitude stretching from pole to pole. It serves to measure distances east (180° East Longitude) and west (180° West Longitude) of the prime meridian (0°). One degree longitude decreases in width with distance poleward from the Equator. *See* Longitude.

Mestizo. A person of mixed European and Indian (aboriginal) ancestry in Latin America.

Metropolis. A large and important city and contiguous built-up area.

Midlatitude. The zone between 35° and 55° north and south latitude, on the poleward side of the subtropics. Seasonal climatic contrasts are strong.

Ministate. Also microstate. A very small sovereign political unit.

Monolith. A single great stone or rock.

Monsoon. A seasonal shift of prevailing winds, onshore in summer and offshore in winter, caused by temperature and barometric pressure changes. It attains fullest form in eastern and southern Asia.

Mortality rate. *See* Death rate.

Natural increase. The excess of births over deaths in a population for a given place and time.

North Atlantic Drift. *See* Gulf Stream.

Oasis. A water source, or watered area, in a desert.

Overpopulation. A nonspecific term used to describe a general situation where a nation, or region within a nation, cannot provide adequate food for its population.

Paddy. A wet field in which rice is cultivated.

Pampas. The midlatitude grasslands of Argentina, much like the prairie of North America, now converted to large-scale agriculture.

Parallel. A line of latitude drawn parallel to and north (for example, 90° North Latitude) and south (for example, 90° South Latitude) of the Equator (0°). Although the concentric circles forming each parallel become smaller to the north and south, one degree of latitude is the same distance everywhere (approximately 70 miles).

Peninsula. A body of land surrounded on three sides by water.

Permafrost. Permanently frozen subsoil, as in the Arctic area.

Piedmont. A zone of rolling topography that adjoins a mountain range and forms a transition between mountains and plains.

Plantation. A large-scale, commercial farm that has a hired labor force and specializes in one or more export crops.

Plateau. An extensive area of relatively level land that is elevated above adjoining areas.

Pluralistic society. A population composed of more than one distinctive ethnic group or subgroup.

Polar latitudes. The zone lying between 66½° North Latitude and the North Pole and 66½° South Latitude and the South Pole. The source region for cold air masses, polar air.

Population density. The average number of persons living in a given land unit, usually a square mile or square kilometer.

Prairie. A tall grassland in moderately humid areas within the midlatitudes.

Prime Meridian. Also Standard Meridian. The great circle that passes through the poles and Greenwich, England, and forms the base line for the system of meridians of longitude.

Rain forest. *See* Tropical rain forest.

Rain shadow. A zone of lighter precipitation on the leeward side of a mountain range; more precipitation occurs on the opposite, windward, side of the range.

Region. A geographical unit of varying size defined by its overall characteristics or functions.

Relative humidity. *See* Humidity.

Savanna. A grassland with scattered trees and shrubs, usually found on the margins of equatorial rainforests where a seasonal wet-dry climate prevails.

Satellite (nation). A nation whose policies are dictated by another, dominant nation.

Steppe. Short, dry grasslands, found in greatest extent in the midlatitudes of the Eurasian interior and other areas of light rainfall.

Strait. A narrow body of water linking two larger water bodies.

Subsistence agriculture. A type of farming where most of the production is for consumption by the producer rather than for sale.

Subtropics. The zone between 23½° and about 35° north and south of the equator (North Latitude and South Latitude) that is adjacent to the tropics but has distinct seasonal climatic change.

Taiga. The coniferous forest that extends across much of subarctic Eurasia and North America.

Tectonic plate. One of a large number of huge segments of the earth's crust that press against one another and generate mountains, earthquakes, volcanos, and the slow, imperceptible movement of the continents and other landmasses.

Temperate climate. A climate marked by seasonal temperature differences, with warm to hot summers and cool to cold winters, and usually found in the mid latitudes.

Third World. Nations whose economies and societies are traditional, nonindustrial, and usually poorer than those of the advanced industrial nations. They are most numerous in Asia, Africa, and Latin America.

Time zone. One of the twenty-four divisions of the earth in which the time is the same. The limits of the zones are set by meridians, but with numerous deviations for political and practical reasons. The time decreases one hour in each of twelve zones westward, and increases one hour in each of twelve zones eastward, from Greenwich, England.

Topography. The configuration of the earth's surface; landforms.

Trade winds. A major wind system of the low latitudes that moves continuously in a general east to west direction. Also called the Easterlies.

Tropical rain forest.   An equatorial forest type marked by a thick canopy of evergreen trees and a great number of flora and fauna species.

Tropics.   The zone between the Tropic of Cancer (23½° North Latitude) and Tropic of Capricorn (23½° South Latitude) that receives the direct rays of the sun, and hence has relatively high temperatures, throughout the year. Tropical refers to locations and conditions within this zone and, popularly, to locations outside the zone having similar climatic conditions.

Tundra.   A treeless zone of grasses, lichens, and shrubs that lies between the poleward tree limit and the polar areas.

Typhoon.   A high-velocity cyclone of tropical and subtropical latitudes, marked by high winds and heavy rainfall, and occurring most frequently in late summer and early fall. The term is usually used in East Asia and Southeast Asia. The hurricane is the same phenomenon in the Caribbean Sea, Gulf of Mexico, and eastern United States.

Vulcanism.   Evidence of volcanic activity in the form of ash, rocks, and lava spewed from a break in the earth's crust.

Uniform Time Coordinated (UTC).   A new name, not yet in widespread use in the United States, for Zulu, or Greenwich Mean Time.

Watershed.   The drainage area of a stream.

Water table.   The upper surface of an underground zone that is saturated by water.

Westerlies.   A major wind system of the midlatitudes that moves continuously in a general west to east direction.

Windward.   Side or direction from which the wind is blowing; side of a mountain getting the wind.

Zulu time.   Greenwich Mean Time.

Index

STUDENT'S
Notebook Atlas
Colorprint®

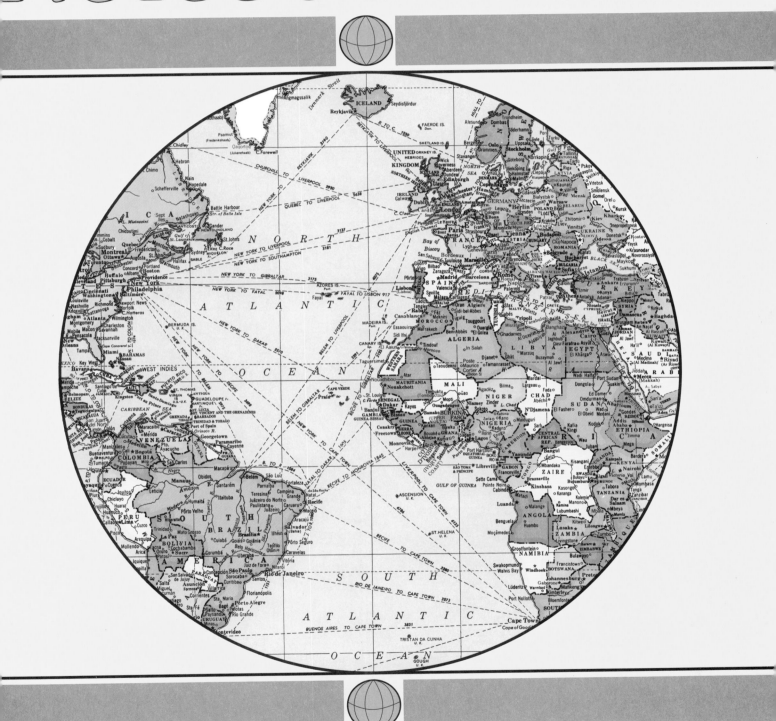

American Map Corporation

Colorprint®

Map of
THE WORLD
Mercator Projection

Scale of Miles at the Equator
0   500   1000   1500   2000

Scale of Kilometers at the Equator
0   1000   2000   3000

AMC
Copyright American Map Corporation

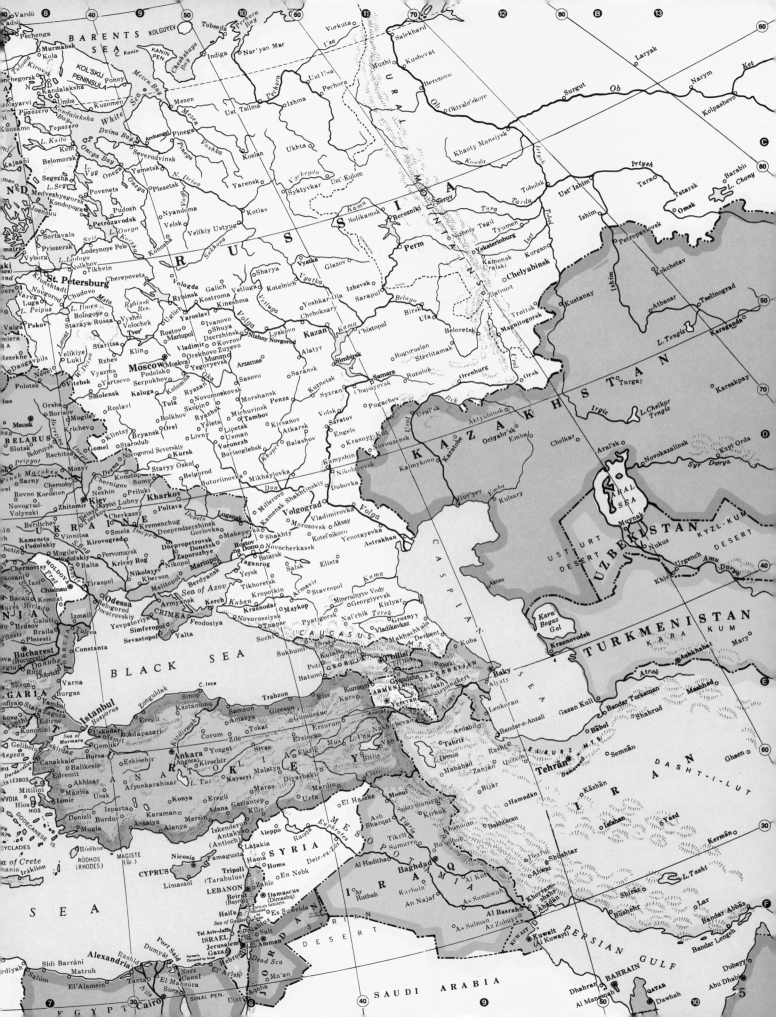

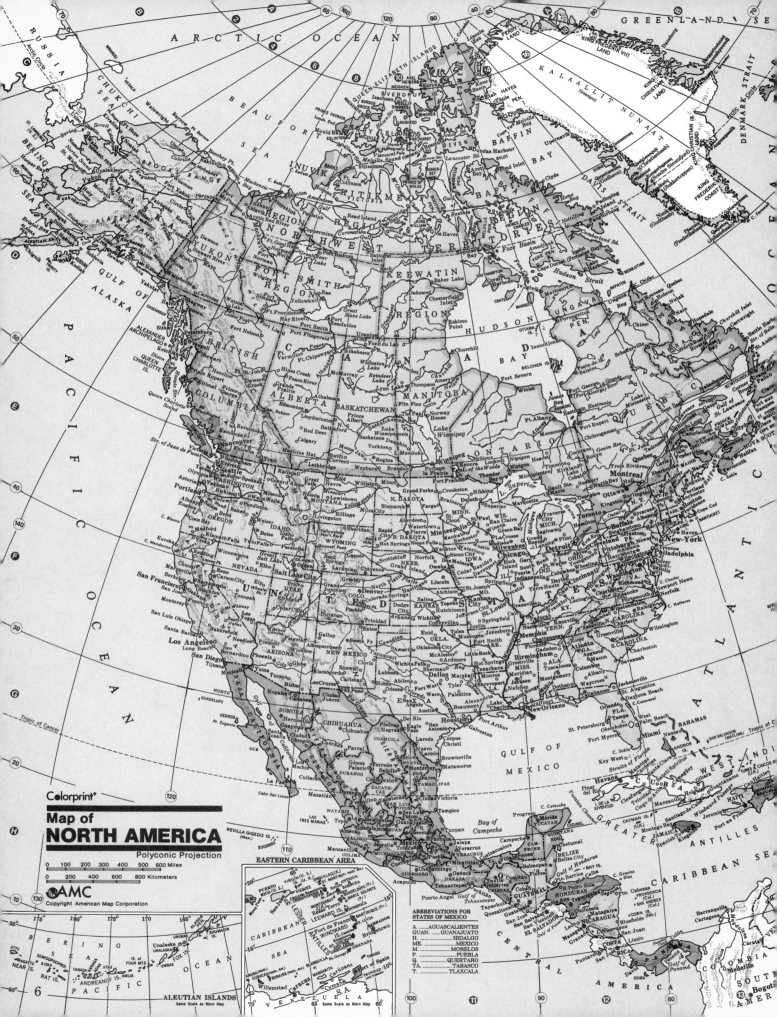

Map of
NORTH AMERICA
Polyconic Projection

Colorprint®

0   100   200   300   400   500   600 Miles
0   200   400   600   800 Kilometers

AMC
Copyright American Map Corporation

ABBREVIATIONS FOR STATES OF MEXICO

A.	AGUASCALIENTES
GUAN.	GUANAJUATO
H.	HIDALGO
ME.	MEXICO
M.	MORELOS
P.	PUEBLA
Q.	QUERETARO
T.	TABASCO
T.	TLAXCALA

EASTERN CARIBBEAN AREA

ALEUTIAN ISLANDS
Same Scale as Main Map

Colorprint®
Map of
ASIA

Azimuthal Equal Area Projection

0   200   400   600   800 Miles

0 200 400 600 800 1000 Kilometers

©AMC
Copyright American Map Corporation

Colorprint®

Map of
AUSTRALIA,
INDONESIA,
NEW ZEALAND

Azimuthal Projection

●AMC

Copyright American Map Corporation

Map of the UNITED STATES

Colorprint®

AMC

Copyright American Map Corporation

100   200   300 Miles

100   200   300   400 Kilometers

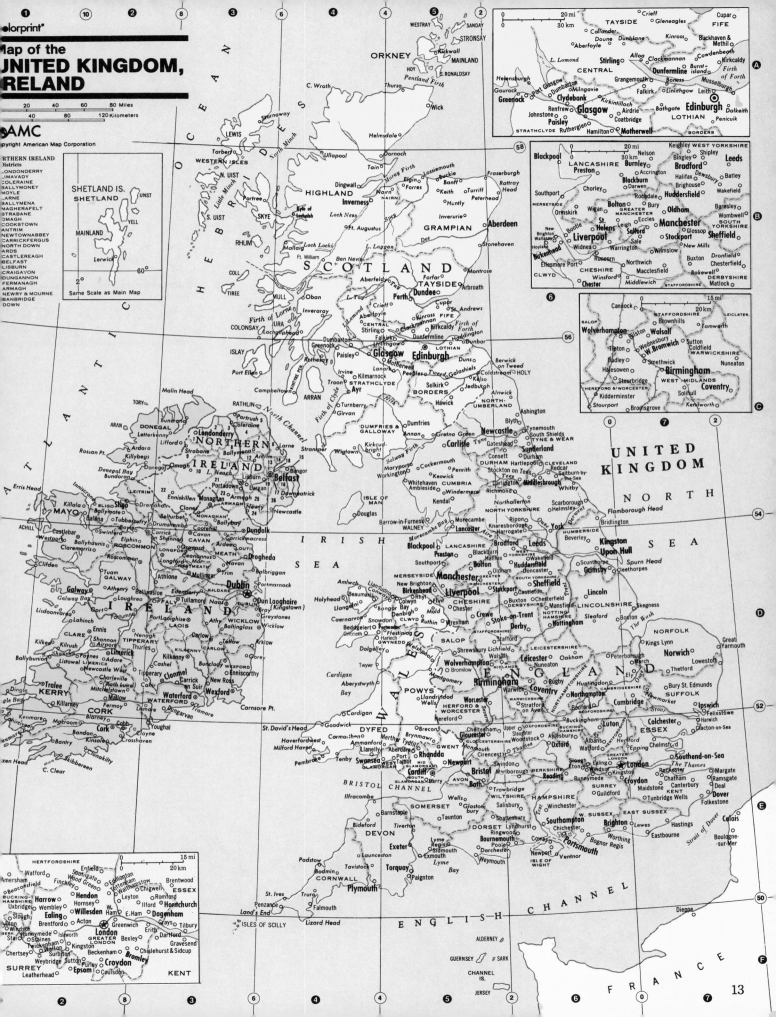

Map of the UNITED KINGDOM, IRELAND

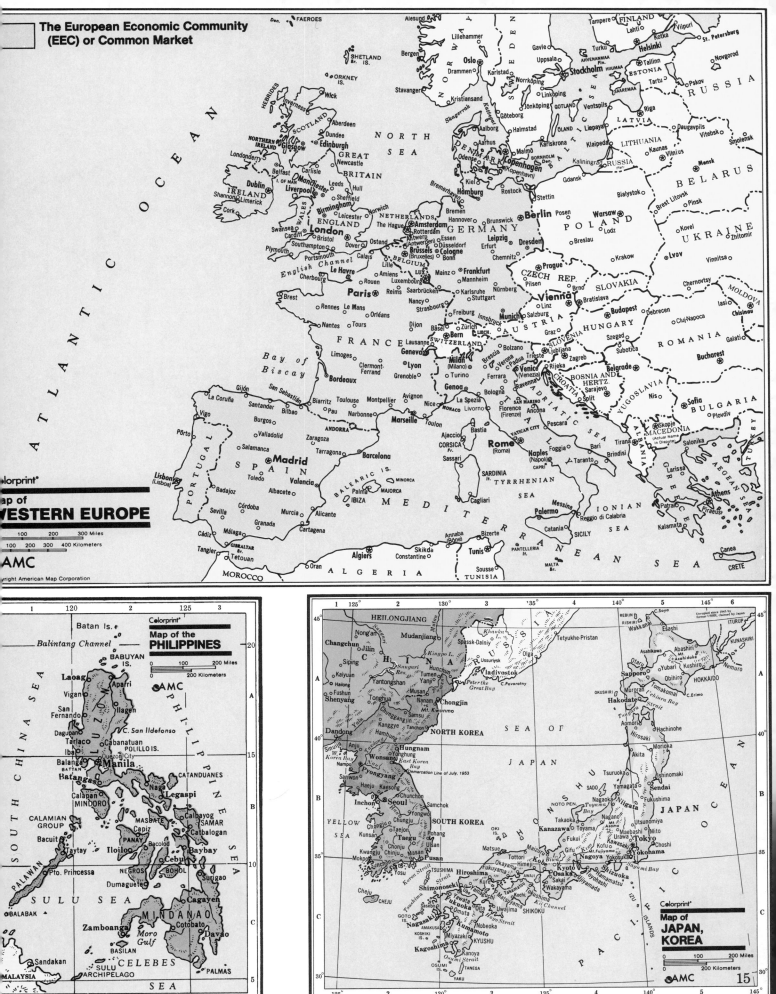

The European Economic Community (EEC) or Common Market

Map of WESTERN EUROPE

Colorprint®

100   200   300 Miles

100   200   300   400 Kilometers

AMC

Copyright American Map Corporation

Map of the PHILIPPINES

Colorprint®

100   200 Miles

200 Kilometers

AMC

Map of JAPAN, KOREA

Colorprint®

100   200 Miles

200 Kilometers

AMC

15

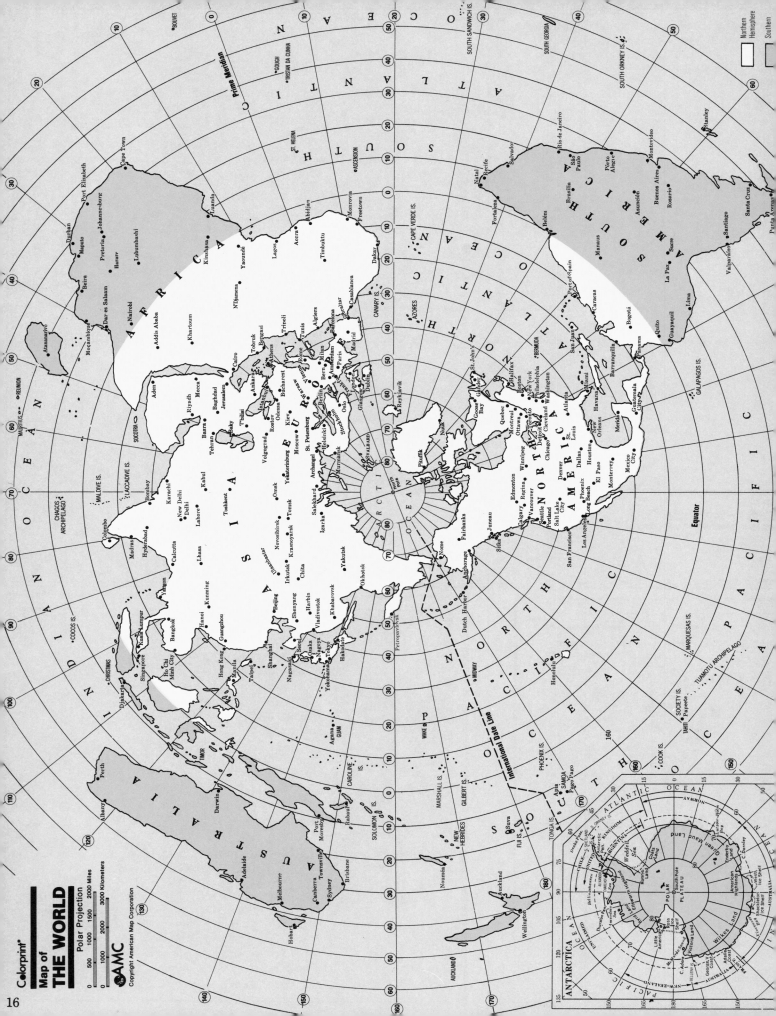

INDEX TO PLACES AND PHYSICAL FEATURES

Explanation of Symbols

CANADA — countries
ALABAMA — political subdivisions
★ ❀ Rome — country capital
⊙ Albany — subdivision capital
○ Jackson — cities/towns

Easter I.
Etna Mt. — physical features
Amazon R.

— — — — international boundary
— — — subdivision boundary
- - - - - - - border under dispute
Ⓔ grid numbers & letters
⑩ latitude or longitude

* not on map due to space limitations
1km² = .386 square miles

List of abbreviations used on map and in index

Adm.	Administration	N.Z.	New Zealand
Austr.	Australia	Pen.	Peninsula
Br. Comm.	British Commonwealth	Port.	Portuguese
		Prot.	Protectorate
Col.	Colony	R.	River
Dep.	Dependency	Sp.	Spain
Fr.	French, France	Str.	Strait
Gr.	Greece	Terr.	Territory
I.	Island	Trust	Trusteeship
It.	Italy	U.K.	United Kingdom
Mt.	Mountain		
N/A	Not Available	U.S.A.	United States of America
Neth.	Netherlands		

All figures following the entries are population figures unless otherwise noted. Population figures are given in full when available. Area figures are in km². Area figures below 10,000 are given in full. Area figures above 10,000 are rounded to the nearest thousand.

Feature — **Population** — **Pg.** — **Grid**

A

Aachen, Germany 231,986 4 *C-5
Abadan, Iran 294,068 9 C-4
Aberdeen, Scotland, U.K. 211,196 13 B-5
Aberdeen, S. Dak. 24,927 11 A-7
Abidjan★, Côte d'Ivoire 109,515 8 E-3
Abilene, Tex 109,110 11 D-7
Abu-Dhabi★, United Arab Emirates 242,975 9 C-4
Accra★, Ghana 564,194 8 E-3
Aconcagua, Mt., Argentina, 7,040m 7 F-2
ACRE, Brazil, ⊙Rio Branco, Area 150,000 417,200 7 C-2
Adana, Turkey 972,318 5 E-8
Adan (Aden)⊙, Yemen 275,373 9 D-4
Addis Ababa★, Ethiopia 1,739,130 8 E-7
Adelaide, Australia 1,013,000 10 F-5
Aden, Gulf of, Africa-Asia 9 D-4
Admiralty Is., Bismarck Archipelago 10 C-6
Adriatic Sea, Europe 4 D-6
Ad Dawhah (Doha)★, Qatar 276,000 9 C-4
Aegean Sea, Europe 5 D-7
AFGHANISTAN, Asia, ★Kabul, Area 652,090 13,051,358 9 C-5
AFRICA, Continent, Area 30,300,000 794,749,000 8
Agalega Is., Indian Ocean 3 F-17
Agana⊙, Guam 896 10 A-6
Agra, India 694,191 9 C-5
AGUASCALIENTES, Mexico, ⊙Aguascalientes, Area 5,000 719,650 14 C-4
Aguascalientes, Mexico 293,000 14 C-4
Ahaggar Mts., Africa 8 C-4
Ahmadnagar, India 143,937 9 C-5
Ahmadabad, India 2,059,725 9 C-5
Air Force I., Canada 12 B-8
Ajmer, India 375,593 9 C-5
Akita, Japan 299,683 15 B-5
Akola, India 225,412 9 C-5
Akron, Ohio 221,510 11 B-10
ALABAMA, U.S.A., ⊙Montgomery, Area 133,000 4,040,587 11 D-9
ALAGOAS, Brazil, ⊙Maceió, Area 28,000 2,229,764 7 C-6
Alamagordo, N. Mex 27,596 11 D-5
ALASKA, U.S.A., ⊙Juneau, Area 1,514,000 550,043 6 C-5
Alaska, Gulf of 11 E-4
Alaska Range, Mts. 11 E-3
ALBANIA, Europe, ★Tiranë, Area 29,000 3,268,000 4 D-7
Albany, Ga 83,540 11 D-10
Albany⊙, New York 94,540 11 B-12
Albany, Oreg. 29,462 11 B-2
Al Basrah, Iraq 310,950 9 *C-4
ALBERTA, Canada, ⊙Edmonton, Area 661,000 2,237,724 12 C-4
Albuquerque, N. Mex 384,736 11 C-5
Aleppo, Syria 1,308,000 5 E-8
Aleutian Is., Alaska 6 J-8
Alexander Archipelego, Alaska 6 D-7
Alexandria, Egypt 2,893,000 8 B-6
Alexandria, La 50,180 11 D-8
ALGERIA, Africa, ★Algiers, Area 2,380,000 20,841,000 8 C-4
Algiers★, Algeria 1,552,300 8 B-4
Alicante, Spain 265,810 4 E-4
Allahabad, India 616,051 9 C-6
Allentown, Pa. 105,200 11 B-11
Almaty★, Kazakhstan 975,000 9 B-5
Alps, Mts., Europe 4 D-5
Altai Mts., Asia 9 B-6
Altoona, Pa. 52,800 11 B-11
Amagaski, Japan 502,974 15 *C-4
AMAPA, Brazil, ⊙Macapá, Area 140,000 256,000 7 B-4
Amarillo, Tex. 157,615 11 C-6
Amazon R., S. America, 6,300km 7 C-4
AMAZONAS, Brazil, ⊙Manaus, Area 960,000 2,001,800 7 C-3
AMERICAN SAMOA, Oceania, (Terr., U.S.A.), ⊙Pago Pago, Area 197 32,297 2 F-6
Amiens, France 130,880 4 D-5
Amman★, Jordan 900,000 5 E-8
Amristar, India 594,884 9 C-5
Amsterdam★, Netherlands 693,209 4 C-5
Amu Darya, R., Asia, 2,625km 9 C-5
Amund Ringnes, I., Canada 6 B-11
Amur R., Asia, 4,300km 9 B-8
Anadyr Mts., Asia 9 A-10
Anchorage, Alaska 226,338 6 C-6
Ancona, Italy 105,562 4 D-6
ANDAMAN AND NICOBAR IS., Bay of Bengal, Indian Ocean (Terr., India), ⊙Port Blair, Area 8,000 188,741 9 D-6
Andaman Sea, Asia, Area 790,000 9 D-6
Andes Mts., S. America 7 C-2
Andizhan, Uzbekistan 288,000 9 B-5
ANDORRA, Europe, ★Andorra, Area 452 50,213 4 D-5
Andreanoff Is., Aleutian Is. 6 J-8
Aneto, Mt., Spain, 3,404m 4 D-4
Angara R., Asia, 1,850km 9 B-7
Angarsk, Russia 262,000 9 B-7
Angers, France 137,760 4 D-4
ANGOLA, Africa, ★Luanda, Area 1,246,000 8,802,000 8 G-5
ANGUILLA, W. Indies, Area 900 7,000 14 D-12
ANHUI, China, ⊙Hefei, Area 134,000 56,750,000 9 C-7
Ankara★, Turkey 2,541,899 5 E-8
Annaba, Algeria 239,975 8 B-4
Annapolis⊙, Md. 33,187 11 C-11
Annapurna, Mt., Nepal, 8,075m 9 *C-6
Anshan, China 1,195,580 9 B-8
Antananarivo★, Madagascar 650,000 8 G-8
ANTARCTICA, Continent, Area 14,000,000 16
ANTIGUA and BARBUDA, W.Indies, ★St. Johns, Area 443 64,000 14 D-12
Antofagasta, Chile 203,067 7 E-2
Antwerp (Antwerpen), Belgium 483,199 4 C-5
Anzhero-Sudzhensk, Russia 112,000 9 B-6
Aomori, Japan 293,020 15 A-5
Apeldoorn, Netherlands 146,804 4 *C-5
Apia★, Western Samoa 32,090 2 F-6
Apo, Mt, Philippines, 3,250m 9 D-8
Appalachian Mts., N. America 11 C-10
Appennines, Mts., Europe 4 D-6
Arabian Sea, Asia 9 D-5
Aracaju, Brazil 361,544 7 D-6
Arad, Romania 185,892 4 D-7
Arafura Sea, Oceania 10 C-5
Aral Sea, Asia, Area 24,288 9 B-4
Ararat, Mt, Turkey, 5,165m 5 E-9
Archangel, Russia 416,000 5 B-9
ARCTIC OCEAN, Area 14,438,000 2 A-4
Ardmore, Okla 23,073 11 D-7
Arequipa, Peru 612,100 7 D-2
ARGENTINA, S. America, ★Buenos Aires, Area 2,777,000 31,534,099 7 F-3
Arhus, Denmark 195,152 4 C-6
ARIZONA, U.S.A., ⊙Phoenix, Area 295,000 3,665,228 11 D-4
ARKANSAS, U.S.A., ⊙Little Rock, Area 138,000 2,350,725 11 C-8
Arkansas R., N. America, 2,400km 11 C-8
Armavir, Russia 172,000 5 D-9
ARMENIA, Asia/Europe, ★Yerevan, Area 30,000 3,283,000 5 D-9
Arnhem, Netherlands 128,526 4 *C-5
Aruba, I, Neth. Antilles, ⊙Oranjestad, Area 178 253,000 14 E-10
Asahigawa, Japan 364,401 15 A-5
Ascension I., S. Atlantic Ocean (Dep. St. Helena), ⊙Georgetown, Area 88 1,179 8 F-2
Asheville, N.C. 61,607 11 C-10
Ashgabat★, Turkmenistan 382,000 9 C-4
ASHMORE AND CARTIER IS. (Terr. Austr.) Area 5 0 10 D-4
ASIA, Continent, Area 43,950,000 2,993,970,000 9
Asmera★, Eritrea 344,101 8 D-7
Astoria, Oreg. 10,069 11 A-2
Astrakhan, Russia 509,000 5 D-9
Asunción★, Paraguay 454,881 7 E-4
Asyût, Egypt 291,000 8 C-7
Atchison, Kan. 10,656 11 C-7
Athabasca, Lake, N. America, Area 8,000 12 C-5
Athens★, Greece 885,737 5 E-7
Atlanta⊙, Ga. 394,017 11 D-10
Atlantic City, N.J. 37,986 11 C-12
ATLANTIC OCEAN, Area 83,000,000 3
Atlas, Mts., Africa 8 B-3
Auckland, New Zealand 150,000 10 E-2
Auckland Is., N.Z. 2 H-5
Augsburg, Germany 245,563 4 D-6
Augusta, Ga. 44,634 11 D-10
Augusta⊙, Me. 21,325 11 B-13
Austin, Minn. 21,907 11 B-8
Austin⊙, Tex. 465,622 11 D-7
AUSTRALIA, Continent, S.W. Pacific Ocean, ★Canberra, Area 7,685,000 16,531,929 10 E-5
AUSTRALIAN CAPITAL TERRITORY, Australia, ⊙Canberra, Area 2,432 281,700 10 F-6
AUSTRIA, Europe, ★Vienna, Area 84,000 7,617,779 4 D-6
Avellaneda, Argentina 650,000 7 *F-4
Axel Heiberg I., Canada, Area 36 6 A-11
AZERBAIJAN, Asia, ★Baky, Area 86,000 7,029,000 5 D-9
AZORES IS., N. Atlantic Ocean (Port.), ⊙Ponta Delgada, Area 2,000 292,000 8 B-1
Azov, Sea of, Ukraine, Area 36,000 5 D-8

B

Badajoz, Spain 123,658 4 E-4
Baffin Bay, N. America 6 B-14
Baffin I., N. America 6 B-13
Baghdad★, Iraq 1,984,142 5 E-9
BAHAMAS, W. Indies, ★Nassau, Area 14,000 232,070 14 B-9
BAHIA, Brazil, ⊙Salvador, Area 560,000 11,738,000 7 D-5
Bahia Blanca, Argentina 256,832 7 F-3
BAHRAIN, Asia, ★Manama, Area 622 488,548 5 F-10
BAJA CALIFORNIA NORTE, Mexico, ⊙Mexicali, Area 70,000 1,657,927 14 B-2
BAJA CALIFORNIA SUR, Mexico, ⊙La Páz, Area 74,000 317,326 14 B-2
Baker, Oreg. 9,140 11 B-3
Bakersfield, Calif. 174,820 11 C-3
Baky★, Azerbaijan 1,741,000 5 D-9
BALEARIC IS., Mediterranean (Spain), ⊙Palma, Area 5,200 468,342 4 E-5
Bali, Indonesia, ⊙Denpasar, Area 5,100 2,100,200 10 C-3
Balkhash, Kazakhstan 132,000 9 B-5
Balkhash, Lake, Asia, Area 18,000 9 B-5
Baltic Sea, Europe, Area 415,000 4 C-6
Baltimore, Md. 736,014 11 C-11
Baluchistan, Region, Pakistan 9 C-5
Bamako★, Mali 650,000 8 D-3
Banda Sea, Indonesia 10 C-4
Bandar, India 112,612 9 D-6
Bandar Seri Begawan★, Brunei 49,902 10 B-3
Bandung, Java, Indonesia 1,462,637 10 C-2
Bangalore, India 2,628,593 9 D-5
Banghazi, Libya 137,295 8 B-6
Bangkok★, Thailand 4,697,001 9 D-7
Bangor, Me. 33,181 11 B-13
BANGLADESH, Asia, ★Dhaka, Area 143,000 104,722,888 9 C-6
Bangui★, Central African Republic 473,817 8 E-5
Banjarmasin, Kalimantan, Indonesia 381,286 10 C-3
Banjul★, Gambia 49,181 8 D-2
Banks I., Canada, Area 62,000 12 A-3
Baoding, China 495,140 9 C-7
Baoji, China 341,240 9 C-7
Baotou, China 149,400 9 B-7
BARBADOS, W. Indies, ★Bridgetown, Area 430 253,881 14 E-13
Barcelona, Spain 1,667,699 4 D-5
Bareilly, India 386,734 9 C-5
Barents Sea, Europe 9 A-3
Bari, Italy 368,896 4 D-6
Barnaul, Russia 596,000 9 B-6
Baroda, India 734,873 9 C-5
Barquisimeto, Venezuela 661,265 7 A-3
Barranquilla, Colombia 917,486 7 A-2
Barrow, Pt., Alaska 6 B-5
Basel, Switzerland 169,600 4 D-5
Bass Is., Oceania 2 G-7
Basse-Terre⊙, Guadeloupe 14,161 14 D-12
Batan, Is., Philippines 9 C-8
Bathurst I., Canada 12 A-5
Baton Rouge⊙, La. 219,419 11 D-8
Baykal, Lake, Asia 9 B-7
Beaufort Sea, N. America 6 B-6
Beaumont, Tex. 114,323 11 D-8
Beijing★, China 5,531,460 9 C-7
Beirut★, Lebanon 474,870 5 E-8
BELARUS, Europe, ★Minsk, Area 208,000 10,200,000 5 C-7
Belém, Brazil 1,120,777 7 C-5
Belfast⊙, N. Ireland, U.K. 303,800 13 C-4
BELGIUM, Europe, ★Brussels, Area 31,000 9,255,872 4 C-5
Belgrade★, Yugoslavia 1,087,915 4 D-7
BELIZE, Central America, ★Belmopan, Area 23,000 179,814 14 D-7
Belize City, Belize 39,050 14 D-7
Bellingham, Wash. 52,179 11 A-2
Belmopan★, Belize 40,000 14 D-7
Belo Horizonte, Brazil 2,122,073 7 D-5
Benares (Varanasi), India 708,634 9 C-6
Bend, Oreg. 20,467 11 B-2
Bengal, Bay of, Asia 9 D-6
BENIN, Africa, ★Porto-Novo, Area 113,000 4,304,000 8 E-4
Berdichev, Ukraine 133,000 5 D-7
Berezniki, Russia 200,000 5 C-10
Bergamo, Italy 102,512 4 D-5
Bergen, Norway 210,463 4 B-5
Bering Sea 2 C-5
Bering Str., Alaska 6 C-4
Berkeley, Calif. 102,724 11 C-2
Berlin★, Germany 3,334,777 4 C-6
BERMUDA, W. Indies (U.K.), ⊙Hamilton, Area 54 56,652 6 F-14
Bern★, Switzerland 135,718 4 D-5
Besancon, France 114,040 4 D-5
Bhagalpur, India 225,062 9 C-6
Bhaunager, India 307,121 9 C-5
Bhopal, India 671,018 9 C-5
BHUTAN, Asia, ★Thimphu, Area 47,000 734,000 9 C-6
Bialystok, Poland 227,116 4 C-7
Bielefeld, Germany 309,000 4 *C-5
Bikaner, India 280,366 9 C-5
Bikini Atoll, Marshall Is. 10 A-8
Bilbao, Spain 351,276 4 D-4
Billings, Mont. 81,151 11 A-5
Binghamton, New York 53,008 11 B-11
Birkenhead, England, U.K. 99,529 13 D-5
Birmingham, Ala. 265,968 11 D-9
Birmingham, England, U.K. 993,695 13 D-6
Bisbee, Ariz. 6,288 11 D-5
Biscay, Bay of, Europe 4 D-4
Bishkek★, Kyrgyzstan 622,000 9 B-5
Bismarck⊙, N. Dak. 49,256 11 A-6
Bismarck Archipelago, Oceania 10 C-7
Bismarck Sea, Oceania 10 C-6
Bissau★, Guinea-Bissau 109,214 8 D-2
Biysk, Russia 231,000 9 B-6
Bizerte, Tunisia 62,900 8 B-4
Blackburn, England, U.K. 134,445 13 D-5
Blackpool, England, U.K. 143,817 13 D-5
Black Sea, Europe 5 D-8
Blantyre, Malawi 331,588 8 G-7
Bloemfontein, S. Africa 104,381 8 H-6
Bochum, Germany 386,895 4 *C-5
Bogor, Java, Indonesia 247,409 10 C-2
Bogotá★, Colombia 4,176,769 7 B-2
Boise⊙, Idaho 125,738 11 B-3
BOLIVIA, S. America, ★Sucre, ★La Paz, Area 1,099,000 6,020,200 7 D-3
Bologna, Italy 445,139 4 D-6
Bolton, England, U.K. 263,641 13 D-5
Bombay, India 8,243,405 9 D-5
Bonaire, Neth. Antilles, ⊙Kralendijk, Area 259 8,087 14 E-11
BONIN IS., N. Pacific Ocean (Japan), Area 70 1,670 9 C-9
Bonn, Germany 279,718 4 C-5
Bordeaux, France 205,960 4 D-4
Borden I., Canada 6 B-9
Borneo, I., See Kalimantan, Indonesia-Malaysia 10 C-3
BOSNIA and HERZEGOVINA, ★Sarajevo, Area 51,129 4,364,574 4 D-6
Bosporus, Str., Turkey 5 D-7
Boston⊙, Mass. 574,283 11 B-12
Bothnia, Gulf of, Europe 4 B-7
BOTSWANA, Africa, ★Gaborone, Area 600,000 1,255,749 8 H-6
Bottrop, Germany 115,308 4 *C-5
Bougainville I., Papua New Guinea, Area 10,000 10 C-7
Boulder, Colo. 83,312 11 B-5
Bournemouth, England, U.K. 154,823 13 E-5
BOUVET I., S. Atlantic Ocean (Dep. Norway), Area 57 0 3 H-15
Bradford, England, U.K. 464,149 13 D-5
Brahmaputra, R., Asia, 2,895km 9 C-6
Braila, Romania 234,600 5 D-7
Brainerd, Minn. 12,353 11 A-8
Braisilia★, Brazil 1,576,000 7 D-5
Brandenburg, Germany 99,600 4 *C-6
Bratislava, ★Slovakia 432,267 4 D-6
Braunschweig, Germany 252,948 4 *C-6
BRAZIL, S. America, ★Brasilia, Area 8,550,000 144,428,000 7 D-5
Brazzaville★, Congo 596,200 8 F-5
Bremen, Germany 533,809 4 C-5
Bremerhaven, Germany 126,605 4 C-5
Brescia, Italy 203,187 4 D-6
Brest, France 154,020 4 D-4
Bridgeport, Conn. 141,686 11 B-12
Bridgetown★, Barbados, W. Indies 102,000 14 E-13
Brighton, England, U.K. 149,220 13 E-6
Brisbane, Australia 1,215,300 10 E-7
Bristol, England, U.K. 377,735 13 E-5
BRITISH COLUMBIA, Canada, ⊙Victoria, Area 948,000 2,744,467 12 C-3
BRITISH INDIAN OCEAN TERR., (Col. U.K.), ⊙Victoria, Area 26 3 F-18
Brno, Czech Republic 388,901 4 D-6
Brock I., Canada 6 B-9
Brooks Range, Mts., Alaska 11 E-3
Brownsville, Tex. 84,997 11 E-7
BRUNEI, Asia, ★Bandar Seri Begawan, Area 6,000 36,000 10 B-3
Brussels (Bruxelles)★, Belgium 976,536 4 C-5
Bryansk, Russia 445,000 5 C-8
Bucaramangá, Colombia 351,687 7 B-2
Bucharest★, Romania 1,975,508 5 D-7
Budapest★, Hungary 2,109,173 4 D-6
BUENOS AIRES, Argentina, ⊙Buenos Aires 12,582,321 7 F-4
Buenos Aires★, Argentina 2,960,976 7 F-4
Buffalo, N.Y. 328,123 11 B-11
Bujumbura★, Burundi 215,243 8 F-6
Bukavu, Zaire 171,064 8 F-6
Bukhara, Uzbekistan 220,000 9 C-5
Bulawayo, Zimbabwe 429,000 8 H-6
BULGARIA, Europe, ★Sofia, Area 112,000 8,971,358 5 D-7
BURKINA FASO (Upper Volta), Africa, ★Ouagadougou, Area 274,000 7,746,651 8 D-3

Burlington, Vt. 39,127 11 B-12
Bursa, Turkey 775,388 5 D-7
Buru I., Moluccas, Area 8,000 10 C-4
BURUNDI, Africa, ★Bujumbura, Area 28,000 5,068,792 8 F-6
Butte, Mont. 33,363 11 A-4
Bydgoszcz, Poland 374,466 4 C-6
Bylot I., Canada, Area 13,000 12 A-8
Bytom, Poland 239,516 4 C-6

C

CABINDA, Angola, Area 7,000 21,124 8 F-5
Cádiz, Spain 154,181 4 E-4
Caen, France 115,180 4 D-4
Cagliari, Sardinia, Italy 224,508 4 E-5
Cairo★, Egypt 6,052,836 8 C-7
Cairo, Ill. 4,846 11 C-9
Calais, France 101,000 4 C-5
Calcutta, India 3,305,006 9 C-6
Calgary, Alberta 592,740 12 C-4
Cali, Colombia 1,369,331 7 B-2
Calicut (Kozhikode), India 394,447 9 D-5
CALIFORNIA, U.S.A., ⊙Sacramento, Area 411,000 29,760,021 11 C-2
California, Gulf of, Mexico 14 B-2
Callao, Peru 515,200 7 D-2
Camagüey, Cuba 279,598 14 C-9
CAMBODIA, Asia, ★Phnom Penh, Area 180,000 6,249,000 9 D-7
Cambridge, England, U.K. 101,200 13 D-7
Cambridge, Mass. 95,802 11 *B-2
Camden, N.J. 87,492 11 C-11
CAMEROON, Africa, ★Yaoundé, Area 475,000 10,446,409 8 E-5
CAMPECHE, Mexico, ⊙Campeche, Area 51,800 528,824 14 D-6
CANADA, N. America, ★Ottawa, Area 9,975,000 26,218,500 12
CANARY IS., N. Atlantic Ocean (Sp.), ⊙Las Palmas, Area 8,000 1,047,370 8 C-2
Canaveral, Cape, Fla. 11 E-10
Canberra★, Australia 289,000 10 F-6
Canton, Ohio 84,161 11 B-10
CANTON AND ENDERBURY IS., Oceania (U.S.A.-U.K.), Area 70 0 2 F-6
CAPE OF GOOD HOPE, S. Africa, ★Cape Town, Area 677,000 5,543,506 8 J-5
Cape Town★, S. Africa 776,617 8 J-5
CAPE VERDE, N. Atlantic Ocean, ★Praia, Area 3,000 347,000 3 E-13
Caracas★, Venezuela 1,246,677 7 A-3
Cardiff⊙, Wales, U.K. 283,909 13 E-5
Caribbean Sea, Central America, Area 1,960,000 14 D-10
Carlsbad, N. Mex. 24,952 11 D-6
CAROLINE IS., N. Pacific Ocean, Area 1,000 10 B-6
Carpathian Mts, Europe 4 D-7
Carson City⊙, Nevada 40,443 11 C-3
Cartagena, Colombia 309,428 7 A-2
Cartagena, Spain 168,596 4 E-4
Casablanca, Morocco 1,371,330 8 B-3
Casper, Wyo. 46,742 11 B-5
Caspian Sea, Area 430,000 9 B-4
Castries★, St. Lucia 56,147 14 E-12
CATAMARCA, Argentina, ⊙Catamarca, Area 111,000 265,571 7 E-3
Catania, Sicily, Italy 379,039 4 E-6
Caucasus Mts., Europe 5 D-9
Cayenne★, Fr. Guiana 38,093 7 B-4
CAYMAN IS., W. Indies (Col. U.K.), ⊙Georgetown, Area 240 25,535 14 D-8
CEARA, Brazil, ⊙Fortaleza, Area 150,000 6,471,800 7 C-6
Cebu, Philippines 613,184 15 B-2
Cedar City, Utah 13,443 11 C-4
Cedar Rapids, Iowa 108,751 11 B-8
Celebes see Sulawesi, Indonesia 10 C-4
Celebes Sea, Oceania 10 B-4
CENTRAL AFRICAN REPUBLIC, Africa, ★Bangui, Area 625,000 2,607,800 8 E-5
Ceram I., Moluccas, Area 18,000 10 C-4
Ceuta, Sp. No. Africa 76,048 8 B-3
CHACO, Argentina, ⊙Resistencia, Area 98,000 838,303 7 E-3
CHAD, Africa, ★N'Djamena, Area 1,290,000 5,064,000 8 D-5
Chad, Lake, Africa, Area 18,000 8 D-5
Chagos Archipelago, Indian Ocean 3 F-18
Chang Jiang, R., Asia, 5,519km 9 C-7
Changchun, China 1,747,410 9 B-8
Changsha, China 1,066,030 9 C-7
Changzhou, China 533,940 9 C-7
CHANNEL IS., Europe (U.K.), ⊙St.Helier, Area 194 4 D-4
Charleston, S.C. 80,414 11 D-11
Charleston⊙, W.Va. 57,287 11 C-10
Charlotte, N.C. 395,934 11 C-10
Chatham Is., Oceania (N.Z.), Area 965 500 2 H-6
Chattagram, Bangladesh 1,388,476 9 C-6
Chattanooga, Tenn. 152,466 11 C-9
Chelyabinsk, Russia 1,119,000 5 C-11
Chemnitz, Germany 317,696 4 C-6
Chengdu, China 2,499,000 9 C-7
Cherbourg, France 85,485 4 D-4
Cheremkhovo, Russia 107,000 9 B-7
Chernovtsy, Ukraine 254,000 5 D-7
Cherskogo Mts., Asia 9 A-9
Cheyenne⊙, Wyo. 50,008 11 B-6
CHIAPAS, Mexico, ⊙Tuxtla Gutiérrez, Area 73,400 3,203,915 14 D-6
Chicago, Ill. 3,005,072 11 B-9
Chiclayo, Peru 409,600 7 C-2
Chico, Calif. 40,079 11 C-2
CHIHUAHUA, Mexico, ⊙Chihuahua, Area 247,100 2,439,954 14 B-3
Chihuahua, Mexico 385,953 14 B-3
CHILE, S. America, ★Santiago, Area 757,100 12,961,032 7 F-2
Chiloe I., Chile, Area 10,000 7 G-2
Chimborazo, Mt., Ecuador, 6,700m 7 C-2
Chimkent, Kazakhstan 389,000 9 B-5
CHINA, People's Republic, Asia, ★Beijing (Peking), Area 9,560,000 1,433,330,000 9 C-7
Chisinau★, Moldova 668,000 5 D-7
Chita, Russia 349,000 9 B-7
Choiseul I., Solomon Is., Area 2,000 10 C-7
Chongqing, China 2,121,000 9 C-7
Christchurch, New Zealand 67,700 10 F-2
CHRISTMAS I., Oceania (Terr. Austr.), Area 137 3,018 10 D-2
CHUBUT, Argentina, ⊙Rawson, Area 214,000 356,587 7 G-3
Chukchi Sea 2 B-6
Churchill R., N. America, 1,609km 12 C-5
Cincinnati, Ohio 364,040 11 C-10
Cirebon, Java, Indonesia 223,776 10 C-2
Citlaltepetl, Mt., Mexico, 6,200m 14 D-5
Ciudad Juárez, Mexico 625,040 14 A-3
Clermont-Ferrand, France 148,040 4 D-5
Cleveland, Ohio 505,616 11 B10
Clovis, N. Mex. 30,954 11 D-6
Cluj-Napoca, Romania 309,843 5 D-7
COAHUILA DE ZARAGOZA, Mexico, ⊙Saltillo, Area 150,000 1,971,344 14 B-4
Cochabamba, Bolivia 403,000 7 D-3
Cod, Cape, Mass. 11 B-12
Coeur d'Alene, Idaho 24,564 11 A-3
Coffeyville, Kans. 12,917 11 C-7
COLIMA, Mexico, ⊙Colima, Area 5,500 424,656 14 D-4
Cologne, Germany 940,200 4 C-5
COLOMBIA, S. America, ★Bogotá, Area 1,140,000 27,837,932 7 B-2
Colombo★, Sri Lanka 609,000 9 D-5
COLORADO, U.S.A., ⊙Denver, Area 269,100 3,294,394 7 C-5
Colorado R., N. America, 2,300km 11 C-4
Colorado Springs, Colo. 281,140 11 C-6
Columbia⊙, S.C. 98,052 11 D-10
Columbia R., N. America, 2,011km 6 E-9
Columbus, Ga. 178,681 11 D-10
Columbus⊙, Ohio 632,910 11 B-10
COMOROS, Africa, ★Moroni, Area 2,000 335,150 8 G-8
Conakry★, Guinea 197,627 8 E-2
Concepción, Chile 280,713 7 F-2
Concord⊙, N.H. 36,006 11 B-12
CONGO, Africa, ★Brazzaville, Area 340,000 1,909,248 8 F-5
Congo, R., Africa, 4,660m 8 F-5
CONNECTICUT, U.S.A., ⊙Hartford, Area 13,000 3,287,116 11 B-12
Constanta, Romania 323,236 5 D-7
Constantine, Algeria 378,668 8 B-4
COOK IS., Oceania (Assoc. Terr., N.Z.), ⊙Avarua, Area 240 17,754 2 G-7
Cook, Mt., N.Z., 3,700m 10 F-2
Coos Bay, Oreg. 15,076 11 B-2
Copenhagen (Kobenhavn)★, Denmark 969,706 4 C-6
Coral Sea, Oceania 10 D-7
CORAL SEA IS. TERR., (Austr.), Area 22 0 10 D-7
CÓRDOBA, Argentina, ⊙Córdoba, Area 169,000 2,764,176 7 F-3
Córdoba, Argentina 1,134,086 7 F-3
Córdoba, Spain 305,490 4 E-4
Cordova, Alaska 2,100 6 C-6
Corfu, I., Ionian Sea 4 E-6
Cork, Ireland 133,271 4 C-4
Cornwallis I., Canada 12 A-6
Corpus Christi, Tex. 257,453 11 E-7
CORRIENTES, Argentina, ⊙Corrientes, Area 89,000 795,021 7 E-4
Corsica, Mediterranean (Dep., Fr.), ⊙Ajaccio, Area 8,100 289,842 4 D-5
COSTA RICA, Central America, ★San José, Area 52,300 2,488,749 14 E-8
CÔTE D'IVOIRE (Ivory Coast), Africa, ★Abidjan, Area 322,000 12,070,000 8 E-3
Cotopaxi, Mt., Ecuador, 5,898m 7 C-2
Coventry, England, U.K. 306,231 13 D-6
Craiova, Romania 275,098 5 D-7
Cremona, Italy 75,547 4 *D-5
Crete I., Mediterranean Sea 5 E-7
CRETE, Mediterranean (Gr.), ⊙Iraklion, Area 8,000 502,270 5 E-7
Crimea, Pen., Ukraine 5 D-8
CROATIA, Europe, ★Zagreb, Area 56,538 4,760,344 4 D-6
Crookston, Minn. 8,119 11 A-7
CUBA, W. Indies, ★Havana, Area 115,000 10,468,661 14 C-9
Cúcuta, Colombia 223,868 7 B-2
Curaçao, Neth. Antilles, Area 445 145,500 14 E-10
Curitiba, Brazil 1,285,027 7 E-5
Cuzco, Peru 181,604 7 D-2
Cuttack, India 269,950 9 C-6
CYPRUS, Mediterranean, ★Nicosia, Area 10,000 708,000 5 E-8
CYRENAICA, Region, Libya 8 C-6
CZECH REPUBLIC, Europe, ★Prague, Area 78,000 10,363,000 4 D-6
Czestochowa, Poland 254,887 4 C-6

D

DAITO IS., N. Pacific Ocean (Japan), Area 47 2,319 9 C-8
Dakar★, Senegal 798,792 8 D-2
Dallas, Tex. 1,006,877 11 D-7
Damanhur, Egypt 226,000 8 B-7
Damascus★, Syria 1,343,000 5 E-8
Danube R., Europe, 2,816km 4 D-6
Dar es Salaam★, Tanzania 757,000 8 F-7
Darling R., Australia, 1,866km 10 F-6
Darmstadt, Germany 138,633 4 *D-5
Darwin, Australia 73,000 10 D-5
Dasht-e-Lut, Desert, Iran 9 C-4
Davao, Philippines 819,525 15 C-3
Davenport, Iowa 95,333 11 B-8
Davis Str., Canada 12 B-10
Dayton, Ohio 182,044 11 C-10
Daytona Beach, Fla. 61,921 11 E-10
Dearborn, Mich. 89,286 11 *B-10
Debrecen, Hungary 218,308 4 D-7
Decatur, Ala. 48,761 11 D-9
Decatur, Ill. 83,885 11 C-9
DELAWARE, U.S.A., ⊙Dover, Area 5,000 666,168 11 C-11
Delhi, India 4,884,234 9 C-5
Del Rio, Tex. 30,705 11 E-6
Demavend, Mt., Iran, 5,670m 9 C-4
DENMARK, Europe, ★Copenhagen (Kobenhavn), Area 44,000 5,127,024 4 C-5
Denmark Str., Greenland 6 C-18
Denver⊙, Colo. 492,200 11 C-6
Derby, England, U.K. 215,376 13 D-6
Des Moines⊙, Iowa 193,187 11 B-8
Detroit, Mich. 1,027,974 11 B-10
Devon I., Canada, Area 55,000 12 A-7
Dhaka★, Bangladesh 3,458,602 9 C-6
Dijon, France 140,900 4 D-5
DISTRICT OF COLUMBIA, U.S.A., ★Washington, Area 158 606,900 11 C-11
DISTRITO FEDERAL, Argentina, Area 192 2,960,976 7 F-4
DISTRITO FEDERAL, Brazil, Area 6,000 1,664,200 7 D-5
DISTRITO FEDERAL, Mexico, Area 1,499 8,236,960 14 D-5
DJIBOUTI, Africa, ★Djibouti, Area 22,000 337,000 8 D-2
Djibouti★, Djibouti 62,000 8 D-8
Dnepr R., Europe, 2,265km 5 D-8
Dneprodzerzhinsk, Ukraine 279,000 5 D-8
Dnepropetrovsk, Ukraine 1,182,000 5 D-8
Dnestr R., Europe, 1,387km 5 D-7
DODECANESE, Aegean Sea (Gr.), ⊙Rhodes, Area 3,000 120,000 5 E-7
Dodge City, Kans. 21,129 11 C-6
DOMINICA, W. Indies, ★Roseau, Area 751 73,795 14 D-12
DOMINICAN REPUBLIC, W. Indies, ★Santa Domingo, Area 49,000 5,430,879 14 D-10
Don R., Europe, 1,962km 5 D-9
Donetsk, Ukraine 1,090,000 5 D-8
Dortmund, Germany 584,595 4 C-5
Dothan, Ala. 53,589 11 D-9
Douala, Cameroon 1,029,731 8 E-4
Douglas⊙, Isle of Man 20,368 13 C-3
Dover⊙, Del. 27,630 11 C-11
Dover, England, U.K. 106,336 13 E-7
Drakensberg, Mts, Africa 8 H-7
Dresden, Germany 515,892 4 C-6
Dublin★, Ireland 502,749 4 C-4
Duisburg, Germany 525,090 4 *C-5
Duluth, Minn. 85,493 11 A-8
Dundee, Scotland, U.K. 174,255 13 B-5
Durango, Colo. 12,430 11 C-5
DURANGO, Mexico, ⊙Durango, Area 114,000 1,352,156 14 C-3
Durban, S. Africa 634,301 8 H-7
Dushanbe★, Tajikistan 582,000 9 C-5
Düsseldorf, Germany 567,372 4 C-5
Dzerzhinsk, Russia 281,000 5 C-9
Dzhugdzhur Mts., Asia 9 B-8

E

Eagle Pass, Tex. 20,651 11 E-6
East China Sea, Asia, Area 1,243,000 9 C-8
East London, S. Africa 119,727 8 J-6
East Siberian Sea, Asia 2 B-5
Easter I., S. Pacific Ocean (Chile), Area 116 2,000 2 G-9
Eau Claire, Wis. 56,856 11 B-8
ECUADOR, S. America, ★Quito, Area 284,000 9,922,514 7 C-2
Edinburgh⊙, Scotland, U.K. 433,480 13 C-5
Edmonton, Alberta 532,246 12 C-4
EGYPT, Africa, Asia, ★Cairo, Area 1,000,000 48,205,049 8 C-7
Eindhoven, Netherlands 190,867 4 *C-5
Elbe, R., Europe, 1,165 4 C-6
Elbert, Mt., Colo., 4,398m 11 C-5
Elbrus, Mt., Russia, 5,633m 5 D-9
Elgon, Mt., Kenya-Uganda, 4,300m 8 E-7
Elizabeth, N.J. 110,002 11 *B-12
Elko, Nev. 14,736 11 B-3
Ellef Ringnes I., Canada, Area 10,000 6 B-10
Ellesmere I., Canada, Area 213,000 6 A-13
El Mansura, Egypt 250,000 8 B-7
El Paso, Tex. 515,342 11 D-5
EL SALVADOR, Central America, ★San Salvador, Area 21,000 4,845,588 14 E-7
Ely, Nev. 4,756 11 C-4
Emi Koussi, Mt., Chad, 3,400m 8 D-5
ENGLAND, Europe (U.K.), ★London, Area 151,000 49,154,000 13
English Channel, Europe, Area 75,000 4 D-4
Enid, Okla. 45,309 11 C-7
Enschede, Netherlands 144,959 4 *C-5
Entebbe, Uganda 21,096 8 E-7
ENTRE RIOS, Argentina, ⊙Paraná 1,022,865 7 F-4
EQUATORIAL GUINEA, Africa, ★Malabo, Area 29,000 943,000 8 E-4
Erfurt, Germany 212,035 4 C-6
Erie, Pa. 108,718 11 B-10
Erie, Lake, N. America, Area 26,000 11 B-10
ERITREA, Africa, ★Asmera, Area 125,000 3,500,000 8 D-7
Eskisehir, Turkey 415,831 5 E-8
ESPIRÍTO SANTO, Brazil, ⊙Vitória, Area 42,000 2,523,900 7 D-6
Essen, Germany 619,981 4 C-5
ESTONIA, Europe, ★Tallinn, Area 44,000 1,466,000 5 C-7
ETHIOPIA, Africa, ★Addis Ababa, Area 1,097,000 46,013,235 8 E-7
Etna, Mt., Italy, 3,277m 4 E-6
Eugene, Oreg. 112,669 11 B-2
Euphrates R., Asia, 2,770km 9 C-4
Eureka, Calif. 27,025 11 B-2
EUROPE, Continent, Area 10,520,000 702,300,000 4-5
Evans, Mt., Colo. 11 C-5
Evansville, Ind. 26,272 11 D-9
Everest, Mt., China-Nepal, 8,840m 9 D-6
Everett, Wash. 69,961 11 A-2
Eyre, Lake, Australia, Area 10,000 10 E-5

F

FAEROE IS., N. Atlantic Ocean (Denmark), ⊙Thórshavn, Area 1,000 45,000 4 B-4
Fairbanks, Alaska 30,843 6 C-6
FALKLAND IS., S. Atlantic Ocean (Adm., U.K.--claimed by Argentina), ⊙Stanley, Area 12,000 1,800 7 H-4
Fargo, N. Dak. 74,111 11 A-7
FERNANDO DE NORONHA, Brazil, Area 26 1,295 7 C-6
Ferrara, Italy 146,735 4 D-6
Fes, Morocco 321,460 8 B-3
Fezzen, Region, Libya 8 C-5
FIJI, Oceania, ★Suva, Area 18,000 716,740 10 D-9
FINLAND, Europe, ★Helsinki, Area 337,000 4,932,123 5 B-7
Finland, Gulf of, Finland 5 C-7
Flagstaff, Ariz. 45,857 11 C-4
Flensburg, Germany 86,000 4 C-5
Flint, Mich. 140,761 11 B-10
Florence, Ala. 36,426 11 D-9
Florence (Firenze), Italy 438,304 4 D-6
Flores I., Indonesia 10 C-4
Flores Sea, Indonesia 10 C-4
FLORIDA, U.S.A., ⊙Tallahassee, Area 152,000 12,937,926 11 E-10
Florida, Straits of, N. America 11 F-10
Foggia, Italy 157,595 4 D-6
FORMOSA, Argentina, ⊙Formosa, Area 72,000 404,367 7 E-3
Fortaleza, Brazil 1,588,709 7 C-6
Fort-de-France⊙, Martinique 97,849 14 E-12
Fort Myers, Fla. 45,206 11 E10
Fort Smith, Ark. 72,786 11 C-8
Fort Wayne, Ind. 173,072 11 B-9
Fort Worth, Tex. 477,619 11 D-7
Fox I., Aleutian Is. 6 J-9
FRANCE, Europe, ★Paris, Area 547,000 56,303,985 4 D-5
Frankfort⊙, Ky. 25,968 11 C-9
Frankfurt (am Main), Germany 623,724 4 C-5
Frankfurt (an der Oder) 88,100 4 C-6
FRANZ JOSEPH LAND, Arctic Ocean, Russia, Area 18,000 3 A-17
Frederiksberg, Denmark 87,616 4 *C-6
Freetown★, Sierra Leone 469,776 8 E-2
Freiburg, Germany 181,991 4 D-5
FRENCH GUIANA, S. America (Overseas Dept., Fr.), ★Cayenne, Area 91,000 54,454 7 B-4
FRENCH POLYNESIA, S. Pacific Ocean (Terr. Fr.), Area 4,000 148,000 2 F-7
Fresno, Calif. 354,202 11 C-3
FUJIAN, China, ⊙Fuzhou, Area 122,000 30,087,000 9 C-7
Fuji, Mt., (Fujiyama), Japan, 3,778m 15 B-4
Fukui, Japan 253,234 15 B-4
Fukuoka, Japan 1,203,729 15 C-3
Fukushima, Japan 275,009 15 B-5
Funafuti★, Tuvalu 3,000 10 C-9
Funchal⊙, Madeira Is. 100,000 8 B-2
Fuzhou⊙, China 1,111,550 9 C-7

G

GABON, Africa, ★Libreville, Area 267,000 1,069,000 8 F-5
Gaborone★, Botswana 119,586 8 H-6
Gadsden, Ala. 42,536 11 D-9
GALAPAGOS IS., Pacific Ocean (Ecuador), ⊙Pto. Baquerizo, ⊙San Cristóbal, Area 8,000 2,000 2 F-10
Galati, Romania 238,292 5 D-7
Galdhopiggen, Mt., Norway, 2,469m 4 B-5
Gallup, N. Mex. 19,154 11 C-5
Galveston, Tex. 59,070 11 E-8
GAMBIA, Africa, ★Banjul, Area 11,000 687,817 8 D-2
Gambier Is., Fr. Polynesia 2 G-8
Gander, Newfoundland 10,207 12 D-10
Ganges R., Asia, 2,510km 9 C-6
Gangtok, India 12,200 9 *C-6
Gannett Peak, Wyo., 4,200m 11 B-5

19

Kyoto, Japan	1,474,507	15	C-4 -
KYRGYZSTAN, Asia, ★Bishkek, Area 199,000	4,291,000	9	B-5
Kyushu, I., Japan, Area 36,000		15	C-3

L

LABRADOR, Region, Newfoundland, Canada		12	C-9
La Coruña, Spain	243,673	4	D-4
La Crosse, Wis.	51,003	11	B-8
Ladoga, Lake, Europe, Area 18,000		5	B-8
Lagos★, Nigeria	1,060,848	8	E-4
Lahore, Pakistan	2,952,609	9	C-5
LAKSHADWEEP IS., Arabian Sea (India), Area 207	40,249	9	D-5
Lake Charles, La.	70,580	11	D-8
Lansing, Mich.	127,321	11	B-10
Lanús, Argentina	450,000	7	*F-4
Lanzhou, China	1,364,480	9	C-7
LAOS, Asia, ★Vientiane, Area 235,000	3,600,000	9	D-7
LA PAMPA, Argentina, ⊙Santa Rosa, Area 143,000	260,034	7	F-3
La Paz★, Bolivia	976,000	7	D-3
LAPLAND, Region, Europe		4	B-7
La Plata, Argentina	630,260	7	F-4
Laptev Sea, Asia		9	A-8
Laramie, Wyo.	26,687	11	B-5
Laredo, Tex.	122,899	11	E-7
LA RIOJA, Argentina, ⊙La Rioja, Area 92,000	220,739	7	E-3
Las Cruces, N. Mex.	62,126	11	D-5
Las Palmas⊙, Canary Is.	76,246	8	C-2
La Spezia, Italy	111,980	4	D-5
Lassen Peak, Calif., 3,189m		11	B-2
Las Vegas, Nev.	258,295	11	C-3
LATVIA, Europe, ★Riga, Area 65,000	2,521,000	5	C-7
Lausanne, Switzerland	123,344	4	D-5
LEBANON, Asia, ★Beirut, Area 10,000	3,340,000	5	E-8
Leeds, England, U.K.	709,584	13	D-6
LEEWARD IS., W. Indies		14	D-12
Legnica, Poland	101,098	4	C-6
Le Havre, France	199,220	4	D-5
Leicester, England, U.K.	278,538	13	D-6
Leiden, Netherlands	108,574	4	*C-5
Leipzig, Germany	538,860	4	C-6
Le Mans, France	147,140	4	D-5
Lena R., Asia, 4,260km		9	A-8
León, Mexico	593,000	14	C-4
LESOTHO, Africa, ★Maseru, Area 31,500	1,216,815	8	H-6
LESSER ANTILLES, W. Indies		14	E-12
Lewistown, Mont.	6,051	11	A-5
Lexington, Ky.	225,366	11	C-10
Lhasa⊙, Xizang, China	343,240	9	C-6
LIAONING, China, ⊙Shenyang Area 200,000	39,670,000	9	B-8
LIBERIA, Africa, ★Monrovia, Area 111,000	2,644,000	8	E-3
Libreville★, Gabon	57,000	8	E-5
LIBYA, Africa, ★Tripoli, Area 1,759,000	4,206,000	8	C-5
Libyan Desert, Egypt		8	C-6
LIECHTENSTEIN, Europe, ★Vaduz, Area 157	27,714	4	D-5
Liège, Belgium	201,746	4	C-5
Ligurian Sea, Europe		4	D-5
Lille, France	164,900	4	C-5
Lilongwe★, Malawi	233,973	8	G-7
Lima★, Peru	6,233,800	7	D-2
Limoges, France	139,320	4	D-5
Lincoln⊙, Nebr.	191,972	11	B-7
LINE IS., Oceania (U.K., U.S.A.)		2	E-7
Linz, Austria	199,190	4	D-6
Lipetsk, Russia	465,000	5	C-8
Lisbon★, Portugal	807,167	4	E-4
LITHUANIA, Europe, ★Vilnius, Area 65,000	3,398,000	4	C-7
Little Rock⊙, Ark.	175,795	11	D-8
Liuzhou, China	581,980	9	C-7
Liverpool, England, U.K.	469,642	13	D-4
Livingston, Mont.	6,701	11	A-4
Livorno(Leghorn), Italy	176,051	4	D-5
Ljubljana★, Slovenia	274,817	4	D-6
Llullaillaco, Mt., Argentina-Chile, 6,735m		7	E-3
Lodz, Poland	957,485	4	C-6
Lofoten Is., Norway		4	B-6
Logan, Utah	32,762	11	B-4
Logan, Mt., Canada, 6,050m		12	B-1
Loire, R., Europe, 1,040km		4	D-5
Lombok I., Indonesia, Area 5,000		10	C-3
Lomé★, Togo	148,156	8	E-4
London★, England, U.K.	6,735,353	13	E-5
London, Ontario	254,280	12	D-7
Long Beach, Calif.	429,433	11	D-3
Los Alamos, N. Mex.	11,455	11	C-5
Los Angeles, Calif.	3,485,398	11	D-3
Louisiade Archipelago, Oceania		10	D-7
LOUISIANA, U.S.A., ⊙Baton Rouge, Area 125,000	4,219,973	11	D-8
Louisville, Ky.	269,063	11	C-9
Lowell, Mass.	103,437	11	B-12
LOYALTY IS., Oceania (Fr.)		10	E-8
Luanda★, Angola	475,328	8	F-5
Lubbock, Tex.	186,206	11	D-6
Lübeck, Germany	210,425	4	C-6
Lublin, Poland	337,977	4	C-7
Lubumbashi, Zaire	543,268	8	G-6
Lucknow, India	1,895,721	9	G-6
Ludhiana, India	607,052	9	C-6
Ludwigshafen, Germany	158,020	4	*D-5
Lugansk, Russia	509,000	5	D-8
Luoyang, China	951,610	9	*C-7
Lusaka★, Zambia	535,830	8	G-6
Luton, England, U.K.	167,623	13	E-5
LUXEMBOURG, Europe, ★Luxembourg, Area 3,000	369,500	4	D-5
Luxembourg★, Luxembourg	79,160	4	D-5
Luzern, Switzerland	60,600	4	D-5
Luzon, I., Philippines, Area 106,000		15	A-2
Lvov, Ukraine	767,000	5	D-7
Lyon, France	408,860	4	D-5
Lyallpur, Pakistan	1,104,209	9	C-5

M

MACAO, Asia (Port.), ⊙Macao, Area 16	400,000	9	C-7
Macao★, Macao	241,813	9	C-7
MACEDONIA (actual name in dispute), Europe, ★Skopje, Area 25,713	2,033,964	4	D-7
Maceió, Brazil	376,479	7	C-6
Mackenzie R., N. America, 4,030km		6	C-8
Mackenzie King I., Canada		6	B-9
Mackenzie Mts., N. America		12	B-2
Macon, Ga.	106,612	11	D-10
MADAGASCAR, Africa, ★Antananarivo, Area 587,000	11,802,000	8	G-8
MADEIRA IS., N. Atlantic Ocean (Port.), ⊙Funchal, Area 798	270,000	8	B-2
Madeira, R., S. America, 3,360km		7	C-3
Madison⊙, Wis.	191,262	11	B-9
Madras, India	4,289,347	9	D-6
Madrid★, Spain	2,991,223	4	D-4
Madurai, India	820,091	9	D-5
Maebashi, Japan	283,567	15	B-4
Magdeburg, Germany	290,422	14	C-6
Magellan, Str. of, Chile		7	H-3
Magnetic Pole, North		6	B-10
Magnitogorsk, Russia	430,000	9	B-4
Mahajanga, Madagascar	60,000	8	G-8
MAINE, U.S.A., ⊙Augusta, Area 86,000	1,227,978	11	A-13
Mainz, Germany	173,738	4	D-5
Majuro★, Marshall Is.	N/A	10	B-9
Makeyevka, Ukraine	455,000	5	D-8
Makhachkala, Russia	320,000	5	D-9
Malabo★, Equat. Guinea	34,980	8	E-4
Malacca, Malaysia	481,491	10	B-2
Málaga, Spain	605,366	4	E-4
Malaita I., Solomon Is., Area 5,000		10	C-8
Malang, Java, Indonesia	511,780	10	C-3
MALAWI, Africa, ★Lilongwe, Area 118,000	7,982,607	8	G-7
Malawi, Lake, Africa, Area 30,000		8	G-7
MALAYA, Malaysia, Area 132,000	14,943,000	10	B-2
MALAYSIA, Asia, ★Kuala Lumpur, Area 333,000	18,193,000	10	B-2
MALDIVES, Republic of, Indian Ocean, ★Male, Area 69,	180,088	9	D-5
Male★, Maldives	55,130	9	D-5
MALI, Africa, ★Bamako, Area 1,240,000	8,089,522	8	D-3
Mallorca, I., Balearic Is.		4	E-5
Malmö, Sweden	230,838	4	C-6
MALTA, Mediterranean (Br. Comm.), ★Valletta, Area 316	349,014	4	E-6
Managua★, Nicaragua	608,020	14	E-7
Manama★, Bahrain	108,684	5	F-10
Manaus, Brazil	834,541	7	C-3
Manchester, England, U.K.	445,927	13	D-5
Manchester, N.H.	99,567	11	B-12
Mandalay, Myanmar	532,949	9	C-6
Mangalore, India	172,252	9	D-5
Manila★, Philippines	1,856,375	15	B-2
MANITOBA, Canada, ⊙Winnipeg, Area 650,000	1,026,241	12	C-6
Manitoba Lake, N. America, Area 5,000		6	D-11
Manizales, Columbia	238,365	7	B-2
Mankato, Minn.	31,477	11	B-8
Mannheim, Germany	298,767	4	D-5
Maputo★, Mozambique	882,601	8	H-7
Maracaibo, Venezuela	1,124,432	7	A-2
Maracay, Venezuela	496,662	7	A-3
MARANHAO, Brazil, ⊙Sao Luis, Area 340,000	5,181,800	7	C-5
Mar del Plata, Argentina	503,799	7	F-4
Mariupol', Ukraine	529,000	5	D-8
MARQUESAS IS., S. Pacific Ocean (Fr.), ⊙Atuona, Area 1,000	5,419	2	F-8
Marquette, Mich.	21,977	11	A-9
Marrakech, Morocco	330,400	8	B-3
Marsala, Sicily, Italy	79,175	4	E-6
Marseille, France	867,280	4	D-5
Marshall, Tex.	23,683	11	D-8
MARSHALL IS., N. Pacific Ocean, ★Majuro, Area 182	43,000	10	B-9
MARTINIQUE, W. Indies (Overseas Dept., Fr.), ⊙Fort-de-France, Area 1,000	313,648	14	E-12
MARYLAND, U.S.A., ⊙Annapolis, Area 27,000	4,781,468	11	C-11
Marysville, Calif.	12,324	11	C-2
Maseru★, Lesotho	13,312	8	H-6
Mashad, Iran	1,463,508	9	C-4
Masqat (Muscat)★, Oman	5,081	9	C-4
MASSACHUSETTS, U.S.A., ⊙Boston, Area 21,000	6,016,425	11	B-12
Masulipatnam, India, See Bandar			
Matamoros, Mexico	188,745	14	B-5
MATO GROSSO, Brazil, ⊙Cuiabá, Mato Grosso Do Sul, Area 1,260,000	1,797,000	7	D-4
Matsumoto, Japan	199,950	15	*B-4
Matsuyama, Japan	437,829	15	C-3
Matterhorn, Mt., Italy-Switzerland, 4,500m		4	*D-5
Mauna Loa, Mt., Hawaii, 4,167m		11	*E-6
MAURITANIA, Africa, ★Nouakchott, Area 1,031,000	2,038,000	8	C-3
MAURITIUS, Indian Ocean, ★Port Louis, Area 2,000	1,016,596	3	G-17
Mayotte, Indian Ocean (Overseas Dept. Fr.), Area 373	53,000	8	G-8
Mbabane★, Swaziland	44,000	8	H-7
Mbandanka, Zaire	125,263	8	E-5
McAlester, Okla.	16,376	11	D-7
McKinley, Mt., Alaska, 6,370m		6	C-5
Mecca (Makkah), Saudi Arabia	366,801	9	C-4
Medan, Sumatera, Indonesia	1,378,955	10	B-1
Medellín, Colombia	1,452,392	7	B-2
Medford, Oreg.	46,951	11	B-2
Mediterranean Sea, Area 2,965,000		4	E-6
Meknès, Morocco	244,520	8	B-3
Mekong R., Asia, 4,500km		9	D-7
MELANESIA, Pacific Is., Oceania		10	C-7
Melbourne, Australia	2,965,600	10	F-6
Melilla, (Sp), No. Afr.	80,758	8	B-3
Melville I., Australia, Area 5,000		10	D-5
Melville I., Canada, Area 42,000		12	A-4
Memphis, Tenn.	610,377	11	C-9
Mendoza, Argentina	706,909	7	F-3
MENDOZA, Argentina, ⊙Mendoza, Area 150,000	1,414,058	7	F-3
Menorca, I., Balearic Is.		4	E-5
Mensk★, Belarus	1,377,000	5	C-7
Mérida, Mexico	400,142	14	C-7
Meridian, Miss.	35,644	11	D-9
Mesopotamia, Region, Asia		5	E-9
Messina, Sicily, Italy	264,848	4	E-6
Metz, France	113,360	4	D-5
Mexicali, Mexico	341,559	14	A-1
MEXICO, N. America, ★Mexico City, Area 1,973,000	81,140,922	14	C-4
Mexico City★, Mexico	9,815,901	14	D-5
Mexico, Gulf of, N. Atlantic Ocean, Area 1,813,000		14	B-7
Miami, Fla.	358,548	11	E-10
MICHIGAN, U.S.A., ⊙Lansing, Area 151,000	9,795,297	11	B-10
Michigan, Lake, N. America, Area 57,000		11	B-9
MICHOACAN DE OCAMPO, Mexico, ⊙Morelia, Area 60,000	3,534,042	14	D-4
Middlesbrough, England, U.K.	143,157	13	C-6
MICRONESIA, FEDERATED STATES OF, Oceania, ★Palikir, Area 700	105,000	10	B-7
MIDWAY IS., N. Pacific Ocean (Terr. U.S.A.), Area 5	2,200	2	D-6
Milan (Milano), Italy	1,548,580	4	D-5
Miles City, Mont.	8,461	11	A-5
Milwaukee, Wis.	628,088	11	B-9
MINAS GERAIS, Brazil, ⊙Belo Horizonte, Area 587,000	15,831,800	7	D-5
Mindanao, I., Philippines, Area 96,000		15	C-2
Mindoro I., Philippines, Area 10,000		15	B-2
Minneapolis, Minn.	368,383	11	A-8
MINNESOTA, U.S.A., ⊙St. Paul, Area 217,000	4,375,099	11	A-8
Minot, N. Dak.	34,544	11	A-6
Miquelon, I., Canada, see St. Pierre			
MISIONES, Argentina, ⊙Posadas, Area 30,000	789,677	7	E-4
Miskolc, Hungary	208,817	4	D-7
MISSISSIPPI, U.S.A., ⊙Jackson, Area 124,000	2,573,216	11	D-9
Mississippi R., N. America, 3,781km		11	D-8
Missoula, Mont.	42,918	11	A-4
MISSOURI, U.S.A., ⊙Jefferson City, Area 178,000	5,117,073	11	C-8
Missouri R., N. America, 4,000km		11	B-7
Mitchell, Mt., N.C., 2,042m		11	C-10
Mobile, Ala.	196,278	11	D-9
Modena, Italy	178,657	4	D-5
Mogadishu★, Somalia	230,000	8	E-8
Mogilev, Belarus	359,000	5	C-8
Mokpo, S. Korea	221,814	15	C-2
MOLDOVA, Europe, ★Chisinau, Area 34,000	4,341,000	5	D-7
Moluccas, Is., Indonesia, ⊙Ambon		10	C-4
Mombasa, Kenya	442,309	8	F-7
MONACO, Europe, ★Monaco, Area 2	27,063	4	D-5
Monchengladbach, Germany	251,551	4	*C-5
MONGOLIA, Asia, ★Ulaanbaatar, Area 1,565,000	2,043,400	9	*B-7
Monroe, La.	54,909	11	D-8
Monrovia★, Liberia	421,058	8	E-2
MONTANA, U.S.A., ⊙Helena, Area 380,000	799,065	11	A-5
Mont Blanc, France		4	D-5
Monterey, Calif.	31,954	11	C-2
Monterrey, Mexico	1,064,269	14	B-4
Montevideo★, Uruguay	1,251,647	7	F-4
Montgomery⊙, Alabama	187,106	11	D-9
Montpelier⊙, Vt.	8,247	11	B-12
Montreal, Quebec	980,350	12	D-8
MONTSERRAT, Leeward Is. (Col., U.K.), ⊙Plymouth, Area 8	11,600	14	D-12
Moradabad, India	330,051	9	C-5
Morelia, Mexico	297,544	14	D-4
MORELOS, Mexico, ⊙Cuernavaca, Area 5,000	1,195,381	14	D-5
Morioka, Japan	231,373	15	B-5
MOROCCO, Africa, ★Rabat, Area 446,000	20,449,551	8	B-3
Moroni★, Comoros	20,000	8	G-8
Moscow★, Russia	8,818,000	5	C-8
Mosul, Iraq	310,313	5	E-9
Moulmein, Myanmar	219,961	9	D-6
MOZAMBIQUE, Africa, ★Maputo, Area 783,000	14,548,400	8	G-7
Mudanjiang, China	151,400	9	B-8
Mulhacen, Mt., Spain, 3,580km		4	E-4
Mülheim, Germany	175,237	4	*C-5
Mulhouse, France	107,480	4	D-5
Multan, Pakistan	732,070	9	C-5
Munich, Germany	1,206,394	4	D-6
Münster, Germany	246,699	4	C
Murcia, Spain	315,378	4	E
Murmansk, Russia	432,000	5	E
Muroran, Japan	129,833	15	A
Murray R., Australia, 2,580km		10	F
Muskogee, Okla.	37,708	11	C
MYANMAR, Asia, ★Yangon, Area 680,000	38,541,119	9	C
Mysore, India	447,175	9	D

N

Nagano, Japan	343,200	15	E
Nagaoka, Japan	184,574	15	E
Nagasaki, Japan	447,535	15	C
Nagoya, Japan	2,147,667	15	E
Nagpur, India	1,302,066	9	C
Naha, Okinawa, Japan	305,987	9	C
Nairobi★, Kenya	1,162,189	8	F
Namangan, Kyrgyzstan	291,000	9	E
Namcha Barwa, Mt., China, 7,818m		9	C
Namib Desert, Africa		8	H
NAMIBIA, Africa, ★Windhoek, Area 825,000	1,400,000	8	H
Nanchang, China	1,075,710	9	C
Nancy, France	96,000	4	D
Nanda Devi, Mt., India, 7,817m		9	C
Nanjiang⊙, China	2,091,400	9	C
Nanning, China	819,790	9	C
Nantes, France	242,340	4	D
Naples (Napoli), Italy	1,207,750	4	D
Nashville⊙, Tenn.	488,374	11	C
Nassau★, New Providence I., Bahamas	3,233	14	E
Natal, Brazil	521,421	7	C
NATAL, S. Africa, ⊙Pietermaritzbug, Area 88,000	5,722,215	8	H
Natchez, Miss.	19,460	11	D
NAURU, Oceania, ★Yaren, Area 21	9,000	10	C
NAYARIT, Mexico, ⊙Tepic, Area 26,000	816,112	14	C
N'Djamena★, Chad	179,000	8	D
NEBRASKA, U.S.A., ⊙Lincoln, Area 200,000	1,578,385	11	E
Needles, Calif.	5,191	11	D
Negro R., S. America, 2,250km		7	C
Negros, I., Philippines, Area 13,000		15	C
NEI MONGOL (Inner Mongolia), China, ⊙Huhhot, Area 450,000	19,274,279	9	E
NEJD, Saudi Arabia		9	C
Nelson R., N. America, 2,655km		12	C
NEPAL, Asia, ★Kathmandu, Area 140,000	17,143,503	9	C
NETHERLANDS, Europe, ★Amsterdam, ★The Hague, Area 40,000	14,760,067	4	C
NETHERLANDS ANTILLES, W. Indies, (Neth.), ⊙Willemstad, Area 995	253,300	14	E-
NEUQUEN, Argentina, ⊙Neuquén, Area 93,000	388,934	7	F
NEVADA, U.S.A., ⊙Carson City, Area 286,000	1,201,833	11	C
Nevis I., see St. Christopher			
Newark, N.J.	275,221	11	B-
New Bedford, Mass.	99,922	11	B-
New Britain, I., Papua New Guinea, Area 39,000		10	C
NEW BRUNSWICK, Canada, ⊙Fredericton, Area 73,000	696,403	12	D
NEW CALEDONIA, Oceania (Overseas Terr. Fr.), ⊙Nouméa, Area 119,000	134,500	10	E
Newcastle, Australia	419,200	10	F
Newcastle, England, U.K.	276,625	13	C
New Delhi★, India	273,036	9	C
NEWFOUNDLAND, Canada, ⊙St. John's, Area 404,000	567,681	12	C
Newfoundland, I., Canada, Area 111,000		12	D-
New Guinea, I., Oceania, Area 830,000		10	C
NEW HAMPSHIRE, U.S.A., ⊙Concord, Area 24,000	1,109,252	11	B-
New Haven, Conn.	130,474	11	B-
NEW HEBRIDES, See Vanuatu			
New Ireland, I., Papua New Guinea, Area 3,000		10	C
NEW JERSEY, U.S.A., ⊙Trenton, Area 21,000	7,730,188	11	B-
NEW MEXICO, U.S.A., ⊙Santa Fe, Area 315,000	1,515,069	11	D
New Orleans, La.	496,938	11	E
Newport, England, U.K.	128,107	13	E
Newport, R.I.	28,227	11	B-
Newport News, Va.	170,045	11	C-
New Siberian Is., Russia		9	A
NEW SOUTH WALES, Australia, ⊙Sydney, Area 800,000	5,797,100	10	F
New York, N.Y.	7,332,564	11	B-
NEW YORK, U.S.A., ⊙Albany, Area 128,000	17,990,455	11	B-
NEW ZEALAND, Oceania, ★Wellington, Area 269,000	3,325,900	10	F
Niagara Falls, N.Y.	61,840	11	B-
Niamey★, Niger	225,314	8	D
NICARAGUA, Central America, ★Managua, Area 130,000	2,732,520	14	E
Nicaragua, Lake, Central America, Area 8,000		14	E
Nice, France	335,240	4	D
Nicobar Is., India, see Andaman			
Nicosia★, Cyprus	166,900	5	E
NIGER, Africa, ★Niamey, Area 1,267,000	7,691,000	8	D
Niger R., Africa, 4,160km		8	D

22

STUDENT'S
Notebook Atlas Colorprint®

- **Fits 3-ring binder**
- **24 pages**
- **Full-color maps**
- **Completely indexed**
- **Accurate and up-to-date**
- **An extraordinary value**

For more than 60 years, American Map Corporation has been recognized for its unique ability to combine cartographic excellence with affordability. Whether it's a simple 8½" x 11" black and white outline map or a lush 9' x 6' full-color laminated map in a deluxe frame, American Map offers the very finest example of the cartographer's skill.

Our Colorprint® brand comprises a comprehensive selection of accurate, authoritative, and up-to-date maps and atlases. Each has been meticulously detailed to show cities, towns, rivers, mountains, lakes, and a wealth of other important data. The judicious choice of colors enhances understanding by making political boundaries clear and readable. Whether you're a student, educator, business person, or inquisitive adult, you'll find Colorprint today's best map value.

Design of our Cleartype® brand maps has been guided by the principle that "less is more." Cleartype maps eliminate physical features normally found on maps but extrinsic to business people focusing on state and county boundaries, population densities, and economic centers. Fidelity to this principle has yielded a product that is cleanly designed, scrupulously researched, and realistically priced.

American Map products are available in map, stationery, book, department, and drug stores throughout the country. If your local retailer does not have the map you wish, have him contact us, or contact us directly.

A-CT-NRP-10099

ISBN 0-8416-9608-X

50295

EAN

9 780841 696082

American Map

Part of the Langenscheidt Publishing Group

46-35 54th Road, Maspeth, New York 11378